"Chuck Kelley's heartbeat is evangelism, and this book reflects the powerful focus of his life."

—**Dr. Robert E. Coleman, Distinguished Senior Professor of Evangelism and Discipleship, Gordon-Conwell Theological Seminary, former dean of the Billy Graham International Schools of Evangelism, director of the Billy Graham Center Institute of Evangelism at Wheaton College, and author of** *The Master Plan of Evangelism*

"Dr. Chuck Kelley has set an example of urgency in personal evangelism throughout his entire ministry. I've been with him numerous times when he began a conversation to share his hope in Jesus. His commitment is exemplary to all of us. In this book written in honor of Dr. Kelley by several faculty members who have served under his leadership at New Orleans Baptist Theological Seminary, the authors lay out practical tools to help you share the gospel with your friends, family, coworkers, and neighbors."

—**Dr. J. D. Greear, lead pastor, The Summit Church, Raleigh-Durham, NC, and president, Southern Baptist Convention**

"I am extremely honored to endorse this book *Engage: Tools for Contemporary Evangelism* because of several reasons:

1. The book is dedicated to Dr. Chuck Kelley, who is retiring as president of NOBTS, the longest-serving president of this seminary. If you cut Dr. Kelley, he bleeds evangelism. He has taught it, preached it, wrote about it, and lived it all his life.
2. Because of my relationship with the authors and their desire to see lost sinners come to repentance.
3. This book truly has all the tools necessary to equip anyone to be effective in evangelism. Whether they live in the inner city or in the suburbs this book—if applied and practiced—are the ABCs to reaching this generation.

I highly recommend *Engage: Tools for Contemporary Evangelism* to everyone who is serious about changing our society through evangelism."

—**Fred Luter Jr., pastor, Franklin Avenue Baptist Church, New Orleans, LA, and former president, Southern Baptist Convention**

"If the gospel we believe is true, then what could possibly be more important than to be able to effectively share it with others? Yet most believers never do. This wonderful book will be the resource you need to help you *Engage* others with this life-changing message and introduce them to a life-changing Savior. You will find in these pages more than information—you will find real tools to help you share the good news in this challenging and changing culture. I'm so thankful for this powerful tool for my own life!"

—**Dr. John Avant, president, Life Action**

"These pages include a firm view of the role of the Holy Spirit in evangelism that is often missed. The faculty at NOBTS has given us a volume filled with solid biblical theology and urgent evangelistic strategy. It is up to us to share the gospel in every possible way, and we have been given a remarkable path to follow."

—**Dr. Jimmy Draper, president emeritus, LifeWay**

"What a terrific compilation of teachings on evangelism! *Engage: Tools for Contemporary Evangelism* provides strong biblical and historical reasoning for reaching people with the message of the gospel. It also addresses many of the theological issues that have kept Christian leaders from winning people to Christ and helping them to grow in their walk with him. However, it doesn't just provide theoretical conclusions. It gives practical help in doing evangelism. It's a great resource that needs to be in the toolbox of every pastor and Christian leader. What a great honor for Dr. Chuck Kelley to have this compiled as a gift for his service in God's kingdom through New Orleans Baptist Theological Seminary. And what a great gift to the body of Christ at this moment in history! Read it, and be blessed. Then apply it and reach the world for Christ!"

—**Dr. Sammy Tippit, author, international evangelist, and president of Conference of Southern Baptist Evangelists**

"I love this book! *Engage: Tools for Contemporary Evangelism* is a tremendous resource for anyone interested in the Great Commission. It is well written, engaging, and practical. In a time that desperately needs to reclaim the value and importance of evangelism, this book shows us how we can be involved in God's great work of saving sinners. Read this book and benefit from the guidance, scholarship, and passion that it provides. I'm praying God uses this book to make an eternal impact!"

—**Dr. Doug Munton, senior pastor, First Baptist Church, O'Fallon, IL, author, and online professor of preaching and evangelism**

"Evangelism, as an academic discipline, began among Southern Baptists shortly after the turn of the twentieth century. From that time to the present, names like Scarborough, Autrey, Drummond, Leavell, Fish, and Miles have become synonymous with evangelism in Southern Baptist academies, churches, and the Convention. Without a doubt, Dr. Charles S. Kelley Jr. belongs among these men's ranks and reputations. Just as with Drs. Drummond, Fish, and Miles, faculty members and former students have determined upon Dr. Kelley's retirement that his evangelistic ministry, writings, and work are so monumental that they have complied essays in order to compose a Festschrift entitled *Engage: Tools for Contemporary Evangelism*. *Engage* is a comprehensive resource on evangelism that will fuel the fire of passionate soul-winning, assist believers by presenting the gospel and then declaring to unbelievers, 'Here's hope,' and elicit in readers, as it did in me, an exuberant, 'Wow!'"

—**Dr. Matt Queen, associate professor and L. R. Scarborough Chair of Evangelism ("The Chair of Fire"), associate director of doctoral programs, Southwestern Baptist Theological Seminary, Fort Worth, TX**

"It is fitting that a Festschrift in honor of Dr. Chuck Kelley represent the clear passion of his life—evangelism. Each essay displays Dr. Kelley's passion tied to the local church, taught by his colleagues, and tethered to an invitation—*Engage!* I strongly recommend this book as a valuable and practical resource for training in church evangelism."

—**Dr. Thomas P. Johnston, professor of evangelism, Midwestern Baptist Theological Seminary and Spurgeon College**

"With the rapid change of culture, scholars in the academic classroom as well as congregants in the local church long desperately to possess a resource for engaging their culture through the Great Commission. Continuing in the evangelistic zeal of Dr. Kelley, this timely Festschrift, written in his honor, provides biblical and historical foundations necessary for effective soul-winning, addresses theological issues germane to the modern-church, yet delivers practical assistance to the local church. *Engage: Tools for Contemporary Evangelism* rightly underscores the unity between the motivations for evangelism and the practice of it. After reading this work, you are sure to have the necessary tools to engage in contemporary evangelism."

—**Dr. Carl J. Bradford, assistant professor of evangelism, Southwestern Baptist Theological Seminary, Fort Worth, TX**

ENGAGE

TOOLS FOR CONTEMPORARY EVANGELISM

A Festschrift Presented upon the Retirement of Dr. Charles S. "Chuck" Kelley Jr. in Honor of His Life and Work

WM. CRAIG PRICE
GENERAL EDITOR

NEW ORLEANS
BAPTIST THEOLOGICAL SEMINARY

ANSWERING GOD'S CALL

New Orleans, LA

Published in conjunction with Iron Stream Media
100 Missionary Ridge
Birmingham, AL 35242
IronStreamMedia.com

© 2019 by New Orleans Baptist Theological Seminary
All rights reserved. First printing 2019.

No part of this publication may be reproduced, stored in a retrieval system, or transmitted in any form or by any means—electronic, mechanical, photocopying, recording, or otherwise—without the prior written permission of the publisher.

Names: Kelley, Charles S., honouree. | Price, Wm. Craig, editor.
Title: Engage : tools for contemporary evangelism : a festschrift presented upon the retirement of Dr. Chuck S. Kelley Jr. in honor of his life and work / Wm. Craig Price, general editor, New Orleans Baptist Theological Seminary, New Orleans, Louisiana.
Description: First [edition]. | Birmingham : Iron Stream Media, 2019. | Includes bibliographical references and index.
Identifiers: LCCN 2019019013 | ISBN 9781563093173 (permabind)
Subjects: LCSH: Missions. | Evangelistic work. | Witness bearing (Christianity)
Classification: LCC BV2030 .E54 2019 | DDC 269/.2--dc23
LC record available at https://lccn.loc.gov/2019019013

All Scripture quotations, unless otherwise indicated, are taken from the New American Standard Bible®, Copyright © 1960, 1962, 1963, 1968, 1971, 1972, 1973, 1975, 1977, 1995 by The Lockman Foundation Used by permission.

Scripture quotations marked (KJV) are taken from The Holy Bible, King James Version.

Scripture quotations marked (NIV) are taken from the Holy Bible, New International Version®, NIV®. Copyright © 1973, 1978, 1984, 2011 by Biblica, Inc.™ Used by permission of Zondervan. All rights reserved worldwide. www.zondervan.com The "NIV" and "New International Version" are trademarks registered in the United States Patent and Trademark Office by Biblica, Inc.™

Scripture quotations marked (NKJV) are taken from the New King James Version®. Copyright © 1982 by Thomas Nelson. Used by permission. All rights reserved.

Scripture quotations marked (NLT) are taken from the *Holy Bible*, New Living Translation, copyright © 1996, 2004, 2007, 2013 by Tyndale House Foundation. Used by permission of Tyndale House Publishers, Inc., Carol Stream, Illinois 60188. All rights reserved.

Scripture quotations marked (ESV) are from The Holy Bible, English Standard Version® (ESV®), copyright © 2001 by Crossway, a publishing ministry of Good News Publishers. Used by permission. All rights reserved.

ISBN: 978-1-56309-651-8
Ebook: 978-1-56309-318-0

1 2 3 4 5—23 22 21 20 19

Contents

Contributors x
Foreword xi
    Blake Newsom
Preface xiii
    Wm. Craig Price
A Short Biography of Dr. Charles S. "Chuck" Kelley Jr.. xviii
A List of Publications by Dr. Charles S. Kelley Jr. xxv

Part 1: Biblical and Historical Basis for Contemporary Evangelism

Biblical Basis

    Motivations for Fulfilling the Great Commission 3
        Preston Nix
    The Role of the Holy Spirit in Evangelism: Aspects of
    Lukan Pneumatology 15
        Wm. Craig Price and Mario Melendez
    Evangelism and Context in the New Testament 33
        William Warren
    The Role of Evangelism in Missions: The Relationship
    of Word and Deed 48
        Ken Taylor

Historical Basis

> The History of Evangelism............................61
> > Archie England and Ronnie McLellan
>
> The Blood of Christians Is Seed: Christian Suffering and Evangelism in Early Christianity and the Contemporary World...................................83
> > Rex D. Butler

Part 2: Theological Issues in Contemporary Evangelism

> The Theology of Evangelism..........................107
> > Steve W. Lemke
>
> A Biblical Theology of Salvation......................131
> > Adam Harwood
>
> Is Jesus Really the Only Savior? Critiquing Common Objections to Christian Particularism...................149
> > Robert B. Stewart
>
> Engaging Mere Morality in Evangelism.................165
> > Jeffrey Riley
>
> Worship and Evangelism.............................177
> > Gregory A. Woodward

Part 3: Practical Applications for Contemporary Evangelism

Personal Evangelism

> Leading People to Jesus..............................203
> > Bo Rice
>
> Counseling and the Great Commission...................216
> > Brooke Osborn and Lorien Fleener

Evangelism Strategy

> The Role of Prayer in Evangelism......................225
> > Jeffrey C. Farmer

The Pastor as Evangelist............................241
  Reggie Ogea
Strategize to Evangelize..............................260
  Jake Roudkovski
Outreach and Evangelism through Sunday School
and Small Group Ministry............................279
  Randall Stone

Target Group Evangelism

Evangelism and Children............................303
  Donna Peavey and Stephanie Cline
Evangelizing Youth and College Students...............317
  David Odom
Men and Women in Evangelism: Keys to Relational
Outreach and Disciplemaking.........................335
  Jody Dean and Emily Dean
Evangelism and Senior Adults........................346
  Bill Day
Evangelism through Social Work Ministries..............360
  Loretta Rivers and Jeanine Bozeman

Multicultural Evangelism

Evangelism, Church Planting, and the New Testament....371
  Damian Emetuche
What Kind of Neighbor Am I?........................390
    A Sermon by David Fleming, Pastor of
    Champion Forest Baptist Church
Transitioning a Monocultural Church to a Multicultural
Ministry..405
    An Interview with the Pastor and Executive Team Members
    of Champion Forest Baptist Church, Houston, Texas

Evangelism Resources

 Utilizing Library Resources Effectively for Evangelistic
 Research, Writing, and Application.....................429
  Eric Benoy and Jeff Griffin

Part 4: Preaching and Contemporary Evangelism

 The Soul of the Evangelistic Expository Sermon: From
 Broadus and Criswell to Rogers and Kelley..............445
  Adam Hughes

 Decisional Preaching: Essential Elements of
 the Evangelistic Sermon...............................464
  Preston Nix

 Invitations with Integrity............................480
  Mark Tolbert

Author Index..493

Scripture Index...499

Subject Index...506

Contributor Biographies.....................................513

ENGAGE

Contributors

Eric Benoy	Blake Newsom
Jeanine Bozeman	Preston Nix
Rex Butler	David Odom
Stephanie Cline	Reggie Ogea
Bill Day	Brooke Osborn
Emily Dean	Donna Peavey
Jody Dean	Wm. Craig Price
Damian Emetuche	Bo Rice
Archie England	Jeffrey Riley
Jeffrey C. Farmer	Loretta Rivers
Lorien Fleener	Jake Roudkovski
Jeff Griffin	Robert B. Stewart
Adam Harwood	Randall Stone
Adam Hughes	Ken Taylor
Mark Johnson	Mark Tolbert
Steve Lemke	William Warren
Ronnie McLellan	Gregory A. Woodward
Mario Melendez	

Foreword

Blake Newsom

Christianity in America is struggling. As morality decreases and spiritual desperation increases, passion for the gospel among God's people seems to be in hibernation. Christians are less interested in sharing the message of Jesus even as more people need to hear the message of Jesus. As the statistics of a rising demographic of people uninterested in Christianity weary us, the church is busier than ever, but about less essential matters.

In times such as these, we need messengers sent from God to keep us focused in a world of distractions. Dr. Charles S. Kelley Jr. is such a man, one who has given his life to the spread of the gospel and, consequently, has had a profound impact on the Southern Baptist community. Dr. Kelley's sermons have inspired generations to make evangelism a priority, and his lectures on contemporary issues in evangelism have impacted scores of students and professors. When others have gotten sidetracked or off track, Dr. Kelley has been a faithful and steady voice reminding us to return to the Great Commission. However, his passion for evangelism isn't reserved for a pulpit or lectern, and his burden for souls isn't theoretical or devoid of practicality. I have personally seen his passion and theory overflow into practice, engaging people individually with the gospel in a loving, sincere manner.

During his tenure as president of New Orleans Baptist Theological Seminary (NOBTS), Dr. Kelley assembled passionate and gifted scholars and practitioners to equip churches in fulfilling the Great Commission. It has been my great honor to serve alongside the scholars and practitioners responsible for this book's content, which is filled with the overflow of wisdom that will benefit the scholar and student as well as the pastor and practitioner. The contributors have a heart for the Lord, the church, and the lost. Their students and churches throughout the world have been blessed by their wisdom and expertise, and I have no doubt the readers of this work will be blessed by their contributions as well.

Within thirty years, the New Testament church pierced the heart of Rome with the life-changing gospel of Jesus. The modern church needs a reawakening of that first-century passion to propel a new surge of gospel revolutionaries into the highways and alleys of the world. My prayer is this book will provide the spark and material for a movement that will turn the world upside down with the message of Jesus. I could think of no better way to honor the life and legacy of Dr. Charles Kelley.

PREFACE

Wm. Craig Price

I first met Dr. Charles S. Kelley Jr. while attending the 2004 Annual Evangelical Theological Society Meeting in Austin, Texas. He was interviewing me for the position of dean of students for NOBTS. During our interview conversation, Dr. Kelley expressed a concept I have never forgotten. With great excitement he talked about changing the world through the evangelistic work and ministry of NOBTS. Dr. Kelley lives, breathes, preaches, and teaches evangelism. Evangelism is his passion, his focus, and his life.

This book is a Festschrift—a "celebration writing"—to honor Dr. Kelley on the occasion of his retirement after more than four decades of faithful service to the Lord at NOBTS. All of the contributing authors are associated with Dr. Kelley through some aspect of NOBTS. The chapters are written by current or recent faculty members, doctoral students, pastors, staff members, counselors, church planters, and evangelists who are all committed to evangelism within the context of their own disciplines and callings. They are women and men with a variety of credentials from a diversity of cultures, ethnicities, and academic disciplines. This collection of authors represents Leavell College of NOBTS and each division in the graduate school of NOBTS. This group of authors is knit together by our belief in and commitment to evangelism and by our deep love and respect for Dr. Kelley.

As Christians, we believe the most effective way to change the world is by sharing the good news of Jesus Christ with all who have not heard this message or have not yet believed it. We have all observed how Christ transforms people's lives from brokenness into wholeness. We have witnessed the power of the gospel to change the world by changing people, one life at a time. This plan has been in the heart of our God since the beginning of time, and evangelism is his method for accomplishing the plan—the plan of salvation. We share a deep-seated conviction that the church must strive to be effective and relevant in our current society and culture. To accomplish this goal, we must engage our society and culture with the most effective tools and knowledge available. Hence, the title of this book is *Engage: Tools for Contemporary Evangelism*.

Part One of this book lays the biblical and historical foundations critical for effective, contemporary evangelism. The prominent components of a biblical foundation for evangelism begin with the motivation of the Great Commission, the role of the Holy Spirit, the context of New Testament evangelism, and the missional crossing of cultural barriers with the gospel. Next, a historical foundation for evangelism is presented with a comprehensive, historical review of evangelism from the time of Jesus to the present. The suffering of the early Christians by persecution provides us with a perspective of their convictions and the cost they paid for following Christ. All these elements combine to provide the foundations for evangelism today.

Part Two consists of articles engaging current theological issues and some of the cultural challenges to contemporary evangelism. Theology matters in evangelism, and included is an accurate overview of the key theological components necessary for every evangelistic encounter. Next, a "whole-Bible view" is outlined for a biblical, theological understanding of the major biblical terminology related to the work of salvation. The modern evangelist will most certainly confront a vast array of philosophical and ethical challenges in our society. How should believers interact with a person who questions, "Is Jesus *really* the only Savior?" How do believers answer questions pertaining to the ethical and moral demands of Christianity without resorting to the extremes of legalism or license? How do we retain the biblical focus of evangelistic fervor and remain healthy in our contemporary worship experience? These chapters will inform and challenge our efforts to share our faith with theological soundness and balance.

Part Three is the largest portion of the book and contains articles written to provide practical help for pastors, staff members, and church members alike. The first section provides the reader with information related to personal evangelism for all believers. It provides a clear understanding of the spiritual power available to every believer and the practical and indispensable components of an evangelistic encounter. It also addresses the multiple daily situations where church members can reach out to other people in their brokenness—from the homeless to the hospitalized, from our local schools to our own spiritual development. We are called by the Great Commission to be prepared to minister to all people.

The second section includes articles that will help the local church engage in strategic planning for building an evangelistic church ministry. Prayer evangelism is not only biblical, but it is foundational for this purpose. Evangelistic churches do not just happen. They are most effective when the pastor takes the lead in evangelism. Next, churches must develop intentional, informed, and spiritual strategies to carry out effective and comprehensive church evangelism. These elements are enhanced and reinforced when the internal structure of the small groups and Sunday School interaction is focused for outreach and evangelism. Effective practices that lead to success are presented.

The third section develops the concept of target group evangelism. Experts who have spent years in practical ministry offer their advice, wisdom, and tips for reaching children, youth and college students, men and women, senior adults, and, broadening the scope, the community through social ministries. Each of these chapters contains helpful tactics for structuring evangelism in any local church setting.

American demographics are changing so rapidly that urban and suburban churches must reexamine how to engage all cultures and ethnicities with a multicultural perspective of ministry. We are now a diverse nation ethnically and culturally. In the Great Commission Jesus commanded that we take the gospel to all nations—and God is bringing the nations to us! How do we reach them? Failure to negotiate these changes will have a detrimental effect upon our churches. If we fail to reach out to all ethnicities and cultures, we risk becoming irrelevant in our cause for Christ, and we could miss our opportunity for affecting change in our society and culture through the power of the gospel. Our number of baptisms is and has been on the decline in the Southern Baptist Convention. How do we turn this trend around?

The fourth section addresses and answers this question with one of the most culturally relevant needs of our time . . . multicultural ministry. The first chapter in this section begins with the topic of planting new churches in multicultural settings. The author presents the statistical data for why we must discard old church planting strategies and replace them with multicultural strategies and approaches. You will find vital information for helping your church understand the trends and the need for this change. Next, we include a sermon on multicultural ministry from a prominent Southern Baptist pastor who issues a challenge to us from the Gospel of Luke: "Who Is *Not* My Neighbor?" This sermon challenges the unbiblical thinking and attitudes that neglect reaching out to different ethnicities who live in the "shadow of our steeples." Following this sermon, we include the full transcription from an interview with this pastor and his multicultural staff. Read how this Houston pastor led his predominantly white, monocultural church to transition successfully and peacefully into a thriving, exciting multicultural, multi-campus ministry that is fulfilling the Great Commission by reaching "the nations" for Christ. This section closes with a chapter on how to navigate modern library systems in order to discover their vast treasure of resources and knowledge on evangelism.

Part Four appropriately rounds out the book with a section on contemporary, evangelistic preaching. Here the preacher will find resources for expository preaching, "decisional preaching," and how to call the hearers in our congregations—with integrity—to make a decision for Christ.

We hope and pray that every person who reads this book will receive practical help, inspiration, and a challenge to engage in reaching all unbelievers in his or her ministry. We have expressed our hearts and expertise in these pages because we believe in the power of the gospel of Jesus Christ to "change the world" through evangelism in any context. Collectively, we offer this gift of scholarship to honor and pay tribute to Dr. Charles S. Kelley Jr. who has sought tirelessly to fulfill his own personal ministry and calling at NOBTS to "do the work of an evangelist" (2 Tim 4:5).

A Short Biography of Dr. Charles S. "Chuck" Kelley Jr.

Family Background

Charles Seymoure Kelley Jr. (affectionately called Chuck) was born July 27, 1952, to Charles Seymoure Kelley and Doris Rae Weisiger Kelley. Chuck was their fourth child and first son. Later, a fourth daughter was born, giving them four daughters and one son. Firstborn daughter Dorothy Jean Kelley Patterson married Dr. Paige Patterson, retired from three presidencies in theological institutions, and lives in Dallas, Texas. Kathleen Rae Kelley is a retired schoolteacher living in Las Vegas, Nevada. Charlene Sue Kelley Coe married Greg Coe and is a retired nurse living in Dallas, Texas. Chuck married Rhonda Harrington Kelley and served as president of the New Orleans Baptist Theological Seminary. Eileen Marie Kelley Turrentine married Rev. Steve Turrentine, a retired pastor, and lives in Tyler, Texas.

Charles S. Kelley Sr. was partner and later owner of the Kelley-Hixson Funeral Home in Beaumont, Texas, where his wife Doris worked faithfully as his bookkeeper after the children completed their high school education. Growing up, Chuck worked in his father's business and was expected to take leadership of the company in the future. Acknowledging Chuck's call to the ministry, Charles sold the funeral home when he retired in 1991 after forty-two years in the funeral business and moved with his wife to Dallas, Texas, to undergo cancer treatments.

Chuck was born and reared in Beaumont, Texas, where his family was faithful members of First Baptist Church. His father was a deacon, and his mother directed a Sunday School department and worked in missionary organizations. Chuck likes to say he "started going to church nine months before he was born." Chuck was involved in all age-level organizations for children including Sunbeams, Royal Ambassadors, choir, and Bible Drill competition.

Chuck attended Sally Curtis Elementary School in Beaumont from kindergarten through sixth grade. He then attended George Marshall Junior High School in Beaumont from the seventh through ninth grades. He began playing football in junior high and continued playing for Forest Park High School. He played offensive center and defensive lineman. As though it had just happened yesterday, Chuck vividly retells the story of the football game when he intercepted the ball and ran for a touchdown to win the game for the Trojans!

Chuck made a personal profession of faith and surrendered to the ministry during his high school years. He preached his first sermon at his home church on Christmas Eve of his senior year in high school. Chuck was president of his senior high school class at Forest Park and was asked to give the graduation commencement speech—the first student to ever be invited to speak for graduation. Also, during Chuck's senior year of high school, evangelist Bob Harrington, "The Chaplain of Bourbon Street," conducted a crusade in Beaumont. Chuck was instrumental in getting Bob Harrington into his high school to speak where he introduced "Brother Bob" to a general assembly of the entire student body. Brother Bob talked about his daughters Rhonda and Mitzi, whom Chuck would meet later at university.

College

When the time came for Chuck to decide where to go to college, he knew he wanted to go anywhere but Baylor University. However, God had a different plan and led him clearly in that direction. He loaded up all his worldly possessions in his Chevy Impala and drove five hours to Waco, Texas. As a freshman, he lived in Penland dormitory and became involved in the Baptist Student Union (BSU). He pledged the fraternity Kappa Omega Tau specifically to be a witness.

During his sophomore year, Chuck pastored a very small church in Ireland, Texas. Then he was asked to join the staff of the BSU as the freshman director. He discipled college men in the dorms during the week and was instrumental in reinventing the Baylor back-to-school retreat for freshmen students. During college, he also began his itinerant ministry preaching revivals and lead youth camps around the state of Texas. It was during college Chuck felt his call to ministry was specifically to evangelism. He majored in philosophy and minored in religion and received a Bachelor of Arts degree in 1974.

Marriage

Chuck met Rhonda Harrington at the first meeting of the freshmen BSU. He was elected president, and she was elected vice president. They got to know each other by serving together in leadership. Rhonda asked Chuck on a date in January of their freshman year for a special event when the female students were expected to extend the invitation to the male students. They began dating during their freshman year at Baylor, started "going steady" in their sophomore year, got "pinned" their junior year (Chuck gave Rhonda his fraternity pin in a formal ceremony), and became engaged their senior year. They truly had a fairytale romance.

Chuck and Rhonda were married at First Baptist Church of New Orleans, Louisiana, on Friday, June 21, 1974, at 8:00 p.m. He jokingly says it was truly the longest day of the year. After their marriage they returned to Waco, Texas, for Rhonda to complete her masters in speech pathology and for Chuck to work full time with the BSU. Their plans were to head to seminary in Fort Worth where most of their ministry friends were going. However, just weeks before it was time to move, the Lord spoke separately to each of them, redirecting them to New Orleans Baptist Theological Seminary (NOBTS) for the purpose of evangelism and missions outside the Bible Belt where Chuck had always lived.

Seminary and Evangelism Ministry

In August 1975, Chuck and Rhonda moved to New Orleans and into student housing on the campus of NOBTS. Chuck began working in the French Quarter for the ministry of Rhonda's father as the crusade logistics coordinator until Bob's ministry ended with a moral failure. When Bob left his marriage, his family, and the ministry, Chuck was forced to reconsider his call to the ministry. God affirmed Chuck's personal call to evangelism, and he and Rhonda began their itinerant ministry called Innovative Evangelism during those seminary years. Chuck has spoken in hundreds of churches, evangelism conferences, state convention meetings, associational meetings, and evangelism training experiences. Rhonda has spoken at hundreds of events relating to ministry to and through the women of the church. Together they have led a number of marriage enrichment conferences.

While Chuck was in seminary, Rhonda was a speech pathologist at the Children's Hospital of New Orleans. She continued "putting her husband through school" by working as a speech pathologist in private practice until she was hired by Ochsner Clinic in 1978 to start their speech pathology program. She received her doctor of philosophy degree in special education and speech pathology from the University of New Orleans in 1983 and became director of the Division of Communicative Disorders at Ochsner Clinic, serving as the only woman and only PhD on a medical staff with one hundred and ninety-nine male medical doctors. Rhonda continued at Ochsner until 1996. Later the Lord led her toward focusing on women's ministry, and she became a nationally known speaker and author in this area.

Chuck received his master of divinity in Biblical studies from NOBTS in 1978 and felt called to enter the doctoral program. He received a doctor of theology in preaching in 1983 and was surprised with an invitation by the provost to join the faculty of NOBTS. While his ministry call had always been to evangelism, Dr. Kelley began to see God was redirecting him to equip ministers for the task of evangelism.

He joined the faculty in August 1983 and was the youngest faculty member at that time.

NOBTS Faculty Member and President

Dr. Kelley continued preaching revivals and leading evangelism conferences as he taught at the seminary. He became a professor of evangelism and later the Roland Q. Leavell Professor of Evangelism, the director of the Leavell Center for Evangelism and Church Growth, and the chairman of the Division of Pastoral Ministries. He authored a number of books and articles on evangelism, as well as developed effective witnessing tools for the church. His teaching specializations have included evangelism and church growth. In 1996, Dr. Kelley was again surprised by the leadership of the Lord when he was approached by the NOBTS presidential search committee.

On March 1, 1996, Dr. Kelley became the eighth president of NOBTS, following the twenty-year tenure of Dr. Landrum P. Leavell II, who had hired and mentored him. He was the first faculty member to become president of a Southern Baptist Convention (SBC) seminary. God gave Dr. Kelley a clear vision to lead his beloved School of Providence and Prayer.

- **Our Mission**—The mission of NOBTS is to equip leaders to fulfill the Great Commission and the Great Commandments through the local church and its ministries.
- **Our Target: Healthy Churches**—The health of a seminary is determined by the health of the churches its graduates lead.
- **Our Core Values**:

    Doctrinal Integrity—Knowing the Bible is the Word of God, we believe it, teach it, proclaim it, and submit to it.

    Spiritual Vitality—We are a worshipping community emphasizing both personal spirituality and gathering together as a seminary family for the praise and adoration of God and instruction in His Word.

Mission Focus—We are not here to get an education or to give one. We are here to change the world by fulfilling the Great Commission and the Great Commandments through the local church and its ministries.

Characteristic Excellence—What we do, we do to the utmost of our abilities and resources as a testimony to the glory of our Lord and Savior Jesus Christ.

Servant Leadership—We follow the model of Jesus and exert leadership and influence through the nurture and encouragement of those around us.

The first few months of Dr. Kelley's presidency were extremely busy with a ten-year accrediting visit and hosting the Southern Baptist Convention in New Orleans with the alumni luncheon on campus. The NOBTS president's home was renovated in a short three-month period and hosted the May 1996 graduation reception as well as an alumni open house during the SBC. The inauguration ceremony was held later that October.

By God's providence, NOBTS has accomplished many milestones under Dr. Kelley's leadership as president, including:

- More than doubling student enrollment.
- More than doubling endowment gifts.
- Increasing and diversifying faculty.
- Enlarging the scholarship program to include specific assistance for minorities, PhD students, and others.
- Launching the Caskey Center for Church Excellence providing full scholarships and other support for those serving in the typical (smaller) churches of the SBC.

- Developing and implementing a church-centered curriculum for undergraduate and graduate studies through a multiple delivery system.
- Twice rebuilding campus, once due to extensive damage by Formosan termites and once due to damage from flooding after Hurricane Katrina.
- Weathering the worst natural disaster in the history of the United States and continuing classes without a campus as well as faculty and students scattered across the country.
- Construction of forty-nine new buildings, including new housing for students, faculty, and staff.
- Launching seminary education programs in maximum-security prisons with transformational effect in the prison culture.
- Celebrating NOBTS's one-hundredth anniversary during the 2017–2018 academic year with numerous special events and campaigns.
- Realizing faculty dreams with the creation of centers of specialized study (H. Milton Haggard Center for New Testament Textual Studies, Greer-Heard Point/Counterpoint Lecture, Michael and Ginger Moskau Institute for Archaeology, among others).
- Developing the Mission Lab program to host more than 2,500 people a year to New Orleans for the purpose of volunteer mission work all over the city.

Dr. Kelley announced his retirement in October 2018. He served as chancellor during the remainder of the 2018–2019 academic year. In retirement, he is eager to return to focusing on his beloved field of evangelism. Burdened by the decline of baptisms in the Southern Baptist Convention, Dr. Kelley desires to help lead churches to refocus on evangelism.

A List of Publications by Dr. Charles S. Kelley Jr.

Doctoral Dissertation

Kelley, Charles S., Jr. "An Investigation of the Changing Role of the Revival Meeting in the Southern Baptist Program of Evangelism,1947–1980." ThD diss., New Orleans Baptist Theological Seminary, 1983.

Books

Kelley, Charles S., Jr. *Fuel the Fire: Lessons from the History of Southern Baptist Evangelism*. A Treasury of Baptist Theology, edited by Paige Patterson and Jason G. Duesing. Nashville, TN: B&H Academic, 2018.

———. "Back to the Future: An Analysis of Southern Baptist Evangelism." *Baptist Why or Why Not Revisited*. Edited by Timothy George and Richard Land, Vol. 12. Library of Baptist Classics. Nashville, TN: Broadman & Holman, 1997.

Kelley, Charles S., Jr., Richard D. Land, and R. Albert Mohler Jr. *The Baptist Faith and Message*. Nashville, TN: LifeWay Press, 2007.

Kelley, Charles S., Jr. "How to Get A Piece of the Power." *Fifty Great Soul-Winning Motivational Sermons*. Compiled by Jack R. Smith. Atlanta, GA: Home Mission Board of the SBC, 1994.

———. *Learning to Share My Faith*. Nashville, TN: LifeWay Press, 1994.

———. *How Did They Do It? The Story of Southern Baptist Evangelism.* New Orleans, LA: Insight Press, 1993.

———. *Interstate Hope: Adult Roman Road Witness Training Learner's Guide.* Atlanta, GA: Home Mission Board of the Southern Baptist Convention, 1993.

———. "Training for Evangelism." *Evangelism Today & Tomorrow.* Compiled by Charles L. Chaney and Granville Watson. Nashville, TN: Broadman Press, 1993.

———. *Show Me the Way! Solid Answers to Hard Questions about the Bible.* Nashville, TN: Convention Press, 1991.

———. "My Calling: Evangelism." In *How God Called.* Compiled by Alice Magill. Nashville, TN: Convention Press, 1986.

Editing Collaboration

Towns, Elmer L., ed. *Evangelism and Church Growth: A Practical Encyclopedia.* Ventura, CA: Regal Books, 1995. (Charles Kelley served on Editorial Committee).

Journal Articles

Kelley, Charles S., Jr. "Five Essentials of Evangelistic Growth." *Growing Churches* 8, no. 4 (Summer 1998): 20–23.

———. "Back to the Future: An Analysis of Southern Baptist Evangelism." *The Theological Educator* 51 (Spring 1995): 149–57.

———. "Involving people in your sermons." *Church Administration* 37, no. 4 (January 1995): 11–13.

———. "Baby Boomers: A Pastor's Bibliography." *The Theological Educator* 45 (Spring 1992): 31–35.

———. "Ethical Issues in Evangelism: A Pyramid of Concerns." *The Theological Educator* 46 (Fall 1992): 33–40.

———. "Reaching the Children of the Boomer." *Youth Ministry Update* 2, no. 4 (January 1992): 5–6.

———. "Ten of My Top Ten." *Evangelism* 5, no. 2 (February 1991): 92–96.

———. "A Theological-Historical Look at Revivalism in the SBC." *Search* 20, no. 3 (Spring 1990): 29–37.

———. "Issues in Evangelism." *The Theological Educator* 41 (Spring 1990): 166–75.

———. "Training for Evangelism: How to Select & Design a Program." *Evangelism* (August 1989): 145–50.

———. "Excellence: Exploring a Commitment." *The Theological Educator* 33 (Spring 1986): 3–5.

NOBTS News Magazine Articles

Kelley, Charles S., Jr. "Dear NOBTS Friends and Family." *Vision*, Fall 2018.

———. "Providence & Prayer." *Vision*, Spring 2018.

———. "Foundations Matter." *Vision*, Fall 2017.

———. "Happy Birthday, NOBTS!" *Vision*, Spring 2017.

———. "God's Problem, God's Solution." *Vision*, Fall 2016.

———. "The Great Commission: Where Are We Now?" *Vision*, Spring 2016.

———. "Answering the Call." *Vision*, Fall 2015.

———. "Who Are We?" *Vision*, Fall 2014.

———. "And Then God Laughed." *Vision*, Spring/Summer 2014.

———. "Everyone Matters." *Vision*, Fall 2013.

———. "School of Providence and Prayer." *Vision*, Spring/Summer 2013.

———. "What Does Providence Look Like?" *Vision*, Fall 2012.

———. "A Tale of Two Seminaries." *Vision*, Spring 2012.

———. "Just Imagine . . ." *Vision*, Fall 2011.

———. "Approaching the Rubicon." *Vision*, Spring 2011.

———. "Five Memories of Katrina." *Vision*, Fall 2010.

———. "A Great Commission Resurgence, New Orleans Style." *Vision*, Spring/Summer 2010.

———. "Bang for the Buck: Southern Baptists and the Problem of World Missions." *Vision*, Fall 2009.

———. "Through a Glass Darkly." *Vision*, Spring/Summer 2009.

———. "Happy Birthday to NOBTS." *Vision*, Winter 2008.

———. "A Celebration of Greatness." *Vision*, Fall 2008.

———. "President's Perspective." *Vision*, Summer 2008.

———. "The Economic Impact of Hurricane Katrina on New Orleans Seminary." *Vision*, Spring 2008.

———. "President's Perspective." *Vision*, Holiday 2007.

———. "President's Perspective." "How is the seminary doing?" *Vision*, Fall 2007.

———. "President's Perspective." *Vision*, Spring/Summer 2007.

———. "President's Perspective." *Vision*, Holiday 2006.

———. "President's Perspective." *Vision*, Katrina Special Edition, Fall 2006.

———. "Thank You! NOBTS Is Back!" *Vision*, Hurricane Katrina Special Edition, Spring 2006.

———. "A Christmas Like No Other." *Vision*, Holiday 2005.

———. "Why I am a Southern Baptist, Part 2." *Vision*, Spring 2005.

———. "President's Perspective." *Vision*, Holiday 2004.

———. "Living Inside a Miracle." *Vision*, Summer 2004.

———. "Yesterday, Today and Tomorrow." *Vision*, Fall 2004.

———. "Building a Legacy." *Vision*, Spring 2003.

———. "Greetings in the Name of Our Lord and Savior Jesus Christ!" *Vision*, Holiday 2003.

———. "Transforming to Preserve our Heritage." *Vision*, Summer 2003.

———. "Changing the Course of History." *Vision*, Summer 2002.

———. "Season of the Family." *Vision*, Spring 2002.

———. "Spiritual Vitality Foundational to Preparing Next Generation of Southern Baptist Leaders." *Vision*, Holiday 2002.

———. "President's Perspective." *Vision*, Fall 2001.

———. "A Word from the President: New Dawning Reveals New Horizons." *Vision*, New Horizons Issue 2001.

———. "Count Your Blessings." *Vision*, Fall 2000.

———. "It's Happening!" *Vision*, Spring 2000.

———. "Knee Deep in Miracles." *Vision*, Holiday 2000.

———. "Kelley Recounts Pilgrimage to Presidency." *Vision*, 1996 Special Edition.

———. "The President's Perspective." *Vision*, 1996 Special Edition

Denominational Curriculum

Kelley, Charles S., Jr., gen. ed. "Genesis 25–50," *Explore the Bible*. (Winter 2018–2019).

———. "The Witnessing Muscle." *Adult Leadership* (September 1991).

———. "What Is Your Story?" *Adult Leadership* (August 1991).

———. "Taking Steps to Meet Jesus." *Adult Leadership* (July 1991).

———. "Sharing the Gospel with Our Teens." *Adult Leadership* (July 1991).

———. "Telling Our Children." *Adult Leadership* (June 1991).

———. "Mapping the Way." *Adult Leadership* (May 1991).

———. "The ABC's of Salvation." *Adult Leadership* (April 1991).

———. "Working Together." *Adult Leadership* (April 1991).

———. "Is God a Stranger to You?" *Adult Leadership* (February 1991).

———. "Introducing God." *Adult Leadership* (February 1991).

———. "Your Secret Ally." *Adult Leadership* (January 1991).

———. "A Tool for Witnessing." *Adult Leadership* (December 1990).

———. "Begin with Prayer." *Adult Leadership* (November 1990).

———. "Highway to Heaven." *Adult Leadership* (October 1990).

———. "News to Lost Adults." *Adult Leadership* (October 1990).

———. "A Transformed Life-style." *Baptist Youth* (April, May, June 1986).

———. "Relating to Others." *Baptist Youth* (April, May, June 1986).

———. "Keeping the Word." *Baptist Youth* (April, May, June 1986).

———. "From Milk to Meat." *Baptist Youth* (April, May, June 1986).

Pamphlets

Kelley, Charles S., Jr. *A Program of Cooperation: A Rejoinder to David Hankins's The Relation of the Southern Baptist Convention to Its Entities*. New Orleans, LA: New Orleans Baptist Theological Seminary, 2005.

———. *Roots of a Dilemma: SBC Entities and the Cooperative Program*. New Orleans, LA: New Orleans Baptist Theological Seminary, 2005.

———. *The Baptist Way: A Personal Perspective*. New Orleans, LA: New Orleans Baptist Theological Seminary, 2004.

———. *Why I am a Southern Baptist: The Baptist Way, Part 2*. New Orleans, LA: New Orleans Baptist Theological Seminary, 2004.

Witnessing Materials

Kelley, Charles S., Jr. *Here's Hope Roman Road Witnessing Tract*. North American Mission Board, 1994.

———. *Here's Hope Roman Road Witness Training Program*. North American Mission Board, 1994.

———. *Here's Hope Roman Road Witness Training Video*. North American Mission Board, 1994.

———. "Learning to Share My Faith." A Witness Training Module, Baptist Sunday School Board (1990; 1994).

PART 1

Biblical and Historical Basis for Contemporary Evangelism

Biblical Basis

MOTIVATIONS FOR FULFILLING THE GREAT COMMISSION

Preston Nix

God's chosen human instrument for fulfilling the Great Commission is the church. Immediately prior to his ascension, the Lord Jesus gave the church "marching orders" for carrying out his ministry of reaching the world with the saving message of the gospel. Those "marching orders" are recorded in the New Testament in the four Gospels and the book of Acts. Although the most familiar of those passages is Matt 28:18–20, Jesus also commissioned his disciples to proclaim the gospel to the whole world in Mark 16:15, Luke 24:46–48, John 20:21, and Acts 1:8. All five of these passages comprise the Great Commission of Christ to his church. Clearly Jesus expected his followers to partner with him in communicating his saving message to the lost world. The term "Great Commission" itself indicates a joint effort between two parties. The church is called to engage in a joint mission effort, a "co-mission" with Christ, to evangelize and disciple the nations.[1]

In order for the Great Commission to be fulfilled, the church and the individual members who comprise the church must be motivated

---

[1] See Preston Nix, "Commentary on Article 10: The Great Commission," in *Anyone Can Be Saved: A Defense of "Traditional" Southern Baptist Theology*, eds. David L. Allen, Eric Hankins, and Adam Harwood (Eugene, OR: Wipf & Stock, 2016), 143–145, 155.

to carry out the Great Commission. Motivation certainly is a major factor in accomplishing anything worthwhile in life. Being motivated is absolutely essential for the church and its members to carry out the "marching orders" of Christ to reach the world with the gospel. People are motivated by many factors such as guilt, fear, love, reward, recognition, and duty. What are the motivating factors that should compel the church and its members to fulfill the Great Commission? In this chapter, the answer to that question will be explored by identifying and discussing the biblical motivations for fulfilling the Great Commission. As Dr. Alvin Reid observed, "Given the recalcitrance of so many believers to share their faith, the question of why we should be interested in sharing the good news matters. ... We need a clear understanding of the why [of evangelism]."[2] Further, the hope is the content of this chapter will be used by the Holy Spirit to motivate churches to carry out the Great Commission in the communities in which the Lord has strategically placed them as well as to other parts of the world as they are obedient to engage in evangelism and missions. Dr. Will McRaney asserted, "Few churches across America are truly focused on the Great Commission. Most are focused primarily on the internal needs of their church."[3] If his assessment is accurate, that reality highlights the great need for churches to respond to the biblical motivations for fulfilling the Great Commission and reengage in the proclamation of the gospel both locally and globally.

The Commandment of Christ

The first motivation for fulfilling the Great Commission is the commandment of Christ. Put simply, the church should be motivated to

---

[2] Alvin Reid, *Evangelism Handbook: Biblical, Spiritual, Intentional, Missional* (Nashville, TN: B&H Publishing, 2009), 34.
[3] Will H. McRaney Jr. "Considering Approaches to a Great Commission Church," in *Mobilizing a Great Commission Church for Harvest: Voices and Views from the Southern Baptist Professors of Evangelism Fellowship*, ed. Thomas P. Johnston (Eugene, OR: Wipf & Stock, 2011), 42.

carry out the Great Commission first and foremost because Jesus commanded his church to do so. This motivation is one of obedience and duty. Jesus began the Great Commission passage as recorded in Matthew's Gospel account by stating, "All authority has been given to Me in heaven and on earth" (Matt 28:18). With these words, Jesus established his divine prerogative to issue the command to his followers to spread the gospel to the whole world.[4] If someone with all authority tells someone else to do something, the only appropriate response is for the person to obey the directive. Jesus commanded his disciples, "Go therefore and make disciples of all nations" (Matt 28:19), and, "Go into all the world and preach the gospel to all creation" (Mark 16:15). To the Gadarene demoniac who wanted to travel with him after being delivered from the legion of demons, Jesus said, "Go home to your people and report to them what great things the Lord has done for you, and how He had mercy on you" (Mark 5:19). In the parable of the dinner, Jesus related the words of the master to the slave, "Go out into the highways and along the hedges, and compel them to come in, so that my house may be filled" (Luke 14:23). In all these instances, the message is crystal clear. Jesus wants his followers to "go and tell" others about him and how they can know him. The Great Commission is not simply a good option for the church and its members to consider. Dr. Alvin Reid emphasized the critical "importance of heeding and obeying" what God commanded believers to do in His Word, particularly as it relates to the Great Commission, when he stated, "The Great Commission is not the Great Suggestion."[5] The Great Commission is a commandment from Christ to be carried out by every church and every Christian.

The primary motivation for fulfilling the Great Commission is the commandment of Christ. "This command alone should motivate

---

[4] Nix, "The Great Commission," 145.
[5] Reid, *Evangelism Handbook*, 38.

Christians to evangelize faithfully."[6] This truth was impressed strongly upon the mind of Dr. Waylon Bailey who related the following incident that occurred early in his ministry.

> A few weeks after my eighteenth birthday I became pastor of a small rural church. Soon after, I was asked to preach on a Sunday afternoon at the Associational Church Training Meeting. I preached on why the church and the individual believer should be evangelistic. Some of the reasons I gave were that people are lost without Christ, sinful, on the way to hell, and in need of a new birth. All of these reasons seemed convincing to me. At the conclusion of my message, our Director of Missions walked slowly toward the pulpit and in a deliberate manner said: "Brethren, it seems to me that we ought to be witnesses because Jesus told us to."
>
> The Director of Missions was exactly right, and I have never forgotten the lesson that I learned that day. While all the reasons that I had mentioned are valid, we should seek to reach people for Christ just because Jesus told us to do it. That is reason enough, and it should be motivation enough. If Jesus' command will not prompt us to share our faith, nothing will.[7]

If the commandment of Christ was the only motivation given in the Bible for the church to fulfill the Great Commission, as stated above, that "should be motivation enough." Although Jesus' command is the primary motivation for the church to carry out the Great Commission,

---

[6] John Mark Terry, *Church Evangelism* (Nashville, TN: Broadman & Holman Publishers, 1997), 7.
[7] Waylon Bailey, *As You Go: Biblical Foundations for Evangelism* (New Orleans, LA: Insight, 1981), 6–7.

Scripture contains other important considerations for fulfilling the Great Commission.

The Compassion for Christ

The second motivation for fulfilling the Great Commission is compassion for Christ. Jesus said, "If you love Me, you will keep My commandments" (John 14:15). In one of his post-resurrection appearances to his disciples on the shore of the Sea of Galilee, Jesus restored the relationship he shared with Peter in a conversation in which he asked Peter three times, "Do you love Me?" When Peter responded in the affirmative after each question, Jesus' three responses to Peter were, "Tend My lambs ... Shepherd My sheep ... Tend My sheep" (John 21:15–17). These two passages of Scripture illustrate the truth that a person's profession of love is proved by his practice of love. If a person really loves Jesus, he will demonstrate his love by doing what Jesus tells him to do.

While the first motivation for fulfilling the Great Commission covered in this chapter is a motivation of duty, this motivation is one of devotion. A believer's compassion for Christ should compel him to meet the needs of others who Jesus loves. Jesus referred to those in need as sheep. Of course, the greatest need any lost sheep has is to be found. Jesus graphically illustrated this truth in the parable of the lost sheep. He related how the shepherd with a flock of one hundred left the ninety-nine in order to find the one lost sheep that had wandered away from the rest of the flock (Luke 15:3–7). As the Great Shepherd, Jesus came "to seek and to save that which was lost" (Luke 19:10) and he has commanded his church to follow his example in bringing the hope of the gospel to a lost world. In the encounter of Jesus and Peter on the shore of the Sea of Galilee, Jesus did not ask Peter if he loved sheep. Jesus asked Peter, "Do you love Me?" Jesus then commanded Peter to take care of his sheep (John 21:15–17). If the church and the members of the church truly love Jesus, they will minister to and witness to the lost who need Christ out of their love for him. "The love of Christ living in believers moves them to have compassion on those who are lost and doomed to hell. True New Testament Christians love Jesus, and that love motivates them to witness and minister in His name."[8] Compassion for Christ should be a major motivation for the church to fulfill the Great Commission.

The Compassion of Christ

The third motivation for fulfilling the Great Commission is the compassion of Christ. Jesus loves lost people. Because Jesus loves lost people, the church should also love lost people enough to share the love of Christ with them. Jesus demonstrated he loved lost people during his earthly ministry. Jesus engaged lost people in many ways. He conversed with lost people. He spent time with lost people. He ate meals with lost people. Jesus was known as a friend of sinners and was highly criticized by the religious establishment of the day for associating with sinful people. In a summary passage of Jesus's ministry in Galilee, the Bible states, "Seeing the people, He felt compassion for them, because they were distressed and dispirited like sheep without a shepherd" (Matt 9:36). The Greek word translated "felt compassion" is one of the strongest words that could be employed for the love a person feels for another human being. The word literally means "intense feeling from one's bowels," indicating the love Jesus felt for lost people was from the innermost depths of his being.[9] Jesus declared to his disciples, "Greater love has no one than this, that one lay down his life for his friends" (John 15:13). Jesus then went to the cross and gave his life as a substitute for the sinners he loved supremely.

The greatest message the church can share with lost people is God loves them, and he wants them to repent of their sin and place their

---

[8] Terry, *Church Evangelism*, 12. See also Bill Bright, *Witnessing without Fear: How to Share Your Faith with Confidence* (Orlando, FL: NewLife Publications, 2003), 40, 50.
[9] John MacArthur, *Matthew 8–15*, The MacArthur New Testament Commentary (Chicago, IL: Moody Press, 1987), 109.

faith in his Son for their salvation. The reality of God's love for the lost was emphasized by Dr. Alvin Reid with his simple yet profound statement, "People are the objects of divine love."[10] Two familiar verses from the Bible reveal the truth of God's love for the lost. First, "But God demonstrates His own love toward us, in that while we were yet sinners, Christ died for us" (Rom 5:8). Second, "For God so loved the world, that He gave His only begotten Son, that whoever believes in Him shall not perish, but have eternal life" (John 3:16). Since the Bible declares how much both the Father and the Son love the lost, the church ought to love the lost as well and attempt to lead them to faith in Christ. As believers are to follow the example of Christ in all ways, we should have a heart of compassion for lost people and share his love with them in order that they can be saved from their sin (2 Cor 5:14).

The Coming of Christ

The fourth motivation for fulfilling the Great Commission is the coming of Christ. The Bible makes clear the fact that Jesus will return to the earth one day to judge all humankind. The Gospel writer Matthew recorded:

> But when the Son of Man comes in His glory, and all the angels with Him, then He will sit on His glorious throne. All the nations will be gathered before Him; and He will separate them from one another, as the shepherd separates the sheep from the goats; and He will put the sheep on His right, and the goats on His left. ... Then He will also say to those on His left, "Depart from Me, accursed ones, into the eternal fire which has been prepared for the devil and his angels." (Matt 25:31–33, 41)

---

[10] Reid, *Evangelism Handbook*, 42.

The apostle John wrote in the book of Revelation:

> Then I saw a great white throne and Him who sat upon it, from whose presence earth and heaven fled away, and no place was found for them. And I saw the dead, the great and the small, standing before the throne, and books were opened; and another book was opened, which is the book of life; and the dead were judged from the things which were written in the books, according to their deeds. ... And if anyone's name was not found written in the book of life, he was thrown into the lake of fire. (Rev 20:11–12, 15)

According to these passages, those who never trust in the atoning work of Christ on the cross of Calvary will be separated from God forever in a place of punishment and torment called hell when Christ returns to the earth in judgment. This serious and sobering truth of the separation of the people from God for eternity should compel the church and its members to proclaim the gospel to lost and dying sinners. "The reality that all outside of Christ are without hope for salvation and face certain judgment should move believers to witness."[11]

The reference in the previous paragraph is to the second coming of Christ and the final judgment of sinners at the end of the age. However, the coming of Christ can also refer to his coming at the time of death and his subsequent judgment of every person who failed to trust him for salvation. The Bible declares, "Inasmuch as it is appointed for man to die once and after this comes judgment" (Heb 9:27). Further, the Bible states, "For we will all stand before the judgment seat of God," and, "So then each one of us will give an account of himself to God" (Rom 14:10, 12). Everyone has a date with death and needs to be prepared to stand before the Judge of the universe. No one has

---

[11] Ibid.

to suffer the wrath of God because by his mercy and grace he has provided the way whereby lost sinners can be saved. That salvation is found exclusively in Jesus Christ, and members of the church should declare boldly to their family and friends the message of hope found in the gospel.

The Condition of People without Christ

The fifth motivation for fulfilling the Great Commission is the condition of people without Christ. A verse previously mentioned in the section on the compassion of Christ for the lost also indicates how Jesus saw people who had no relationship with God. "Seeing the people, He felt compassion for them, because they were distressed and dispirited like sheep without a shepherd" (Matt 9:36). The words *distressed* and *dispirited* were picturesque words in the Greek language. *Distressed* had the meaning of being mangled by a wild beast while *dispirited* had the meaning of someone who was prostrate on the ground due to drunkenness or a mortal wound.[12] The portrait painted by these words is one of people devastated by sin as well as people groping to find answers to their problems and seeking meaning and purpose in life. In Jesus' day, sheep with no shepherd would be prey to predators and would face certain death. The description of people as sheep without a shepherd meant they were helpless and hopeless. Jesus saw people as devastated by their sin with no solution for their condition and with no hope apart from the forgiveness only He could provide. The church can help people find forgiveness of sin as well as the meaning and purpose in life for which they are searching by sharing with them the saving gospel of Jesus Christ.

---

[12] Archibald Thomas Robertson, *Word Pictures in the New Testament*, Vol. 1: *The Gospel according to Matthew, The Gospel according to Mark* (New York: Harper & Brothers Publishers, 1930), 1:76.

Further, people without Christ are spiritually dead and are under the wrath of God. (Eph 2:1, 3, 5 and John 3:36).[13] The Bible declares, "For all have sinned and fall short of the glory of God" (Rom 3:23), and, "For the wages of sin is death" (Rom 6:23). The penalty for sin is both physical and spiritual death. Spiritual death is separation from God in this life. According to Scripture, when a person dies without Christ, he will experience the second death, which is eternity in hell (Rev 2:11; 20:6, 14; 21:8). Jesus described hell as the place of "outer darkness" where there will be "weeping and gnashing of teeth" (Matt 8:12). People are lost without hope apart from Christ in this life and will suffer in a devil's hell separated from Christ for eternity. That fact alone should motivate the church and its members to reach out to lost people in their communities and around the world with the gospel.

> Most believers can quote John 3:16, but many forget that John 3:18 says, "Whoever does not believe stands condemned already because he has not believed in the name of God's one and only Son." Hell is not a popular topic in North American pulpits today. Still, we cannot escape its existence; ignoring it will not make it go away. Jesus often spoke of hell, and he warned people of the danger of going there. Pastors and churches must warn people of their precarious position.[14]

Because the Lord Jesus Christ is the only solution to the sin problem of mankind and is the only way a person can go to heaven, the church must declare that truth to all the peoples of the world.

---

[13] For a brief discussion on the wrath of God as both eternal and temporal, see Scott Dawson, "Introduction: Why or Why Not Witness?" in *The Complete Evangelism Guidebook: Expert Advice on Reaching Others for Christ*, ed. Scott Dawson (Grand Rapids, MI: Baker Books, 2006), 15–16.

[14] Terry, *Church Evangelism*, 11.

Conclusion

The necessity of motivation in order for the church to carry out the "marching orders" of Christ to fulfill the Great Commission cannot be overstated.[15] Clearly the church and its members must be motivated in order to take the gospel into their local communities and the rest of the world. A church can have proper theology, clear vision, sound strategy, and even be aware of proven methodology for fulfilling the Great Commission. However, without motivation that leads to action, the church and its members will never reach out to those who desperately need to hear the message of the gospel. The commandment of Christ, the compassion for Christ, the compassion of Christ, the coming of Christ, and the condition of people without Christ are clear biblical motivations that can be used by the Holy Spirit to compel believers to join with Christ in fulfilling the Great Commission given to his church.

---

[15] For further analysis of biblical motivations for fulfilling the Great Commission, see Thomas P. Johnston, *Evangelizology: A Biblical-Historical Perspective on Evangelism*, Vol. 1: *Motivation and Definition* (Liberty, MO: Evangelism Unlimited, Inc., 2011), 1:132–51.

BIBLIOGRAPHY

Bailey, Waylon. *As You Go: Biblical Foundations for Evangelism.* New Orleans, LA: Insight, 1981.

Bright, Bill. *Witnessing without Fear: How to Share Your Faith with Confidence.* Orlando, FL: NewLife Publications, 2003.

Dawson, Scott. "Introduction: Why or Why Not Witness?" In *The Complete Evangelism Guidebook: Expert Advice on Reaching Others for Christ*, ed. Scott Dawson, 13–16. Grand Rapids, MI: Baker Books, 2006.

Johnston, Thomas P. *Evangelizology: A Biblical-Historical Perspective on Evangelism*, Vol. 1: *Motivation and Definition.* Liberty, MO: Evangelism Unlimited, Inc., 2011.

MacArthur, John. *Matthew 8–15.* The MacArthur New Testament Commentary. Chicago, IL: Moody Press, 1987.

McRaney, Will H., Jr. "Considering Approaches to a Great Commission Church." In *Mobilizing a Great Commission Church for Harvest: Voices and Views from the Southern Baptist Professors of Evangelism Fellowship*, ed. Thomas P. Johnston, 35–50. Eugene, OR: Wipf & Stock, 2011.

Nix, Preston. "Commentary on Article 10: The Great Commission." In *Anyone Can Be Saved: A Defense of "Traditional" Southern Baptist Theology*, eds. David L. Allen, Eric Hankins, and Adam Harwood, 143–56. Eugene, OR: Wipf & Stock, 2016.

Reid, Alvin. *Evangelism Handbook: Biblical, Spiritual, Intentional, Missional.* Nashville, TN: B&H Publishing, 2009.

Robertson, Archibald Thomas. *Word Pictures in the New Testament*, Vol. 1: *The Gospel according to Matthew, The Gospel according to Mark.* New York: Harper & Brothers Publishers, 1930.

Terry, John Mark. *Church Evangelism.* Nashville, TN: Broadman & Holman Publishers, 1997.

Biblical Basis

The Role of the Holy Spirit in Evangelism: Aspects of Lukan Pneumatology

Wm. Craig Price and Mario Melendez

The Holy Spirit is prominent in the books of Luke and Acts and is closely associated with several key Old Testament (OT) prophecies.[1] These prophecies are related to evangelism in the Gospel of Luke and also in the book of Acts. To understand the role of the Holy Spirit in Luke and Acts we will examine first the use of "Spirit" in the OT with a focus on the prophecies of Isa 61:1–2 and Joel 2:28–32. Next, we will examine the work of the Holy Spirit in the New Testament (NT) specifically in the Gospel of Luke and then in the book of Acts. We will examine the role of the Holy Spirit in the life and ministry of Jesus and also in the life of the early church. From these examples we will draw theological principles for the work of evangelism today.

Use of "Spirit" in the OT

Luke utilizes two prominent Old Testament prophetic texts to focus on the Holy Spirit. The first text is Isa 61:1–2 in Luke 4:18–19. The second text is Joel 2:28–32 in Acts 2:17–21. The OT speaks of the Spirit of the Lord "coming upon" individuals. The word *rúah* translated

---

[1] The Holy Spirit is mentioned no less than fifty-four times in Luke and Acts.

as *spirit* in its literal sense means "breath" or "wind." The essence of Spirit is Yahweh's power, such as the storm in Jonah 1:4 or the Spirit that moved the sea in Exod 15:8. So when the Spirit of Yahweh comes upon a person, they are receiving power for a task. The Spirit of Yahweh came upon people who were to serve as: leaders, priests, and prophets. These three groups are *māšîaḥ*, meaning "ordained" or "anointed with oil" (anointed here after). "The externally flowing oil represents the internal reality of the Spirit's filling."[2] Thus, one could say these offices are called: anointed "Prophet," anointed "Priest," and anointed "King."[3]

The first office to consider is that of leaders on whom the Spirit "came upon."[4] The second office is priests who were often anointed with the Spirit. Aaron and his sons are anointed with oil in Lev 8:2–30. Though this is, indeed, the ritual that empowered them to perform the task of the priests, there is no explicit mention of the Spirit. The later mentioned priest, Zechariah, is clothed with the Spirit in 2 Chron 24:20.

The third office to have the Spirit upon them is the most pertinent for the study at hand—prophets. In Num 11:29, Moses stated, "Would that all the LORD's people were prophets, that the LORD would put His Spirit upon them!"[5] Numbers 11—12 sets the stage for how things

---

[2] Wilf Hildebrandt, "Spirit of Yahweh," in *Dictionary of the Old Testament Prophets*, eds. T. Desmond Alexander and David W. Baker (Downers Grove, IL: InterVarsity Press), 752.
[3] Robert Jamieson, Andrew Fausset, and David Brown, *Commentary Critical and Explanatory on the Whole Bible*, vol. 1 (Oak Harbor, WA: Logos Research Systems, Inc., 1997), 499.
[4] The list of leaders is impressive: Joseph (Gen 41:38), Moses (Num 11:25), elders including Joshua (11:25), Othniel (Judg 3:10), Gideon (6:34), Jephthah (11:29), Samson (14:6, 19, 15:4), King Saul (1 Sam 10:1, 10), and King David (1 Sam 16:13).
[5] "Prophets are concerned with the events and circumstances of their own times and with influencing people in their own societies. Many prophets speak about future events, but they do so as part of their interest in persuading their contemporaries to adopt a course or attitude that best represents the will of God and the best interest of the people." Marvin A. Sweeney, *The Prophetic Literature* (Nashville, TN: Abingdon Press, 2005), 23.

would change after the destruction of Solomon's Temple. McComiskey states:

> Key vocabulary from Numbers 11—12 is repeated: God's people will prophesy (Num 11:25–29; Joel 3:1); the revelatory means that characterize prophets (dream and vision—Num 12:6) will characterize all (Joel 3:1[2:28]). The Spirit will possess "young men" (Joel 3:1; Num 11:28). Possession by God's Spirit will not be the privilege of the few, but the experience of all (Num 11:25; 12:6; Joel 3:1[2:28]).[6]

Therefore, the office of prophet was not specifically a temple position. The Spirit of Yahweh empowered all anointed persons to minister apart from the temple.

When the Spirit of Yahweh came "upon" a person, it denoted a unique function among the Israelites as an anointed leader, priest, and/or prophet. First, the leaders delivered, led, obtained power, and/or executed justice on behalf of Yahweh's covenant people.[7] Second, the Spirit of Yahweh led the anointed to prophesy. For example, the elders in Num 11, King Saul, and King David all prophesied after the Spirit came upon them (1 Sam 10:6, 10; 11:6; 19:20, 23; 2 Sam 23:2). Like the noted role of leaders, the worship and words of the prophets and priests were always in service to the covenant.

The OT Context of Isa 61:1–2 and Joel 2:28–32

Isaiah and Joel ministered in the eighth century BCE. The eighth century was replete with corruption within Judea and culminated with the Babylonian invasion of 722 BCE. Thus, Isaiah and Joel gave testimony to the rebelliousness and unrighteousness of the pre-exilic and

---

[6] Thomas McComiskey, *The Minor Prophets* (Eugene, OR: Wipf & Stock, 2014), 1:294.
[7] Lee Roy Martin, "Power to Save!? The Role of the Spirit of the Lord in the Book of Judges," *Journal of Pentecostal Theology* 16.2 (2008), 22.

post-exilic nation. Isaiah is organized in three phases. Chapters 1—39 contain messages of the pending exile. Chapters 40—55 contain messages of an enduring exile. Finally, chapters 56—66 contain post-exilic. The book of Joel contains seventy-three verses with two clear sections; the preview of the day of the Lord (1:1—2:17) and the day of the Lord (2:18—3:21).[8]

Prior to the Babylonian exile, the people lost sight of the covenant relationship and proper covenant worship. Ezekiel recounted the glory (*kavod*) of God's Spirit leaving the temple as a physical picture (10:18–19*a*). Thus, Isaiah's and Joel's audiences would have understood the Spirit coming upon someone as a message of hope. Hanson says:

> The future of those who have suffered at the hands of this world's tyrants is in the hands of a personal sovereign who not only enacts laws but loves justice, who not only decrees punishments for misdeeds but hates robbery and wrongdoing. Israel's future does not depend on divine caprice but is guided by God's faithful adherence to the covenant relationship.[9]

Thus, Isaiah offered words of encouragement to the nation that in the end, Yahweh through His Spirit would gather the nation back together (Isa 34:16).

Content of Isaiah and Joel

The prophetic works of Isaiah and Joel may have encouraged Babylonian exiles, but they also empowered NT believers. Mason stated, "There may be no more influential Old Testament work for

---

[8] Kendell H. Easley, *Holman QuickSource Guide to Understanding the Bible*, Holman Reference (Nashville, TN: Holman, 2002), 182.
[9] Paul D. Hanson, *Isaiah 40–66* (Louisville, KY: Westminster John Knox Press, 2012), 226.

understanding the contours of the gospel than the book of Isaiah."[10] Similarly, Joel is equally crucial for grasping the work of the Holy Spirit through the church in Acts. This prompts one to ask, "Who are these people that Yahweh's Spirit comes upon?" Secondly, "What are these people empowered to do/be?"

Isaiah 61 is located after the "servant songs" (42:1–9; 49:1–13; 50:4–11; 52:13–53:12). The chapter begins with the phrase, "The Spirit of the Lord GOD is upon me." Chisholm concludes that the "me" of the verse is the divine servant of Isaiah.[11] He states, "This mission of deliverance and justice is a distinctly royal task that links the speaker with the royal figure of the first two servant songs and with the ideal just king portrayed in Isaiah 11."[12] Another possibility is Isaiah could be including the concept of a corporate servant. In this view the prophet and the community were *both* anointed to the office of prophet, priest, and leader in the exilic and post-exilic periods. Hanson concludes, "The ambiguity was intentional ... the servant was set forth as a model for both an individual and the community."[13] He argues the individual and the community accepted the calling to be agents of God's reign of compassionate righteousness. The result is the anointing of the Spirit came for the twofold purpose of proclamation and consolation.

---

[10] Steven D. Mason, "Getting a 'Handle' on Holistic Christian Mission: The Contribution of Isaiah 61 as a Discrete Old Testament Voice," *Missiology*. 40.3 (2012): 296. Pennington contends Isaiah is the fifth Gospel. Jonathan T. Pennington, *Reading the Gospels Wisely: A Narrative and Theological Introduction* (Grand Rapids, MI: Baker Academic, 2012), 14.

[11] Robert B. Chisholm Jr., *Handbook on the Prophets: Isaiah, Jeremiah, Lamentations, Ezekiel, Daniel, Minor Prophets* (Grand Rapids, MI: Baker Academic, 2002), 130. James E. Smith, *The Major Prophets*, Old Testament Survey Series (Joplin, MO: College Press, 1992), Isaiah 61:1–3. James E. Carter and Peter McLeod, "Isaiah," in *The Teacher's Bible Commentary*, ed. H. Franklin Paschall and Herschel H. Hobbs (Nashville: Broadman and Holman Publishers, 1972), 426.

[12] Ibid., 130.

[13] Hanson, *Isaiah 40–66*, 223–24.

Joel began his message with a locust plague depicting Yahweh's punishment of their covenant sin. After they endured the plague, the recipients were comforted with the day of the Lord as a restorative day. Similar to Isaiah, Joel's message contained a twofold blessing: a physical blessing (2:18–27) and a spiritual blessing (2:28–32). Using a plural pronoun, Joel stated all flesh shall receive the Spirit. McComiskey contends, "There can be little doubt in this context that Joel intended 'all flesh' to refer to Israel alone. The phrase 'all flesh' is explicated as your sons and daughters, slaves, young and old; the fortunes of Judah are contrasted to those of the Gentiles (4:1–17 [3:1–17])."[14] It should be noted Joel's message of all receiving the Spirit is consistent with Isaiah's message, for he spoke of a singular prophet receiving the Spirit (Isa 11:1–5; 42:1; 61:1–5) and a second anointing being upon the restored covenant people (Isa 4:4; 32:15; 44:3).[15]

Both of these passages were utilized in the NT in an "eschatological motif."[16] In the OT, however, these passages described the ministry of Isaiah, the community, or Cyrus the Great.[17] While the contemporary application may be debated among scholars, these two passages worked in harmony. Hübner says, "In Isaiah 11 the Spirit of Yahweh is the quasi-eschatological gift to the prophetically proclaimed new King as representative of the Old Testament People of God. In Joel 2 the Spirit is the eschatological gift to the people itself (post-exilic situation!)."[18]

---

[14] McComiskey, *The Minor Prophets*, 1:295.

[15] Matthew Steven Godshall, "The Messiah and the Outpouring of the Holy Spirit: The Christological Significance of Jesus as Giver of the Spirit in Luke–Acts" (PhD diss., The Southern Baptist Theological Seminary, 2013), 69.

[16] "The important word in verses 28–29 is 'afterward,' which indicates that the prophet is now speaking about what the Lord will do in the far distant future." James Limburg, *Hosea–Micah* (Atlanta: Westminster John Knox, 1988), 69–70.

[17] See 2 Chron 36:22 and Isa 45:1.

[18] Hans Hübner, "The Holy Spirit in Holy Scripture," *The Ecumenical Review* 41.3 (1989): 329.

Though the temple lay in ruins, and though the later temple lay empty, the Spirit of the Lord will be upon his chosen for the purpose of demonstrating his relationship with them and demonstrating his character to the world. No longer shall the Spirit be upon the few or contained in a building, but all (sons and daughters) will function as prophets and "have access to the words of Yahweh and to communion with him."[19]

Implications

Though the temple may be void of the Spirit of Yahweh, the OT promises the Spirit will return upon His covenant people. As such, the anointing of Isaiah 61 yields a direct relationship with Yahweh and a calling for all to accomplish covenant actions throughout the earth, not just in Jerusalem.[20] No longer does one watch the anointed perform the acts of prophet, priest, and leader, but all will one day share in this title. Ezekiel 36:26–27 testifies, "The Spirit of Yahweh 'transforms' the human spirit to motivate a new and favorable response to the covenant."[21]

The following implications may be drawn: (1) The office of prophet, priest, and leader required divine anointing, even though not every person was described as having received the Spirit. (2) The Spirit of the Lord was always for the purpose of empowering covenant ministry. (3) The anointing of the Spirit upon all individuals resulted in the declaration of the good news of total restoration (physical, spiritual, national, and covenantal). (4) The anointing of the Spirit spoke of the "priesthood," "prophethood," and "leaderhood" of the believer because this is what Isa 61 and Joel 2 were

---

[19] Hildebrandt, "Spirit of Yahweh," 755.
[20] Limburg, *Hosea–Micah*, 71.
[21] Hildebrandt, "Spirit of Yahweh," 754.

calling their hearers to.²² The result of Isa 61 and Joel 2 in context is the beginning of an answer for Moses's prayer that all may become prophets with the Spirit (Num 11:29). As such, the Spirit upon Old Testament believers provides a means for all to see the Lord is both with them and has blessed them.²³

Jesus and the Holy Spirit[24]

The "glory of the Lord" departed from the temple because of Israel's sin and apostasy (Ezek 10:18–19). The nation experienced a deep spiritual drought with the passing of Haggai, Zechariah, and Malachi. They longed for the return and restoration of the Spirit.²⁵ Luke chronicles the return of the work of the Spirit with the advent of the Messiah. The Holy Spirit is central in Luke's narrative of salvation history.²⁶ A key to understanding the importance of the work of the Holy Spirit is found in the notion of "fullness" (Greek *plērēs*). Turner notes the term, "full of the Holy Spirit," is a Lukanism "normally characterizing an endowment of some duration . . . to mark the

---

[22] McComiskey, *The Minor Prophets*, 1:295. In Christian circles we often speak of the "priesthood of the believers," for we have the spirit.

[23] Hanson, *Isaiah 40–66*.

[24] Horn calls Luke "the theologian of the Spirit." F. W. Horn, "Holy Spirit," *The Anchor Yale Bible Dictionary*, 277. For comprehensive discussion on the OT רוח "spirit" and the NT πνεῦμα "spirit," see: David Hill, *Greek Words and Hebrew Meanings: Studies in the Semantics of Soteriological Terms* (London: Cambridge University Press, 1967), 202–300. Of the ninety references in the NT to the "Holy Spirit," fifty-four of these are found in Luke and Acts—thirteen in Luke and forty-one in Acts.

[25] Goldingay argues Joel 2:28 does not indicate "YHwh's [sic] spirit was no longer present and active in Israel, but it does set before people the prospect of a great new outpouring of God's spirit." John Goldingay, *Old Testament Theology: Israel's Gospel*, Vol. 1. (Downers Grove, IL: IVP Academic, 2015), 795. See Jeremias's section: "The Return of the Extinct Spirit." Joachim Jeremias, *New Testament Theology*, trans. John Bowden (London: S.C.M. Press, 1971), 81.

[26] Richard J. Bauckham, "The Role of the Spirit in the Apocalypse," *EQ* 52.2. April/June (1980): 73. Bauckham defines the "Spirit of Prophecy" in post-biblical Judaism as "the Spirit which speaks through the prophets" functioning as the means of communication between God and people.

person concerned as one in whose life the Spirit was regularly and powerfully felt."[27]

In Luke's first reference to the Holy Spirit, the Angel of the Lord announced John the Baptist was "filled with the Holy Spirit while yet in his mother's womb" (Luke 1:15). He was a "forerunner before Him in the spirit and power of Elijah, to turn the hearts of the fathers back to the children, and the disobedient to the attitude of the righteous, so as to make ready a people prepared for the Lord" (v. 17). Next, the angel visited Mary and explained the Holy Spirit would come upon her and the power of the Most High would overshadow her. She would give birth to the "Son of God" (v. 35). When Elizabeth and Mary met, "the baby leaped in her womb; and Elizabeth was filled with the Holy Spirit" (v. 41). Simeon was led by the Spirit to the temple (Luke 2:25–27) where he met and held the Christ child proclaiming the coming of the Lord's salvation—a light for the gentiles and the glory of Israel (vv. 29–32). The Holy Spirit returned to Israel at the same place He had departed—the temple in Jerusalem.

Luke continued to highlight the work of the Holy Spirit as John the Baptist baptized in the Jordan River and announced Jesus would baptize with the "Holy Spirit and fire" (Luke 3:16). In prophetic tradition, Luke specified the "Holy Spirit descended upon" Jesus (v. 22). Confirmation from heaven followed as God declared, "You are My beloved Son, in You I am well-pleased" (v. 22). Lukan narrative described Jesus as "full of the Holy Spirit ... led around by the Spirit in the wilderness" (Luke 4:1) and returned from the wilderness to Galilee in the "power of the Spirit" (v. 14). These references to the Spirit culminated in the inauguration of Jesus's earthly ministry. Jesus stood in the synagogue and read Isa 61:1–2 declaring: "The Spirit of the LORD is upon Me, because He anointed Me to preach the gospel to the poor.

---

[27] Max Turner, *Power from on High: The Spirit in Israel's Restoration and Witness in Luke–Acts* (Sheffield, England: Sheffield Academic Press, 2000), 202.

He has sent Me to proclaim release to the captives, and recovery of sight to the blind, to set free those who are oppressed, to proclaim the favorable year of the LORD" (vv. 18–19).[28] This anointing is significant from the OT passages as observed previously. Luke recognized Jesus as the anointed Messiah who came in the OT conventions of prophet, priest, and leader king.

Jesus: Prophet, Priest, and King

Wayne Grudem argues for the superiority of Jesus in all three of these roles.[29] As a prophet, Jesus is the one *of whom* Israel's prophets predicted. As priest, Jesus offered Himself as the perfect sacrifice. As king, He refused earthly military and/or political power. In a transcendent sense, Jesus is fulfilling each of these three roles in the Lukan narrative.

First, Luke portrayed Jesus as the anointed prophet in the city of Nain where He touched a coffin and raised a dead man (Luke 7:11–23). The large crowd of onlookers was gripped with fear and began glorifying God saying, "'A great prophet has arisen among us!' and 'God has visited His people!'" (v. 16). When the report of the incident reached John the Baptist, he sent two disciples to inquire of Jesus, "Are You the Expected One, or do we look for someone else?" (v. 19). Jesus answered them and said, "Go and report to John what you have seen and heard: the blind receive sight, the lame walk, the lepers are cleansed, and the deaf hear, the dead are raised up, the poor have the gospel preached to them" (v. 22). Collectively, these miracles fulfilled

---

[28] Note the minor textual differences from the LXX in Luke where he does not follow the Masoretic Text. See Turner, *Power from on High*, 221. Luke omitted "to heal the broken hearted" and added "to set at liberty the oppressed." He changed the LXX infinitive "to call" (Greek *kalesai*) to the NT verb "to preach" or "to proclaim" (Greek *kēruksai*), most likely to conform to Christian nomenclature. These changes are relatively minor and do not detract from the prophetic tradition of Isa 61:1–2. See also Jesus's anointing in Acts 1:16.

[29] Wayne A. Grudem, *Systematic Theology: An Introduction to Biblical Doctrine* (Grand Rapids, MI: Zondervan, 1994), 624–39.

the prophecy of Isa 61:1–2, which Jesus quoted and applied to himself in Luke 4:18. Turner is correct to identify Jesus as a prophet like Moses rather than Elijah.[30]

Second, as priest, Jesus was offered as the perfect sacrifice for sins. While Hebrews provides us our most comprehensive view of Christ as priest, Luke referenced the tearing of the veil in the temple as a simultaneous event to Jesus's death (Luke 23:45). Grudem argues this rending of the veil symbolized open access to the holy of holies for all who worship Christ.[31]

Third, Luke reported numerous references to Jesus as king during the passion week. At the triumphal entry to Jerusalem, Luke added the title of *king* to his quotation of Ps 118:38: "Blessed is the *King* who comes in the name of the LORD" (Luke 19:38, emphasis added). The Jews accused Jesus of claiming rivalry to Rome as a king at his arraignment before Pilate.[32] This prompted Pilate to ask Jesus, "Are You the King of the Jews?" and he answered, "It is as you say." Pilate found no fault in Jesus, pronounced him guiltless, and attempted to pass him off to Herod's jurisdiction (Luke 23:2–3, 7). At the crucifixion, the soldiers mocked him, "If you are the King of the Jews, save Yourself!" (vv. 36–37). Luke noted the inscription above Jesus on the cross, "This is the King of the Jews" (v. 38). Thus we observe Luke attributed to Jesus the anointed qualities of prophet, priest, and king.

---

[30] Turner argues rabbinic exegesis erroneously associated Elijah (1 Kgs 17) with the messianic promises. Turner, *Power from on High*, 238–41. This popular Elijianic belief is reflected by the disciples' answer to Jesus's question, "Who do the people say that I am?" (Luke 9:18–19). Luke associated the Messiah with Moses (Acts 3:22; 7:37). For a typological exegesis concluding with Moses, see Jindřich Mánek, "New Exodus in the Books of Luke," *Novum Testamentum* 2.1 (1957): 8–23.

[31] Grudem, *Systematic Theology*, 627.

[32] There were three charges: (1) Jesus was disturbing the Jewish peace by claiming he was the Son of God (Luke 22:70); (2) he forbade the paying of taxes to Caesar (Luke 23:2); and (3) this final charge contending rivalry toward Rome, thus alluding to his messianic claims.

The Church and the Holy Spirit: Prophets, Priests, Leader-Kings

Luke cited Joel's prophecy of the outpouring of the "Spirit upon all flesh" (Acts 2:17 KJV). For Joel, "all flesh" referred to the covenant people of Judah, but Luke expanded this meaning to include believing Jews *and* gentiles.[33] Luke ended with, "And it shall be that everyone who calls on the name of the LORD will be saved" (v. 21; see also Joel 2:32, Rom 10:13).

Turner notes the Holy Spirit in Luke and Acts was "the power of preaching" that provided argument/exhortation, corroborating signs, and convincing power for the speaker that impacted the hearers.[34] The Holy Spirit remains the "power of preaching" for missions and evangelism (Acts 1:8). In a real sense, the modern evangelist shares in the roles of prophet, priest, and leader king, but in a much more subordinated fashion. Grudem argues we imitate Christ in each of these roles until his return.[35]

The Holy Spirit in Evangelism Today

What is the relationship of the Holy Spirit to evangelism today? The filling of the Spirit characterizes every evangelistic effort. By cross-referencing the Holy Spirit with evangelistic episodes in Luke and Acts we observe the following:

1. *The Holy Spirit Supplies Divine Power for Evangelistic Witness*

    Luke was quite clear that the Holy Spirit's anointing precedes evangelistic witnessing to unbelievers. Without the Holy Spirit,

---

[33] Barrett interprets "all flesh" as "world-wide in its scope." C. K. Barrett, *A Critical and Exegetical Commentary on The Acts of the Apostles* (Edinburgh: T & T Clark, 1994), 1:156. Luke's inclusion of Joel 2:32 and Rom 10:13 clearly focuses the fulfillment of Joel's prophecy on all believers—Jew or gentile.

[34] Turner, *Power from on High*, 431–32. See also Max Turner, "The Spirit of Prophecy and the Power of Authoritative Preaching in Luke–Acts: A Question of Origins," *NTS* 38 (1992), 68–72, 87–88.

[35] Grudem, *Systematic Theology*, 549. Pennington believes the gospels were written for the purpose of emulating the character of Christ and other virtue-forming aspects. Pennington, *Reading the Gospels Wisely*, 33–35.

all evangelism is powerless to win the lost.[36] Just as the anointing and equipping of the Holy Spirit was vital and indispensable in the life of Jesus, it remains so for all evangelism today.[37] In Acts 1:8, Jesus promised his disciples, "You will receive power when the Holy Spirit has come upon you; and you shall be My witnesses both in Jerusalem, and in all Judea and Samaria, and even to the remotest part of the earth."

2. *The Holy Spirit Emboldens the Evangelist in Times of Opposition and Hardship*

Peter was "filled with the Holy Spirit" when on trial before the rulers, elders, and scribes in Jerusalem (Acts 4:5–12). Even though he was before Annas the high priest and the priestly descendants Caiaphas, John, and Alexander, Peter was emboldened to speak evangelistically in the face of possible death and imprisonment. Even under persecution, he declared salvation could come by "no other name under heaven that has been given among men by which we must be saved" (v. 12). This same power for boldness equips the evangelistic witness in times of persecution and opposition to the gospel witness.

3. *The Holy Spirit Gives Victory over All Forms of Spiritual Darkness*

From the anointing of the Holy Spirit, Jesus demonstrated divine power over all spiritual darkness: "to proclaim release to the captives and recovery of sight to the blind, to set free those who

---

[36] Moody writes, "There is no use in running before you are sent; there is no use in attempting to do God's work without God's power. A man working without this unction, a man working without this anointing; a man working without the Holy Ghost upon him, is losing time after all." Dwight Lyman Moody, *Secret Power* (Gainesville, Fla.: Bridge-Logos, 2006), 32.

[37] Anthony C. Thiselton, *The Holy Spirit: In Biblical Teaching, through the Centuries, and Today*, (Grand Rapids, MI: William B. Eerdmans Publishing Company), 47.

are oppressed" (Luke 4:18).[38] In Luke and Acts, we witness this same anointing upon believers for spiritual warfare against darkness.[39] The disciples had divine power over evil spirits, but Jesus reminded them the end result of evangelism is the presence of the Spirit of God: "Nevertheless, do not rejoice in this, that the spirits are subject to you, but rejoice that your names are recorded in heaven" (Luke 10:20). The victory and proclamation of "the favorable year of the LORD" had arrived (Luke 4:19).

4. *The Holy Spirit Provides Growth: Peace, Edification, Fear of the Lord, and Comfort*

    Luke recorded the church "enjoyed peace, being built up; and going on in the fear of the Lord and the comfort of the Holy Spirit, it continued to increase" (Acts 9:31). The main clause here is "it continued to increase." The components of that increase were peace (Greek *irene*), edification, (Greek *oikodomeia*), reverence (Greek *fobio*) for the Lord, and comfort (Greek *paraklesis*) of the Holy Spirit.[40] The overall effect of this growth was a flourishing of healthy, spiritual qualities. These same healthy qualities are brought through the Holy Spirit to the church today, and evangelism is a key component to this spiritual health.

5. *The Holy Spirit Is Indispensable for Every Evangelistic Effort*

    The Holy Spirit led the evangelists in every evangelistic effort (see Acts 13:4; 15:28; and 19:21). Sometimes the Holy Spirit led the evangelist into difficulty and hardship (see Acts 7; 13; 19:21; 20:23; and 21:11). Sometimes, the Holy Spirit did not permit the evangelists to share a witness (Acts 16:6–13).

---

[38] Release to the captives (Luke 4:36; 6:18; 7:21; 8:2, 29; 9:42; 13:11); sight to the blind (Luke 18:35; Acts 9:18; 26:18); freedom to the oppressed (Luke 13:12–14; Acts 10:38).
[39] Luke 10:20 and Acts 10:38–47.
[40] Luke used "to comfort" (Greek *parakaleō*) here. Jesus used its noun form in John 16:7 to describe the Holy Spirit as "Helper" or "Comforter."

Thiselton reminds us of the importance of retaining our Trinitarian perspective that includes the Holy Spirit in our understanding of the work of Christ and the early church.[41]

We have sought to show in this chapter how the Spirit was a key concept in the OT for prophet, priest, and king. In the NT we see the Holy Spirit as vital and indispensable in the life and work of Christ as well as the early church. The roles of prophet, priest, and leader king could not be fulfilled without the work of the Holy Spirit. In conclusion, the anointing of the Holy Spirit is essential in the life of every Christian, every church, and every denomination—but most especially so in the work of evangelism. Kelley concludes his "lessons" from the history of evangelism in the Southern Baptist Convention by reminding us, "Effort is not enough." He quotes from the old hymn, "All is vain unless the Spirit of the Holy One comes down!"[42] Luke would agree!

---

[41] Thiselton, *The Holy Spirit*, 47–48.
[42] Charles S. Kelley Jr., *Fuel the Fire: Lessons from the History of Southern Baptist Evangelism*, a Treasury of Baptist Theology, eds. Paige Patterson and Jason G. Duesing (Nashville, TN: B&H Academic, 2018), 223–25.

Bibliography

Barrett, C. K. *A Critical and Exegetical Commentary on The Acts of the Apostles*. Vol. 1. Edinburgh: T & T Clark, 1994.

Bauckham, Richard J. "The Role of the Spirit in the Apocalypse." *EQ* 52.2. April/June (1980): 66–83.

Burke, Trevor J., and Keith Warrington, eds. *A Biblical Theology of the Holy Spirit*. London: SPCK, Society for Promoting Christian Knowledge, 2014.

Carter, James E., and Peter McLeod. "Isaiah." In *The Teacher's Bible Commentary: A Concise, Thorough Interpretation of the Entire Bible Designed Especially for Sunday School Teachers*, edited by H. Franklin Paschall and Herschel H. Hobbs. Nashville, TN: Broadman and Holman Publishers, 1972.

Chisolm, Robert B., Jr. *Handbook on the Prophets: Isaiah, Jeremiah, Lamentations, Ezekiel, Daniel, Minor Prophets*. Grand Rapids, MI: Baker Academic, 2002.

Easley, Kendell H. *Holman QuickSource Guide to Understanding the Bible*. Holman Reference. Nashville, TN: Holman, 2002.

Godshall, Matthew Steven. "The Messiah and the Outpouring of the Holy Spirit: The Christological Significance of Jesus as Giver of the Spirit in Luke–Acts." PhD diss., The Southern Baptist Theological Seminary, 2013.

Goldingay, John. *Old Testament Theology: Israel's Gospel*. Vol. 1. Downers Grove, IL: IVP Academic, 2015.

Grudem, Wayne A. *Systematic Theology: An Introduction to Biblical Doctrine*. Grand Rapids, MI: Zondervan, 1994.

Hanson, Paul D. *Isaiah 40–66*. Louisville, KY: Westminster John Knox Press, 2012.

Hildebrandt, Wilf. *An Old Testament Theology of the Spirit of God.* Peabody, MA: Hendrickson Publishers, 1995.

———. "Spirit of Yahweh." In *Dictionary of the Old Testament Prophets*, edited by Mark J. Boda and J. Gordon McConville. Downer's Grove, IL: InterVarsity Press, 274–257.

Hill, David. *Greek Words and Hebrew Meanings: Studies in the Semantics of Soteriological Terms.* London: Cambridge University Press, 1967.

Horn, F. W. "Holy Spirit." *The Anchor Yale Bible Dictionary.*

Hübner, Hans. "The Holy Spirit in Holy Scripture." *The Ecumenical Review* 41.3 (1989): 324–38.

Jamieson, Robert, Andrew Fausset, and David Brown. *Commentary Critical and Explanatory on the Whole Bible*, vol. 1. Oak Harbor, WA: Logos Research Systems Inc., 1997.

Jeremias, Joachim. *New Testament Theology.* Translated by John Bowden. London: S.C.M. Press, 1971.

Kelley, Charles S., Jr. *Fuel the Fire: Lessons from the History of Southern Baptist Evangelism.* A Treasury of Baptist Theology, edited by Paige Patterson and Jason G. Duesing. Nashville, TN: B&H Academic, 2018.

Limburg, James. *Hosea–Micah.* Atlanta: Westminster John Knox, 1988.

Mánek, Jindřich. "New Exodus in the Books of Luke." *Novum Testamentum* 2.1 (1957): 8–23.

Martin, Lee Roy. "Power to Save!? The Role of the Spirit of the Lord in the Book of Judges." *Journal of Pentecostal Theology* 16.2 (2008): 21–50.

Mason, Steven D. "Getting a 'Handle' on Holistic Christian Mission: The Contribution of Isaiah 61 as a Discrete Old Testament Voice." *Missiology* 40.3 (2012): 295–313.

McComiskey, Thomas. *The Minor Prophets.* Vol. 1. Eugene, OR: Wipf & Stock, 2014.

Moody, Dwight Lyman. *Secret Power.* Gainesville, FL: Bridge-Logos, 2006.

Pennington, Jonathan T. *Reading the Gospels Wisely: A Narrative and Theological Introduction.* Grand Rapids, MI: Baker Academic, 2012.

Smith, James E. *The Major Prophets.* Old Testament Survey Series. Joplin, MO: College Press, 1992.

Sweeney, Marvin A. *The Prophetic Literature: Interpreting Biblical Texts.* Nashville, TN: Abingdon Press, 2005.

Thiselton, Anthony C. *The Holy Spirit: In Biblical Teaching, through the Centuries, and Today.* Grand Rapids, MI: William B. Eerdmans, 2013.

Turner, Max. *Power from on High: The Spirit in Israel's Restoration and Witness in Luke–Acts.* Sheffield, England: Sheffield Academic Press, 2000.

———. "The Spirit of Prophecy and the Power of Authoritative Preaching in Luke–Acts: A Question of Origins." *NTS* 38 (1992): 66–88.

Wood, Leon James. *The Holy Spirit in the Old Testament.* Contemporary Evangelical Perspectives. Grand Rapids, MI: Zondervan Pub. House, 1976.

Wright, Christopher J. H. *Knowing the Holy Spirit through the Old Testament.* Downers Grove, IL: IVP Academic, 2006.

Biblical Basis

EVANGELISM AND CONTEXT IN THE NEW TESTAMENT

William Warren

"Location, location, location!" That's the motto for real estate sales in that everything depends on the location of the property. To a large extent, the same motto should be remembered when interpreting the Bible in that "context, context, context" is one of the most important considerations for understanding the historical meaning of the biblical text and likewise the possible modern applications of the text. So how would a context-centered approach to the topic of evangelism in the New Testament (NT) look? In what follows, the topic of evangelism will be examined from the perspective of the social contexts in order to highlight aspects of the presentation of the message in light of the social makeup of both the target group for evangelism and the larger surrounding culture.[1]

To clarify, Jesus ministered in a predominantly Jewish context with a Jewish culture forming the primary backdrop for both Jesus and his audiences in the Israel setting. But Paul ministered primarily in a culture dominated by the Roman Empire with a message from a minority

---

[1] See David Watson, *I Believe in Evangelism* (Grand Rapids: Eerdmans, 1976). Watson, in his chapter on "Personal Evangelism," gives a detailed overview of the encounter between Jesus and the Samaritan woman at the well, noting aspects of the approach and overall evangelistic encounter. This chapter helped spark my interest in looking more at the NT evangelistic encounters, an interest later augmented by missionary work in Colombia, Cuba, Venezuela, Mexico, and Malawi, and then study in the field of anthropology.

Jewish group built on the Old Testament (OT). So how do these different contexts impact the approaches to evangelism? That question will be addressed in what follows.

Before looking at some of the contexts represented in the NT, an understanding of what is meant by "contexts" is warranted. The percentage of the total population a specific social group represents in their setting is a general guide for weighing the contexts. For example, if Capernaum is being considered or the larger Galilee setting outside of perhaps the two cities of Sepphoris and Tiberius, the largest social group consists of Jews. And this indeed is the context the gospels represent as primary for the ministry of Jesus in Galilee. In this social context, Jesus ministered as part of the majority group to the majority group. On the other hand, Paul was Jewish and although he often started by going to the Jewish synagogues, the larger group in his ministry was not Jewish. Paul especially ministered as part of a minority group to the non-Jewish majority group. In a somewhat different context, James was Jewish and addressed his letter to the predominantly Jewish-Christian diaspora groups, but those groups were within the larger Roman Empire. In this case, James was part of a minority group writing to a minority group within the larger majority culture.

Jesus's Ministry in Galilee: A Majority Jewish Context in the Majority Jewish Culture

As Mark 1:14–15 notes about the ministry of Jesus after John's imprisonment, Jesus was "preaching the good news from God and saying, 'The time has been fulfilled and the kingdom of God has come near'" so his hearers should "repent and pledge faithfulness to the good news."[2] The message was based on the fulfillment of an already

---

[2] All translations are the author's own unless otherwise noted and are based on the text of the Nestle-Aland 28th edition: *Novum Testamentum Graece*, Nestle-Aland, 28th Revised Edition. Institut fur Neutestamentliche Textforschung Munster/Westfalen, eds. Barbara and Kurt Aland, Johannes Karavidopoulos, Carlo M. Martini, Bruce M. Metzger. Deutsche Bibelgesellschaft Stuttgart, 2012.

present expectation of a coming kingdom of God within Judaism and built on the consistent call from OT prophets and John the Baptist that God's people need to repent and renew their commitment to God in preparation for God's movement among them. Mark 1:16–20 details the calling of the first disciples mentioned in Mark, namely a call to "follow" Jesus. In other words, the call was for them to step into the future that had already been announced in their context through the OT. They were to become actively involved as this future now became reality by following Jesus who was ushering in the kingdom. In their majority Jewish culture, the disciples were expected to understand the call of Jesus from that perspective as they were invited to take part in the kingdom of God that was dawning in Jesus's person and ministry.

While the message of the kingdom of God might not make sense to a non-Jew, especially not as a kingdom promised from times past through the prophets, such a message made total sense to Jews who shared a knowledge base and contextual heritage that "knows the language" Jesus was speaking. In this case, the call was for those listening to become part of what God was doing by becoming "followers of Jesus" as he accurately explained the ways of God and actively engaged in the work of God.

Another text where the Jewish context was prominent is the parable of the prodigal son in Luke 15. The introduction to the parable (Luke 15:1–2) sets the stage by mentioning two groups: (1) the tax collectors and sinners represented by the younger son and (2) the Pharisees and scribes represented by the older son. The tax collectors were Jews who actively made money by fraud and abuse. They charged excess taxes that went to their own pockets as well as to those over them (higher level tax collectors or government officials). The "sinners" group was not simply everyone in the Pauline sense of Rom 3:23 where "all have sinned and have fallen short of the glory of God." This group was a specific Jewish social group that openly did not live a Torah-observant life or seek to be obedient to God. As the parable developed about the prodigal son, the son sought his inheritance early, before his father had even died. This in and of itself was an affront to the entire honor system for the family, and in this case the message was clear these tax collectors and sinners had lived their lives in a way that was an insult to their God—the God of Abraham, Isaac, and Jacob. This group, like the younger son, had also squandered their inheritance, the inheritance they had as part of the people of God, as Jews who had a blessed place in God's plan. But even as the son "comes to himself" and realizes his need to go back to his father in repentance, the tax collectors and sinners also were finally coming to their senses as seen in their coming to Jesus. They were thereby seeking to restore their relationship with God. In other words, the story of the prodigal son spoke about the tax collectors and sinners coming to Jesus to realize their true heritage in the God of Abraham, Isaac, and Jacob.

The older son saw his younger brother as one who wasted his inheritance, with the parallel being the Pharisees and scribes saw the tax collectors and sinners as ones who had wasted their Jewish heritage. Their call was to realize their value to God and their role to bring the family together by promoting healing in the family versus sowing discord and strife. They were being called to get "on-board" with God instead of becoming jealous that others were being restored to God.

In the ministry of Jesus with a Jewish message in a majority Jewish context, the call to fellow Jews was for them to get right with the God they already knew about and to come back to a faith their ancestors knew and proclaimed in the OT. The call was not one for switching gods but rather to come back to the one true God their heritage proclaimed. Repentance and a pledge of faithfulness to God are central.

The Sermon on the Mount also highlights the importance of context. The Jewish context can be seen clearly in Matt 5:20 where the scribes and Pharisees are mentioned as not having a sufficient "righteousness." In Matthew, righteousness is firmly anchored in Judaism as the doing of the will of God, meaning being Torah observant in life and thereby pleasing to God. The problem was the Pharisees and scribes had twisted the definition of righteousness in ways that favored them and failed to achieve the will of God. Jesus therefore challenged their understanding throughout the Sermon on the Mount. In particular Matt 6:1–18 involves three practices often seen as indicating a high level of spirituality in the sense of obedience to God— almsgiving, prayer, and fasting. In a majority culture, external spiritual practices can become means of gaining public acclaim instead of ways to draw near to God, and that was what had happened to at least some of the Pharisees and scribes in their practices of almsgiving, prayer, and fasting. They sought the public acclaim of being considered good practitioners of Judaism instead of sincerely worshipping God and seeking to do his will. In this setting, Jesus called for people (Jewish listeners and followers in this context) to return to an authentic worship of God. This call was in contrast to that of the Pharisees who represented the option of performing culturally expected external acts that might validate those involved in the eyes of the majority culture but that all too often failed to represent a true faithfulness to and focus on God.

What does this say about evangelism? The main takeaway is the call for people to repent and return to the faith of their heritage, the faith they were raised in, born into, and called to embrace. Jesus is calling Jewish people to come back to the God they have often heard about and who is reflected in their culture through the Jewish festivals, the dominant religious social groups, their gatherings in the synagogues, and their temple worship experiences. Their entire culture was shaped by their religious heritage, and so evangelism in this context was a call back to a faith those in the setting had already heard and knew about.

For today, a parallel might be the Bible Belt as a culture (to be sure, a waning culture in the USA) or homes that over generations have instilled Christian values and practices in their family life and celebrated Christian events like the birth of Jesus and His death and resurrection. The celebrations continue but the reality of the Christian focus may wane in such a context. Likewise, the increased attendance at many, if not most, churches on days like Easter Sunday reflects the presence of this underlying Christian heritage, but the drop in attendance at other times of the year reveals the lack of a deeper understanding of God's call and of the message that forms the backdrop to the Christian heritage. The result is cultural religion—people who claim their role within the heritage, and even benefit from it, while often not appreciating the undergirding reality of that heritage with an authentic relationship with God. In such a context, the approach to evangelism in Jesus's ministry is a call for repentance and a faith commitment to Jesus that brings one back to the God who has already been proclaimed in the context, whether accurately or not. The call is to go beyond cultural religion to a reality of a relationship with God that transforms both the person's life and their religious and cultural heritage.

Jewish Ministry to Mixed Groups: A Majority Jewish Context in a Larger Non-Jewish Culture

The setting in some parts of the NT includes the proclamation of the message either as a call for faithfulness to a minority subgroup within the larger context or as a call for reaching out to others outside the group in defiance of the prevailing attitudes within the majority group. This context can be found in multiple places in the NT. The Gospel of John and the books of 1, 2, and 3 John all seem to reflect a Jewish Christian context that was no longer living in Israel but rather was part of the larger Roman context. Acts 8—12 likewise reflects this type of context with the inclusion of the Samaritans in Acts 8 and then Cornelius in Acts 10. Two other NT settings for this type of context are found in James and some parts of the Synoptic Gospels where non-Jews were addressed, with Luke having more of that emphasis than Mark or Matthew.

In Luke, the parable of the good Samaritan is a primary example of an outside group from the larger culture while also addressing a Jewish majority context. In the parable, Jesus answered an intentionally conflictive question from a Jewish expert in the Torah (law): "Teacher, I will inherit eternal life by doing what?" (Luke 10:25). Jesus reversed the conversation by turning the question back onto the Torah expert, who then replied by giving the twofold focus of the Great Commandment about loving God and loving one's neighbor. After Jesus affirmed this answer and told the Torah expert to do what these commandments said, the expert asked Jesus a follow-up question in order to justify himself: "And who is my neighbor?" (v. 29). Jesus replied by telling this parable. The story broke outside the majority Jewish context by having a Samaritan as the hero. After telling the parable, Jesus asked the Torah expert about which of the three—the priest, the Levite, or the Samaritan—was a good neighbor to the man who fell among the thieves. The expert was left with no other option but to admit the Samaritan was the one who was a good neighbor. But rather than use the term *Samaritan*, he replied: "The one practicing mercy with him" (v. 37). The point is a true neighbor is anyone who needs someone to be a good neighbor to them. The focus is on the other person's need versus the desires of the one who might offer help with those needs. The net result is to emphasize that faith is to be practiced even for outsiders (and may even be practiced by them) regardless of what the majority religious culture says.

In the Epistle of James, James wrote to a context where the majority of his recipients were Jews, with no evidence of gentiles at all among the recipients. This setting reflected a cultural Judaism where the profession of faith was a badge for belonging to the group by identifying as one who worshipped the God of Abraham, Isaac, and Jacob. But the tendency in this cultural Judaism was to adopt the faith of the culture without living it on a daily basis. What James then emphasized was the need for faith to be seen and not just professed, for "faith without works is dead" (Jas 2:26).

The argument in James is that the second half of the Great Commandment, "love your neighbor as yourself" (cited in v. 8), is essential, even as the parable of the good Samaritan likewise emphasized. The difficulty with the first part of the Great Commandment is that loving God with all of one's being is hard to verify in any concrete way. One can say they love God, but if the words come from a cultural religion context where such a profession is expected, the profession may carry little weight in everyday life. The verification aspect of the Great Commandment comes with the second part about loving one's neighbors—something that can indeed be verified. In this context, evangelism would need to include a call for repentance and faith in Christ that called for concrete demonstrations in everyday life of the commitment to follow Jesus. The resulting evangelism focus was not unlike that for a majority Jewish context like in the ministry of Jesus in Galilee, but an outreach component is sometimes included.

In thinking about how the context in these two settings helps for understanding evangelism, in the context in Luke, one evidence of a true faith is that it will seek the good of others, no matter whether they are part of the in-group or not. Even the larger outside group will be considered, and sometimes one of the outside groups may even provide a challenge to the in-group to reevaluate their own living out of God's will and their relationship with God. Indeed, James goes so far as to say a correct verbal profession about God without living it out in concrete actions does not get to the level of a saving faith, for "even the demons believe and shudder" (v. 19).

Perhaps the lesson in these two cases is that, on the one hand, cultural religion has to be challenged to become more than that by becoming a relationship that shows itself in concrete actions of good to others in ways that go way passed simply being a reflection of the dominant culture of the in-group. On the other hand, the realization of explicit "good neighbor" actions of helping others in need may open the door for God to become "real" to others due to seeing visible actions that go beyond the cultural religious veneer. When coming from a cultural religion context, evangelism may need to be validated more by actions in order to communicate more than just the prevailing cultural religion. The message needs to be both proclaimed and visibly seen in actions of kindness and love.

Paul's Ministry: A Majority Non-Jewish Context in a Larger Non-Jewish Culture

As Paul launched more and more into a non-Jewish audience and ministry, his context shifted dramatically, with the end result being he had a minority message about a Jewish Messiah to proclaim to the larger non-Jewish culture. Part of his struggle was to find how the larger non-Jewish group fit into the story of the smaller Jewish group without having to become part of the Jewish culture that marked that group as distinct. And he had to find a way to communicate the message of a Jewish Messiah who was the fulfillment of Israel's story to a group that had received the implicit if not explicit message they were not part of Israel's story since they were not Jews.

An easy path would have been to require the non-Jewish group to become Jews so there would not be any need for more transitioning within the Jewish Christian group. But that would never have worked in the long term. One reason is the non-Jewish element would come to eventually so outnumber the original Jewish group the identity of the Jewish group would have been threatened, if not lost. Also, conflict would have resulted between the two groups as they vied for leadership and control. Furthermore, the vast majority of non-Jews would not have been drawn to the gospel message due to rejecting the Jewish context of the Jewish group with its difficult entry requirements for non-Jews. The solution was not to be found in making the non-Jewish audience fit into the larger Jewish context and culture (larger during the stages of church history). What was needed was a way to respectfully communicate with the non-Jewish culture. The non-Jewish group needed to be addressed in its own cultural context in ways that kept the integrity of the gospel message, stayed true to Israel's story, and presented the gospel message in ways that persuaded non-Jews to respond to the message.

As an example of this context, Gal 2 shows the struggle Peter and Paul had over making the shift from the dominant Jewish culture to one open to non-Jews while being true to the gospel message. Peter came to Antioch where Paul was and openly mixed with the believers who were not Jews and who therefore were not observing the Jewish dietary rules. At this point, Peter had crossed over from the dominant Jewish culture of the Jewish Christian group to participate in the majority culture of non-Jewish believers with regard to dietary rules. Paul said Peter "ate with the Gentiles" (Gal 2:12) until some of James's group came. At that time, Peter reverted back to Jewish dietary rules, separating himself from the non-Jewish group in order to be with the Jewish group.

What then ensued was Paul rebuked Peter for his hypocrisy, reminding Peter that as Jewish Christians, they knew a person was "justified not by the works of the law, but only through faith in Jesus Christ, and we ourselves believed in Christ Jesus" (vv. 15–16). Paul used this foundation in his evangelistic appeal to the gentiles as the way to validate their acceptance by God without adopting the minority culture of the Jewish followers of Jesus, even though at the time Jewish culture was the majority culture for Jewish Christians. The battle was both theological and cultural. The theological battle was about a faith commitment to Jesus as the only requirement for being made right with God and to be part of God's plan for this world. And the cultural battle was about whether or not the dominant culture of the Jewish Christian group and of Jesus as a Jewish messiah was a requirement for being a Jesus follower.

From the standpoint of evangelism, both battles are of vital importance. Paul's solution on the first front was to go to Gen 15:6 where Abram[ham] "trusted [believed] God and it was credited to him for righteousness." Paul placed the gentiles within the Jesus followers as the fulfillment of Gen 15, which was before the covenant based on circumcision in Gen 17, and a prior covenant is not voided by the later covenant. So gentiles were accepted by faith only, as was Abraham himself, and Jewish believers were likewise accepted by faith only based on Gen 15. Of course, Jewish believers were free to continue practicing the Gen 17 requirement within their own group, but they were not free to impose that covenant and in-group practice on non-Jews. A parallel might be a given church group that has its own internal requirements for membership, but the group needs to be very careful not to confuse those requirements with the essential truth of salvation by faith in Christ alone.

Acts: God's Expansion of the Jesus Followers

The tendency of Jewish Christians in Paul's day to see Jewish culture as an essential part of worshipping the God of Abraham, Isaac, and Jacob, the God Jewish people had so long worshipped and proclaimed, was one of the more difficult hurdles for the early church to overcome. In fact, this hurdle led to the Jerusalem meeting in Acts 15. Needless to say, this battle for both continuity with the past and outreach to the present generation remains a struggle point today. How is a proper balance to be found between keeping the positive aspects of a culture that have historically reflected many gospel values and maintaining the foundational call of faith in Christ alone as the requirement for those who don't come from or share that culture? Some examples from Acts may be instructive for finding this balance.

In Acts, the hurdle for accepting non-Jews and nontraditional Jews (like the Samaritans) into the Jesus group was overcome only with the special intervention of God. In Acts 8, the Samaritans responded to Philip's proclamation of the gospel and were baptized. But some underlying questions still had to be answered. Would the home group of Jesus followers accept these rivals who also worshipped the God of Abraham, Isaac, and Jacob? Or, in light of the difficulties between Jews and Samaritans, would more be required of them before they were accepted? Would the Samaritan converts be required to come back into the fold of traditional Judaism in order to be part of the Jewish followers of Jesus in Jerusalem, including the

Apostles? God intervened through Peter and John who were sent to Samaria by the Jerusalem group to investigate and validate what had happened there. What followed was that the Samaritans received the Holy Spirit, which was God's full validation of their repentance and conversion. No further requirement could be placed on the Samaritans about changing their culture to that of the Jewish Christians in Jerusalem since God had already fully accepted them and validated that acceptance.

In Acts 10, with the conversion of Cornelius and his household, a major hurdle was crossed in several ways. First, Peter's vision of the non-kosher food coming down set the stage for him to understand God alone decides what is acceptable and permitted, including with respect to people. A major cultural and theological boundary was being crossed. Second, Cornelius, a God-fearer who already worshipped the God proclaimed by the Jewish people, crossed a major cultural boundary by being willing to ask for help from a non-Roman, one with no official role of authority in the culture and one who would most likely reject his request. But because of God's call, Cornelius sent men to get Peter. Third, Peter crossed a cultural boundary by inviting Cornelius's men into the house and even allowing them to lodge there (v. 23). Fourth, Peter entered Cornelius's house (v. 25), the house of a non-Jew (v. 28), and presented the gospel to Cornelius and his family and friends who had gathered (v. 24). In the midst of the preaching, God showed his acceptance of Cornelius and those with him by way of a dramatic event. God gave Corneluis and those with him a similar experience to that of Peter and the disciples on the day of Pentecost. This made it impossible for Peter to deny that God had accepted these gentile hearers without having them convert first to Judaism (vv. 45–47). If God had said yes to these being part of the Jesus group without becoming Jews, who was Peter to dispute with God? The evangelism pattern involved the proclamation of the message and a response to the message without any cultural demands.

Implications for Evangelism Today

When looking at the contexts for the Christian message in the NT, each one yields helpful insights for the practice of evangelism today. In the dominant Jewish context of Galilee, the call to those in a Jewish culture that already proclaimed the one true God centered on an appeal for them to repent and come back to the true roots of their godly heritage by becoming Jesus followers. In such a context, the culture of the dominant group may become threatening when challenged, for sometimes the majority group can cause havoc for dissenters and those promoting change, even as seen in what happens to Jesus.

In the midst of cultural religion like in James, the call is for a godly life based on a verifiable walk with God that supersedes the cultural religious context. The culture and the individuals of the dominant group need to be brought back into faithfulness to God. As seen in the parable of the good Samaritan, breaking out of that monolithic religious cultural outlook may very well include a call to see those outside the group through godly eyes versus merely cultural stereotypes.

For Paul in a non-Jewish context, the call is for people to make a total conversion from false gods to worship the God who is in Christ reconciling the world to himself (2 Cor 5:18–20). This is a total change of pathways, a shift from pagan gods to following Jesus. The call was not to come back to a God previously proclaimed in the setting but rather to change gods and now to live in a relationship with the true God. Paul had to insist that the culture of the dominant Jewish Christian group should not be part of the requirements of the gospel. The call was to change gods by entering a faith relationship with the one true God in Christ. Certain aspects of Jewish culture (the dominant group) could not be added as requirements for salvation.

While the basic message for evangelism is always about Jesus and involves a call to repentance and faith in Him, the context in which the message is proclaimed should have an impact on how it is proclaimed. The goal is to reach as many as possible with the gospel. If a more effective means for accomplishing this can be accomplished by considering the context in which the proclamation is being made, then that needs to be taken into account. Hopefully the end result will be that those from different backgrounds and cultures will find the unifying presence of Christ, "For he is our peace, the one who made the two groups one and tore down the dividing wall of hostility by means of his own flesh" (Eph 2:14). May the proclamation of the gospel bring this about, starting with an evangelism that is faithful to the message and sensitive to the context.

Bibliography

Bailey, Kenneth. *Jesus through Middle Eastern Eyes: Cultural Studies in the Gospels*. Downer's Grove, IL: InterVarsity Press, 2011.

———. *Paul through Mediterranean Eyes: Cultural Studies*. Downer's Grove, IL: InterVarsity Press, 2008.

Brusco, Elizabeth E. *The Reformation of Machismo: Evangelical Conversion and Gender in Colombia*. Austin, TX: University of Texas Press, 2010.

Buckser, Andrew, and Stephen D. Glazier. *The Anthropology of Religious Conversion*. Lanham, MD: Rowman and Littlefield, 2003.

Burge, Gary M. *Encounters with Jesus: Uncover the Ancient Culture, Discover Hidden Meanings*. Grand Rapids, MI: Zondervan, 2010.

Burge, Gary M., Lynn H. Cohick, and Gene L. Green. *The New Testament in Antiquity: A Survey of the New Testament within Its Cultural Context*. Grand Rapids, MI: Zondervan, 2009.

deSilva, David. *Honor, Patronage, Kinship and Purity: Unlocking the New Testament Culture*. Downer's Grove, IL: InterVarsity Press, 2012.

McKnight, Scot. *Turning to Jesus: The Sociology of Conversion in the Gospels*. Louisville, KY: Westminster John Knox Press, 1992.

Richards, E. Randolph, and Brandon J. O'Brien. *Misreading Scripture with Western Eyes: Removing Cultural Blinders to Better Understand the Bible*. Downers Grove, IL: IVP Books, 2012.

Watson, David. *I Believe in Evangelism*. London: Hodder and Stoughton, 1976.

Biblical Basis

THE ROLE OF EVANGELISM IN MISSIONS: THE RELATIONSHIP OF WORD AND DEED

Ken Taylor

Evangelism is sharing the message of Christ with the goal of seeing people accept him as Lord and Savior. In its simplest form, missions is crossing one or more cultural barriers in an effort to see people accept Jesus as Savior. In defining these terms in this way, we can see evangelism is always a part of missions, but evangelism does not always include missions. Evangelism without missions can be seen when a Christian shares the message of Christ with someone nearby who is very similar in background and culture. When a Christian from Louisiana goes to Asia and attempts to share Christ with an Asian, his journey involves missions and evangelism. The latter illustration includes taking the message of Christ across one or more cultural barriers.

Just what constitutes evangelism on the mission field? Is starting a medical clinic in a chronically underserved mission field evangelism? A statement often attributed to St. Francis of Assisi is, "Preach the gospel at all times, and if necessary use words." It cannot be documented that this statement came from St. Francis. The emphasis of the statement also has problems. Certainly, living a Christian life and doing good deeds is important. But these are never substitutes for a verbal witness of the gospel of Jesus Christ. In the late nineteenth century and early twentieth century, the Social Gospel Movement became prominent. This movement asserted personal salvation should not be the sole concern of the church. The individual should be saved, but society needed saving as well. Indeed, there were many ills in society that needed to be addressed, like child labor, prison reform, the plight of the poor, and working conditions in factories. Secular organizations addressed these issues, but many ministers and churches also began advocating for improvements.

In a number of mainline Protestant denominations, emphasis on the social gospel became so great that any emphasis on sharing the gospel message and personal salvation was almost eliminated. For these, the role of the church was seen primarily as to impact society by improving the social condition of the population. More conservative denominations did not get so caught up in this movement. Later in the twentieth century, the Social Gospel Movement faded in influence but continued to exert a negative influence on conservative churches. For many conservative churches, any involvement in ministry to the whole person, beyond a sharing of the gospel for personal salvation, was tainted with being associated with the Social Gospel Movement. This kept many churches from ministering in ways that would have opened the door to a verbal witness.

Fortunately, fear of being labeled liberal for ministering to physical and social needs began to lessen as the twentieth century drew to a close. Many churches and mission organizations instituted ministries that helped provide nutrition, tutoring, English as a second language classes, assistance to released prisoners to help them adapt to life out of prison, as well as many other ways of ministering to the whole person. Some of these, like First Baptist Church of Leesburg, Florida, under the leadership of pastor Charles Roesel, were able to see large increases in baptisms through using social ministries that provided opportunities for sharing the gospel. The priority of sharing the gospel was maintained with a passion. Many conservative churches began ministries with a joint goal of ministering to human needs and winning individuals to Christ. Terms such as *service evangelism* and *ministry-based evangelism* were adopted to describe these activities. Most churches taking part in this type of work held to the belief that winning souls to Christ was the most important goal. Ministering to other needs was important, but evangelism that resulted in personal salvations was at the centerpiece of the ministry.

Many have described a proper balance between proclamation and social action as holistic ministry. Sider, Olson, and Unruh sought to lessen the gap between proponents on opposite sides of this issue: "Holistic ministry overcomes this long-standing divide by reaching out with the whole gospel in both word and deed. ... Without social ministry, evangelism can be perceived as just 'so much mouth.' Without the gospel, social activism is stripped of the Holy Spirit's transforming power."[1] A longtime leader of Southern Baptist missions said the following: "From the beginning, Southern Baptist foreign missions ministries have been holistic; that is, they have addressed the whole person in an actual life situation, not just the soul."[2]

Christians in the early church were involved in social ministry. In fact, many were led to view Christians differently because they reached out to the poor and needy with practical help beyond sharing the saving message of Christ. Throughout Christian history, followers of Christ have sought to minister to the spiritual and physical needs of the lost. Christians have historically been involved in addressing the issues in society that do not reflect the Christian worldview. When William Carey, the father of modern missions, arrived in India in the late eighteenth century, he quickly became aware of a societal ill in India he felt compelled to address. It was a common tradition among Hindus to burn alive the wife of a deceased husband on his funeral pyre. Carey began advocating for the outlaw of this practice of *suttee*. Carey and his missionary associates preached the gospel, started schools and

---

[1] Ronald J. Sider, Philip N. Olson, and Heidi Rolland Unruh, *Churches That Make a Difference: Reaching Your Community with Good News and Good Works* (Grand Rapids: Baker Books, 2002), 45–46.
[2] Winston Crawley, *Global Mission: A Story to Tell: An Interpretation of Southern Baptist Foreign Missions* (Nashville: Broadman, 1985), 21.

churches, translated the Bible, and fought for the ruling British government of India to outlaw *suttee*. After decades of advocacy, the practice was finally made unlawful.

With the beginning of the modern mission movement, near the beginning of the nineteenth century, western missionaries and mission agencies began to go into all the world with the message of Christ and with a desire to improve the lot of those without Christ. The gospel was shared widely as was good works. Countless schools, of all levels, were started. Hospitals were built and staffed by mission organizations to treat the physical ills of the populations of mission fields. Orphanages were opened in order to minister to orphans. Agricultural missionaries taught improved farming practices so hunger would be less of a problem. Unfortunately, some missionaries and mission agencies gradually replaced sharing the gospel with more and more social and physical ministries. For some, the task of evangelism faded so it could no longer be found in their work. Some saw evangelism and social action as equally important.

Referring back to the quote often attributed to Saint Francis of Assisi, can one actually be active in missions and evangelism through deeds only? W. Stanley Mooneyham referred to four views on the relationship between evangelism and engagement with social issues (social action). He distinguished between providing some sort of social help for individuals, few or many, without a verbal witness of the saving power of Jesus and, on the other hand, a direct witness with the goal of leading individuals to Christ. The views discussed are as follows:

1. social concern *or* evangelism,
2. social concern *is* evangelism,
3. social concern *for* evangelism, and
4. social concern *and* evangelism.[3]

---

[3] W. Stanley Mooneyham, "Evangelism and Social Action," in *Evangelism: The Next Ten Years*, ed. Sherwood Eliot Wirt, (Waco, TX: Word Books, 1978), 44–45.

Mooneyham noted the first view is clearly wrong as there can be no either/or when it comes to these two activities. He eliminated the second option because clearly the two activities are not the same. Mooneyham noted such a view would eliminate evangelism as a necessity. As to the third view, he eliminated it because he saw it as manipulative and as lessening the importance of social ministry. He adopted the fourth view as the proper one since we have an obligation to win people to Christ and to minister to our neighbor.[4]

In Matt 25 Jesus spoke of the obligation to minister to others. Jesus said, "For I was hungry, and you gave Me something to eat; I was thirsty, and you gave Me something to drink; I was a stranger, and you invited Me in; naked, and you clothed Me; I was sick, and you visited Me; I was in prison, and you came to Me" (Matt 25:35–36). He went on to say that when we do these things, we do them to him and, when we do not do these things for others, we do not do them to him. Clearly we have an obligation to be of aid to those who have physical needs. This concept is reinforced by what Jesus called the two greatest commandments. When asked what the greatest commandment was, Jesus answered, "The foremost is, 'Hear, O Israel! The Lord our God is one Lord; and you shall love the Lord your God with all your heart, and with all your soul, and with all your mind, and with all your strength.' The second is this, 'You shall love your neighbor as yourself.' There is no other commandment greater than these" (Mark 12:29–31). The command to love our neighbor as we love ourselves necessitates doing more than sitting idly by while our neighbor is in need.

And just who our neighbor is was taught by Jesus in the parable of the good Samaritan (Luke 10:25–37). The proper Jewish religious leaders did not do what was right, but the Samaritan who, seeing the man who had been robbed, beaten, and left for dead beside the road, ministered to him. Jesus was teaching that even a Samaritan could know the proper action when faced with a person in such need.

---

[4] Ibid., 44–47.

Jesus set an example of ministry to the needs brought before him. However, his teachings show his priority was communicating the truth about the kingdom of God. When crowds in Capernaum looked for him to perform more miracles and his disciples came to find him on behalf of the throngs of people, Jesus responded, "Let us go somewhere else to the towns nearby, so that I may preach there also; for that is what I came for" (Mark 1:38). In Matt 9:35 it is recorded Jesus went through "all the cities and villages, teaching in their synagogues and proclaiming the gospel of the kingdom, and healing every kind of disease and every kind of sickness." Verse 36 indicates Jesus had compassion on the crowds he saw because they "were distressed and dispirited like sheep without a shepherd." In the next verse, Jesus pointed out the shortage of workers for a plentiful harvest. Finally in verse 38, Jesus told his followers to pray the Lord of the harvest would "send out workers into His harvest." It is interesting Jesus did not tell his disciples to pray for those who would bring healing from disease but for those who would reap the harvest. This involves sharing the good news of the kingdom of God—the message of Jesus Christ. This instruction of Jesus indicates the superior role evangelism had over other types of ministry.

In John 6, Jesus referred to himself as the Bread of Heaven. The crowds followed him because he had just miraculously fed them. Jesus recognized they had again come to him because they wanted to continue to be fed material bread. He then shared with them a message that was difficult for them to hear. They wanted bread; he told them that he was the true bread: "I am the living bread that came down out of heaven; if anyone eats of this bread, he will live forever; and the bread also which I will give for the life of the world is My flesh" (John 6:51). The crowds did not understand, so Jesus made the truth even starker: "Truly, truly, I say to you, unless you eat the flesh of the Son of Man and drink His blood, you have no life in yourselves" (v. 53). Our Lord made it clear he had not come to feed people's stomachs but rather to give himself for the benefit of those who would trust him fully. As Jesus completed this teaching in the synagogue in Capernaum, many of those who had been following him left him. Jesus did not want followers who were disciples simply for the material benefits they would receive. He wanted them to be born again by accepting what he had come to do for them, dying for their sins.

In Matt 5, Jesus described kingdom kind of people as both salt and light. Kingdom kind of people are to add flavor and be a preservative in our world. We are to reflect the light of Christ around us. One way of doing this is to show Jesus by the way we live our lives. This is so people may see the Lord in our lives. Jesus said, "Let your light shine before men in such a way that they may see your good works, and glorify your Father who is in heaven" (Matt 5:16). A real living out of this command should involve both word and deed. We ought to exemplify Christian character, seek to be good neighbors by serving others, and tell the world that it is because of Jesus we do these things. By doing so, we will glorify God and point people toward a saving faith in Jesus Christ.

In Acts 3, Peter and John were walking to the temple in Jerusalem. A lame man saw them approaching and began to ask them for money. The response was telling, "But Peter said, 'I do not possess silver and gold, but what I do have I give to you: In the name of Jesus Christ the Nazarene—walk!'" (v. 6). Immediately the man was healed and began to praise God. Peter and John could have found alms to give to the lame man, but instead they ministered to him in a much more significant way. He was healed in the name of Jesus. There was a life-changing impact on this man. And as a result of this healing, the name of Jesus was spread, and proclamation was extended. Peter had a ready audience so he could explain what really happened. He made it clear it was not his power that raised this man, but it was the Lord who did this. Peter was then able to preach a powerful sermon. It got Peter and John arrested, but all of this helped get the proclamation of who Jesus was to more and more people. Proclamation was essential; material possessions were not.

Ronald Sider addressed the question of whether the proclamation of Jesus as Savior and Lord must be shared before we begin to address great material needs:

> I know of no one who would argue that today. In times of emergency, it is entirely proper to feed the starving and cloth the naked without speaking of Christ. At other times, it will be just as appropriate to invite people to accept our Lord before any social action is undertaken. It all depends on the circumstances.[5]

Sider discussed arguments about which—proclamation or missions—should have priority. He did not come up with a formula for deciding how we should divide our time and resources between proclamation and good works. He did state, however, "But if we truly follow Jesus, then Christian congregations and denominations will enthusiastically devote large amounts of resources to both evangelism and social action."[6]

While proclamation is essential, proclamation is often made possible by ministry before the proclamation. Years ago, in the New Orleans neighborhood where Gentilly Baptist Church is located, an evangelism team from our seminary was assigned to visit. I was working with our supervised ministry office and had the responsibility of receiving reports from the teams working in the city. I remember that week after week as the team working in this neighborhood turned in their reports of evangelistic activity, the results were almost always the same. Few people allowed the team to share the gospel and rarely did anyone accept Christ. Years later, Hurricane Katrina devastated much of the city of New Orleans. The building where my church met was

---

[5] Ronald J. Sider, *Good News and Good Works: A Theology for the Whole Gospel* (Grand Rapids: Baker Books, 1993), 18.
[6] Ibid., 170–71.

rendered permanently unusable and had to be demolished. The kind people of Gentilly Baptist invited our church to meet in their building. Our two churches merged, and we continued to meet in that building. The Arkansas Baptist Convention needed a headquarters for the massive rebuilding ministry they planned for our city. They chose the Gentilly Baptist facility. For several years, volunteers poured into our community rebuilding homes and churches, visiting in neighborhoods, mowing yards, planting shrubbery, and, at times, providing food, clothing, paint, and household goods to our community.

The attitudes of those of our neighborhood were changed toward a gospel witness. People became receptive. Many people made professions of faith. I remember visiting one home and mentioning I was from Gentilly Baptist Church. I remember being almost dragged into the home because the family that lived there had such a positive view of what people working out of our church had done for the community. Truly, the tragedy of Katrina had been heartbreaking. But the opportunity to do so much ministry in the community after the flood opened many doors and caused an increase in the proclamation of the good news of Jesus.

Donald Atkinson and Charles Roesel wrote of the responsibility of the church, saying, "Winning persons to faith in Jesus Christ is the priority of many, if not most evangelical churches. However, evangelism that does not minister to the needs of the whole person falls short of the New Testament standard."[7] Stanley Mooneyham stated, "It is not divinely ordered that the word should follow the deed or that the service should precede the witness. They interact with each other—naturally, wholesomely, redemptively."[8] R. H. Graves, a medical missionary who had the longest missions career of any missionary with what is now the International Mission Board of the Southern Baptist

---

[7] Donald A. Atkinson and Charles L. Roesel, *Meeting Needs, Sharing Christ: Ministry Evangelism in Today's New Testament Church* (Nashville: Lifeway Press 1995), 3.

[8] Mooneyham, "Evangelism and Social Action," *Evangelism*, 7.

Convention, noted the connection he saw between proclamation and good works: "We find medical work of special service in preparing the way for the preaching of the word and the founding of new churches … In China, we find it especially useful in opening new stations, by overcoming the prejudices of the people and showing the benevolent aspect of Christianity in a way that the simplest may understand."[9]

Jeff Palmer, head of Baptist Global Response, an organization involved in relief and development ministries internationally, noted several ways relief and development can advance missions and evangelism. These included making it easier to get into hostile areas, giving a platform for outsiders to gain access to an area, giving long-term access, and overcoming negative attitudes toward Christians.[10]

In *Mission Drift: The Unspoken Crisis Facing Leaders, Charities, and Churches*, the authors addressed a danger so often faced by churches and missionaries. An organization can be formed with a Christ-centered purpose and continue with that central purpose for years. Little by little, the mission begins to drift away from the initial purpose. Many factors can lead to this drift. Organizations must realize missional drift is always a danger. Hard decisions often have to be made. "If an organization is drifting far from its initial purpose, then God can empower leaders to turn it around, but it often requires desperate measures. Pain avoidance is the fastest way for Mission Drift to devastate an organization's Christ-centered identity."[11] Individuals, churches, and mission organizations can easily allow mission drift to move them from the Christ-centered goal of sharing Christ always.

---

[9] R. H. Graves, *Forty Years in China or China in Transition* (Baltimore: R. H. Woodward Company, 1895), 224–25.
[10] Jeffrey Palmer, "Human Needs Ministry," in *Missiology: An Introduction to the Foundations, History, and Strategies of World Missions*, 2nd ed., ed. John Mark Terry (Nashville: B&H Publishing Group, 2015), 44.
[11] Peter Greer and Chris Horst, *Mission Drift: The Unspoken Crisis Facing Leaders, Charities, and Churches* (Minneapolis: Bethany House, 2014), 4.

Years ago, a large homeless shelter received large quantities of food donations from several grocery stores. The largest quantity of food included all kinds of bread and pastries. The shelter could not use all the donated food for their meals. The shelter contacted me to see if our church wanted to come pick up the items they could not use. I felt this would be a great blessing to many of the lower socio-economic people we ministered to in the inner city. Some Saturday mornings, I would pick up several hundred pounds of bread and other items in our church van. This ministry was physically demanding and very time consuming. I would travel inner city streets and make stops along the way, making distributions in areas where we did evangelistic outreach and often used our van to pick up youth and children for church.

It did not take long at all for people to begin looking for me on Saturday mornings. There was so much bread I would rush from one spot to another to give the maximum amount of bread away. I did not want to be left with bread that had to be thrown away. It was a hectic time, but people were getting some much-needed food. I remember thinking about how rushed I was on those bread delivery runs and how the rush prevented me from being able to share the gospel as often as I once had on these same streets. One day, I heard an individual yell down the street as I drove up, "The bread man is here." This gave me pause. I was used to a number of titles that reflected my line of work, such as "preacher man," but being called the "bread man" caused me to begin assessing whether or not giving out bread, certainly a good thing, was actually the best thing that I could be doing with my time and energy. Had my mission drifted from ministering to people in a way that would give me opportunities to share Christ to simply providing for people to be able to fill their stomachs? I had experienced mission drift.

I did not have to make any hard decisions. At least one grocery store that was donating food items to the shelter went out of business. Soon the shelter had no excess food to give away, and I was no longer the "bread man." Some people missed the distributions, but I do not feel our ministry had been hurt. In fact, I was then able to focus more on the main thing—sharing the good news of Jesus.

While some equate the roles of evangelism and social action, a more biblical approach is prioritism—a view that spiritual transformation is the most important work of the church. Little says prioritism "asserts, in line with the Lausanne Covenant (paragraph 6), that the priority of the church in mission should be the proclamation of the gospel."[12]

Samuel Hugh Moffett concluded his magisterial two-volume work on the history of missions in Asia with the following account. Decades after the time of Adoniram Judson, Christian Karen tribesmen in Burma were suffering from lack of food because an outbreak of rats had devoured their rice crops. The Karens were forced to eat the rats. Missionaries working with the Karen people were preparing to move to another part of the country to seek to reach another people group, the Ka-Khyen. A Karen Christian brought the missionaries a small gift of money from their church to help with the new work. The missionary at first refused the gift, telling him they should keep the money to help prevent them from starving. The Karen believer refused the offer noting they could survive by eating rats, but the Ka-Khyen could not survive unless they received the gospel.[13]

We ought to do all that we can to add material and social aid to our sharing of the gospel, but we must remember that without Christ people have no hope and that our Savior said, "I am the way, and the truth, and the life; no one comes to the Father but through Me" (John 14:6).

---

[12] Christopher R. Little, "Breaking Bad Missiological Habits," in *Discovering the Mission of God: Best Missiological Practices for the 21st Century*, eds. Mike Barnett and Robin Martin (Downers Grove, IL: IVP Academic, 2012), 41.

[13] Samuel Hugh Moffett, *A History of Christianity in Asia*, vol. 2: 1500–1900 (Maryknoll, NY: Orbis Books, 2005), 26.

BIBLIOGRAPHY

Atkinson, Donald A., and Charles L. Roesel. *Meeting Needs, Sharing Christ: Ministry Evangelism in Today's New Testament Church*. Nashville, TN: LifeWay, 1995.

Crawley, Winston. *Global Mission: A Story to Tell; An Interpretation of Southern Baptist Foreign Missions*. Nashville, TN: Broadman, 1985.

Graves, R. H.. *Forty Years in China or China in Transition*. Baltimore: R. H. Woodward Company, 1895.

Greer, Peter, and Chris Horst. *Mission Drift: The Unspoken Crisis Facing Leaders, Charities, and Churches*. Minneapolis: MN: Bethany House, 2014.

Little, Christopher R. "Breaking Bad Missiological Habits." In *Discovering the Mission of God: Best Missiological Practices for the 21st Century*, edited by Mike Barnett and Robin Martin. Downers Grove, IL: IVP Academic, 2012.

Miles, Delos. *Evangelism and Social Involvement*. Nashville, TN: Broadman Press, 1986.

Moffett, Samuel Hugh. *A History of Christianity in Asia*. Vol. 2: 1500–1900. Maryknoll, NY: Orbis Books, 2005.

Mooneyham, W. Stanley. "Evangelism and Social Action." In *Evangelism: The Next Ten Years*, edited by Sherwood Eliot Wirt. Waco, TX: Word Books, 1978.

Palmer, Jeffrey. "Human Needs Ministry." In *Missiology: An Introduction to the Foundations, History, and Strategies of World Missions*, edited by John Mark Terry, 2nd edition. Nashville, TN: B&H Publishing Group, 2015.

Sider, Ronald J. *Good News and Good Works: A Theology for the Whole Gospel*. Grand Rapids, MI: Baker Books, 1993.

Sider, Ronald J., Philip N. Olson, and Heidi Rolland Unruh. *Churches That Make a Difference: Reaching Your Community with Good News and Good Works*. Grand Rapids, MI: Baker Books, 2002.

Historical Basis

THE HISTORY OF EVANGELISM

Archie England and Ronnie McLellan

Dr. Kelley spent much of his scholarly pursuits on the history of evangelism in the Southern Baptist Convention. Kelley's dissertation in 1983 focused upon the developments in revival meetings in the Southern Baptist Convention between 1947 and 1980. Ten years later, he published the book, *How Did They Do It?*, to recount the storied history of evangelism in the denomination. Just before announcing his retirement in 2018, Kelley released *Fuel the Fire* as an update to his earlier SBC evangelism history. The following contents honor Kelley's scholarship in this area with a history of evangelism beginning with Jesus and spanning to the present.

Jesus (AD 26–30)

Prior to Jesus's public ministry, announcements of the Messiah's birth proceeded from the mouths of angels, wise men, and shepherds (Matt 1:20–21; 2:2; Luke 1:28–35; 2:9–20). Proclamation of the gospel in earnest came through John the Baptist, Jesus's cousin, as he "preached the gospel to the people" (Luke 3:18). After John baptized Jesus, the Holy Spirit descended upon Jesus as he also would descend upon the disciples at Pentecost to empower them for the task of evangelism (Luke 2:21–22; Acts 2:1–4).[1]

---

[1] Gerald L. Stevens, *Acts: A New Vision for the People of God* (Eugene, OR: Pickwick Publications, 2016), 168.

Jesus traveled through villages, healed the sick, and called for a response of repentance and belief in the gospel message (Matt 4:23; 9:35; Mark 1:14–15). Jesus preached he was the gospel and the fulfillment of Isaiah's prophecies: "The Spirit of the Lord is upon me, because he anointed me to preach the gospel to the poor. He has sent Me to proclaim release to the captives, and recovery of sight to the blind, to set free those who are oppressed, to proclaim the favorable year of the Lord" (Luke 4:18–19; see also Isa 61:1–2).

Jesus also practiced personal evangelism. He offered personal invitations to the twelve disciples (Matt 4:19; 9:9; John 1:43), Zacchaeus (Luke 19:1–9), Nicodemus (John 3:1–16), and the Samaritan woman at the well (John 4:1–42). While many were converted through Jesus's personal evangelism, He also suffered rejection on several occasions. The rich young ruler declined Jesus's invitation because "he owned much property" (Matt 19:22). Only one of the ten lepers Jesus healed returned to express thanks and receive salvation (Luke 17:11–18). While one of the criminals crucified alongside Jesus confessed faith, the other mocked him (Luke 23:32–43). Further, many of Jesus' outer band of disciples deserted him after they found his teaching offensive, foreshadowing the ultimate betrayal by Judas who was one of the Twelve (John 6:60–71; Matt 26:47–56; Acts 1:16–20).

Jesus's personal evangelism may serve as a model for the contemporary church as well. He offered the gospel to the least likely candidates for salvation. Zacchaeus and the Samaritan woman at the well represented those normally shunned because their sins were unacceptable to society, while Jesus could have considered Nicodemus a lost cause because of his association with the antagonistic Pharisees. Also, his example of perseverance despite constant rejection challenges a Western culture that is often noncommittal.

Acts (AD 30–53)

Jesus's substitutionary death on the cross and his resurrection became the gospel message his disciples preached when they were empowered by the Holy Spirit during Pentecost and beyond. They excelled in proclaiming the gospel in neutral locations. Peter's Spirit-filled message at Pentecost in Jerusalem resulted in three thousand new believers (Acts 2:41). Paul's open-air preaching met mixed results as Lydia's conversion helped Paul establish a church in Philippi (Acts 16:14–15). Paul's preaching in Lystra (Acts 14:8–20), Athens (Acts 17:22–34), and Ephesus (Acts 19:9–10), resulted in few initial converts, and he instead received threats of execution, apathy, and rioting. Paul also engaged in synagogue preaching throughout his missionary journeys. Michael Green identified three points in these messages to dispersed Jews: Israel's history and the expectation of the Messiah; the message of Jesus as the fulfillment of Old Testament prophecies; and an offer of forgiveness through Jesus's death and resurrection.[2]

While Peter and Paul's gospel ministries dominated much of the biblical witness in Acts, the contributions of less-known and anonymous individuals should not be ignored. In fact, most conversions in the early centuries of the Christian church happened through lay witnesses. Stephen and Philip were among seven Hellenistic Jews who were chosen to serve during a crisis in the Jerusalem church. Stephen's apologetic before Jewish leaders led to a martyr's death that resulted in the dispersion of Christians to Samaria. Philip's ministry in Samaria flourished during Saul's persecution as many Samaritans trusted in Jesus, and Philip's obedience to the Holy Spirit resulted in the first gentile convert who was an Ethiopian eunuch. Ananias, described as a "disciple in Damascus," obeyed the Lord's calling through a vision and visited Saul, which led to Saul/Paul's conversion and prolific ministry (Acts 9:10–18). Anonymous believers had a great impact in Antioch as "men of Cyprus and Cyrene, who came to Antioch and began speaking to the Greeks also, preaching the Lord Jesus. ... and a large number who believed turned to the Lord" (Acts 11:20–21). The contemporary

---

[2] Michael Green, *Evangelism in the Early Church*, rev. ed., (Grand Rapids, MI: William B. Eerdmans Publishing Company, 2004), 301–302.

church, unlike the New Testament church, has depended upon both its hired clergy and its official church buildings for the task of evangelism. Green observed the Roman "imperial government was very allergic to large meetings in public places," and that "the Christians did not own any (buildings) until the third century ... I have a feeling we could learn from them."[3]

Growth by Persecution (AD 100–300)

During the second and third centuries, the early Christian church experienced growth as a result of persecution much like the growth that followed Stephen's death in Acts. The martyrdom of Polycarp (156) and Justin Martyr (166) both resulted in significant numbers of conversions for Christianity. Polycarp championed the gospel as the bishop of Smyrna in modern-day Turkey. He refused to recant his faith and suffered death by dagger after the executioners failed to burn him at the stake. Likewise, Justin was beheaded in Rome after he affirmed his faith in Christ. Irenaeus (130–202), a disciple of Polycarp, led the defense of the gospel against Gnosticism with his writing, *Against Heresies*. He led revival in Lyons, now France, and sent missionaries to modern-day Spain in Gaul.[4]

Origen (184–253) defended the gospel against the pagan philosopher Celsus in his writing, *Contra Celsus*. Celsus attacked Christianity regarding the common arguments that the Christian love feasts were immoral and that the meetings Christians hosted were secret societies. Origen also persuaded Gregory Thaumatargus (213–270) to become a Christian. Gregory "the Miracle Worker" became Bishop of Lyons and led most of the city to Christian faith. By AD 300, the gospel took

---

[3] Michael Green, *Thirty Years that Changed the World: The Book of Acts for Today* (Grand Rapids, MI: William B. Eerdmans Publishing Company, 2004), 1477–81, Kindle.
[4] Justin Martyr, *Ante-Nicene Fathers*, ed. Philip Schaff, vol. 1 (Grand Rapids, MI: Christian Classics Ethereal Library, 1885), 124, 832, accessed February 18, 2019, http://www.ccel.org/ccel/schaff/anf01.pdf.

root in every city of the Roman Empire. Emperor Diocletian slowed the Christian church's advance through persecution in 303, but the move backfired as the gospel spread to the countryside instead of cities as a result.[5]

Missionary Movements and Reform in the Middle Ages (AD 400–1500)

Once the Christian church had been established in the Roman Empire, missionary movements advanced the gospel in other pagan nations. Native Scot Patrick (389–461) landed in Ireland in 432 after being kidnapped by pirates at the age of sixteen. Patrick was converted to Christianity and spread the gospel to more than 120,000 Irishmen and started 365 churches in nearly thirty years. More than a century later, Irish native Columba (521–597) returned the favor by bringing the gospel to the island of Iona off the Scottish coast.[6] The charge across the United Kingdom continued when Augustine of Canterbury (545–605), not Hippo, spread the gospel across England with the conversion and blessing of King Ethelbert. From England, Boniface (675–754) brought the gospel to Germany and Belgium. He confronted pagans in the area by felling a sacred tree dedicated to the god Thor. When Thor failed to exact retribution on Boniface, many Germans converted to Christianity.[7]

The evangelists in the middle of the Middle Ages tended toward preaching bands and orders rather than an individual approach. Peter Waldo took a vow of poverty and refused to live in a monastery. Instead, he lived among the poor in Lyons, France, and preached

---

[5] Justo L. Gonzalez, *The Story of Christianity: The Early Church to the Dawn of the Reformation*, vol. 1 (New York, NY: HarperCollins Publishers, 1984), 91–108.

[6] Philip Schaff, *History of the Christian Church: Mediaeval Christianity. A.D. 590–1073* (Grand Rapids, MI: Christian Classics Ethereal Library, 1998), 42–53; http://www.ccel.org/ccel/schaff/hcc4.pdf.

[7] John Mark Terry, *Evangelism: A Concise History* (Nashville, TN: Broadman & Holman Publishers, 1994), 846–887, Kindle.

the gospel. The Bishop of Lyons opposed him, and at the Third Lateran Council, Waldo and his band of followers were prohibited from preaching without the bishop's consent. This group became known as the Waldensians and preached across Europe after being expelled from Lyons. Similarly, Francis of Assisi (1181–1226) also chose poverty to minister to the poor in Italy. He gained a following for the purpose of gospel ministry, which became known as the Franciscan order.[8]

The latter Middle Ages produced evangelists who foreshadowed the coming Reformation. In England, John Wycliffe (1320–1384) gained popularity with the monarchy because he opposed the Roman papacy's practice of collecting tributes from other nations. Wycliffe also charged the monastic orders with corruption. Rome retaliated and pressured English royalty to end Wycliffe's attacks against the church. However, Wycliffe's favor with those in high position spared his life and his ministry, and he published the first English translation of the Bible in 1382. John Huss (1369–1415), a priest appointed in Prague (now the Czech Republic), was influenced greatly by the writings of Wycliffe, and he preached in the common language despite opposition from Rome. Huss died as a martyr after refusing to recant his faith.[9] Jerome Savonarola (1452–1498) followed Huss, denouncing the Roman church for simony and sexual immorality. Savonarola became a force both politically and spiritually in Florence, Italy. He too was executed for his dissent against Rome, but not in vain.[10] These pioneers of reform set the table for the Reformation of Martin Luther, Ulrich Zwingli, and John Calvin.

---

[8] Ibid., 903–912, 1029–1078.
[9] Ellen Gould White, *The Great Controversy* (Grand Rapids, MI: Christian Classics Ethereal Library, 1994), 50–55, 60–67; accessed February 18, 2019, http://www.ccel.org/ccel/white/controversy.pdf.
[10] Philip Schaff, *History of the Christian Church: The Middle Ages. A.D. 1294–1517* (Grand Rapids, MI: Christian Classics Ethereal Library, 1998), 553–574.

The Reformation (AD 1500–1650)

Martin Luther (1486–1546) became disenchanted with the Roman church's doctrine of salvation by works along with its corrupt practice of selling indulgences. In 1517, Luther nailed his *Ninety-Five Theses* to the door of the Castle Church in Wittenberg, Germany. Like his predecessors, Luther emphasized faith instead of works in the doctrine of salvation. He also affirmed the sole authority of the Scriptures and published a German translation of the New Testament in 1522 and completed the Old Testament in 1534.[11]

In Switzerland, Ulrich Zwingli published sixty-seven theses against the Roman Catholic Church in 1523. Among Zwingli's differences with the Catholic Church, he held that the Lord's Supper and baptism were symbolic rather than sacramental, championed predestination, and viewed Scripture as the sole authority for the Christian life. Some of Zwingli's more conservative followers splintered from his group in 1525 because they opposed infant baptism and other practices of the Roman Catholic Church that Zwingli still embraced. The dissenters formed the Anabaptist movement, which spread across Europe after being opposed in Switzerland.

French theologian John Calvin completed the cycle of the Reformation as he expounded upon and defended the doctrine of predestination in his writing *Institutes of the Christian Religion* in 1534. Because of his unpopular doctrinal positions, Calvin relocated to Geneva, Switzerland, but he reached the people of his homeland by sending eighty-eight missionaries to evangelize France between 1555 and 1562, which resulted in more than one-hundred thousand converts.[12]

Pietism & Puritanism (AD 1580–1740)

After the Thirty Years War in Germany (1618–1648), Lutheranism suffered a schism. A dissenting group known as Pietists rejected infant

---

[11] Terry, *Evangelism*, 1250–1320.
[12] Ibid., 1355–1444.

baptism, which the Lutherans still practiced, but they also desired religious fervor that was lacking in the preaching and evangelism of Lutheran churches. Philip Jakob Spener pioneered the official Pietism movement when he published *Pious Desires* in 1675. He emphasized more intense Bible study, lay leadership, higher moral standards, and intentional evangelism in the lives of believers.[13] Spener's method of intensive group Bible study resembles modern-day cell groups or Sunday School classes. He termed these groups *"ecclesiolae in ecclesiae* (Latin: 'little churches within the church')."[14] Nickolaus von Zinzendorf established the Moravian Brethren as part of the Pietism movement. The Moravians mobilized their disciples for a worldwide missionary movement that included journeys to America.[15]

In England, a desire to see the Anglican church employ the theology of Calvin led to the rise of Puritanism. However, Queen Elizabeth I and King James I thwarted these attempts in an effort to solidify political control through the state church. Separatist churches were formed out of the Puritanism movement, and the General and Particular Baptist churches in England resulted. Puritan leader William Bradford led a group of pilgrims to America in search of religious freedom and to escape religious persecution. They landed in Plymouth Rock, Massachusetts, and were the forerunners of the Awakening in America.[16]

The Great Awakenings (AD 1725–1830)

The open-air preaching of George Whitefield (1714–1770) and John Wesley (1703–1791) began to stir souls of the common people in England after Whitefield was banned from preaching in Anglican churches due to his emphasis of salvation by grace alone. Whitefield, who had

---

[13] Ibid., 1507–82.
[14] Alister E. McGrath, *Christian History: An Introduction* (West Sussex, UK: John Wiley & Sons Ltd., Publication, 2013), 6425, Kindle.
[15] Terry, *Evangelism*, 1590–1607.
[16] Robert A. Baker and John M. Landers, *A Summary of Christian History*, 3rd ed. (Nashville, TN: B&H Academic, 2005), 4202–342, 5479–87, Kindle.

established an orphanage in the American colony of Georgia, passed the baton to the older Wesley in order to continue the open-air meetings in England. Whitefield's preaching drew crowds as large as forty-thousand people in Bristol, Gloucester, and London. John and his brother Charles Wesley also had ties to the Georgia colony through Moravian missionaries and experienced conversion in 1738. While Whitefield pioneered the preaching method, Wesley organized the large number of converts into tiered groups for the purpose of discipleship. Although Wesley desired these groups as a means of revival for the Anglican church, the public dubbed this group as the Methodist Church beginning in 1759.[17]

The First Great Awakening in America began with the ministry of Theodore Frelinghuysen (1691–1747). The Dutch Reformed Church appointed Frelinghuysen, a German native, to pastor four churches in New Jersey. When he arrived in 1719, Frelinghuysen confronted the cultural, dead, religious habits of the congregations with the call for a personal commitment to Christ, and the movement began a ripple effect in 1726. Gilbert Tennent, who served a Presbyterian church in New Jersey, shared Frelinghuysen's desire for revival and confronted many of the same problems in his congregation.[18]

In New England, the Holy Spirit utilized the polar personalities of Jonathan Edwards (1703–1758) and George Whitefield. Edwards, a Congregationalist, was concerned for the moral purity of younger members in his congregation at Northampton, Massachusetts. His methods of evangelism included home visitation and a highly intellectual style of preaching from written manuscripts. A revival movement began at Edwards's church where three hundred people were converted and spread to forty towns in Massachusetts and Connecticut between 1734 and 1737 in what became known as the Valley Revival.

---

[17] Terry, *Evangelism*, 1736–1829.
[18] Ibid., 2008–40.

After the revival fires cooled, Whitefield stirred the embers with his itinerant preaching ministry in New England between 1740 and 1742. Unlike Edwards, Whitefield preached extemporaneously, and he continued his method of open-air preaching because church buildings could not house the large crowds he drew.[19]

After the Revolutionary War in America, the Second Great Awakening began with student-led revivals in 1786 on the campuses of Hampden-Sidney College in Virginia and Washington College in Maryland. The movement poised the Presbyterians for evangelistic growth as many of the students became ministers in the denomination. Conversely, Yale president Timothy Dwight confronted his students with the gospel, many of whom had fallen prey to agnosticism with the influence of the Enlightenment. Dwight tilled the ground of revival for seven years through his lectures and chapel sermons before one-third of Yale's student population confessed Christ in 1802.[20]

Although Kentucky and Tennessee are considered Southern states in modern American history, they were considered the Western frontier following the Revolutionary War. Fifty years before Tennessee whiskey distiller Jack Daniel was born, the people of this new frontier had fallen into the vice of drunkenness because of their taste for homemade whiskey. Presbyterian revivalist James McGready (1763–1817) desired to see a move of the Holy Spirit similar to what he experienced at Hampden-Sydney College in Virginia.[21] He initiated the revival with Kentucky's common people after being rejected by elite congregations in North Carolina. McGready partnered with fellow Presbyterian, Baptist, and Methodist ministers. The Cane Ridge Camp Meeting in August 1801 near Paris, Kentucky, launched the Great Revival (or the South's Second Great Awakening) as a movement. Many of the characteristics of this movement between 1799 and 1806 may be seen

---

[19] Ibid., 2040–2106.
[20] Ibid., 2306–15.
[21] Ibid., 2331–40.

in traditional evangelical churches in the South today such as upbeat gospel hymns, an individualistic approach to conversion, a theology more bent toward Arminianism than Calvinism, and protracted revival meetings.[22]

Charles G. Finney (1792–1875) became the most well-known preacher of the Second Great Awakening. His conversion took place in 1821 at the age of twenty-nine while studying to become a lawyer. He entered the preaching ministry in 1824, and his evangelistic messages proved fruitful in New York State. He saw the greatest number of conversions in Rochester where revival fell from the fall 1830 to spring 1831. In addition to his role as an evangelist, Finney also served as a pastor in local churches and as a professor at Oberlin College in Ohio, where he eventually became president from 1851 to 1866.[23] Finney also implemented new techniques during his revival meetings, which his critics called "New Measures."[24] Many of these techniques have persisted in modern revivals such as protracted revival meetings, the popularization of the altar call, utilizing music to set a mood conducive to evangelism, and the advertisement of revival meetings.

The Layman's Prayer Revival (AD 1857–1858)

The Layman's Prayer Revival of 1857–1858 began with the commissioning of businessman Jeremiah Lanphier from the North Dutch Reformed Church on Fulton Street in New York City. During his private prayer time after a day of ministering, Lanphier heard God's call to begin a weekly prayer meeting for businessmen during the lunch hour. The group grew from a half-dozen men in one meeting to twenty separate daily prayer meetings across New York City two months later. The ground rules

---

[22] John B. Boles, *The Great Revival: Beginnings of the Bible Belt* (Lexington, KY: The University of Kentucky Press, 1996), 41–43; 53–82; 125–39.
[23] Charles Finney, *The Works of Charles Finney: Volume 1* (Seattle, WA: Amazon Digital Services, LLC, 2012), 198, 72982–97, Kindle.
[24] Terry, *Evangelism*, 2535.

allowed for any attendee to speak or pray for a maximum of five minutes with the meetings lasting exactly one hour from noon to 1 p.m. The prayer movement caught fire in major cities across the United States.[25]

This revival movement took place concurrently with an economic crisis in America—the Business Revulsion of 1857. The crisis caused the majority of banks nationwide to shut down for nearly two months.[26] This evangelism movement differed from the Great Awakenings that preceded it because the leading personalities were laymen instead of renowned preachers. In addition to the prayer meetings, the leaders also carried out systematic home visitation programs and distributed tracts. Historians of the revival estimated that between 300,000 and one million people converted to Christianity as a result.[27]

The Welsh Revival and the Azusa Street Revival (AD 1904–1906)

In 1903 Dean David Howell, a leader in the Anglican Church, called the country of Wales to pray for a much-needed revival. He died before the prayer was answered, but evangelist Seth Joshua began to pray a preacher would be raised from the common coal miners. Robert Evans, a coal miner raised in a Welsh Calvinist Methodist church, heard the call to ministry and became the answer to Joshua's prayer. After hearing Joshua's message, "Lord, Bend Us," in a 1903 meeting, Roberts quit his formal ministry training and pursued itinerant evangelistic ministry. Roberts reported seeing a vision of the number 100,000 written on paper. He began to pray for that same number of conversions. While Roberts became the public face of the revival, the majority of

---

[25] Mark Alan Carpenter, "An Interpretive Analysis of the Layman's Prayer Revival of 1857–1858" (PhD diss., Mid-America Baptist Theological Seminary, 2006), 30–34, 46–48, accessed February 18, 2019, https://search.proquest.com/docview/304933587/abstract/ DC0DA0BE911D4CD7PQ/1.
[26] Ibid., 35–45.
[27] John D. Hannah, "Layman's Prayer Revival of 1858," in *Bibliotheca Sacra* 134, no. 533 (January 1977): 59–73, accessed February 15, 2019, http://search.ebscohost.com/login.aspx?direct=true&db=rfh&AN=ATLA0000759731&site=ehost-live.

the evangelists were little known. Historians have estimated the number of conversions ranged between 80,000 and 162,000.[28]

While the Welsh revival has been credited with Pentecostalism movements in India, Korea, and Africa, many Pentecostals in North America have traced their beginnings to the Azusa Street revival in Los Angeles. Before William Seymour's ministry on the West Coast, he sat under the tutelage of Charles Parham, who taught about a second baptism of the Holy Spirit evidenced by speaking in tongues. Seymour, an African-American preacher, and Parham, a Caucasian, met in Houston, Texas. While Parham advocated segregation in worship, Seymour's movement in Los Angeles saw the Holy Spirit's baptism as an eschatological event in which all human divisions, including racism, were broken in preparation for Christ's return.[29] Most Pentecostal congregations in North America derive either from Parham or Seymour. Parham established the Apostolic Faith Movement, predominant in the Midwestern and Southwestern United States and in Chicago-area congregations. While Parham confined his influence to regions where he resided, Seymour drew Christians from across the country to experience Pentecostalism in Los Angeles through his publication *Apostolic Faith*. The influence of Azusa Street may be seen in established denominations such as the Church of God in Christ, the Pentecostal Holiness Church, and the Church of God (Cleveland, Tennessee).[30]

---

[28] Wolfgang Reinhardt, "'A Year of Rejoicing': The Welsh Revival 1904–05 and Its International Challenges," *Evangelical Review of Theology* 31, no. 2 (April 2007): 100–126, accessed February 16, 2019, http://search.ebscohost.com/login.aspx?direct=true&db=rfh&AN=ATLA0001659700&site=ehost–live.

[29] Edith L. Blumhofer, "Azusa Street Revival," *The Christian Century* 123, no. 5 (March 7, 2006): 20–22, accessed February 16, 2019, http://search.ebscohost.com/login.aspx?direct=true&db=rfh&AN=ATLA0001503067&site=ehost–live.

[30] Joe Creech, "Visions of Glory: The Place of the Azusa Street Revival in Pentecostal History," *Church History* 65, no. 3 (September 1996): 405–24, accessed February 18, 2019, http://search.ebscohost.com/login.aspx?direct=true&db=rfh&AN=ATLA0000910922&site=ehost–live.

Evangelistic Preaching in the Nineteenth and Twentieth Centuries (AD 1870–2018)

Finney became a dominating personality during the Second Great Awakening, but his "New Measures" influenced the evangelistic preaching of the nineteenth and twentieth centuries. Dwight L. Moody (1837–1899) became the first evangelist to partner with a prominent singer as he toured with Ira Sankey.[31] Moody's friend Charles Spurgeon (1834–1892) exemplified evangelistic pastoral preaching in London's Metropolitan Tabernacle and printed his sermons for the public.[32] Meanwhile, Moody's protégé J. Wilbur Chapman (1859–1918) innovated the simultaneous evangelistic campaigns in which several revival meetings would be held at the same time across one city,[33] and Chapman's advance man Billy Sunday (1862–1935), a professional baseball player turned preacher, became well-known for his revivals in urban centers.[34]

While Billy Sunday faded from the scene, Billy Graham was preparing for ministry. Graham became perhaps America's most beloved evangelist because of his willingness to work across denominational lines. This practice shifted from Graham's upbringing and early ministry connected to fundamentalist churches. Graham's 1949 Los Angeles

---

[31] David W. Bebbington, "How Moody Changed Revivalism," *Christian History* 9, no. 1 (February 1990): 22, accessed February 16, 2019, http://search.ebscohost.com/login.aspx?direct=true&db=khh&AN=9604244218&site=ehost-live.

[32] Craig Skinner, "The Preaching of Charles Haddon Spurgeon," *Baptist History and Heritage* 19, no. 4 (October 1984): 16–26, accessed February 18, 2019, http://search.ebscohost.com/login.aspx?direct=true&db=rfh&AN=ATLA0000926087&site=ehost-live.

[33] Scott Sterling Hobbs, "The Contributions of J. Wilbur Chapman to American Evangelism" (PhD diss., Southwestern Baptist Theological Seminary, 1997), 34–37; 97; 120–77, accessed February 16, 2019, https://search.proquest.com/docview/304384733/abstract/B85C754 F4E594916PQ/1.

[34] Preston Lamont Nix, "A Critical Analysis of the Organizational Methodology in Selected Evangelistic Campaigns of William Ashley (Billy) Sunday" (PhD diss., Southwestern Baptist Theological Seminary, 1992), 285–300, accessed February 16, 2019, https://search.proquest.com/docview/304022958/abstract/D1D945074F0F490EPQ/1.

Crusade became the first in which he included churches from multiple denominations and launched his ministry into the limelight.[35] Graham's use of technology set him apart from other evangelists as he broadcasted the "Hour of Decision" radio program, televised many of his crusades, published *Christianity Today* magazine, and continued his work after his official retirement in 2005 by posting vidoes of his sermons to his website through the "My Hope" campaign from 2013 to 2016. His son Franklin Graham has carried on his legacy and ministry since the 1990s and continues to do so since his father's death in 2018 through the Billy Graham Evangelistic Association.

Greg Laurie is the most current and well-known revivalist. Laurie is the founder and pastor of Harvest Christian Fellowship in Riverside, California. He established Harvest Crusades in 1990, which modeled the style of Billy Graham's crusades in a contemporary fashion. Also, Laurie was the product of the Jesus Movement—the last large-scale revival in America. During this movement of the 1960s and 1970s, teens and young adults known as hippies rebelled against the establishments of government, society, and religion through the empty pleasures of drugs, sexual encounters, and rock and roll music. Many found their answer in the gospel of Jesus through open-air preaching on beaches, Bible studies on high school campuses, and Christian songs palatable to the hippie culture. While many traditional churches rejected these new believers for cultural reasons, leaders such as Billy Graham and Bill Bright of Campus Crusade for Christ encouraged established churches to embrace these "Jesus freaks," as they were referred to by non-Christian hippies. As a result, the converts of the Jesus Movement birthed contemporary Christian music and seeker-sensitive services.[36]

---

[35] Thomas Paul Johnston, *Examining Billy Graham's Theology of Evangelism* (Eugene, OR: Wipf and Stock, 2003), 309–311, Kindle.
[36] Gregg Laurie and Ellen Vaughn, *Jesus Revolution: How God Transformed an Unlikely Generation and How He Can Do It Again Today* (Grand Rapids, MI: Baker Books, 2018), 154–195, Kindle.

The Church Growth Movement

Pastors and church members in evangelical churches may not be familiar with missiologist Donald McGavran, but many of the pragmatic methods utilized for outreach and evangelism in the contemporary Christian church derived from McGavran's research. As a missionary to India, McGavran noticed that churches within the same contexts could thrive or decline based on certain principles. After he retired, McGavran began applying his research in the mission field to churches in America. The homogeneous unit principle became McGavran's most popular and most controversial finding. McGavran stated, "People like to become Christians without crossing racial, linguistic, or class barriers."[37] Critics of McGavran's research have pointed toward this principle to further segregate the church. However, McGavran and his protégé C. Peter Wagner claimed the principle described reality rather than prescribed an evangelistic method.

In a broader sense, the Church Growth Movement applied social research to discover the most pragmatic evangelistic methods for particular ministry contexts. Rick Warren, pastor of Saddleback Church in California, popularized this approach to evangelism in *The Purpose Driven Church* as he described how a church should decide on its target audience. Warren's philosophy echoed the homogeneous unit principle: "While your church may never be able to reach everyone, it is especially suited to reaching certain types of people. Knowing who you're trying to reach makes evangelism much easier."[38] Warren utilized church growth principles to build some of the largest megachurches in the United States through seeker-sensitive and even seeker-driven worship services.

---

[37] Donald A. McGavran, *Understanding Church Growth*, ed. C. Peter Wagner, 3rd ed. (Grand Rapids, MI: William B. Eerdmans Publishing Company, 1990), 163.
[38] Rick Warren, *The Purpose Driven Church: Growth without Compromising Your Message and Mission* (Grand Rapids, MI: Zondervan, 1995), 157.

The theological foundations for these pragmatic evangelistic practices have been questioned in the twenty-first century. While the research of this movement proved helpful, others such as Mark Dever, pastor of Capitol Hill Baptist Church in Washington, DC, have offered a correction to the Church Growth Movement known as Church Health.[39]

The influence of the Church Growth Movement also may be seen in the pragmatic methods of personal evangelism training through memorized gospel presentations. D. James Kennedy, former pastor of Coral Ridge Presbyterian Church in Fort Lauderdale, Florida, developed a method eventually labeled "Evangelism Explosion" after his church had dwindled to seventeen attendees. Kennedy trained his members to share the gospel by asking a diagnostic question and sharing a gospel presentation with memorized Scripture. His church grew to more than two thousand attendees as a result. Kennedy launched this program nationally and internationally, and his work continues today even after his death.[40] Southern Baptists implemented similar methods through programs such as *Continuing Witness Training, FAITH Evangelism, The NET,* and most recently *The Three Circles*. Parachurch ministries geared toward evangelizing certain age groups and demographics also may be seen as another outgrowth of the Church Growth Movement. Such ministries included Campus Crusade for Christ, Youth for Christ, the Navigators, and Promise Keepers. These groups developed both methods of mass and personal evangelism.

Evangelism in the Southern Baptist Convention (AD 1845–2018)

Since its inception in 1845, member churches of the Southern Baptist Convention had agreed upon a cooperative effort toward world missions. The SBC founded the Foreign Mission Board to accomplish foreign

---

[39] Mark Dever, *Nine Marks of a Healthy Church*, 3rd ed. (Wheaton, IL: Crossway, 2013).
[40] "History," Evangelism Explosion, accessed June 19, 2019, https://evangelism explosion.org/about–us/history/.

missions and the Domestic Mission Board to accomplish missions in the United States (renamed the International Mission Board and North American Mission Board in 1997). While Southern Baptists practiced evangelism through local churches, the first attempt at denominational cooperation in the conventions took place between 1904 and 1906. W. W. Hamilton became the first secretary of evangelism at the Home Mission Board and emphasized the method of revivalism.[41]

After some setbacks during the 1920s and 1930s, the SBC's evangelism department gained traction under the leadership of C. E. Mathews in the 1940s and 1950s. He prioritized evangelism in the local churches through leadership in evangelism at the state and association levels, which funneled to each local church through its own evangelism church council. The SBC baptized one million more converts during a decade of Mathews's leadership than in the previous decade.[42]

During the SBC's greatest evangelistic effectiveness, Kelley identified what he considers the four distinctives of an evangelism strategy in most Southern Baptist Churches: decisional preaching with a public invitation at the conclusion of the sermon, personal evangelism through a church visitation program, Sunday School,[43] and at least one week of revival services each year as the culmination of a church's evangelism efforts.[44]

While the SBC's baptism numbers declined and spiked several times between 1960 and 2000, the SBC's number of baptisms has

---

[41] Charles S. Kelley Jr., *Fuel the Fire: Lessons from the History of Southern Baptist Evangelism*, a Treasury of Baptist Theology, eds. Paige Patterson and Jason G. Duesing (Nashville, TN: B&H Academic, 2018), 9–26.

[42] Ibid., 36–38.

[43] An emphasis on Sunday School or small group Bible study has been a focus of the SBC since 1863 when the Sunday School Board was founded. It was reestablished in 1891 as the Sunday School Board and renamed LifeWay Christian Resources in 1998. See J. M. Frost's *The Sunday School Board Southern Baptist Convention: Its History and Work* (Nashville, TN: Sunday School Board, 1914), 7–8, accessed February 17, 2019 https://digital.library.sbts.edu /bitstream/handle/10392/630/frost_ss.pdf?sequence=1.

[44] Ibid., 115–17.

declined steadily in the first two decades of the twenty-first century.[45] Kelley attributed the decline to the lack of church health and the absence of significant discipleship in established SBC churches.[46] At the denominational level, Kelley noted the North American Mission Board in 2016 "no longer included" evangelism "as a primary focal point for the entity charged with reaching North America with the gospel."[47] After an evangelism task force recommended NAMB hire leadership in the area of evangelism at the 2018 annual meeting of the SBC, NAMB president Kevin Ezell named Johnny Hunt, an evangelistic and tenured pastor of First Baptist Church of Woodstock, Georgia, as senior vice president of evangelism and leadership.[48]

Kelley offered five simple practices for SBC churches to revive their evangelism ministries: praying for the unevangelized, setting annual baptism goals, teaching members to share an evangelistic testimony, teaching members a gospel presentation, and training members to turn conversations toward the gospel.[49] Just as Heb 11 has become known as the "Hall of Faith" for believers, Southern Baptists are known for having a "Hall of Evangelists" with well-known personalities such as Billy Graham, George W. Truett, W. A. Criswell, Jerry Falwell, Chuck Colson, Lottie Moon, Annie Armstrong, and Adrian Rogers. More likely the future of evangelism in the SBC will resemble the unnamed heroes of Hebrews 11 "of whom the world was not worthy" (v. 38). These heroes will be pastors who train their congregations to share the gospel, men and women who share their testimonies of how Christ made the difference, and students who love Jesus by leading their friends to do the same.

---

[45] Charles S. Kelley Jr., "The Great Commission: Where Are We Now?," *Dr. Chuck Kelley* (blog) accessed February 17, 2019, http://www.drchuckkelley.com/2016/04/04/the-great-commission-where-are-we-now/.
[46] Kelley, *Fuel the Fire*, 176–91.
[47] Ibid., 47.
[48] "Johnny Hunt to Lead NAMB Evangelism and Leadership Group," NAMB, accessed February 17, 2019, https://www.namb.net/news/johnny-hunt-to-lead-namb-evangelism-and-leadership-group/.
[49] Kelley, *Fuel the Fire*, 206–15.

BIBLIOGRAPHY

Baker, Robert A., and John M. Landers. *A Summary of Christian History*. 3rd ed. Nashville, TN: B&H Academic, 2005. Kindle edition.

Bebbington, David W. "How Moody Changed Revivalism." *Christian History* 9, no. 1 (February 1990): 22. http://search.ebscohost.com/login.aspx?direct=true&db=khh&AN=9604244218&site=ehost-live.

Blumhofer, Edith L. "Azusa Street Revival." *The Christian Century* 123, no. 5 (March 7, 2006): 20–22. http://search.ebscohost.com/login.aspx?direct=true&db=rfh&AN=ATLA0001503067&site=ehost-live.

Boles, John B. *The Great Revival: Beginnings of the Bible Belt*. Lexington, KY: The University of Kentucky Press, 1996.

Carpenter, Mark Alan. "An Interpretive Analysis of the Layman's Prayer Revival of 1857–1858." PhD, Mid-America Baptist Theological Seminary, 2006. https://search.proquest.com/docview/304933587/abstract/DC0DA0BE911D4CD7PQ/1.

Creech, Joe. "Visions of Glory: The Place of the Azusa Street Revival in Pentecostal History." *Church History* 65, no. 3 (September 1996): 405–24. http://search.ebscohost.com/login.aspx?direct=true&db=rfh&AN=ATLA0000910922&site=ehost-live.

Dever, Mark. *Nine Marks of a Healthy Church*. 3rd ed. Wheaton, IL: Crossway, 2013.

Evangelism Expolsion. "History." About EE. Accessed June 19, 2019. https://evangelismexplosion.org/about-us/history/.

Finney, Charles. *The Works of Charles Finney*. Vol. 1. Seattle, WA: Amazon Digital Services, LLC, 2012. Kindle edition.

Frost, J. M. *The Sunday School Board Southern Baptist Convention: Its History and Work*. Nashville, TN: Sunday School Board, 1914. https://digital.library.sbts.edu/bitstream/handle/10392/630/frost_ss.pdf?sequence=1.

Gonzalez, Justo L. *The Story of Christianity: The Early Church to the Dawn of the Reformation*. Vol. 1. New York, NY: HarperCollins Publishers, 1984.

Green, Michael. *Evangelism in the Early Church*. Revised. Grand Rapids, MI: William B. Eerdmans Publishing Company, 2004.

———. *Thirty Years That Changed the Word: The Book of Acts for Today*. Grand Rapids, MI: William B. Eerdmans Publishing Company, 2004. Kindle edition.

Hannah, John D. "Layman's Prayer Revival of 1858." *Bibliotheca Sacra* 134, no. 533 (January 1977): 59–73. http://search.ebscohost.com/login.aspx?direct=true&db=rfh&AN=ATLA0000759731&site=ehost-live.

Hobbs, Scott Sterling. "The Contributions of J. Wilbur Chapman to American Evangelism." PhD diss., Southwestern Baptist Theological Seminary, 1997. https://search.proquest.com/docview/304384733/abstract/B85C754F4E594916PQ/1.

"Johnny Hunt to Lead NAMB Evangelism and Leadership Group." NAMB, February 19, 2019. https://www.namb.net/news/johnny-hunt-to-lead-namb-evangelism-and-leadership-group/.

Johnston, Thomas Paul. *Examining Billy Graham's Theology of Evangelism*. Eugene, OR: Wipf and Stock Publishers, 2003. Kindle edition.

Kelley, Charles S., Jr. *Fuel the Fire: Lessons from the History of Southern Baptist Evangelism*. A Treasury of Baptist Theology, edited by Paige Patterson and Jason G. Duesing. Nashville, TN: B&H Academic, 2018.

———. "The Great Commission: Where Are We Now?" *Dr. Chuck Kelley* (blog). http://www.drchuckkelley.com/2016/04/04/the-great-commission-where-are-we-now/.

Laurie, Gregg and Ellen Vaughn. *Jesus Revolution: How God Transformed an Unlikely Generation and How He Can Do It Again Today*. Grand Rapids, MI: Baker Books, 2018.

Martyr, Justin. *Ante-Nicene Fathers*. Edited by Philip Schaff. Vol. 1. Grand Rapids, MI: Christian Classics Ethereal Library, 1885. http://www.ccel.org/ccel/schaff/anf01.pdf.

McGavran, Donald A. *Understanding Church Growth*. Edited by C. Peter Wagner. 3rd ed. Grand Rapids, MI: William B. Eerdmans Publishing Company, 1990.

McGrath, Alister E. *Christian History: An Introduction.* West Sussex, UK: John Wiley & Sons Ltd., Publication, 2013. Kindle edition.

Nix, Preston Lamont. "A Critical Analysis of the Organizational Methodology in Selected Evangelistic Campaigns of William Ashley (Billy) Sunday." PhD diss., Southwestern Baptist Theological Seminary, 1992. https://search.proquest.com/docview/304022958/abstract/D1D945074F0F490EPQ/1.

Reinhardt, Wolfgang. "'A Year of Rejoicing': The Welsh Revival 1904-05 and Its International Challenges." *Evangelical Review of Theology* 31, no. 2 (April 2007): 100–126. http://search.ebscohost.com/login.aspx?direct=true&db=rfh&AN=ATLA0001659700&site=ehost-live.

Schaff, Philip. *History of the Christian Church: Mediaeval Christianity. A. D. 590–1073.* Grand Rapids, MI: Christian Classics Ethereal Library, 1998. http://www.ccel.org/ccel/schaff/hcc4.pdf.

———. *History of the Christian Church: The Middle Ages. A.D. 1294–1517.* Grand Rapids, MI: Christian Classics Ethereal Library, 1998. http://www.ccel.org/ccel/schaff/hcc6.pdf.

Skinner, Craig. "The Preaching of Charles Haddon Spurgeon." *Baptist History and Heritage* 19, no. 4 (October 1984): 16–26. http://search.ebscohost.com/login.aspx?direct=true&db=rfh&AN=ATLA0000926087&site=ehost-live.

Stevens, Gerald L. *Acts: A New Vision for the People of God.* Eugene, OR: Pickwick Publications, 2016.

Terry, John Mark. *Evangelism: A Concise History.* Nashville, TN: Broadman & Holman Publishers, 1994. Kindle edition.

Warren, Rick. *The Purpose Driven Church: Growth without Compromising Your Message and Mission.* Grand Rapids, MI: Zondervan, 1995.

White, Ellen Gould. *The Great Controversy.* Grand Rapids, MI: Christian Classics Ethereal Library, 1994. http://www.ccel.org/ccel/white/controversy.pdf.

Historical Basis

THE BLOOD OF CHRISTIANS IS SEED: CHRISTIAN SUFFERING AND EVANGELISM IN EARLY CHRISTIANITY AND THE CONTEMPORARY WORLD

Rex D. Butler

Tertullian, the Carthaginian teacher who bore witness to Christian martyrdom, stated in his well-known dictum on persecution and martyrdom: "The blood of Christians is seed." From this church father's perspective, the early church not only survived but thrived in spite of persecution and martyrdom. In fact, he wrote, "The oftener we are mown down by you, the more in number we grow."[1] Although Tertullian was given to exaggeration, history seems to bear out his rhetoric. According to educated estimates, in the Roman Empire, the number of Christians during Tertullian's time, 200 AD, was 200,000, or less than one percent of the population. A century later, just ahead of Constantine's conversion and the end of persecution, the number had grown to more than a million, or ten percent of the population. At that time, Christians could be found from all walks of life and social classes in all the major cities and many smaller towns all around the Mediterranean.[2]

---

[1] Tertullian, *Apology* 50.13, in *Early Christian Martyr Stories: An Evangelical Introduction with New Translations* by Bryan M. Lifton (Grand Rapids, MI: Baker, 2014), 123.
[2] Robert Wilken, *The First Thousand Years: A Global History of Christianity* (New Haven, CT: Yale University Press, 2012), 65–66.

Similar phenomena can be found today around the globe as the church grows even where the forces of the enemy inflict persecution and martyrdom on Christ's followers. The church is growing fastest in China and Cuba, two Communist countries, and in Muslim Iran. Elsewhere, however, persecution has had a negative impact on the churches. Even so the stories of Christian suffering and perseverance serve to inspire believers who give heed to them.

One goal of this research project is to examine early Christian martyr stories and to compare them with contemporary accounts of persecution according to the martyrs or confessors, the persecutors, the methods of persecution, and the outcomes. After such an examination, the second goal is to apply the findings toward an understanding of evangelism and church growth in the midst of Christian suffering.

Tertullian's Apology

At the turn of the third century, Tertullian famously wrote: "Yet nothing whatsoever is accomplished by your cruelties, even when each is more heinous than the last. Instead they serve as an enticement to our religion. Indeed, we supply a greater yield whenever you cut us down. The blood of Christians is seed!"[3] More recently, during a visit to NOBTS, a pastor from Bangladesh expressed a similar sentiment: "Persecution is the rain that causes the church to grow." He said this in spite of, or because of, his loss of employment, his property, and his family due to persecution from Muslims. He also reported a house church pastor had been hanged because of his faith in Jesus Christ.

Ronald Boyd-Macmillan, a modern reporter of persecution, relates an interesting story that illustrates the point made by Tertullian and the Bangladeshi pastor. In 1990, he was in Beijing to meet covertly with three elderly Chinese Christians. He was surprised when they offered up a toast "in memory of the man who did more than any other to bring to our beloved China the largest scale revival in the

---

[3] Tertullian, *Apology* 50.13, trans. Bryan M. Litfin, *Early Christian Martyr Stories*, 123.

history of Christianity! To Mao Zedong!" They explained: "He closed the churches, jailed the pastors, burned the Bibles—annihilated the visible church. Many Christians died. It was a horrible time." But, after Mao's death, "The few evangelists that were left ... began to go and preach the gospel in the countryside." Those who heard the gospel realized Mao could not save them—because he died—but Jesus, who rose from the dead and lives, is the true Savior. Boyd-Macmillan concluded the story: "We laughed. We almost felt sorry for Mao, doing his worst to finish the church off and all the while laying the foundation for the world's biggest revival." Then he added the statistics of the revival in China are impossible to determine, but "whatever figure you use, it still constitutes the largest numerical revival in the history of Christianity."[4]

The Martyrdom of Polycarp

Other parallels, although not as exact, can be found between accounts of martyrdom in the early church and the contemporary world. About forty years before Tertullian penned *Apology*, Polycarp, the elderly bishop of Smyrna, was burned at the stake for his faith in Jesus Christ. When commanded to deny Christ or face a cruel death, Polycarp declared: "For eighty-six years I have been his servant, and he has done me no wrong. How can I blaspheme my King who saved me?"[5] Aged pastors are still martyred, such as Paulos Faraj Rahho, the sixty-five-year-old Catholic Chaldean archbishop of Mosul, Iraq. In 2008, a gang of Islamist criminals abducted him from his church, and, two weeks later, his body was found in a shallow grave. The archbishop is remembered for his dynamic leadership, his hope, and his service to the young and old of his Christian community. Like Polycarp, Rahho was a symbol of Christianity in his community. In the words of Johan

---

[4] Ronald Boyd-MacMillan, *Faith That Endures: The Essential Guide to the Persecuted Church* (Grand Rapids, MI: Revell, 2006), 7–12.
[5] *Martyrdom of Polycarp* 9.3, trans. Litfin, *Early Christian Martyr Stories*, 60.

Candalin, executive director of the Religious Liberty Commission of the World Evangelical Alliance, "An archbishop is more than one ordinary clergyman. He is a symbol of the whole church. And when he is killed in this brutal way it is a very clear signal to all Christians that this is what could happen to any of you."[6]

When Polycarp was arraigned before the governor of Smyrna, he was urged on several occasions to say, "Caesar is lord," to swear by the divine spirit of the emperor, and to curse the name of Christ. Such declarations would have secured his release from martyrdom. However, in the center of the arena, surrounded by pagans, he refused boldly.[7] Other, more recent political leaders have demanded worship and obedience, and many pastors have continued to refuse. Such a pastor was Richard Wurmbrand, who today is a symbol of the persecuted church. When the Communists took over Romania, they convened a "Congress of Cults," attended by four thousand priests and pastors, who chose Joseph Stalin honorary president. During the congress, many religious leaders succumbed to the Communists' seductive language, praised Communism, and pledged the loyalty of their churches. Sabina Wurmbrand said to her husband: "Richard, stand up and wash away this shame from the face of Christ! They are spitting in his face." Richard reminded her, "If I do so, you lose your husband." She replied, "I don't wish to have a coward as a husband." With the same kind of courage exhibited by Polycarp, Wurmbrand went to the podium and declared to the congress that their loyalty was due not to murderers of Christians but to Christ and God. Not only did those in attendance hear Wurmbrand's confession of faith, but his speech was also broadcast throughout the whole country. As a result

---

[6] "Death of Christian Leader in Iraq, Ominous Sign for Believers," in *Mission Network News* (March 14, 2008), http://www.mnnonline.org/article/11006, cited by Paul Marshall, Lela Gilbert, and Nina Shea, *Persecuted: The Global Assault on Christians* (Nashville, TN: Thomas Nelson, 2013), 225–26.

[7] *The Martyrdom of Polycarp* 8.2, 9.2, 10.1. Perpetua also was urged to perform a sacrifice for the welfare of the emperors, but she refused. *The Passion of Perpetua* 6.2–3.

of Wurmbrand's faithfulness, three years later, he was imprisoned and tortured for Christ.[8]

The Acts of Justin and His Companions

About a decade after Polycarp's martyrdom, the Christian apologist Justin Martyr came to the attention of the imperial authorities of Rome. In a public debate, Justin bested Crescens, a Cynic philosopher who had the ear of Emperor Marcus Aurelius. Humiliated and angered, Crescens and the intellectual elites of Rome plotted to bring Justin and six of his companions before the Roman prefect, Junius Rusticus.[9] According to the trial record, which was preserved, Justin revealed he presided over a congregation that met in his apartment above a bathhouse and that there were a number of meeting places throughout the city because Christians were too numerous to gather in a single location.[10] Elsewhere, Justin described the worship conducted in his house church. The president, or pastor, led the small congregation in Scripture reading from both the Old and New Testaments, teaching, praying, singing, the Eucharist, and an offering.[11]

A common feature of stories of persecution not only in the early church but also in the contemporary world is the house church.

---

[8] Richard Wurmbrand, *Tortured for Christ* (Middlebury, IN: Living Sacrifice Books, 1985), 15–16. When Wurmbrand was released from prison, he left Romania and came to the United States, where he founded the organization known as Voice of the Martyrs. This ministry of advocacy for the persecuted church has as its mission the words of Heb 13:3 (KJV), "Remember them that are in bonds, as bound with them; and them which suffer adversity, as being yourselves also in the body."

[9] Litfin, "Justin Martyr: Apologetics at the Ultimate Price," in *Early Christian Martyr Stories*, 65–66.

[10] "The Martyrdom of Saints Justin, Chariton, Charito, Euelpistos, Hierax, Paion, Liberian, and Their Comrades" 3.1–3, in *The Acts of the Christian Martyrs*, trans. with an introduction by Herbert Musurillo (Oxford: At the Clarendon Press, 1972), 45.

[11] Justin Martyr, *First Apology* 67, trans. by Marcus Dods and George Reith, in *The Ante-Nicene Fathers*, vol. 1, ed. Alexander Roberts and James Donaldson (Edinburgh: T. and T. Clark, 1873; reprint, Peabody, MA: Hendrickson, 2012), 185–86.

Globally, house churches facilitate both the numbers of Christians and, more importantly, secrecy.

Perhaps the most famous house church movement is the one in China. In the aftermath of the Communist revolution, churches were divided between those who were loyal to the state and those who insisted the union of church and state hindered the gospel message and mission. The "Dean of the House Churches," Wang Mingdao, resisted the state-sponsored, state-controlled church and was ostracized, arrested, and imprisoned for twenty years. As one biographer, Thomas Alan Harvey, expressed it: "His life, resistance, suffering, and perseverance bear the marks of the Chinese church. Even as his arrest and imprisonment marked the end of public defiance of the government, how much more did his reemergence from the Chinese gulag twenty years later embody a Christian faith that has not only survived but grown stronger in spite of its official banishment."[12]

The house church movement in China is known also as the underground church, so by its very nature, its numbers are impossible to gauge. Estimates of the total number of Christians in China range from 2.3 million to 200 million. According to the Lausanne Global Analysis, perhaps a reasonable estimate is closer to 100 million, a number that includes Protestant and Catholic, registered and unregistered churches.[13] As John Allen points out, "Protestantism took off after the expulsion of foreign missionaries, so most of this expansion has been home-grown."[14] Furthermore, according to Paul Marshall, Lela Gilbert, and Nina Shea, "Most of the explosive increase of Christians

---

[12] Thomas Alan Harvey, *Acquainted with Grief: Wang Mingdao's Stand for the Persecuted Church in China* (Grand Rapids, MI: Brazos Press, 2002), 9. See also Roy Stults, "Stubborn Saint: Wang Mingdao and the Birth of the Chinese House Church Movement," *Christian History* 109 (2014): 21–24.

[13] Marshall, Gilbert, and Shea, *Persecuted*, 29–30. See also John L. Allen Jr., *The Global War on Christians: Dispatches from the Front Lines of Anti-Christian Persecution* (New York: Image, 2013), 68–69.

[14] Allen, *The Global War on Christians*, 69.

in China has taken place in house churches (or underground churches), which are usually Evangelical in theology and practice. In the last thirty years, these church networks have experienced the largest pattern of church growth in world history. In no other country, at no other time, have tens of millions of people come into the Christian faith at such a pace."[15]

Because of the sheer numbers of house churches, the Communist authorities have been challenged to regulate them and to force them to register. The pastors of underground churches, however, resist registration because, as one Baptist pastor explained, provincial governors can censor the sermons preached in churches under his control. Subjects such as the Holy Spirit and the Second Coming of Christ seem threatening to a regime that fears direction of its subjects from a divine source and the idea that the Communist kingdom will not endure forever.[16] As a rule, authorities will not interfere with house churches if they follow three guidelines: (1) they must not be subversive to the government; (2) they must not develop networks with other churches; and (3) they must not receive support from foreign entities.[17]

However, there are numerous instances of persecution against house churches and their pastors. Mark Shan of China Aid reports: "House Church always face persecution, especially church leaders are facing danger of even being sent to prison, though different regions in different times have different degree of persecutions."[18] Since 2013, when Xi Jinping became president of the People's Republic of China, the Communist Party has intensified religious persecution

---

[15] Marshall, Gilbert, and Shea, *Persecuted*, 35.
[16] In September 2013, I had the opportunity to teach pastors of unregistered churches in China, and I asked one of them why he chose not to register with the government.
[17] Because of this last guideline, a group of pastors "smuggled" me into a church in order to teach Christian doctrines. An acquaintance, who has worked with registered churches in China for over twenty years, explained to me these guidelines for house churches.
[18] Mark Shan, cited by Marshall, Gilbert, and Shea, *Persecuted*, 36.

as Christianity's popularity has grown at what the Communists perceive to be alarming rates. The crackdown on Christianity is the worst since the Cultural Revolution under Mao Zedong thirty years ago. In 2018, local governments closed hundreds of underground churches. In other churches, Communist officials removed crosses from buildings, displayed Chinese flags and pictures of Xi Jinping, and forbade attendance by children. Online sales of Bibles are no longer permitted, and the next step is to retranslate the Bible to make it compatible with Chinese Communism. Xi Jinping's goal is to "Sinicize" Christianity—to conform it to the ideals of the Communist Party.[19]

In December 2018, the well-known house church, Early Rain Covenant Church, located in Chengdu, experienced the persecution revived by Xi Jinping. The pastor Wang Yi and his wife Jiang Rong were arrested and charged with subversion, a crime that carries the penalty of up to fifteen years in prison. Over one hundred church members were also arrested; many others went into hiding; still others were evicted from the city.[20] Before his arrest, Wang Yi wrote "My Faithful Declaration of Obedience," to be published in the event of his arrest. In his declaration, this faithful pastor recognized the unexpected blessings that come from persecution: "If God decides to use the persecution of this Communist regime against the church to help more Chinese people to despair of their futures, to lead them through a wilderness of spiritual disillusionment and through this to make them know Jesus, if through this he continues disciplining and building up his church, then I am joyfully willing to submit to God's plans, for his plans are always benevolent and good."

Wherever the church is persecuted, house church movements will grow. One other notable site is Iran, where house churches are among

---

[19] Lily Kuo, "In China, They're Closing Churches, Jailing Pastors—and Even Rewriting Scripture," *The Guardian*. https://www.theguardian.com/world/2019/jan/13/china-christians-religious-persecution-translation-bible (accessed January 24, 2019).
[20] Ibid.

the very few options for Muslim-background believers to worship. Established churches, such as the Assyrian Church of the East and Armenian Orthodox Church, are prohibited from allowing Muslim-background believers to participate. The numbers are much smaller than they are in China, but still they are encouraging: estimates suggest there are 100,000 Iranian believers meeting in house churches in their country. One former pastor, Ali Akbar, worked with thirty-five house churches in a dozen different locations before multiple arrests forced him to leave his country.[21]

House church movements, such as the one described by Justin Martyr, continue to provide opportunities for worship, evangelism, and discipleship. In many cases, house churches can also enable believers to gather in secret, but, as has been seen all too often, persecuting authorities can penetrate the defenses and impose various levels of suffering on underground believers.

The Martyrs of Lyons and Vienne

In AD 177, a little over a decade after Justin Martyr's death, an extensive persecution broke out against Christians in Lyons and Vienne in Gaul. This persecution was not instigated by an emperor's edict, although the governor of the province oversaw the imprisonments, tortures, and executions, but it was the residents of these towns who rose up in mob violence against their Christian neighbors. The violence lasted for six days, during which dozens of Christians endured unimaginable tortures—scourged, stretched on the rack, roasted in a red-hot chair, attacked by wild beasts, impaled on a stake. The Christians who survived the persecution of the mob prayed that, although they did not have the privilege to die for their faith, they would live out their witness with boldness before their neighbors.

---

[21] David Garrison, *A Wind in the House of Islam: How God Is Drawing Muslims Around the World to Faith in Jesus Christ* (Monument, CO: WIGTake Resources, 2014), 140.

Persecution instigated by individuals or mobs operating out of hatred and ignorance toward Christianity rather than by government officials is not uncommon. One such incident of individual violence against Christians occurred in December 2002 at the Jibla Baptist Hospital in Yemen. A Muslim militant, incensed by Christian influence in his country, infiltrated the hospital, shot and killed three Southern Baptist medical missionaries, and wounded a pharmacist. In the aftermath of this killing, Yemenis who appreciated the ministry of the medical missionaries poured out their grief over their deaths. In the years ahead, Southern Baptists and other Christians continued the medical mission of the hospital, renamed Peace Hospital. The widow of one victim appealed for mercy for the man who killed her husband.[22]

An incident of mob violence occurred in Malatya, Turkey. Officially, Turkey is a secular Islamic state, but the government does not recognize Protestant Christianity. In April 2007, three Protestants were attacked, tortured, and killed in a Christian publishing house. Two of the victims were Turkish converts, and the third was a German missionary; two were married and the other was engaged. The five men arrested for the murders have been tied to ultranationalist groups who teach that Turkey is for Islam. Soon after the deaths of these three Christians, the two wives and the fiancée appeared on national television to voice forgiveness for the murderers of the men they loved.[23]

In these two contemporary stories of martyrdom, the survivors were able to forgive the persecutors. In doing so, they were following Jesus' directive: "But I say to you who hear, love your enemies, do good to those who hate you, bless those who curse you, pray for those who mistreat you" (Luke 6:27).

Back in Lyons in the second century, the eyewitness of the persecution reported: "Our adversary the Devil, giving us a foretaste of

---

[22] Erich Bridges and Jerry Rankin, *Lives Given, Not Taken: 21st Century Southern Baptist Martyrs* (Richmond, VA: International Mission Board, SBC, 2005), 25–26, 97–100.
[23] Allen, *The Global War on Christians*, 70; Marshall, Gilbert, and Shea, *Persecuted*, 25–26.

his final appearance, which is surely very close, fell upon us with all his might. He used every trick available to prepare and train his followers to attack God's servants."[24] Boyd-MacMillan agrees: "It is the devil, the demonic hatred that is behind all anti-Christian violence." The devil is "waging his cosmic battle of spite against Jesus Christ."[25] The early Christians who faced persecution held the same view that their ultimate enemy was not the Roman government or the mob but rather Satan. For this reason, Christians of all ages are able to forgive their persecutors, because their enemy is Satan, not those who act out their hatred for Christ and for Christians.

The Passion of Perpetua and Felicitas

The Scillitan martyrs were the earliest known Christians of the North African church, which was called by one historian, "the church of the martyrs."[26] Just over two decades later, another faithful group of Christians gave their lives for their faith in Jesus Christ, and their story is told in *The Passion of Perpetua and Felicitas*. Although the martyrs included five catechumens, three men and two women, along with their teacher, the two heroines are immortalized in the title of the *Passion*. The narrator introduced Perpetua as "a woman nobly born, educated in the liberal arts, and respectably married. She had a father and a mother and two brothers ... as well as an infant son, who was still nursing. Perpetua was about twenty-two years old." Felicitas was a slave, who was eight months pregnant at the time of their arrest. The prominence given to the women in the *Passion* troubled Augustine, who preached three extant sermons about the Carthaginian martyrs. He addressed the unspoken question about why the day was named for two women

---

[24] Liftin, "The Martyrs of Lyons and Vienne: A Crown of Many Flowers" 5.1, in *Early Christian Martyr Stories*, 73.
[25] Boyd-MacMillan, *Faith That Endures*, 36.
[26] W. H. C. Frend, "The North African Cult of Martyrs: From Apocalyptic to Hero-Worship," in *Jenseitsvorstellungen in antike und Christentum: gedenkschrift für Alfred Stuiber* (Münster Westfalen: Aschendorffshe Verlagsbuchhandlung, 1982), 154.

with a pun on their names: "Obviously, Perpetua and Felicitas are the names of two of them but the reward of all of them. And indeed, all the martyrs suffered bravely for that time in a struggle of pain and confession of faith only to rejoice in perpetual felicity."[27]

Throughout church history, the role of women in the church has been debated. In the arena of Christian suffering, however, women have always had a prominent place in the annals of martyrs. Reading through early Christian martyr stories, several women stand out: Agathonice; Blandina and her mistress; the five women of Scillium; Potamiaena; Marcella; Crispina; and these two, Perpetua and Felicitas, perhaps the best known of all.

Women continue to suffer for Christ's sake around the globe. Two women reminiscent of Perpetua and Felicitas are Maryam Rostampour and Marziyeh Amirizadeh, who were arrested in March 2009 by Iranian security forces and imprisoned in the infamous Evin Prison in Tehran. When interrogated about their alleged apostasy, they answered: "Yes, we are Christians;" "We have no regrets;" "We will not deny our faith." Thankfully, they were released in November of the same year.[28]

Another Christian woman who has gained international attention for her suffering is Asia Bibi. In Pakistan, in 2009, this farm worker and mother of five was imprisoned after being accused of blasphemy. Her crime was to drink from a cup belonging to Muslim coworkers, who complained she made the cup "impure." As she was arrested, Bibi's arm was broken, and a Muslim mob cried out, "Death to the

---

[27] Augustine, *Sermon* 282.3. See also Augustine, *Sermon* 281.3: "I mean to say here that the name of the two women was the gift of all the martyrs. For why do martyrs endure all things to the end except that they might glory in perpetual felicity? Therefore, these women were called that to which the entire body is called. And, for that reason, although there was a numerous company in that contest, the enduring memory of them all is signified and the annual festival of them all is designated by the names of these two women" (my translations).

[28] For more of Maryam and Marziyeh's story, see *Captive in Iran: A Remarkable True Story of Hope and Triumph amid the Horror of Tehran's Brutal Evin Prison* (Carol Stream, IL: Tyndale Momentum, 2013).

Christian!" During eight years of imprisonment, Bibi was moved from prison to prison, often facing death threats and attempts to take her life. Even two men who advocated for her were assassinated.[29] Finally, on October 31, 2018, she was acquitted by the Pakistani Supreme Court, but her acquittal generated protests that brought the country almost to a standstill. Due to threats from Islamic extremists, Bibi went into hiding in Pakistan, her daughters immigrated to Canada, and her husband sent out requests for asylum throughout the western world. On January 29, 2019, the Pakistani Supreme Court upheld its acquittal of Bibi, paving the way for her to leave the country and be reunited with her family.[30]

Often women suffer equally with their husbands. Three years after her husband Richard was imprisoned in Communist Romania, Sabina Wurmbrand was placed in work camps and remained there for over two years. Richard described her ordeal: "Christian women suffer much more than men in prison. ... The mockery, the obscenity is horrible. The women were compelled to work at hard labor at a canal which had to be built, and they had to fulfill the same work load as men. They shoveled earth in winter. ... My wife has eaten grass like cattle to stay alive. ... One of the joys of the guards on Sundays was to throw women into the Danube and then fish them out, to laugh about them. ... My wife was thrown in the Danube in this manner."[31] Sabina survived her imprisonment to serve alongside her husband throughout their ministry on behalf of Christians suffering around the world.

---

[29] Sheraz Khan, "Imprisoned over a Glass of Water: Persecution of Christians in the Islamic World," *Christian History* 109 (2014): 38. See also Asia Bibi and Anne-Isabelle Tollet, *Blasphemy: A Memoir: Sentenced to Death over a Cup of Water* (Chicago: Chicago Review Press, 2013).

[30] Ben Farmer, "Asia Bibi's Daughters Take Refuge in Canada Ahead of Court Blasphemy Ruling," *The Telegraph*, January 25, 2019 https://www.telegraph.co.uk/news/2019/01/25/asia-bibis-daughters-take-refuge-canada-ahead-court-blasphemy/.

[31] Wurmbrand, *Tortured for Christ*, 47–48.

In Communist China, Wang Mingdao's wife, Liu Jingwen, was imprisoned twice at the same times as her husband. She endured her second sentence for fifteen years, from 1959 to 1974.[32] These several women serve only as token reminders of the thousands of "Perpetuas" and "Felicitases" who have suffered for their faith in Christ. As Augustine pointed out regarding the "manliness" of these women: "But this is the highest glory of him, in whom believers and in whose name faithful and zealous combatants are found, according to the inner person, neither male nor female."[33]

One more interesting feature of *The Passion of Perpetua and Felicitas* was the witness of the imprisoned Christians to Pudens, the jailer. According to Perpetua, "The junior officer in charge of the prison, named Pudens, began to honor us because he recognized the spiritual power at work in us."[34] Saturus continued to evangelize Pudens, even in the arena. Before Saturus faced the leopard, he said to Pudens: "It has all come down to this, exactly as I foresaw and predicted. Until this moment I haven't been touched by any of the beasts. So believe me now with all your heart. Watch and see, I'm going back in there to be finished off by one bite of a leopard." Indeed, Saturus was dealt a death blow by the leopard, and his final encounter with Pudens was recorded by the eyewitness: "'Farewell! Remember me and my faith. Don't let these things dismay you. Be strengthened instead!' As Saturus was speaking, he asked Pudens for his finger ring, which he dipped in his wound and handed back as an inheritance. In this way Saturus left behind a symbol and reminder of his bloody martyrdom."[35]

Faithful Christians who suffer today continue in the tradition of Saturus and the Carthaginian martyrs to witness to those around them,

---

[32] Roy Stults, "Stubborn Saint," *Christian History* 109, 24.
[33] Augustine, *Sermon* 280.1 (my translation).
[34] *The Passion of Perpetua and Felicitas* 9.1, trans. Bryan M. Litfin, *Early Christian Martyr Stories*, 99.
[35] *The Passion of Perpetua and Felicitas* 21.1–5, Ibid., 108.

whether their jailers or their fellow prisoners. One example is the Chinese Christian, Brother Yun, known as "The Heavenly Man." In the 1980s, Brother Yun was arrested multiple times for leading several house churches, secretly preaching and baptizing in Communist China. During his second imprisonment, he conducted a seventy-four-day fast without food or water. At the conclusion of the fast, although he had been tortured by the prison guard and was weak from deprivation, he was able, through the power of the Holy Spirit, to stand and preach to his fellow inmates. According to Brother Yun's account, "After I spoke it was as though a bomb dropped on the men! They couldn't help themselves. The cell leader was the first to come and fall on his knees. ... The other prisoners also knelt down, including the Muslim. They cried out in a loud voice, 'What must we do to be saved?' Every one of those sin-hardened men received the Lord Jesus Christ, repenting of their sins with many tears." Because there was very little water available, Brother Yun baptized each of the men with a few drops. A prison guard witnessed these events and was amazed to hear Brother Yun's message and to see the prisoners' conversions.[36]

The faithful witnesses of martyrs—from Perpetua and Saturus to Brother Yun and countless others—brings us full circle to the earlier discussion of Tertullian's famous dictum: "The blood of Christians is seed!" The very name "martyr" comes from the Greek word that means "witness." The witness that began with the persecution and martyrdom of the early church continues today in the contemporary suffering of Christians around the globe.

Christian Suffering and Evangelism in the Early Church and Contemporary World

Selected principles about evangelism and church growth can be gleaned from the testimonies of early and contemporary Christians who have

---

[36] Brother Yun, *The Heavenly Man: The Remarkable True Story of Chinese Christian Brother Yun*, with Paul Hattaway (London: Piquant, 2003), 132–34.

suffered and died for their faith in Jesus. Michael Green, expert on evangelism in the early church, expressed it this way: "Evangelism was the very life blood of the early Christians: and so we find that 'day by day the Lord added to their number those whom he was saving' [Acts 2:47]. It could happen again if the church were prepared to pay the price."[37]

If contemporary Christians follow the example of their early brothers and sisters, then old and young, men and women will become involved in evangelism. Bishop Polycarp was at least eighty-six years old when he testified to his faith in Christ. Only twenty-two years old, the young mother Perpetua declared at her trial, "I am a Christian!"

In order to become effective evangelists, Christians, especially in contemporary America, must be willing to truly suffer for their faith in Jesus. And yet, American Christians equate suffering with liberal opposition to biblical stances on abortion and homosexuality, infringements on religious liberty, or even the "war on Christmas." True persecution, however, is directly related to evangelism.[38] The number-one cause of persecution is people turning to Jesus. Therefore, obedience to the Great Commission will bring about persecution and suffering. Conversely, the absence of persecution and suffering in a Christian community indicates a lack of evangelism and discipleship.

One of the most effective tools in evangelism and church growth is the discipline of apologetics—not apologizing for being a Christian but rather defending the Christian faith. Justin Martyr and Tertullian were cutting-edge apologists in the second century, and they were joined in this vital work by other early church fathers such as Origen, Tatian, Theophilus, and Minucius Felix. In today's increasingly skeptical and hostile society, this discipline has been revived by a number of Christian theologians, philosophers, ethicists, historians, and scientists.

---

[37] Michael Green, *Evangelism in the Early Church* (Grand Rapids, MI: Eerdmans, 1970), 280.
[38] Nik Ripken, *The Insanity of Obedience: Walking with Jesus in Tough Places* (Nashville: B&H Books, 2014), 133.

Christian universities and seminaries are offering a variety of degrees and sponsoring numerous conferences that cover such topics as cosmology, the existence of God, creation, the problem of good and evil, the reliability of Scripture, and other issues that speak to a world that needs answers to spiritual questions. The goal of apologetics is to train Christians "to make a defense to everyone who asks you to give an account for the hope that is in you" (1 Pet 3:15).

Another tool in evangelism and church growth is the house church movement. House churches were the norm in early Christianity, as Justin Martyr testified. In recent years, house churches continue to be effective both in America and around the globe for different reasons. As noted, in regions where persecution of Christians is rampant, house churches provide secret spaces for worship, evangelism, and discipleship. In America, especially among the more impersonal megachurches, small groups meeting in homes provide similar benefits for church members as well as safe spaces for unbelieving friends and neighbors. Church plants also depend upon homes and storefront spaces for small meeting places. These contemporary house churches conduct worship much the same as Justin's church—Scripture reading, teaching, praying, and singing.

Lessons taught repeatedly by stories of Christians suffering for their faith in Jesus include the necessity of praying for persecutors, forgiving them, and witnessing to them. As Boyd-MacMillan reminds his readers, "It is the devil, the demonic hatred that lies behind all anti-Christian violence. ... The devil's ire is directed at Christ."[39] Earthly persecutors are not Christians' enemies—Satan is. For this reason, Jesus instructed His disciples: "Love your enemies, do good to those who hate you, bless those who curse you, pray for those who mistreat you" (Luke 6:27–28). The persecutors are victims of Satan's malice, and they need our prayers. Often, the persecutors turn to Christ as a result of their victims' prayers and witness as seen in the stories of Perpetua and Brother Yun.

---

[39] Boyd-MacMillan, *Faith that Endures*, 36.

The final application about evangelism to learn from these stories of Christian suffering is the need to pray for our persecuted brothers and sisters around the world. Persecuted believers, however, do not ask that we pray *for* them that persecution will end, but instead to pray *with* them that they will be faithful witnesses through persecution. Because persecution is a result of evangelism and conversions and because Satan attacks when the kingdom of God is growing, to pray for the end of persecution is to pray for the end of kingdom growth. As American believers pray for persecuted believers around the world, we unite ourselves with them in their work and become a part of their struggle and witness.[40] Boyd-MacMillan reminds us: "Western Christians require an encounter with the persecuted church to recover essential insights into their own faith, especially the biblical truth that there is no such thing as a *nonpersecuted* believer."[41]

What words of encouragement to evangelism would suffering but victorious Christians speak to us today? Hear Perpetua's words to new believers who witnessed her martyrdom: "Stand firm in the faith, and all of you must love one another! Don't let our martyrdom be a stumbling block to you!" And her teacher Saturus imparted his last words to the jailer, Pudens, who converted through the martyr's witness: "Farewell! Remember me and my faith. Don't let these things dismay you. Be strengthened instead!"[42] Finally, an Eastern European Christian exhorted Nik Ripken—and all American Christians—with these instructions: "Don't you steal my joy! I took great joy that I was suffering in my country, so that you could be free to witness in your country. Don't ever give up in freedom what we would never have given up in persecution! That is our witness to the power of the resurrection of Jesus Christ!"[43]

---

[40] Nik Ripken, *The Insanity of God: A True Story of Faith Resurrected* (Nashville: B&H Books, 2013), 304–06; Ripken, *The Insanity of Obedience*, 88–89.
[41] Boyd-MacMillan, *Faith that Endures*, 15–16 (his emphasis).
[42] *The Passion of Perpetua* 20.10, 21.4.
[43] Nik Ripken, *The Insanity of God*, 195–96.

Bibliography

Allen, John L., Jr. *The Global War on Christians: Dispatches from the Front Lines of Anti-Christian Persecution.* New York: Image, 2013.

Agustine. "Sermon 282.3." In *Early Christian Martyr Stories: An Evangelical Introduction with New Translations*, by Bryan M. Liftin. Grand Rapids, MI: Baker, 2014.

Bibi, Asia, and Anne-Isabelle Tollet. *Blasphemy: A Memoir: Sentenced to Death over a Cup of Water.* Chicago, IL: Chicago Review Press, 2013.

Boyd-MacMillan, Ronald. *Faith That Endures: The Essential Guide to the Persecuted Church.* Richmond, VA: International Mission Board, 2005.

Bridges, Erich, and Jerry Rankin. *Lives Given, Not Taken: 21st Century Southern Baptist Martyrs.* Richmond, VA: International Mission Board, 2005.

Brother Yun. *The Heavenly Man: The Remarkable True Story of Chinese Christian Brother Yun.* With Paul Hattaway. Carlisle, UK: Piquant, 2003.

Farmer, Ben. "Asia Bibi's Daughters Take Refuge in Canada Ahead of Court Blasphemy Ruling." *The Telegraph.* Accessed January 25, 2019. https://www.telegraph.co.uk/news/2019/01/25/asia-bibis-daughters-take-refuge-canada-ahead-court-blasphemy/.

Frend, W. H. C. "The North African Cult of Martyrs: From Apocalyptic to Hero-Worship." In *Jenseitsvorstellungen in antike und Christentum: gedenkschrift für Alfred Stuiber*, 154–67. Münster Westfalen: Aschendorffshe Verlagsbuchhandlung, 1982.

Garrison, David. *A Wind in the House of Islam: How God Is Drawing Muslims Around the World to Faith in Jesus Christ.* Monument, CO: WIGTake Resources, 2014.

Green, Michael. *Evangelism in the Early Church.* Grand Rapids, MI: Eerdmans, 1970.

Harvey, Thomas Alan. *Acquainted with Grief: Wang Mingdao's Stand for the Persecuted Church in China.* Grand Rapids, MI: Brazos Press, 2002.

Justin Martyr. "First Apology." In *The Ante-Nicene Fathers*, edited by Alexander Roberts and James Donaldson, translated by Marcus Dods and George Reith, Reprint. Vol. 1. Peabody, MA: Hendrickson, 2012.

Khan, Sheraz. "Imprisoned over a Glass of Water: Persecution of Christians in the Islamic World." *Christian History* 109 (2014): 38–40.

Kuo, Lily. "In China, They're Closing Churches, Jailing Pastors—and Even Rewriting Scripture." *The Guardian*. Accessed January 24, 2019. https://www.theguardian.com/world/2019/jan/13/china-christians-religious-persecution-translation-bible.

Litfin, Bryan M. *Early Christian Martyr Stories: An Evangelical Introduction with New Translations.* Grand Rapids, MI: Baker, 2014.

Marshall, Paul, Lela Gilbert, and Nina Shea. *Persecuted: The Global Assault on Christians.* Nashville, TN: Thomas Nelson, 2013.

Musurillo, Herbert. *The Acts of the Christian Martyrs.* Oxford: Clarendon, 1972.

Ripken, Nik. *The Insanity of God: A True Story of Faith Resurrected.* Nashville, TN: B&H Books, 2013.

———. *The Insanity of Obedience: Walking with Jesus through Tough Places.* Nashville, TN: B&H Books, 2014.

Rostampour, Maryam, and Marzieh Amirizadeh. *Captive in Iran: A Remarkable True Story of Hope and Triumph amid the Horror of Tehran's Brutal Evin Prison.* Carol Stream, IL: Tyndale Momentum, 2013.

Stults, Roy. "Stubborn Saint: Wang Mingdao and the Birth of the Chinese House Church Movement." *Christian History* 109 (2014): 21–24.

Tertullian. "Apology." In *The Ante-Nicene Fathers*, edited by Alexander Roberts and James Donaldson, translated by S. Thelwall, 3:17–55. Edinburgh: T&T Clark, 1873.

Wilken, Robert. *The First Thousand Years: A Global History of Christianity*. New Haven, CT: Yale University Press, 2012.

Wurmbrand, Richard. *Tortured for Christ*. Middlebury, IN: Living Sacrifice Books, 1985.

Part 2

Theological Issues in Contemporary Evangelism

THE THEOLOGY OF EVANGELISM

Steve W. Lemke

The apostle Paul began his letter to the Galatian Christians admonishing these believers to communicate the *true* gospel, not a false one. Paul had proclaimed the gospel of grace to them, but they had modified it to be a false gospel of good works:

> I am amazed that you are so quickly deserting Him who called you by the grace of Christ, for a *different gospel*; which is really not another; only there are some who are disturbing you and want to distort the gospel of Christ. But even if we, or an angel from heaven, should preach to you a gospel contrary to what we have preached to you, he is to be accursed! As we have said before, so I say again now, if any man is preaching to you a gospel contrary to what you received, he is to be accursed! (Gal 1:6–9, italics added)

Likewise in the Old Testament, God upbraided the so-called friends of Job who purported to bear witness of the ways of God to Job. As God said to Eliphaz the Temanite, "My wrath is kindled against you and against your two friends, because *you have not spoken of Me what is right* as My servant Job has" (Job 42:7, cf. v. 8, italics added).

These disparate accounts from different situations in the two Testaments both assert that as believers we are accountable to tell others accurately who God is and what his gospel is. In other words, *theology matters*. This is nowhere more evident than in evangelism as we share the good news of Jesus Christ with unbelievers. How can we be effective ambassadors for Christ and agents of reconciliation if we do not present God and his gospel accurately (2 Cor 5:20)?

Scripture repeats numerous warnings about the dire consequences of believers who promulgate false doctrine (Jas 3:1; 1 Tim 4:1–16; 6:1–4; 2 Tim 2:15–19; 3:13; 4:3–4; 2 Pet 2:1–22). To be a good witness, we must communicate the truths of God's word *accurately*. This article will propose a sound theological foundation for evangelism, reflecting how the doctrines of revelation, theology, Christology, pneumatology, anthropology, soteriology, and ecclesiology provide a proper framework for evangelism.[1]

Revelation: The Doctrine of Scripture

The first question one must address is the source of truth and authority for evangelism. The apostle Paul asserts in Rom 1:18–21 that persons are held accountable to reason from creation itself to the existence of the Creator and, in Rom 2:12–16, that the existence of the human conscience should point persons to the Divine Lawgiver. This way of knowing about God is called *general revelation*. But knowing God personally requires *special revelation*, which is revealed in the Bible. The most fundamental theological presupposition of evangelism is the divine inspiration and authority of the Bible—more specifically, from the conviction that Scripture is *theopneustos*, i.e., "God-breathed" (2 Tim 3:16 NIV). The Bible reflects the very words of God written by the human author under the inspiration of the Holy Spirit. As Peter described this process, "For no prophecy was ever made by an act of human will, but men moved by the Holy Spirit spoke from God" (2 Pet 1:21). If Scripture is not divinely inspired, there is no real

---

[1] Excellent works in the theology of evangelism include C. E. Autry, *The Theology of Evangelism* (Nashville, TN: Broadman, 1966); Lewis Drummond, *The Word of the Cross: A Contemporary Theology of Evangelism* (Nashville, TN: Broadman, 1992); and Alvin L. Reid, "Truth Matters: The Theology of Evangelism," chap. 5 in *Introduction to Evangelism* (Nashville, TN: Broadman & Holman 1998).

authority in Scripture for evangelism. A Bible that is just a compilation of human ideas and wisdom has little authority and offers little help. Only a divinely inspired Scripture provides an authoritative basis for evangelism. The Bible is not just a collection of good ideas or lofty human thoughts; it is the word of God. In Jesus's parable of the sower, the seed being sown is the word of God (Mark 4:14). We do not make up the content of our evangelism; the gospel is found in the word of God. Paul instructed the young minister Timothy to "preach the word" (2 Tim 4:2–5) and to read and exposit Scripture in teaching sound doctrine (1 Tim 4:11–16).

The particular view of the inspiration of Scripture being described here is normally called the *plenary verbal* view of inspiration. For inspiration to be "verbal" means God's inspiration extends not just to general concepts and ideas but also to the very words of Scripture. To be *"plenary* verbal" means inspiration is *fully* verbal, extending God's inspiration to each and every word. The Holy Spirit so superintended the process of inspiration that every word accurately reflects the word of God, even though it is within the vocabulary and worldview of the human author. If a believer does not believe in plenary verbal inspiration, then Scripture might be understood to communicate merely broad, general ideas about God. In this perspective, each word may or may not actually communicate the word of God, and thus one could not have absolute confidence in the truth of every statement in Scripture. However, if each word is divinely inspired, the grammatical details of the words matter. The proper interpretation of a text might depend upon the tense or some other grammatical detail. Biblical evangelism presupposes that *every* word in Scripture is inspired by God, and thus important insights may depend upon a proper understanding of the words of Scripture.

The inerrancy of Scripture is also foundational for evangelism. If Scripture is not true, the basis for evangelism is merely the shifting sand of opinion—an unworthy foundation for life. However, if the word of God is the bedrock of truth, it gives authority and credibility to evangelism (Matt 7:24–29). When faithfully proclaimed, God's word will not return void but will accomplish God's purpose effectively (Isa 55:11).

A commitment to the divine inspiration and inerrancy of the Bible demands good hermeneutics. Incumbent upon the faithful witness who believes each word of Scripture is divinely inspired is not to handle the word of God "deceitfully" (2 Cor 4:2) but to divide rightly the word of truth (2 Tim 2:15). Utilizing sound hermeneutics, the Bible student exegetes the Scripture verse by verse, seeking the true meaning of the text. Good exegesis seeks to discover what the Holy Spirit intends to communicate in a text of Scripture, aided by the illumination of the Holy Spirit.

Perhaps some might think such an assertion about biblical inerrancy and authority is unnecessary. Unfortunately, it is not. Each generation must affirm for itself the truthfulness of Scripture. As G. K. Chesterton famously said, to keep a white fence looking white, you can't just leave it as it is. You have to keep repainting it white over and over again to keep it looking the same.[2] If we are going to keep Southern Baptists and other evangelicals believing the Bible is the inerrant, infallible word of God, we're going to have to keep repainting that fence in every generation. We should not only hold to scriptural authority in our hearts but also teach it diligently to the next generation over and over again (cf. Deut 6:4–9).

There is room in evangelism to utilize a number of tools, particularly personal testimony. Sharing personal testimonies about our own experience with Christ can encourage unsaved persons that they too can be saved. But witness without use of Scripture is incomplete. As important as our own experiences with God are to us, we should present Scripture to unbelievers. It is in the pages of the Bible that we hear the "words of life." Evangelism without the Bible is like trying to play baseball without a bat. All the witnesses in the New Testament

---

[2] G. K. Chesterton, *Orthodoxy* (New York: John Lane, 1908), 212.

referred to the Old Testament Scriptures as they shared with others about Christ. Since we also have the New Testament that even more clearly focuses on Christ, it would be negligent not to share with the lost what God's word says about salvation through Jesus Christ.

Theology: The Doctrine of God

When believers accord divine revelation its appropriate role as the proper source for authority and truth in evangelism, and good hermeneutics are applied in its interpretation, it should lead the witness to a correct theology (the doctrine of God). Theology is the proper content of evangelism—more specifically, God as revealed in Scripture as the Trinity of God, namely the Father, Jesus Christ the Son, and the Holy Spirit. Christian witnesses do not share their own ideas about God; they proclaim what the Bible says about who God is and what he has done.

What does the Bible reveal about God that is foundational to evangelism? God reveals himself in Scripture as a *self-revealing* God. Although there is much about God that transcends human understanding (Isa 55:8–9), God has revealed to us the most important aspects of his nature through Scripture and through the incarnation of his Son Jesus Christ.[3] God is personal, and he communicates with humans. He is not the distant god of Deism, separate and transcendent from the world. In Christ, God became flesh and got his hands dirty in the world. The Word became flesh and dwelt among us (John 1:14). We need not speculate about God's character or what his will is for our lives. God has taken the initiative in revealing himself to us and communicating who he is and what he is about in our world.

The Bible reveals God is perfect in every way. He is all-powerful (omnipotent), all-knowing (omniscient), all-present (omnipresent), all-wise

---

[3] Francis A. Schaeffer, *He Is There and He Is Not Silent* (Wheaton, IL: Tyndale House, 1972); Carl F. H. Henry, *God, Revelation, and Authority: God Who Speaks and Shows*, 6 vols. (Waco, Word: 1976–1983).

(omnisapient), and all-loving (omnibenevolent).[4] He is the Creator of the universe and sustains it through his providential care. He is the sovereign Lord who reigns over all creation. No power or being can stand against his sovereign power. The Bible reveals God as expressed in the Trinity of three Persons—God the Father, God the Son, and God the Holy Spirit—"with distinct personal attributes, but without division of nature, essence, or being."[5]

What does the Bible reveal about the *character* of God? Scripture reveals God is a perfectly moral being, not merely an impersonal force. One important aspect God has revealed to us about his moral character is He *is love* (1 John 4:7–8). Any depiction of God that does not characterize him as loving is unbiblical. Indeed, despite God's hatred of sin because of his holiness and righteousness, through his holy and sovereign love, the Bible makes it clear God loves everyone in the world:[6]

> For *God so loved the world*, that He gave His only begotten Son, that whoever believes in Him shall not perish, but have eternal life. For God did not send the Son into the world to judge the world, but that *the world might be saved through Him*. (John 3:16–17, italics added)

---

[4] "The Baptist Faith and Message 2000," Article II, "God," Southern Baptist Convention. Article II of the Baptist Faith and Message twice describes God as "all powerful" and "all knowing," and adds, "His perfect knowledge extends to all things, past, present, and future, including the future decisions of his free creatures." It also describes God as "all wise" and "all loving," "infinite in holiness and all other perfections." See also Millard Erickson, *God the Father Almighty: A Contemporary Exploration of the Divine Attributes* (Grand Rapids, MI: Baker Academic, 2003).
[5] Ibid.
[6] The Baptist Faith and Message affirms not only that God the Father is "all loving" but also that "He is fatherly in His attitude toward all men." "The Baptist Faith and Message 2000," Article II A: "God the Father," Southern Baptist Convention.

> The Lord is not slow about His promise, as some count slowness, but is patient toward you, not wishing for any to perish but for *all to come to repentance.* (2 Pet 3:9, italics added)
>
> And He Himself is the propitiation for our sins; and *not for ours only, but also for those of the whole world.* (1 John 2:2, italics added)
>
> Beloved, let us love one another, for love is from God; and everyone who loves is born of God and knows God. The one who does not love does not know God, for *God is love.* By this *the love of God was manifested in us,* that God has sent His only begotten Son into the world so that we might live through Him. In this is love, not that we loved God, but that *He loved us* and sent His Son to be the propitiation for our sins. ... We have come to know and have believed *the love which God has for us. God is love,* and the one who abides in love abides in God, and God abides in him. (1 John 4:7–10, 16, italics added)

Scripture also describes another aspect of God's moral character—God is *holy and righteous.* This aspect of God's character is expressed by his moral perfection and his commandments for us to live up to his standards (Matt 5:48; Rom 12:2). God's holiness is also revealed in his holy wrath against all manner of sin.

A believer does well to maintain the balance of these two key aspects of God's nature—both his love and his holiness. While one cannot explain everything about God in a brief conversation, it is the responsibility of each believer to balance our message with both the holiness and righteousness of God with the love of God. An overly strong focus on the holiness of God presents the hearers with a God who is righteous and "wholly other," so transcendent He has little or no interaction with humans. An overly strong focus on the love of God, however, presents the image of a kind God who has no real objective standards. The Bible reveals the truth about God is somewhere between these two extremes, proclaiming the love of God while upholding God's high moral standards without compromise. Applied to evangelism, God's holiness and righteousness leads him to find human sinfulness as unacceptable. Unfortunately, since we are sinners, we are unable to save ourselves. Therefore, in God's grace and love, he sent his only Son Jesus to pay the price for our sins on the cross (John 3:16; Eph 2:16). Salvation thus comes only to those who repent of their sins and claim Jesus Christ as their Savior and Lord (Acts 2:38; 16:31; Rom 10:9–10).

Christology: The Doctrine of Christ

We know God through Jesus Christ, for he is the Savior sent by God. A sound Christology is thus necessary for effective evangelism. As the Baptist Faith and Message words it, "All Scripture is a testimony to Christ, who is himself the focus of divine revelation."[7] We should always heed the example of the apostle Paul to focus our message on Jesus Christ, for he said, "We do not preach ourselves but Christ Jesus as Lord, and ourselves as your bond-servants for Jesus' sake (2 Cor 4:5). Jesus told the devout Nicodemus, "As Moses lifted up the serpent in the wilderness, even so must the Son of Man be lifted up; so that whoever believes will in Him have eternal life" (John 3:14–15). Jesus also promised, as he entered Jerusalem to face his crucifixion, "'And I, if I am lifted up from the earth, will draw all men to Myself.' But He was saying this to indicate the kind of death by which He was to die" (John 12:32–33). It is crucial we believe in the life-changing power of the gospel. As the apostle Paul said, "For I am not ashamed of the gospel, for it is the power of God for salvation to everyone who believes, to the Jew first and also to the Greek" (Rom 1:16). As we share the gospel with others, we must proclaim Jesus Christ as the

---

[7] "The Baptist Faith and Message 2000," Article I, "The Scriptures," Southern Baptist Convention.

Son of God who was born of a virgin, lived a sinless life, taught divine truth and performed miracles, was crucified on the cross as a substitutionary atonement for our sins, is risen and ascended to the right hand of God to make intercession for us, and is coming again to take us to heaven with him. That gospel message is what our world is hungry to hear, whether they realize it or not.

Jesus is not just one way among others to God; he is the *only* way to God. Jesus himself said: "I am the way, and the truth, and the life; no one comes to the Father but through Me" (John 14:6). This Christ-centeredness was also highlighted in the preaching of the New Testament church: "And there is salvation in no one else [than the name of Jesus Christ]; for there is no other name under heaven that has been given among men by which we must be saved" (Acts 4:12).

God sent Jesus to this world to offer salvation to all who would repent of their sins and trust Christ as their Savior. It is a repeated theme in the New Testament that Jesus's atonement is sufficient for *all* who trust in him:

> He came to His own, and those who were His own did not receive Him. But *as many as received Him*, to them He gave the right to become children of God, *even to those who believe in His name*. (John 1:11–12, italics added)

> As Moses lifted up the serpent in the wilderness, even so must the Son of Man be lifted up; so that *whoever believes* will in Him have eternal life. For *God so loved the world*, that He gave His only begotten Son, that whoever believes in Him shall not perish, but have eternal life. For God did not send the Son into the world to judge the world, but that the *world might be saved through Him*. (John 3:14–17, italics added)

> This is good and acceptable in the sight of God our Savior, who *desires all men to be saved* and to come to the knowledge of the truth. For there is one God, and one mediator

also between God and men, the man Christ Jesus, who gave Himself as *a ransom for all*, the testimony given at the proper time. (1 Tim 2:3–6, italics added)

The Lord is not slack concerning His promise, as some count slackness, but is longsuffering toward us, *not willing that any should perish but that all should come to repentance*. (2 Pet 3:9 NKJV, italics added)

And he is the propitiation for our sins: and *not for ours only, but also for the sins of the whole world*. (1 John 2:2 KJV, italics added)

Paul maintained this focus on the crucifixion of Christ by practicing gospel-focused *kerygmatic* preaching (gospel preaching focused on the cross of Christ). The *kerygma* is the proclamation of the essential details of the gospel—that Jesus is the promised Messiah, the Son of God, whose coming was prophesied in the Old Testament; that His identity was confirmed by his teachings and miracles during his ministry in this world; that he was crucified and resurrected according to God's eternal plan; that he is exalted to the right hand of God; that those who repent of their sins and trust in Christ as Lord and Savior can receive forgiveness and eternal life; and that he is coming again to save his own and judge the sin of the world (Acts 2:22–39; 3:13–26; 4:10–12; 10:36–43; 13:17–41; 1 Cor 15:1–11).[8]

The focus of the *kerygma* is the cross of Christ. Paul told the Corinthian church that "I determined to know nothing among you except Jesus Christ, and Him crucified" (1 Cor 2:2). Although the Jews sought confirmation of the message by miraculous signs and gentiles sought wisdom through philosophy, Paul asserted that "we preach Christ crucified, to Jews a stumbling block and to Gentiles foolishness, but

---

[8] C. H. Dodd, *The Apostolic Preaching and Its Developments* (New York: Harper and Row, 1964), 7–35.

to those who are the called, both Jews and Greeks, Christ the power of God and the wisdom of God" (1 Cor 1:23–24). A witness should always be focused on the cross of Christ, for this crucial moment in history has the power to change lives even today.

Pneumatology: The Doctrine of the Holy Spirit

The Holy Spirit plays an indispensable and irreplaceable role in evangelism. A sound pneumatology is thus a key to effective evangelism because, first of all, the Holy Spirit inspired the scriptural text that is being shared (2 Pet 1:21). Since He inspired the text of Scripture, the Spirit is the best source for its proper interpretation. The Spirit illumines the spiritually discerning reader of Scripture (John 16:7–14).

The Holy Spirit convicts and convinces the hearers, not the human witness alone. Jesus said that the Spirit "will convict the world concerning sin and righteousness and judgment; concerning sin, because they do not believe in Me; and concerning righteousness, because I go to the Father and you no longer see Me; and concerning judgment, because the ruler of this world has been judged" (John 16:8–11). Persons are not saved by mere human words but by the conviction and prompting of the Holy Spirit.[9] The Baptist Faith and Message highlights the crucial role the Holy Spirit plays in conversion, sanctification, and Christian service:

> [The Holy Spirit] convicts men of sin, of righteousness, and of judgment. He calls men to the Saviour, and effects regeneration. At the moment of regeneration He baptizes every believer into the Body of Christ. He cultivates Christian

---

[9] Some describe the Spirit's work in leading a person to salvation as the "solicitous call," as "prevenient grace," or as "enabling grace." See Richard Land, "Congruent Election: Understanding Salvation from an 'Eternal Now' Perspective," in *Whosoever Will: A Biblical-Theological Critique of Five-Point Calvinism*, eds. David Allen and Steve Lemke (Nashville, TN: B&H Publishing Group, 2014), 59.

character, comforts believers, and bestows the spiritual gifts by which they serve God through His church. He seals the believer unto the day of final redemption. His presence in the Christian is the guarantee that God will bring the believer into the fullness of the stature of Christ. He enlightens and empowers the believer and the church in worship, evangelism, and service.[10]

Only the believer who witnesses in the power of the Spirit will see the life-changing results the Spirit alone can work in someone's life. The Bible records that just before the disciples began witnessing to the world about the truth of Christ, they were "filled with the Holy Spirit" (Acts 2:4) as they met together in prayer. From that experience they went out into the streets of Jerusalem to tell others about Jesus Christ. People from all over the world were in Jerusalem that day of Pentecost to celebrate the Feast of Pentecost, and this small group of believers, filled with the Sprit, shared Christ with everyone they met, leading three thousand people to faith in Christ that day (Acts 2:41). Dependence upon the Holy Spirit is an essential for effective evangelism. A witness can have a skillful presentation of the gospel, but without being filled with the Holy Spirit one will not be effective in transforming lives.

Anthropology: The Doctrine of Persons

Why do human beings need salvation? We need salvation through Christ because we cannot save ourselves. We are sinners. As Rom 3:23 asserts, "For all have sinned and fall short of the glory of God." Although we were born with the image of God within us (Gen 1:27), our human natures are inclined toward sin. Since the first couple Adam and Eve sinned, each human being who is born has a sinful nature, and when

---

[10] "The Baptist Faith and Message 2000," Article II C, "God the Holy Spirit," Southern Baptist Convention.

they reach the age of accountability, they will inevitably sin. As the Baptist Faith and Message puts it, "Through the temptation of Satan man transgressed the command of God, and fell from his original innocence whereby his posterity inherit a nature and an environment inclined toward sin. Therefore, as soon as they are capable of moral action, they become transgressors and are under condemnation."[11] We are thus not born guilty of Adam's sin (hence the need for infant baptism), but inevitably we all sin and become accountable for our sins because our fallen human natures and environment are both inclined toward sin. When we sin ourselves (when we come to the point in life at which we are morally accountable), we come under condemnation for our sins. At that point we cannot save ourselves. But even as fallen humans, we retain enough of the image of God that, under the conviction of the Holy Spirit, we can throw ourselves on the mercy of God. Anyone who repents of their sins and trusts Jesus Christ as Savior and Lord can be saved (John 1:11–12; 3:16–17). Jesus paid for our sins on the cross by his blood, and through him our sins can be forgiven and we can be reconciled to God (Rom 5:10; 2 Cor 5:11–20; Eph 2:16; Col 1:19–21; 1 John 1:8–10).

Soteriology: The Doctrine of Salvation

Of course, the doctrine that most directly impacts evangelism is soteriology—the doctrine of salvation. The Christian doctrine of salvation focuses on the *gospel* of our Lord Jesus Christ. Just what is the gospel? The word *gospel* literally means "good news." The gospel, although it involves deep truths, is nonetheless rather clear and specific. It is not confusing or complex or vague. It does not involve various ethical positions or political stances. The gospel has *implications* for these things but should not be confused with the gospel itself. The *gospel* is simply the good news that forgiveness of sin and eternal life are made

---

[11] "The Baptist Faith and Message 2000," Article III, "Man," Southern Baptist Convention.

available to everyone who puts their faith in Jesus Christ as Savior and Lord. Through his sinless life, substitutionary death, and glorious resurrection, Jesus Christ made a way for anyone to be saved. Redemption through Jesus Christ was God's plan for salvation from the beginning of time (Acts 2:22–24).

Salvation comes through Christ Jesus *alone*, by faith believing in the name of the Lord Jesus Christ (John 1:11–12; 3:16–18; 14:6; Acts 4:12; 16:31; Rom 1:16; 1 John 3:23; 5:5; 5:10). Jesus called himself the "Door" of the sheep. All would-be alternative ways to God he described as "thieves and robbers" (John 10:1–2, 7–8). Simon Peter confessed the truth about Jesus when he said, "You are the Christ, the Son of the living God" (Matt 16:16). All believers must come to God through faith in Christ: "If you confess with your mouth Jesus as Lord, and believe in your heart that God raised Him from the dead, you will be saved; for with the heart a person believes, resulting in righteousness, and with the mouth he confesses, resulting in salvation. For the Scripture says, 'Whosoever believes in Him will not be disappointed.' … for 'Whosoever will call on the name of the Lord will be saved'" (Rom 10:9–13). As Peter proclaimed on the day of Pentecost, "Repent, and each of you be baptized in the name of Jesus Christ for the forgiveness of your sins; and you will receive the gift of the Holy Spirit" (Acts 2:38). The atonement provided by Jesus through the cross is sufficient for all; no further payment is needed (Rom 6:10; 1 Tim 2:3–6; 2 Pet 3:18; Jude 3; Heb 7:27; 9:28; 10:10).[12]

To summarize, anyone and everyone is potentially savable, but not everyone will be saved. In fact, more will be lost than will be saved (Matt 7:13–14). Biblically, therefore, we must reject the doctrine of universalism that everyone will be saved. Only those who trust in Christ as Savior and Lord will be saved. But salvation through Christ is available

---

[12] For a further development of this argument, see Allen and Lemke, eds. *Whosoever Will*.

to anyone and everyone who believes in Jesus as their Savior.[13] The twelfth century theologian Peter Lombard is usually credited for being the first to say an oft-repeated theological dictum—the atonement of Christ is sufficient for all, but efficient just for the elect.[14] Jesus's atonement is sufficient for everyone, but it functions or is "efficient" just for those who are elect. How does one become elect? According to the New Testament, election comes as a result of the perfect foreknowledge of God of who is going to trust Christ as their Savior (Rom 8:29–30; 11:2; 1 Pet 1:1–2). Those who will not meet that condition of personal faith cannot be saved.

Some question such a teaching, saying it somehow limits God's sovereignty for salvation to be dependent on a human response. But this concern is misplaced. Who else should have the right to determine the conditions for salvation but our Sovereign Lord, who purchased that salvation at the dear price of his own Son's life? If God has required that only those who trust Christ as their Savior are to be saved, and that is precisely what the New Testament repeatedly teaches about salvation (John 1:11–12; 3:14–17; 10:1-10; 14:6; Acts 2:38; 4:12; 16:31; Rom 10:9–15; 1 Tim 2:3–6; 2 Pet 3:9; 1 John 2:2; 3:23; 5:5, 10), then who are we to question God's sovereign choice? Of course, none of us alone makes the decision to follow Christ. The Holy Spirit convicts and convinces us to trust Christ through what some call "prevenient" or "enabling" grace. But some persons reject the work of the Spirit in their lives (Matt 1:31; Acts 7:51; Rom 1:18–24; Eph 4:17–19). In the end, unless we trust Christ personally, we will not be saved.

Salvation through Christ is not free, and it is not easy. Our salvation cost our Savior his life and cost God the Father the painful

---

[13] David Allen, Eric Hankins, and Adam Harwood, *Anyone Can Be Saved: A Defense of "Traditional" Southern Baptist Soteriology* (Eugene: Wipf and Stock, 2016).

[14] Peter Lombard, *The Sentences: Book 3; On the Incarnation of the Word*, 3.20.3, trans. G. Silano, Mediaeval Sources in Translation 45 (Toronto: Pontifical Institute of Medieval Studies, 2008), 86.

death of his Son. Although the atonement of Christ is offered freely to believers, it is not easy. True believers must repent of their sins, trust Christ as their Savior and Lord, and lay aside their own self-centered life to begin living the Christ-centered life. This momentous decision is probably harder for some adults than for most children, because adults have a longer pattern of living without God in their lives. Perhaps C. S. Lewis best described this battle when as an adult he reluctantly came to believe in God:

> You must picture me alone in that room in Magdalen, night after night, feeling, whenever my mind lifted even for a second from my work, the steady, unrelenting approach of Him whom I so earnestly desired not to meet. That which I greatly feared had at last come upon me. In the Trinity Term of 1929 I gave in, and admitted that God was God, and knelt and prayed: perhaps, that night, the most dejected and reluctant convert in all England.[15]

Later Lewis took the further step of trusting Christ as his Savior:

> To accept the incarnation was a further step in the same direction. It brings God nearer, or near in a new way. And this, I found, was something I had not wanted. But to recognize the ground for my evasion was of course to recognize both its shame and its futility. I know very well when, but hardly how, the final step was taken. I was driven to Whipsnade one sunny morning. When we set out I did not believe that Jesus Christ is the Son of God, and when we reached the zoo I did.[16]

---

[15] C. S. Lewis, *Surprised by Joy: The Shape of My Early Life* (London: Geoffrey Bles, 1955), 215.
[16] Ibid., 223.

Lewis thus wrestled about becoming a Christian for quite some time. But while Lewis was reluctantly led to Christianity, he never regretted that decision. He resisted the work of the Holy Spirit in his life, but eventually he capitulated to the conviction and convincing of the Holy Spirit (see Matt 23:37; John 16:8–11; Acts 7:51; Eph 4:30).

The good news of salvation through Jesus Christ is so surprising and so undeserved that it is a stumbling block or foolishness from the perspective of the world (1 Cor 1:18–25; 2 Cor 4:1–6). The word translated "stumbling block" in 1 Cor 1:23 is *skandalon*, from which we get the English word *scandal*. The world sought salvation by intellectual enlightenment or human good works, but God provided salvation as a gift of grace through the atoning sacrifice of Christ on the cross. Salvation is not based in any way on our own works; it is entirely provided by the grace of God through faith (Eph 2:8–10).

Not only is the message of the gospel surprising and scandalous, but Scripture ties salvation closely to hearing God's word. Paul expressed to the church at Rome the crucial role that sharing the gospel with unbelievers plays in salvation:

> For whoever will call on the name of the Lord will be saved. How then will they call on Him in whom they have not believed? How will they believe in Him whom they have not heard? And how will they hear without a preacher? How will they preach unless they are sent? Just as it is written, "How beautiful are the feet of those who bring good news of good things!" (Rom 10:13–15)

That such an incredible treasure as the forgiveness and eternal life offered through the gospel could be communicated through the vehicle of fallible humans is both amazing and sobering. Paul recognized the supreme irony of the transcendent treasure of the gospel being communicated though human "earthen vessels" or "clay jars": "But we have this treasure in earthen vessels, so that the surpassing greatness of the power will be of God and not from ourselves" (2 Cor 4:7, cf. 1 Cor 1:18–21). Paul called upon Timothy to "do the work of an evangelist" to "fulfill your ministry" (2 Tim 4:5). Focusing on soteriology is not a task just for evangelists, but is a crucial responsibility for all Christians (Matt 28:19–20; Acts 1:8).

Merely proclaiming how to be saved, however, is still incomplete. Incumbent in sharing the gospel is the duty to appeal to and exhort the hearers for a response. Note the appeal given by Peter at the end of the sermon at Pentecost: "And with many other words he solemnly testified and kept on *exhorting* them, saying, 'Be saved from this perverse generation!' So then, those who had received his word were baptized; and that day there were added about three thousand souls" (Acts 2:40–41, italics added). The word translated "exhorting" here is variously translated "strongly urged" (HCSB), "entreated" (Weymouth), "pleaded" (NIV), or "begged" (New Century). The word translated "exhort" is *parekalei*, meaning to invite or summon someone to a decision, to beseech or implore someone, or to plead with or call someone to a decision.[17] The same meaning applies to all six other usages of *parekalei* in the New Testament. It is used to describe the poor servant pleading for mercy from his creditor (Matt 18:29). The same word *parekalei* is used twice in Mark 5, both when Legion, the demon who was tormenting the Gerasene demoniac, pled with Jesus not to send him out of the area (Mark 5:10), and when the delivered former demoniac begged Jesus for permission to go with him (Mark 5:18). It is the word used describing the loving father pleading with his elder son to join in the celebration of the prodigal son having returned home (Luke 15:28). It is used to describe Barnabas exhorting the church at Antioch (Acts 11:23) and Paul urging his fellow passengers in a storm-tossed ship to eat to keep up their strength

---

[17] Gerhard Kittel and Gerhard Friedrich, eds., *Theological Dictionary of the New Testament*, 10 vols., trans. Geoffrey W. Bromiley (Grand Rapids, MI: Eerdmans, 1986), 5:773–79, 793–94.

(Acts 27:33). Thus in all seven times that the word *parekalei* is used in the New Testament, it clearly means to make an urgent appeal, to persuade, to exhort, or to plead with someone. It means going beyond merely announcing and proclaiming the gospel to actually making an urgent appeal for decision and response. As the apostle Paul said, "For we must all appear before the judgment seat of Christ, so that each one may be recompensed for his deeds in the body, according to what he has done, whether good or bad. Therefore, knowing the fear of the Lord, *we persuade men*" (2 Cor 5:10–11). Paul used a word that appears only here in the New Testament—*peithomen*, meaning to persuade or convince someone, to try to win someone over to your point of view.[18]

John Stott has affirmed the crucial importance in preaching of neglecting neither proclamation nor appeal:

> It is not enough to expound a thoroughly orthodox doctrine of reconciliation if we never beg people to come to Christ. Nor is it right for a sermon to consist of an interminable appeal that has not been preceded by an exposition of the gospel. The rule should be "no appeal without a proclamation, and no proclamation without an appeal."[19]

Mere proclamation without invitation leads to frustration. Mere appeal without proclamation produces confusion. Whether in relation to justification or sanctification, a fully orbed gospel ministry must include both proclamation and appeal for decision.

Evangelism is focused on helping lead persons to an initial salvation experience with Christ (*justification*), but believers should mature in salvation toward *sanctification*. In the Great Commission, Jesus commanded the church not just to baptize new believers but also to

---

[18] Kittel and Friedrich, *Theological Dictionary of the New Testament*, 6:1–2.
[19] John Stott, *The Cross of Christ*, 20th anniversary ed. (Downers Grove, IL: InterVarsity, 2008), 198.

"make disciples of all nations" by "teaching them to observe all that I commanded you" (Matt 28:19–20). Evangelism is incomplete without discipleship. The apostles discipled the early church in Jerusalem with their teaching (Acts 2:42). In his last message to the elders of the church at Ephesus, the apostle Paul reminded them, "I did not shrink from declaring to you the whole purpose of God. … Night and day for a period of three years I did not cease to admonish each one with tears" (Acts 20:27, 31). Ephesus was Paul's longest pastorate, and the apostle dedicated his preaching ministry to discipling the Ephesian church. The giftedness of pastors is described as being a "pastor/teacher" (Eph 4:11), being "apt to teach" is one of the qualifications for pastors (1 Tim 3:2; 2 Tim 2:24), and feeding the flock of God with sound doctrine is one of the key responsibilities of pastors (1 Tim 3:2; 5:17; 2 Tim 2:24; 4:1–4; Titus 1:9–6; 2:1; 1 Pet 5:2). Paul instructed Timothy, "Until I come, give attention to the public reading of Scripture, to exhortation and teaching" (1 Tim 4:13).

One of the first steps in discipling new believers is to lead them into an assurance of their salvation. Those who genuinely trust Christ as their Savior and Lord are saved forever and thus should not be constantly anxious that they might lose their salvation. We are saved by God, not by ourselves (Eph 2:8–9), and it is God who secures our salvation (John 15:16; 10:27–29; Rom 8:29–30; Eph 1:13–14; 1 Pet 1:3–5; 1 John 4:19; Jude 1:24–25). We cannot lose salvation because we never earned it or deserved it in the first place. It was the gift of God in the first place, and it is protected by the promise of God. For all these reasons teaching believers sound doctrine is a significant part of the responsibility of every church.

Ecclesiology: The Doctrine of the Church

Who should proclaim the gospel and where should the primary locus be for Christian proclamation? The doctrine of the church (ecclesiology) is foundational for evangelism because sharing the gospel is the responsibility of all believers (Matt 28:19–20; Acts 1:8). The church in

Jerusalem was launched on the Day of Pentecost with Peter preaching the sermon at Pentecost (Acts 2:14–41), reinforced by individual believers sharing their faith with persons in the crowd. The church's *witness* brought a harvest of three thousand souls into the church on the day of Pentecost and continued thereafter (Acts 2:37–41, 47). As persons were saved, they were led into *discipleship* by the teaching of the apostles (Acts 2:42). Unfortunately, baptisms in Southern Baptist churches have been declining now for more than twenty years. Although we have many more churches than we did seventy years ago, we are now baptizing fewer people than in the 1950s. We need a return to personal evangelism done by every member of the church.[20] A great need exists in our churches for a rediscovery of Bible-based, God-honoring, Christologically focused, Spirit-empowered, and doctrinally sound evangelism.

Eschatology

One of the strongest motivations for sharing our faith is what the Bible teaches about heaven and hell. Heaven is the place of eternal fellowship with God promised to those who trust Christ as the Way (John 14:1–6). Gehenna, or hell, is the place of eternal punishment for unbelievers (Mark 9:42–48; 13:24–30; Luke 16:19–31; 2 Pet 2:4–10; Rev 20:11–15). Although talking about heaven and hell have come to be out of fashion with some contemporary believers, Jesus spoke about heaven and hell consistently in the gospels. Jesus taught that only a small number would find the narrow way that leads to salvation, while many will follow the broad way that leads to destruction (Matt 7:13–23). He described the last judgment as separating believers (the sheep) from unbelievers (the goats) (Matt 25:31–46). Jesus asserted he would say to believers, "Come, you who are blessed of My Father, inherit the kingdom prepared for you from the foundation of

---

[20] J. E. Conant and Roy Fish, *Every Member Evangelism for Today: An Updating of J. E. Conant's Classic Every Member Evangelism*. (Eugene, OR: Wipf and Stock, 2009).

the world" (v. 34). The sentence given to unbelievers will be, "Depart from Me, accursed ones, into the eternal fire which has been prepared for the devil and his angels" (v. 41). Jesus concludes this discussion by asserting that unbelievers "will go away into eternal punishment, but the righteous into eternal life" (v. 46). What greater motive could we have for evangelism? Leading an unbeliever to faith in Jesus changes their lives for all eternity. We are therefore under obligation to share the gospel with people we encounter about how to have eternal life through faith in Jesus Christ (Rom 1:13–17; 1 Cor 9:20–23).

BIBLIOGRAPHY

Allen, David, and Steve W. Lemke, eds. *Whosoever Will: A Biblical-Theological Critique of Five-Point Calvinism.* Nashville: B&H Academic, 2010.

Allen, David, Eric Hankins, and Adam Harwood. *Anyone Can Be Saved: A Defense of "Traditional" Southern Baptist Soteriology.* Eugene: Wipf and Stock, 2016.

Autry, C. E. *The Theology of Evangelism.* Nashville, TN: Broadman, 1966.

Chesterton, G. K. *Orthodoxy.* New York: John Lane, 1908.

Conant, J. E., and Roy Fish. *Every Member Evangelism for Today: An Updating of J. E. Conant's Classic Every Member Evangelism.* Eugene, OR: Wipf and Stock, 2009.

Dodd, C. H. *The Apostolic Preaching and Its Developments.* New York: Harper and Row, 1964.

Drummond, Lewis. *The Word of the Cross: A Contemporary Theology of Evangelism.* Nashville, TN: Broadman, 1992.

Erickson, Millard. *God the Father Almighty: A Contemporary Exploration of the Divine Attributes.* Grand Rapids, MI: Baker Academic, 2003.

Henry, Carl F. H. *God, Revelation, and Authority: God Who Speaks and Shows.* 6 vols. Waco, TX: Word, 1976.

Kittel, Gerhard, and Gerhard Friedrich, eds. *Theological Dictionary of the New Testament.* Translated by Geoffrey W. Bromiley. 10 vols. Grand Rapids, MI: Eerdmans, 1986.

Land, Richard. "Congruent Election: Understanding Salvation from an 'Eternal Now' Perspective." In *Whosoever Will: A Biblical-Theological Critique of Five-Point Calvinism*, edited by David Allen and Steve Lemke, 45–59. Nashville, TN: B&H Publishing Group, 2014.

Lewis, C. S. *Surprised by Joy: The Shape of My Early Life.* London: Geoffrey Bles, 1955.

Lombard, Peter. *The Sentences: Book 3; On the Incarnation of the Word*, 3.20.3. Translated by G. Silano, Mediaeval Sources in Translation 45. Toronto: Pontifical Institute of Medieval Studies, 2008.

Reid, Alvin L. "Truth Matters: The Theology of Evangelism." Chap. 5 in *Introduction to Evangelism*. Nashville, TN: Broadman & Holman 1998.

Schaeffer, Francis A. *He Is There and He Is Not Silent*. Wheaton, IL: Tyndale House, 1972.

Southern Baptist Convention. "The Baptist Faith and Message: The 2000 Baptist Faith and Message." Southern Baptist Convention. Accessed February 9, 2019. http://www.sbc.net/bfm2000/bfm2000.asp.

Stott, John. *The Cross of Christ*. 20th anniversary edition. Downers Grove: InterVarsity, 2008.

A BIBLICAL THEOLOGY OF SALVATION

Adam Harwood

The Bible contains no inspired list of key words or definitions for salvation. Brenda Colijn observes, "The New Testament does not develop a systematic doctrine of salvation. Instead, it presents us with a variety of pictures taken from different perspectives."[1] Colijn is correct. The New Testament provides various *images* of salvation. Those images, or pictures, of salvation can be discerned in the biblical plotline, not only in the New Testament but also in the entire Bible. Unfortunately, few studies attempt to craft a biblical view of salvation across both testaments.[2] Some of the literature on the doctrine of salvation focuses almost exclusively on the New Testament while neglecting the Old Testament.[3] A biblical theology of any

---

[1] Brenda B. Colijn, *Images of Salvation in the New Testament* (Downers Grove: IVP Academic, 2010), 13–14.

[2] See, as examples, Jan G. van der Watt, ed. *Salvation in the New Testament: Perspectives on Soteriology*, Supplements to *Novum Testamentum* 121 (Leiden: Brill, 2005); Colijn, *Images of Salvation in the New Testament*; Charles H. Talbert and Jason A. Whitlark, *Getting Saved: The Whole Story of Salvation in the New Testament* (Grand Rapids: Eerdmans, 2011); and Victor Kuligin, *The Language of Salvation: Discovering the Riches of What It Means to Be Saved* (Wooster, OH: Weaver, 2015). Although the title of Kuligin's book does not limit the study to the New Testament, the content effectively does so. His book grew out of his study on the book of Romans (pp. 20–21), and the content of each chapter focuses primarily on New Testament verses and themes.

[3] This emphasis on the New Testament rather than the Old Testament when considering the doctrine of salvation makes sense because Christians live under the new covenant rather than the old, and the New Testament provides the clearest revelation of this doctrine. Even so, it is important to notice the continuity between the Old Testament and the New Testament on salvation by God's grace through faith.

topic, however, must account for truths revealed in both the Old and the New Testaments and provide a whole-Bible view of God's work of salvation by exploring key biblical words and images to answer the question, what is salvation?[4]

To develop a biblical view of salvation, one should engage in a rigorous study of the Bible. First, attempt to account for every major term related to salvation. Those who can work in the biblical languages can identify the Hebrew and Greek terms; others should consult exhaustive concordances keyed to a modern Bible translation to aid their study. Check occurrences of each key word, noting the context, frequency, and genre (such as wisdom literature, or Paul's letters). Those studying any doctrine would benefit from engaging in this kind of Bible study *before* looking at theology books because theological systems sometimes subtly guide one's thinking about a doctrine in a different direction from the Scriptures. Then, work diligently to identify what the Scriptures say about salvation without saying things the Scriptures do *not* say about salvation. Those who write and teach about God and his ways must give careful attention to the Scriptures.

A note of explanation is in order. Salvation can be conceived in a broad or narrow sense. In a broad sense, the doctrine of salvation includes salvation accomplished (also called atonement, the work of Christ, salvation provided, or redemption accomplished), as well as salvation applied (also called the application of the atonement, salvation received, or redemption applied). In a narrow sense, the doctrine of salvation concerns only salvation applied. To limit the scope of this study, I will survey the Bible for key words and images that reveal

---

[4] Three important issues are beyond the scope of this essay: defending the legitimacy of developing a biblical theology of salvation, explaining the theological method, and addressing *how* a person is saved.

salvation in the narrow sense, salvation applied. Also, I will presuppose traditional Christian views of the person and work of Christ.[5]

The method for selecting the list of terms following was a combination of a biblically formed intuition as well as consulting biblical-theological resources to look for frequently occurring words and prominent images for salvation in the Bible.[6] The selection of key words and images following reflects a composite of that effort and will answer the question, what is salvation?

What Is Salvation?

One biblical term for salvation is, unsurprisingly, the Hebrew and Greek words translated into English as *salvation* or *to save*. The primary Hebrew noun is *yeshuah* ("salvation"). At the end of his life, Jacob gathered his sons and prayed, "For Your salvation I wait, O LORD" (Gen 49:18). When the people of God were trapped between Pharaoh's army and the Red Sea, Moses told the Israelites, "Do not fear! Stand by and see the salvation of the LORD which He will accomplish for you today" (Exod 14:13). Hannah turned to the Lord in her barrenness and distress and vowed to dedicate to the Lord a son if he would give her one (1 Sam 1:10–11). Hannah conceived and gave birth to Samuel, weaned him, and fulfilled her vow, taking him to Eli at the temple. Hannah worshipped the Lord, saying, "I rejoice in Your salvation" (1 Sam 2:1). These examples illustrate three of the seventy-eight

---

[5] Traditional Christian views of the person and work of Christ include a Chalcedonian definition of his person (Jesus was and is truly divine and truly human, two natures in one person) and that he gave his life on the cross as a sacrifice and substitute for sinners and was raised to life to justify and reconcile sinners to God.

[6] The resources consulted include James Leo Garrett Jr., *Systematic Theology: Biblical, Historical, and Evangelical* (Grand Rapids: Eerdmans, 1995), 2:221–454; Christopher J. H. Wright, *Salvation Belongs to Our God: Celebrating the Bible's Central Story* (Downers Grove: IVP Academic, 2007); Gerald Cowen, *Salvation: Word Studies from the Greek New Testament* (Nashville: Broadman, 1990); Colijn, *Images of Salvation in the New Testament*; and Kuligin, *The Language of Salvation*.

occurrences of the noun in the Old Testament; the verb *yasha* occurs 178 times.[7]

Salvation involves a rescue from crisis or danger. God rescued his people from the Egyptians (Exod 3:7–8), saved Hezekiah from physical death (Isa 38:20), and promised to rescue Jeremiah from the hands of his oppressors (Jer 15:20–21). In these instances, God's salvation included rescue from physical circumstances. In the New Testament, *sōzō* and *sōtēria* are used to refer to salvation from drowning (Matt 8:24–25; 14:30), physical disease (Matt 9:21–22), terminal illness (John 11:12), and physical death (Luke 23:35–39). In other texts, references to salvation concern the soul or the afterlife. Peter revealed the goal of our faith is the salvation of our souls (1 Pet 1:9), and the writer of Hebrews says Jesus will appear again to bring salvation to those who wait for him (Heb 9:28). Rather than conceiving of salvation as either God's act of rescuing from earthly circumstances *only* or God's act of rescuing in the afterlife *only*, the Bible's testimony of God's work of salvation concerns *both* the present life and the afterlife.

The angel's comment about baby Jesus's name in the infancy narrative revealed his mission. The Hebrew noun *yeshuah* ("salvation") echoes the name *yeshu* (Hebrew "Joshua," literally "Yahweh saves"; Greek *Iēsous*, "Jesus"), who "will save His people from their sins" (Matt 1:21). Chris Wright observes seven salvation terms embedded in Luke's infancy narrative: in Mary's song (Luke 1:47); Zechariah's song (vv. 69, 71, 77); the angel's announcement (Luke 2:11); Simeon's song (v. 30); and Luke's quotation of Isaiah (Luke 3:6). Wright concludes, "This newborn Jesus is above all else, the salvation of God arrived on earth."[8]

---

[7] Another verb is *natsal* ("to deliver"). Joel Hamme observes, "God can rescue (*nāṣal*) people, but no one can deliver (*nāṣal*) people from God's hand (Deut 32:39)." Joel T. Hamme, "Salvation," in *Lexham Theological Wordbook*, Lexham Bible Reference Series, eds. Douglas Mangum et al. (Bellingham, WA: Lexham Press, 2014).

[8] Wright, *Salvation Belongs to Our God*, 28–29.

Entrance into God's Kingdom

In the Bible, salvation is sometimes pictured as entrance into or the coming of God's kingdom (Greek *basileia*). In the Old Testament, God was called King (Ps 97:1), but his reign was not always acknowledged. Thus, God acted to reassert his rule over creation. Jesus taught his followers to pray for God's kingdom to come (Matt 6:10), and he said those who want to enter the kingdom should receive it like a child (Mark 10:15). Jesus equated the kingdom with inheriting eternal life (Mark 10:17–23), and his disciples equated the kingdom with being saved (Mark 10:24–26). Jesus said a person must be born again to see the kingdom (John 3:3, 5), and Paul described salvation as being rescued from Satan's domain and transferred to the kingdom of God's Son (Col 1:13). Paul referred to the behavior of those who will *not* inherit the kingdom (1 Cor 6:9–10; Gal 5:21; Eph 5:5), revealing that citizenship in God's kingdom requires holy living. Jesus's followers, who are citizens of heaven (Phil 3:20–21), should work diligently and prepare for his return (Matt 25:1–13). If God's kingdom is both a present and future reality of God's reign in the world, then God's kingdom is the goal of salvation.[9]

New Life

Salvation is sometimes described as new life. The word *life* (Greek *zōē*) is used by every New Testament author and usually refers to a quality of life that is genuine, full, and beyond physical life only (Matt 7:14; Mark 9:43; John 10:10).[10] The phrase "eternal life" (Greek *aiōnios zōē*) occurs forty-three times in the New Testament. John used the phrase three times in John 3. In verse 15, John stated whoever believes in Jesus will have eternal life. Verse 16 makes the same statement, and verse 36 sums up the matter, "He who believes in the Son has eternal

---

[9] Colijn, *Images of Salvation in the New Testament*, 66–84.
[10] Exceptions to this definition include a reference to *physical* life (Acts 8:33) and Paul's remark, "We shall be saved by His life" (Rom 5:10).

life; but he who does not obey the Son will not see life, but the wrath of God abides on him."

The language of new birth is used almost exclusively by John. He quoted Jesus saying a person must be *gennaō anōthen* ("born again" or "born from above") to see the kingdom of God (John 3:3). The language of creation and new creation, however, is used almost exclusively by Paul. Believers are "created [Greek *ktizō*] in Christ Jesus for good works" (Eph 2:10). And anyone in Christ is a new creation (Greek *kainē ktisis*, 2 Cor 5:17). Regeneration (Greek *palingenesia*) is related to new life because the word is from *palin* ("again") and *genesis* ("birth" or "origin"). The word for regeneration occurs twice in the New Testament, once about all things (Matt 19:28) and once about believers (Titus 3:5). Salvation, whether described as life, eternal life, new birth, or new creation, is pictured in the New Testament as new life.

Belonging to God's Family

Salvation is sometimes pictured in the Bible in familial terms, either as a marriage relationship with God or as God adopting people into his family. For example, the prophets sometimes referred to Israel's unfaithfulness to the Lord as prostituting themselves to false gods and idols rather than covenant faithfulness (Ezek 16:20; also Jas 4:4). Hosea enacted this prophetic message through his marriage to Gomer. In the New Testament, Paul referred to the relationship between Christ and the church as a husband and his bride (Eph 5:22–33).

Ezekiel 16:1–7 referred to God's relationship to Israel using some of the same terminology for adoption as the Code of Hammurabi, suggesting God became Israel's father through adoption.[11] Paul used

---

[11] Meir Malul, "Adoption of Foundlings in the Bible and Mesopotamian Documents: A Study of Some Legal Metaphors in Ezekiel 16:1–7," *Journal for the Study of the Old Testament* 46 (1990): 98–99 and Jack Miles, "Israel as Foundling: Abandonment, Adoption, and the Fatherhood of God," *Hebrew Studies* 46 (2005): 7–24, in Michelle J. Morris, "Adoption," in *The Lexham Bible Dictionary*, eds. John D. Barry et al. (Bellingham, WA: Lexham Press, 2016).

the word *huisothesia* ("adoption" or "sonship") to refer to becoming children of God (Rom 8:15), a believer's future bodily resurrection (v. 23), and Israel's relationship to Yahweh (Rom 9:4). Adoption brings one into God's family and includes one as an heir of God (Gal 4:4–7). Similarly, believers are called children of God (John 1:12; Rom 8:16) and "sons of God through faith in Christ Jesus" (Gal 3:26). Jesus calls those he sanctifies "brothers" (Heb 2:11), for he was made like people in every way to atone for their sin (Heb 2:17). Adoption is by God as Father (Gal 4:6; Rom 8:15) due to his love (Eph 1:5; 1 John 3:1) through Christ (Gal 3:26; Eph 1:5), transfers one from slavery to freedom (Gal 4:5, 7; Rom 8:15), and involves the leadership and testimony of the Holy Spirit that we belong to God (Rom 8:14, 16).[12] Salvation means being included in God's family.

Forgiveness of Sin

Scripture envisions salvation as forgiveness of sin. The two main words for forgiveness in Hebrew are *slh* ("to forgive, pardon") and *nasa* ("to lift up, bear, or forgive"), but God is always the subject of *slh*. Under the sacrificial system, the people were forgiven because the priests made atonement as prescribed by God (Lev 4—5). People are in need of God's forgiveness (Ps 51:1–5; Isa 6:1–5; Rom 3:9, 23; 1 John 1:8–10). Just as blood is required for forgiveness under the old covenant (Heb 9:22), so too blood is required under the new covenant for forgiveness. Jesus identified his blood with the new covenant, "poured out for many for the forgiveness of sins" (Matt 26:28; see also Luke 22:20). Paul stated the same truth in Eph 1:7 that Jesus's blood provides *aphiēmi*, which means, "to remove the guilt resulting from wrongdoing."[13] Forgiveness in both testaments presupposes God's loving desire to be in fellowship with the people he created as well

---

[12] Garrett, *Systematic Theology*, 290.
[13] Johannes P. Louw and Eugene Albert Nida, *Greek-English Lexicon of the New Testament: Based on Semantic Domains* (New York: United Bible Societies, 1996), 502.

as their alienation from their holy Creator due to their sin. The good news is God forgives sinners through the blood of Jesus.

Forgiveness of sin is illustrated in two familiar stories: the prodigal son (Luke 15:11–24) and the adulterous woman (John 8:3–11). The son funded a sinful lifestyle with his inheritance until the money ran out and he came to his senses. The son realized and confessed his sin against God and his earthly father. The father enthusiastically received the son, lavishing gifts and kisses on this son who was dead but was now alive. The woman caught in adultery deserved, under the old covenant, to be killed by people throwing large stones at her. When Jesus called for the sinless person among them to throw the first stone, they scattered. Jesus told her he did not condemn her, then told her to end her lifestyle of sinful behavior. Neither the son nor the woman deserved God's forgiveness, but neither does anyone. Forgiveness of sin is not a thing one deserves. Rather, forgiveness of sin—salvation—is freely and graciously given to undeserving people by God through Christ.

Reconciliation to God

Reconciliation to God is another image of salvation. The Greek word *allassō* means "change" or "exchange" and concerns a change in the relationship between God and a person or between people with one another. Reconciliation presupposes a broken relationship and alienation that needs to be repaired. The problem is not with God but with people. Paul stated in Rom 5:6–11 that Christ died for us while we were helpless, ungodly sinners. Also, God reconciled us to himself through the death of Jesus while we were still his enemies. In freedom and love, the holy and only true God initiated this change in relationship through the death of his Son for sinners. And God commands those who have been reconciled to him to declare to others the message of reconciliation (2 Cor 5:19–20). Although the language of reconciliation was used in Jewish and Greek literature outside of and near the time of the first century, Paul's two uses of the image in the New

Testament carried unique elements. The biblical distinctions between the extra-biblical and biblical usage highlight the significant features of the image.[14] Reconciliation means that as a result of God's love, Christ died for sinners to change their status from enemy to friend.

Redemption from Sin

Salvation is sometimes pictured in Scripture as costly redemption. Under the old covenant, a firstborn person or animal could be redeemed (Hebrew *padah*) at the cost of the life of another animal or monetary payment (Exod 13:13; Num 18:15–16). One could also redeem (Hebrew *gaal*) property. In the book of Ruth, Boaz acted as the kinsman-redeemer (Hebrew *goel*, Ruth 2:20), the nearest relative who paid money to restore the land to its original family. Providentially, the law of Levirate marriage also resulted in Boaz marrying Ruth. The death of Jesus redeemed those sins committed under the old covenant (Heb 9:15), redeemed (Greek *exagorazō*) sinners from the curse of the law (Gal 3:13), and brought redemption (Greek *apolytrōsis*, "to release or set free") through his blood (Eph 1:7). Also, redemption is a future event (Rom 8:23; Eph 4:30). These biblical terms paint a portrait of salvation as redemption at a cost, namely God in Christ paid the cost to redeem people from their sin.

When salvation is viewed as redemption purchased at a cost, the redemption is enjoyed with a grateful remembrance of its cost. Perhaps the presence of the Lamb in the heavenly vision of the multitude around God's throne (Rev 7:9) is explained by grateful remembrance. In Scripture, the Lamb of God is a composite picture of sacrifice that culminates in the cross of Christ, in which Jesus is the Lamb of God who takes away the sin of the world (John 1:29). At the cross, God provided for himself the sacrifice he required. The multinational

---

[14] For a detailed analysis of the extra-biblical and Pauline usage of the terms, see Cilliers Breytenbach, "Salvation of the Reconciled (With a Note on the Background of Paul's Metaphor of Reconciliation)," in *Salvation in the New Testament*, 271–86.

crowd cries out, "Salvation to our God who sits on the throne, *and to the Lamb*" (Rev 7:10, italics added). Salvation is redemption at a cost, and the redeemed will thank throughout eternity the One who purchased their redemption.

Deliverance

Deliverance is another picture of salvation. The greatest Old Testament story of deliverance is the release of the Israelites after four hundred years of Egyptian captivity. At the burning bush, the Lord told Moses he had heard their cries and was aware of their suffering, and he would deliver (Hebrew *natsal*) them from the hand—or power—of the Egyptians (Exod 3:7–8). The story of the Passover and exodus is a story of God delivering his people from bondage. In the Old Testament, God is the deliverer. Jacob asked God to deliver (*natsal*) him from the hand of his brother, Esau (Gen 32:11). God used Joseph to keep the people alive by a great deliverance (Hebrew *peletah*, Gen 45:7). In the story of Esther, Mordecai warned that if she remained silent, deliverance (Hebrew *hatsalah*) would arise from another place (Esth 4:14). The psalmist asked God to deliver (*natsal*) him from his enemies (Pss 25:20; 143:9). The Old Testament is a story of God delivering people.

In the New Testament, Jesus taught his disciples to ask God to deliver (Greek *rhyomai*) them from evil (Matt 6:13). Also, his disciples would know the truth, and the truth would deliver them or set them free (Greek *eleutheroō*, John 8:32). A dramatic depiction of deliverance occurred in a Gerasene cemetery. A man with unclean spirits lived among the tombs naked, chained, screaming, and cutting himself (Mark 5:1–5). Jesus delivered the man from the spirits, and the man was clothed and in his right mind (v. 15). The man desired to travel with Jesus. Interestingly, Jesus told him no. Instead, Jesus told him to go home and tell people what the Lord had done for him. That story ends with the statement that the delivered man proclaimed in the region the "great things Jesus had done for him; and everyone was amazed" (Mark 5:20).

Christ set us free (*eleutheroō*) for freedom (*eleutheria*), Paul wrote. Thus, we should not submit to a yoke of slavery (Gal 5:1). Formerly, we were slaves to sin and free from the control of righteousness (Rom 6:20). But the situation has been reversed for those who have been baptized into Christ. We have been freed from sin and are now slaves of God (Rom 6:18, 22). Those who have been delivered should freely serve God and others in his name.

Sanctification

The holy God calls and causes his people to be holy. In Lev 19:2 and 1 Pet 1:15–16, God's holiness is paired with a call for God's people to live holy lifestyles. For people to be holy means they are set apart for special use, such as the priests or objects set apart for use in worship during the old covenant (Exod 29:21). Those objects were sprinkled with the blood of an animal; they were not to be used for common purposes but only in worship. Similarly, believers have been sprinkled by the blood of Jesus (figuratively in 1 Pet 1:2) and are called to live holy lives, dedicated to God. Also, God's people are addressed as "those who have been sanctified [Greek *hagiazō*] in Christ Jesus" (1 Cor 1:2). The verb in 1 Cor 1:2 is in the passive voice, which means the subject is acted upon. In other words, sanctification—or being set apart—is a thing that happens *to* a person, not a thing a person does. God sanctifies. He sets apart and makes holy those he has called to live holy and separate lives. Although God is the one who sanctifies people, he calls them to action. In Phil 2:12–13, Paul explained, "Work out your salvation with fear and trembling; for it is God who is at work in you, both to will and to work for His good pleasure." The verb translated "work out" is *katergazomai*, which means "to do something with success or thoroughness." What did Paul tell the Philippian believers to work out? Their *sōtēria*, or "process of being saved."[15] Salvation is pictured as the

---

[15] Louw and Nida, *Greek-English Lexicon of the New Testament*, 511 and 241.

holy God calling his people to be set apart for holy living, which he works in us as we work out our salvation.

Transformation

Salvation is transformation. In his fascinating study on idolatry, Greg Beale makes a case from the language of Scripture that people become what they worship, whether for their benefit or ruin.[16] For example, when the people of God worshipped idols that were described as deaf and dumb, the people assumed those traits. The opposite is true. People who worship God are transformed to be like him. Paul taught this concept when he described Moses coming down the mountain, wearing a veil on his face because his face shone with the glory of God (2 Cor 3:7–8). Paul then stated we who approach the Lord with unveiled faces reflect the Lord's glory and "are being transformed into the same image" (2 Cor 3:18). This image of transformation is significant. The verb is *metamorphoomai*, which is similar in form and meaning to the word *metamorphosis*, meaning, "to change form." Also, the verb is passive, which means this transformation is something that happens *to us* rather than something we do. The point is only God can transform people. They can position themselves to be in the Lord's presence by reading his word, humbling themselves before him, submitting to him, and setting aside time to speak to him in prayer. Even after doing all those things, though, only God can transform a person. And he does so because of his love for fallen creatures. Max Lucado correctly writes, "God loves you just the way you are, but He refuses to leave you that way. He wants you to be just like Jesus."[17]

Those who look to the Lord are changed by the Lord. In this way, salvation is transformation. This transformation begins during the lifetime of the believer and is not complete until the return of Christ. The

---

[16] G. K. Beale, *We Become What We Worship: A Biblical Theology of Idolatry* (Downers Grove: IVP Academic, 2008).

[17] Max Lucado, *Just Like Jesus* (Nashville: Word, 1998), 3.

apostle John wrote, "When He appears, we will be like Him, because we will see Him just as He is" (1 John 3:2). As promised in Rom 8:30, God predestined believers (those God foreknew) to be conformed to the image of his Son. Believers will one day look like Jesus. Salvation is transformation because God is at work to remake his people to be more like Jesus, and God promises to complete that transformation at the return of his Son.

Righteousness

Righteousness is both a picture and a means of salvation. The English terms *justification, justify, righteous,* and *righteousness* share the same root in both Hebrew (*tsdq*) and Greek (*dikai*).[18] In the Old Testament, God and his ways are called righteous (Deut 32:4; Ps 11:7; Jer 12:1; Dan 9:14). Also, some individuals are called righteous. For example, we learn in Gen 6:9, "Noah was a righteous [*tsaddiq*] man, blameless in his time; Noah walked with God." In the next chapter, God told Noah, "You alone I have seen to be righteous before Me in this time" (Gen 7:1). Noah, unlike others in his generation, enjoyed a right relationship with God. According to the author of Hebrews, Noah's righteousness was by faith (Heb 11:7). When God restated his promise to make Abram the father of a nation, God pointed Abram to the sky and said his children would outnumber the stars. Genesis 15:6 states Abram "believed in the LORD" and the Lord "reckoned it to him as righteousness." Abram believed God, and for that reason, God counted him to be righteous.[19] Moses said if the people obeyed God's commands, they would be righteous (Deut 6:25), and Ezekiel stated a person would be righteous who does justice and righteousness and observes the commands of the law (Ezek 18:5–9). The people of

---

[18] This section draws from Michael F. Bird, "Righteousness," in *The Lexham Bible Dictionary*, eds. John D. Barry et al. (Bellingham, WA: Lexham Press, 2016).
[19] "Abram believed the LORD, and the LORD counted him as righteous because of his faith" (Gen 15:6 NLT).

God were called righteous when they were faithful to their covenant with God.

In the New Testament, some individuals are called righteous, such as Zechariah and Elizabeth (Luke 1:5–6), Simeon (Luke 2:25), Joseph of Arimathea (Luke 23:50), and Cornelius (Acts 10:22). Also, Jesus blesses those who hunger and thirst after righteousness (Matt 5:6). Yet Jesus clarified he came for sinners, not the righteous (Matt 9:13; Mark 2:17; Luke 5:32). Perhaps Jesus was referring here to those who depend on their own righteousness rather than those who call out to God for mercy and are justified (see Luke 18:9–14). Paul noted no person is righteous (Rom 3:10), meaning no person is right with God by his own effort. However, like Abraham—who believed God and was credited righteousness (Rom 4:3, 9, 22; Gal 3:6)—those who believe in Jesus will be credited righteousness (Rom 4:24; Gal 3:21–22).

Salvation is a picture of righteousness in the Old and the New Testaments because the God who is righteous and acts righteously calls people who are faithful to him in a covenant relationship righteous. Believing God has always been the condition for righteousness, and the New Testament equates believing God with believing in his Son.

Participation

Participation is the idea in Scripture that because God became a human, humans can be transformed, by the Holy Spirit, to become like God and participate for eternity in the life of God. Participation overlaps with other images of salvation, such as sanctification and transformation, but is distinct in its emphasis on the incarnation enabling this transformation as well as the ongoing communion with God. The author of Hebrews explained, "Since the children share in flesh and blood, He Himself likewise also partook of the same" (Heb 2:14). In other words, at the incarnation, the eternal Son partook of flesh and blood. The incarnation involved participation of God with humanity in a new way. Previously, God created people. At the incarnation, he became a person to reveal the Father and redeem people. Perhaps more shocking than God partaking of humanity is that through the cross of Christ, humans can partake of divinity. Peter wrote, "For by these He has granted to us His precious and magnificent promises, so that by them you may become partakers of the divine nature, having escaped the corruption that is in the world by lust" (2 Pet 1:4). Believers become "partakers" (Greek *koinōnos*) of "the divine nature" (Greek *theias physeōs*) in the sense they participate, or join with, God's nature. This participation between the believer and the triune God begins at one's confession of faith in Jesus Christ, culminates at his return, and continues into eternity. Although this view, also called *theosis* and divinization, is frequently associated with the Eastern Orthodox view, advocates can be found throughout the wider Christian tradition.[20] Salvation as participation is an important complement to the other images, which focus on salvation from the punishment of sin or God's judgment. Without denying those other images, participation focuses on union and communion with the triune God through the incarnation of the Son.

Conclusion

There are twelve key biblical terms and images for salvation. These words and images are: salvation, entrance into God's kingdom, new life, belonging to God's family, forgiveness of sin, reconciliation to God, redemption from sin, deliverance, sanctification, transformation, righteousness, and participation. More could be said than what was stated in this chapter. Also, what was said in this chapter could have been better articulated at points. Nevertheless, this chapter was intended to highlight and summarize salvation as revealed in the Bible.

Identifying key biblical terms for salvation is helpful but does not resolve theological differences. For example, this survey highlighted

---

[20] For a history of *theosis* in the wider Christian tradition, see *Partakers of the Divine Nature: The History and Development of Deification in the Christian Traditions*, ed. Michael J. Christensen and Jeffrey A. Wittung (Grand Rapids: Baker Academic, 2007).

the many instances in the New Testament of people believing in Christ but did not attempt to answer *how* they came to believe. *How* one comes to believe in Christ is sometimes a topic of dispute among Christians. Do people believe in Christ because God caused them to be born again, or are people born again precisely *because* they believe in Christ? Consider also that believers are referred to as called, predestined, or chosen more than one hundred times in the New Testament. Although it is clear those who believe in Christ are called the elect, the nature of election remains disputed. Did God, before the foundation of the world, select some individuals for salvation? Or did God, before the foundation of the world, select Christ to be the Savior of all who freely repent of sin and believe in Him? Questions such as the order of salvation or nature of election deserve consideration, but this chapter focused on identifying key biblical words and images of salvation to answer, what is salvation, rather than considering the various issues and questions concerning *how* people are saved. Such questions usually require one to consider differing (faithful) interpretations of Scripture.

Despite the shortcomings of this chapter and the issues it did not address, this summary is offered as a foundation for future study as well as an offering of praise to God for his saving work among sinners like me who are helpless and hopeless apart from God's grace toward us in Jesus Christ.

BIBLIOGRAPHY

Beale, G. K. *We Become What We Worship: A Biblical Theology of Idolatry.* Downers Grove, IL: IVP Academic, 2008.

Bird, Michael F. "Righteousness." In *The Lexham Bible Dictionary*, edited by John D. Barry, David Bomar, Derek R. Brown, Rachel Klippenstein, Douglas Mangum, Carrie Sinclair Wolcott, Lazarus Wentz, Elliott Ritzema, and Wendy Widder. Bellingham, WA: Lexham Press, 2016.

Breytenbach, Cilliers. "Salvation of the Reconciled (With a Note on the Background of Paul's Metaphor of Reconciliation)." In *Salvation in the New Testament*, edited by Jan G. van der Watt, 121:271–86. Supplement to *Novum Testamentum*. Leiden: Brill, 2005.

Christensen, Michael J., and Jeffrey A. Wittung, eds. *Partakers of the Divine Nature: The History and Development of Deification in the Christian Traditions.* Grand Rapids, MI: Baker Academic, 2007.

Colijn, Brenda B. *Images of Salvation in the New Testament.* Downers Grove, IL: IVP Academic, 2010.

Cowen, Gerald. *Salvation: Word Studies from the Greek New Testament.* Nashville, TN: Broadman, 1990.

Garrett, James Leo, Jr. *Systematic Theology: Biblical, Historical, and Evangelical.* Vol. 2. Grand Rapids, MI: Eerdmans, 1995.

Hamme, Joel T. "Salvation." In *Lexham Theological Wordbook*, Lexham Bible Reference Series, edited by Douglas Mangum, Derek R. Brown, Rachel Klippenstein, and Rebeccah Hurst. Bellingham, WA: Lexham Press, 2014.

Kuligin, Victor. *The Language of Salvation: Discovering the Riches of What It Means to Be Saved.* Wooster, OH: Weaver, 2015.

Louw, Johannes P., and Eugene Albert Nida. *Greek-English Lexicon of the New Testament: Based on Semantic Domains.* New York: United Bible Societies, 1996.

Lucado, Max. *Just Like Jesus*. Nashville, TN: Word, 1998.

Malul, Meir. "Adoption of Foundlings in the Bible and Mesopotamian Documents: A Study of Some Legal Metaphors in Ezekiel 16:1–7." *Journal for the Study of the Old Testament* 46 (1990): 98–99.

Miles, Jack. "Israel as Foundling: Abandonment, Adoption, and the Fatherhood of God." *Hebrew Studies* 46 (2005): 7–24.

Morris, Michelle J. "Adoption." In *The Lexham Bible Dictionary*, edited by John D. Barry, David Bomar, Derek R. Brown, Rachel Klippenstein, Douglas Mangum, Carrie Sinclair Wolcott, Lazarus Wentz, Elliott Ritzema, and Wendy Widder. Bellingham, WA: Lexham Press, 2016.

Talbert, Charles H., and Jason A. Whitlark. *Getting Saved: The Whole Story of Salvation in the New Testament*. Grand Rapids, MI: Eerdmans, 2011.

van der Watt, Jan G. ed. *Salvation in the New Testament: Perspectives on Soteriology*. Supplements to *Novum Testamentum* 121. Leiden: Brill, 2005.

Wright, Christopher J. H. *Salvation Belongs to Our God: Celebrating the Bible's Central Story*. Downers Grove, IL: IVP Academic, 2007.

Is Jesus Really the Only Savior? Critiquing Common Objections to Christian Particularism

Robert B. Stewart

There are few things more offensive to our postmodern, post-Christian, post-truth culture than the traditional Christian claim that Jesus is the only Savior of the world. Theologians refer to this position as Christian particularism. In this article, I will respond to some of the most common objections to Christian particularism.

Objection #1: Christian Uniqueness Is Intolerant

The first objection is that claims of Christian uniqueness are offensive because they are intolerant. Notice this objection does not claim it is *false* Jesus is the only Savior, or even merely *irrational* to believe such a claim, but rather that making such a claim is immoral.

Far too often in contemporary culture, personal attacks take the place of reasoned discussion of issues. This is in keeping with the concept of "post-truth." In 2016, Oxford Dictionaries designated the term "post-truth" as the word of the year. "Post-truth" is an adjective "relating to or denoting circumstances in which objective facts are less influential in shaping public opinion than appeals to emotion and personal belief."[1] The word *post* is not meant to function as a chronological marker in the sense of being "after" truth, as opposed

---

[1] "Word of the Year," Oxford Living Dictionaries, accessed January 29, 2019, https://en.oxforddictionaries.com/word-of-the-year/word-of-the-year-2016.

to "simultaneous with" truth or "before" truth, but rather to signify there are contexts in which the notion of truth is irrelevant. Sadly, for many today, religion appears to be one of these post-truth contexts.

Still, something must occupy the space left behind when we jettison truth; we need something to direct our decisions. For some, it will be pragmatism; others will prefer power. When it comes to religion, many make tolerance the supreme virtue. An example would be this comment from Rabbi Shmuley Boteach: "I am absolutely against any religion that says that one faith is superior to another. I don't see how that is anything different than spiritual racism. It's a way of saying that we are closer to God than you, and that's what leads to hatred."[2]

Apparently Boteach is oblivious to the fact he has implicitly stated religions that don't say they are superior to other religions are superior to those that do.

Not all Jews agree with Boteach. Jewish New Testament scholar Amy-Jill Levine of Vanderbilt University thinks differently:

> Exclusivism should not be "morally dubious," … What I would find more "morally dubious" is my insisting to another that his or her reading or presuppositions, because they are not pluralistic, are somehow wrong. … The evangelical Christian should be free to try to seek to convert me to Christianity: such an attempt is biblically warranted and consistent with evangelical (exclusivist) theology. I remain free to say "thank you, but no thanks." I would not want someone telling me that my "cherished confessional traditions" have only limited value. I would not presume to do the same to another.[3]

---

[2] "Should Christians Stop Trying to Convert Jews?" *Larry King Live*, CCN.com Transcripts, aired January 12, 2000, http://transcripts.cnn.com/TRANSCRIPTS/0001/12/lkl.00.html.

[3] Amy-Jill Levine, "Homeless in the Global Village," in *Moving Beyond New Testament Theology? Essays in Conversation with Heikki Räisänen*, eds. Todd Penner and Caroline Vander Stichele (Helsinki: University of Helsinki Press, 2005), 195–96.

Tolerance is not saying all religious views are equally correct. Tolerance is respecting someone's right to disagree with you; intolerance is insisting they not disagree with you. In fact, *tolerance demands disagreement.* You can't be tolerant without disagreeing. We don't tolerate opinions we agree with—we agree with them.

How did we get to this point? Answering this question fully would require extensive social analysis and thus more space than this article allows because the reasons are varied and complex. But surely some of the reason has to do with how truth is thought of by many today. Allow me to offer some examples.

One frequently hears the canard there is no such thing as truth. The reply to this statement should be, "Really, is that true?" Is it not obvious if there's no such thing as truth, then it's not true there's no such thing as truth? If it's not true there's no such thing as truth, then it seems to be true that truth exists.

Therefore, frequently this dodge will be changed to, "Nobody can know the truth." But again this reasoning is shown to be obviously flawed simply by asking once again: "Really, is that true?" After all, if nobody can know the truth, then how can anybody know that nobody can know the truth?

These oft-repeated bits of rhetoric are not even believed by those who use them. We all know there is such a thing as truth and that it can be known. I don't have to appeal to any complicated philosophical analysis of the nature of knowledge and how it is obtained to demonstrate this is the case. I simply have to ask, "Have you ever been lied to?" Everyone knows they have been lied to, even those who deny there is such a thing as truth or argue nobody can know the truth. But when one analyzes what a lie is—an intentionally false statement meant to deceive—one must realize that if there is no such thing as truth then there can be no such thing as a lie.

The way we live reveals that deep down we all really know there is such a thing as truth. When I go to the pharmacist and hand over my prescription, I trust the pharmacist will actually give me what the doctor has prescribed rather than simply looking around for some pretty pills he or she thinks match my complexion or personality. When I take my W-2 tax form to my accountant, I expect her to supply the IRS with accurate information—i.e., the truth about my pay and withheld taxes, etc. How we actually live reveals all of us really do believe in truth.

Denying truth leads to absurdity. I remember well a doctoral seminar in cultural anthropology that I took at a large state university. After going over the syllabus with us, the professor lectured for about ten minutes. The first line of the first lecture on the first day of class was the following: "Rationality and will are illusory." I was so stunned at this assertion I wrote it across the top of the syllabus. Understand the implications of rationality and will being illusory. He was saying to us that, although we thought we were rational people who could assess evidence and arguments, that was but an illusion. He was also saying we thought we were free to choose for ourselves, but that sense of freedom was also an illusion. Rationality and will were simply social constructs. My question for him afterward was, "If rationality and will are illusory, then on what basis will we be graded in this seminar?" His answer told me he wasn't really doubting his own rationality, just ours. Truth is undeniable. We can't live without it; we don't live without it.

What people generally mean is it's often impossible to be certain what you believe is true. Fortunately, most of the time, one doesn't need to be certain as to what one believes to know the truth. To be rational, our beliefs should be reasonably held (evidence-based or properly formed), but reason doesn't require certainty. This is true even in the case of our most important and existentially significant commitments. For instance, a jury isn't required to conclude a defendant is guilty beyond the shadow of any doubt but merely beyond a reasonable doubt.

Several years ago, one of my colleagues asked me to join him and his college-age son for lunch because his son was going through a crisis of faith. This young man had been raised in a Christian home, attended Bible-believing churches, and was frequently exposed to the best of evangelical theology and apologetics. But he was genuinely doubting the foundation of the Christian faith. We went to lunch, and I began to ask him questions as to where he was with regard to his faith and why. (Note well: this is what we should do in evangelism and apologetics: find out where those we minister to actually are and why they believe what they believe.) Pretty quickly, I thought I could identify his basic issue. The conversation that followed went like this:

> ME: If I'm understanding you, you think there's pretty good evidence for God, Christianity, and things like the resurrection of Jesus, but you're troubled because you can't be 100 percent certain these things are true while Christianity calls for a 100 percent commitment of your life. Am I reading you right? (Notice again: I made certain I was actually addressing his issue, not simply repeating a stock apologetic answer!)
>
> HIM: Yes, exactly.
>
> ME: Do you want to get married?
>
> HIM: Oh yeah, I'm going to get married.
>
> ME: Okay. When you get married, would you like to have a wife who is faithful to you 100 percent of the time, or would it be okay if she cheated on you from time-to-time, like once every leap year?
>
> HIM: I want a wife who is always faithful to me!
>
> ME: But how could you ever be certain that she was faithful to you 100 percent of the time?
>
> HIM: [After a pause] I guess I couldn't be 100 percent certain.
>
> ME: So I guess you're never going to get married.
>
> HIM: I'm going to get married.
>
> ME: But you can't be certain.
>
> HIM: I'm going to get married.
>
> ME: But marriage requires a total, 100 percent commitment of your life—just like Christianity.

At that moment I could see the light bulb come on as the realization hit him that 100 percent existential commitments don't require 100 percent logical certainty. I need to be clear at this point as to what I am not saying. I am not saying we don't have to examine relevant evidence when and if it is brought forward to challenge our beliefs. I am also not saying we shouldn't examine arguments (including our own) to assess their merits. I am saying somebody else having a different opinion on a matter is evidence *of* a difference of opinion—it is not evidence *for* one opinion over the other, nor is it an argument. It is certainly not proof that both views are equally correct.

There is an Internet lie that is frequently repeated: "Extraordinary claims require extraordinary evidence." This is simply not true. The evidence for some claims is extraordinary, but no belief requires extraordinary evidence (as though what it would mean for evidence to be "extraordinary" were obvious). Beliefs require sufficient evidence. After all, the assertion that extraordinary claims require extraordinary evidence seems pretty extraordinary to me. So where is the evidence for it? It's even shown to be false when we look at the world around us. In science, we frequently see the most extraordinary claims made (like the cosmological case for an inflationary multiverse) on the barest and most indirect line or lines of evidence. Yet the hypothesis of an inflationary multiverse is widely viewed among cosmologists as a serious scientific theory.

Obviously there are committed religious believers in other religions who hold their beliefs with equal or greater seriousness than we do. We should respect their sincerity, but their sincerity alone provides us with no reason to doubt our own well-supported beliefs. Nor should it cause us to think our beliefs require certainty.

Another fruit of the (misguided) quest for certainty is this question: "How do you know your religion is the only true religion? Have you investigated every religion?" When one first hears this, one is tempted to think it is a reasonable question. But closer examination shows it to be anything but.

First, nobody can actually examine every religion. In fact, nobody can even name them all. There are far too many (and new religions are birthed virtually every day). But the good news, once again, is we don't need to do this.

Perhaps another story will demonstrate what I mean. In 1998, I joined the faculty at NOBTS. Around 3:00 a.m. one morning, the phone on our kitchen wall rang. I stumbled out of bed and answered it. It was a campus security officer with some questions for me.

> SECURITY: Do you have a dog?
>
> ME: Yes.
>
> SECURITY: Is your dog in your house?
>
> ME: No, she's an outside dog.
>
> SECURITY: Is your dog in your backyard?
>
> ME: She's supposed to be.
>
> SECURITY: Would you check and see?
>
> At this point, I got dressed and went out in our backyard.
>
> ME: No, she's not in our backyard.
>
> SECURITY: Look on your carport, and see if the dog on your carport is your dog.
>
> ME: Why didn't you start right there?

If I had seen my dog on my carport, I would have known my dog was not in my backyard because I would have had evidence my dog was somewhere else, namely on my carport. We can do something similar in comparing religions. If we have good evidence Christianity is true, then we have good reason to believe anything contrary is false. This doesn't mean we don't have to consider counterevidence that would serve to undermine or defeat our belief in Christianity. It does mean counterevidence is not required. Until or unless we are provided some evidence to the contrary, we are rationally entitled to believe

Christianity is true and that religions based on truth claims contrary to those of Christianity are false. Anything else is just epistemic paranoia.

We don't ask someone who says that 17−7=10, "How do you know? Have you checked all the other equations?" In fact, we routinely say we know the truth and disagree with others who say anything contrary to what we believe to be true. We do it in mathematics and chemistry; we even do it in history and ethics. The difference is we frequently lack consensus in history and ethics. But a lack of consensus does not entail that mutually exclusive claims are both true. When we disagree about history or ethics, we disagree precisely because we believe historical truth (e.g., Luther nailed his Ninety-five Theses on the Wittenberg chapel door in 1517, not 1715) and ethical truth (e.g., it is wrong to torture infants simply for your individual enjoyment) exist.

These sorts of thought stoppers are not actually about truth and whether or not it exists or can be known. They are really about us. Many in our postmodern culture tend to view insisting someone else is mistaken or living the wrong way as intolerant. But this is exactly what those advocating for Christian particularism must do. If Jesus is the only Savior, then every other so-called savior is a false savior. Others are free to disagree, but it is unreasonable for either party to argue that both parties are right in the same sense at the same time because it is unreasonable to agree with opinions contrary to one's own beliefs.

Truth is always and necessarily exclusive. Truth excludes its opposite, falsehood. The two are mutually exclusive. This is so, however, not for ethical or social reasons but because of the nature of truth. A true statement is an accurate description of the way the world (or a part of it) actually is. Truth therefore is grounded in reality, not in perception, regardless of who the one perceiving it is.

We don't say a physician is arrogant for telling those diagnosed with cancer they need treatment. In fact, we insist doing so is morally required. In some cases, it is unethical not to voice your disagreement.

A video blog by the well-known illusionist, Penn Jillette, provides us an example. In the video, Jillette tells of a Christian approaching him after a show and giving him a marked New Testament that included his personal contact information. Jillette commended this anonymous believer for his effort. He said, "How much do you have to hate somebody to believe that everlasting life is possible and not tell them that?"[4] What is worse than arrogance is knowing something can save a life and not sharing it with those who need to know it.

Sharing information that you think can save a life with someone who believes differently from you is not arrogant. Arrogance is not saying that one thing is true and anything contrary is false; arrogance is mistreating people who disagree with you. It's certainly not arrogant to say I was blind, but now I see, or you need to admit you're wrong just like I admitted I was wrong. This is, in fact, what every convert has done.

Objection #2: All Religions Are the Same at Their Core

Another set of objections to Christian particularism is based on the supposed similarity between religions. The crudest form is simply to say, "All religions are the same." One problem with this claim is it's impossible to define religion. You might think all religions have a god, but that's wrong. Or that all religions have holy books, but that's wrong. Or that all religions believe in an afterlife or a soul, but that's wrong. Or that all religions have ethical codes, but that's also wrong. Religions have one thing in common with pornography—you can't define what religion is but you know a religion when you see one. Religions do, however, have family resemblances. Identifying a religion is thus somewhat like diagnosing rheumatoid arthritis (RA).

In 2002, when I was diagnosed with RA, I was surprised to learn there was no objective test for RA. I discovered there were seven symptoms characteristic of RA and anyone who had four of the seven symptoms for two months was considered to have RA. Obviously this allows for a great deal of variation of symptoms between diagnosed

---

[4] "Penn Jillette Gets a Bible," Vimeo, accessed April 30, 2019, https://vimeo.com/147280375/.

individuals. Person A could have symptoms 1–4, Person B have symptoms 4–7, Person C have symptoms 1, 3, 5, and 7, while Person D had symptoms 2, 4, 6, and 7, and each of these persons would in fact have RA. In short, religions are analogous to RA, in that there are recognizable family resemblances between religions, but no single trait is required of any religion in order for that religion to be a religion.

Sometimes one hears all religions teach the same basic or core doctrines, although they use different terms, symbols, and narratives to do so. The problem with this position is it is obviously false. If no religion necessarily has any single religious trait, then it cannot be the case that all religions have the same core beliefs or practices. Furthermore, this requires reducing primary beliefs to secondary beliefs. Consider as a case in point two of the world's largest and most significant religions: Christianity and Islam. The Christian doctrine of the Trinity is certainly a core doctrine for Christians—it's not Christianity if it's not Trinitarian. But the doctrine of the Trinity is anathema to the Muslim. Both Christianity and Islam teach that God exists, yet most forms of Buddhism hold that God does not exist. Clearly, it is not true all religions teach the same core doctrines.

Other pluralists, following the late John Hick, argue many other religions have the same goal as Christianity, which is salvation, or liberation, that results in individuals being transformed in such a way they move from self-centeredness to reality-centeredness.

> There are, first, important ideas within the different traditions which on the surface present incompatible alternatives but which can be seen on deeper analysis to be different expressions of the same more fundamental idea: thus the Christian concept of salvation and the Hindu and Buddhist concepts of liberation are expressions of the more basic notion of the realization of a limitlessly better possibility for human existence.[5]

---

[5] John Hick, *An Interpretation of Religion: Human Responses to the Transcendent*, 2nd ed. (New Haven: Yale University Press, 2004), 374.

Some religions have somewhat similar goals. Other religions don't, but so what? The issue is not what the goal of a religion is but whether what a religion teaches is true or, at the very least, if what that religion is supposed to offer is achievable by the means that religion advocates.

Others assert all religions are legitimate but incomplete ways to speak about reality. Frequently those who do so will appeal to the analogy of the blind men and the elephant. The analogy involves a story in which six blind men are asked independently to describe an elephant. The first blind man touches the tusk of the elephant and says that an elephant is like a spear. The second blind man touches the trunk of the elephant and says an elephant is like a snake. The third blind man touches the ear of the elephant and says an elephant is like a large leaf. The fourth blind man pushes against the side of the elephant and, when it doesn't budge, says an elephant is like a boulder. The fifth blind man grasps the leg of the elephant and says an elephant is like a pillar. The sixth blind man grasps the tail of the elephant and says an elephant is like a rope. The point of the story is supposed to be that all of the blind men are correct in part. But in order for the story to make any sense at all, one has to understand what an elephant is like in its entirety. In other words, one has to affirm the very thing the story denies. The story is supposed to prove nobody has a comprehensive or "God's-eye" view of reality, but it depends upon a comprehensive view of reality, at least so far as an elephant is concerned. Furthermore, analogies, like the blind men and the elephant, depend upon the two things that relate to one another, in this case an elephant and God, or the whole of reality, being sufficiently alike. Is an elephant really sufficiently like God? I for one am extremely doubtful that such is the case.

Others will insist all religions have some truth but that no religion has all truth. This is true—there is some truth in all religions. No religion that was false in everything it affirmed could possibly be taken seriously by anyone. Christianity, however, does not teach that all other religions are entirely false but rather that Jesus is the only Savior and all people need saving. Christianity also teaches all God's word is true, but that's not the same as saying no other religion is right about anything.

The question is not whether there is "some truth" in other religions; it's whether or not there is "saving truth" in anyone other than Jesus.

Another question must be answered: "Is any other religious figure equal to Jesus?" Not according to Jesus. Jesus said in John 14:6 he was the way, the truth, and the life, and that no one could come to the Father but by him. The important thing to note here is not only that Jesus claims to be a Savior but he also claims to be the *only* Savior. This sets Jesus apart. If he is the only Savior, then he cannot be lowered to the level of those who don't claim to be saviors. If he is not the only Savior, then he cannot be raised to their level as spiritual teachers.

Objection #3: It's Unfair of God to Send People to Hell Who've Never Heard of Jesus.

The third type of objection is it is unfair of God to send people who've never heard of Jesus to hell simply for not believing in Jesus. I agree; it would be unfair of God to send a person who has never heard of Jesus to hell *merely* for not believing a message he has never heard. But is this actually something Christian particularists teach God does?

There is a hidden premise in this objection, namely that people become separated from God, and thus condemned by God, because they don't believe in Jesus. The Bible does not teach that people *become* lost because they reject Jesus. Instead the Bible teaches people *remain* lost if they reject Jesus. To think that people become lost because they reject Jesus would make the gospel bad news, not good news. Furthermore, it would make evangelism and missions absurd.

Why then are people lost—i.e., separated from God? Paul answered this question in Rom 1. In verses 18–23, Paul did not say people are lost for rejecting the truth that they don't know but for rejecting the truth they do know.

> For the wrath of God is revealed from heaven against all ungodliness and unrighteousness of men who suppress the truth in unrighteousness, because that which is known

about God is evident within them; for God made it evident to them. For since the creation of the world His invisible attributes, His eternal power and divine nature, have been clearly seen, being understood through what has been made, so that they are without excuse. For even though they knew God, they did not honor Him as God or give thanks, but they became futile in their speculations, and their foolish heart was darkened. Professing to be wise, they became fools, and exchanged the glory of the incorruptible God for an image in the form of corruptible man and of birds and four-footed animals and crawling creatures.

Notice the terms we find in this brief passage that imply knowledge: "revealed" (v. 18); "truth" (v. 18); "known" (v. 19); "evident" (twice in v. 19); "clearly seen" (v. 20); "understood" (v. 20); "knew" (v. 21); and "wise" (v. 22). Simply put, there is a whole lot of knowing going on in Rom 1:18–23.

The problem is not what people *know* but what people *want*. Human beings apart from the grace of God revealed through the gospel don't reject Jesus the Savior, God the Son, but rather they reject God the Father, the Creator of heaven and earth.

Some will object that adherents to other religions are just as sincere and spiritual as any Christian. This is, of course, true. But sincerity is not the issue. Neither is spirituality. I have no doubt people in other religions have real spiritual experiences, but are these spiritual experiences true spiritual experiences with God? The New Testament over and over again warns us to test the spirits because many false teachers have gone out into the world (1 John 4:1). It is possible for an experience to be real but not true.

Still, some people hear the gospel numerous times in their lives while some others never do. Some would insist this is unjust. The hidden premise in this is a misunderstanding of grace. Justice is giving people what they deserve. Injustice is denying them what they deserve or giving them less than they deserve. Grace is giving people better than they deserve. But it is absurd to claim God is unjust for not being better toward particular sinners than those sinners deserve, even if God has been better to other sinners than those sinners deserve. Grace is something by definition that cannot be required of anyone.

Asking why God saves some but not others is not the right question. Nobody is saved because of how good, moral, intelligent, or spiritual he or she is. If God gave us what we deserve, none of us would be spared. Salvation is God's free work of grace, not something we earn because of our behavior. The question is not, "Why are only some sinners saved?" but rather, "Why is any sinner ever saved?" God's standard for righteousness is not how well we do when compared to other people—it is his nature as revealed through conscience, creation, his word, and his Spirit.

We can trust God to deal righteously with all people. If they respond to the light they have, God can be trusted to give more light. Note: I did *not* say they were saved by their initial response to the light they have but rather if they respond correctly to the light they have, then God will give them more light (if there actually are any who do respond in this way).

We have two New Testament examples of God sending a gospel messenger to individual gentiles in the book of Acts: the Ethiopian eunuch in Acts 8 and Cornelius in Acts 10. Both men had some knowledge of the God of Israel. The eunuch had at least some of the book of Isaiah and had been to Jerusalem to worship. Cornelius had some contact with Jews, gave many alms, and prayed to God continually. Neither, however, knew what he needed to be saved.

Do such things still happen? Indeed. A friend of mine is a military chaplain who was stationed in Afghanistan. Once when leading a Bible study for a group of soldiers and American contractors, one of the contractors shared that a man from Afghanistan was waiting for him in his office that morning when he arrived. The man asked the contractor if he was an American. The contractor replied he was. Then the man shared how he'd had a dream in which he saw a man with wounds in his hands and feet. When he asked who he was, he was told: "Find an American, and he will tell you about me." The American contractor then shared how he had led this man from Afghanistan to faith in Christ.

Note both the eunuch and Cornelius—and the man from Afghanistan—were responding to the light of special revelation, not to the light of general revelation. General revelation is the sort of knowledge of God available to all persons in all places and all times through creation and conscience. Special revelation is the sort of knowledge of God available to particular persons in particular places and particular times. Such knowledge comes to individuals through God's written word, worship, incarnation, or through God-ordained special circumstances such as a vision or a dream. We have no clear instance in Scripture of anyone responding appropriately to the light of general revelation.[6] Still, I think it a legitimate inference that if anyone were to respond appropriately to the light of general revelation, then God could be trusted to provide that individual more light in whatever way God chose. I am (skeptically) agnostic as to whether or not anyone actually honors God or gives thanks on the basis of general revelation. I am not, however, in the dark as to God's righteousness and desire for all to be saved. He will not condemn the faithful along with the unfaithful. Though I am skeptical about anyone responding appropriately to the light of general revelation, I am convinced those who respond appropriately to the light they have can trust God to give them more light.

The gospel proclamation of the substitutionary death of Jesus Christ for sinners, his resurrection from the dead, and his acceptance of all who call upon his name in faith is good news. Our God is good, and it is our job to share this good news with all who need it everywhere until Christ in God's good time returns.

---

[6] Nor do we have any unambiguous statement saying nobody responds in faith to the light of general revelation; we don't read of the eunuch or Cornelius that they weren't given some special revelation after an initial favorable response to general revelation. I think Paul intended to condemn all humanity in Rom 1—3, but I am also well aware this is a debatable interpretation with which some other sincere, fair-minded Christians disagree.

BIBLIOGRAPHY

Hick, John. *An Interpretation of Religion: Human Responses to the Transcendent.* 2d edition. New Haven, CT: Yale University Press, 2004.

Larry King Live. "Should Christians Stop Trying to Convert Jews?" CNN.com Transcripts. Aired January 12, 2000. http://transcripts.cnn.com/TRANSCRIPTS/0001/12/lkl.00.html.

Levine, Amy-Jill. "Homeless in the Global Village." In *Moving Beyond New Testament Theology? Essays in Conversation with Heikki Räisänen*, edited by Todd Penner and Caroline Vander Stichele. Helsinki: University of Helsinki Press, 2005.

Oxford Living Dictionaries. "Word of the Year." Accessed January 29, 2019. https://en.oxforddictionaries.com/word-of-the-year/word-of-the-year-2016.

Vimeo. "Penn Jillette Gets a Bible." Vimeo Accessed April 30, 2019. https://vimeo.com/147280375/.

ENGAGING MERE MORALITY IN EVANGELISM

Jeffrey Riley

The Christian faith makes moral demands. Christianity is, after all, a confession of faith and a way of living. Today we see an uncoupling of belief about God from morality that distorts a proper understanding of the relationship between God and human beings. The distortions tend to go in two general directions—either legalism or license. For those who see through legalistic lenses, the God of Christianity is unloving and unkind, a hard taskmaster who rules by threat and fear. For those who see through permissive lenses, the God of Christianity overlooks the behavior and beliefs of individuals and wishes only happiness for everyone. These are, of course, caricatures; but similar corrupted understandings of God and morality obscure the gospel, much like Paul's description in 2 Cor 4:3–4: "And even if our gospel is veiled, it is veiled to those who are perishing, in whose case the god of this world has blinded the minds of the unbelieving so that they might not see the light of the gospel of the glory of Christ, who is the image of God."

The good news regarding the life, death, and resurrection of Jesus Christ is the power of God to save, particularly when declared by those who handle the word of God rightly, renounce shameful behavior, and live according to the truth. In this way, Christians commend themselves morally "to every man's conscience in the sight of God" (v. 2). Said another way, the Christian ethic matters for sharing the gospel because the message received by faith ought to transform the way a person thinks and acts—a person's ethic and morality. As such, Christians cannot avoid thinking about the relationship between ethics and evangelism. In fact, in many evangelistic encounters, the non-Christian is often the first to question what the Bible teaches and Christians believe about specific moral issues. How should we answer? How should we prepare?

Preparing to Answer Moral Questions

The way to prepare is not simply to know what the Bible says about myriad ethical issues. Frankly, the Bible says little about many twenty-first-century issues, not to mention that few of us have the time or mental discipline to become experts on all of the issues. However, Scripture does orient believers to the will and way of God so they might respond wisely to contemporary moral questions. In some sense, there is nothing new under the sun (Eccl 1:9). God is still God; human beings are still fallen and in need of redemption; basic human needs and desires are unchanged; people still have a sense of right and wrong; God is still pleased to grant wisdom to those who ask (Jas 1:5).[1] Evangelistic encounters still need the conviction of God's Spirit and the persuasiveness of God's wisdom, particularly when, for various reasons, nonbelievers want to know what Christians think about sex, marriage, abortion, bioethics, race, war, and so forth.

To be ready to respond appropriately to ethical questions, Christian witnesses need to prepare not only by knowing about contemporary issues but also by understanding what it means to be ethical. Ethics is as much about *being* human as it is about *doing* right and wrong. Because we ought to live in the world as Christians, we ought to evaluate moral issues as Christians. Consequently, a good way to get "ready to make a defense to everyone who asks you to give an account for the hope that is in you" is to approach questions on particular issues as one who first

---

[1] C. S. Lewis builds an apologetic on the fact that a sense of right and wrong is common to being human. See *Mere Christianity* (New York: HarperOne, 1980) and *The Abolition of Man* (New York: HarperOne, 1974). Paul disclosed the theological significance of this common human sense of right and wrong in Rom 2:12–16.

understands how the Christian faith encompasses and defines ethics (1 Pet 3:15).

Defining Christian Ethics

Christian ethics is the integration of character and conduct that glorifies God, practices biblical faith, values moral truth, and reflects the virtues of Christ Jesus. The Bible reveals much about character and conduct—of God and humans. For example, one could argue the entire Sermon on the Mount is a call to integrity—what we do mirrors who we are, and the God who always acts consistently and rightly according to his holy character is the standard (Matt 5—7)! Said another way, the heart produces acts, and acts reveal the heart. In the sermon, Jesus attacked explicitly the hypocrisy displayed by religious leaders and false teachers, the outward acts of self-righteousness that hide the sinful character of the person. Jesus recurrently used the analogy of a tree and its fruit to correlate character and conduct (Matt 7:15–20; 12:33–37; 15:15-20; Mark 7:14–23). After teaching that eating certain foods does not defile a person, Jesus explained, "That which proceeds out of the man, that is what defiles the man. For from within, out of the heart of men, proceed the evil thoughts, fornications, thefts, murders, adulteries, deeds of coveting and wickedness, as well as deceit, sensuality, envy, slander, pride and foolishness. All these evil things proceed from within and defile the man" (Mark 7:20–23). As my pastor used to say, "What's in the well comes up in the bucket."

Understanding the Relationship between God and Sinful Individuals

Morality is a window to the soul. According to the New Testament, the character of the human heart directs the way a person thinks and talks about right and wrong and ultimately shapes the way a person acts. The relationship between the heart and behavior is not a trivial matter, and neither is the way people speak, post, or tweet about moral issues. In Matt 12:33–37, Jesus rebuked the Pharisees, demanding they "either make the tree good and its fruit good, or make the tree bad and its fruit bad" (v. 33). He then warned them, "The good man brings out of his good treasure what is good; and the evil man brings out of his evil treasure what is evil" (v. 35). On the day of judgment, every person will have to give an account for every careless word, "For by your words you will be justified, and by your words you will be condemned" (v. 37). What we think, say, and do not only reveals the character of our hearts, but also, over time, shapes our identity—we don't just think bad thoughts and do bad things; we *are* sinners. Outside of his grace, Christ Jesus will judge human beings for who they really are and for what they actually have thought, said, and done. The good news of the gospel, however, is Jesus will judge those who trust him on the basis of his own righteousness and in light of what he accomplished on the cross—the forgiveness of sin and sinners.

That God forgives our sins does not mean we now can believe and do whatever we want without fear of judgment. To be both just and justifier, Jesus paid a high price—death by crucifixion (Rom 3:23–6). This demonstration of God's love toward us, even though we are guilty of sin and enemies of God, exposes the gravity of the unrighteousness and ungodliness of humans. Individuals, groups, communities, institutions, and states alike exchange the truth of God for lies, cling to lusts of the heart, pursue degrading passions, and rouse depraved minds so they do what they ought not to do and support those who practice immoral behaviors (Rom 1:24–32). The fallen state of humanity is not just Christian dogma; it is a reality experienced by all, which accounts for the ubiquity of community mores, laws, cultural taboos, moral expectations, criminal punishments, and so forth. Arguing in defense of a "law of nature," which he defined as the reality of right and wrong and as decent behavior known to all peoples, C. S. Lewis concluded, "First, that human beings, all over the earth, have this curious idea that they ought to behave in a certain way, and cannot really get rid of it. Secondly, that they do not in fact behave in that way. These two facts are the foundation of all clear thinking about ourselves and the universe we live in."² This being the case, the offer of salvation is always a concurrent challenge to unrighteousness in general and personal immorality in particular.

In 1 Cor 6:9–10, the apostle Paul listed the kinds of characters who cannot expect to be welcomed by God: "Neither fornicators, nor idolaters, nor adulterers, nor effeminate, nor homosexuals, nor thieves, nor *the* covetous, nor drunkards, nor revilers, nor swindlers, will inherit the kingdom of God." Paul closed his list of nefarious characters with a liberating reminder: "Such were some of you; but you were washed, but you were sanctified, but you were justified in the name of the Lord Jesus Christ and in the Spirit of our God" (v. 11). The good news is Jesus not only forgives sins but also transforms sinners. The evangelistic encounter confronts core beliefs about personal identities, lifestyle choices, and political views, even when the one presenting the gospel avoids addressing moral issues. The invitation to follow Jesus and the confession that Jesus is Lord compel a rethinking of oneself and the world and a redirection of life to follow a path marked out by the Word of God. The transformation is so dramatic only the language of new birth or a life raised from the dead adequately captures the change. No wonder people so often ask about ethics when approached with the gospel. Even non-Christians sense that the life, death, and resurrection of Jesus Christ challenges their moral values.

The Gospel and Moral Transformation

That Jesus Christ challenges individual and cultural values should not surprise Christians. Jesus taught his disciples that the Holy Spirit would convict individuals about the way they live (morality) and the way they think they ought to live (ethics), calling for repentance while revealing the truth about right living and right thinking in the face of God (John 16:5–15). Said another way, the nature of redemption necessitates ethical enlightenment and assessment because it presumes moral

---

² Lewis, *Mere Christianity*, 8.

transformation. This enlightenment and assessment are a work of God the Spirit, who helps those related to God rightly understand his word. Consequently, the moral demands consonant with the Christian faith are placed primarily on followers of Jesus Christ—the church—though the presence of the church in the world should be a constant reminder to non-Christians that their lives are not the way they are supposed to be.[3] Jesus redeems for himself a morally peculiar people who are to represent him in this world, a world in rebellion against God. The evangelist still proclaims the good news to individuals, who respond to the message delivered. Those who respond by faith become children of God and join with others as the church to mature as disciples of Jesus Christ. As Lewis said, "God wants people of a particular sort."[4]

Of course, many recoil at the thought of ethical judgments and the call for moral transformation, viewing them as malicious, unseemly, and hateful. Oliver O'Donovan argues to the contrary, however, asserting that an ethic that arises from the gospel "rejoices the heart and gives light to the eyes because it springs from God's gift to mankind in Christ Jesus."[5] We do not become ethical to be forgiven and reconciled to God; we become ethical and address moral issues of the day because we have been forgiven and reconciled to God. Christians ought to hold moral positions on sexuality, marriage, wealth, social justice, violence, racism, and so forth, under the weight of humility, remembering we are all forgiven recipients of eternal life. Moreover, we all desperately need the Spirit of God to instruct us in the Word of God.

Redeemed to a Rewarding Way of Life

The authors of the New Testament use rich language to describe the way of life expected of those who follow Jesus. Two analogies are

---

[3] This language is borrowed from Cornelius Plantinga Jr., *Not the Way It Is Supposed to Be: A Breviary of Sin* (Grand Rapids, MI: Eerdmans, 1995).
[4] Lewis, *Mere Christianity*, 80.
[5] Oliver O'Donovan, *Resurrection and the Moral Order: An Outline for Evangelical Ethics*, 2nd ed. (Grand Rapids, MI: Eerdmans, 1994), 12.

particularly instructive: John's depiction of Jesus as the light of the world and Paul's entreaty that Christians walk in the Spirit. For the apostle John, Jesus invites us to live in the truth, to leave our dark lives behind and walk in the light. The one who provides light for living is Jesus himself. Comparing the incarnation to the creation story, John introduces Jesus as the true light that comes into the world (John 1:9). Those who reject Jesus ignore or reject the light because it reveals that their way of thinking and living is wrong. Jesus spoke of himself and his mission to Nicodemus the Pharisee:

> For God did not send the Son into the world to judge the world, but that the world might be saved through Him. He who believes in Him is not judged; he who does not believe has been judged already, because he has not believed in the name of the only begotten Son of God. This is the judgment, that the Light has come into the world, and men loved the darkness rather than the Light, for their deeds were evil. For everyone who does evil hates the Light, and does not come to the Light for fear that his deeds will be exposed. But he who practices the truth comes to the Light, so that his deeds may be manifested as having been wrought in God. (John 3:17–21)

A Christian who lives and works in the arts community of New Orleans once told me his friends and neighbors will believe anything and everything—except Jesus. Why? In part because to love Jesus is to obey his commandments, to transfer lordship from self to the Savior who lays claim on the way people live. Those who accept Jesus will walk in the light of life—that is, live according to the word and ways of God (John 8:12). The light of Christ Jesus sets us free to walk with eyes wide open to the beauty of his grace, to marvel at God's plans and purposes, and to understand and grieve over the corruption of immorality.

The moral demands of Christ Jesus are liberating and are compelled by love rather than the imposition of guilt or the madness of vainglory (John 14:15). The way of Christ Jesus sets people free from the bondage of sin and death so they might know and serve God. With a play on words, Jesus, the *Logos* (Word) of God, declares if you love him, then you will obey his *logos* (word). If you do not love him, then you will not keep his *logos* (word), which is the word of the living God (John 14:23–4). In the life and teachings of Jesus, truth always accompanies grace. As John announced when distinguishing the old covenant with the new, "Law was given through Moses; grace and truth were realized through Jesus Christ" (John 1:17). Grace and truth liberate captured souls. Those who hear and respond to the word of God, the truth, are not only empowered to live the way they ought to in this world but are also set free for all eternity from the thrall of death (John 8:31–58).

For the apostle Paul, the redemptive work of Jesus frees Christians to walk in the wisdom and way of God. If Jesus is the liberator, the Spirit is the enabler. A Christian ethic is life in the Spirit, in contrast to life in the flesh. According to Oliver O'Donovan, "Every way of life not lived by the Spirit of God is lived by 'flesh,' by man taking responsibility for himself whether in libertarian or legalistic ways, without the good news that God has taken responsibility for him."[6]

To the Christians in Ephesus, Paul reminded them they were dead in trespasses and sins in which they formerly walked (Eph 2:1). They were no longer to live as non-Christians, who "walk, in the futility of their mind, being darkened in their understanding, excluded from the life of God because of the ignorance that is in them, because of the hardness of their heart; and they, having become callous, have given themselves over to sensuality for the practice of every kind of impurity with greediness. But you did not learn Christ in this way" (Eph 4:17–20). Christians are to live in a manner worthy of their status as God's people (v. 1), which is not a position of vanity and self-importance but of humility, gratitude, and dependence, characterized

---

[6] Ibid.

by the imitation of Christ. Consequently, Christians are to walk in love (Eph 5:1); walk as children of light (v. 8); and walk with wisdom as those filled with the Spirit of God (vv. 15–18).

In his letter to the Galatians, Paul reduced the options to two distinct ways of living: walking by the flesh or walking by the Spirit. The way of the world is the way of the flesh and the way of Christ Jesus is the way of the Spirit, and each way manifests discernible characteristics. The fruit of the flesh is self-evident: sexual "immorality, impurity, sensuality, idolatry, sorcery, enmities, strife, jealousy, outbursts of anger, disputes, dissensions, factions, envying, drunkenness, carousing, and things like these" (Gal 5:19–21). Those whose identities and practices are defined by flesh "will not inherit the kingdom of God" (v. 21). In contrast, "the fruit of the Spirit is love, joy, peace, patience, kindness, goodness, faithfulness, gentleness, self-control … Those who belong to Christ Jesus have crucified the flesh with its passions and desires. If we live by the Spirit, let us also walk by the Spirit" (vv. 22–25). Paul encourages faithful Christians to recognize and reject the temptations of the flesh and be led by the Spirit. Said another way, if Jesus is Lord, "you may not do the things that you please" (v. 17). The New Testament indicates a Christian way of thinking and living is typically incompatible with the world, which accounts for why moral issues often arise when we "talk religion." However, do not miss the nature of the conflict. The gospel, like the crack of dawn, pierces the moral darkness of the human soul to display the ugliness of lusts, guilt of shameful deeds, folly of self-righteousness, and deception of the world's systems of knowledge and power devoid of God. The Lord of heaven and earth, through love displayed, stakes a claim on rebellious individuals, calls for repentance, and transforms hearts and minds. Those who believe and follow Christ Jesus are set on a new way of thinking and living, which requires they seek the counsel and will of God regarding morality, both personal and public. When the light pushes back the darkness and reveals the true way of living, people will surrender, flee, or fight. Unfortunately, the responses that seem most common in a post-Christian West are the latter two.

Declaring the Good News and Defending a Christian Morality

Christians do not have the option to be silent about the good news of Jesus Christ or the moral implication of following him. What does one do, however, when the evangelistic encounter becomes a forum for questions about ethical issues? Listen first, and try to discern why the person is asking questions about morality. People ask questions for four basic reasons: to entrap, evade, exonerate, or engage. Entrapment seeks to make a person speechless or to damage credibility. Evasion seeks to change the subject from the gospel to something else—anything else. Exoneration attempts self-justification for immoral behavior. Engagement seeks genuine answers about the relationship between the Christian faith and personal behavior or positions on moral issues. Discerning the motive behind a person's ethical questions or moral-political statements helps the Christian witness to empathize with the concerns of another and determine the best way to respond for the sake of the other.

The goal of gospel conversations is to communicate the truth about Jesus Christ and invite people to trust and follow him—to become disciples. If the gospel conversation turns to ethics and morality, discern the motive behind the questions, and if possible move the conversation toward engagement. Discuss legitimate moral questions so a person can count the cost of following Jesus, but avoid trying to win political arguments or debate ethical issues superficially. If the opportunity arises, take the counsel of Gregory Koukl, and put a stone of doubt in a person's shoe.[7] Ask strategic questions that make antagonists defend indefensible positions, and allow the serious nature of the gospel to arrest the attention of evaders and exonerators.

---

[7] I first heard Koukl use the phrase, "Put a stone in their shoes," at an apologetics conference at NOBTS. An outstanding source for learning how to communicate Christian convictions skillfully is Gregory Koukl, *Tactics: A Game Plan for Discussing Your Christian Convictions* (Grand Rapids, MI: Zondervan, 2009).

Anticipate the types of moral issues that may come up in any conversation. Defend your position if necessary. In doing so, however, avoid dueling with clichés, slogans, or sound bites. As Paul Copan once quipped, avoid sassy answers to stupid questions. In the end, however, trust the word and Spirit of God. The gospel is the power of God for salvation to all who believe (Rom 1:16). The word of God does not return empty, either spiritually or morally (Isa 55:6–11). Peter, teaching churches to defend the faith, gave the following instructions: "Sanctify Christ as Lord in your hearts" and give the best account of the gospel that you possibly can. Do so "with gentleness and reverence; and keep a good conscience so that in the thing in which you are slandered, those who revile your good behavior in Christ will be put to shame" (1 Pet 3:15–6). The morality of the Christian faith is, after all, a reflection of our Savior. If nothing else, in an evangelistic encounter, let people see Jesus in the way we hold onto moral truth and live the truth with integrity. Let the appeal of our message match an appeal in the way we live.

Many, however, do not want to be exposed to God's light because of what it reveals in their lives. Moreover, they may be threatened by the way we live and by the justifications made for our moral positions because we expose the darkness in their own lives. Jesus said of his disciples, "You are the light of the world. ... Let your light shine before men in such a way that they may see your good works, and glorify your Father who is in heaven" (Matt 5:14, 16). We can force no one to come into the light and believe as we do, but we can tell what Christ Jesus has done for us and how the moral demands of the gospel are nothing compared to the surpassing value of knowing Christ and experiencing fellowship with the living God (Phil 3:8).

BIBLIOGRAPHY

Koukl, Gregory. *Tactics: A Game Plan for Discussing Your Christian Convictions.* Grand Rapids, MI: Zondervan, 2009.

Lewis, C. S. *Mere Christianity.* New York: HarperOne, 1980.

———. *The Abolition of Man.* New York: HarperOne, 1974.

O'Donovan, Oliver. *Resurrection and the Moral Order: An Outline for Evangelical Ethics.* 2nd ed. Grand Rapids, MI: Eerdmans, 1994.

Plantinga, Cornelius, Jr. *Not the Way It Is Supposed to Be: A Breviary of Sin.* Grand Rapids, MI: Eerdmans, 1995.

Worship and Evangelism

Gregory A. Woodward

During my early childhood in the New Orleans area in the 1970s, I could hardly have imagined that my emerging understanding of worship would eventually intersect with a master of divinity student who had recently arrived at NOBTS.[1] Southern Baptist identity in the 1970s reflected the centrality of evangelism to pastoral ministries and church function, as this mantra continues to be the clarion call for any NOBTS grad who allows the flames of evangelism emanating from every foundation on the beautiful campus of 3939 Gentilly Boulevard to gain full sway. But one such foundation remains for me an enduring icon of my New Orleans roots, which inextricably entails my roots as a deep Southern boy brought home from the Baptist hospital to humble campus housing on the NOBTS campus. That symbol is a fixture of curiosity for many who pass through or live in the city for an extended time. The symbol remains at the distance of curiosity unless one takes the Louisa Street exit and finds their way to Leavell Chapel on Providence Place, passing the centennial historical marker of this unlikely institution in a city of New Orleans mystique. If one ventures into our beloved chapel, they might be privileged to hear the organ pipes rumble, taking in the passion of the empty cross draped in crimson.

Thus, two of the primary purposes of the church linger: evangelism and worship. Interestingly, two of the leading tomes on systematic theology reveal distinct areas regarding the primary purpose of the church. Grudem suggests all purposes of the church ultimately serve

---

[1] Charles Kelley arrived on the NOBTS campus as a master of divinity student in 1975.

the purpose of worship while Erickson suggests evangelism plays the primary role, at least during the church's time on earth.[2] Thus, these two great pillars of church purpose have vied for lead position throughout Western history.[3]

What Has Been Done

The ancient liturgy offers a picture of the ideal marriage of these two primary purposes of the church. Burkholder, Grout, and Palisca show that the early liturgy served the purpose of both evangelism and worship, although a clear demarcation was evident as only those who were confirmed were allowed to remain for the Eucharist.[4] Elements of the liturgy in the Eastern church served an apologetic purpose, proclaiming through song the truth of Christ's identity.[5] Luther expanded the relationship between evangelism and worship by making the culture of worship

---

[2] Millard J. Erickson, *Christian Theology*, 2nd ed. (Grand Rapids: Baker Academic, 1983), 1061. Wayne Grudem, *Systematic Theology: An Introduction to Biblical Doctrine* (Grand Rapids, MI: Zondervan, 1994), 867.

[3] The task of the writers for this tribute entailed large areas of church ministry. Although an ongoing conversation remains regarding the relationship of evangelism and worship on an individual basis, this topic is a subcategory of the larger issues addressed in this article, the corporate call to worship versus the corporate call to evangelize.

[4] J. Peter Burkholder, Donald Jay Grout, and Claude V. Palisca, *A History of Western Music*, 8th ed. (New York: W. W. Norton & Company, 2010), 48–49. Burkholder, Grout, and Palisca explain the early Christian liturgy emphasized the key aspects of the gospel, "making clear the path to salvation." They also reveal that "catechumens" received basic teachings in the first part of the liturgy, but the priests dismissed catechumens for the Eucharist. Thus, evangelism occurred as the gospel was proclaimed and taught through liturgy.

[5] Martin Stringer, *A Sociological History of Worship* (New York: Cambridge University Press, 2005), 66; 97–98. Stringer explains that in early church history Constantinople processions represented different factions of theological thought (e.g., Arian versus Orthodox). Originally, Christian processions served as an apologetic "against those of the pagans" (98). Thus, one need not be "surprised" that processions would later represent schools of thought within an emerging Christian community. Furthermore, the processions were "always accompanied by music" (98). Thus, we may logically infer that music served as a critical apologetic role in the early Eastern church.

accessible to the average German. Although his purposes appear to have been more for the nurture of the church than evangelism, he permanently tilted the paradigm of the liturgy toward cultural accessibility.

Kelley traced the impact of nineteenth-century crusade leaders that eventually led to a consistent evangelistic movement.[6] Kelley highlighted Nettleton, Finney, and Moody as hegemonic forces in the emergence of an evangelistic invitation in corporate church gatherings, thus reflecting the wide range of theological influence on this particular aspect of an emerging Baptist liturgy.[7] In so doing, with a broad sweep Kelley substantiates that the "public invitation" became a permanent aspect of the Southern Baptist liturgy: "The time of response gradually became a characteristic feature of Southern Baptist preaching and worship."[8]

Although the influence of the evangelistic giants of the nineteenth century contributed to Baptist worship most specifically by substantiating the public invitation, a more general cultural change in how music was used in the Sunday morning gathering also transformed the corporate evangelistic worship experience. Hustad chronicled the emergence of the music evangelist in the nineteenth century, noting Phillip Phillips was likely the first full-time music evangelist.[9] Phillip P. Bliss, among others, soon followed playing various roles—singer, congregational leader, and in many cases choral conductor, ultimately

---

[6] Charles S. Kelley Jr., *Fuel the Fire: Lessons from the History of Southern Baptist Evangelism*, A Treasury of Baptist Theology, eds. Paige Patterson and Jason G. Duesing (Nashville, TN: B&H Academic, 2018), 59.

[7] Ibid. Kelley specifically notes Nettleton is Calvinistic. Although he does not comment on Finney's theological disposition, Kelley's careful balance of perspectives is apparent and reflects the type of leadership he provided throughout his presidency at NOBTS, welcoming the value of all legitimate voices in the Southern Baptist identity.

[8] Ibid. The use of the phrase "preaching and worship" is equivalent to saying Southern Baptist liturgy. Wisely, Kelley is reticent to use the world *liturgy*, of which Southern Baptists self-identify as free form.

[9] Don Hustad, *Jubilate II: Church Music in Worship and Renewal* (Carol Stream, IL: Hope Pub., 1993), 394.

playing a "master of ceremonies" role.[10] Moody's crusade movement empowered the gospel hymn, which had previously been used solely in Sunday School.[11] Ira Sankey, Moody's pastoral partner in music ministry, introduced gospel hymns to large crusade crowds on his portable reed organ[12] and became the "archetype" in this era in which music was fused with evangelistic zeal at unprecedented levels.[13]

Throughout the twentieth century, the church's use of music as an evangelistic tool increasingly permeated the evangelical landscape. Thus, the desire to connect culturally with nonbelievers increasingly obscured the purpose of the worship gathering as a distinct and necessary purpose of the church. However, a countermovement began in the latter half of the twentieth century. Tozer, Wiersbe, and Webber, among others, led the evangelical church to discover the "missing jewel" of the evangelical movement—worship.[14] These three influential voices for worship renewal initiated a reset of the purpose of worship in the evangelical church.

What Has Been Said

However, in more recent years, there appears to be a growing desire to make sure the potential of the worship gathering to engage culture is

---

[10] Ibid., 394.
[11] Harry Eskew and Hugh T. McElrath, *Sing with Understanding: An Introduction to Christian Hymnody*, rev. ed. (Nashville, TN: Church Street Press, 1995), 198–99.
[12] Ibid., 199.
[13] Ibid., 395.
[14] A. W. Tozer, *Worship: The Missing Jewel* (Camp Hill, PA: Christian Publications, 1992), 10, 12, 23. Robert E. Webber, *Ancient-Future Worship: Proclaiming and Enacting God's Narrative* (Grand Rapids, MI: Baker Books, 2008), 90–91. Warren W. Wiersbe, *Real Worship: Playground, Battleground, or Holy Ground?*, 2nd ed. (Grand Rapids, MI: Baker Books, 2000), 11–16. Tozer warns against a "neo-rationalism" that seeks to "explain" all "mystery out of worship." Thus, he calls for a return to the "missing jewel, the jewel of worship," suggesting, "Worship is the missing jewel in modern evangelicalism." Webber reviewed how worship as a primarily corporate experience became a more personal journey in the Reformation and how the clergy's passion was turned from worship to "argumentative" sermons. Although Wiersbe does not specifically refer to Tozer's call to a return to the "missing jewel," his indictment of what was missing in his own life and evangelical churches in general in the 1980s parallels Tozer's call for a return to the missing jewel, worship, in the 1960s.

not forgotten. Thus, David Wheeler and Vernon M. Whaley offered a civil dialogue as professors representing these two primary functions of the church.[15] They poignantly expressed an increasing concern in the evangelical church that one can define the Christian experience as worship to the exclusion of evangelism:

> The sad part is that so-called leaders appear to be content with this disconnect in reference to their faith, thus allowing for outward expressions of worship with little regard to what it means to be a multiplying disciple of Christ. After generations of allowing this anemic expression of worship to exist with little or no challenge from Christian leaders, the result has been the normalizing of an impotent faith that ignores the Great Commission in favor of reducing worship to an emotional act of personal expression.[16]

Mark Powers also sought to emphasize the potential of worship to affect missions; he expresses a similar sentiment to Wheeler and Whaley:

> And today, as we face the decline of the evangelical church, worship-discipleship-mission is the key to restoring the intent and purpose of our churches. If we want our worship heightened and our discipleship deepened, we must be on mission all the time.[17]

---

[15] David Wheeler and Vernon M. Whaley, *The Great Commission to Worship: Biblical Principles for Worship-Based Evangelism* (Nashville, TN: B&H Academic, 2011).
[16] Ibid., 7–8.
[17] Mark C. Powers, *Going Full Circle: Worship That Moves Us to Discipleship and Missions* (Eugene, OR: Wipf & Stock Publications, 2013), 6, 53–56. Powers describes a cyclical relationship among worship, discipleship, and missionary zeal in the life of Paul in a chapter titled "The Circle of Missional Living: Worship-Discipleship-Mission" (6).

Will Bishop reminds us that Christian youth musical "mission tours gave birth to today's modern short-term missions movement."[18]

Pushback in the spirit of Tozer remains strong as well. Scott Aniol warns the church to be careful of cultural influence in the worship gathering.[19] Among recent authors exploring the relationship

---

[18] William Robert Bishop, "Christian Youth Musicals: 1967–1975" (PhD diss., New Orleans Baptist Theological Seminary, 2015), 406, accessed March 6, 2019, ProQuest Dissertations & Theses.

[19] Scott M. Aniol, "The Mission of Worship: A Critique of and Response to the Philosophy of Culture, Contextualization, and Worship of the North American Missional Movement" (PhD diss., Southwestern Baptist Theological Seminary, 2013), 45–65, accessed February 2, 2019, ProQuest Dissertations & Theses. Darrell Guder, *Be My Witnesses: The Church's Mission, Message, and Messengers* (Grand Rapids, MI: Wm. B. Eerdmans, 1985), 96, 157, 175. Ed Stetzer, *Planting Missional Churches* (Nashville, TN: Broadman & Holman, 2006), 260, 368, Scribd. John Piper, *Let the Nations Be Glad: The Supremacy of God in Missions*, 3rd ed. (Grand Rapids, MI: Baker Academic, 2010), 35. Aniol reviews the relationship between the missional mindset of the evangelical church and corporate worship practice with an awareness of evangelistic elements in corporate worship. His study reveals that some of the most careful reflections on the relationship between worship and evangelism may be found among missiologists. His review is particularly helpful in showing the complexity of distinguishing evangelism and worship. For example, Aniol revealed the challenge Gruder faced in distinguishing a "seeker" service from a worship service for believers that is culturally sensitive, and Aniol notes that Stetzer argued for the use of corporate worship for unbelievers being called to salvation, while he concluded the "purpose of church planting" is "corporate worship" and not *vice versa*. Furthermore, Aniol substitutes the word *missions* for *church planting* in his summary of Stetzer's thoughts on the balance of missions and worship, yet he reflects Stetzer's own juxtaposition of the two terms as Stetzer seeks to substantiate his statement regarding the purpose of church planting with Piper's often quoted quip: "Missions still exists because worship does not exist everywhere." Aniol's reference to the reverse logic of worship not being about missions, by which he appears to mean evangelism, appears to be his own thought and not that of Stetzer. Scott Aniol, "How Does the Church's Ministry Relate to Worship," part five of "Worship and the Missio Dei," Religious Affections Ministries, last modified April 25, 2013, accessed February 1, 2019, http://religiousaffections.org/articles/articles-on-worship/how-does-the-churchs-mission-relate-to-worship/. In this more informal writing, Aniol rightly points out that what is meant by *missions* by Piper in a discussion of the relationship between worship and missions in Piper's *Let the Nations Be Glad*, referenced previously, is actually worship and evangelism. Stetzer also uses the word *mission* in a manner equivalent to evangelism as he discusses the relationship between mission and worship in *Planting Missional Churches*, referenced above.

between worship and evangelism, Stetzer and Schattauer present perhaps the broadest conception of the unified purpose of evangelism and worship by surrendering both to the *imagio dei* of the mission of God:

> We are called to please God. This includes the edification of believers, but the true purpose of the church is as broad as the purposes of God. It is the *missio Dei*—the mission of God. It includes all that God includes because we are an extension of his work in the world. The *missio Dei* includes worship but also evangelism, ministry, encouragement, and pastoral care.[20]

What Lies Ahead?

How shall the church press forward with evangelistic fervor while remaining healthy in its worship? I suggest three areas for continued conversation for these two foundational purposes of the church. The first area for consideration, biblical scholarship, is always the wellspring of creative thought and the beginning point for balancing kingdom priorities. In a review of the history of hymnological and worship studies, Woodward and Bishop advanced that particularly early church studies on worship are receiving increased attention.[21] While acknowledging the historians' (e.g., liturgists) influence on such studies, they suggested the "most fruitful" area of future

---

[20] Stetzer, *Planting Missional Churches*, 368. Aniol, 56–57. Thomas H. Schattauer, *Inside Out: Worship in an Age of Mission* (Minneapolis, MN: Fortress Press, 1999), 56–57. Aniol credits Schattauer in presenting a similar conception of *missio Dei*. Schattauer presents three categories through which missions and worship might be related: worship leading to missional activity, a missional mindset in the worship gathering that equates missions with evangelism as noted previously, and the broad conception of *missio Dei* in agreement with Stetzer's view. Aniol also seems to use the term *mission* interchangeably with *evangelism* in the category 3 description.

[21] Gregory A. Woodward and William Bishop, "The Current State of Research as Related to Worship," *The Journal of Research in Worship Ministries*, no. 1 (Spring 2014): 12, http://www.worshipjournal.org/resources/PDF/HIstory%20Article.pdf.

research may be found among biblical scholars.[22] Such a movement continues to emerge, perhaps because of personal interest by world-class biblical scholars on the topic of worship, such as Wright's and Witherington's offerings to the topic of worship.[23] A second fruitful area in regard to a holistic view of worship and evangelism may be found in recent calls for biblical justice to be integrated into the evangelism narrative, a category of evangelism dialogue that Charles Kelley has begun in earnest. Finally, a more thoughtful approach to the worship gathering that entails evangelism is desperately needed in our churches, so consideration of the relationship between worship and apologetics will be briefly addressed.

Biblical Scholarship as a Way Forward

A holistic view of worship and evangelism may be found most profoundly in the echo of ancient Hebrew text in early church worship. Jesus, the head of the church, infuses the standard Hebrew book of worship, the Psalms, with grand messianic vision. The reality that Ps 110 is the most quoted Old Testament chapter in the New Testament ties the eternal proclamation of Christ as Lord inextricably to worship. Thus, Jesus, playing a rabbinic role, set the paradigm for

---

[22] Ibid., 13–15. Woodward and Bishop particularly highlighted the third quest for the historical Jesus as an area contributing to early worship practice studies. However, as noted in the following text, historical Jesus studies necessarily include Second Temple studies, which ultimately lead to a revival of interest in the full scope of Scripture for the church's ongoing need for worship renewal.

[23] Ben Witherington, *Psalms Old and New: Exegesis, Intertextuality, and Hermeneutics* (Minneapolis, MN: Fortress Press, 2017). Ben Witherington, *We Have Seen His Glory: A Vision of Kingdom Worship* (Grand Rapids, MI: Wm. B. Eerdmans, 2010). N. T. Wright, *The Case for the Psalms: Why They Are Essential* (New York: HarperOne, 2013). Larry W. Hurtado, *At the Origins of Christian Worship: The Context and Character of Earliest Christian Devotion* (Grand Rapids, MI: Eerdmans Publishing, 1999). Hurtado's important work on the reality of Jesus worship in the first century was a critical precursor to serious biblical scholarship on the topic of worship.

infusing a high Christology in the Psalms.[24] The Catholic church captured this paradigm by juxtaposing psalm tones, a basic intonation of various psalms in corporate worship, with the *Gloria Patri*.[25] Isaac Watts provided a path for evangelicals to sing psalms with a high Christology in what was and remains perhaps the most seamless settings of psalms with a high Christology in church history (e.g., "Joy to the World").[26] More recently, Keith and Kristyn Getty have inaugurated a project to once again turn the church to the psalms for profound gospel proclamation.[27] Thus, what was predicted by Woodward and Bishop regarding biblical scholarship on the topic of worship appears to be unfolding in ways that are more basic and far-reaching than the scope of worship scholarship.

However, the dialogue with biblical scholars remains a priority. Two rich bodies of biblical research related to worship may provide helpful dialogue points with evangelism scholarship. For example, a potentially rich body of biblical scholarship for worship may be found in Second Temple era studies. N. T. Wright showed how careful research of the

---

[24] Craig S. Keener, *The Gospel of Matthew: A Socio-Rhetorical Commentary* (Grand Rapids, MI: Eerdmans, 2009), 532. Gregory A. Woodward and Wm. Craig Price, "The Royal Psalms and the New Perspective," (paper presented at the annual Southwest Regional Meeting of the Evangelical Theological Society, Fort Worth, Texas, March 31, 2017). Woodward and Price showed, "Keener emphasized the rabbinic nature of Jesus' reference to Psalm 110. Keener explained that Jesus used a 'haggadic antinomy,' meaning 'both sides of a question were correct but their relationship needed to be resolved.'"

[25] Burkholder, Grout, Palisca, *A History of Western Music*, 54.

[26] Eskew and McElrath, *Sing with Understanding*, 132–33. Eskew and McElrath provide a concise review of the two types of hymns Watts produced, one of which is a "Christian content" psalm setting.

[27] Keith Getty, *Sing! Psalms* (The Getty Music Worship Conference, Nashville, TN, 2018). Building upon Calvin's emphasis of the Psalms, the 2018 conference featured several new psalm settings, and Keith Getty explained they plan to complete a new psalter setting. Although the Calvin Institute recently completed a psalter, representing a rigorous hymnological approach, the Getty movement appears to have a much broader reach.

Second Temple era could inform one's view of the historical Jesus. For example, Wright references Ps 2 particularly as indicative of the mindset of Second-Temple Jews who "hoped for the new exodus, seen as the final return from exile."[28]

The rise of the penitential prayer during the Second Temple era should be considered alongside the rise in importance of the messianic psalm. The penitential prayer emerged as the biblical response to the just punishment of Israel before the building of the Second Temple.[29] Ezra demonstrated the appropriate prayer response based on the teaching of the Torah in Leviticus. Namely, when God finds Israel to be unfaithful (מָעַל *ma'al*), collective confession is required.[30] Collective

---

[28] N. T. Wright, *Jesus and the Victory of God*, Christian Origins and the Question of God, vol. 2, (Minneapolis, MN: Fortress Press, 2013), 209–212. In this portion of Wright's argument, he shows the heightened apocalyptic mindset, distinctly contradicting the work of the Jesus Seminar and John Dominic Crossan in proximity to *Jesus and the Victory of God*; Wright accused these thinkers of a generic hellenization of any distinct Jewish apocalyptic view. See also N. T. Wright, *Paul and the Faithfulness of God*, Christian Origins and the Question of God, vol. 4; (Minneapolis, MN: Fortress Press, 2013), 119. Wright reiterated the connection between the promise of Davidic rule in a range of psalms, particularly Ps 2, and the covenant with Abraham.

[29] Samuel E. Balentine, "I Was Ready to Be Sought Out by Those Who Did Not Ask," in *The Origins of Penitential Prayer in Second Temple Judaism*, ed., Mark J. Boda, Daniel K. Falk, and Rodney A. Werline, vol. 1, *Seeking the Favor of God*, ed., Mark J. Boda, Daniel K. Falk, and Rodney A. Werline, *Early Judaism and Its Literature*, no. 23, ed. Judith H. Newman (Atlanta, GA: Society of Biblical Literature, 2006), 7.

[30] Mark J. Boda, "Confession as Theological Expression: Ideological Origins of Penitential Prayer," in *The Origins of Penitential Prayer in Second Temple Judaism*, ed., Mark J. Boda, Daniel K. Falk, and Rodney A. Werline, vol. 1, *Seeking the Favor of God*, ed., Mark J. Boda, Daniel K. Falk, and Rodney A. Werline, *Early Judaism and Its Literature*, no. 23, ed. Judith H. Newman (Atlanta: Society of Biblical Literature, 2006), 34. Boda explains a collective confessional response to unfaithfulness was one of two primary responses to the exile. This collective confessional response is rooted in the "priestly tradition," whereas the Deuteronomic tradition emphasized "a return to the observance of Torah as covenant document that fosters the eternal relationship between God and his people."

prayer is by definition the genesis point of worship renewal, and the spirit of congregational confessional prayer, particularly rooted in Second Temple *ma'al*, may well have been the ancient Jewish context for Jesus's call for worship renewal at the temple: "My house shall be called a house of prayer" (Matt 21:13). Furthermore, the establishment of penitential prayer as a consistent liturgical aspect of Second Temple Judaism is the clear precursor to the Kyrie.

Congregational confession of sin and total dependence on God matches well with messianic expectation. One could even argue that penitential prayer leads to messianic expectation.[31] Liturgists typically trace a good and right confession of the church to the Kyrie, a fifth century expression of confession,[32] but in fact, as we have seen, the roots of confession for the people of God are deeper, reaching to

---

[31] I am proposing messianic expectation as the logical result of penitential prayer as a key development in Second Temple Judaism up to the time of Christ; evidence for this supposition may be found ultimately in combining the important messianic expectation research by scholars such as N. T. Wright, referenced previously, and the work of penitential prayer scholars. Balentine, "I Was Ready to Be Sought Out by Those Who Did Not Ask," 2. Balentine reminds the church that Paul may be the originator of the conception of certain psalms as confessional psalms because of the free use of these psalms in building an argument for the reality of the wrath of God in Romans. Thus, Paul's use of penitential psalms may be the connection point between penitential prayer and the fulfillment of messianic expectation in the early church.

[32] Paschal Botz, "Kyrie Eleison: Our Advent Prayer," *Orate Fratres* XX, no. 1, (December 1945): 1, EBSCOhost. S. J. P. van Dijk, "The Bible in Liturgical Use," in *The Cambridge History of the Bible*, ed., G. W. H. Lampe, vol. 2, *The West from the Father to the Reformation* (New York: Cambridge University Press, 1963), 241. Botz speculated in a reasonable manner that the Kyrie Eleison could likely be traced to the Jerusalem church, he acknowledged that the first documented record of the lyrics appearing in Western churches is the fifth century, which he states is a century later than the prayer's appearance in the Greek liturgy. Dijk concurred Christians used the prayer "long before" the text was used in the liturgy, and he also placed the text in the Western liturgy in the fifth century. Furthermore, Dijk noted the phrase *kyrie eleison* may be found throughout Psalms.

a liturgical paradigm in Leviticus.[33] Confession in the context of the emergence of Jesus as Messiah may be traced more specifically to the penitential prayers of Ezra, Nehemiah, and penitential psalms.[34] Furthermore, the consistent proclamation of Jesus as Messiah from the context of collective confessional prayer carries certain implications for action in the church. Namely, Brueggemann, a lead scholar on the emergence of the penitential prayer,[35] recognizes the potential for the disenfranchised to gain a sense of kingdom clarity in regard to justice.[36]

---

[33] Claus Westermann, *Praise and Lament in the Psalms* (trans. Keith R. Crim and Richard N. Soulen: Atlanta: John Knox, 1981), 171–72, 206. Balentine, "I Was Ready to Be Sought Out by Those Who Did Not Ask," 5. Boda, "Confession as Theological Expression: Ideological Origins of Penitential Prayer," 35–36. Balentine, in reviewing scholarship on penitential prayer, explained, based on the work of Westermann, that "the way" Israel prayed changed as penitnetial prayer emerged; thus, I use the word *liturgy* to represent this shift but not necessarily as a documentation of change in temple liturgy. Balentine's willingness to call Westermann's establishment of penitential prayer as a "form-critical foundation" may also justify the use of the word *liturgy*.

[34] Balentine, "I Was Ready to Be Sought Out by Those Who Did Not Ask," 2. As noted in the previous note, Balentine provides a concise review of the importance of penitential psalms (6, 32, 38, 51, 102, 130, 133) on Christian doctrine. Revealing the importance of these psalms, he also begins his review of "Previous Scholarship on Penitential Prayer" with Cassiodorus, a sixth century Latin priest "who may have the distinction" of originally treating these psalms as a distinct group.

[35] Balentine, "I Was Ready to Be Sought Out by Those Who Did Not Ask," 6. Westermann, *Praise and Lament in the Psalms*, 171–72, 203, 206–207, and 274. Balentine emphasized Brueggemann's substantial work in answering Westermann's charge to see lament restored to Christian worship. Westermann contended that only in so doing would there be a healthy recognition of human tragedy. Balentine argued, "Brueggemann goes further, however, to argue that lament is also vital, because it keeps the possibility that status quo political and religious systems . . . can be questioned and changed."

[36] Walter Brueggemann, *Israel's Praise: Doxology Against Idolatry and Ideology* (Philadelphia: Augsburg Fortress Publishers, 1988), 3, 13–36. The essence of Brueggemann's argument in relationship to the power of collective confession is captured in the following statement: "My argument is based on the conviction that the church has acute problems concerning ethical responsibility because our worship has not been critiqued or understood as a social act" (3).

Biblical Justice Serving Evangelism Empowered by Worship

Brueggemann's supposition provides a potentially important segue into the rising tide of calls for evangelism to be combined with biblical justice issues. Although Evangelicals have understandably distanced themselves from an unholy alliance of such humanitarian efforts and gospel proclamation,[37] they are increasingly recognizing that demonstrating love through social action adds integrity to evangelism. Kevin Brown, a sociology professor at NOBTS, articulates the need for collective confession in a manner that both aligns with the lamentation model discussed and resonates with recent calls for evangelism to be combined with social justice issues:

> Recognizing our propensity to enact evil against others, the Book of Leviticus codifies the way Israel was to live, and this perspective was both individual and systematic. When Israel was called to repentance, it was not simply a call for individuals to repent but also for the nation to engage in corporate penance. The nation of Israel was also called to periodically recalibrate their economic system and enact a Year of Jubilee.[38]

---

[37] Eric Metaxas, *Bonhoeffer: Pastor, Martyr, Prophet, Spy*, Repeat ed. (Minneapolis, MN: Thomas Nelson, 2011), 44–45, 102, 332–33. Metaxas reviews how social justice issues emerged early in the twentieth century in a dangerous combination with a heretical gospel. Harry Emerson Fosdick's departure from First Presbyterian Church to pastor a church funded by Rockefeller Foundation resulted in Riverside Church, located in proximity to Union Seminary in New York. Riverside Church was rooted in a less-than-divine Jesus, yet perpetuated innovative humanitarian efforts in tandem with the liberal controlling camp of Union Seminary. This pivotal historical development in the American church provided the paradigm for consistent combinations of a weak gospel with social justice action. Thus, evangelicals have been reticent to embrace the combining of humanitarian efforts with gospel proclamation without ample justification that the gospel plays the lead role in such efforts.

[38] Kevin Brown, "Racism and Our Definitional Challenge: Is Sin Simply an Individual Act?" *North American Association of Christians in Social Work Quarterly Newsletter* (Spring 2019).

Kelley demonstrated his understanding of the need for biblical justice leaders to dialogue with leading evangelists, creating the opportunity for highly visible conversations. Furthermore, he courageously determined to align his ongoing legacy as an evangelist educator with certain trusted social justice gospel advocates. Adjunct NOBTS professor and prominent New Orleans church planter Page Brooks, Kelley, and John Perkins participated in a critical conversation regarding the intersection of social justice and gospel proclamation in fall 2018. A key statement from this dialogue came from Perkins: "To achieve true racial reconciliation in the church, gospel proclamation must remain the central theme."[39] While such conversations may serve as incredible signs of hope for a twenty-first century evangelistic movement seeking to draw the passion of young leaders, it could be that a logical worship response to such a rising tide holds the greatest potential for sustaining such a movement. Thus, it could be that the combination of a consistent collective confession of how far short we have fallen in regard to the current state of American culture matched with a consistent proclamation of the lordship of Christ is the beginning point for exploring just causes and calling for biblically ordained action in the local church.

Ultimately, Brueggemann ties the needs of society to the proclamation of God as King, suggesting each generation has a need to return to the psalms for a reordering of society.[40] Brueggemann reminds the church that the idea of gospel proclamation is deeply rooted in the psalms.[41] For example, Ps 96 tells the Israelite community to declare his salvation. In relationship to the phrase, "tell of his salvation" (Ps 96:2 ESV), Brueggemann emphasized the connection between the Hebrew word, *basar*, and the Greek word, *euaggelizesthe*,[42] and added the nominal form of the

---

[39] Gary Myers, "Perkins: The Gospel Leads to Gospel Proclamation," *New Orleans Baptist Theological Seminary News*, Nov. 5, 2018, accessed February 1, 2019, http://www.nobts.edu/news/articles/2018/Perkins2018.html.
[40] Brueggemann, *Israel's Praise*, 35–40.
[41] Ibid., 31.
[42] Ibid.

Greek word means "gospel."[43] Furthermore, Brueggemann emphasized the emergence of a "gospel of Yahweh": "The gospel of Yahweh, which is to be sung and recounted among the nations, is that Yahweh is to be feared above all the gods."[44] Thus, a golden thread of evangelism begins to emerge in the ancient worship book of Israel, the Psalter.

Although declaring his salvation in the worship gathering is not equivalent to proclaiming such realities to a lost world, perhaps this biblical command is a healthy starting point for keeping the Great Commission in sync with worship. Although I can't prove the connection, I suspect there is a relationship between this New Orleans boy's zeal to sing strong the songs of the church—so strong at Highland Baptist Church in Metairie, Louisiana, that my parents had to encourage me to sing a bit softer—perhaps this same zeal eventually spilled over into a willingness to share the good news of Jesus Christ with a lost world. Thus, we begin to teach our children to evangelize, to "declare his glory among the nations" (Ps 96:3 ESV), when we equip them to sing of his truth from an early age in our churches.[45]

Worship and Apologetics as a Way Forward

The final area to be explored in terms of an ideal integration of worship and evangelism is informed by the fields of theology and apologetics. Charles Kelley created an appropriately curious atmosphere for reflection and dialogue in his long tenure at NOBTS. One of the highlights of each academic year is the apologetics conference, titled Defend the Faith, inaugurated and sustained by world-class apologist, Robert Stewart. In conversation with one of the key presenters

---

[43] Ibid.
[44] Ibid., 31, 33. Although Brueggemann's connection of Psalms's emphasis on Yahweh as King to Jesus as King is somewhat lacking, his rich exegesis of Ps 96 remains an excellent starting point for connecting worship to evangelism.
[45] Certainly, a good number of leading evangelicals do not have such an experience in childhood. The encouragement offered is toward an ideal development of evangelism and worship in the life of the church.

at Defend the Faith, I suggested a reasonable or reflective liturgy that holds the potential of both feeding the church in worship and starting a gospel conversation with a lost world.[46] A reasonable liturgy seeks not to dismiss the possibility that at a given evangelistic event it might be possible to perform some hip Jesus songs, preach the gospel, and then call for decisions with a new or old song of invitation; rather, a reflective liturgy challenges pastors who might be in the mindset of seeing their Sunday morning gathering tilted more toward evangelism than others, to give new thought to how rich and thoughtful music and liturgy might serve that purpose.

Boa and Bowman present a four-part taxonomy on apologetics: (1) classical, (2) Reformed, (3) evidentialism, and 4) fideism.[47] Classical apologists present a two-step tango in which the gospel presenter first seeks to establish a monotheistic view of God and then seeks to show that this God is in fact the historical/biblical Jesus.[48] Within the two primary streams of modern Reformed theology and apologetic method, presuppositionalism, conceived by Cornelius Van Til, was the eventual landing point.[49] The strictest form of the method does not allow for arguments from science or other academic fields but rather takes the high position that only those enlightened by God to see the truth will grasp what is being presented anyway, and thus the approach is integrated

---

[46] Gregory A. Woodward, "Reconciling Evangelistic Methods with Worship Models: A Consideration of Apologetic Approaches in the Worship Framework," *The Journal for Baptist Theology and Ministry* 7, no. 1 (Fall 2010): 93–104, accessed February 1, 2019, http://baptistcenter.net/journals/JBTM_7-2_Fall_2010.pdf#page=96.

[47] Kenneth D. Boa and Robert M. Bowman, *Faith Has Its Reasons: Integrative Approaches to Defending the Christian Faith* (Waynesboro, GA: Authentic, 2001).

[48] Ibid., 163, 173–95.

[49] Ibid., 373–95. Boa and Bowman label the two modern streams of Reformed thought as Scottish Calvinism and Dutch Calvinism. Key figures under the label Scottish Calvinism are Thomas Reid and Charles Hodge; Abraham Kuyper and Herman Dooyeweerd were highlighted under the category Dutch Calvinism. Although Boa and Bowman determine presuppositionalism to be the landing point of these two streams, this is not to say every Reformed apologist is a presuppositionalist.

with a high view of Scripture.⁵⁰ Evidentialists are ever mindful of the preeminence of the resurrection as the primary evidence for belief, so although they might use a range of evidences to prove the supernatural (e.g. ghost stories),⁵¹ they are ever moving toward the evidence of the resurrection to prove the lordship of Christ.⁵² Fideism may be traced to Tertullian, Pascal, and Luther, but Boa and Bowman show that Kierkegaard provided a modern defensible framework for the system.⁵³ Ultimately, Kierkegaard's response to the rising tide of modernism was to call for belief beyond reason and science.⁵⁴ Boa and Bowman connect this category to a more "personal" approach to sharing the gospel based in relational aspects of God's revelation of himself.⁵⁵

---

[50] Ibid., 65, 70, 398. Cornelius Van Til, *The Defense of the Faith*, 3rd ed. (Nutley, N.J. and Philadelphia, PA: Presbyterian & Reformed, 1967), 99. Boa and Bowman were careful to show Van Til's approach is more academic than may be apparent at first glimpse. Van Til argued that ultimately only the Christian system of thought truly allows for anything to be known. Thus, all other perspectives are doomed to end in "irrationalism" (398). This summation of Van Til, as well as other summations throughout this review of Boa and Bowman's work, is also informed by Bowman's numerous appearances at NOBTS for Defend the Faith.

[51] Gary Habermas and Michael Shermer, "Is There Life After Death: A Dialogue between Gary Habermas and Michael Shermer" (Greer-Heard Point-Counterpoint Forum, April 13, 2012). Gary Haberman, a leading evangelical evidentialist, used out-of-body documentation and ghost stories to argue for "life after death," representing evangelicals in opposition to noted atheist, Michael Shermer, founder of Skeptics Society. Habermas's primary work in the field of apologetics has related to the resurrection.

[52] Boa and Bowman, *Faith Has Its Reasons*, 80, 240, 256–57, 264, 278, 297–98, 302, 317.

[53] Ibid., 543–53, 554–62, 585–86, 600–601.

[54] Ibid., 585–86, 594, 600–603, 604–605

[55] Ibid., 572, 587, 588, 632, 665–66. Karl Barth, *Church Dogmatics*, trans., T. H. L. Parker, W. B. Johnston, Harold Knight, J. L. M. Haire, ed. Geoffrey T. Bromiley and Thomas F. Torrance, vol 1, part 2 (New York: T. & T. Clark, 1957, 2004), 330–31. Boa and Bowman placed Karl Barth under the category fideism and highlighted his conclusions regarding the priority of love. In addition to describing this approach to apologetics as "personal," Boa and Bowman describe Jesus as "personal" and "gracious" in their summary of the strengths of the fideist approach, thus rooting the quality of this apologetic approach to the nature of Christ.

I have sought to show that a movement from transcendence (i.e., an emphasis on big attributes of God: God is holy; God is Creator) to immanence (the gospel) in the worship liturgy marries well to classical apologetics.[56] Presuppositionalism also matches this liturgical model well, with perhaps a greater emphasis on Scripture in an approach that is presuppositionally friendly. Evidentialism may be the hardest to align with a worship model, although perhaps the greatest connection point is the recognition of the possibility of the miraculous in our worship, which is always most importantly the conversion of a soul. And perhaps evangelicals are ready for the possibility, after five hundred years of reflection, that a Lord's Supper service can be uniquely powerful without giving way to the notion of transubstantiation. I contend that, for a lost person observing a powerful Lord's Supper, the service provides much to be contemplated in terms of the possibility of the gospel becoming reality in their lives. Fideism was a category that had little appeal for me upon my initial observations of the Boa and Bowman text, but after further reflection I concluded what is to be gained in considering fideism is not primarily content but an "infrastructure" for delivery.[57] Boa and Bowman support the fideist idea of infrastructure in a different sense: a life lived for Christ, particularly characterized with love, should be an important aspect of our apologetic.[58] I would suggest this high view of ethics be compared to infrastructure in the

---

[56] Woodward, "Reconciling Evangelistic Methods with Worship Models," 93–104.

[57] Ravi Zacharias, "Is Atheism Dead, Is God Alive: Part One," *Just Thinking* (podcast), Ravi Zacharius International Ministries, July 30, 2018, https://www.rzim.org/listen/just-thinking/is-atheism-dead-is-god-alive-part-1. Ravi refers to an "infrastructure of the arts."

[58] Boa and Bowman, *Faith Has Its Reasons*, 758, 773, Scribd. John M. Frame, *The Doctrine of the Knowledge of God: A Theology of Lordship* (Phillipsburg, NJ: Presbyterian and Reformed, 1987), 357. Boa and Bowman connect Frame's call for love "as one of the strongest (i.e., most persuasive) arguments" to fideism, Frame, 357. Frame, 11, 40, 202, 211, 231. They also cast Frame's "existential perspective" that emphasizes "truth" as "something we do" in the fideist mold. Frame connects the "existential" to a sequence of thought that enables our biblical ethical conclusions, 231.

sense that our ethic is not the message itself. A potentially fruitful area for future discussion may be found by integrating the need for corporate confession as a call for social justice, presented previously, to the fideist approach.

Here we stand at the end of a whirlwind tour of the integration of worship and evangelism, and I am once again reminded of that powerful enduring image in this Baptist boy's heart, Leavell Chapel. Could even this symbol help us reconcile our commitment to these ever-important areas of evangelism and worship? Recently, on a mission trip to the NOBTS satellite campus in Miami, our music and worship students listened intently as a Cuban NOBTS gradudate sought to explain tearfully that the same feeling we might have felt in our hearts when we saw Disney World for the first time as kids overwhelms his heart each time he tops the "High Rise" entering New Orleans and sees that chapel ever beckoning to a desperately lost city. Was it worship that first caused this pang of emotion for my friend Carlos? Or is this emotion a precursor to evangelism as he can't help but declare his ever-new freedom in Christ to all to whom he comes in contact? It shall ever be both and yet one purpose for a kingdom citizen and for the church until his return, at which time we rest from our evangelistic labors forever and ever in the glory of his presence—may we burn brightly for him until that time.

BIBLIOGRAPHY

Ackroyd, P. R. In *The Cambridge History of the Bible*, edited by P. R. Ackroyd. Cambridge: University Press, 1963.

Aniol, Scott M. "How Does the Church's Ministry Relate to Worship," part five of "Worship and the Missio Dei." Religious Affections Ministries, April 25, 2013. http://religiousaffections.org/articles/articles-on-worship/how-does-the-churchs-mission-relate-to-worship/.

———. "The Mission of Worship: A Critique of and Response to the Philosophy of Culture, Contextualization, and Worship of the North American Missional Movement." PhD dissertation, Southwestern Baptist Theological Seminary, 2013.

Balentine, Samuel E. "I Was Ready to Be Sought Out by Those Who Did Not Ask." In *The Origins of Penitential Prayer in Second Temple Judaism*, edited by Mark J. Boda, Daniel K. Falk, and Rodney A. Werline. Early Judaism and Its Literature 23. Atlanta, GA: Society of Biblical Literature, 2006.

Barth, Karl. *Church Dogmatics*. Edited by Geoffrey T. Bromiley and Thomas F. Torrance. Translated by T. H. L. Parker, W. B. Johnson, Harold Knight, and J. L. M. Hire. Vol. 1 Part 2. New York: T&T Clark, 2004.

Bishop, William Robert. "Christian Youth Musicals: 1967–1975." PhD diss., New Orleans Baptist Theological Seminary, 2015. Accessed March 6, 2019. ProQuest Dissertations & Theses.

Boa, Kenneth D., and Robert M. Bowman. *Faith Has Its Reasons: Integrative Approaches to Defending the Christian Faith*. Waynesboro, GA: Authentic, 2001.

Boda, Mark J. "Confession as Theological Expression: Ideological Origins of Penitential Prayer." In *The Origins of Penitential Prayer in Second Temple Judaism*, edited by Mark J. Boda, Daniel K. Falk, and Rodney A. Werline, Vol. 1 Seeking the Favor of God. In

Early Judaism and Its Literature 23. Edited by Judith H. Newman. Atlanta, GA: Society of Biblical Literature, 2006.

Botz, Paschal. "Kyrie Eleison: Our Advent Prayer." *Orate Fratres XX* no. 1 (December 1945): 1–11.

Brown, Kevin J. "Racism and Our Definitional Challenge: Is Sin Simply an Individual Act?" *North American Association of Christians in Social Work Quarterly Newsletter*, 2019.

Brueggemann, Walter. *Israel's Praise: Doxology Against Idolatry and Ideology*. Philadelphia, PA: Augsburg Fortress Press, 1988.

Burkholder, J. Peter, Donald Jay Grout, and Claude V. Palisca. *A History of Western Music*. 8th ed. New York, NY: W. W. Norton & Company, 2010.

Erickson, Millard J. *Christian Theology*. Edited by Grand. 2nd ed. Grand Rapids, MI: Baker Academic, 1983.

Eskew, Harry, and Hugh T. McElrath. *Sing with Understanding: An Introduction to Christian Hymnody*. Rev. ed. Nashville, TN: Christian Street Press, 1995.

Frame, John M. *The Doctrine of the Knowledge of God: A Theology of Lordship*. Phillipsburg, NJ: Presbyterian and Reformed, 1987.

Getty, Keith. *Sing! Psalms*. The Getty Music Worship Conference. Nashville, TN, 2018.

Grudem, Wayne. *Systematic Theology: An Introduction to Biblical Doctrine*. Grand Rapids, MI: Zondervan, 1994.

Guder, Darrell. *Be My Witnesses: The Church's Mission, Message, and Messengers*. Grand Rapids, MI: Wm. B. Eerdmans, 1985.

Habermas, Gary, and Michael Shermer. "Is There Life After Death: A Dialogue between Gary Habermas and Michael Shermer." Presented at the Greer-Heard Point-Counterpoint Forum, New Orleans, LA, April 13, 2012.

Hurtado, Larry W. *At the Origins of Christian Worship: The Context and Character of Earliest Christian Devotion*. Grand Rapids, MI: Eerdmans Publishing, 1999.

Hustad, Don. *Jubilate II: Church Music in Worship and Renewal*. Carol Stream, IL: Hope Publishing, 1993.

Keener, Craig S. *The Gospel of Matthew: A Socio-Rhetorical Commentary*. Grand Rapids, MI: Eerdmans, 2009.

Kelley, Charles S., Jr. *Fuel the Fire: Lessons from the History of Southern Baptist Evangelism*. A Treasury of Baptist Theology, edited by Paige Patterson and Jason G. Duesing. Nashville, TN: B&H Academic, 2018.

Metaxas, Eric. *Bonhoeffer: Pastor, Martyr, Prophet, Spy*. Minneapolis, MN: Thomas Nelson, 2011.

Myers, Gary. "Perkins: The Gospel Leads to Gospel Proclamation." *New Orleans Baptist Theological Seminary News*. November 5, 2018. http://www.nobts.edu/News/articles/2018/Perkins2018.html.

Piper, John. *Let the Nations Be Glad: The Supremacy of God in Missions*. 3rd edition. Grand Rapids, MI: Baker Academic, 2010.

Powers, Mark C. *Going Full Circle: Worship That Moves Us to Discipleship and Missions*. Eugene, OR: Wipf & Stock Publications, 2013.

Schattauer, Thomas H. *Inside Out: Worship in the Age of Missions*. Minneapolis, MN: Fortress Press, 1999.

Stetzer, Ed. *Planting Missional Churches*. Nashville, TN: Broadman & Holman, 2006.

Stringer, Martin. *A Sociological History of Worship*. New York: Cambridge University Press, 2005.

Tozer, A. W. *Worship: The Missing Jewel*. Camp Hill, PA: Christian Publications, 1992.

Van Dijk, S. J. P. "The Bible in Liturgical Use." In *The Cambridge History of the Bible*, edited by G. W. H. Lampe, Vol. 2. The West from the Father to the Reformation. New York: Cambridge University Press, 1963.

Van Til, Cornelius. *The Defense of Faith*. 3rd edition. Nutley, NJ: Presbyterian & Reformed, 1967.

Webber, Robert. *Ancient-Future Worship: Proclaiming and Earning God's Narrative*. Grand Rapids, MI: Baker Books, 2008.

Westermann, Claus. *Praise and Lament in the Psalms*. Translated by Keith R. Crim and Richard N. Soulen. Atlanta, GA: John Knox, 1981.

Wheeler, David, and Vernon M. Whaley. *The Great Commission to Worship: Biblical Principles for Worship-Based Evangelism*. Nashville: B&H Academic, 2011.

Wiersbe, Warren W. *Real Worship: Playground, Battleground, or Holy Ground?* 2nd ed. Grand Rapids, MI: Baker Books, 2000.

Witherington, Ben. *Psalms Old and New: Exegesis, Intertextuality, and Hermeneutics*. Minneapolis, MN: Fortress Press, 2017.

———. *We Have Seen His Glory: A Vision of Kingdom Worship*. Grand Rapids, MI: Wm. B. Eerdmans, 2010.

Woodward, Gregory A. "Reconciling Evangelistic Methods with Worship Models: A Consideration of Apologetic Approaches in the Worship Framework." *The Journal for Baptist Theology and Ministry* 1, no. Fall (2010): 93–104. http://baptistcenter.net/journals/JBTM_7-2_Fall_2010.pdf.

Woodward, Gregory A. and William Bishop. "The Current State of Research as Related to Worship." *The Journal of Research in Worship Ministries*, no. 1 (Spring 2014): 1–28. Accessed March 6, 2019. http://www.worshipjournal.org/resources/PDF/HIstory%20Article.pdf.

Woodward, Gregory A., and Wm. Craig Price. "The Royal Psalms and the New Perspective." Presented at the Southwest Regional Meeting of the Evangelical Theological Society, Fort Worth, TX, March 31, 2017.

Wright, N. T. *Jesus and the Victory of God*. Christian Origins and the Question of God. Vol. 2 Minneapolis, MN: Fortress Press, 1992.

———. *Paul and the Faithfulness of God.* Christian Origins and the Question of God. Vol. 4. Minneapolis, MN: Fortress Press, 2013.

———. *The Case for the Psalms: Why They Are Essential.* New York: HarperOne, 2013.

Zacharias, Ravi. "Is Atheism Dead, Is God Alive." *Just Thinking* (podcast), Ravi Zacharias International Ministries.

———. "Is Atheism Dead, Is God Alive: Part One." *Just Thinking* (podcast), Ravi Zacharias International Ministries. July 30, 2018. https://www.rzim.org/listen/just-thinking/is-atheism-dead-is-god-alive-part-1.

PART 3

Practical Applications for Contemporary Evangelism

Personal Evangelism

LEADING PEOPLE TO JESUS

Bo Rice

The call for every believer to make disciples is made clear in the Great Commission. Matthew 28:18–20 states, "And Jesus came up and spoke to them, saying, 'All authority has been given to Me in heaven and on earth. Go therefore and make disciples of all the nations, baptizing them in the name of the Father and the Son and the Holy Spirit, teaching them to observe all that I commanded you; and lo, I am with you always, even to the end of the age.'"

In Acts, the gospel spread rapidly and miraculously. No megachurches, seminaries, Christian book publishers, or gospel witnessing tools existed. Yet the gospel spread powerfully. How might one be able to explain this? While extraordinary, the answer is quite simple. Jesus promised His disciples: "You will receive power when the Holy Spirit has come upon you; and you shall be My witnesses both in Jerusalem, and in all Judea and Samaria, and even to the remotest part of the earth" (Acts 1:8). Extraordinary power filled the disciples, who were ordinary people. Combined with frequent prayer and everyday gospel conversations, the gospel advanced rapidly to the nations. Jimmy Scroggins notes, "There was no power on earth that would stop them from sharing the good news that Jesus died for their sins, was buried, and God raised Him from the dead. They were put in prison, beaten, exiled, and martyred because they refused to stop telling people about Jesus."[1] Acts 4:13

---

[1] Jimmy Scroggins and Steve Wright, *Turning Everyday Conversations into Gospel Conversations* (Nashville, TN: B&H Publishing Group, 2016), 87.

notes how the people of the day viewed these disciples: "Now as they observed the confidence of Peter and John and understood that they were uneducated and untrained men, they were amazed, and began to recognize them as having been with Jesus." It was through these uneducated and untrained disciples the gospel went forth.

The power that equipped disciples in the early church equips and propels the church today. Scroggins noted, "This same fire has spread the gospel from Peter's first sermon in Acts 2 until today. It's ordinary people filled with the extraordinary power of God's Spirit who obey Jesus' command to go and make disciples. We are not ashamed of the gospel because we know it's the power of God for salvation (Rom 1:16)."[2] With such clear scriptural evidence of spiritual empowerment, one would think modern-day believers would feel as empowered and emboldened to accomplish the task of evangelism without hesitation. However, there still remains much fear and uncertainty.

A recent Barna Group report revealed a great concern about evangelism. The report stated, "A number of factors are curbing many Christians' enthusiasm for faith-sharing, including the decline of religion in America, a spreading apathy toward spiritual matters and a growing cultural suspicion of people of faith."[3] Surprisingly, this report revealed, "Christian Millennials feel especially conflicted about evangelism—and, in fact, almost half believe it is wrong to share their faith."[4] Interestingly, many of the generational respondents said they felt adequately equipped to share the gospel. Millennials were at the top of the list of those who felt equipped, with 73 percent saying they were confident in their ability to share their faith. However, almost half of this same group (47 percent) felt "at least somewhat that it is

---

[2] Ibid.
[3] "Almost Half of Practicing Christian Millennials Say Evangelism Is Wrong," Barna Group, accessed February 5, 2019, https://www.barna.com/research/millennials-oppose-evangelism/.
[4] Ibid.

wrong to share one's personal beliefs with someone of a different faith in hopes that they will one day share the same faith."[5] The report further stated, "Three out of five Christian Millennials believe that people today are more likely than in the past to take offense if they share their faith (65%) ... Millennials are also either two (Gen X) or three (Boomers and Elders) times more likely than any other generational group to believe that disagreement means judgment."[6]

What does this research reveal? Unfortunately, we see a growing number of Americans who identify as Christians and yet do not believe in practicing evangelism. The answer? David Kinnaman, president of Barna Group, says, "Even after they are committed to sustaining resilient faith, we must persuade younger Christians that evangelism is an essential practice of following Jesus ... As much as ever, evangelism isn't just about saving the unsaved, but reminding ourselves that this stuff matters, that the Bible is trustworthy and that Jesus changes everything."[7] Every believer must be reminded of Rom 10:14 and 17: "How then will they call on Him in whom they have not believed? How will they believe in Him whom they have not heard? And how will they hear without a preacher? ... So faith comes from hearing, and hearing by the word of Christ."

Barna Group's research points to fear as being the greatest barrier to evangelism today. The fear of the unknown, failure, and rejection has been typical in the past. However, the fear of manipulation is rising among evangelicals. Many point to this perceived manipulation by others as the reason they overcorrect and do not evangelize at all. Matt Queen stated, "Manipulation is a matter of the heart much more than it is a matter of practice. By guarding their own hearts, these believers can minimize their risk of manipulating others, who desperately need

---

[5] Ibid.
[6] Ibid.
[7] Ibid.

to hear the gospel proclaimed to them personally."[8] At this point, we must note the difference between manipulation and persuasion. Obviously, the use of manipulation in evangelism should be avoided. However, the Bible clearly states we should attempt to persuade people to place their faith in Christ. Paul wrote: "Therefore, knowing the fear of the Lord, we persuade men, but we are made manifest to God; and I hope that we are made manifest also in your consciences. ... Therefore, we are ambassadors for Christ, as though God were making an appeal through us; we beg you on behalf of Christ, be reconciled to God" (2 Cor 5:11, 20). *Persuade* in verse 11 can be translated as "to convince, or to win over." This desire to convince people to place their trust in Christ led Paul to beg people to be reconciled to God. His burden to convince people with the gospel must be recovered by the church today if we are to see a change in evangelism.

The lack of fear in a Holy God also affects evangelism. Queen stated, "All believers must embrace the fear of God, especially in terms of their witness for Christ."[9] In his commentary on 2 Corinthians in the *New American Commentary* series, David Garland remarked that the fear of the Lord in 2 Cor 5:11 refers to "a religious consciousness, a reverential awe of God, that directs the way one lives."[10] Paul desired to persuade others to be reconciled to God because he knew he would one day stand before the Lord and give an account for what he had done with the truth of the gospel. Queen stated, "Believers consistently living devoid of the fear of God, at best, will end in forfeiture of heavenly rewards and, at worst, will generate apathy for the lost."[11] The remedy to all fear in evangelism is reminding believers of the power found in the word of God and in the presence of the Holy Spirit in their lives.

---

[8] Matt Queen, *Everyday Evangelism* (Fort Worth, TX: Seminary Hill Press, 2015), 38.
[9] Ibid., 39.
[10] David Garland, *2 Corinthians*, New American Commentary (Nashville, TN: B&H, 1999), 269–70.
[11] Queen, *Everyday Evangelism*, 39.

When the believer is reminded of the power in God's word and the presence of the Holy Spirit, the importance of evangelism is pushed to the front of his or her personal walk with the Lord. This results in a desire to see people repent of their sins and place their faith in Christ for salvation. The issue then becomes how to practice evangelism in a natural and effective way. At this point, we must remember personal evangelism happens most naturally in the context of conversations. Believers must be intentional in starting conversations with people with the intent of sharing the gospel. These conversations occur naturally in relationships and in times of serving a person's needs. However, gospel conversations must occur if there is a desire to see people place their faith in Christ. That leaves us with the question: "What do we say in evangelism?"

Essential Elements of Gospel Conversations

Through the years, many resources have been created to offer simple approaches and methods of presenting the gospel in a clear manner. Some are shorter than others; some are simpler than others; some are more rigid than others. Yet most add value to the preparation of believers for evangelism. What matters most is that each resource is sound in biblical doctrine. I believe there are certain truths that must be shared in every conversation for it to qualify as a true gospel conversation.

Gospel conversations must begin with the reality of a holy God who created humankind in his image. This holy God desires a personal relationship with every human, but something prevents that personal relationship. At this point, a gospel conversation must reveal the problem of sin.[12] Every individual must face the reality that their sin separates them from God. The gospel is good news because it provides the remedy for sin. The good news message of the gospel is that Jesus

---

[12] John MacArthur, *Evangelism: How to Share the Gospel Faithfully* (Nashville, TN: Thomas Nelson, 2011), 151–63. The outline that follows is adapted from MacArthur's chapter, "Jesus as Lord: Essential Components of the Gospel Message."

Christ conquered sin. Through this conquering of sin, Christ offers an escape from punishment, free forgiveness, and the promise of everlasting life in the presence of God in heaven.

In order for sin to be conquered in the life of individuals, they must understand the call to repentance and obedience. Jesus declared, "Repent and believe in the gospel" (Mark 1:15). Paul wrote, "If you confess with your mouth, Jesus as Lord, and believe in your heart that God raised Him from the dead, you will be saved" (Rom 10:9). Peter preached at Pentecost, "Repent, and each of you be baptized in the name of Jesus Christ for the forgiveness of your sins; and you will receive the gift of the Holy Spirit" (Acts 2:38). As believers who practice evangelism, our conversations must be marked by telling sinners to turn from their sin.

Everyone has sinned, and that must be noted in a gospel conversation. This lets everyone involved in the conversation know no one is deserving of a relationship with God. As a result of our sins, no one deserves true peace with God. In fact, sin makes each of us worthy of death. Paul wrote, "For the wages of sin is death, but the free gift of God is eternal life in Christ Jesus our Lord" (Rom 6:23). Because of our sins, no one can earn salvation. This results in all of us remaining in a hopeless state. Fortunately, there is good news in the gospel—news about who Jesus is and what he has done for guilty sinners. Believers should tell the story of how God bridged the divide between his holiness and the sinfulness of man.

Every sinner needs to understand who Christ is in order to fully understand what God has done. Jesus is God, who has always existed: "In the beginning was the Word, and the Word was with God, and the Word was God. He was in the beginning with God. All things came into being through Him, and apart from Him nothing came into being that has come into being. ... And the Word became flesh, and dwelt among us, and we saw His glory, glory as of the only begotten from the Father, full of grace and truth" (John 1:1–3, 14). This reveals Jesus (as part of the Trinity) brought the world into existence with God during creation. Jesus then became a man so He could come to earth among sinners. Paul wrote of Jesus: "Who, although He existed in the form of God, did not regard equality with God a thing to be grasped, but emptied Himself, taking the form of a bond-servant, and being made in the likeness of men" (Phil 2:6–7). Though Jesus came in the likeness as man, He was without sin. Peter wrote of Jesus, "Who committed no sin, nor was any deceit found in His mouth" (1 Pet 2:22). Yet he chose to die on the cross even though he was without sin. Again, Paul wrote, "Being found in appearance as a man, He humbled Himself by becoming obedient to the point of death, even death on a cross. For this reason also, God highly exalted Him, and bestowed on Him the name which is above every name" (Phil 2:8–9).

This is the good news of the gospel. The sinless Son of God became a sacrifice for our sin even though he himself had no sin! Paul wrote, "He made Him who knew no sin to be sin on our behalf, so that we might become the righteousness of God in Him" (2 Cor 5:21). His death on the cross is what provided us a way to have salvation from our sins. Peter explained, "He Himself bore our sins in His body on the cross, so that we might die to sin and live to righteousness; for by His wounds you were healed" (1 Pet 2:24). The sin of mankind led Jesus to the cross. Yet the good will of God rose him from the dead. Paul wrote, "For I delivered to you as of first importance what I also received, that Christ died for our sins according to the Scriptures, and that He was buried, and that He was raised on the third day according to the Scriptures" (1 Cor 15:3–4). Through the death, burial, and resurrection of Christ, sinners are brought into reconciliation with God. Peter emphasized, "For Christ also died for sins once for all, the just for the unjust, so that He might bring us to God, having been put to death in the flesh, but made alive in the spirit" (1 Pet 3:18).

At this point, believers must tell others what God demands in order to receive forgiveness of sins and salvation. Sinners must be called to repent of their sins, place their faith in Jesus Christ, and trust him as Savior and Lord. The essential elements to every gospel conversation are as follows: understanding who God is; moving to the problem of sin; explaining the salvation that is provided in Christ through his death, burial, and resurrection; and calling sinners to repent of their sins and place their faith in Christ.

A Gospel Conversation Starter Guide

A simple way to explain all these truths is found in a gospel presentation known as the Roman Road. Dr. Kelley shared, "When the Holy Spirit led Paul the apostle to write the letter we call Romans, one of His purposes seems to have been to provide a thorough discussion of salvation. Perhaps more than any other book of the Bible, Romans seeks to explain what salvation is, why salvation is necessary, and how salvation happens. This concern with salvation has made Romans a popular book to use in telling others about Jesus."[13] What follows is an outline that is easy to remember while incorporating it into everyday gospel conversations, referred to most often as the Roman Road:[14]

1. Rom 1:20–21: "For since the creation of the world His invisible attributes, His eternal power and divine nature, have been clearly seen, being understood through what has been made, so that they are without excuse. For even though they knew God, they did not honor Him as God or give thanks, but they became futile in their speculations, and their foolish heart was darkened."

   We must acknowledge God as the creator of everything and understand how mankind fits into that creation.

2. Rom 1:16: "For I am not ashamed of the gospel, for it is the power of God for salvation to everyone who believes, to the Jew first and also to the Greek."

---

[13] Charles S. Kelley Jr., *Learning to Share My Faith: A Practical Guide for Successful Witnessing* (Nashville, TN: LifeWay Press, 1994), 20.
[14] Adapted from Kelley's *Learning to Share My Faith*.

God's power can make us secure. This verse teaches us there is a power in Christ that is great enough to bring salvation and deliverance.

3. Rom 2:4: "Or do you think lightly of the riches of His kindness and tolerance and patience, not knowing that the kindness of God leads you to repentance?"

   God's power results in change. In the Bible, this change is known as repentance. Repentance is allowing God to change the direction of our lives.

4. Rom 3:23: "For all have sinned and fall short of the glory of God."

   Every person has a problem. The Bible refers to that problem as sin. Sin makes change necessary. We must realize we all are sinners and we need forgiveness. None of us are worthy under God's standards. We may do a lot that is good, and we may try to avoid doing what is bad. However, none of us can ever measure up to God's standard of always doing what is right.

5. Rom 5:8: "But God demonstrates His own love toward us, in that while we were yet sinners, Christ died for us."

   The amazing truth of the gospel is God still loves us despite our sin. God revealed his love for us while knowing our sin and knowing it would result in the death of his Son. The sacrificial love of Christ overcame our problem with sin.

6. Rom 6:23: "For the wages of sin is death, but the free gift of God is eternal life in Christ Jesus our Lord."

   Scripture is clear that God is the judge of man. As judge, he cannot ignore the problem of sin in our lives. We deserve the rightful penalty of death because of our sin. In fact, since everyone sins, everyone deserves death and eternal separation from God. However, the good news of the gospel breaks through our deserving penalty. Though we deserve death, "the free gift of God is eternal life in Christ Jesus our Lord." The death of Jesus on the cross took our penalty. He took our guilt of sin upon himself so his death would take the judgment of God away from us. Jesus was our substitute! Our works earn us death, but his grace has granted us eternal life. This is a precious gift indeed.

7. Rom 10:9–10: "If you confess with your mouth Jesus as Lord, and believe in your heart that God raised Him from the dead, you will be saved; for with the heart a person believes, resulting in righteousness, and with the mouth he confesses, resulting in salvation"

Only those who recognize who Jesus is, what he did, and trust in him receive the free gift of salvation mentioned in Rom 6:23. Confessing him as Lord involves recognizing his rightful authority over us. This confession involves believing in his death in our place and placing our faith in him. Confessing him as Lord also involves repenting of our sins. Repentance means we turn away from our sin in order to follow Jesus. Believing in Jesus entails trusting in him by having confidence that the death and resurrection of Jesus are enough to secure our salvation. Belief in Jesus involves putting your life, both physically and spiritually, into his hands.

8. Rom 10:13: "Whoever will call on the name of the Lord will be saved."

Calling on the name of Jesus involves asking him for forgiveness of sin and trusting him alone for salvation. When you call on him, you are acknowledging him as your Lord and expressing your intention to live a life of obedience and service.

At this point, you will want to ask the person hearing the gospel if he or she wants to call on the Lord and be saved. If the person says yes, help them to understand how they can simply pray for salvation. Help him or her consider the cost of following Jesus even though the gift of salvation is absolutely free. If the person does pray to receive Christ . . .

9. Rom 8:16–17, 38–39: "The Spirit Himself testifies with our spirit that we are children of God, and if children, heirs also, heirs of God and fellow heirs with Christ, if indeed we suffer with Him so that we may also be glorified with Him. ... For I am convinced that neither death, nor life, nor angels, nor principalities, nor things present, nor things to come, nor powers, nor height, nor depth, nor any other created thing, will be able to separate us from the love of God, which is in Christ Jesus our Lord."

When we trust in Christ for salvation, God adopts us as his children, and the Holy Spirit assures us we are part of his family. Verses 38–39 tell us we are eternally children of God because the work of Christ was complete in defeating all evil forces. Nothing can separate us from God's love in Christ Jesus our Lord.

10. Rom 12:1–2: "Therefore I urge you, brethren, by the mercies of God, to present your bodies a living and holy sacrifice, acceptable to God, which is your spiritual service of worship. And do not be conformed to this world, but be transformed by the renewing of your mind, so that you may prove what the will of God is, that which is good and acceptable and perfect."

According to Rom 12:1–2, we should strive to live for Christ when we become a Christian. We can expect our lives to be different. God desires for believers to look less like the world and more like Jesus as we live for him. God brings about such change. He transforms us, making it possible to live a life that brings him glory. Continued trust in Jesus will help us to look and live like a child of God.

The Need to Lead People to Jesus

The need to lead people to Jesus is as great today as ever before. The call to practice evangelism is crucial for the church in America. Yet there are many people who profess to be Christians who do not believe it is good to do so. We must be reminded that the call to make disciples has never changed since Christ first commanded his followers to spread the gospel. There is an apparent need for the church to be constantly reminded of who God is and the salvation he has provided through Christ. Believers must be adequately equipped with the truth of God's word while learning to live out the truth of the gospel in an increasingly hostile world. Fear of rejection and the use of wrongful manipulation must not prevent the church from fulfilling the Great Commission. Learning to share the truth of the gospel in everyday conversation is as critical today as ever before. The world will continue to say that the practice of evangelism is wrong, but the church of Jesus Christ must never forget that the gospel is the power of God unto salvation to everyone who believes. But "how then will they call on Him in whom they have not believed? How will they believe in Him whom they have not heard? And how will they hear without a preacher?"

BIBLIOGRAPHY

Barna Group. "Almost Half of Practicing Christian Millennials Say Evangelism Is Wrong." Accessed February 5, 2019. https://www.barna.com/research/millennials-oppose-evangelism/.

Garland, David. *2 Corinthians*. New American Commentary. Nashville, TN: B&H, 1999.

Kelley, Charles S., Jr. *Learning to Share My Faith: A Practical Guide for Successful Witnessing*. Nashville, TN: LifeWay Press, 1994.

MacArthur, John. *Evangelism: How to Share the Gospel Faithfully*. Nashville, TN: Thomas Nelson, 2011.

Queen, Matt. *Everyday Evangelism*. Fort Worth, TX: Seminary Hill Press, 2015.

Scroggins, Jimmy, and Steve Wright. *Turning Everyday Conversations into Gospel Conversations*. Nashville, TN: B&H Publishing Group, 2016.

Personal Evangelism

COUNSELING AND THE GREAT COMMISSION

Brooke Osborn and Lorien Fleener

We live in a world of unprecedented suffering and brokenness. These human conditions include different types and levels of social and psychological suffering, which are often minimized, neglected, or, because they are beyond what local people can cope with at a given time, left unattended or addressed from out-of-context perspectives. These omissions are both unjust and costly to individuals and communities. Virtually all of the major public health problems in the world have a psychosocial component. A comprehensive approach to health is not possible without physical, communal, and psychological health.

    C. S. Lewis once said, "Mental pain is less dramatic than physical pain, but it is more common and also more hard to bear. The frequent attempt to conceal mental pain increases the burden: it is easier to say 'My tooth is aching' than to say 'My heart is broken.'"[1] According to John 16:33, we will not escape trouble in this world, so we must find ways to navigate the difficulties of life. The Chinese language can be complex and difficult to read and understand. What is interesting is the Chinese character for crisis is composed of two characters signifying danger and opportunity. This combination is seemingly appropriate

---

[1] C. S. Lewis, *The Complete C. S. Lewis Signature Classics* (New York: Harper Collins, 2002), 646.

considering we have two options when we encounter a crisis. We can choose to give in to despair or see it as an opportunity for growth and change.[2]

The church is one of the first places people, both believers and nonbelievers, consult when they are struggling. This gives the church an invitation to gather with those stuck in their darkest moments and introduce them to the light of the world. Many churches and ministry organizations are engaged actively in compassion ministries. These ministries come alongside those who are suffering, offer sympathy, and meet basic needs.[3] Some common examples of compassion ministries in our local churches are prison ministries and homeless ministries. When we look beneath the surface of those who are serving time in prison or those who are sleeping under the bridge, we see a common denominator, which is often mental illness. Around a quarter of those in prison and those who are homeless have a recent history of a mental health condition or are currently living with a serious mental illness.[4]

Like other organizations, many prisons lack the resources to properly rehabilitate those who have been incarcerated. The lack of resources leads to segregation. Our society is content to lock people up where we do not interact with them on a regular basis. We struggle to reconcile the sanctification process with the crimes people have committed. We desire to avoid pain and suffering at all costs, and this makes it disconcerting to hear the stories many of these people carry.

When dealing with the homeless, many believe they brought it on themselves. We are comfortable with that belief system because it means we can avoid the same situation. However, those in prison, those who are homeless, and those in a multitude of other difficult life circumstances,

---

[2] H. Norman Wright, *The Complete Guide to Crisis and Trauma Counseling: What to Do and Say When It Matters Most* (Ventura, CA: Regal, 2011), 128.
[3] Elise Mae Cannon, *Social Justice Handbook: Small Steps for a Better World* (Downers Grove, IL: InterVarsity Press, 2009), 35.
[4] "Mental Health by the Numbers," National Alliance of Mental Illness, accessed January 24, 2019, https://www.nami.org/learn-more/mental-health-by-the-numbers.

could be helped if we were to address the issue of mental illness in our society.

To address these problems and a multitude of others, the church must go beyond compassion and meeting basic needs. Instead, we should look below the surface and deal with the root cause of the issue. Addressing mental health needs and connecting people with resources will open even more doors for churches to share the gospel. In this way, churches can leave an eternal impact rather than a consumable need that will be gone quickly and forgotten easily.

Consider other opportunities that are available with the reality of living in a fallen world. Parents who are at their wits' end with their children seek guidance from their pastor. If a teenager commits suicide, the school reaches out to a local pastor to come and debrief with the students. A natural disaster occurs and churches mobilize to help those who have been caught in the devastation. In each of these situations, the church has an opportunity to take the gospel into a local home, a local school, across the nation, and in some cases, to the ends of the earth.

Many of these scenarios mentioned previously are the norm for churches and ministry organizations even if they are not equipped adequately for the task. During these times of crises, the question becomes, what type of impact does the church want to have in someone's time of suffering? A pastor may share some words of encouragement and offer some referral sources for the parents of a wayward teenager. But what happens weeks and months down the road when the counseling is not going well? Or maybe the parents struggled to connect with anyone on the pastor's referral list with any availability for counseling. The church has the opportunity to train, equip, and place people in each of these situations who are prepared to go the distance in meeting needs, showing compassion, and sharing the gospel.

The pastor, along with a few staff members, may go down to the local high school to visit one afternoon with some teenagers who have lost a dear friend to suicide. The school and the students appreciate their time and concern. Then, weeks or months down the road, students are struggling to accept the new normal or are still reeling from the guilt of how they could have helped their friend. A hurricane hits and ministries come in ready to offer food, clothing, and water to those who have lost everything. They may even gut out a house or two to help others rebuild. People are often in survival mode in the first few weeks after a natural disaster. What happens down the road when all of the resources have pulled out of the disaster? The full weight of what has happened hits the survivors. They are overwhelmed and no one else is around to offer comfort or support.

In each of the situations mentioned, pastors and church members have the opportunity to make a brief impact on those to whom they are ministering. We want to encourage those who are already doing the hard work to consider ways to extend their presence and impact potential in these situations. Staying the course with others during times of crisis will strengthen our relationship with them and deepen our conversations.

For the pastor who has made himself available to the school where suicide has taken place, why not continue to follow up with the students and the school after time has passed? When people are grieving and trying to come to terms with traumatic events that have taken place, they are often in a state of shock and disbelief. The real struggle may begin when the reality of what has occurred sets in, which is often the very time when resources are gone and others may have moved on and forgotten, even though those involved directly are struggling still.

In this situation, the church could continue the relationship by reaching out to the school. Church members could make themselves available on a regular basis to visit with the students and staff. The continual availability can lead to relationships and opportunities for gospel conversations. Making the most of these opportunities involves an internalized sense of awareness.[5] In our age of technology and instant

---

[5] Cannon, *Social Justice Handbook*, 106.

gratification, our lives can be so fast-paced we can be oblivious to those around us who are hurting and in need of help. This makes it easy for us to be task-oriented in our helping methods, rather than thinking about a long-term impact.

Church members are more likely to be involved in these ministry opportunities if they have been equipped. Some of these situations may require training and support for ministering to those who have experienced grief, crisis, or trauma. Training people in advance allows for them to be ready when something happens. Then, when a natural disaster occurs, not only can the church come prepared to gut houses and offer meals, but they can also come prepared to meet mental and emotional needs. Churches and ministry organizations should prioritize building a network of mental health and trauma-informed professionals who are prepared to equip and mobilize various ministry groups.

In working with those in crisis, it is important to determine the location of the people with whom we are working. Dr. Ian Jones stresses the necessity of helpers locating a person's relationship to self, God, and others when walking alongside someone facing a crisis. A better understanding of where they come from, the major influences in their lives, and how they arrived at their current season of life will help us meet them where they are.[6]

Discussions of worldview are a great foundation for effective evangelism and counseling. It is our held beliefs about how we see God, ourselves, and others that truly impact how we evaluate our lives in light of truth. These beliefs impact how we think, how we feel, and how we act. Gospel conversations allow the opportunity to understand a person's worldview and challenge them to consider the truths of Christ.

---

[6] Ian Jones, *The Counsel of Heaven on Earth: Foundations for Biblical Christian Counseling* (Nashville, TN: Broadman & Holman, 2006), 33–35.

For some, moments of crisis involve a time of searching. In many of these situations, there are three groups of people. The first group is comprised of those who have never believed but think there must be more to life than this. The second group involves those who have turned from their faith. They may have grown up in the church, but the circumstances of this life became so difficult they were not able to trust a God who would allow this to happen, so they walked away. The third group involves those who are believers and are wrestling with their faith.

With nonbelievers, their unbelief can often be traced back to a negative experience with faith. Maybe it was a person of faith who should have been trustworthy but who broke that trust. Perhaps it was a negative life circumstance, such as growing up in poverty or a series of traumatic events that left a lifetime of scars. Our earliest life experiences often provide the lens through which we view the world. These negative experiences may be a major obstacle in coming to Christ. Permitting nonbelievers to process past events may allow for a new perspective and help them to grasp the love God has for them.

Mary Jo Sharp noted, "Our actions flow from what we really believe. Thus, if a person hasn't deeply examined his or her current beliefs and compared them to what the Bible has to say, it is possible for him or her to act contrary to the Christian ethic."[7] A crisis may be the point at which we become aware our beliefs do not match our response. Adjusting to the unexpected turns that life takes may prompt us to examine the difference between our beliefs and actions. In other words, what are we really holding onto for life?

Unfortunately, our held beliefs and our actions are often in conflict. We may assent mentally to a truth but fail emotionally to let it impact our living. Moments of crisis open a door for those providing counseling to help a person's head and heart align. These types

---

[7] Mary Jo Sharp, *Defending the Faith: Apologetics in Women's Ministry* (Grand Rapids, MI: Kregel, 2012), 13.

of reflective discussions move the searching unbeliever to look for reconciliation between the thought that there is no God and a stirred heart that is convinced there must be something more. They provide moments for the person who left the church to see God once again as he truly is instead of through the heartbreak and disappointment of past circumstances. These discussions also encourage the faithful believer to grow, learn to suffer well, and live more fully in the face of life situations that do not make sense.

We see this conflict demonstrated in the events leading up to the cross. Peter boldly proclaimed he would not deny Christ, but Jesus saw his heart. Before the rooster crowed, Peter's actions did not match his intentions. The seemingly brave Peter, willing to wield a sword in defense of Christ, found fear in the driver's seat that overwhelmed his ability to follow through consistently with his beliefs. He was devastated. The fear that drove his actions resulted in shame, disappointment, and despair. Peter's sinful humanity revealed a disparity between head and heart that required the redemption of Christ.

While fear and shame crushed Peter in the midst of this crisis, redemption and hope would rebuild. The resurrected Christ guided Peter into healing and restoration. Returning to a charcoal fire, Peter received an invitation to follow Christ obediently with his head and heart. An evaluation of his beliefs not only restored but also prepared him for future difficulties.

In a chapel address at the NOBTS, Dr. Kelley said, "Aggressive evangelism without aggressive discipleship will eventually undo itself."[8] While choosing to follow Christ is the first step in the process, this worldview conversation can continue through discipleship. The great commission begs for more than decisions. It commands the development of disciples. Conversations in counseling allow for believers to

---

[8] Charles S. Kelley Jr., "The New Methodists" (chapel address, New Orleans Baptist Theological Seminary, New Orleans, LA, March 3, 2009).

examine their worldview in such a way that they move closer to living a consistent life in the truth Scripture reveals.

One of the most important things we can do is help believers grow and develop their spiritual lives. For most believers, this process involves refining. It is important for us to know what we believe and why we believe it. Our worldview "helps us understand where we come from, our heritage of who we are, our identity; why we exist on this planet, our purpose; what drives us, our motivation; and where we are going, our destiny."[9]

Modern media makes it impossible to escape the fact that individuals, groups, and even entire countries face seemingly unbearable crises daily. It can be easy to turn away or give into numbness as we sit bewildered by the trauma faced by those all too aware of the realities of this fallen world. But the call of Christ begs his church to respond differently. The traumatized need hope, healing, and the redeeming love of their Savior. The Great Commission commands Christ followers to meet the hurting with the gospel while the example of the Wonderful Counselor invites believers to learn how to sit in the trenches with the broken as he heals and restores. The work of counseling provides a great opportunity to address the issue of trauma through the intersection of the Great Commission with the work of the Wonderful Counselor. In fact, Diane Langberg, noted counselor and advocate for worldwide trauma work, asserts trauma could be one of the primary mission fields of the twenty-first century.[10]

---

[9] Armand Nicholi, *The Question of God: C. S. Lewis and Sigmund Freud Debate God, Love, Sex, and the Meaning of Life* (New York: Free Press, 2002), 7.
[10] Diane Langberg, *Suffering and the Heart of God: How Trauma Destroys and Christ Restores* (Greensboro, NC: New Growth Press, 2015), 9.

BIBLIOGRAPHY

Cannon, Mae Elise. *Social Justice Handbook: Small Steps for a Better World.* Downers Grove, IL: InterVarsity Press, 2009.

Jones, Ian. *The Counsel of Heaven on Earth: Foundations for Biblical Christian Counseling.* Nashville, TN: Broadman & Holman Publishers, 2006.

Kelley, Charles S., Jr. "The New Methodists." Chapel address of New Orleans Baptist Theological Seminary, New Orleans, LA, March 3, 2009.

Langberg, Diane. *Suffering and the Heart of God: How Trauma Destroys and Christ Restores.* Greensboro, NC: New Growth Press, 2015.

Lewis, C. S. *The Complete C.S. Lewis Signature Classics.* New York: Harper Collins, 2002.

"Mental Health by the Numbers." National Alliance of Mental Illness. January 24, 2019. https://www.nami.org/learn-more/mental-health-by-the-numbers

Nicholi, Armand. *The Question of God: C. S. Lewis and Sigmund Freud Debate God, Love, Sex, and the Meaning of Life.* New York: Free Press, 2002.

Sharp, Mary Jo. *Defending the Faith: Apologetics in Women's Ministry.* Grand Rapids, MI: Kregel, 2012.

Wright, H. Norman. *The Complete Guide to Crisis and Trauma Counseling: What to Do and Say When It Matters Most.* Ventura, CA: Regal, 2011.

Evangelism Strategy

THE ROLE OF PRAYER IN EVANGELISM

Jeffrey C. Farmer

One of the great evangelistic preachers of the modern age was Charles Spurgeon who was known to have said, "If sinners be damned, at least let them leap to hell over our dead bodies. And if they perish, let them perish with our arms about their knees, imploring them to stay. If hell must be filled, at least let it be filled in the teeth of our exertions, and let not one go unwarned and unprayed for."[1] Spurgeon emphasized the compassionate zeal all Christ followers must exhibit in order to make disciples of all nations.

Previous chapters have examined methods to keep sinners from going unwarned. This chapter will look at the importance of keeping sinners from going unprayed for. The most productive witnesses for Christ are those who devote significant attention to prayer. I often tell my students, "If evangelism is a car, prayer is the fuel." Prayer is so important for the believer who is engaged in gospel conversations. It aligns our hearts and minds with God. It makes us receptive to the Holy Spirit, who speaks through us to proclaim the gospel message. Believers can have all the evangelistic training, skill, and opportunity at hand, but without prayer, the power just will not be there. Ken Hemphill cautioned, "Prayer is in no way a squeaky wheel designed to manipulate God into remembering us."[2] He

---

[1] Charles H. Spurgeon, *Spurgeon at His Best*, compiled by Tom Carter (Grand Rapids, MI: Baker, 1991), 67.
[2] Ken Hemphill, *The Prayer of Jesus: The Promise and Power of Living in the Lord's Prayer* (Nashville, TN: Broadman & Holman, 2001), 10.

went on to say, "Prayer is not about answers. Prayer is about reward."[3] The reward is being brought into the Father's presence.

What is prayer evangelism? It is praying for the souls of the lost people in the world. What is church prayer evangelism? It is a group of believers gathered in unity (Matt 18:19–20), being taught how to pray (Luke 11:1), and praying in faith (Matt 21:22; Mark 11:24) for the lost (Rom 10:1–3, 1 Tim 2:1–8), who are their "neighbors" (Luke 10:25–37) lovingly by name (Exod 33:17; Isa 43:1), regularly and persistently (Luke 18:1–8), recording the answers and building faith (1 Chron 16:4).

Why does prayer evangelism work? Because prayer aligns our hearts with the heart and mind of God. We do not pray so God knows what we want or need. We pray so we might know God. Prayer wrestles against the powers and principalities (Eph 6:10–20) that keep people in spiritual bondage (Eph 2:1–4; 4:17–19) and which can deceive them away from the truth (1 Tim 4:1–4). Prayer also opens people's spiritual eyes (Col 1:9; Eph 1:17–19) and assists with the Holy Spirit's work of convicting them of sin, righteousness, and judgment (John 16:8). We are instructed to pray in faith and expect answers (Matt 21:22; Mark 11:24). The Scriptures tell us to pray believing we have received (1 John 5:14–15). Faith and holy expectation reach heaven. Finally, we are to pray lovingly by name for people. Names are important to God who knows us by name (Exod 33:17) and redeems us by name (Isa 43:1), and for some reason names have great power in the spiritual realm. Prayer directed personally and lovingly, in faith, on the basis of redemption of a soul, is powerful.

Promise

Jesus promised his disciples and his church that if we abide in him we will bear fruit. Jesus said in John 15:4, "Abide in Me, and I in you. As the branch cannot bear fruit of itself unless it abides in the vine,

---

[3] Ibid.

so neither can you unless you abide in Me." Christ followers abide in Christ through prayer and Scripture. It is by being so connected with Christ we are able to bear fruit. Prayer is essential to our abiding in Christ. Without our connection to Christ, our efforts will not bear fruit. This is true of internal fruit as well as external fruit. We would not display the fruit of the Spirit, which comes through the process of sanctification. We also would not have effectiveness in our witness. More likely, the non-praying Christian would not have a witness at all.

Jesus continued to describe what happens to those who do not abide in him: "If anyone does not abide in Me, he is thrown away as a branch and dries up; and they gather them, and cast them into the fire and they are burned" (v. 6). Lack of prayer is equal to ignoring God. The example of a non-praying Christian is not what God wants to bless. How unfortunate it would be for the church if the model of a Christ follower was one who does not pray! God will empower the believer who is faithfully following him.

Priest

A key function of Christ followers is to be priests. Within the Southern Baptist doctrinal tradition is the understanding of the priesthood of every believer. First Peter 2:5 states the church was "being built up as a spiritual house for a holy priesthood, to offer up spiritual sacrifices acceptable to God through Jesus Christ." Even further, Peter wrote, "But you are a chosen race, a royal priesthood, a holy nation, a people for God's own possession, so that you may proclaim the excellencies of Him who has called you out of darkness into His marvelous light; for you once were not a people, but now you are the people of God; you had not received mercy, but now you have received mercy" (vv. 9–10).

As a nation of priests, our job is to be intermediaries. We are to represent God before humankind since humanity has been cut off from the King of kings. We are also to represent man before God for the very same reason. Christ followers have access to the King of kings that the rest of the world does not have. While humanity searches for significance in the face of general revelation, Christ followers call the creator *Abba*—Father.

As representatives for Christ, our priestly mediator role requires we proclaim the good news to humanity. As representatives of humanity, we are to intercede on behalf of those who do not have access to the throne room. This intercession is our prayers. We are instructed in Scripture to pray for workers in the harvest (Matt 9:38), missionaries (Acts 13:3), public officials (1 Tim 2:2), unity in the church (1 Tim 2:8), and those who do not know Christ as Savior (Rom 10:1).

Prayer of Salvation

The chief end of all prayer is union with God. It can also be said that the beginning of union with God is through prayer. The humble supplication of a person under the conviction of the Holy Spirit leads to rebirth as an eternal child of God. The first step of salvation is to acknowledge sin, seek forgiveness through the grace of Jesus Christ, and serve him as Lord of all. This is accomplished through prayer.

Paul noted in Rom 10:9–10, "That if you confess with your mouth Jesus as Lord, and believe in your heart that God raised Him from the dead, you will be saved; for with the heart a person believes, resulting in righteousness, and with the mouth he confesses, resulting in salvation." The initial confession is to God. Subsequent confessions before the church and the world are also necessary, but first the new believer must confess Jesus as Lord to God.

In recent years, there has been controversy over the idea of the "Sinner's Prayer." The controversy is not because a sinner praying for forgiveness is wrong. The problem with the Sinner's Prayer is because of the abuse or misuse of a model prayer. Paul Chitwood traced the history of the Sinner's Prayer to early twentieth-century revivalism.[4] It

---

[4] Paul Chitwood, "The Sinner's Prayer: A Historical and Theological Analysis" (PhD diss., The Southern Baptist Theological Seminary, 2001), 61.

evolved into the sample prayer due to efforts in mass evangelism to make training simple.

There is nothing wrong with the content of the prayer itself. An example of the Sinner's Prayer can be found in the gospel tract, "Your Life: A New Beginning." It says, "Dear Jesus, I want to follow You. I turn from my sin and place my trust in You alone and ask for Your forgiveness. Right now, I receive Your gift of eternal life and confess You as Lord. Thank You for loving me and dying for me. Thank You for giving me new life. In Jesus' name, Amen."[5] Someone who genuinely prays this prayer will no doubt find salvation. The problem arises when the believer leads someone to recite the prayer with no understanding or meaning attached.

Since Christ followers are called to make disciples *and* teach them to obey the commands and teachings of Christ, teaching a new believer to pray is a natural first step. When a person states their need and desire for salvation, the evangelist should joyfully share that the first step to salvation is to pray. I always counsel the person how to pray and then encourage them to pray to God what is in their heart to say. The sweetest prayers of contrition are offered from the heart of a person experiencing the grace of God for the first time.

Rather than ask someone to repeat a series of phrases, we should counsel how to pray. Even the disciples sought instruction on how to pray. It is at the same time the simplest and hardest thing for a person to do. For some, there is an awkwardness in speaking to God face-to-face yet not seeing Him. For others, there is fear they might say the wrong thing. We should help the new believer by reassuring him or her that these thoughts and fears are not only normal but also unnecessary. As a father is excited to hear his child call his name, God is just as excited to hear from us.

---

[5] North American Mission Board, *Your Life: A New Beginning* (Nashville, TN: LifeWay, 2001), 9.

What counsel can we offer a new believer on prayer? My first lesson on prayer for someone who would like to repent is to say:

> The way that we receive God's gift of salvation is through prayer. Prayer is simply talking with God. You tell him what is on your mind and listen to his response. Romans 10:9–10 says, "If we confess with our mouth Jesus as Lord, and believe in your heart that God raised Him from the dead, you will be saved; for with the heart a person believes, resulting in righteousness, and with the mouth he confesses, resulting in salvation." This means you need to confess Jesus as Lord to God himself. Pray and acknowledge your sinful nature. Ask for God's forgiveness as it is available through the sacrifice of Jesus Christ. Then submit to God as the ruler of your life. If anything else comes to your mind to say, feel free to tell God.[6]

More often than not, the person will ask that I listen to them and help. I love to listen to these prayers! Teaching brand-new believers how to speak to their Savior is a blessing. Do not miss it by asking people to recite something from rote memory.

Prayer Instruction

As important as it is to teach new believers to pray, it is also necessary to instruct Christ followers on a regular basis. Prayer requires intentionality and persistence. Ole Hallesby wrote:

> Prayer is a fine, delicate instrument. To use it right is a great art, a holy art. There is perhaps no greater art than the art of prayer. The other fine arts require a great deal of native ability, much knowledge, and a great deal of money to cover the cost of a long and expensive period of training. Fortunately, such is not the case with the art of prayer. It requires neither

---

[6] This is a general summary of my instruction to new believers. While the conversation may vary to a certain extent, this is a good representation.

great native ability, much knowledge, nor money. The least gifted, the uneducated, and the poor can cultivate the holy art of prayer. However, certain requirements must also be met, if the art of prayer is to be acquired. In the main, they are two: practice and perseverance.[7]

Teaching Christ followers, new and old, how to pray is a valuable endeavor. One of the key lessons is to pray often.

Another lesson is the structure of prayer. There are many different approaches. Some use prayer outlines such as these:

ACTS Personal Prayer Format (Acrostic):
- **A**doration
- **C**onfession
- **T**hanksgiving
- **S**upplication

Personal Prayer Format:
- Listening
- Praise
- Thanksgiving
- Confession
- Intercession
- Petition

Prayer Walking Format:
- Worship—Praise, magnify God
- Welcome—Prayers of hope and vision. What do you want to see happen there?
- Weep—Cry for God's mercy for pre-believers.
- Warfare—Pray for deliverance

---

[7] O. Hallesby, *Prayer*, updated version, (Minneapolis, MN: Augsburg Press, 1994), 42.

Others pray as a running conversation with God throughout their day. There is a story of a teacher at a boarding school who was known for his devout prayer life. One night, the boys in his hall snuck into the teacher's room to hear his personal prayer time. As the teacher finished preparing for bed, he prayed, "Well, I'm done. I'll see you in the morning." He then turned out his lamp and went to sleep. The point is that while there are guidelines for prayer, it is intensely personal. Hallesby noted, "Prayer life has its own laws, as all the rest of life has. The fundamental law in prayer is this: Prayer is given and ordained for the purpose of glorifying God. Prayer is the appointed way of giving Jesus an opportunity to exercise His supernatural powers of salvation. And in so doing He desires to make use of us."[8] The most important rule about prayer is that we must pray!

Church Prayer Strategies

Instruction in prayer is often neglected in the church. Perhaps church leaders believe prayer is a discipline that should be caught rather than taught. I believe both modeling and instruction should be pursued. Church growth expert Kirk Hadaway noted, "Growing congregations are not only evangelistic and outreach oriented. They also place a greater emphasis on prayer."[9] Essentially, evangelistic and growing churches emphasize prayer as much or more than evangelism training or outreach efforts. Hemphill indicts the modern church's lack of prayer as an indication for declining churches: "We spend more time praying to keep dying saints who are prepared to die out of heaven than we do to keep sinners out of hell. There is little passion to our praying and little confidence that it really does matter."[10] In order for

---

[8] Hallesby, *Prayer*, 129.
[9] C. Kirk Hadaway, *Church Growth Priniciples: Separating Fact from Fiction* (Nashville, TN: Broadman Press, 1991), 163.
[10] Ken Hemphill, *The Antioch Effect: 8 Characteristics of Highly Effective Churches* (Nashville, TN: Broadman & Holman, 1994), 61.

the church to accomplish its purpose, it must help its members be more effective pray-ers.

In addition to preaching on the topic of prayer or teaching a Bible study on prayer, church leaders should schedule prayer times and events. These can include prayer chains, prayer partners, prayer groups, seasons of prayer for certain occasions, the development of prayer rooms, prayer retreats, prayer request cards, and prayer walking. The goal is to create an environment of prayer within the church to enable the church to reach out to the world.

Prayer Groups within the Church

Different types of prayer groups within the church are helpful for modeling and instruction at various comfort levels. Some believers thrive better in an intimate setting (i.e., prayer partners, prayer chains, or prayer small groups), while others find larger groups or events most helpful. These events could be midweek prayer meetings, but the prayer would need to be directed. Too often, midweek prayer meetings devolve into gossip sessions of who is sick or in the hospital. Prayer meetings must be intentional. Devote time for interceding for the lost people known in the church. It would even be helpful to develop a church-wide list of people who need to hear the gospel. I call this the church's "Most Wanted" list. Leading a church to pray for an individual's salvation creates an evangelistic atmosphere within the church.

Another type of prayer event within the church includes seasons of prayer. Some of these seasons may include a time of fasting. The leadership of the church must be clear in the purpose of the season of prayer. Why is the church devoting time to praying, for what are they praying, and how are they praying together (specific time, place)? If fasting is involved, the pastor must instruct the church on what fasting is and is not. Fasting is not just abstaining from food. We are to replace the time devoted to eating with prayer.

Prayer rooms and prayer retreats serve similar functions. Often a prayer room is set aside within a church to give church members a place to quietly reflect on Scripture and pray. These rooms can be very helpful, but the church leadership needs to regularly promote use of the room. Otherwise, the room will remain empty or end up being a storage room. Prayer retreats serve the same function as the prayer room—to withdraw from distractions in order to focus on prayer. I encourage a church to host prayer retreats in preparation for major initiatives (i.e., evangelistic campaigns, revivals, pastor searches, capital campaigns). It is important to seek the Lord's guidance before devoting time, attention, and resources to an endeavor.

Prayer Strategies outside the Local Church: Prayer Walking

Prayer walking is praying on site with insight. It entails praying in the exact place where you expect God to answer the prayer. It is praying for the community in the community.

There are several types of insight involved when we engage in prayer walking. First is responsive insight, which is praying with your eyes wide open. It is praying about what you observe in your community. As you walk through the community, you will undoubtedly notice indicators there.

For instance, on a recent prayer walk in a local neighborhood, I passed one house with kids' toys scattered in the yard, one house that was immaculately landscaped, one house that had bars on the windows, and one house that was in an advanced stage of neglect. For these houses, I prayed for the homeowners and families in specific ways. For the house with toys, I prayed the parents knew Christ and were leading their children to worship the Lord. I also prayed they were healthy and had energy to parent the child or children in that house. For the house with the immaculately landscaped yard, I prayed God would reveal himself there. I acknowledged the person took pride in their house and expressed concern to God that this homeowner was not materialistic—searching for joy in possessions. For the house with bars on the windows, I prayed they would know the peace of God. It was apparent the residents were living with fear. Christ is the only source of lasting peace and comfort. Finally, for the neglected house, I prayed the situation in the owner's life was not dire and that the residents were not living in turmoil.

The second type of insight utilized in prayer walking is research insight, praying specifically about what you have discovered about your community. If you want to knowledgeably pray for a community, utilize all types of research to understand what is going on in that community. Research includes reading newspaper articles about events in the community, talking with public officials, and talking with residents. Often many of the issues and concerns of a community are a matter of public record. This could be the crime rate, new schools or businesses, potential legislation, or various other issues that may arise when people deal with people. The church can prayer walk effectively with the knowledge that a bit of research will provide.

Finally, the third type of insight utilized in prayer walking is revealed insight, which is when you pray what the Holy Spirit reveals to you about your community as you walk through the community. The Holy Spirit assists believers as we offer up our prayers to God. Paul shared the promise of the Holy Spirit in Rom 8:26–27: "In the same way the Spirit also helps our weakness; for we do not know how to pray as we should, but the Spirit Himself intercedes for us with groanings too deep for words; and He who searches the hearts knows what the mind of the Spirit is, because He intercedes for the saints according to the will of God." God wants to guide us in prayer, and he provides us the means of praying in the Spirit by revealing how to pray.

Results of Prayer Walking

What are the results of prayer walking? First, prayer walking can engage the entire church in the community. Mature and immature believers alike can participate in prayer walking. In fact, it is a great tool to help new believers learn how to pray for the lost in their neighborhood. Prayer walking also opens our eyes to the realities in the community. Too often we are blinded by our own "bubble" within the community. This is particularly true in situations where you do not work in the same community where you live. People often are consumed with their own lives to the point they are unaware of what is going on around them.

Since people are often oblivious to the concerns in their community, prayer walking has another effect in that it enlarges our hearts for the community. I cannot fathom how a person could earnestly pray for another person and it not create compassion in the heart of the one offering the prayer. When we pray for the lost, the hurting, and the marginalized in our communities, we emulate the compassion of Christ. This prayer changes us in a fundamental way. It helps us to view others through the eyes of Christ.

Another result of prayer walking is that it cultivates a kingdom mentality and a passion to win the community to Christ. When our hearts have been refocused on the plight of the community and we see people the way Christ sees them, we love the people the way Christ loves us. It grieves us to know that the people we have been praying for—the people whose community we have prayer walked—are bound for hell. The idea that someone in the community is bound for hell because he or she has not heard the gospel is unacceptable for a Christ follower. We have received a mandate to make disciples of all the people on earth.

Finally, prayer walking prepares the way of the Lord in the community. By praying specifically for the needs of the community, and empowered by the Holy Spirit, the church will see God blessing people within the community. This will lead to changes in the community as God overcomes the harm done by generations of evilness.

How to Prayer Walk

The first step to prayer walking is to form a team of believers. This team needs to be small. Arriving in a neighborhood with a large group may cause fear or concern. Mobs are scary whether they are religious or not. If you gather a large group of believers for your prayer walk, make sure to split into smaller groups of three or four people. Then instruct the groups to prayer walk areas separately (one group per street or block).

The next step to prayer walking is to identify a territory. You will want to cover a small area slowly and expand from there. There is not a rush to cover ground. Take your time to walk and pray over an area. The area could be as small as a single street, a city block, or a neighborhood. Geography will play a part in determining the size, but always follow the guidance of the Holy Spirit.

Next you will follow a topic. Once your team is assembled on site, begin by reading verses of Scripture. Pray those verses over the community as you walk. Most importantly allow the Holy Spirit to guide you in the topic of prayer. I encourage prayer-walking teams to follow a similar prayer format. The format listed earlier is helpful (Worship, Welcome, Weep, Warfare), but any format can be used.

Finally, finish with a talk. Debrief with your group about what they learned during the prayer walk. Ask questions like: What did you learn? What did the Holy Spirit reveal to you? What further prayer effort does God want? Determine the next step for the community. Continue to pray, but allow God to guide you toward the next step. How could you present the gospel in the community? What needs exist within the community that your church can address? Remember that prayer walking is only one of the evangelistic tools to use in the community. Ultimately, you must proclaim the gospel there.

Personal Prayer Evangelism Strategies

While praying within the context of the local church is highly important, all believers own the commission to make disciples. Therefore, all believers should develop a personal strategy of evangelistic prayer. Two possible strategies are the *Oikos* Prayer Strategy and the Lighthouse of Prayer Strategy.

Oikos Prayer Strategy

The *Oikos* Prayer Strategy is a simple approach to develop a prayer list of the people within one's sphere of influence who are not Christ followers. *Oikos* is the Greek term for "household." For the purpose of this prayer strategy, *oikos* refers to all the people within a person's sphere of influence. The steps to developing an *Oikos* Prayer Strategy list are simple.

Begin by setting aside approximately two hours to prayerfully develop your list. Pray God will bring people to mind who are within your sphere of influence—people you know but you are not sure whether they are believers or not. Spend the next two hours writing down the names of everyone who comes to mind. The only people to exclude from your list are those people who you are absolutely certain of their testimonies. If you end up having a Christ follower on your list, that is fine. I doubt any believer would be upset you are praying for their walk with Christ. Strive to have at least one hundred names on your list.

Once you have your list of one hundred or more people, pray for the people on the list each day. You do not have to pray for the entire list each day, pray for as many as you feel led. I tend to pray for about ten people per day. Pray God would reveal himself to these people and that they would be receptive to hearing and believing the gospel of Jesus Christ. Pray for the Christ followers who interact with these people every day.

The next step is to select three to five people each week and find an opportunity to have a gospel conversation with them. Then, boldly proclaim the gospel to these people. If you find that one of the people on your list professes to be a Christian, ask them to share their testimony with you. Christ followers learn to share the gospel across contexts when they are familiar with different testimonies. As you listen to the testimony, pray for discernment. Many times, people profess to be Christian, but they do not have an appropriate understanding of what that means. Sometimes, some will say they are Christian because they grew up attending a church. Once I had someone tell me he was a Christian because he was an American citizen. If the person is legitimately a believer, celebrate his or her story and encourage one another to faithfully proclaim the gospel. If not, share the gospel.

As people on your list become Christ followers, note the date and the circumstances in your prayer journal. This is always a good practice so you can read back over the answered prayers at a later date. Whenever I am discouraged, there is great comfort in reading my personal accounts of God answering my prayers.

Finally, as you pray through your list, share the gospel, and meet people, keep adding to the list. The *Oikos* Prayer List is not a static, one-time document. It is dynamic. Add people as you meet them; remove people once they are saved.

Lighthouse of Prayer Strategy

In Matt 5:14–16, Jesus said, "You are the light of the world. A city set on a hill cannot be hidden; nor does anyone light a lamp and put it under a basket, but on the lampstand, and it gives light to all who are in the house. Let your light shine before men in such a way that they may see your good works, and glorify your Father who is in heaven." The Lighthouse of Prayer Strategy is based on your house being a gospel light in your neighborhood. Begin by praying for your neighbors: across the street, to the right, to the left, and directly behind you. Pray God will reveal himself to them, that they would be receptive to the gospel, and that you would have the opportunity to present the gospel and a Christ-honoring witness to them.

As you pray for these neighbors, look for opportunities to show God's love to them. Find ways to show you care for them. Perhaps you could mow their lawn if they've been too busy to do so. Maybe you can take care of a pet or collect their mail. Bringing a hot meal when your neighbor is sick is a possibility. There are infinite ways to show that you care.

By praying and caring for your neighbors, you are building relationships and creating opportunities to have gospel conversations. Following the Prayer-Care-Share formula is a simple reminder to be incarnational with your neighbors. As those immediate neighbors become Christ followers, expand your efforts to the next house out. As the light from the lighthouse penetrates further into the darkness, let your prayer efforts do the same.

BIBLIOGRAPHY

Chitwood, Paul. "The Sinner's Prayer: A Historical and Theological Analysis." PhD diss., The Southern Baptist Theological Seminary, 2001.

Hadaway, C. Kirk. *Church Growth Principles: Separating Fact from Fiction.* Nashville, TN: Broadman Press, 1991.

Hallesby, O. *Prayer.* Updated Version. Minneapolis: MN: Augsburg Press, 1994.

Hemphill, Ken. *The Antioch Effect: 8 Characteristics of Highly Effective Churches.* Nashville, TN: Broadman & Holman Publishers, 1994.

———. *The Prayer of Jesus: The Promise and Power of Living in the Lord's Prayer.* Nashville, TN: Broadman & Holman Publishers, 2001.

North American Mission Board. *Your Life: A New Beginning.* Nashville, TN: LifeWay Press, 2001.

Spurgeon, Charles H. *Spurgeon at His Best.* Edited by Tom Carter. Grand Rapids, MI: Baker, 1991.

Evangelism Strategy

THE PASTOR AS EVANGELIST

Reggie Ogea

The personal context for this article distills forty-two years of pastoral ministry and denominational leadership experience in a Southern Baptist Convention (SBC) setting. All my vocational ministry experience encompasses the field of pastoral leadership and pastoral ministry. The apostle Paul's last challenge before his death captures the role and function of pastoral leadership:

> I solemnly charge you in the presence of God and of Christ Jesus, who is to judge the living and the dead, and by His appearing and His kingdom: preach the word; be ready in season and out of season; reprove, rebuke, exhort, with great patience and instruction. For the time will come when they will not endure sound doctrine; but wanting to have their ears tickled, they will accumulate for themselves teachers in accordance to their own desires, and will turn away their ears from the truth and will turn aside to myths. But you, be sober in all things, endure hardship, do the work of an evangelist, fulfill your ministry. (2 Tim 4:1–5)

Nine imperatives in the text frame the role and function of a faithful pastoral leader and preacher. This article will address the eighth imperative—"do the work of an evangelist."

The noun *euangelistes* (evangelist) occurs only two other times in the New Testament—Paul's list of church leadership gifts (Eph 4:11) and the reference to Philip the evangelist (Acts 21:8). This third occurrence in 2 Tim 4 differs from the other two. Paul did not designate Timothy as an evangelist but challenged him "to do the work of an evangelist." However, the related verb *euangelizo* (to evangelize) and its derivatives are referenced fifty-four times, and the noun *euangelion* (gospel, good news) is utilized seventy-six times. John MacArthur affirmed both words are used "not only in relation to evangelists but also in relation to the call of every Christian to witness for Christ and of the responsibility of every preacher and teacher to proclaim the gospel of salvation."[1]

In *Fuel the Fire: Lessons from the History of Southern Baptist Evangelism*, Dr. Kelley lamented, "As I write these words, the SBC is in year 16 of the longest decline in baptisms in its history."[2] While doing the work of an evangelist does not define the primary and exclusive function of pastoral leadership, those of us who serve as pastors of churches must take some of the personal responsibility for this decline in evangelistic results. Dr. Bill Day, distinguished research professor at NOBTS, frequently shares his research results with the seminary faculty. During a week of faculty prayer meetings, Dr. Day concluded that if every member of clergy in the SBC would lead one more person to be baptized in a twelve-month period, the number of baptisms for that year would be the largest number in the history of the SBC.

Vocational Challenges

The role and function of a pastor consumes enormous volume and time constraints. The responsibilities of pastoral leadership, pastoral

---

[1] John MacArthur, *2 Timothy: The John MacArthur Commentary* (Chicago, IL: Moody Press, 1995), 185.
[2] Charles S. Kelley Jr., *Fuel the Fire: Lessons from the History of Southern Baptist Evangelism*, A Treasury of Baptist Theology, eds. Paige Patterson and Jason G. Duesing (Nashville, TN: B&H Academic, 2018), 1.

ministry, and pastoral care can consume all the pastor's time so little is left for family and personal enrichment. Time management then becomes the greatest vocational challenge for a pastor. The pastor must either control his time and schedule, or his time and schedule will control him. Growing demands upon a pastor's time increases the pressure to establish priorities.

Establishing Priorities

Every pastor struggles with what comes first, what must be done if nothing else gets done, and what constitutes an emergency. Unless and until a pastor settles priorities, life in the pastorate evolves into more reactive response instead of proactive action. No one Scripture defines the role and function of pastoral leadership better than the apostle Peter's exhortation in 1 Pet 5:1–4:

> Therefore, I exhort the elders among you, as your fellow elder and witness of the sufferings of Christ, and a partaker also of the glory that is to be revealed, shepherd the flock of God among you, exercising oversight not under compulsion, but voluntarily, according to the will of God; and not for sordid gain, but with eagerness; nor yet as lording it over those allotted to your charge, but proving to be examples to the flock. And when the Chief Shepherd appears, you will receive the unfading crown of glory.

Peter used the terms *elder* (respected leader), *shepherd* (pastor), and *overseer* (bishop) interchangeably for the same person—the leader of the congregation. This leadership exhortation confirms only two pastoral proficiencies: shepherding the flock and exercising oversight. Tracing the shepherd motif throughout Scripture verifies the main role and function of the pastor as the one who feeds the sheep. Shepherding certainly involves more than feeding, but feeding is the most critical function for the shepherd. In congregational life, that priority mandates the pastor's preparation to teach and preach God's word. In most congregations, that responsibility occurs multiple times a week, not just a Sunday sermon. Whatever else happens during a week of a pastor's life, he must be prepared to preach and teach God's word every week. I would add to the weekly sermon and Bible study preparation to include conducting weddings and funerals. Most weddings are planned and most funerals are unplanned. Weddings and funerals provide pastors unique opportunities to shepherd the flock.

Exercising oversight is the second pastoral proficiency. A pastor must give visionary direction to the church and assume ultimate responsibility as the respected leader. Oversight means assuming responsibility; it does not mean doing all the pastoral ministry and pastoral care alone. One person cannot meet all the ministry needs of a church. Even in smaller congregations, one pastor cannot grant every request for an appointment, visit every evangelistic prospect, see everyone with health issues, extend compassion to the homebound, tend to every benevolent situation, attend every meeting, and accept every speaking engagement. The shepherding function can be shared in larger congregations with multiple ministerial staff, but in most of the small and medium-sized churches, the pastor fills that role exclusively. However, in a church of any size, a pastor's effectiveness will be determined by how well he delegates, equips, and empowers others in shared ministry.

John Maxwell identified establishing priorities as the key to leadership.[3] As a pastor for twenty-one years in three churches of different sizes and demographic contexts, creating balance between family priorities, ministry/church priorities, and personal priorities defined my most constant and challenging struggle.

Family must be the pastor's first priority. Your family is your ministry. To be absolutely blunt, if you lose your family, you lose your ministry. Carving time for husband/wife relationships and parent/children/

---

[3] John Maxwell, *Developing the Leader Within You* (Nashville, TN: Thomas Nelson, 1993), 19–34 and *The 21 Irrefutable Laws of Leadership* (Nashville, TN: Thomas Nelson, 1998), 207–218.

grandchildren relationships must be first priority. One of the biblical qualifications for pastoral leadership implies family priority. The apostle Paul's list of pastoral qualifications in 1 Tim 3 includes this implication: "He must be one who manages his own household well, keeping his children under control with all dignity (but if a man does not know how to manage his own household, how will he take care of the church of God?)" (vv. 4–5). Ministry and church functions must never crowd out family priorities.

Balancing ministry functions and church activities involves difficult choices. Determine a weekly schedule and be disciplined to stick to it. Seek God's wisdom and your spouse's affirmation. Allow your personality and family rhythm to shape your schedule. Be wise to not overschedule, leaving no room for interruptions. Crises need immediate and urgent attention. I agree with John Bisagno: "People never *interrupt* our ministry; they *are* our ministry ... what might seem like 'just another interruption' to your day might be life and death to the person on the other end of the line."[4]

Often lost in the balancing act of establishing priorities is time for personal wellness and enrichment. In *Building Blocks for Longer Life and Ministry*, Tommy Yessick warned, "A coming dilemma for the church as a whole is brought on from two fronts (1) the expectations of the congregation placed on the minister and (2) the minister's neglect of self-care as a substitute or excuse for being a caregiver for others."[5] Yessick's warning of a *coming* dilemma has now become a *common* dilemma. Yessick asserted a balance of six dimensions of personal well being to

---

[4] John Bisagno, *Pastor's Handbook* (Nashville, TN: B&H Publishing Group, 2011), 78.
[5] Tommy Yessick, *Building Blocks for Longer Life and Ministry* (Nashville, TN: Convention Press, 1997). See also H. B. London Jr. and Neil B. Wiseman, *Pastors at Greater Risk* (Ventura, CA: Regal Books, 2003), first published as *Pastors at Risk*, 1993. On a personal note, as director of the professional doctoral programs at NOBTS since 2003, we utilize Yessick's Wellness Assessment Tool in our required Mid-Career Assessment Workshop. This workshop for professional doctoral students receives the highest evaluation of all of our workshops and seminars every year.

reverse this ministerial neglect of self-care: spiritual, emotional, intellectual, physical, social, and vocational. A wise pastoral leader will give close attention to all of these dimensions of wellness.

By now, you may be wondering, "What does establishing priorities have to do with the pastor as evangelist?" Well, glad you asked. In the midst of creating balance between family, ministry/church, and personal priorities, a pastor must work into that priority balance a strategy for both personal evangelism and church evangelism. For a pastor to "do the work of an evangelist" requires a sense of urgency.

A Sense of Urgency

Space will not permit a lengthy discussion of a theology of evangelism contained within soteriology (doctrine of salvation) and ecclesiology (doctrine of the church). In my first pastorate, as a seminary student, I wrestled with and settled three convictions that framed my commitment to do the work of an evangelist. A conviction is a strong persuasion beyond reasonable doubt.

First, no one gets to heaven without an encounter with Jesus. Two biblical declarations bookend this conviction: The words of Jesus Himself in John 14:6—"I am the way, and the truth, and the life; no one comes to the Father but through Me," and the deposition of Simon Peter in Acts 4:11–12—"[Jesus] is the stone which was rejected by you, the builders, but which became the chief corner stone. And there is salvation in no one else; for there is no other name under heaven that has been given among men by which we must be saved."

Second, no one has an encounter with Jesus apart from preaching and personal witness. With the craft of an experienced defense attorney, the apostle Paul asserted the centrality of preaching in the salvation experience in Rom 10:13–17:

> "Whoever will call on the name of the Lord will be saved."
> How then will they call on Him in whom they have not believed? How will they believe in Him whom they have not

heard? And how will they hear without a preacher? ... So faith comes from hearing, and hearing by the word of Christ.

While preaching provides the public forum for the salvation experience, personal witnessing produces the incubation for an encounter with Jesus. Personal witnessing is every Christian's responsibility. However, a church is not likely to be evangelistic unless "the pastor is personally committed to the task—there must be in the heart of the undershepherd a burning desire to see people saved."[6]

Third, no one is beyond the reach of God's hand. Three Scripture passages capture this powerful reminder:

- Isa 59:1: Behold, the LORD's hand is not so short that it cannot save; nor is His ear so dull that it cannot hear.
- 1 Tim 2:3–4: This is good and acceptable in the sight of God our Savior, who desires all men to be saved and to come to the knowledge of the truth.
- 2 Pet 3:9: The Lord is not slow about His promise, as some count slowness, but is patient toward you, not wishing for any to perish but for all to come to repentance.

Jesus modeled one-on-one encounters with individuals, many who were considered beyond the reach of God's hand.[7] The second half of the book of Acts narrates witnessing encounters with individuals who represented people groups beyond the reach of God's hand.[8]

---

[6] Joe H. Cothen, *The Pulpit Is Waiting: A Guide for Pastoral Preaching* (Gretna, LA: Pelican Publishing, 1998), 128.
[7] See G. Campbell Morgan, *The Great Physician: The Method of Jesus with Individuals* (Old Tappan, NJ: Fleming H. Revell, 1937); Robert E. Coleman, *The Master Plan of Evangelism* (Grand Rapids, MI: Revell, 1963); Jerry Vines, *Interviews with Jesus* (Nashville: Broadman Press, 1981); and Delos Miles, *How Jesus Won Persons* (Nashville, TN: Broadman Press, 1982).
[8] Philip and the Ethiopian eunuch, Acts 8; Ananias and Saul of Tarsus, Acts 9; Peter and Cornelius, Acts 10; Paul and Silas and the Philippian jailor, Acts 16; Paul's testimony before Felix, Festus, and King Agrippa, Acts 24—26.

These three convictions must be settled beyond reasonable doubt in order to maintain a sense of evangelistic urgency. Without evangelistic urgency, a pastor's personal evangelism strategy will either be nonexistent or "hit and miss" at best. My colleague and professor of evangelism at NOBTS, Mark Tolbert, reminds us often, "Pastors don't naturally drift *toward* evangelism—they drift *away* from evangelism."

Viable Competencies

Framed by the vocational challenges of establishing priorities and maintaining a sense of urgency, what are some viable competencies every pastor can develop to do the work of an evangelist? Competency defines skill development, and skill development takes time and practice. Competencies must be filtered through the personality and spiritual giftedness of the individual pastor. I had to learn how to be "comfortable in my own skin." Allow me to share three competencies with some personal examples.

Personal Evangelism Competencies

Learning to share Jesus with those personally lost and spiritually unchurched never came natural for me. I forced myself to learn numerous personal witnessing techniques, such as sharing my personal salvation testimony in two minutes or less; utilizing gospel tracts, such as the Roman Road, the Four Spiritual Laws, and How to Have a Full and Meaningful Life; and learning and participating in extensive evangelism programs, such Lay Evangelism Schools (LES), Witness Involvement Now (WIN), Evangelism Explosion (EE), Continuous Witness Training (CWT), Building Witnessing Relationships (BWR) and FAITH Evangelism, and One-Day Soul-Winning Workshops. Eventually, I settled on a personal method, which borrowed from all of these techniques. Sometimes I use the Roman Road. Sometimes I pose a question, like the one from CWT, "If you were to stand before God and he were to ask you, 'Why should I let you into my heaven,' what would you say to Him?" Sometimes I shared my brief personal testimony, involving my life before Christ, how I received Christ, and my life since receiving Christ. No one method worked well all of the time. Each individual encounter called for contextualization.[9]

Friendship Evangelism Competencies

While a seminary student in the late 1970s, Wayne McDill's book *Making Friends for Christ* radically shaped my pastoral evangelistic approach. McDill's friendship evangelism strategy hinged on the principle that "evangelism will be effective toward making disciples in direct proportion to its dependence on the establishment and cultivation of meaningful relationships."[10]

Since then, I have kept a friendship hit list—a list of individuals and families with whom I am intentionally building relationships with the view of winning them to Christ. One of my greatest joys is to mark people off the list when they make that decision. And that's the only way they get marked off the list![11]

Ministry Evangelism Competencies

One of the hardest evangelistic ministries, but also one of the richest, is what Delos Miles and Robert Dale called "evangelizing the hard-to-reach." They described categories of unchurched persons and outreach approaches tailored to their particular needs: the Left-Outs, the Drop-Outs, the Locked-Outs, and the Opt-Outs.[12] These are the

---

[9] These resources have encouraged and mentored me in developing my personal evangelism competencies. Murray Downey, *The Art of Soul-Winning* (Grand Rapids, MI: Baker Book House, 1957); Paul E. Little, *How to Give Away Your Faith* (Downers Grove, IL: Intervarsity Press, 1966); Bill Bright, *Witnessing Without Fear* (San Bernardino, CA: Here's Life Publishers, 1987); William Fay, *Share Jesus Without Fear* (Nashville, TN: B&H Publishing, 1999).

[10] Wayne McDill, *Making Friends for Christ: A Practical Approach to Relational Evangelism* (Nashville, TN: Broadman Press, 1979), 6. See also Joseph C. Aldrich, *Gentle Persuasion: Creative Ways to Introduce Your Friends to Christ* (Portland, OR: Multnomah Press, 1988).

[11] This strategy proved effective in reaching lost and unchurched men. See the section "Reaching Men" later in this article.

[12] Robert D. Dale and Delos Miles, *Evangelizing the Hard-To-Reach* (Nashville, TN: Broadman Press, 1986).

people Jesus challenged his disciples to reach out to—"the least of these" (Matt 25:31–46).

My passion as a pastor doing the work of an evangelist moved me to seek out Christians who had a passion for the hard-to-reach. Some of those Christians were members of the churches I served as pastor. Some of those Christians were involved in other churches and faith-based organizations. When a Christian with a passion for ministry to an unchurched demographic approached me, my response was usually, "I'll be praying God will give you wisdom about starting that ministry. When you find at least two other people who share your passion, the three of you come back and talk to me and, together, we'll get started." That statement exposed the seriousness of the person. Many times, I never heard back from the individual. But sometimes he or she would return with their passionate friends, ready to get started. Most of my ministry evangelism initiatives started that way, and as their pastor, I became their greatest cheerleader.[13]

Every pastor interested in ministry evangelism should read Charles Roesel's book *It's a God Thing*.[14] Dr. Roesel's personal testimony and the powerful stories from First Baptist Church, Leesburg, Florida, should motivate every pastor to do "least of these" evangelism and should challenge every church to engage in ministry evangelism.

Volitional Commitments

Vocational challenges and viable competencies enable the pastor-evangelist to focus on specific areas of intentional evangelism. These

---

[13] Space in this article will not permit me to share the stories of a teen center for drug and alcohol recovery, a lay-counseling ministry for troubled marriages, an after-school program for single-parent children, an ESL ministry to several ethnic groups, a Christmas party for children of incarcerated fathers, church plants to reach Laotians and Hispanics, partnering with the Gideons in various Bible distribution projects, etc., etc., etc.

[14] Charles L. Roesel, *It's a God Thing: The Powerful Results of Ministry Evangelism* (Abbotsford, WI: Life Sentence Publishing, 2014).

volitional commitments should merge personal proficiencies with ministry context. Three areas of impact produced effective evangelistic results in my ministry journey.

Evangelizing Children

Even a casual reading of the gospels confirms Jesus welcomed children: "But Jesus said, 'Let the children alone, and do not hinder them from coming to Me; for the kingdom of heaven belongs to such as these'" (Matt 19:14).[15] Therefore, a pastor must determine his theological position on the salvific potential of children. Can children personally profess their faith in Jesus Christ? Is there an acceptable "age of accountability"? What depth of understanding should we accept to validate a profession of faith? Can a childhood salvation experience endure for a lifetime?

My personal testimony informed my theology and practice of evangelizing children. I experienced the privilege of being raised in a Christian home by Christian parents who practiced their faith. I never knew a time in my childhood when church attendance and spiritual formation was not a high family priority. Our family attended church weekly and were involved in worship attendance and age-group Bible study. My earliest memory can recall a knowledge of biblical characters and content as a result of weekly Bible classes and pastoral sermons. I remember distinctly as my eighth birthday approached struggling with questions: Did Jesus really die on the cross to save me from my sins? If I died before acknowledging Jesus as Lord and Savior, would I be doomed to hell? Was I too young to be saved? Although I could not theologically describe my decision, one Sunday night in our small Baptist church, I walked forward when my pastor extended a gospel invitation and activated my personal profession of faith in Jesus Christ. Baptized soon after that Sunday evening decision, I lived the duration of my childhood and teenage years without any critical challenges to my faith.

---

[15] Literally, "heaven is of such ones." See also Mark 10:15 and Luke 18:17.

However, as a high school senior, I wrestled with doubts and uncertainties. Had I really received salvation at age eight? How could I be sure? Were these doubts and questions an indication my childhood salvation experience had not been real? Since my knowledge of theological terms and life experience now advanced far beyond my childhood, and to seek to eliminate all doubt and uncertainty, I marched forward during a revival service at another church and pledged my profession of faith all over again. I will be grateful for all eternity to my wise father who insisted I speak with our pastor about my decision to be "saved again."

I remember that Saturday morning like it happened yesterday. Our pastor, though seminary trained, served as a pastor of small churches for the entirety of his vocational ministry. He could have rejoiced in my decision and proceeded to baptize me again for the second time. However, he opened his well-worn Bible and read to me the words of Jesus from John 10:27–28: "My sheep hear my voice, and I know them, and they follow Me. And I give eternal life to them, and they will never perish; and no one will snatch them out of My hand." He further explained when a person volitionally and willfully professes their faith in Jesus Christ, from that point forward, God is holding onto them and keeping their salvation secure. He asked me directly, "Do you trust the grip of God to hold onto your salvation?" He then explained to me that assurance of salvation and eternal security meant trusting by faith that God's grip would be strong enough to hold onto my salvation, through any life situation, challenging circumstance, and even the doubts and discouragements hurled at me by Satan himself.

I believe in evangelizing children because I am a product of childhood salvation. The same God who can deliver adults from the worst of sins and circumstances can also protect children from the worst of sins and circumstances. I would rather be saved *from* a life of sin and chaos than saved out of a life of sin and chaos.[16]

---

[16] See Adam Harwood and Kevin Lawson, *Infants and Children in the Church: Five Views on Theology and Ministry* (Nashville: B & H Academic, 2017) and Tony Evans, *Raising Kingdom Kids* (Carol Stream, IL: Tyndale House, 2014).

When I became a father, I wanted my children to experience assurance of salvation and eternal security. I could not bear the thought that I would hinder my children from a meaningful relationship with Jesus Christ. All three of my children experienced childhood salvations followed by believer's baptism. And now as a grandparent, that desire is even stronger for my grandchildren. As I write this article, five of our six grandchildren have experienced childhood salvations and followed through in believer's baptism. Our youngest grandchild is only five, but we are confident that in due time he will personally profess his faith in Jesus. I cannot bear the thought of standing before God one day and lamenting that I failed to evangelize my own children and grandchildren.[17]

My personal experience led me as a pastor to maximize ministries for the purpose of evangelizing children. Weekly Bible study groups for children and youth, Vacation Bible School, and preteen summer camps provide rich potential and opportunity to evangelize children. These ministries demand leadership development, strategic planning, and financial resources. Equip and train spiritually mature volunteer leaders to facilitate weekly small groups and mentor children. Strategically plan and execute a gold standard Vacation Bible School every summer, one that not only impacts the church kids but involves families of unchurched children.

The senior pastor should be the best evangelist in his congregation. Schedule time periodically with the weekly children's Bible studies to share the gospel. I may be biased, but I believe the pastor should be the worship leader of the Vacation Bible School and should schedule a time to share the basics of salvation, especially with the older children's groups. Develop an annual process of preteen summer camps, where the fourth through sixth graders can experience a concentrated week of fun, activity, and worship. Embed in the camp worship venue

---

[17] See Dr. Kelley's sobering indictment: "An analysis of SBC baptisms during the decline reveals that biggest issue driving the decline. Southern Baptists stopped reaching their own children." *Fuel the Fire*, 218.

opportunities for children to experience salvation. Subsidize the cost of the camp through the church budget and scholarships.

Healthy churches intentionally evangelize children. Theologically sound churches will not hinder the children from coming to Jesus. Every pastor can do the work of an evangelist by evangelizing children.

Reaching Men

By biblical design, God created male and female and designated unique function for them in a marriage relationship. (See Eph 5:21–33; Col 3:18–21.) The Baptist Faith and Message states the marriage relationship "models the way God relates to His people. A husband is to love his wife as Christ loved the church. He has the God-given responsibility to provide for, to protect, and to lead his family."[18] When a husband and father embraces his God-given responsibility to lead his family, the strong implication exists that to reach families starts with reaching the husbands and fathers of the families.

With rare exception, churches will be populated with more godly wives and mothers who involve their children in spiritual formation than godly men who lead their families. Pastors must not only model by example the biblical function of husbands and fathers but must also create an atmosphere and attitude within the church that encourages men to be servant leaders of their families. Reaching men must become an intentional initiative for the pastor-evangelist. I agree with Steve Farrar:

> God knows the importance of family chains because He invented the family chain. And that's why God puts such importance on each father successfully anchoring his line in the family chain. I'm responsible to take care of my link, and you are responsible to take care of yours."[19]

---

[18] "The Baptist Faith and Message 2000," Article XVIII, "The Family," Southern Baptist Convention.
[19] Steve Farrar, *Anchoring the Family Chain* (Nashville: Thomas Nelson Publishers, 1998), 3–5. See also Patrick Morley, *No Man Left Behind: How to Build and Sustain a Disciple-Making Ministry for Every Man in Your Church* (Chicago, IL: Moody Publishers, 2006).

Reaching men involves building strong relationships. The pastor's unique position in a congregational context allows him access to the husbands and fathers of those families who are active in the congregation. Start there, and seek to build bridges of friendship where evangelistic opportunity exists. For example, when children personally profess their faith in Christ and desire Christian baptism, make their baptismal event a family event. Husbands and fathers who previously indicated little or no spiritual interest will respond positively to those moments. I have witnessed the initial spiritual journey of husbands and fathers beginning with the spiritual interest of their wives and children.

Special events that target men produce relationship building and provide opportunities to reach men. Wild-game suppers, first-responder/law enforcement appreciation banquets, sports venues, men's retreats, and car shows are just some of the ways to target the interests of men. Identify what would attract men in your community context and create events of connection. The pastor should equip and empower the men of the congregation to plan and promote these events and then be involved as an active participant.

Community Involvement

The pastor's involvement in community organizations will unveil unique evangelistic opportunities. Civic clubs provide unbelievable opportunity to build relationships with key business leaders in the community. Most civic clubs meet regularly as a social event, enabling the pastor to build peer-to-peer relationships with the club members. Most civic clubs also participate in several community events during the year as service projects. In two of my pastorates, I negotiated as part of my compensation for the church to pay my dues in the local Rotary Club. In both of these instances, I was the only clergy in the club, so I immediately earned the respect of the other club members. These business leaders became my friends and in time would consult me for spiritual counsel and advice in their personal lives. Some of these relationships resulted in gospel conversations, some of the gospel conversations led to salvation experiences, and some of the salvation experiences produced baptism and church membership.

If civic club memberships are not available, the pastor can offer his service in other community endeavors. In addition to my civic club involvement, I served as chaplain for the local high school football team, preached weekly in a jail ministry, conducted nursing home services, and served meals at a faith-based food kitchen. Some of my most fruitful evangelistic opportunities developed as a result of my involvement in these community organizations.

Doing the work of an evangelist is hard work, consistent work, consuming work, rewarding work, and eternal work. Hard work requires effort. Consistent work calls for intentionality. Consuming work necessitates commitment. Rewarding work entails persistence. Eternal work demands focus.

Evangelistic skills and competencies are taught, but evangelistic passion and zeal are caught. Effective pastoral leadership is always leadership from the front. Leadership from the front requires a pastor to set an example for the congregation. To say it plainly and clearly: I could never expect from the congregation what I was not willing to do. However, when I effectively modeled for the congregation doing the work of an evangelist, then I could expect that some of what they saw me doing would rub off on them and challenge them to join me in doing the work of an evangelist.

BIBLIOGRAPHY

Aldrich, Joseph C. *Gentle Persuasion: Creative Ways to Introduce Your Friends to Christ*. Portland, OR: Multnomah Press, 1988.

Armstrong, Richard Stroll. *The Pastor as Evangelist*. Philadelphia, PA: Westminster Press, 1984.

Barna Group. *Gen Z: The Culture, Beliefs, and Motivations Shaping the Next Generation*. Ventura, CA: Barna Group, 2018.

Bisagno, John. *Pastor's Handbook*. Nashville, TN: B&H Publishing Group, 2011.

Bright, Bill. *Witnessing Without Fear*. San Bernardino, CA: Here's Life Publishers, 1987.

Bryant, James W., and Mac Brunson. *The New Guidebook for Pastors*. Nashville, TN: B&H Publishing, 2007.

Coleman, Robert E. *The Master Plan of Evangelism*. Grand Rapids, MI: Revell, 1963.

Cothen, Joe H. *The Pulpit Is Waiting: A Guide for Pastoral Preaching*. Gretna, LA: Pelican Publishing, 1998.

Dale, Robert D., and Delos Miles. *Evangelizing the Hard-To-Reach*. Nashville, TN: Broadman Press, 1986.

Downey, Murray. *The Art of Soul-Winning*. Grand Rapids, MI: Baker Book House, 1957.

Evans, Tony. *Raising Kingdom Kids*. Carol Stream, IL: Tyndale House, 2014.

Farrar, Steve. *Anchoring the Family Chain*. Nashville, TN: Thomas Nelson Publishers, 1998.

Fay, William. *Share Jesus Without Fear*. Nashville, TN: B&H Publishing Group, 1999.

Green, Michael. *Evangelism in the Early Church*. Grand Rapids, MI: Eerdmans, 1970.

Harrison, Rodney A., Jeffrey A. Klick, and Glenn A. Miller. *Pastoral Helmsmanship: A Pastor's Guide to Church Administration*. Kansas City, MO: Institute for Church Management Publishing, 2015.

Harwood, Adam, and Kevin Lawson. *Infants and Children in the Church: Five Views on Theology and Ministry*. Nashville, TN: B&H Academic, 2017.

Kelley, Charles S., Jr. *Fuel the Fire: Lessons from the History of Southern Baptist Evangelism*. A Treasury of Baptist Theology, edited by Paige Patterson and Jason G. Duesing. Nashville, TN: B&H Academic, 2018.

Kilbreth, Leon. *How to Win Souls*. Herrin, IL: Leon Kilbreth Evangelistic Association, 1970.

Little, Paul E. *How to Give Away Your Faith*. Downers Grove, IL: Intervarsity Press, 1966.

London, H. B., Jr., and Neil B. Wiseman. *Pastors at Greater Risk*. Ventura, CA: Regal Books, 2003.

MacArthur, John. *2 Timothy: The John MacArthur Commentary*. Chicago, IL: Moody Press, 1995.

Maxwell, John. *Developing the Leader Within You*. Nashville, TN: Thomas Nelson, 1993.

———. *The 21 Irrefutable Laws of Leadership*. Nashville, TN: Thomas Nelson, 1998.

McDill, Wayne. *Making Friends for Christ: A Practical Approach to Relational Evangelism*. Nashville, TN: Thomas Nelson, 1979.

Miles, Delos. *How Jesus Won Persons*. Nashville, TN: Broadman Press, 1982.

Morgan, G. Campbell. *The Great Physician: The Method of Jesus with Individuals*. Old Tappan, NJ: Fleming H. Revell, 1937.

Morley, Patrick. *Left Behind: How to Build and Sustain a Disciple-Making Ministry for Every Man in Your Church*. Chicago, IL: Moody Publishers, 2006.

Phillips, Jere L. *Pastoral Ministry for the Next Generation*. Collierville, TN: Innovo Publishing, 2014.

Roesel, Charles L. *It's a God Thing: The Powerful Results of Ministry Evangelism*. Abbotsford, WI: Life Sentence Publishing, 2014.

Sanderson, Leonard. *Personal Soul-Winning*. Nashville, TN: Convention Press, 1958.

Southern Baptist Convention. "The Baptist Faith and Message: The 2000 Baptist Faith and Message." Southern Baptist Convention. Accessed June 19, 2019. http://www.sbc.net/bfm2000/bfm2000.asp.

Stanfield, Vernon L. *Effective Evangelistic Preaching*. Grand Rapids, MI: Baker Book House, 1965.

Vines, Jerry. *Interviews with Jesus*. Nashville, TN: Broadman Press, 1981.

Yessick, Tommy. *Building Blocks for Longer Life and Ministry*. Nashville, TN: Convention Press, 1997.

Evangelism Strategy

STRATEGIZE TO EVANGELIZE

Jake Roudkovski

William E. Hull defines strategy as "plotting the direction in which an organization should move to position itself to carry out its mission most effectively."[1] Aubrey Malphurs delineates strategy as "the process that determines how a ministry or organization will accomplish its mission."[2] Effective evangelistic strategy involves providing direction and establishing a process for evangelism in the local church.

In his seminal work on Southern Baptist evangelism, Dr. Kelley underscored the genius of Southern Baptist evangelism in "the development of an integrated process" that incorporated decisional preaching, systematic outreach, weekly Bible study, and revivalism into the evangelistic climate and culture of the local church.[3] Unfortunately, many churches have departed from viewing evangelism as an integrated process. Many churches seem to have fifty-two disconnected Sundays during the year with limited intentionality toward direction and an evangelism process. The purpose of this chapter is to encourage church leadership to analyze contextual and institutional factors

---

[1] William Hull, *Strategic Preaching: The Role of the Pulpit in Pastoral Leadership* (Atlanta, GA: Chalice Press, 2006), 2.
[2] Aubrey Malphurs, *Advanced Strategic Planning: A New Model for Church and Ministry Leaders* (Grand Rapids, MI: Baker Books, 2005), 17.
[3] Charles S. Kelley Jr., *Fuel the Fire: Lessons from the History of Southern Baptist Evangelism*, A Treasury of Baptist Theology, eds. Paige Patterson and Jason G. Duesing (Nashville, TN: B&H Academic, 2018), 117.

in order to develop an intentional, informed, and spiritual evangelistic strategy. Such elements as plowing, sowing, watering, harvesting, and multiplication will be explored to serve as the foundational base for a contextual evangelistic strategy in the local church.

As church leadership determines to develop an evangelistic strategy for the church, an analysis of the community in which that church functions and ministers may be invaluable. An analysis of contextual factors provides better understanding of the community. Contextual factors include those external to a church over which a congregation has little or no control. On the local level, such factors may involve neighborhood changes, population shifts, and local economic trends. One can analyze contextual factors from demographics and psychographics of the selected community. Demographics is the study of population based on factors such as age, gender, race, educational level, etc. Psychographics is the study of people according to their attitudes, aspirations, preferences, etc. Churches can obtain a community profile that includes demographic and psychographic trends from the Leavell Center for Evangelism and Church Health at NOBTS.

In addition to contextual factors, an analysis of institutional factors may offer helpful insights in the development of an evangelistic strategy. Institutional factors deal with the internal life of the church and involves programs, leadership composition, internal structure, spiritual dynamics, etc. Reports addressing institutional factors such as growth and decline, giving, participation in worship, etc. may be available from a state convention and/or the Leavell Center for Evangelism and Church Health. Other information such as internal structures, leadership composition, spiritual health, etc. may have to be discerned through interviews with church leadership and membership. By examining contextual and institutional factors, one develops community and church profiles necessary for an effective evangelistic strategy. Understanding one's geographical, cultural, and church contexts provides necessary information that may be used in developing an informed evangelistic strategy.

Equipped with an understanding of the church and community, church leaders may develop an evangelistic strategy based on agricultural concepts of plowing, sowing, cultivation, harvesting, and multiplication. Before the farmer scatters seeds for sowing, the field must be prepared. In Jer 4:3, the people of Judah were challenged to "break up your fallow ground," evoking the concept of plowing. In my personal opinion, plowing addresses the spiritual foundation for evangelistic strategy. Several elements of spiritual preparation may need to be considered.

First of all, church leaders need to embrace the scriptural imperative of evangelism. It may be helpful at this point to define the word *evangelism*. The word *evangelism* comes from the Greek verb *euangelidzō*, meaning "to announce, proclaim or bring good news." The verb form is found thirty-three times in the New Testament. The noun form *euangelion*, meaning "gospel, good news, or evangel" is found seventy-six times in the New Testament. Evangelism is sharing of the good news.

Jesus began his proclamation ministry with sharing of the good news in Mark 1:14–15, calling people to "believe in the gospel." Later in verse 17, Jesus called Simon and Andrew to follow him, promising he would make them "fishers of men." Christ exemplified what it meant to be fishers of men by sharing the good news. Leighton Ford highlighted thirty-five evangelistic encounters of Jesus in the gospels.[4] In John 3, Jesus engaged in an evangelistic encounter with Nicodemus. In John 4, Christ witnessed to the Samaritan woman who came to believe in Jesus as the text explicitly revealed in John 9:38. In John 18, Jesus testified to Pilate who rejected his witness. In addition to embodying what it means to be fishers of men, Christ provided training opportunities for his followers to share the good news. In Luke 10:1–12, Christ sent seventy of his followers to engage people with the gospel. In the same context, Jesus encouraged his disciples

---

[4] Leighton Ford, *The Christian Persuader: A New Look at Evangelism Today* (Philadelphia, PA: Westminster Press, 1966), 67.

to pray for more harvest workers, implying that the workers of the kingdom were those that shared the good news. Before his ascension, Christ issued the Great Commission that demanded sharing of the good news (Matt 28:18–20; Mark 16:15; Luke 24:46–49; John 20:21; and Acts 1:8). Paul later defined the good news as the death, burial, and resurrection of Jesus Christ (1 Cor 15:1–5). Leading a congregation to understand the biblical imperative of evangelism may be a good place to start in developing an intentional strategy for church evangelism.

Prayer is the second element in plowing and preparing the church field for evangelistic harvest. Without consistent prayer for lost people, a local church will not be able to reach its evangelistic potential. Charles Spurgeon defined the church's goal in regard to prayer in the following way, "If sinners will be damned, at least let them leap to hell over our bodies. And if they will perish, let them perish with our arms about their knees, imploring them to stay. If hell must be filled, at least let it be filled in the teeth of our exertions, and let not one go there unwarned and unprayed for."[5] The goal of any church is for every person in its circle and sphere of influence to be prayed for in regard to his or her salvation.

Another ingredient in spiritual preparation in evangelistic strategy is the absolute necessity of relying upon the Holy Spirit. The church leadership who are developing a strategy for evangelism should rely upon the Holy Spirit as they pursue holiness in their lives and seek insights in how best to reach their respective community for Christ. In addition, efforts must be undertaken to teach the congregation that the Holy Spirit is indispensable to the task of evangelism. Without the Holy Spirit, a lost person cannot come to faith in Christ since the Holy Spirit brings conviction (John 16:8) and a new birth (John 3:1–6). It is not the role of a believer to bring conviction to the lost; that role is reserved for the Holy Spirit.

---

[5] Charles H. Spurgeon, *Spurgeon at His Best*, compiled by Tom Carter (Grand Rapids, MI: Baker, 1991), 67.

The church leadership and church membership will be freed from fears and anxieties when they realize the Holy Spirit is at work in the lives of all lost people (John 16:7–10). Before the believer speaks to the unbeliever about Jesus, the Holy Spirit has already been working in the life of the unbeliever. The Holy Spirit may have spoken to that person through a general revelation of God through nature and/or a passage of Scripture and/or the Holy Spirit may have placed other people who witnessed to the unbeliever and/or the Holy Spirit may have created circumstances that allowed that person to be more sensitive to spiritual realities. A helpful tool in illustrating the aforementioned concept is the Spider Principle.[6] The work of the Holy Spirit is to create a web drawing people to salvation. The Holy Spirit connects our message to that of other believers, circumstances, general revelation through nature, and specific revelation through the word of God. When the believer shares the good news of Christ with the unbeliever, they are adding another strand to the web that the Holy Spirit of God has been working on to draw the unbeliever to faith in Christ.

When the church leadership works on developing a process for church evangelism, the following questions need to be answered in the plowing stage of the strategy: How is the church going to educate the congregation in the biblical imperative of evangelism? What is the church going to do in the area of evangelistic prayer? How is the church going to emphasize the necessity of relying upon the Holy Spirit in evangelism and personal holiness?

The second stage of the strategy is sowing (Ps 126:5–6; Luke 8:4–15). When the church leadership and membership share the good news with the community through the variety of contextual ways and methods, they are sowing the seeds of the gospel in the lives of people in their community. Dr. Kelley lamented the fact that many contemporary churches attempted "to harvest in an unseeded" context. If churches

---

[6] Charles S. Kelley Jr., *Adult Roman Road Witnessing Training Teacher's Guide* (Nashville, TN: Home Mission Board of the Southern Baptist Convention, 1993), 8.

want to see the harvest of souls, they need to sow the seeds of the gospel in their communities. One of the most effective ways to sow the seeds of the gospel in the lives of the lost is through personal evangelism. It is my strong conviction that the senior pastor and ministerial staff must lead in personal evangelism. Paul encouraged Timothy to do "the work of an evangelist" (2 Tim 4:5). In my doctoral dissertation involving research of 314 pastors, the practice of personal evangelism was the strongest predictor for evangelistic growth of the church as evidenced by baptisms.[7] Even though teaching church members how to witness and preaching messages that encouraged church members to be intentionally evangelistic were correlated with more baptisms, it was what the pastor did in the area of personal evangelism that seemed to have a greater impact upon evangelistic effectiveness of the church. The practice of personal evangelism provided credibility to pastoral efforts in equipping church members in personal evangelism skills.

When the pastor shares Christ with others, he may want to incorporate some of his experiences into his sermons. When the pastor shares how he may have overcome his fears and relied on the Holy Spirit for witnessing, his transparency and authenticity provide inspiration and motivation for church members to be intentional about sharing the good news with others. As the pastor leads his people in personal evangelism, he should consider teaching a witnessing class periodically. Such resources as *One on One: Evangelism Made Simple*[8] and *3 Circles Evangelism Kit*[9] may help the pastor train his church members how to share the good news. In providing a class for witnessing, the pastor and church leaders may need to consider providing hands-on opportunities for class participants to share Christ with the lost.

---

[7] Jake Roudkovski, "An Investigation into a Relationship between Pastoral Personal Evangelism and Baptisms in Selected Southern Baptist Churches" (PhD diss., New Orleans Baptist Theological Seminary, 2004), 121.

[8] *One on One: Evangelism Made Simple*, Personal Evangelism Kit (Alexandria, LA: Evangelism/Church Growth Team), 2017.

[9] *3 Circles Evangelism Kit* (Atlanta, GA: North American Mission Board), 2012.

In the sowing stage of the strategy, the local church should consider prioritizing reaching children and youth. Since around 80 percent of people come to know Christ before they turn twenty,[10] the small church must be willing to prioritize reaching this receptive audience. The church must be willing to invest time, efforts, and resources into reaching children and youth in order to reach maximum evangelistic effectiveness. It is beyond the scope of the chapter to have a comprehensive discussion on the age and the stage of moral accountability.[11] It is my personal conviction that when a child enters the stage of moral awareness, he or she may come to faith in Christ.

Several New Testament passages have informed this conviction. From 2 Tim 3:15, the implication can be made that Timothy followed Christ from childhood. Jesus said, "Let the little children come to me, and do not hinder them, for the kingdom of God belongs to such as these" (Mark 10:14 NIV). In Matt 18:6 (KJV), Jesus warned those who "offend one of these little ones which believe in me." The word Jesus employs for *believe* in the verse is the same one used in John 3:16, Acts 16:31, and Rom 10:9–10. According to Christ, children can believe in Christ. Church leaders will do well to heed the encouragement of Charles Spurgeon, "Let none despise the stirrings of the Spirit in the hearts of the young. Let not boyish anxieties and juvenile repentances be lightly regarded. I, at least, can bear my personal testimony to the fact that grace operates on some minds at a period almost too early for recollection."[12] Any church that does not desire to disregard the work of the Holy Spirit in the lives of children should be willing to invest time and efforts in reaching children and youth.

---

[10] Thom Rainer, *The Bridger Generation* (Nashville, TN: Broadman and Holman, 1997), 23.
[11] For a more detailed discussion on the topic, see Alvin Reid, *Evangelism Handbook: Biblical, Spiritual, Intentional, Missional* (Nashville, TN: B&H Publishing Group, 2009), 411–16.
[12] W. Y. Fullerton, *Charles Haddon Spurgeon: A Bibliography* (Create Space Independent Publishing Platform, 2014), 22.

Several practical actions may enable churches to be more intentional in reaching children and youth. Parents need to be equipped to reach their children for Christ. Even though Christian parents tend to bring their children to their pastor or ministerial staff for conversion conversations, the pastor and ministerial staff over a period of time need to develop a church culture that encourages direct transmission of faith from parents to their children. Many parents have expressed their deepest appreciation to me for equipping them to lead their children to Christ. As parents who led two of our children to faith in Christ, my wife and I feel the experience is as precious as our own conversion. In addition to equipping parents in evangelistic skills, a wise pastor and ministerial staff members would want to equip leaders who work with children and youth. Sunday School teachers, Bible study leaders, VBS workers, and leaders of other youth-oriented organizations will benefit from evangelism training as they seek to reach children for Christ.

In addition to equipping parents and children's workers, the church may need to provide appropriate opportunities for children and youth to hear and embrace the good news. Some of those opportunities may include Awana, Upward Sports, Children's Night, and Youth Night at evangelistic meetings. Vacation Bible School has been one of the more widely used tools affording opportunities for children to hear and respond to the good news. The Vacation Bible School methodology has been employed effectively by many churches to reach children for Christ. As a pastor, I would typically schedule one day during VBS to speak to children about Christ in an age-appropriate manner. For those children who are spiritually ready for a wholehearted commitment to Christ, the church should schedule a visit with their parents to clarify the child's spiritual readiness and provide an opportunity for parents to witness their child making a commitment to follow Christ as his or her Savior and Lord.

As the church leadership addresses the sowing stage of the evangelistic strategy, the following questions need to be examined: "In what ways will the pastor, church staff, and church leadership prioritize personal evangelism in their lives and the ministry of the church?" and "In what specific ways will the church be intentional about reaching children and youth?"

The third stage of the evangelistic strategy is watering (1 Cor 3:5–8). Once the field has been plowed and the seeds have been scattered and sowed, watering and cultivation of the field need to occur. Watering may be accomplished through intentional cultivation of relationships with the lost. According to one study, when participants were asked what influenced them most with their decision for Christ, the two methods with the highest response percentage included conversation with a family member (38.6 percent) and conversation with a friend (14.9 percent).[13] The two methods comprise more than 50 percent of the total responses suggesting that one of the most effective ways of leading others to faith in Christ is simply having a spiritual conversation with a person one knows well. When church members are encouraged, equipped, and deployed to have spiritual conversations with their friends and family members, the church deals with the watering stage of the intentional evangelistic strategy.

Another effective way to cultivate relationships with the lost is to provide opportunities for small groups in the local church to host fellowship events. From my personal observation, unchurched are more likely to come to a fellowship event than a local church service. In addition, several churches have encouraged their church members to host nonbelievers in their homes for a meal or meeting at a neutral site for coffee. Rosaria Butterfield challenged churches to invite lost friends and neighbors to their homes from a perspective that views homes not as "our own, but as God's tools for furtherance of his kingdom."[14]

---

[13] Gary L. McIntosh, *Growing God's Church: How People Are Actually Coming to Faith Today* (Grand Rapids, MI: Baker Books, 2016), 105.
[14] Rosaria Butterfield, *The Gospel Comes with a House Key: Practicing Radically Ordinary Hospitality in Our Post-Christian World* (Wheaton, IL: Crossway, 2018), 10.

Butterfield's story of coming to faith in Christ as a result of a Christian couple befriending her and spending time with her in their home has served as an inspiration for churches to prioritize friendships and hospitality in evangelism. When considering cultivation of relationships with the lost, church members need to be encouraged to view nonbelievers not as mere church prospects but as individuals for whom Jesus died on the cross.

Ministry evangelism may be employed in the watering stage of an intentional evangelistic strategy. Ministry evangelism calls for churches to meet various felt needs in the community with a purpose of reaching people for Christ. Charles Roesel describes ministry evangelism as "walking alongside those in need, building ongoing relationships; providing aid, friendship and mentoring; and explaining God's mercy and grace."[15] The prominent pastor offered more than one hundred ideas for ministry evangelism for any size church, such as parents' day out, parenting seminars, tutoring, adult day care, home meal delivery, lawn care, car repair, health screenings, athletic events, income tax assistance, disaster relief, and grief support groups. Ministry evangelism provides opportunities for church members to develop and cultivate relationships with the lost.

In the watering stage of the evangelistic strategy, the following priorities must be addressed. How will church members be encouraged and equipped to have spiritual conversations with their unchurched friends and family members? In what ways will the church members be challenged to use hospitality in evangelism? What are some ways the local church can use ministry evangelism ideas in their context?

The fourth stage of the evangelistic strategy is harvesting (John 4:34–38). When the field has been plowed, sowed, and cultivated, opportunities for harvesting need to be present. In harvesting, church members need to be equipped not just with sharing the gospel but in providing

---

[15] Charles Roesel, *It's a God Thing: The Powerful Results of Ministry Evangelism* (Abbotsford, WI: Life Sentence Publishing, 2014), 28–29.

opportunities for lost people to say yes or no to Jesus Christ. Another opportunity for harvesting occurs every Sunday morning during a worship service in many churches. By issuing a public invitation, the preacher gives an opportunity for people in the audience to respond to the good news. Analyzing the different views in relation to the public invitation is beyond the scope of the article.[16] My personal conviction is that a biblical message demands a call for action. Vines and Shaddix listed and discussed the following models in calling for a response to the message: verbal appeal, physical relocation, post-meeting ministry, written record, physical gesture, and a multiple approach.[17] Not every message the pastor preaches will be evangelistic, but every message should include an evangelistic appeal.

Mass evangelism is another viable tool for harvesting. One of the more popular tools in many churches have been revival meetings. It is beyond the scope of this chapter to provide a comprehensive analysis of revival meeting methodology[18] but I will outline several principles gleaned from revival meetings that may be transferable for other mass evangelism events.

When church leadership begins to sense God is leading them to schedule a revival meeting, they need to ask what the purpose of such an event should be. Will it be primarily for evangelism or revitalization of a local congregation? The purpose will dictate a strategy for preparation. Even though a church selects the primary purpose as evangelism, the church may experience a spiritual renewal among the membership. In turn, a church with the primary purpose as revitalization may reach people for Christ along the way. A clear purpose will

---

[16] For further discussion on the subject, see Alan Streett, *The Effective Invitation: A Practical Guide for the Pastor* (Grand Rapids, MI: Kregel, 1995).

[17] Jerry Vines and Jim Shaddix, *Power in the Pulpit: How to Prepare and Deliver Expository Sermons* (Chicago, IL: Moody Press, 1999), 214–15.

[18] For a more comprehensive discussion on revival meetings, see Thomas Johnston, ed. *Mobilizing a Great Commission Church for Harvest: Voices and Views from the Southern Baptist Professors of Evangelism Fellowship* (Eugene, OR: Wipf and Stock, 2011), 85–96.

enable church leadership to be more proactive in matching the purpose with a strategy for preparation and resources.

Once the primary purpose is established, the church leadership should prayerfully select a revival team. I have to confess for the first ten years as a pastor, I invited my pastor friends to preach revival meetings. However, I came to a conclusion that if I really believed an evangelist was God's gift to the church, I should be willing to use vocational evangelists. The Conference of Southern Baptist Evangelists is a group of full-time evangelists who serve as an excellent resource for selecting leaders to preach and lead music in revival meetings. Many churches benefit greatly from the giftedness of vocational evangelists, and the meetings are blessed with people coming to Christ and believers being renewed in their faith.

Another consideration in relation to the revival teams should be clarity about finances. It has been my practice as a pastor to initiate the conversation about finances with an evangelist. Typically, we budget the money for expenses (travel, food, lodging, and incidentals) and use a love offering to provide honorarium for the revival team. If you choose this method, make sure the love offering will be given to the team in its entirety. Some churches budget an entire amount for expenses and honorariums. Regardless of the approach, the church leadership and the revival team must be clear about finances at the onset of the process. If the church decides to use the love offering method to reimburse the revival team, the pastor needs to plan a thoughtful and prayerful love offering. For full-time evangelists, this money is the way God provides for their families. In addition, church leaders should be gracious hosts to the revival team. Church members observe how pastors and staff treat the revival team and in many instances that is how church members learn how to treat their leaders!

After the church leadership establishes the purpose and secures a spiritually gifted revival team, they are ready to develop a strategy for preparation. Several state conventions publish manuals on revival preparation.[19] The church must begin preparations three to six months in advance. Church leadership should share enthusiastically with the church council, deacons, teachers, and other key leaders about the upcoming revival. The more church members are involved in preparation of the revival meeting, the more they will be willing to attend and invite their friends to come. Revival manuals provide concrete ways for how to involve church membership in preparation and participation in revival meetings. The goal should be to involve as many church members as possible in various tasks associated with revival preparation and the revival meeting itself.

One critical aspect of revival preparation is publicity. The most effective way of publicity is personal invitation. A business card with information about the event may be printed and distributed to church members to use in inviting their family, friends, coworkers, and neighbors. We have found out that distributing such a card one month to two months in advance created excitement, provided focus in prayer, and gave church members a tangible way to invite others. Church media such as a newsletter, worship guide, and website should provide pertinent information about the event. Publicity via social media and other online marketing strategies by the church and church members can generate a buzz in the community and beyond.

One often-neglected aspect of revival preparation is what to do with children. In one church I served as pastor, I became concerned about an apparent lack of participation by young couples. When asked, they responded by pointing to the fact the church did not have anything for children during the revival week. From that day forward, in addition to typical childcare, we provided a specialized program for children during revival services. When young couples knew their children were taken care of spiritually, they were more inclined to participate and invite their lost friends and family members to attend.

---

[19] *Revival Preparation Manual* (Atlanta, GA: North American Mission Board, 2009), 10.

In preparation for revival meetings, post-event follow-up should not be overlooked. Training on post-event follow-up may be incorporated into the training for commitment counselors. As commitment counselors are taught how to lead people to Christ, provide assurance of salvation, and explore issues of church membership, an emphasis can be placed on taking accurate records of those making spiritual commitments. As soon as the revival meeting concludes, names of those who made spiritual commitments can be distributed among deacons and/or Bible study group members for further follow-up. In the churches I have pastored, we continued to baptize people who were identified as potential prospects months after the conclusion of the revival meetings.

The most significant aspect of revival meetings must be prayer. A genuine revival can be brought only by God. Only God can save individuals through the Holy Spirit. As the church leadership and membership engages in prayer, they acknowledge their dependence on God. Church leaders should set aside personal time to pray for genuine revival in their church as well as provide opportunities for church members to pray for God's movement in their church. Among various avenues for engaging membership in prayer for revival, some churches employ cottage prayer meetings in the home of church members, while other churches open up their prayer rooms for continual prayer for revival, and some others assemble prayer chains for the purpose of praying for revival.

Although some have pronounced local church revival meetings "dead," they are much alive in many churches. It is my conviction that the effectiveness of revival meetings will depend on the stewardship of that methodology by the local church. The more churches are willing to prepare, the more they place themselves in the position before God to reach people for Christ. Churches should not be afraid to employ mass evangelistic events when appropriate! The aforementioned matters, such as establishment of the purpose, spiritually gifted team, publicity, adequate preparation, post-event follow-up, and the priority of prayer, may be emulated with other mass evangelistic events including wild game suppers, Power Team ministries, community widow and widowers' banquets, etc.

When the church leadership considers harvesting in developing an evangelistic strategy, the following areas need to be considered: How will church members be equipped in personal evangelism? In what ways will the pastor of the church enhance and use his skills in giving public evangelistic invitations? What mass evangelistic events may be employed by the local church?

The last stage for effective evangelistic strategy is multiplication (Matt 13:1–23). When people respond to the good news and become followers of Christ, the church should provide immediate follow-up for new believers. Waylon Moore recommended follow-up with a new believer should begin within forty-eight hours of his or her profession of faith.[20] Four methods may be used for immediate follow-up with a new believer. The first method is personal contact. In the contemporary context, the church members should be willing to make a visit, place a phone call, or text a new believer offering encouragement and prayer. Information about baptism and further steps for spiritual growth is best communicated through personal contact. The second method is personal prayer. In the past two churches I served as interim pastor, we listed new believers on our prayer list on Wednesday night and prayed for them as a church.

The third method is personal representatives. The pastor may not be able to provide immediate follow-up to every new believer, but he may equip other faithful church members for follow-up. The fourth method is personal correspondence. In the modern context, the church leaders can provide follow-up encouragement and instruction via letters, emails, texts, and social media. Several goals for immediate follow-up may be established as the church uses the four methods of follow-up. The goals for new believers include following Christ in

---

[20] Waylon Moore, *New Testament Follow-Up: For Pastors and Laymen* (Grand Rapids, MI: Eerdmans Publishing Company, 1963), 23.

the believer's baptism, becoming acquainted with initial spiritual disciplines, and taking active part in a vibrant small group.

In addition to providing ways for immediate follow-up, the church leadership should consider using a new members' class for follow-up and initial discipleship. Thom Rainer listed the following twenty-one most common topics included in the new members' classes after surveying approximately three hundred evangelistic high-assimilation churches arranged by the frequency of their appearance from highest to the lowest: doctrine of the church, polity, church constitution, the Lord's Supper and baptism, church covenant, policies for church discipline, expectation for members, history of the church, tour of church facilities, denominational information, plan of salvation, financial support of the church, requirement for membership, current opportunities for service, training in spiritual disciplines, introduction to church staff and leadership, explanation of church's mission, inventory of spiritual gifts, support for missions, and training for witnessing and evangelism.[21] Each church should determine the content and duration of new members' classes based on the ministry context. One cannot possibly provide all the information and instruction new believers need about being followers of Christ in a new members' class, but new membership classes assist a new believer with an intentional direction as he or she begins to grow in Christ in the context of the local church.

In the multiplication stage of evangelistic strategy, church leadership should address how the church will provide immediate follow-up to new believers by using personal contact, prayer, representatives, and correspondence. Furthermore, the church leadership may need to prioritize offering new members/new believer's classes on a regular basis.

In bringing the elements of the strategy together, a six- to twelve-month evangelistic calendar may be useful. I fully recognize the impossibility of scheduling such actions as reliance on the Holy Spirit;

---

[21] Thom Rainer, *High Expectations: The Remarkable Secret of Keeping People in Your Church* (Nashville, TN: Broadman and Holman Publishing, 1999), 109–110.

however, many spiritual activities and events may be planned. The pastor may look at sermons to preach on the biblical mandate for evangelism as the Holy Spirit leads and place them on calendar. When the pastor, church staff, and church leadership schedule time to pray for the lost and for personal evangelism, intentionality and accountability for evangelism are cultivated in their lives. In the area of reaching children and youth, seasonal events such as VBS and Upward Sports, as well as regular ministries such as Sunday School and Awana, etc., will need to be added to the evangelistic calendar. Mass evangelistic events with preparation and post event follow-up activities should be placed on the calendar. New members' class may be placed on the calendar along with training opportunities for those designated with responsibilities of follow-up.

As the church leadership plans evangelistic direction of the church, they should carefully consider events and activities that address plowing, watering, sowing, harvesting, and multiplication phases of the strategy. Before and during the process of strategy and calendar planning, the pastor, staff, and church leadership should be praying and depending on the Holy Spirit for insights. Granted, the church may not address every eventuality and complexity associated with the ministry in the church, but a workable evangelistic strategy will provide a workable blueprint for the church.

BIBLIOGRAPHY

3 Circles Evangelism Kit. Atlanta, GA: North American Mission Board, 2012.

Butterfield, Rosaria. *The Gospel Comes with a House Key: Practicing Radically Ordinary Hospitality in Our Post-Christian World.* Wheaton, IL: Crossway, 2018.

Ford, Leighton. *The Christian Persuader: A New Look at Evangelism Today.* Philadelphia, PA: Westminster Press, 1966.

Fullerton, W. Y. *Charles Haddon Spurgeon: A Bibliography.* Scotts Valley, CA: Create Space Independent Publishing Platform, 2014.

Hull, William. *Strategic Preaching: The Role of the Pulpit in Pastoral Leadership.* Atlanta: Chalice Press, 2006.

Johnston, Thomas, ed. *Mobilizing a Great Commission Church for Harvest: Voices and Views from the Southern Baptist Professors of Evangelism Fellowship.* Eugene, OR: Wipf & Stock, 2011.

Kelley, Charles S., Jr. *Adult Roman Road Witnessing Training Teacher's Guide.* Nashville, TN: Home Mission Board of the Southern Baptist Convention, 1993.

———. *Fuel the Fire: Lessons from the History of Southern Baptist Evangelism.* A Treasury of Baptist Theology, edited by Paige Patterson and Jason G. Duesing. Nashville, TN: B&H Academic, 2018.

Malphurs, Aubrey. *Advanced Strategic Planning: A New Model for Church and Ministry Leaders.* Grand Rapids, MI: Baker Books, 2005.

McIntosh, Gary L. *Growing God's Church: How People Are Actually Coming to Faith Today.* Grand Rapids, MI: Baker Books, 2016.

Moore, Waylon. *New Testament Follow-Up: For Pastors and Laymen.* Grand Rapids, MI: Eerdmans Publishing Company, 1963.

One on One: Evangelism Made Simple. Personal Evangelism Kit. Alexandria, LA: Evangelism/Church Growth Team, 2017.

Rainer, Thom. *High Expectations: The Remarkable Secret of Keeping People in Your Church.* Nashville, TN: B&H Publishing Group, 1999.

———. *The Bridger Generation.* Nashville, TN: Broadman and Holman, 1997.

Reid, Alvin. *Evangelism Handbook: Biblical, Spiritual, Intentional, Missional.* Nashville, TN: B&H Publishing Group, 2009.

Revival Preparation Manual. Atlanta, GA: North American Mission Board, 2009.

Roesel, Charles. *It's a God Thing: The Powerful Results of Ministry Evangelism.* Abbotsford, WI: Life Sentence Publishing, 2014.

Roudkovski, Jake. "An Investigation into a Relationship between Pastoral Personal Evangelism and Baptisms in Selected Southern Baptist Churches." PhD diss., New Orleans Baptist Theological Seminary, 2004.

Spurgeon, Charles H. *Spurgeon at His Best.* Compiled by Tom Carter. Grand Rapids, MI: Baker, 1991.

Streett, Alan. *The Effective Invitation: A Practical Guide for the Pastor.* Grand Rapids, MI: Kregel, 1995.

Vines, Jerry, and Jim Shaddix. *Power in the Pulpit: How to Prepare and Deliver Expository Sermons.* Chicago, IL: Moody Press, 1997.

Evangelism Strategy

OUTREACH AND EVANGELISM THROUGH SUNDAY SCHOOL AND SMALL GROUP MINISTRY

Randall Stone

For the past two decades, local congregations have seen a shift in the purpose and focus of small groups away from outreach and evangelism to other perceived needs. A casual inquiry of pastoral staff, key leaders, small group leaders, and group participants reveals a disagreement about the purpose and priorities of small groups. Teachers and small group leaders indicate Bible teaching is the paramount task of the small group gathering. Group members and participants are more likely to report fellowship or pastoral care as the most important tasks of small groups. Finally, appropriately trained staff members and key leaders understand the fundamental need for small groups to be the primary outreach and evangelism arm of the church.

No other ministry or organization within the church has the involvement, organization, relationships, or devotion to fulfill the Great Commission better than Sunday Schools or other forms of small group ministry. Many churches have failed to utilize the very ministry designed to accomplish the task of outreach and evangelism by the body of Christ.

In the following pages, major themes are presented in four sections. First, we will consider a foundational framework for small group ministry. Second, we will explore ten foundational principles with suggested effective practices. The third section will identify essentials for success, predictions about the future, and possibilities of small group ministry in local congregations.

Foundational Framework

Biblical Mandate

The Bible clearly communicates a mandate and mission to reach the lost, make disciples, and teach the truth. Most obvious is the Great Commission (Matt 28:18–20). Believers in their quest to follow Christ fully must also share in his mission as declared by the New Testament writers. Luke declared: "For the Son of Man has come to seek and to save that which was lost" (Luke 19:10). Similarly the mission is reinforced in John's Gospel, "So Jesus said to them again, 'Peace be with you; as the Father has sent Me, I also send you'" (John 20:21). Steve Gladen, small group pastor at Saddleback Church, affirmed, "Evangelism is a duty all Christians share. It is not optional; it is required."[1]

Jesus did not come to bring condemnation and judgment; rather, motivated by love, Jesus came to bring deliverance and salvation (John 3:16–18). The call is to be witnesses of the gospel that God became flesh, lived among people, died a gruesome death, and rose from the dead to bring repentance and forgiveness for all nations (Luke 24:44–48). Christ followers empowered by the Spirit give witness of this glorious and life-giving truth (Acts1:8). We would do well to follow Paul's admonition in his pastoral letter to the church. "We proclaim Him, admonishing every man and teaching every man with all wisdom, so that we may present every man complete in Christ. For this purpose also I labor, striving according to His power, which mightily works within me" (Col 1:28–29).

---

[1] Steve Gladen, *Small Groups with Purpose: How to Create Healthy Communities* (Grand Rapids, IL: Baker Books, 2011), 105.

Vital Relationships

All small group ministries are built on and around vital relationships. In order for small groups to function, individuals must initiate and cultivate meaningful relationships. Believers and church members must be proactive in starting conversations or creating social situations that promote interactions. Initiating contact and developing connections that lead to spiritual conversations must be embedded in the small group ethos and value system. Pursuit of manufactured and manipulated conversations will reap nothing. Genuine connections motivated by a concern for others far from God and needful of redemption and reconciliation reap eternal rewards.

Leaders within the ministry must forge deeper relationships with members and one another. Relationships built on genuine love and trust foster an environment that allows others to learn to lead. As leaders define and communicate responsibilities and priorities, the entire small group systems grows into a community of sincere care, an incubator for future leaders, and a fruitful field for evangelism.

Effective Teaching

"Poor and ineffective Bible teaching will drive away more people than a good outreach program can bring in!" The genesis of the quote has been long forgotten, but the sentiment is still true. Congregations with zealous members and intentional outreach efforts can identify and reach their lost and unchurched community. However, the greatest concern expressed by many pastors and Sunday School or small group ministry leaders is how to deal with ineffectual Bible study leaders. Certainly addressing effective Bible instruction is paramount. The study of God's word as a central part of group experiences and encounters is a distinguishing characteristic of evangelistic groups as compared to other types of affinity groups. Evangelistic small groups allow the Bible to speak to the character, lifestyle, and needs of Christ followers. Keeping Bible study an essential element of group meetings serves as a guideline and reminder of God's work. A task force appointed by the

Southern Baptist Convention determined Bible engagement in small groups is essential to the larger disciple-making process.[2]

Sunday School leader Darryl Wilson lamented, "We are not teaching them how to study God's Word. We are not teaching them how to listen to His still small voice. We are not teaching them how to read His Word in search of truth that needs to be applied to daily life. We are not teaching them how to open God's Word to encounter a great God and realize our insignificance."[3] Effective Bible study involves two key characteristics: proper exegesis and application of the biblical text. Prepared Bible study leaders are able to read, understand, and communicate the truths contained in the Bible. Christ followers and the lost need to hear the word presented accurately, personally, and systematically. Additionally, prepared Bible study leaders are able to engage a variety of learners. By understanding learning styles and maintaining awareness of learner needs, effective Bible teachers can lead participants to understand and apply the biblical truths in their daily lives.

Teachers need to know their students so they can connect the lesson to life. Teachers need to know their culture so they can connect life to the lesson. Teachers need to know the word so they can learn the lesson. Teachers need to know the Master Teacher so they can live the lesson.

Work of the Holy Spirit

Perhaps the most neglected or misunderstood ingredient of small group life is the work of the Holy Spirit. The Holy Spirit is active and engaged at all levels of outreach, evangelism, teaching, and caring. As Harrington and Absalom observed, "Our part, as disciples, is to

---

[2] Robby Gallaty, "Disciple-making Task Force Report: Bible engagement, follow up key to discipleship," North American Mission Board, June 21, 2018, https://www.namb.net/news/disciple-making-task-force-report-bible-engagement-follow-up-to-key-discussion/.

[3] Darryl Wilson. *Disciplemaking Encounters: Revolutionary Sunday School* (Abbotsford, WI: Aneko Press, 2014), 105.

show up, be consistent, and open our hearts to the Spirit of God living inside us. God's part is to work within us and guide the process."[4]

Church leaders are gifted uniquely by the Holy Spirit to serve the body. Some possess speaking gifts of teaching, exhortation, or prophecy to edify and enrich the body of Christ. Other members manifest serving gifts of leadership/administration, giving, serving, and mercy. As believers cooperate with one another in ministry teams and exercise their respective gifts, they are able to reach the unchurched, cultivate an openness to gospel conversations, and extend an invitation to follow Christ.

The Holy Spirit works actively in the lives of lost and unchurched individuals. He convicts of sin, judgment, and righteousness (John 16:8–11). As listeners and learners fall under the conviction of the Holy Spirit, he prompts them to respond by following Christ.

The Holy Spirit teaches Christ followers to understand the word of truth. Likewise, he convicts believers when they disregard and disobey spiritual truths. He leads to wisdom and understanding. The Holy Spirit stirs up faith and empowers believers to be witnesses of Jesus and the transformed life available in him. The work of the Spirit is indispensable in leading and serving in an evangelistic small group ministry.

Foundational Principles and Effective Practices

Principle 1: Discover and Maintain Records of Unreached People

Long-time church growth specialist John Sisemore noted, "Searching for unreached persons is not only essential to the growth of the Sunday School, it is the very lifeline of the church."[5] What was true four decades ago remains true today. Most evangelistic-minded groups

---

[4] Bobby Harrington and Alex Absalom, *Discipleship That Fits: The Five Kinds of Relationships God Uses to Help Us Grow* (Grand Rapids, MI: Zondervan, 2016), 139.
[5] John T. Sisemore, *Church Growth Through the Sunday School* (Nashville, TN: Broadman Press, 1983), 101.

embed a process to identify and reach new members. Every church and group should collect the names and current contact information of the lost, unchurched, and dechurched in the sphere of their influence. Possessing names, addresses, emails, and phone numbers represent possibility to reach people, not just pad numbers. Leaders must have access to relevant contact information. Efforts to identify guests or first-time attendees and maintain the records must be the foremost task of a staff member and designated group leaders.

Where do you find future group members? Names and contact information can be gathered in a plethora of ministry encounters. First-time guests in worship services are usually the most consistent source. Vacation Bible School still draws many guests and generates a significant number of potential members. Special events, such as music presentations or youth and children's activities, are prime for prospect discovery. The most obvious and efficacious is personal invitation by group members. Individual members can identify friends, family, acquaintances, neighbors, and business associates who are lost, unchurched, or not actively involved in a Bible study group.

The goal is to engage prospects in meaningful Bible study with a group of devoted followers of Christ. Interestingly, for every three new people enrolled in the Bible study program the organization will see one baptism in the following year. For example, if a church enrolls or engages one hundred new people in group life, they can reasonably expect to baptize 33 people during the next year. Be advised, the principle applies across the entire organization, not to a specific group.

Practice: Contemporary data information systems allow sharing between groups and church offices. Every church should possess a digital database or a paper file maintained by a file manager, outreach-evangelism director, or designated group leader.

The following four actions make the file a valid source of evangelistic opportunities: (1) Review the list of new additions and prospective members regularly for numeric and contact information accuracy. (2) Assign each guest to a selected small group for follow up. (3) Assign staff, group leaders, or group members to contact all assigned prospects in a scheduled and rotating process. (4) Collect contact reports and comments and update the database. Repeating these basic actions will reap solid results.

Some churches prefer to assign or assimilate new attendees through connection events.[6] Conducting and hosting planned events are opportunities to introduce inquirers, worship attendees, and ministry participants to small groups. Web portals that allow inquirers to find and connect with groups based on time, life stage, affinity, or geography are popular, but their efficiency is not validated. Harrington and Absalom recommend new members try multiple groups and "third space" group meetings to lower barriers and enhance connections.[7]

Principle 2: Select the Right Leaders

The selection of leaders in the small group ministry is key to success. Mentor to many successful small group leaders, Carl George wrote, "The central task of the Church after hearing from God is to develop leaders."[8] Not every leader has to be an all-star, but leaders must exhibit essential characteristics. Small group leaders must be committed to Christ, the mission of the church, and the goals of the local congregation. Leaders should be teachable and willing to work together to fulfill the vision and reach the goals of the local body of Christ. Stetzer and Geiger highlighted the importance of leader selection, observing that while many leaders in the congregation exhibit a variety of skills and gifts, "Matching leadership qualities with the strategy you have selected for your church can make or break your group strategy."[9]

---

[6] "Small Group Connection Process" Downloads, Small Group Ministries, accessed March 1, 2019, https://smallgroups.net/download/connection-strategy/.
[7] Harrington and Absalom, *Discipleship that Fits*, 221.
[8] Carl George, *Nine Keys to Effective Small Group Leadership: How Lay Leaders Can Establish Dynamic and Healthy Cells, Classes, or Teams* (Taylors, SC: CDLM 2013), 46.
[9] Ed Stetzer and Eric Geiger, *Transformational Groups: Creating a New Scorecard for Groups* (Nashville, TN: B&H Publishing, 2014), 119.

Small groups should have leaders committed to outreach and evangelism. The group leader or Sunday School class director should enlist a team of leaders responsible for outreach, prayer, and care. All small group leaders need be to intentional about inviting prospective members, including them in group or class activities, and responding to spiritual needs, thus creating an openness for spiritual conversations and responsiveness to the work of the Spirit.

Practice: Evangelistic and growing groups have fruitful leaders. Pastors and staff must employ a culture of leader growth by spending time getting to know potential leaders and creating a consistent enlistment process. Recommended steps to enlistment:

1. Schedule a face-to-face meeting to invite a potential leader to serve. (Be prepared to present a job description, responsibilities, resources, training opportunities, and support system.)
2. Allow leaders to prayerfully consider serving.
3. Follow-up (usually within a week) with a conversation to get a sense of the potential leader's interest.
4. Provide basic training for the task.
5. Allow new enlistees opportunities to gain experience under supervision by another experienced leader.
6. Assign a new leader to group/task with the greatest possibility for success.
7. Conduct a checkup and evaluation based on the job description after a prescribed time (three months, for example.)
8. Write appreciation notes and perform continued evaluation.

Principle 3: Start New Groups Regularly

Groups are a powerful force in the expansion of the gospel. According to Rick Howerton, popular small group coach and trainer, "Groups that make the greatest impact see beyond themselves and realize they can influence more people with the gospel as well as generations to come if they are strategically and purposefully involved in being unapologetically and powerfully evangelistic by birthing new groups."[10]

New groups reach and assimilate new people more effectively than established groups. In fact, once a group has existed for more than eighteen months, it frequently functions as a closed group. Relationship circles, space, or leader capacity can limit the addition of new members and prospects. An intentional plan to launch new groups is the best strategy to connect with prospects, assimilate attenders, and create serving opportunities. As you consider new groups, you identify clusters of unreached groups within the church.

Average group size is between eight and twelve. Every church possesses a collection of groups that reach a variety of people and relate to each other and the leaders. To determine the average group size, divide the average weekly group attendance by the number of groups. Small churches typically will be closer to eight, and larger congregations tend to be nearer to twelve. After insuring church records are accurate, calculate the total number of needed classes by adding the number of resident church members and the number of valid prospects in the data file and dividing by the church group size (eight to twelve). The new group goal will also determine the number of new leaders needed to reach your prospects and inactive church members.

Starting new units reaps a number of benefits. Wayne Poling observed four associated byproducts. He concluded that new units: "bring new life and vitality"; "expand the possibilities for ministry"; "grow the leadership"; and "give a fresh place for new people to join."[11]

Practice: Survey the list of unreached prospects and inactive church members and organize names according to specific common characteristics. Consider creating new groups such as young singles, women of

---

[10] Rick Howerton, *A Different Kind of Tribe: Embracing the New Small-Group Dynamic* (Colorado Springs, CO: NavPress, 2012), 179.
[11] Wayne Poling, *How to Sunday School Manual* (Nashville, TN: LifeWay Press, 2009), 19.

various ages, parents of children, parents of teens, men, and empty nesters. Affinity groups such as golfers, hunters, and selected vocations may interest some prospects. Do not forget to explore shared experiences, such as families with special needs children, job loss, or other concerns. Short-term classes of six to eight weeks in length featuring special topics can be an excellent catalyst to create new classes. Finally, Parkinson reported that campaign-driven small groups may be "the most effective spiritual growth strategy" discovered in research.[12]

Principle 4: Organize for Outreach

Effective organizations exist as a result of intentionality. Ken Hemphill posed, "A good organizational strategy is as critical to church growth as any other component. Without it much of the hard work that goes into outreach, assimilation, and teaching will be dissipated."[13] Creating an operational structure that allows for expansion is important for fulfilling the small group task.[14] Organization of the entire ministry or individual group should point toward identifying and connecting with lost, dechurched, and unchurched in a community. Important tasks require high capacity people dedicated to accomplishing the big goals. A high capacity leader positioned to promote and guide regular outreach and evangelistic efforts is critical.[15] Effective outreach and evangelism results from right actions borne of a passion for lost people and a zeal to serve Christ faithfully.

In the same manner, each small group should have members designated to lead the follow-up process while motivating and encouraging group members to do the same. As each group organizes with small

---

[12] Cally Parkinson, *Rise: Bold Strategies to Transform Your Church* (Colorado, CO: NavPress, 2015), 165.
[13] Ken Hemphill, *Revitalizing the Sunday Morning Dinosaur: A Sunday School Growth Strategy for the 21st Century* (Nashville, TN: Broadman & Holman, 1996), 67.
[14] Ibid., 84–85.
[15] Allan Taylor, *Sunday School in HD: Sharpening the Focus on What Makes Your Church Healthy* (Nashville, TN: Broadman & Holman, 2009), 52.

group leaders, commit to reach, pray, care, and teach in order to ensure the shared work of outreach and evangelism is fruitful.

Practice: Write simple but clear job descriptions for each position within the small group and larger organization. Make sure each person accepts his or her role and responsibility seriously. Communicate consistently with all key leaders about organizational goals and information sharing. Conduct regular training for new and experienced small group leaders.

Principle 5: Cultivate Relationships

Perhaps the greatest need of contemporary Americans is meaningful relationships. "Great groups and thriving Christians encourage a deepening relationship with God and relationships of integrity with other people."[16] Recent studies demonstrate that even though young people connect through social media, they are more depressed, lonely, and isolated than previous generations. Relationships have always been important. Small groups provide a unique environment to cultivate deeper and more significant relationships.

America observed a unique sociological shift in the past quarter century as families and individuals moved from interconnected communities to compartmentalized communities. For example, schools, churches, and neighborhoods once served as shared spaces in local communities. However, the emergence of private and magnet schools, the decline in church participation, the rise in segmented and gated neighborhoods, the separation of competitive sports teams, and the escalation of individualized hobbies have diminished or extinguished natural relationships. As a result, the need and desire for deeper and more meaningful relationships has grown. Carving out time and creating opportunities for group members to form and deepen relationship must become part of the small group strategy. In recent years many

---

[16] Brett Robbe, *Connect, Grow, Serve, Go: Moving Toward a Balanced Approach to an Adult Ministry*, with Dwayne McCrary (Nashville, TN: LifeWay Press, 2010), 11.

churches have made a concerted effort to create a small group system, often replacing a traditional Sunday School model. The underlying motivation is to "meet this need for personal relationship."[17]

To start and maintain groups a number of factors must be considered. First, members need time to talk and interact at group meetings. Therefore, optimal group time seems to be sixty to ninety minutes in length.[18] Traditional Sunday School groups incorporate social encounters in addition to the regular meetings. Groups are doing "life together. Successful groups encourage members to socialize outside the weekly gatherings."[19] Such extensive social life is contrarian to the typical American lifestyle. Nevertheless, groups must schedule and plan times for member to grow to care about one another.

Second, individuals need and want friendships (a term men find preferable to "relationships"). Friendships are forged over time and with proximity. Group life should include gatherings that allow members to be near one another. As members spend time in the same place, they deepen friendships. Third, the care factor is important. Guiding members to respond to one another's needs prayerfully and practically spawns genuine affection between members. Ministry between members becomes more natural as group members become friends rather than strangers or disconnected attendees.

Small group veteran Eddie Mosely advocates for regular outreach events. He wrote, "The small groups are expected to have parties once a quarter and invite these new friends. People want to know about you before they make such a radical decision to attend church with you or step across the line of faith."[20]

---

[17] Harrington and Absalom, *Discipleship That Fits*, 135.
[18] Jim Egli, "How Long Should Your Group Meetings Last?" *Christianity Today*, accessed March 3, 2019, https://www.smallgroups.com/articles/2013/how-long-should-your-group-meetings-last.html.
[19] Gladen, *Small Groups with Purpose*, 66.
[20] Eddie Mosley, *Connecting in Communities: Understanding the Dynamics of Small Groups* (Colorado Springs: CO, NavPress, 2012), 75.

Practice: Plan plenty of outside socials if your groups meet on campus for Bible study. Tailgating before the big game, cookouts at the park, soup nights, and similar activities make excellent gatherings for members and prospects to get to know one another. Select activities based on the age and interest of the group and prospective members. Plan socials and gatherings around the times and locations that best accommodate your members. Schedule them ahead of time and be sure to invite everyone.

If you meet in home-based groups, consider having monthly invite nights to include friends and new members. Serve a meal or dessert around the group meeting to allow time for casual conversation. Consider hobby nights where the entire group participates together.

Promote conversations within the Bible study or social encounters. Plan discussion questions or triadic groups that allow members to share their personal stories, spiritual journeys, or individual struggles in a more intimate venue.

Principle 6: Space and Facilities Influence the Small Group Ministry Design

Most American churches assemble for worship, discipleship, and teaching weekly. Most provide some building or facility to host these vital functions. Facilities can enhance or restrict the design of the small group ministry. Traditional churches with campus-based groups typically offer excellent educational environments but may limit the relational dynamics within groups.

New and nontraditional congregations feature off-campus or home-based groups. Joel Comisky, a cell ministry advocate, suggests a biblical rationale for home-based small groups.[21] Home-based groups often are more relational, but must contend with limited teaching resources and childcare challenges. An ongoing debate exists between the two camps. However, Scripture seems to support the importance of both environments. Act 5:42 (NIV) says, "Day after day, in the temple courts and from house to house, they never stopped teaching and

---

[21] Joel Comisky, *2000 Years of Small Groups: A History of Cell Ministry in the Church*. (Moreno Valley, CA: CCS Publishing, 2015), 17–26.

proclaiming the good news that Jesus is the Messiah." Gatherings in large assemblies at a place of worship and in smaller groups in homes each have distinctive value. A both/and approach provides a biblical and philosophical anchor on which to build a group ministry.

Practice: Campus-based groups must intentionally plan and provide "off-campus" or "in-home" fellowships and socials that allow members to build relationships. Home-based groups will find regular times of teaching and special instruction at the place of worship meaningful as they engage with other groups and generations. Both approaches have strengths that must be recognized and incorporated. Both approaches have weaknesses that must be identified and addressed.

Because home-based groups can weary hosts and leaders over time, consider converting existing education space to "living spaces" with more casual seating and a warmer atmosphere. Providing space with food preparation and service space creates a terrific venue that can be used multiple times throughout the week.

Cally Parkinson found providing space on campus removed some of the barriers for small groups. Coupling on-campus space with supervised childcare contributed to group success.[22]

Principle 7: Contact all Current and Potential Group Members Regularly

Weekly or monthly personal contact with all group members and associates secures two major benefits. First, prospective members who receive consistent calls or visits sense genuine concern from God's people. Over extended time, relationships with associates can be developed and result in openings for deeper and more fruitful spiritual dialogue. Second, members receive a call from a care leader and are able to share personal needs and prayer concerns. Regular calls promote relationships and foster greater community as group members pray for shared concerns, serve one another, and communicate consistently. Personal calls and visits are critical. Connections are made easily in an

---

[22] Parkinson, *Rise*, 169.

age of social media and electronic communication. However, digital connections have limitations. One-way exchanges fail to capture information critical for cultivating individuals toward an evangelistic appeal. Similarly, social media interactions can be superficial and even artificial. Only as we spend time with others do we penetrate the façade and discover the real person, real perceptions. Generational Sunday School leader Bill Taylor emphasized "Caring about those without Christ means taking the time to get involved in their lives."[23]

Practice: Consider using this simple sample script when contacting members, absentees, and prospects. A group leader should make this call monthly ... preferably weekly.

> *Hello I'm* _____ *(give them your name) from* _____ *Church. May I speak with* _____ *(person's name)? How are you doing today? I'm calling on behalf of* _____ *(group name). How can we pray for you? (Listen for need.) May I share your need with others who will pray for you? I also want to personally invite you to (give them information about a class social, church-wide event, discipleship group, etc.). We'd love for you to join us.*

After you have made a number of calls and established yourself as a caring friend, you will gain rapport and ultimately permission to ask them about their spiritual condition. Ask the following question, which is not threatening but is revealing. *How would you describe where you are on your spiritual journey?*

Principle 8: Teach an Evangelistic Lesson Regularly

An intentional presentation of the gospel accompanied with an invitation to respond should be scheduled consistently. When small group

---

[23] Bill Taylor, *21 Truths, Traditions, and Trends: Propelling the Sunday School into the 21st Century* (Nashville, TN: Convention Press, 1996), 84.

Bible teachers seek to keep the gospel at the center of all Bible teaching, a monthly or quarterly lesson with an appeal to follow Christ will yield results. Dr. Kelley, an ardent student, teacher, and champion for church evangelism said, "People who are identified as prospects and involved in worship are cultivated through the Sunday School (small group Bible study). ... As prospects are involved in studying the Bible, they receive more and more exposure to the gospel."[24] Purposeful prayer, outreach visitation, and personal calls would be worthwhile efforts to couple with teaching preparation in the weeks preceding the evangelistic lesson day. Members and participants can be encouraged to invite lost friends, family, or associates.

Practice: Preview lessons in the curriculum to determine the best days to teach evangelistic lessons. Some printed curriculum contains prescribed evangelistic lessons. If you write or design your curriculum, make sure to include some gospel elements in your weekly lessons and present a clear gospel message on the evangelistic lesson day. Be sure to present the message and material accurately, address the spiritual needs of students, and expect a commitment to the gospel message. Consider a response card, counseling time, or sharing time as part of the group experience. You may want to "seed" the experience with individual group members sharing their own conversion stories in the weeks prior to the commitment day. The church or preaching calendar may be conducive for evangelistic lessons. Coordinate whenever possible.

Principle 9: Celebrate Victories

Jesus encouraged his followers that the angels in heaven rejoice when a sinner repents (Luke 15:10). Organizational success, spiritual victories, and life transformation deserve to be celebrated as a congregation. Celebrations not only encourage the church, but they reinforce the priority of evangelism, demonstrate shared ministry, and prompt

---

[24] Charles S. Kelley Jr., *Fuel the Fire: Lessons from the History of Southern Baptist Evangelism*, a Treasury of Baptist Theology, eds. Paige Patterson and Jason G. Duesing (Nashville, TN: B&H Academic, 2018), 116.

leadership enlistment. Sensitive pastors and leaders recognize the birth of new groups, the salvation and baptism of new believers, successful ministry actions by specific groups, and numeric and spiritual growth.

Practice: Schedule celebrations into training times by recognizing successful groups. Seek to find multiple points of success so multiple groups can be acknowledged. Provide a venue for leaders to report spiritual victories, numeric gains, multiplication efforts, new leader development, and other metrics. Setting goals in these areas at the beginning of a new year or ministry cycle allows leaders to pursue goals with greater purpose and intent. Recognitions may be as simple as public expression of appreciation or more elaborate as special gifts. Be sensitive to the best way to affirm servant leaders, some prefer private recognition with a personal note or lunch meeting with a pastor or key leader.

Principle 10: Undergird Ministry with Prayer

Prayer is essential for outreach and evangelistic success. Prayer is an irreplaceable component of the outreach and evangelism process. Evangelist and teacher Oscar Thompson reminded us, "The one indispensable ingredient in a great church … in a close walk with God is know how to pray."[25] Matters of prayer include individuals who need restoration and regeneration, leaders who need anointing and encouragement, members who need to exercise spiritual giftedness, witnesses who need open doors to share the good news of Jesus, and lost souls who need receptivity to the message of the gospel. Too often the focus of prayer is the physical healing or financial needs of members when a more intense need is for the spiritual redemption of people far from God. Jesus gave attention to the needs of the outcasts, disenfranchised and marginalized members of his society. Personalized prayer connects people with Jesus in a supernatural way.

---

[25] W. Oscar Thompson, *Concentric Circles of Concern: From Self to Others through Life-Style Evangelism* (Nashville, TN: Broadman Press, 1981), 65.

Practice: Ask the following three questions as part of your group evaluation process.

- Does your group have an evangelistic prayer list?
- Do you take time to pray (fervently) for the names on the list?
- Do you allow time for members to share their concerns for lost friends or family?

Provide each group member with an instruction guide to pray continually and fervently for individuals to come to Christ. Prayer prepares the heart of the witness and the receiver.

Essentials for Success

Successful small groups exhibit other important qualities and characteristics. While many more could be introduced, three are critical.

Groups succeed when the pastor champions the ministry. Congregants and attendees respond to the pulpit ministry and proclamation. When a pastor shares his heart for people, presents a compelling vision, and supports the work of group leaders publicly, the ministry cannot help but grow. However, when a pastor is silent about group life, avoids the ministry, and fails to articulate the purpose and direction of groups, the ministry languishes.

Modeling is the paramount teaching method. It is hard to explain internal motivations, but church members and attenders replicate in their church activity the patterns of the leaders. Hemphill said teachers "must have a clear testimony of a personal relationship with Jesus Christ and be one who actively shares that faith. It will be virtually impossible to develop a strong evangelistic climate in the Sunday School class if the teacher doesn't embody the biblical principles related to witnessing."[26] At both the congregational and group level, followers do what the leader does. Therefore, when the small group

---

[26] Hemphill, *Revitalizing the Sunday Morning Dinosaur*, 133.

leader neglects participation in outreach events or fails to invite others to the group, members do likewise. The pastor's absence from evangelistic visitation liberates members to imitate him. The result is evangelistic apathy. Leaders at all levels must model right living, right doing!

Finally, growing evangelistic churches exude enthusiasm. Two axioms drive an evangelistic small group ministry.

1. "When people feel good about their church or group they will invite people to come."
2. "When people are excited about their relationship with Jesus they will invite people to come."

Both axioms in effect are simultaneous multipliers. "When people feel good about their church or group *and* they are excited about their relationship to Christ, they will *really* invite people to come."[27] Conversely, when the opposite describes a church or group, the opposite results can be expected. Leaders must take care to allow the Spirit freedom to stimulate spiritual zeal and purposeful passion among believers. God desires to work; the task of leaders is to remove barriers that hinder the work of God and movement of the Spirit.

Future and Possibilities

Pastors and leaders often ask which should we do: Sunday School or small groups? The answer to the question depends on what you expect to happen in the meetings. Just labeling your ministry a small group or determining to meet on or off campus based on space is insufficient. The name and structure are subservient to the experience people have in the group. For example, millennials have high, and maybe unrealistic,

---

[27] Randall Stone, "5 Catalytic Actions to Rejuvenate Sunday School/Bible Teaching Ministry," conference presentation. Leadership Training, Gulf Coast Baptist Association, Gulfport, MS, February 2, 2019.

expectations of small groups.[28] Dr. Kelley prophetically stated, "Perhaps the greatest challenge for the denomination is to keep the Sunday School focused on evangelism rather than nurture as it primary focus."[29] The challenge is even greater and more important for small group ministry today.

Small group ministry is at a crossroads in many congregations. Churches that embrace either Sunday School or small groups as their primary strategy to equip members to serve, empower their leaders to lead, and open their doors to the lost and dying world will experience renewal and revitalization. Small groups afford an opportunity for the world to see authentic spiritual living and experience the transforming power of Christ.[30]

Churches that allow their small groups to become "holy huddles" of self-righteous or self-centered Christians can expect a slow decline in membership, resources, and ultimately spiritual fervor. Leaders and congregations that dismiss or reject the life-giving power of Christ as demonstrated in the church, the body of Christ, make themselves vulnerable to the slow, painful death of an organization. Allowing the group ministry of the church to languish in the face of such great need seems so unnecessary. With confidence we can proclaim, "God is sovereign and head of the church. He will preserve his people, build his church, and advance his kingdom!"

---

[28] "10 Things Millennials Are Looking For In Small Groups," Vanderbloemen, January 29, 2018, https://www.vanderbloemen.com/blog/millennials-looking-for-small-groups.

[29] Charles S. Kelley Jr., *How Did They Do It? The Story of Southern Baptist Evangelism* (Covington, LA: Insight Press, 1993), 98.

[30] Howerton, *A Different Kind of Tribe*, 159–166.

BIBLIOGRAPHY

Bilezikian, Gilbert. *Community 101: Reclaiming the Church as Community of Oneness.* Grand Rapids, MI: Zondervan Corp, 1997.

Boren, M. Scott, and Don Tillman. *Making Cell Groups Work: 8 Stages for Navigating the Transition to the Cell-Based Church.* Houston, TX: Touch Publications, 2002.

Cloud, Henry, and John Townsend. *How People Grow: What the Bible Reveals About Personal Growth.* Grand Rapids, MI: Zondervan, 2001.

Coleman, Robert. *The Master Plan of Evangelism.* Grand Rapids, MI: Revell, 2010.

Comisky, Joel. *2000 Years of Small Groups: A History of Cell Ministry in the Church.* Moreno Valley, CA: CCS Publishing, 2015.

Donahue, Bill. *Leading Life-Changing Small Groups.* Grand Rapids, MI: Zondervan, 2002.

Donahue, Bill, and Russ Robinson. *Building a Church of Small Groups: A Place Where Nobody Stands Alone.* Grand Rapids, MI: Zondervan, 2001.

Early, David, and Rod Dempsey. *Disciplemaking Is: How to Live the Great Commission with Passion and Confidence.* Nashville, TN: B&H Academic, 2013.

Egli, Jim , "How Long Should Your Group Meetings Last?" *Christianity Today*, accessed March 3, 2019, https://www.smallgroups.com/articles/2013/how-long-should-your-group-meetings-last.html.

Estep, James R., Michael J. Anthony, and Gregg R. Allison. *A Theology for Christian Education.* Nashville, TN: B&H Publishing Group, 2008.

Gallaty, Robby."Disciple-making Task Force Report: Bible engagement, follow up key to discipleship," North American

Mission Board, June 21, 2018, https://www.namb.net/news/disciple-making-task-force-report-bible-engagement-follow-up-to-key-discussion/.

Geiger, Eric, Michael Kelley, and Phillip Nation. *Transformational Discipleship: How People Really Grow*. Nashville, TN: B&H Publishing Group, 2012.

George, Carl F. *Nine Keys to Effective Small Group Leadership: How Lay Leaders Can Establish Dynamic and Healthy Cells, Classes, or Teams*. Taylors, SC: CDLM, 2013.

Gladden, Steve. *Small Groups with Purpose: How to Create Healthy Communities*. Grand Rapids, MI: Baker Books, 2011.

Harrington, Bobby, and Alex Absalom. *Discipleship That Fits: The Five Kinds of Relationships God Uses to Help Us Grow*. Grand Rapids, MI: Zondervan, 2016.

Hemphill, Ken. *Revitalizing the Sunday Morning Dinosaur: A Sunday School Growth Strategy for the 21st Century*. Nashville, TN: Broadman and Holman, 1996.

Hemphill, Ken, and R. Wayne Jones. *Growing an Evangelistic Sunday School*. Nashville, TN: Broadman Press, 1989.

Henderson, D. Michael. *John Wesley's Class Meeting: A Model for Making Disciples*. Nappannee, IN: Francis Asbury Press, 1997.

Howerton, Rick. *A Different Kind of Tribe: Embracing the New Small-Group Dynamic*. Colorado Springs, CO: NavPress, 2012.

Hull, Bill. *The Disciple-Making Church*. Grand Rapids, MI: Fleming H. Revell, 1990.

Icenogle, Gareth Weldom. *Biblical Foundations for Small Group Ministry: An Integral Approach*. Downer's Grove, IL: InterVarsity Press, 1994.

Kelley, Charles S., Jr. *Fuel the Fire: Lessons from the History of Southern Baptist Evangelism*. A Treasury of Baptist Theology, edited by Paige Patterson and Jason G. Duesing. Nashville, TN: B&H Academic, 2018.

Kelley, Charles S., Jr. *How Did They Do It? The Story of Southern Baptist Evangelism.* Covington, LA: Insight Press, 1993.

Martin, Glen, and Gary McIntosh. *Creating Community: Deeper Fellowship Through Small Group Ministry.* Nashville, TN: Broadman & Holman, 1997.

McBride, Neal F. *How to Build a Small Groups Ministry.* Colorado Springs, CO: NavPress, 1995.

Melick, Rick, and Shera Melick. *Teaching That Transforms: Facilitating Life-Change through Adult Bible Teaching.* Nashville, TN: B&H Academic Publishing Group, 2010.

Mosley, Eddie. *Connecting in Communities: Understanding the Dynamics of Small Groups.* Colorado Springs, CO: NavPress, 2012.

Parkinson, Cally, *Rise: Bold Strategies to Transform Your Church*, Colorado Springs: CO: NavPress, 2015

Parr, Steve. *Sunday School That Really Works: A Strategy for Connecting Congregations to Communities.* Grand Rapids, MI: Kregel Publishers, 2010.

Pazmino, Robert E. *Basics of Teaching for Christians: Preparation, Instruction, Evaluation.* Grand Rapids, MI: Baker Book House, 2002.

Poling, Wayne. *How to Sunday School Manual.* Nashville, TN: LifeWay Press, 2009.

Putman, Jim, and Bobby Harrington. *DiscipleShift: Five Steps That Help Your Church.* Grand Rapids, MI: Zondervan, 2013.

Robbe, Brett. *Connect, Grow, Serve, Go: Moving Toward a Balanced Approach to an Adult Ministry.* With Dwayne McCrary. Nashville, TN: LifeWay Press, 2010.

Sisemore, John T. *Church Growth Through the Sunday School.* Nashville, TN: Broadman Press, 1997.

Small Group Ministries. "Small Group Connection Process." Accessed March 1, 2019, https://smallgroups.net/download/connection-strategy/.

Stetzer, Ed, and Eric Geiger. *Transformational Groups: Creating a New Scorecard for Groups*. Nashville, TN: B&H Books, 2015.

Stone, Randall. "5 Catalytic Actions to Rejuvenate Sunday School/Bible Teaching Ministry," n.d. Leadership Training Conference, Gulf Coast Baptist Association, Gulfport, MS, February 2, 2019.

Stone, Randall, John McClendon, and Jim Estep. *Indispensable: Becoming an MVP in Disciplemaking*. Amazon Digital Services LLC, 2018.

Taylor, Allan. *Sunday School in HD: Sharpening the Focus on What Makes Your Church Healthy*. Nashville, TN: Broadman and Holman, 2009.

Taylor, Bill. *21 Truths, Traditions, and Trends: Propelling the Sunday School into the 21st Century*. Nashville, TN: Convention Press, 1996.

Thompson, W. Oscar. *Concentric Circles of Concern: From Self to Others Through Life-Style Evangelism*. Nashville, TN: Broadman Press, 1981.

Vanderbloemen. "10 Things Millennials Are Looking For In Small Groups." Accessed March 3, 2019. https://www.vanderbloemen.com/blog/millennials-looking-for-small-groups.

Welch, Bobby H. *Evangelism Through Sunday School: A Journey of Faith*. Nashville, TN: LifeWay, 1997.

Wilson, Darryl. *Disciple-Making Encounters: Revolutionary Sunday School*. Abbotstord, WI: Aneko Press, Life Sentence Publishing, 2017.

Target Group Evangelism

EVANGELISM AND CHILDREN

Donna Peavey and Stephanie Cline

Children become Christians only through an experience of repentance and faith in Christ. In some way, a regenerate child must be able to express who Jesus is, what he did on his or her behalf, and that he resurrected. Like an adolescent or adult, a child must willingly choose to make a commitment of his or her life to Christ. Some may ask, can conversion of a child be sudden or is it gradual? While sudden conversion is a possibility, Scripture requires intentional spiritual nurturing that prepares a child for conversion. Both nurture and evangelism are necessary; "Nurture prepares the way, evangelism brings the good news that Jesus is the way."[1]

Southern Baptists have a conversionist theology—meaning that the way to become a Christian is by conversion, regardless of age. "Conversionist theology assumes an awareness of alienation from God, a recognition of God's provision for our salvation in Jesus Christ, and the cooperation of the human will with the divine will in effecting a conversion."[2] A child, at a point in time and enabled by God's grace, *becomes* a Christian. While the child's faith and repentance bring about regeneration, God initiates revelation and reconciliation.

Children are of utmost importance to Jesus. Matt 19:13–15 describes probably the most recognized interaction between Jesus and children. Jesus had been teaching about the nature of marriage when "some

---

[1] Gaines Dobbins, *Winning the Children* (Nashville, TN: Broadman, 1953), 52.
[2] William Hendricks, *A Theology for Children* (Nashville, TN: Broadman, 1980), 15.

children were brought to Him so that He might lay His hands on them and pray; and the disciples rebuked them. But Jesus said, 'Let the children alone, and do not hinder them from coming to Me; for the kingdom of heaven belongs to such as these.' After laying His hands on them, He departed from there." The disciples, those closest to Jesus (could this be church leaders today?), rebuked the *adults* who were bringing the children, either because they thought the children would be bothersome to him or were too young to understand. Clearly, Jesus was displeased with his disciples and called the children to himself, demonstrating the value he placed on them. Church leaders must encourage parents and other significant adults in the lives of children to bring them to him.

Before Jesus ascended to heaven, he addressed his followers and issued a final command, commonly known as the Great Commission, to "go therefore and make disciples of all the nations, baptizing them in the name of the Father and the Son and the Holy Spirit, teaching them to observe all that I commanded you" (Matt 28:19–20). All nations means all people, including children. Jesus also quoted from the Shema when he said in Matt 22:37 that the greatest commandment is, "You shall love the Lord your God with all your heart, and with all your soul, and with all your mind." The Shema (Deut 6:4–5) also instructed Israel to teach God's commandments to their children. Jesus joined the Great Commission and the Great Commandment, demonstrating they are inextricably intertwined. Obedience to God's commands is a demonstration of love for him. Nurturing, teaching, and sharing the gospel with children are essential to demonstrating love and obedience to the commands of God.

The nurture, teaching, and evangelism of children must take into account their developmental stage to avoid coercing them into confessing faith in Christ. Parents and church leaders do a disservice to young children when they expect them to understand concepts too complex for their stage of development. Children have spiritual experiences, and many respond to the loving nature of Jesus. This is a step toward faith and should not be equated with a responsible decision for Christ as it does not demonstrate the required understanding of key biblical truths. Faith required for salvation is accompanied by a sense of remorse and repentance.

Considering that such faith is required for salvation, a century-long trend among Southern Baptists that should be given attention is the drop in the average age of baptism. From 1899 to 1916, the average age for conversion and church membership was sixteen, in contrast with churches practicing infant baptism. From 1935 to 1955, the norm for conversion was nine to ten years of age. According to the 1966–67 reports of SBC churches, 48 percent of all baptisms were children age twelve and under. Of that number, 20 percent were age six to eight, with less than 1 percent under six. In 1970, Clifford Ingle predicted that on the basis of the trend, "It is reasonable to expect that children of four or five years of age will be considered as prospects for evangelistic activity."[3] His prediction has come to pass.

In 2014, a task force on evangelism and baptisms reported "the only consistently growing age group in baptisms is age five and under."[4] This is alarming, considering Southern Baptists believe baptism is "an act of obedience symbolizing the believer's faith in a crucified, buried, and risen Savior, the believer's death to sin, the burial of the old life, and the resurrection to walk in newness of life in Christ Jesus. It is a testimony to his faith in the final resurrection of the dead."[5] Are these children truly converted?

Young children can be saved. Yet history has taught us most children who make that decision under the age of seven tend to ask for rebaptism later. Responsible evangelism must be practiced because children are pliable and want to please, so they may yield to pressure from adults and peers to profess conversion. Hugh Wamble, professor of church history at Midwestern Theological Seminary, wrote,

---

[3] Clifford Ingle, "Why the Interest?" in *Children and Conversion*, ed. Clifford Ingle (Nashville, TN: Broadman, 1970), 14–15. Since *Children and Conversion,* no work can be found by Southern Baptist theologians that deals extensively with the nature of the child, accountability, conversion, and the discipleship of children. Dr. Donna Peavey (NOBTS) and Dr. Karen Kennemure (SWBTS) will soon release such a text.
[4] "Pastors' Task Force on SBC Evangelistic Impact and Declining Baptisms," *Baptist Press*, accessed January 25, 2019, http://www.bpnews.net/pdf/SBCTaskForceReport.pdf.
[5] "The Baptist Faith and Message 2000," Southern Baptist Convention, accessed January 25 2019, http://www.sbc.net/bfm2000/bfm2000.asp.

"Baptists have insisted that a church should consist only of regenerate persons admitted by believer's baptism only. But now they admit children to communion and to voting privileges at a younger age than do most Protestant Paedobaptists."[6] A worrying result of baptizing children too young is churches will be filled with unregenerate church members.

The task force also acknowledged a next generation problem, stating that although SBC churches have "increasingly provided programs for children, students and young adults, we are not being effective in winning and discipling the next generation to follow Christ."[7] To address the problem, the task force recommends efforts be made to reach and make disciples of the next generation. Additionally, church leaders must renew their focus on equipping parents and church leaders to communicate the gospel to the next generation.[8] If the children of today are going to embrace Christ as Savior, then Christians must commit to both nurturing and responsible evangelism.

How responsive are children to the gospel message? Children between the ages of five and thirteen are more likely than any other age group to accept Christ as Savior. A 2004 study by the Barna Group revealed just how receptive American children are to the gospel message and the window of opportunity for responsibly and effectively reaching them. Barna found 43 percent of all Americans who accept Jesus Christ as their Savior do so before age thirteen, and of that number, 64 percent make their commitment to Christ before their eighteenth birthday. Furthermore, 40 percent of the born-again people aligned with a Protestant church make their decision as children.[9] Yet, most evangelistic efforts

---

[6] Hugh Wamble, "Historic Practices Regarding Children," in *Children and Conversion*, ed. Clifford Ingle (Nashville, TN: Broadman, 1970), 83.

[7] "Pastors' Task Force on SBC Evangelistic Impact and Declining Baptisms."

[8] Resources available for equipping parents and leaders to share the gospel with children include: LifeWay Kids, *Leading a Child to Christ* Training Pack, (Nashville, TN: LifeWay Press, 2008); Art Murphy, *The Faith of a Child: A Step-by-Step Guide to Salvation for Your Child* (Chicago, IL: Moody Press, 2000).

[9] "Evangelism Is Most Effective Among Kids," Barna Group, accessed January 31, 2019, https://www.barna.com/research/evangelism-is-most-effective-among-kids/.

target adolescents and adults. Research indicates one's spiritual condition at age thirteen is a strong predictor of one's adult spiritual profile. The time has come for Christian parents, ministers, churches, and Christian ministries serving children to recognize that children develop their theological and moral worldviews by the time they are thirteen and to make intentional efforts to share the gospel message with them.

Many parents, pastors, church staff, and children's leaders find it difficult to share the gospel with children. They are unsure about what to say when a child is showing genuine interest and concern over their spiritual condition and how to know when a child is ready to accept Christ. Equipping the saints to share the gospel with children is necessary. There is no one special formula for sharing the gospel with children. In fact, sticking to a presentation outline may cause the evangelist to misread the situation and fail to answer the child's questions.

To illustrate, a crying preteen girl approached a counselor during the invitation at a summer camp worship service. The counselor, who was trained in counseling children, made no assumptions and said, "Tell me what is on your mind. What would you like to talk about?" The child responded she was concerned about her teenage sister's salvation, and so the counselor prayed for the sister with the child. A young boy responded to the invitation at VBS. When the counselor asked why he had come, he responded, "Well, if my brother is a sinner, I must be one too!" This young boy was taking a step toward saving faith, but he was not ready to make a decision.

10 Guiding Principles to Remember When Sharing the Gospel with Children

1. *The gospel is best communicated in the context of a relationship.*

    Barna found of the Christians who embraced Christ as Savior before their teen years, half were led to Christ by their parents, with another one in five led by some other friend or relative.[10]

---

[10] Ibid.

Children develop trust through relationships. When they know and trust the person sharing the gospel, they are more at ease and receptive. At children's camps and Vacation Bible Schools, the gospel presentation is most often shared close to the end of the session after the children have become familiar with the evangelist. Christ uses transformed people, not programs and activities, to touch the life of a child.

2. *Biblical language should be used when sharing the gospel, and the words need to be defined in child-friendly language.*

    The language of the faith is important, and it should be spoken to children. They must hear and use any language in order to understand it and become fluent. Sacred, biblical words that are unfamiliar need to be defined. Children are told that Jesus is the *Savior*—he *saves* them from their sin. They wonder what those words mean. Child-friendly definitions for words commonly used in gospel presentations, such as *Lord, forgive, eternal, repent,* and *confess,* should be developed.

3. *Avoiding Zionese and using clear language increases the child's understanding.*

    Religious vocabulary, often referred to as the language of Zion, consists of words and phrases used by Christians for generations. These terms are meaningful to those who understand them but are confusing to children and others who are unfamiliar with the language. For example, when someone says "Give your heart to Jesus," a child may think, "Why does Jesus need my heart? I need my heart." Instead, the evangelist should say, "Start a relationship with Jesus." Because children connect words they hear with words they already know, they can misinterpret the meaning of what has been stated. When "God is holy" is heard, a child may think, "God is full of holes." The evangelist should say, "God is holy. That means he is good and perfect." Instead of the Zionese phrase, "Jesus saves us from our sin," the evangelist should say "Jesus saves us from the *consequences* of our sin," which expresses more accurately what Jesus accomplished on the cross. Children understand consequences.

4. *Questions elicits responses that reveal a child's level of understanding.*

    Open-ended questions allow children to respond with more information about their understanding, attitudes, and feelings. Instead of asking, "Do you understand what sin is?" the evangelist should ask, "What do you understand about sin?" If a child doesn't understand essential biblical concepts, he should not be pressed into making a decision. Some children are still in the discerning stage and not ready to make a decision.

5. *Leading questions should be avoided in a gospel presentation.*

    Leading questions can manipulate a child and generally prompt a false response. For example, asking a child is she wants to go to heaven and then telling her if she prays the sinner's prayer she will go to heaven does not lead to true conversion. The result is a false positive, as she may believe she is now saved.

6. *The whole gospel should be shared with the child.*

    Galatians 1:7 is clear: "There are some who are disturbing you and want to distort the gospel of Christ." A child can understand the gospel message in its entirety under the leadership of the Holy Spirit who guides the child into *all* truth. The responsible evangelist must share the biblical truths in language on a level children can understand, which takes preparation and practice.

7. *The Holy Spirit should be trusted.*

    He is at work to give understanding, convict of sin, and draw the child to himself. Rom 1:16 states the gospel is "the power of God for salvation to everyone who believes." The evangelist should spend time in prayer before sharing the gospel and be sensitive to the Spirit's leading.

8. *The Bible and other resources should be used when sharing the gospel with children.*

    Children can highlight verses used in the gospel presentation in their Bible and write a list of the verses inside the cover. By doing so, they can return to the gospel presentation and review it.

Gospel tracts may be read by the child during and after the gospel presentation.

9. *Children should have their questions answered.*

    Children often have questions about heaven, hell, and death, among others. The questions they ask give clues as to how the Holy Spirit is working in their life. The wise evangelist takes the time to listen and answer the questions.

10. *Children should express their thoughts and feelings in a prayer of their own words.*

    Conversion is between the child and Jesus. He wants to hear from the child, not the evangelist. Rote and repeat-after-me prayers of salvation are not a biblical model.

Sharing the Gosepl with Children

Before beginning a gospel presentation, the evangelist should tell the child that *gospel* means "good news—telling the message about Christ, the kingdom of God, and salvation."[11] The following presentation emphasizes God's plan of salvation from creation to Jesus.

The Gospel as Presented in The Gospel: God's Plan for Me

- *God Rules*—God created everything, including you and me, and he oversees all he created. Verses to look at include Gen 1:1; Col 1:16–17; and Rev 4:11.[12]

---

[11] LifeWay Kids, *The Gospel: God's Plan for Me*, (Nashville, TN: LifeWay Press, 2012), 1. *The Gospel: God's Plan for Me is* a booklet to help parents and leaders share the gospel with children ages five to twelve. The gospel story is presented in child-friendly language and has applicable Scripture verses. It also includes information about how to respond to the gospel and the steps to take immediately afterwards to tell others.

[12] Easy-to-use translations for children include the Christian Standard Bible (CSB) or the New International Readers Version (NIRV).

- *We Sinned*—When we disobey God, we sin. Sin is an action, attitude, or thought that displeases God. Sin is what separates us from God, and we deserve his punishment of death. Verses to look at include Rom 3:23 and Rom 6:23.
- *God Provided*—Because sin entered the world, God provided his perfect Son Jesus as the way to rescue us from the punishment we deserve. Jesus alone saves us, and we can't earn it on our own. Verses to show include John 3:16 and Eph 2:8–9.
- *Jesus Gives*—Jesus lived a perfect life, died on the cross so we would not have to live separated from God forever, and rose again. Because Jesus died for us, we can live with God forever in heaven. Verses to look at include Rom 5:8; 2 Cor 5:21; Eph 2:8–9; and 1 Pet 3:18.
- *We Respond*—We are given the opportunity to choose to follow Jesus—believe he died on the cross and rose again three days later—repent (turn away) from the sin, and turn to Jesus. When you choose to live for Jesus, tell others what you did. Verses to show children include John 14:6 and Rom 10:9–10, 13.[13]

The ABCs of Responding to the Gospel

The ABCs help a child remember how to respond to the gospel.

A: *Admit* you are a sinner and repent. Repent means to turn around or change direction. We turn away from our sin and toward God.

B: *Believe* Jesus is God's Son and receive his gift of forgiveness from sin.

---

[13] For a more detailed version of explaining the gospel to children, see *The Gospel: God's Plan for Me*.

C. *Confess* to God, and other people, that Jesus is your Savior, and he is Lord of your life.[14]

Engaging Children in Evangelism

Christians must communicate the truth about their faith for boys and girls to understand *and* experience.[15] Once a child has become a Christian, he is to be obedient to the Great Commission and the Great Commandment. Church leaders and parents can equip children to share the gospel and engage children in evangelism through the following ways:

- *Develop a mission-minded attitude.*

  Children should understand God is mission-minded on a local and global scale. Jesus commanded, "Go therefore and make disciples of all the nations, baptizing them in the name of the Father and the Son and the Holy Spirit, teaching them to observe all that I commanded you" (Matt 28:19–20). Children come to understand the needs of their community by being involved with local mission agencies and meeting missionaries around the world.

  Second, parents who are mission-minded model such for their children. The church must equip parents to model mission-mindedness in the home. Children can invite their friends to church—whether it be an event like Vacation Bible School (VBS) or a regular Sunday service. Children may have friends who do not own Bibles. Parents can take children shopping for a Bible their friend may like. In the Bible, the child can write a note or highlight favorite verses, and present it as a gift. In the home, prayer can also be a powerful tool to build a mission-minded focus.[16]

---

[14] Chuck Peters, "Free Resources for Sharing Jesus with Kids," LifeWay Kids Ministry 101, accessed January 24 2019, https://kidsministry.lifeway.com/2016/12/12/free-resources-for-sharing-jesus-with-kids/.

[15] Lawrence O. Richards, *Children's Ministry: Nurturing Faith Within the Family of God* (Grand Rapids, MI: Zondervan, 1988), 78.

[16] Daniel R. Hyde, *Nursery of the Holy Spirit: Welcoming Children in Worship* (Eugene, OR: Wipf and Stock Publishers, 2014), 30.

- *Pray for friends and family.*
  Prayer in the home can start with meal times but can grow into prayer for others.[17] Children can make a list of friends and family with a need for salvation and other needs for which they can pray. Similarly, children can be shown a map of the world and be led to pray for missionaries sharing the gospel in a selected country. Children can be taught how to use a prayer journal or create a prayer board—one side is "prayers"; the other side is "praises." When God answers a prayer, the children can move the "prayer" to the side of "praises." Activities such as the prayer journal and prayer board help children grow in their relationship with Christ, as they look back and see how God worked in the situations. These activities engage the children physically, which reinforces their learning.

- *Equip children to share the gospel.*
  Equipping children to share the gospel with others is crucial to their ability to effectively share the gospel. Children may practice sharing the gospel presentation presented earlier in the chapter. The more the child practices sharing the gospel, the more confident he or she becomes in their ability. Children may practice with family members or peers at church.

- *Help children write and share their testimony.*
  An essential part of evangelism is telling one's story or testimony. All Christians have a testimony of how Jesus changed their life. A testimony involves three sections: what life was like before becoming a Christian, how the choice was made, and what life is like as a Christian. Children should be led to understand that as they mature in their relationship with God, they will be able to add to the third portion of the testimony. Telling their testimony to family and friends helps children become more comfortable in sharing it and will help them share the gospel when taking part in local mission projects and mission trips.

---

[17] Ibid.

- *Involve children in local mission projects.*
  Children can share the gospel message while serving at a food bank, writing cards, and visiting nursing home patients; they can collect toys, nonperishable food items, socks, gloves, and blankets for local shelters. Children are able to take much responsibility for collection drives. Visits to local mission sites provide children the opportunity to share their faith and learn about the needs of others.

- *Involve children in age-appropriate mission trips.*
  Children can share the gospel with others by being involved in local, national, or international mission trips taken with the church or their family. Mission trips are an excellent way for families to serve together. Children of all ages can participate in evangelism on mission trips. Whether they are the ones sharing the gospel or watching their parents do so, children can grow with the experience. Involving children in missions can lay a foundation for a future call.[18] One researcher concluded that one-third of missionaries in the early 1900s recollected their first interest in missions as children.[19] The Woman's Missionary Union (WMU) hosts an annual summer mission trip in the United States for families to participate in together. Age-appropriate mission trips and local projects allow children to grow and see the needs of others while being the hands and feet of Jesus.

The decision to accept Christ as Savior is one every person must make for him or herself, regardless of age. Parents, family members, and church leaders nurture and teach children, working together to bring them to the time when they are ready, able, and willing, to make a decision. While the evangelist must be prepared to share the gospel with children in a manner that is age-appropriate and biblically sound, the Holy Spirit "will convict the world concerning sin and righteousness and judgment" (John 16:8).

---

[18] Ibid., 16.
[19] Ruth Rouse, "A Study of Missionary Vocation," in *The International Review of Missions*, ed. J. H. Oldham (April 1917): 244–57.

BIBLIOGRAPHY

Baptist Press. "Pastors' Task Force on SBC Evangelistic Impact and Declining Baptisms." Accessed January 25, 2019. http://www.bpnews.net/pdf/SBCTaskForceReport.pdf.

Barna Group. "Evangelism Is Most Effective Among Kids." Accessed January 31, 2019. https://www.barna.com/research/evangelism-is-most-effective-among-kids/.

Dobbins, Gaines. *Winning the Children*. Nashville, TN: Broadman, 1953.

Griffiths, Mark. *One Generation From Extinction: How the Church Connects with the Unchurched Child*. Oxford: Monarch Books, 2009.

Hendricks, William. *A Theology for Children*. Nashville, TN: Broadman, 1980.

Hyde, Daniel R. *Nursery of the Holy Spirit: Welcoming Children in Worship*. Eugene, OR: Wipf and Stock Publishers, 2014.

Ingle, Clifford. "Why the Interest?" In *Children and Conversion*, edited by Clifford Ingle. Nashville, TN: Broadman, 1970.

LifeWay Kids. "Leading a Child to Christ." In *Training Pack*. Nashville, TN: LifeWay Press, 2008.

———. *The Gospel: God's Plan for Me*. Nashville, TN: LifeWay Press, 2012.

Murphy, Art. *The Faith of a Child: A Step-by-Step Guide to Salvation for Your Child*. Chicago, IL: Moody Press, 2000.

Peters, Chuck. "Free Resources for Sharing Jesus with Kids." LifeWay Kids Ministry 101. Accessed January 25, 2019. https://kidsministry.lifeway.com/2016/12/12/free-resources-for-sharing-jesus-with-kids/.

Richards, Lawrence O. *Children's Ministry: Nurturing Faith Within the Family of God*. Grand Rapids, MI: Zondervan, 1988.

Rouse, Ruth. "A Study of Missionary Vocation." In *The International Review of Missions*, edited by J. H. Oldham, Vol. 6. New York: Oxford University Press, 1917.

Southern Baptist Convention. "The Baptist Faith and Message: The 2000 Baptist Faith and Message." Southern Baptist Convention. Accessed May 2, 2019. http://www.sbc.net/bfm2000/bfm2000.asp.

Wamble, Hugh. "Historic Practices Regarding Children." In *Children and Conversion*, edited by Clifford Ingle. Nashville, TN: Broadman, 1970.

Target Group Evangelism

EVANGELIZING YOUTH AND COLLEGE STUDENTS

David Odom

Toby is a loud and rambunctious seventh grader who loves video games, sci-fi novels, and pestering girls. He spends his time at school, hanging out with friends, and doing whatever his single mom tells him to do. He's a good kid and mostly stays out of trouble. However, Toby is not a Christian, and he doesn't attend a church. As far as he knows, he doesn't even know anyone who is a Christian or goes to church. To Toby, Sunday is just another day, and God isn't real.

Tamra is a smart, outgoing junior in high school. She enjoys school and spending time with her two best friends. Tamra works part-time at a local fast-food restaurant to help her family make ends meet. She hopes to go to college and become a teacher, but unless she gets a scholarship, that dream may die. Tamra is an unbeliever, but one of her best friends, Samantha, is a Christian. At first, she thought it was odd and ridiculous to believe in Jesus and go to church. However, as she considers her life after high school, she has begun to wonder about life's meaning and purpose.

Junglim is a bright and funny twenty-year-old. She has several good friends, but family is most important to Junglim. She is an engineering major in college and lives on campus but spends weekends at home. She feels pressure to excel in school in order to get into the graduate school she wants. As a result, Junglim does not spend time on anything other than school and family. Although Sue, one of her classmates, has invited her to a campus Bible study, Junglim has never attended. Junglim is not a Christian.

Each of these youth and college students represents someone who needs the gospel. They need someone to take the time to engage them with the message of salvation. They need leaders who will train and mobilize other believers to share their faith with them. They need you.

According to Barna Group, today's youth and college students are part of the first truly post-Christian generation.[1] The term post-Christian refers to a decline in spiritual indicators such as church attendance, belief in God, prayer, and Bible reading. Despite these declines, the teenage and young adult years continue to hold spiritual significance. Most believers become a Christian before age twenty-one.[2] Less than one out of every four accept Christ after their twenty-first birthday.[3] The apostle Paul wrote in Phlm 1:6 (italics added), "I pray that you may be *active in sharing your faith* so that you may know every good thing you have in Christ Jesus."[4] Ministry leaders must clearly communicate the vision and purpose for evangelism and develop a strategic evangelistic process for reaching youth and college students.

A healthy ministry invites young people and college students into a relationship with Jesus Christ and helps them grow toward spiritual maturity. However, a priority on evangelism does not happen automatically. Seventy-five percent of youth leaders view "building relationships" as the main concern while only 20 percent see evangelism as a high priority.[5] Evangelism will only become a core value

---

[1] Barna Group, *Gen Z: The Culture, Beliefs, and Motivations Shaping the Next Generation* (Barna, 2018), 24.
[2] "Evangelism Is Most Effective Among Kids," Barna Group, accessed January, 15, 2019 https://www.barna.com/research/evangelism-is-most-effective-among-kids/.
[3] Ibid.
[4] The Holy Bible, New International Version. Grand Rapids: Zondervan House, 1984.
[5] Barna Group, "The Priorities, Challenges, and Trends in Youth Ministry," April 6, 2016, https://www.barna.com/research/the-priorities-challenges-and-trends-in-youth-ministry/.

when ministers provide "genuine and dramatic leadership in that direction."⁶ The most effective leaders lead by example. John Maxwell says, "People do what people see."⁷ Students and adult leaders need to see healthy evangelism modeled.⁸ The first step in modeling evangelism is an understanding of what makes youth and college students unique.

Know Your Audience

Over the last decade, discussions of young people have centered on Millennials. However, today's teenagers and college students are known by a new name: Generation Z (born 1996–2010). Approximately 1.8 billion Gen Z'ers exist worldwide—the largest youth population ever.⁹ They make up 25.9 percent of the US population.¹⁰

Generation Z is characterized by pluralistic ideology and superficial theology.¹¹ Gen Z has a hard time believing in a good God who would allow evil and pain in the world.¹² Consequently, most people ages eighteen to twenty-five do not have a relationship with Christ and are not prepared for a lifetime of faith.¹³ The faith of most young adults is weak and anemic.

---

⁶ Richard Ross, *Youth Ministry That Lasts a Lifetime* (Fort Worth, TX: Seminary Hill Press, 2017), 164.

⁷ John Maxwell, *The 21 Irrefutable Laws of Leadership: Follow Them and People Will Follow You* (Nashville, TN: Thomas Nelson, 2007), 235.

⁸ Ben Trueblood, *Student Ministry That Matters: Three Elements of Healthy Student Ministry* (Nashville, TN: LifeWay, 2016), 26.

⁹ Steven Edwards, "10 things you didn't know about the world's population," *United Nations Population Fund*, April, 13, 2015, https://www.unfpa.org/news/10-things-you-didn%E2%80%99t-know-about-world%E2%80%99s-population.

¹⁰ Sparks & Honey, "Meet Generation Z: Forget Everything You Learned About Millennials," LinkedIn SlideShare. N.p., 17 June 2014.

¹¹ Tim Elmore, *Marching off the Map: Inspire Students to Navigate a Brand New World* (Atlanta: Poet Gardner, 2017), Kindle.

¹² Barna Group, *Gen Z*, 38.

¹³ Richard Ross, *Accelerate: Parenting Teenagers toward Adulthood* (Bloomington: CrossBooks, 2013), 4.

Here are few more of the findings:

- 57 percent use a smartphone four or more hours a day[14]
- Daily interact with three to five screens (compared to one to two for Millennials)[15]
- Eight hours of total electronic exposure daily[16]
- 94 percent of eighteen- to twenty-four-year-olds watch YouTube[17]
- 57 percent of teens have met a new friend online[18]
- Lower attention span of eight seconds (down from twelve seconds in 2000)[19]
- Open-minded[20]
- Empowered to change institutions (including the church)[21]
- 78 percent believe in God and 41 percent attend weekly religious services[22]
- Twice as likely as adults to be atheists[23]
- Social activists who want to join a cause[24]

---

[14] Barna Group, *Gen Z*, 16.
[15] Sparks & Honey, "Meet Generation Z."
[16] Anthony Turner, "Generation Z: Technology and Social Interest," *Journal of Individual Psychology* 71, no. 2 (2015): 105.
[17] Ibid.
[18] Amanda Lenhart, "Teens, Technology and Friendships," *Pew Internet* August 6, 2015, http://www.pewinternet.org/2015/08/06/teens-technology-and-friendships/.
[19] Ibid.
[20] Corey Seemiller and Meghan Grace, *Generation Z Goes to College* (San Francisco: John Wiley & Sons, 2016), 10.
[21] Ibid., 44.
[22] Ibid., 43.
[23] Barna Group, *Gen Z*, 14.
[24] Donna Vallone, A. Smith, T. Kenney, and Robin Koval. "Agents of Social Change: A Model for Targeting and Engaging Generation Z across Platforms," *Journal of Advertising Research* 56 no. 4 (2016): 418.

Seven out of ten high school students have significant doubts about God and faith.[25] Yet fewer than half talk with either church leaders or peers about their struggles.[26] Recent LifeWay research shows 66 percent of students who were active in church during high school drop out during their college years.[27]

Even if today's youth and college students do not drop out of the church, they are more likely to develope an immature faith. In fact, the faith of many adults in the church is immature. Kenda Creasy Dean explains the problems in youth ministry are representative of problems in the church as a whole: "The religiosity of American teenagers must be read primarily as a reflection of their parents' religious devotion (or lack thereof) and, by extension, that of their congregations."[28] Teens mirror the faith modeled for them by parents and members of the congregation.

Communicating a Vision and Purpose for Evangelism

The greatest need of every teenager and college student is to come to faith in Christ. The Bible provides clear support for an emphasis on evangelism. Evangelism is part of the Great Commission (Matt 28:19–20). God desires for every student to repent and turn to him (John 3:17; 2 Tim 2:3–4; 2 Pet 3:9). Jesus died for everyone (Heb 2:9; 1 Tim 4:10; 1 John 2:2). God will forgive anyone who calls on him (Rom 10:13). Although the biblical imperative is clear, some church leaders struggle with the tension between a focus on discipleship and evangelism.

---

[25] Kara Powell, Brad Griffin, and Cheryl Crawford, *Sticky Faith, Youth Worker Edition: Practical Ideas to Nurture Long-Term Faith in Teenagers* (Grand Rapids, MI: Zondervan, 2011), 143–145.
[26] Ibid.
[27] Ben Trueblood, *Within Reach: The Power of Small Changes in Keeping Students Connected* (Nashville, TN: LifeWay Press, 2018), 11.
[28] Kenda Creasy Dean, *Almost Christian: What the Faith of Our Teenagers Is Telling the American Church* (New York: Oxford University Press, 2010), 4.

The Tension between Discipleship and Evangelism

In some churches today there exists a dichotomy between evangelism and discipleship—between an attraction-based ministry approach (evangelism) and one that focuses on training (discipleship). It is common for a church to emphasize one over the other. Church leaders may feel pressure to focus on ministry and programs for the current members of the congregation.

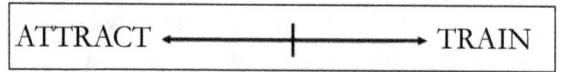

Figure 1. The Tension between Discipleship and Evangelism[29]

However, the tension between these two does not have to exist at all. A healthy church includes evangelism and discipleship along with worship, ministry, and fellowship.[30] "True discipleship leads to making evangelism a priority. And evangelism leads to an even greater desire for discipleship."[31] Ephesians 4:11 describes the role of an evangelist as a vital part of equipping the church.

Pressures to meet the perceived needs of church members are not the only reason churches do not focus on evangelism. Church leaders and volunteers use excuses such as *I'm not outgoing, I'm not good at public speaking,* and *I don't know what to say or how to start a conversation.* These excuses may stem from fear and inexperience. Healthy churches provide training to prepare believers to share their faith. An evangelistic focus is the result of missional culture within the church.

---

[29] Mark Senter, "A Historical Framework for Doing Youth Ministry" in *Reaching a Generation for Christ: A Comprehensive Guide to Youth Ministry* eds. Richard R. Dunn and Mark Senter (Chicago: Moody, 1997), 111.
[30] Mark Cannister, *Teenager Matter: Making Student Ministry a Priority in the Church* (Grand Rapids: Baker Academic, 2013), 35.
[31] Ross, *Accelerate*, 166.

Missional Culture

The mission of the church is the mission of youth and collegiate ministry. It is not enough to focus on evangelizing and discipling youth; leaders must focus on disciples who produce disciples. The goal is replication.[32] Producing disciple makers happens through evangelistic training and discipleship.

Leaders must intentionally engage young people and help them grow toward spiritual maturity.[33] Pastors begin the disciple-making process by leading young people to a saving relationship with Jesus Christ. The next step is providing young people with the spiritual food necessary for growth. They need the spiritual food of God's word. Youth need to learn how to share their faith. In order to spiritually mature, teenagers need regular engagement in both areas because they are cyclical—evangelism leads to Bible study and Bible study informs evangelism.[34]

Some view evangelism from two basic approaches: signposts and sales.[35] Signposts point the way, and salespeople try to close the deal. The problem with this view is that church leaders tend to focus on pointing the way without ever calling for a personal response to the gospel. I believe there is a place for both in today's youth and college ministry. Leaders should develop incarnational relationships with youth and young adults. However, leaders should also develop a strategy that includes explicit gospel presentations and invitations for a response.

---

[32] Dave Keehn, "Youth Ministry from a Family Perspective," in *A Theology for Family Ministry* eds. Michael Anthony and Michelle Anthony (Nashville: B&H Academic, 2011), 232.
[33] Steve Parr and Tom Crites, *Why They Stray: Helping Parents and Church Leaders Make Investments That Keep Children and Teens Connected to the Church for a Lifetime* (Bloomington: WestBow, 2015), 122.
[34] David Odom, "Ministry Leadership with Emerging Adults," in *Together We Equip: Integrating Disciple and Ministry Leadership for Holistic Spiritual Formation* (Bloomington, IL: WestBow Press, 2018), 143.
[35] Duffy Robbins, *Building a Youth Ministry That Builds Disciples: A Small Book about a Big Idea* (Grand Rapids, MI: Zondervan, 2011), 65.

Strategic Evangelistic Process for Youth and College Ministry

Prayer fuels evangelism.[36] Before adopting an evangelistic strategy, wise leaders will pray for a harvest of souls and for insight to lead effectively. A six-step process will help leaders develop a strategy for clearly presenting the gospel to students. First, leaders need to develop relationships with youth and college students. Next, leaders need to build a ministry structure for reaching young people. Third, church leaders must train students and adults to share the gospel. Fourth, leaders should harness the power of personal testimony. Fifth, leaders should share the gospel in multiple contexts. Sixth, ministers must invite a response to the gospel.

1. Develop Relationships

Rather than a program, a leader's priority should be on building godly relationships with teenagers and college students.[37] Jesus focused on relationships. The call to "follow Me" in Matt 4:19 was a relational invitation. Jesus invited his disciples into a relationship with him. True discipleship can only take place in the context of relationships. Leaders must intentionally invest in relationships with young people. God-centered relationships produce faithful and mature disciples.[38]

But church leaders cannot do it alone. They need caring adults who are willing to come alongside youth and college students. Leaders need to build an "environment of care and discipleship" by providing many ways for adults to invest time with young people.[39]

---

[36] Greg Stier, *Gospelize Your Youth Ministry: A Spicy "New" Philosophy (That's 2000 Years Old)* (Arvada, CO: D2S Publishing, 2015), 87.

[37] Greg Ogden, *Transforming Discipleship: Making Disciples a Few at a Time* (Downers Grove, IL: InterVarsity Press, 2003), 121.

[38] David Kinnaman, *You Lost Me: Why Young Christians Are Leaving the Church … and Rethinking Faith* (Grand Rapids: Baker, 2011), 206.

[39] Trueblood, *Student Ministry That Matters*, 29.

The mentor and mentee relationship provide a strong basis for discipleship and disciple-making. Learning from the example of others is an effective model used throughout Scripture. It is still true today. In fact, the strongest predictor of a student staying in church after high school is three or more adults investing in that young person's life between ages fifteen and eighteen.[40]

Leaders must intentionally seek out godly adults willing to mentor young people who often do not have relationships with older and wiser believers.[41] Leaders must recruit disciple-making adults who demonstrate faithfulness, reliability, and dependability.[42] Once leaders have developed relationships, it's time to build a structure for evangelism.

2. Build a Structure for Evangelism

As with any ministry, leaders should begin with the end in mind. What is the goal of evangelism? How will you help youth and college students grow in their faith? What is your process for helping young people move from new believer to a disciple? The apostle Paul talked about the goal of discipleship in his letter to the Ephesians.

> Until we all attain to the unity of the faith, and of the knowledge of the Son of God, to a mature man, to the measure of the stature which belongs to the fullness of Christ. As a result, we are no longer to be children, tossed here and there by waves and carried about by every wind of doctrine, by the trickery of men, by craftiness in deceitful scheming; but speaking the truth in love, we are to grow up in all aspects into Him who

---

[40] Ibid., 27.
[41] Christian Smith, *Lost in Transition: The Dark Side of Emerging Adulthood* (New York: Oxford University, 2011), 235.
[42] Ogden, *Transforming Discipleship*, 179.

is the head, even Christ, from whom the whole body, being fitted and held together by what every joint supplies, according to the proper working of each individual part, causes the growth of the body for the building up of itself in love. (Eph 4:13–16)

Paul explained the process of spiritual growth in developmental terms. He describes it as the natural progression from infancy to adulthood. According to Paul, maturing faith is strong enough to withstand "every wind of doctrine" and "deceitful scheming." He also described a person with maturing faith as one who understands his or her place in the body of Christ. To develop maturing faith in youth and college students, leaders should develop a strategy that begins with evangelism and continues through the discipleship process.

The process of evangelism and discipleship has been illustrated over the years by well-known leaders. In several models, the process incorporates four broad levels of maturity for a believer.[43] Doug Fields, in *Purpose Driven Youth Ministry*, uses community/crowd, congregation, committed, and core.[44] Sonlife Ministries uses outreach, growth, ministry training, and leadership multiplication.[45] At Cru (formerly Campus Crusade for Christ), it is win, build, equip, and send.[46] Jay Sedwick uses curious, convinced, committed, and commissioned.[47] Steve Vandergriff and Richard Brown call their four levels: entry, evangelize, edify, and equip.

---

[43] Jay Sedwick, "In Between: Adolescents" in *Invitation to Educational Ministry: Foundations of Transformative Christian Education*, eds. George M. Hillman Jr. and Sue G. Edwards (Grand Rapids, MI: Kregel Publications, 2018), 165.
[44] Doug Fields, *Purpose Driven Youth Ministry* (Grand Rapids, MI: Zondervan, 2000), 51.
[45] Dann Spader and Gary Mayes, *Growing A Healthy Church* (Chicago, IL: Moody, 1991), 34.
[46] Cru.org.
[47] Sedwick, "In Between: Adolescents" in *Invitation to Educational Ministry*, 165.

The strength of Vandergriff and Brown's approach is a dedicated level of evangelistic intention. While the others imply evangelism in the first or second level, Vandergriff and Brown state the intention of stage two is to see "unsaved students to commit to Christ."[48] Duffy Robbins describes a six-level progression—pool of humanity, come, grow, disciple, develop, and multiplier—that corresponds to three relational ministry levels: contact, connect, and contribute.[49]

Leaders can use one of these models or develop their own. The point is to adopt a process that leads students to evangelize the lost and help them grow toward maturity in Christ. It is not enough to focus on evangelism; leaders must focus on making disciples who produce disciple-makers. The goal is to replicate yourself.[50]

3. Train Students and Adults to Share the Gospel

An effective witness is a trained witness. Students and adults need to know how to share their faith. However, before you train others, you need training. For some leaders, the first step might involve participation in an evangelistic training event for church leaders.

Modeling evangelism is one of the best ways to train others to share their faith.[51] Jesus inspired his followers by offering his life as an example to follow.[52] Leaders can do the same. As leaders make evangelistic visits, they should take youth with them. When preparing for an evangelistic sermon, leaders can invite college students to help plan the message.

---

[48] Steve Vandergriff and Richard Brown, *Student Ministry Essentials: Reaching. Leading. Nurturing.* (Chicago, IL: Moody Publishers, 2015), 181.
[49] Robbins, *Building a Youth Ministry That Builds Disciples*, 118, 173.
[50] Keehn, "Youth Ministry from a Family Perspective," in *A Theology for Family Ministry*, 232.
[51] Ibid., 118.
[52] Dave Rahn and Terry Linhart, *Evangelism Remixed: Empowering Students for Courageous and Contagious Faith* (El Cajon, CA: Youth Specialties, 2009), 30.

In my own ministry, I have used a variety of gospel presentation methods to lead students to faith in Christ. The ABCs of the Gospel is easy to remember—Admit, Believe, and Confess. In the 1990s, I used FAITH—Forgiveness, Available, Impossible, Turn, and Heaven. A tried-and-true method is the Roman Road to Salvation, which uses key verses from the book of Romans (Rom 3:23; 6:23; 5:8; 9:9–10). Another method is a relational approach called Gospel Conversations, which uses the 3 Circles (God's design, brokenness, and gospel) diagram.[53]

In addition to key verses describing how to become a Christian, leaders should also prepare for questions and doubts. Leaders should become familiar with apologetic responses to questions such as: How do we know the Bible is true? Is Jesus the only way to a right relationship with God? Why is baptism important?

A reasoned response is helpful, but a personal relationship of mutual trust is the key. The necessity of mutual trust is why relationships and community are vital. One of the personal characteristics most significantly related to evangelism is "increased honesty about questions and struggles."[54] Relationships provide a safe environment for questions and doubts related to salvation. Leaders must be sensitive to questions and doubts, seeing them as "faith-forming opportunities rather than freak-out moments of failure."[55] Many of today's young people desire a sense of belonging before they believe. Not every gospel conversation has to be an in-depth proclamation of the gospel.[56]

---

[53] Dustin Willis and Aaron Coe, *Life on Mission: Joining the Everyday Mission of God* (Chicago, IL: Moody Publishers, 2014).
[54] Kara Powell, Jake Mulder, and Brad Griffin, *Growing Young: 6 Essential Strategies to Help Young People Discover and Love Your Church* (Grand Rapids, MI: Baker, 2016), 144.
[55] Powell, et al., *Growing Young*, 157.
[56] Robbins, 69.

4. Harness the Power of Testimony

A personal testimony can be a powerful witness. Leaders must encourage students to share their personal stories of God's work in their lives. These testimonies might include conversion experiences, breakthroughs, and stories of God's work in the lives of church members.[57] "When a people can see their story located within God's story, the work of the church gains greater meaning."[58]

A basic testimony outline is: (1) What your life was like before Christ, (2) How you became a Christian, and (3) How Jesus has changed your life. Instruct students to memorize and practice sharing their testimony with friends and family. Once students have mastered their testimonies, they are ready to share with others. I have used student testimonies in worship settings, in beach evangelism, at campus clubs, on mission trips, and during evangelistic visits.

5. Share in Multiple Contexts

Leaders should share the gospel in multiple contexts. For example, in a large group gathering, a leader might present the basics of how to become a Christian using the ABCs of the Gospel method. In a small group setting, a leader could discuss the Roman Road to Salvation. In a one-on-one encounter, a leader might have a Gospel Conversation. Any given week, leaders should plan to engage students in all three contexts. In addition, leaders should train volunteers to engage in all three contexts as well.

6. Invite a Response

A missing ingredient in some evangelistic efforts is a call for response. Church leaders will follow the gospel presentation steps and stop short of inviting youth and college students to accept

---

[57] Powell, et al., 155.
[58] Ibid., 140.

Christ. Yet inviting a response is biblical. Biblical examples of calling for response include:

- Jonah (Jonah 1:1–2; 3:4–5; 4:1–2)
- Elijah (1 Kgs 18:21, 36–39)
- Jesus (Matt 4:12–22; Mark 2:13–14; Luke 19:1–6, 8–10)
- Peter (Acts 2:36–39)
- Paul (Acts 17:1–4)

Some hesitation to calling for response is warranted. Leaders do not want to be manipulative or prey on the emotions of young people.[59] Yet I wonder if part of the reason baptism rates are down is that church leaders have abandoned the use of an invitation to call for a personal response to the gospel. If leaders are concerned about avoiding manipulation, train adults to conduct effective decision counseling and follow-up. Leaders can also invite youth to stay after the service to speak privately instead of a traditional "come forward" invitation. College leaders could ask students to send text messages if they have questions about salvation. There are multiple ways to invite a response—the key is to do it and let the Holy Spirit do his work.

The summer after seventh grade year, Toby attended a sports clinic run by a local church youth ministry. He had a great time and made several new friends. He also made a connection with Jake, a college student who served as one of the clinic coaches. Jake invited Toby and his friends to youth camp. On the last night of camp, Toby made a decision to accept Christ. He is now being discipled by Jake.

Samantha had been praying for weeks for the right opportunity to share with Tamra. She attended evangelism training at her church and memorized her testimony and several key Scripture verses. One day

---

[59] David Evans, "An Analysis of Personal Experiences that Influence Selected Generations to Attend Churches Affiliated with the Tennessee Baptist Convention" (PhD diss., New Orleans Baptist Theological Seminary, 2016), 83.

Tamra and Samantha were looking at college brochures for schools with childhood education degrees. Samantha saw Tamra looking at a brochure with three ABC building blocks on the cover. She reached out and wrote "admit, believe, confess," across the blocks. Tamra asked her what that meant. Samantha spent a few minutes explaining the plan of salvation and then asked Tamra if she wanted to accept Christ. Tamra said she wasn't ready but would think about. Although Samantha was disappointed her friend didn't make a decision that day, she knew God was at work in Tamra's life. Samantha continues to pray for Tamra and for further opportunities to share her faith.

Sue took another approach to evangelism after Junglim rejected the idea of spending time at a campus Bible study. She began to engage Junglim in Gospel Conversations. At first, it was a question about what Junglim believed about global warming and the environment. Sue used the opportunity to share that as a Christian, she believes it is important to care for the planet. Over the course of several weeks, Sue talked with Junglim about her thoughts on God, sin, death, and Jesus. One day after class, Sue shared the 3 Circles evangelistic tool. A week later, Junglim asked Sue to pray with her to receive Christ as Savior.

Jake, Samantha, and Sue all have one thing in common. They each had church leaders who gave them evangelistic training and encouragement to share their faith with others. You can do the same.

Bibliography

Barna Group. *Gen Z: The Culture, Beliefs, and Motivations Shaping the Next Generation*. Ventura: Barna Group, 2018.

Barna Group. "Evangelism Is Most Effective among Kids." *Barna* (2004). Accessed January 15, 2019. https://www.barna.com/research/evangelism-is-most-effective-among-kids/.

Barna Group. "The Priorities, Challenges, and Trends in Youth Ministry" *Barna* (2016). Accessed January 15, 2019. https://www.barna.com/research/the-priorities-challenges-and-trends-in-youth-ministry/.

Berg, Ryan. "Cru: Joining In God's Story." *Cru*. Accessed January 15, 2019. https://www.cru.org/us/en/about/what-we-do/cru-joining-in-gods-story.html

Cannister, Mark. *Teenager Matter: Making Student Ministry a Priority in the Church*. Grand Rapids, MI: Baker Academic, 2013.

Dean, Kenda Creasy. *Almost Christian: What the Faith of Our Teenagers Is Telling the American Church*. New York: Oxford University Press, 2010.

Edwards, Steven. "10 things you didn't know about the world's population." *United Nations Population Fund*, (April, 2015). Accessed January 15, 2019. https://www.unfpa.org/news/10-things-you-didn%E2%80%99t-know-about-world%E2%80%99s-population.

Elmore, Tim. *Marching off the Map: Inspire Students to Navigate a Brand New World*. Atlanta, GA: Poet Gardner, 2017.

Evans, David. "An Analysis of Personal Experiences that Influence Selected Generations to Attend Churches Affiliated with the Tennessee Baptist Convention." (PhD diss., New Orleans Baptist Theological Seminary, New Orleans, 2016).

Fields, Doug. *Purpose Driven Youth Ministry*. Grand Rapids, MI: Zondervan, 2000.

Keehn, Dave. "Youth Ministry from a Family Perspective," in *A Theology for Family Ministry*, edited by Michael Anthony and Michelle Anthony. Nashville, TN: B&H Academic, 2011.

Kinnaman, David. *You Lost Me: Why Young Christians Are Leaving the Church ... and Rethinking Faith*. Grand Rapids, MI: Baker, 2011.

Lenhart, Amanda. "Teens, Technology and Friendships." *Pew Internet* (August 2015). Accessed January 15, 2019. http://www.pewinternet.org/2015/08/06/teens-technology-and-friendships/.

Maxwell, John. *The 21 Irrefutable Laws of Leadership: Follow Them and People Will Follow You*. Nashville, TN: Thomas Nelson, 2007.

Odom, David. "Ministry Leadership with Emerging Adults." In *Together We Equip: Integrating Disciple and Ministry Leadership for Holistic Spiritual Formation*. Bloomington: WestBow Press, 2018.

Ogden, Greg. *Transforming Discipleship: Making Disciples a Few at a Time*. Downers Grove, IL: InterVarsity Press, 2003.

Powell, Kara, Jake Mulder, and Brad Griffin. *Growing Young: 6 Essential Strategies to Help Young People Discover and Love Your Church*. Grand Rapids, MI: Baker, 2016.

_____, Brad Griffin, and Cheryl Crawford. *Sticky Faith, Youth Worker Edition: Practical Ideas to Nurture Long-Term Faith in Teenagers*. Grand Rapids, MI: Zondervan, 2011.

Parr, Steve, and Tom Crites. *Why They Stray: Helping Parents and Church Leaders Make Investments That Keep Children and Teens Connected to the Church for a Lifetime*. Bloomington, IL: WestBow, 2015.

Rahn, Dave, and Terry Linhart. *Evangelism Remixed: Empowering Students for Courageous and Contagious Faith*. El Cajon, CA: Youth Specialties, 2009.

Ross, Richard. *Youth Ministry That Lasts a Lifetime*. Fort Worth, TX: Seminary Hill Press, 2017.

_____. *Accelerate: Parenting Teenagers toward Adulthood*. Bloomington, IL: CrossBooks, 2013.

Robbins, Duffy. *Building a Youth Ministry That Builds Disciples: A Small Book about a Big Idea* Grand Rapids, MI: Zondervan, 2011.

Seemiller, Corey, and Meghan Grace, *Generation Z Goes to College*. San Francisco: John Wiley & Sons, 2016.

Sedwick, Jay. "In Between: Adolescents." In *Invitation to Educational Ministry: Foundations of Transformative Christian Education*, edited by George H. Hillman Jr. and Sue G. Edwards. Grand Rapids, MI: Kregel Publications, 2018.

Senter, Mark. "A Historical Framework for Doing Youth Ministry." In *Reaching a Generation for Christ: A Comprehensive Guide to Youth Ministry*, edited by Richard R. Dunn and Mark Senter. Chicago, IL: Moody, 1997.

Smith, Christian. *Lost in Transition: The Dark Side of Emerging Adulthood*. New York: Oxford University, 2011.

Spader, Dann, and Gary Mayes. *Growing A Healthy Church*. Chicago, IL: Moody, 1991.

Sparks & Honey. "Meet Generation Z: Forget Everything You Learned About Millennials." LinkedIn SlideShare. (June 2014). Accessed January 15, 2019. https://www.slideshare.net/sparksandhoney/generation-z-final-june-17.

Stier, Greg. *Gospelize Your Youth Ministry: A Spicy "New" Philosophy (That's 2000 Years Old)*. Arvada: D2S Publishing, 2015.

Trueblood, Ben. *Student Ministry That Matters: Three Elements of Healthy Student Ministry*. Nashville, TN: LifeWay, 2016.

_____. *Within Reach: The Power of Small Changes in Keeping Students Connected*. Nashville: LifeWay Press, 2018.

Turner, Anthony. "Generation Z: Technology and Social Interest." *Journal of Individual Psychology* 71, no. 2 (2015): 105.

Vallone, Donna, A. Smith, T. Kenney, and Robin Koval. "Agents of Social Change: A Model for Targeting and Engaging Generation Z across Platforms," *Journal of Advertising Research* 56 no. 4 (2016).

Vandergriff, Steve, and Richard Brown. *Student Ministry Essentials: Reaching. Leading. Nurturing*. Chicago, IL: Moody Publishers, 2015.

Willis, Dustin, and Aaron Coe. *Life On Mission: Joining the Everyday Mission of God*. Chicago, IL: Moody Publishers, 2014.

Target Group Evangelism

MEN AND WOMEN IN EVANGELISM: KEYS TO RELATIONAL OUTREACH AND DISCIPLEMAKING

Jody Dean and Emily Dean

When Jesus came in the flesh to bring the gift of the good news of the gospel, he brought his gift of salvation to all people, both men and women. For centuries men and women around the globe have heard and responded to the gospel of Jesus Christ. In Gal 3:28, the apostle Paul points out the gospel is the same for all, while the way in which individuals receive and respond to the gospel may be different based on the unique distinctions in gender.

Why is it that studies in recent decades have found women to be more likely to be involved in the church than men[1], more likely to say religion is very important in their lives, and more likely to pray on a regular basis?[2] While the gender gap is decreasing slightly from the 1980s, the smaller gap can be attributed to an overall decline in church attendance from both men and women. As the religious landscape

---

[1] Pew Research Center, "Religious Landscape Study," Pew Research Center (2018), accessed December 18, 2018, www.pewforum.org/religious-landscape-study/gender-composition/.

[2] Dalia Fahmy, "Christian Women in the U.S. Are More Religious than Their Male Counterparts," Pew Research Center, April 6, 2018, www.pewresearch.org/fact-tank/2018/04/06/christian-women-in-the-u-s-are-more-religious-than-their-male-counterparts/.

in America changes, the decrease is likely a result of the increase in "nones," or those who have no religious affiliation at all.[3] With overall church attendance in decline, opportunities now abound for sharing the gospel to both men and women. If women are more likely to participate in church, then what can the church do to focus greater efforts on reaching men while continuing to reach more women with the gospel?

Relational Outreach among Men

Men who have been connected to a Southern Baptist church for the past several decades likely have memories of brotherhood program, church work days, and wild game dinners. However, the influence of men for the kingdom is broader and should involve men reaching men for Christ. The reality is many in-depth approaches to reach men and begin a discipleship process have not been as strong as those by women in most churches. However, the trend may be changing as churches begin to see a greater desire for men's ministry with a discipleship focus. An emphasis of men mentoring men to grow into the people God has called them to be is vital to evangelism. If we reach men, then we also should have a pipeline for these men to be discipled, find community, and learn to serve using their giftedness through the local church. Natural opportunities for outreach abound as men:

1. *Develop an inclusive spirit.*

    A men's ministry with an inclusive spirit is one that invites all men to come and be a part of the holistic nature of the church. The problem for many men is the awkwardness of feeling connected to a local church. Sometimes it is hard for men to be open and inviting to other men, and this lack of an inclusive spirit can be a

---

[3] Aaron Earls, "Church Attendance Gender Gap Shrinks, But It's Not All Good News," LifeWay Facts and Trends, September 25, 2017, https://factsandtrends.net/2017/09/25/church-attendance-gender-gap-shrinks-but-its-not-all-good-news/.

vulnerable point in reaching other men for Christ. If men move from being worship attenders to being engaged in a small group for discipleship, then opportunities for serving within the body would be a natural result cascading in the relational components of outreach. Community can occur for men in many ways. When we help men find other men with similar interests, whether in sports, food, family, or work, then relational evangelism can naturally occur. Men have to decide how they are going to take their influence among the men they do life with to engage in a gospel conversation.

2. *Invite friends.*

How many men play golf, watch a football game, fish, spend time at the gym, or pursue other hobbies? The idea of inviting others with an inclusive spirit does not add to how we are already living life. The change with having an inclusive spirit is that as we are going, we are intentional to invite others to join. *Experiencing God* highlighted this reality years ago with the concept that God is already at work and invites us to join him in the work.[4] As we invite others, it is amazing to discover how God is already working in the lives of those we invite.

3. *Mentor men.*

We have to remind ourselves many men were not discipled by other men, and thus the concept of having community with others is sometimes a challenge. A great question to ask is: "Are you aligned so that you can minister to people far from God just because you are active in your community?"[5] Mentoring men and teaching them to tell their story of life change through Christ to

---

[4] Henry Blackaby and Claude V. King, *Experiencing God: Knowing and Doing the Will of God* (Nashville: LifeWay Press, 1990), 15.
[5] Eddie Mosley, *Connecting in Communities: Understanding the Dynamics of Small Groups* (Colorado Springs: NavPress, 2011), 22.

other men is powerful. Paul shared with us in his writing of the concept of mentoring others in what we have learned on our faith journey. "The things which you have heard from me in the presence of many witnesses, entrust these to faithful men who will be able to teach others also" (2 Tim 2:2). In America alone, the Center for Fathering estimates 33 percent of children are growing up in a fatherless home.[6] Men need to be reached for Christ and mentored to live out their faith in Christ.

4. *Study together.*

(a) Dive deep into God's word: Many men, if they were invited, would dive into Bible study. A hot topic or interest study can be a great way to get a man engaged in a small group. Lifeway has found Bible engagement is crucial to most all other personal growth metrics.[7]

(b) Center evangelistic outreach around the word: According to Aubrey Malphurs, "An unstated mission in some churches is to win lost people to faith in Christ."[8] Since adults are less likely to come to faith in Christ and many churches have less men than women, the men in our churches have to be trained through the word to reach the lost. If we invite men to come to an outreach group of men around the word, then chances are the men will attend.

5. *Receive training.*

One area that can strengthen the focus for men to reach other men for Christ is training. Many men have not been trained to

---

[6] National Center for Fathering, "The Extent of Fatherlessness," National Center for Fathering, accessed January 30, 2019, http://fathers.com/statistics-and-research/the-extent-of-fatherlessness.

[7] Russ Rankin, "Study: Bible Engagement in Churchgoers' Hearts, Not Always Practiced," LifeWay Research, January 1, 2014, https://www.lifeway.com/en/articles/research-survey-bible-engagement-churchgoers.

[8] Aubrey Malphurs, *Strategic Disciplemaking: A Practical Tool for Successful Ministry* (Grand Rapids, MI: Baker Books, 2009), 15.

share their story to one another about how Christ has changed their life. The powerful story of how one man came to faith in Christ is the first step in training men to share their faith. In addition, men need to be trained beyond their story in how to walk another man through how to be saved and exchange their sinful life for a life of faith in Christ alone. In the fabric of ministries, evangelism needs to become a thread that is continually being woven for men to learn to share their faith.

6. *Think missional.*

We have to think beyond reaching someone for Christ as a one-time event. Both Jesus and Paul are examples in the New Testament who made strategic investments into disciples for long seasons of time.

> Jesus' ministry example was a combination of word and deed. He healed the sick, cast out demons, helped the blind see, and fed people. He realized that sometimes he had to help fill people's stomachs before sharing his message with them. We know more about how Jesus fed the five thousand than the words he spoke on that day. Sometimes people may remember more about how we help them than what we actually say. Helping meet needs is not an option for us but a responsibility from the Lord that allows all our fingers to work together.[9]

Service evangelism may be a great way for men to engage other men as they are geared more toward being active in doing for others. Churches can offer service opportunities focused toward men along with training on how men can be intentionally evangelistic as they serve others. As men intentionally share their faith while serving others, more men will be reached for the gospel.

---

[9] Scott Dawson, *Evangelism Today: Effectively Sharing the Gospel in a Rapidly Changing World* (Grand Rapids, MI: Baker Books, 2009), 69.

Relational Outreach Among Women

While overall Americans are less likely to be joiners than they were during the mid-twentieth century post-World War II culture,[10] women still tend to travel in tribes. Women are relational by nature, and even the most introverted woman needs connections with other women. Perhaps one reason women tend to resonate with the church is it provides a place to belong. They find like-minded people with whom they can share community. While certainly men and women both need relationships, women tend to be more open about expressing and seeking out fulfillment of that need.

Women also need woman-to-woman understanding. Many experiences a woman may encounter are unique to womanhood, such as being a wife and/or a mother, experiencing miscarriage or emotional crises, or being a woman in the workplace. Former LifeWay women's ministry specialist Chris Adams noted, "Women need women who can share emotions and experiences and help round out life's experiences."[11] Those shared experiences can open doors uniquely for women to develop relationships and reach other women.

Relationships in the church, even among women, do not happen automatically. With the busy culture in which women currently live, they may struggle to feel that they cannot add one more commitment to their lives. Women also must be careful to avoid being exclusive.[12] Natural opportunities for outreach abound as women:

1. *Develop an inclusive spirit.*

   Multiple reasons exist why women tend to stay in their own circles, even at church. People are habitual by nature, so sitting in the same

---

[10] Robert D. Putnam, *Bowling Alone: The Collapse and Revival of American Community* (New York: Simon & Schuster, 2000), 25–28.

[11] Chris Adams, "Why Have a Women's Ministry?" in *Women Reaching Women: Beginning and Building a Growing Women's Ministry*, rev. and ex., ed. Chris Adams (Nashville: LifeWay Press, 2015), 25.

[12] Elizabeth Luter and Betty Hassler, "Focusing Outside the Church Walls," in *Transformed Lives: Taking Women's Ministry to the Next Level*, rev. and ex., ed. Chris Adams (Nashville: LifeWay Press, 2015), 70.

pew week after week becomes familiar and comfortable. Sitting in the same place and talking to the same women at Bible study takes less energy and effort than talking to or even inviting someone new. Yet Jesus reached out to anyone and everyone who was willing to follow him, even those despised and neglected (Matt 8:3). To really become Christlike, women must develop an inclusive spirit.

2. *Invite friends.*

With all of the new advances in technology that allow for instant dissemination of information, a personal invitation is still a very effective way to invite someone to participate in a church event or Bible study. Because women tend to travel in groups, they are less likely to attend something if they have to go alone. Certainly, some women will see an event advertised and choose to come by themselves. However, many women want a friend to join them. A personal invitation, whether by text, social media, or phone call, may be just the encouragement a woman needs to attend a church event and hear the gospel. Women can invite their friends.

3. *Mentor women.*

Women mentoring women is a biblical imperative (Titus 2:3–5). Mentoring can occur at various levels with many different topics, which can be a great outreach tool as younger women are looking for role models in multiple aspects of life skills, such as marriage, parenting, budgeting, or career. Disciple-making is a natural outflow of Christian mentoring for spiritual growth. All believers are called to make disciples who ideally will then go and make more disciples (Matt 28:18–20). As the disciple-making cycle continues, multiplication will occur. As LifeWay women's ministry specialist Kelly King noted, "Intentional discipleship results in good evangelism, and good evangelism should result in ongoing discipleship."[13] Through mentoring, women can teach other

---

[13] Kelly D. King, *Ministry to Women: The Essential Guide for Leading Women in the Local Church* (Nashville: LifeWay Press, 2018), 108.

women what it looks like to follow Jesus from the unique perspective of being a woman.

4. *Study together.*

The abundance of women's Bible study resources available in the last few decades speak to the hunger of women to study Scripture. In fact, one reason suggested for the discrepancy between men and women in church involvement is how often women study Scripture.[14] The women's Bible study movement in many churches points out the desire of women to study Scripture together. In outreach to women, one question to consider is whether or not opportunities exist for creating new groups. It can be easy for women to continue attending Bible study after Bible study while seeing little life transformation. To take ownership for reaching out to other women and create new groups is more challenging. Yet when the word of God truly transforms their lives, they will want to share about it with others.

5. *Receive training.*

A recent study conducted by the Southern Baptist Convention Women's Advisory Council of more than 3,600 women across the SBC revealed 71 percent of churches represented did not offer any type of evangelism training specific for women. While a few training resources have been developed specific to evangelism for women, one of the recommendations of the advisory council was for additional training resources to be developed by women to help women share the gospel to women of all different backgrounds. Churches could offer training in evangelism specifically focused on the unique relational aspects of women reaching women.[15]

---

[14] Joe Carter, "Why Are Christian Women More Religious Than Christian Men?" The Gospel Coalition, April 7, 2018, https://www.thegospelcoalition.org/article/christian-women-religious-christian-men/.

[15] SBC Women's Advisory Council, "Women's Advisory Council Final Report," Southern Baptist Convention Executive Committee (2017), 9–10.

6. *Think missional.*

In many regions of the world, women are only allowed to interact with other women. Therefore, women who serve as missionaries in those regions have a unique opportunity to reach women. Female missionaries learn to contextualize their presentations of the gospel through developing relationships with women. While women are not limited to female-only interaction in the United States, the concept is still applicable, regardless of the context in which a woman serves. Women understand the unique relational needs of other women and have unlimited potential to be able to reach women with the gospel.

In conclusion, the biblical model outlined in Titus 2 exhorts men to teach men and women to teach women. Men and women each have unique relational needs that can be met through those discipling relationships. As men disciple men and women disciple women, evangelism will be a natural outflow of discipleship. As churches provide opportunities to foster mentoring and discipling relationships along with training and equipping for sharing one's faith story, both men and women will be reached with the good news of Jesus Christ.

Bibliography

Adams, Chris. "Why Have a Women's Ministry?" In *Women Reaching Women: Beginning and Building a Growing Women's Ministry*. Edited by Chris Adams. Rev. and exp. Nashville, TN: LifeWay Press, 2015.

Blackaby, Henry, and Claude V. King. *Experiencing God: Knowing and Doing the Will of God*. Nashville, TN: LifeWay Press, 1990.

Carter, Joe. "Why Are Christian Women More Religious Than Christian Men." The Gospel Coalition, April 7, 2018. https://www.thegospelcoalition.org/article/christian-women-religious-christian-men/.

Dawson, Scott. *Evangelism Today: Effectively Sharing the Gospel in a Rapidly Changing World*. Grand Rapids. MI: Baker Books, 2009.

Earls, Aaron. "Church Attendance Gender Gap Shrinks, But It's Not All Good News." LifeWay Facts and Trends, September 25, 2017. https://factsandtrends.net/2017/09/25/church-attendance-gender-gap-shrinks-but-its-not-all-good-news/.

Fahmy, Dalia. "Christian Women in the U.S. Are More Religious than Their Male Counterparts." Pew Research Center. April 6, 2018. https://www.pewresearch.org/fact-tank/2018/04/06/christian-women-in-the-u-s-are-more-religious-than-their-male-counterparts/.

Fathers.com. "For Fathering. 'The Extent of Fatherlessness.'" Accessed January 30, 2019. http://fathers.com/statistics-and-research/the-extent-of-fatherlessness.

King, Kelly D. *Ministry to Women: The Essential Guide for Leading Women in the Local Church*. Nashville: LifeWay Press, 2018.

Luter, Elizabeth, and Betty Hassler. "Focusing Outside the Church Walls." In *Transformed Lives: Taking Women's Ministry to the Next Level*. Edited by Chris Adams. Rev. and ex. Nashville, TN: LifeWay Press, 2015.

Malphurs, Aubrey. *Strategic Disciplemaking: A Practical Tool for Successful Ministry*. Grand Rapids, MI: Baker Books, 2009.

Mosley, Eddie. *Connecting in Communities: Understanding the Dynamics of Small Groups*. Colorado Springs, CO: NavPress, 2011.

Pew Research Center. "Religious Landscape Study." Accessed December 18, 2018. https://www.pewforum.org/religious-landscape-study/.

Putnam, Robert D. *Bowling Alone: The Collapse and Revival of American Community*. New York: Simon & Schuster, 2000.

Rankin, Russ. "Study: Bible Engagement in Churchgoers' Hearts,Not Always Practiced." LifeWay Research, January 1, 2014. https://www.lifeway.com/en/articles/research-survey-bible-engagement-churchgoers.

SBC Women's Advisory Council. "Women's Advisory Council Final Report." Southern Baptist Convention Executive Committee, 2017.

Target Group Evangelism

EVANGELISM AND SENIOR ADULTS

Bill Day

Churches across America are in serious decline. The Southern Baptist Convention (SBC), the largest Protestant denomination in the United States, has not been exempt from this trend. In eighteen years (2009 to 2017), the membership in the SBC has declined by 1,300,608 (-14.3 percent).

A primary indicator for the level of the evangelistic zeal in the denomination has been its number of baptisms. In twenty years the annual number of baptisms has declined by 157,905, going from 412,027 in 1997 to 254,122 in 2017. This represents a baptism decline of 157,905 (-38 percent). The seriousness of this decline in the number of baptisms becomes even more apparent when one discovers the number of baptisms in 2017 was the lowest since 1944.[1]

How can these trends be reversed? While there are many answers to this question, almost everyone believes the SBC needs to develop ways to significantly improve its evangelistic methods to children, youth, and young adults, which traditionally have produced a majority of baptisms in the denomination. While this is true, there is an age group that could significantly contribute to overall baptisms but has been relatively ignored—senior adults. Helping increase the number of

---

[1] Data from the Annual Church Profile of the Southern Baptist Convention.

senior adult conversions and baptisms is vital to reversing the decline in baptisms in the SBC.

There are several reasons senior adult evangelism has received little attention. One reason has been that in earlier years, only a small percentage of total baptisms were senior adult baptisms. For example, in 1972, the year the SBC had its highest number of baptisms, the percentage of baptisms for each age group were: children (35.8 percent), youth (30.9 percent), young adults (18.4 percent), adults (13.0 percent), and senior adults (1.9 percent).[2] Thus the argument has been made that we need to focus on the more receptive younger groups. While previous data may tend to support a focus on younger age groups because of their size, more contemporary trends challenge this conclusion. One article recently reported that when looking at the total population of the US, the percentage of children under eighteen is declining while adults are increasing. By 2035 senior adults are projected to outnumber children under eighteen.[3]

Another reason evangelism of senior adults has been ignored is the attitude this age group has had opportunities over many decades to respond to the gospel but have not. Logic then dictates we need to focus on the more receptive younger age groups. An illustration of this argument is when groups of Christians are asked how many of them became Christians before they were twenty years old, and a vast majority raise their hands signifying they were converted and baptized at an early age. The implication has been made that senior adults become more and more hardened to the gospel as they grow older.

In spite of these arguments, the conversion and baptism of senior adults could be a critical factor in changing the decline in baptisms in the Southern Baptist Convention.

---

[2] Ibid.
[3] United States Census Bureau, "An Aging Nation: Projected Number of Children and Older Adults," last modified September 6, 2018, http://www.census.gov/library/visualizations/2018/comm/historic-first.html.

Research Project

Several years ago I conducted a research project on senior adult evangelism. The purpose of the study was to determine if certain variables dealing within a church's community and the actions and attitudes within a church significantly influenced its evangelism of senior adults.[4]

I statistically compared two groups of churches: senior adult evangelism (SAE) churches and evangelistic (EVAN) churches. SAE churches were defined as churches that baptized four or more senior adults in at least two of the three years of the study (1995–97). A total of 164 SBC churches were categorized as SAE churches (0.41 percent). EVAN churches were defined as churches that were in the top 0.5 percent of churches in total baptisms in the SBC while baptizing zero senior adults for any of the three years of the study. A total of 193 SBC churches (0.49 percent) were classified as EVAN churches.

The community context of each church was studied using demographic data. The institutional variables were assessed using a fifty-four-question survey. Prior to its use, the survey was validated and determined to be statistically reliable. The surveys were mailed to the pastors of 323 churches. A total of 186 surveys (57.3 percent) were returned.

Statistical analysis showed that SAE and EVAN churches had two significant contextual differences. This analysis showed the total number of senior adults and the percentage of senior adults in a church's community significantly influenced the number of senior adults a church will evangelize. Statistically influenced means there was a 99 percent probability that the differences between the two types of churches were real. In addition to the two significant contextual variables, twenty-four institutional variables were statistically valid.

---

[4] William H. Day Jr., "The Relationship of Selected Contextual and Institutional Factors to the Evangelism of Senior Adults in Churches of the Southern Baptist Convention" (PhD diss., New Orleans Baptist Theological Seminary, 1999).

Survey Results

Variables arranged according percentage difference in SAE and EVAN churches were:

1. *Evangelistic Training*

    The area in which SAE and EVAN churches differ the most is evangelistic training. Churches that were successful in evangelizing senior adults (SAE churches) were 33.3 percentage points higher than those evangelistic (EVAN) churches that did not evangelize any seniors (52.6 percent versus 19.3 percent).

2. *Targeting Senior Adults*

    Growing churches often target a particular segment of a community for outreach. SAE churches applied this principle by targeting senior adults for evangelism more than the EVAN churches. The proportion of churches targeting seniors is 50 percent for SAE churches and 18 percent for EVAN churches.

3. *Seniors Witnessing to Lost Friends*

    Training senior adults in evangelism is just part of the reason SAE churches exceed EVAN churches in evangelizing senior adults. SAE churches mobilize their seniors more effectively to share their faith with their non-Christian friends (69.5 percent versus 38.6 percent).

4. *Pastoral Vision for Evangelizing Senior Adults*

    Church growth writers emphasize the importance of pastoral leadership to church growth. The vision of the pastor is understood to be a vital part of the pastoral leadership. Pastors of SAE churches are more likely to communicate a vision for reaching senior adults than EVAN pastors (58.3 percent versus 28.1 percent).

5. *Evangelistic Results in Church Senior Adult Programs*

    Many of the churches in the SBC have senior adult programs. However, most of these programs center on fellowship, trips to various locations, and ministry to elderly church members. A major distinction between SAE and EVAN churches is people become Christians through church senior adult programs in higher percentages in SAE churches than EVAN churches (56.9 percent vs. 26.8 percent).

6. *Evangelistic Focus in Church Programs for the Elderly*

An intentional evangelistic focus is one reason more people became Christians through the church senior adult programs in SAE churches than EVAN churches. More SAE than EVAN churches make evangelism a priority in their programs for the elderly (62.7 percent versus 33.9 percent).

7. *Seniors Invite Lost Friends to Church Revivals*

Revivals are not a major means of reaching senior adults in either SAE or EVAN churches. Only 34 percent of the SAE churches and 40 percent of EVAN indicate revivals are a major means of evangelizing senior adults in their church. While the role of revivals in senior adult evangelism is similar in both SAE and EVAN churches, one difference is in how much more seniors in SAE churches support their church revivals than seniors in EVAN churches. More than 71 percent of the SAE churches say their senior adults invite their lost friends to revivals while only 43 percent of EVAN churches make this claim.

8. *Evangelism Is the Top Priority in Senior Adult Programs*

Items six and seven indicate evangelism is a major factor in churches that are successful in senior adult evangelism. This evangelistic focus is highlighted further by the fact that 83 percent of SAE churches say evangelism is the number-one priority in their senior adult programs. Only 59 percent of the EVAN churches make this claim.

9. *Seniors Focus More on Future than Past*

The climate of a church is important to senior adult evangelism. The attitude of the seniors in SAE churches is significantly different from EVAN churches. In 68 percent of the SAE churches, seniors are excited about their church and dream about its future. Only 42 percent of EVAN churches have seniors more focused on their church's future than the past.

10. *Senior Sunday School Classes Well Represented in Church Evangelism Programs*

The senior adult Sunday School classes in 69 percent of the SAE churches are well represented in their church's evangelism program. Only 45 percent of the EVAN churches have senior adult classes similarly involved.

11. *Visitors Warmly Greeted by Senior Adults*

How church members greet guests is important to the overall success of a church's outreach ministry. An unfriendly church can destroy the ability of a church to attract and keep those who visit. Friendly church members who are the same age as those visiting a church add to the evangelistic success of a church. This is also true in senior adult evangelism. More SAE churches (83 percent) than EVAN churches (59 percent) have senior adults who go out of their way to welcome visitors to their church.

12. *Senior Sunday School Workers Trained in Evangelism*

As noted in item one, the number-one difference between SAE and EVAN churches is in the area of training all senior adults in evangelism. In this regard, SAE and EVAN churches also differ in the percentage of their Sunday School workers who are trained to share their faith. A higher percentage of both SAE (69 percent) and EVAN (45 percent) churches indicate their senior adult Sunday School workers are more likely to be evangelistically trained than their senior members in general.

13. *Senior Adult Greeters*

In keeping with item eleven, stationing senior adults within the church to greet guests is important to a church's success in evangelizing the elderly. While only 55 percent of the EVAN churches have senior adult greeters, the percentage is 78 percent for SAE churches.

14. *Priority on Making Friends with Non-Christian Senior Adults*

In addition to being friendly, a church must reach out beyond its walls if it is to make an evangelistic impact upon its community. The problem with many senior adult church members and programs is they focus all their attention on people who are already Christians. Even SAE churches are not immune. Only 53 percent of the SAE churches say their senior adults intentionally seek to form friendships with non-Christians. However, only 32 percent of the EVAN churches have seniors who seek to establish such friendships.

15. *Regular Evangelistic Planning by Senior Adult Sunday School Workers*

In Southern Baptist churches, Sunday School is often the primary organization for planning and organizing a church's outreach to non-Christians. While this may be true for other age groups, this research project indicated that little evangelistic planning is happening in SBC churches related to senior adult evangelism. In SAE churches, only 25 percent of the senior adult Sunday School workers meet regularly for evangelistic planning. However, this level of planning was 21 percentage points better than the EVAN churches. Only 4 percent of the EVAN churches say their seniors meet regularly for evangelistic planning.

16. *Senior Adults Have a Vision for Church Growth*

One of the reasons senior adults in SAE churches tend to dream about their church's future (item 9) is because they envision their church successfully reaching people for Christ. More than 76 percent of the SAE churches note their seniors have a vision for church growth. This percentage contrasted to 56 percent of the EVAN churches.

17. *New Sunday School Classes Willingly Started by Seniors*

    Starting new Sunday School classes is an important part of the growth philosophy of Southern Baptist churches. Unfortunately, for many reasons, some church members resist starting new classes. This resistance tends to be a greater problem among senior adults. A low percentage of both SAE and EVAN churches indicate their senior adults are willing to help start new classes. Only 37 percent of SAE churches and 18 percent of the EVAN churches say their seniors are willing to start new classes.

18. *The Primary Purpose of the Sunday School Is Evangelism*

    While the primary purpose of the Bible teaching program in other denominations may be learning or fellowship, in SBC churches it officially has been evangelism. A majority of both SAE (86 percent) and EVAN (80 percent) churches agree their evangelism program is organized through the Sunday School. However, SAE churches differ significantly from EVAN churches over whether or not the primary purpose of Sunday School is evangelism (83 percent versus 63 percent).

19. *Church's Style of Worship Enjoyed by Senior Adults*

    One potential area of conflict in churches deals with the style of worship. Many seniors resist their church moving to a more contemporary style of worship. Interestingly, both the SAE and EVAN churches report neither had a traditional worship style. The area where both types of churches differed is that 85 percent of the SAE churches indicate their seniors enjoy their church's worship style as opposed to 66 percent for EVAN churches.

20. *Visitor-Friendly Senior Adult Classes*

    Items eleven and thirteen demonstrate one area of significant difference between SAE and EVAN churches deals with the friendliness of their senior adults. This difference in friendliness is also seen in their senior adult Sunday School classes. A high proportion of SAE churches (87 percent) report their senior adult classes are visitor friendly while only 68 percent of the EVAN churches agree.

21. *Sermons Focused on Evangelism*

    Since both SAE and EVAN churches are evangelistic, the preaching in these churches should be expected to have an evangelistic focus. Both SAE (92 percent) and EVAN churches (85 percent) respond that preaching is a major factor in their evangelistic effectiveness. Also both SAE and EVAN churches agree evangelism is the primary focus of their preaching ministry (66 percent versus 51 percent, respectively).

22. *New Seniors Quickly Included and Involved in Church*

    Few people become Christians the first time they visit a church. A period of nurture is needed in a successful evangelistic program. However, even after people attend a church for some time, some churches do a poor job of incorporating newcomers into their fellowship. Over 73 percent of the SAE churches say new senior adults are quickly assimilated, as opposed to 59 percent of EVAN churches.

23. *Seniors Set Evangelism Goals*

    While SAE churches have an evangelistic focus, one area of weakness is in evangelistic planning. Only 26 percent of the SAE churches report their seniors set evangelism goals for reaching other seniors while only 15 percent set these goals in EVAN churches.

24. *Seniors Involved in Prayer Ministries*

    Both SAE and EVAN churches indicate prayer is not just another program in their church (97 percent and 92 percent, respectively). More SAE churches (92 percent) than EVAN churches (86 percent) said their senior adults are well represented in their church's prayer ministries.

Surprises

Several surprising items were revealed in this study. First, revivals by themselves do not appear to be an important factor in distinguishing SAE from EVAN churches. Instead, the important factor is whether or not senior adults support their church's revivals by inviting their lost friends. Second, the style of a pastor's leadership is not important in distinguishing SAE from EVAN churches. One reason leadership seems to be of little importance may be because both SAE and EVAN churches are both evangelistic and consequently have pastors with similar leadership styles. This hypothesis is supported by those items on the survey that show pastors of SAE and EVAN churches generate lots of enthusiasm and are seen as the church's primary catalyst for growth. Third, both church groups equally emphasize the importance of prayer. The distinguishing feature of SAE churches is not the existence of prayer but how well senior adults were represented in this ministry.

Contextual Versus Institutional Variables

Much debate has occurred over whether contextual or institutional variables are more important to the growth of a church. Regarding senior adult evangelism, both prove equally important.

Of significant value are two factors: one contextual and the other institutional. The contextual variable is the percentage of senior adults in the community. The institutional variable relates to the involvement of senior adults in the evangelism program of their church. Two less significant factors are the percentage of senior adults in the church and the involvement of seniors within their church.

Implications

While the percentage of children and youth in the United States is declining, the senior adult population percentage in the United States is growing significantly. If Christians are going to reach our nation for Christ, we cannot continue to ignore senior adults.

Many pastors and denominational leaders are not sensitive to the need of reaching senior adults for Christ. At a time in their lives when one would expect senior adults to have a new openness to the gospel, seniors often have been a forgotten group.

Some have the attitude that senior adults cannot be reached with the gospel. Because so much emphasis has been placed on reaching people at a young age, some think senior adults who have not responded to the gospel during their earlier years are now closed to the gospel. However, the SAE churches in this study demonstrate senior adults can be reached for Christ. While their number is currently small in a denomination with thousands of churches, research is beginning to show their number in the future could increase significantly.

While some of the effects of an ever-increasing senior adult population on the United States are a subject of debate, one effect is obvious. Senior adults will present a tremendous evangelistic challenge and opportunity for our churches. An important factor in the effective evangelism of the elderly will be the mobilization of senior adults themselves to the task of sharing the good news.

Conclusion

Often Christians have on blinders that keep them seeing the evangelistic opportunities all around them.[5] This point is made in a true story about a revival years ago in a Texas church that was planning for a week of revival services. The pastor called a denominational leader and asked if he would preach at his church's revival. The leader said he would be glad to preach at the church's revival services under one condition: the pastor and the leader would make evangelistic visits during the day before each nightly revival service.

---

[5] John Evans, "Soul-Winning Commitment Senior Adult Evangelism: A Little Effort Makes Huge Difference," SBC Life, March 1, 2012, http://www.sbclife.net/article/2088/soulwinning-commitment-senior-adult-evangelism.

After making this requirement, the leader noted there was a long pause by the pastor. Finally the pastor said this requirement would be difficult to achieve since all the unbelievers he knew were either at work or in school.

Whereupon the leader said, "Don't you know any retirees who are not Christians in your community?" The pastor responded, "I guess I might be able to locate a few non-Christians retirees in the church's community." The leader said, "Fine! We will visit these retirees during the week." As a consequence of these visits, the church during this revival had fifteen retirees accept Christ as their Savior who were then baptized in the church. This story shows there were lost seniors all around this pastor's community that could become believers and be baptized if someone had only taken enough interest in them to go and share the gospel. As someone once noted, who in your community is asking the question, "I wonder what will happen to me when I die?" Is it children? Is it youth? Is it young adults? No, it's much more likely to be senior adults.

Very little research has been done on the evangelism of senior adults. One new reason for the absence of further research is the Southern Baptist Convention unfortunately ceased tracking senior adult baptisms after 2010.

Bibliography

Arn, Win, and Charles Arn. *Catch the Age Wave: A Handbook for Effective Ministry with Senior Adults.* Grand Rapids: Baker Book House, 1993.

———. "Why Aren't More Senior Adults Being Evangelized?" *Growing Churches* 4, no. 4 (July–September 1994): 41–43.

Arn, Charles. *White Unto Harvest: Evangelizing Todays Senior Adults.* Monrovia, CA: Institute for American Church Growth, 2003.

Barna, George. *Evangelism That Works: How to Reach Changing Generations with the Unchanging Gospel.* Ventura, CA: Regal Books, 1995.

Carroll, Jackson W., and Wade Clark Roof. *Bridging Divided Worlds: Generational Cultures in Congregations.* San Francisco, CA: Jossey-Bass, 2002.

Cass, Don. *Equipping Senior Adults for Lifestyle Evangelism.* Dallas, TX: Baptist General Convention of Texas, 1972.

Day, William H., Jr. "The Relationship of Selected Contextual and Institutional Factors to the Evangelism of Senior Adults in Churches of the Southern Baptist Convention." PhD diss., New Orleans Baptist Theological Seminary, 1999.

Evans, John. "Soul-Winning Commitment Senior Adult Evangelism: A Little Effort Makes Huge Difference," SBC Life, March 1, 2012, http://www.sbclife.net/article/2088/soulwinning-commitment-senior-adult-evangelism.

Evers, Randy Phillip. "Senior Adults Evangelizing Senior Adults through the First Baptist Church Piedmont, Alabama." DMin project, The Southern Baptist Theological Seminary, 1990.

Gulledge, J. Kirk. "Influences on Clergy Attitudes towards Aging." *Journal of Religious Gerontology* 8, no. 2 (1992): 63–77.

Hammett, Edward H.. and James R. Pierce. *Reaching People Under 40 while Keeping People Over 60: Being Church for All Generations.* St. Louis, MO: Chalice Press, 2007.

Houston, James M. *A Vision for the Aging Church: Renewing Ministry for and by Seniors*. Downers Grove, IL: InterVarsity Press, 2011.

United States Census Bureau, *An Aging Nation: Projected Number of Children and Older Adults*. Last modified September 6, 2018. http://www.census.gov/library/Visualizations/2018/comm/historic-first.html.

Target Group Evangelism

EVANGELISM THROUGH SOCIAL WORK MINISTRIES

Loretta Rivers and Jeanine Bozeman

We acknowledge varying opinions exist about combining evangelism and social work ministries. Our purpose is not to engage in the debate of whether or not evangelism and social work ministries ought to exist together. We write from a Southern Baptist perspective. As such, Southern Baptists have historically combined social work ministries and evangelism and continue to do so. We also teach at a Southern Baptist seminary that offers classes integrating social work ministries and evangelism.

The Baptist Faith and Message contains "doctrines essential to the Baptist tradition of faith and practice."[1] Within that document are doctrinal sections on "Evangelism and Missions" and "The Christian and the Social Order." Evangelism is the responsibility of every Christian: "It is the duty of every child of God to seek constantly to win the lost to Christ by verbal witness undergirded by a Christian lifestyle, and by other methods in harmony with the gospel of Christ."[2] Evangelism is not an option for Christians. In the Great Commission, Jesus

---

[1] "The Baptist Faith and Message 2000," Southern Baptist Convention, accessed January 25, 2019, http://www.sbc.net/bfm2000/bfm2000.asp.

[2] "The Baptist Faith and Message 2000," Article XI, "Evangelism and Missions," and Article XV, "The Christian and the Social Order," Southern Baptist Convention.

commanded his followers, "Go therefore and make disciples of all the nations" (Matt 28:19). In Acts 1:8, believers again are instructed, "You shall be My witnesses," after being empowered by the Holy Spirit.

In addition to addressing spiritual needs, Jesus also addressed physical, emotional, and relational needs. Luke recorded many examples of Jesus meeting needs, as well as Jesus instructing his followers to respond to the needs of others. In Luke 5, Jesus healed the leper and the paralytic. In Luke 9, Jesus fed the five thousand. In Luke 10, Jesus told the parable of the good Samaritan and instructed his followers to show mercy to those in need.

Social work ministries are faith-based ministries that seek to enhance the well-being of persons as individuals in the context of families, groups, and communities through a variety of direct and indirect services. The purpose of social work ministries from a Southern Baptist perspective is meeting needs in the name of Christ through the power of the Holy Spirit so persons might come to a right relationship with God. Southern Baptist social work ministries most often are based within a church or faith-based agency. Ministry to the whole person necessitates physical, emotional, and relational needs be met alongside spiritual needs.

Social work ministries include both social ministry and social action. Social ministry is the practical meeting of human needs: giving food to the hungry and drink to the thirsty, clothing those without clothes, visiting those sick and in prison, and showing hospitality to the stranger. Social action involves seeking justice on behalf of the most vulnerable in society, such as widows, orphans, and the poor. Social action may focus on changing societal structures, social policies, and laws.[3]

Neither evangelism nor social work ministries are optional for Christians. Christians are to be a witness to the world, as well as provide for and advocate for the most vulnerable in our society. Social work ministries use evangelism, and evangelism uses social work ministries.

---

[3] Delos Miles, *Evangelism and Social Involvement* (Nashville: Broadman Press, 1986), 7.

Jesus combined evangelism and social work ministries and "aimed at changing hearts and human society."[4] Social work ministries should be evangelistic, and evangelism can use social work ministries as an avenue to share the gospel. Southern Baptists have combined social work ministries and evangelism in denominational entities, the local church, and faith-based agencies.

Southern Baptist Denominational Entities

Southern Baptist entities intentionally emphasize evangelism through social work ministries.

In 1994, the Woman's Missionary Union (WMU) started Project HELP to raise awareness for social and moral issues, such as human trafficking, HIV/AIDS, poverty, racial injustice, and the global refugee crisis. WMU produces material to educate children, students, and adults about the issues and to suggest ways to engage with these problems.[5] Christian Men's Job Corps and Christian Women's Job Corps are also WMU ministries designed to help people with practical needs and share the gospel. These ministries equip men and women with life skills and prepare them for employment through such activities as Bible study, computer classes, and job readiness skills training. The program also has a mentoring component that provides relational opportunities for sharing the gospel.[6]

The North American Mission Board has a program called SEND Relief that offers help and hope to persons through compassion ministries. Service projects focus on needs in areas like foster care and adoption, crisis response, and poverty. In the midst of helping, volunteers offer hope through witnessing of Christ's love and salvation.[7]

---

[4] Miles, *Evangelism and Social Involvement*, 7.
[5] Project HELP, WMU, September 5, 2018, http://www.wmu.com/?q=article/national-wmu/project-help.
[6] Christian Job Corps, WMU, accessed January 15, 2019, http://www.wmu.com/?q=simple-page/christian-job-corps.
[7] Visit www.sendrelief.org for more information about SEND Relief.

The Ethics and Religious Liberty Commission (ERLC) highlights the Christian's responsibility to address social and moral issues and "is dedicated to engaging the culture with the gospel of Jesus Christ and speaking to issues in the public square for the protection of religious liberty and human flourishing."[8] The ERLC provides resources to raise awareness about issues—such as world hunger and sanctity of human life—and suggests practical ways individuals and churches can make a difference through advocacy and service.[9]

State conventions also work together to share Christ and minister to people. As an example, the Mississippi River Ministry (MRM) is a partnership of eight state conventions: Arkansas, Illinois, Iowa, Kentucky, Louisiana, Mississippi, Missouri, and Tennessee. MRM seeks to address poverty along the Mississippi River through ministries focused on meeting the basic needs of people—food, clothing, and shelter. Along with addressing needs related to poverty, MRM desires to reach those in the region who do not know Christ.[10]

Local Church

First Baptist Church, Covington, Louisiana, is an example of a local church combining evangelism and social work ministries. Associate pastor Jay Johnston has much experience with introducing social work ministries to his church, including ministries called Grief Share and Celebrate Recovery, and is presently involved in starting "To Covington with Love," the local missions strategy for the church in an attempt to discover community needs and enlist persons to minster to local people and share the love of Christ.

---

[8] "Employment," The Ethics and Religious Liberty Commission of the Southern Baptist Convention, accessed January 26, 2019, https://erlc.com/about/employment.
[9] Visit www.erlc.com for more information about the ERLC.
[10] Visit www.mississippiriverministry.com for more information about Mississippi River Ministry.

Jay went to a local elementary school selected as one of the starting points of the ministry and asked, "What is your greatest need?" He was surprised when the principal reported, "Underwear for three hundred kids." Members of First Baptist Covington began collecting the needed items. Other initiatives designed to serve the school include participating in special event days like teacher appreciation day, providing weekend food bags for children who might have insufficient food at home, and stocking school supply closets with needed items.

Jay dreams of having a witness in every school, hospital, cancer center, business, police station, and fire station, as well as the local jail. His goal is to have two persons working together to meet the expressed needs. "To Covington with Love" also includes church members coming alongside of and supporting other local ministries in the community. Each ministry effort is an avenue to demonstrate the love of Christ and share the hope of the gospel while meeting existing needs.[11]

Faith-Based Agencies

Baptist Friendship House (BFH), a faith-based agency in New Orleans operated by the North American Mission Board, was established in 1944. Though the focus of the ministry has changed through the years, the overall purpose of the ministry consistently has been to reach the surrounding community and the Greater New Orleans Area by meeting needs and sharing Christ. Kay Bennett, executive director, shared some of the ways Baptist Friendship House engages in social work ministries and evangelism to assist the homeless, human trafficking survivors, abuse victims, persons with addictions, and persons living in poverty. Examples of ministries include literacy, English as a second language, job readiness skills training, life skills training, psychoeducational groups, case management, emergency food assistance, and

---

[11] Jay Johnston, in discussion with the author, January 2019. Visit www.fbccov.org and www.tocovingtonwithlove.com to learn more about First Baptist Covington and their outreach ministries.

housing. Kay emphasized the importance of building relationships through ministry opportunities.

> At BFH there is really no separation between compassion ministry and evangelism. If we want to help others with our fullest capabilities, it is important to minister to the whole person and not leave a part out. Everyone is different, everyone has experienced different things in life, everyone has different personalities, and everyone has different gifts and abilities. The things we have experienced in life make us uniquely who we are. It is therefore important that we get to know the person that is standing before us, so that we can better help them in life and help them to have a better understanding of who Jesus is.[12]

Many of the people who go to BFH have experienced traumatic events and do not trust easily. Ministry focused on meeting the needs of people builds trust, and a relationship provides evangelistic opportunities. When people see Jesus through workers serving in compassion ministries, they often want to know about how Jesus can transform their lives. Kay recounted one such encounter with a young woman who came to BFH. When Kay opened the door, the first thing she noticed was the lady's T-shirt with ugly words written on it. The lady, who was homeless and had no place to go, asked to use the restroom. Kay let her use the restroom and offered her a new T-shirt. The lady had no idea what the words were on her shirt because she could not read or write. Kay gave her a new T-shirt. These simple acts of compassion helped Kay build a relationship with her and discover her needs. Eventually, the lady learned how to read and write, which opened the door for the workers at BFH to share Jesus with her.

---

[12] Kay Bennett, email message to author, January 10, 2019. Visit www.baptistfriendshiphouse.org for more information.

Guidelines for Evangelism through Social Work Ministries

The ministries previously described have been successful in incorporating evangelism and social work ministries. We offer the following guidelines for consideration to churches and faith-based agencies seeking to be evangelistic through social work ministries.

1. *Recognize the dignity and worth of every person.*

    Each person is made in the image of God (Gen 1:27) and has worth and value. God loves every person. God demonstrated his love by sending Jesus into the world to be the Savior. Because God desires for every person to know him, he commissioned Christians to take the gospel to every person. Christians should treat all persons with respect and demonstrate care and concern.

2. *Listen to people.*

    Listening to another person can be a powerful gift. When we listen, the focus is on the other person rather than on our agenda and ourselves. Truly listening helps us better understand the person's situation and gives insight that can guide us as we seek to help. If we fail to listen to a person, the help we offer may do more harm than good. What we offer may be irrelevant to the person's situation or may be a response to an assumed need rather than a real need.

3. *Build relationships.*

    When we care about others, we are willing to make the time commitment necessary to get to know the person. Social work ministries in faith-based settings often provide the opportunity to develop relationships through ongoing contact with persons. Within the context of a relationship, the person to whom we seek to minister and witness has the opportunity to observe Christ within us through our lifestyle. Therefore, the person can observe whether our lives match our words. When Christians are people of integrity, their authenticity makes their witness more credible and convincing.

4. *Help others without forcing them to attend a religious service or event.*

If attendance at a Bible study, worship service, or some other event is required for assistance, people may come only because they want the help provided and will do anything to get that help. Some people in need may not come because they do not want to participate. Our preferred approach is to help the person in need if the resources are available and then invite them to a religious service or event.

Several years ago, a homeless ministry required persons to attend a chapel service before receiving food and shelter. When the number of participants exceeded the chapel's capacity, the fire marshal required changes to be made. Ministry leaders considered downsizing the ministry or removing the chapel requirement. After much consideration, leaders decided to make chapel attendance voluntary. The result was the persons who chose to attend the chapel service actually wanted to be there and spiritual needs were addressed more effectively.

5. *Do not manipulate people into making a spiritual decision.*

Christians may unintentionally manipulate a person into making a spiritual decision because of their eagerness for the person to experience the life-changing relationship with Jesus they have experienced. Manipulated decisions do not produce lasting commitments.

Jesus gave persons the opportunity to choose to follow him. Jesus said to the disciples, "Follow Me," and they chose to do so (e.g., Matt 4:19; 9:9). Others, like the rich young ruler, chose not to follow (Matt 19:16–26). Jesus wanted people to carefully consider the cost of following him (Luke 9:57–62) and desired commitment and obedience from his followers. Likewise, as helpers, we should never coerce a person to make a decision to follow Christ. If we do so, we may feel good temporarily because of a decision, but we have misrepresented and cheapened Jesus' call to discipleship.

6. *Avoid judging others.*

   Sometimes helpers make false assumptions about the people who seek assistance. Faulty assumptions might be: "It's the person's fault he or she is in this situation"; "People who need help must not be Christians"; "If we help too much, the person will not learn from the situation"; and "People who really need help will take whatever is offered." At the core of these false assumptions are our judgments about others. Judging others takes place from a position of pride. Our helping should be from a position of humility.

7. *Be an intentional witness.*

   Evangelism does not happen without effort. Ministers should witness through words and deeds. Intentional evangelism involves planning and preparation. Planning insures evangelism is an integral part of what we do. Training participants how to share their faith is necessary preparation.

8. *Be concerned about the whole person.*

   God created human beings with spiritual, emotional, physical, and relational needs. If the focus is only on spiritual needs, then the opportunity to address the spiritual need may never come if the person has another need that prevents focusing on the spiritual need. For example, if a person is hungry, the physical need temporarily may supersede any other need.

9. *Be transparent.*

   Persons have the right to know about the church or agency providing help. The mission of the entity should be apparent to every person coming for services. Helpers should not be ashamed of Christ. In Rom 1:16, Paul wrote, "For I am not ashamed of the gospel, for it is the power of God for salvation to everyone who believes, to the Jew first and also to the Greek."

10. *Check your attitude.*

    Christians are Christ's ambassadors to the world (2 Cor 5:20). People who are served should readily know who a minister represents. A negative attitude can hurt a person's witness. Social work ministries can be emotionally, physically, and spiritually draining. When a helper's ministry situation is overwhelming and appropriate self-care is not given, compassion fatigue may arise. A negative attitude, excessive complaints, and a lack of concern for those served can be signs of compassion fatigue.

If Christians follow the example of Jesus, they will engage in both social work ministries and evangelism. Examples of Southern Baptist entities combining social work ministries and evangelism have been given in this chapter. Suggested guidelines for doing evangelism through social work ministries have been provided for consideration.

BIBLIOGRAPHY

Bennett, Kay. E-mail message to author. January 10, 2019.

The Ethics and Religious Liberty Commission of the Southern Baptist Convention. Accessed January 26, 2019. www.erlc.com.

Johnston, Jay. In discussion with the author. January, 2019.

Miles, Delos. *Evangelism and Social Involvement.* Nashville, TN: Broadman, 1986.

Mississippi River Ministry. Accessed January 15, 2019. www.mississippiriverministry.com.

SEND Relief. Accessed January 25, 2019. www.sendrelief.org.

Southern Baptist Convention. "The Baptist Faith and Message: The 2000 Baptist Faith and Message." Southern Baptist Convention. Accessed January 25, 2019. http://www.sbc.net/bfm2000/bfm2000.asp.

To Covington with Love. Accessed January 21, 2019. www.tocovingtonwithlove.com.

WMU. "Christian Job Corps." Accessed January 15, 2019. http://www.wmu.com/?q=simple-page/christian-job-corps

WMU. "Project HELP." Accessed January 15, 2019. http://www.wmu.com/?q=article/national-wmu/project-help.

Multicultural Evangelism

EVANGELISM, CHURCH PLANTING, AND THE NEW TESTAMENT

Damian Emetuche

Probably the unintended consequences of the para-church movements of the 1950s through the 1980s is the idea and practice of being a Christian while not affiliated to a local church. In contemporary America, many claim to be Christians but are unaffiliated and uninvolved with any church. However, the New Testament does not recognize evangelism that does not result in church planting or church growth. To evangelize and reach lost souls without adding them to a local church or gathering them as part of a new church plant is like having babies without families to raise them up. In our culture, we know the consequences of having such children: homelessness, drugs, crimes, incarcerations, fractured and dysfunctional homes, and what medical professionals call "failure to thrive" children.

In Matt 28:18–20 is the biblical justification for both evangelism and church planting. The passage reads, "All authority has been given to Me in heaven and on earth. Go therefore and make disciples of all the nations, baptizing them in the name of the Father and the Son and the Holy Spirit, teaching them to observe all that I commanded you; and lo, I am with you always, even to the end of the age." Other relevant New Testament passages associated with the Great Commission include

---

Part of the materials contained in this chapter have been taken from the author's book, *The Future of Church Planting in North America* (New York: Peter Lang, 2014).

Luke 24:45–47; John 20:21–23; and Acts 1:8. Looking at these texts, the emphasis is placed on making disciples of all nations. As J. D. Payne observed, "The apostolic Church was given the mandate to bear witness to Christ and his resurrection by making disciples of all nations. Though a disciple is made whenever a person places his/her faith in Christ for salvation, discipling is a lifelong process. The best context for both making disciples and discipling—which includes baptism and teaching obedience, is the local community of disciples (i.e., the church)."[1]

The *Contemporary Theologies of Mission* defines mission as "carrying the gospel across cultural boundaries to those who owe no allegiance to Jesus Christ, encouraging them to accept Him as Lord and Savior and to become responsible members of His Church, working, as the Holy Spirit leads, at both evangelism and justice, at making God's will done on earth as it is done in heaven."[2] The *ekklesia* refers to a local assembly convened for some specific purpose in the biblical context and first refers to the congregation of Israel as the people of God. In the New Testament, *ekklesia* speaks of the body of Christ, where Christ is present, and through that body (the church), manifests himself to the world.[3] In the New Testament, while individuals and household believers in obedience to the Great Commission shared their faith, it was not an organization or institution as we have them today but an organism. People were transformed through their relationship with Christ and were willing to have radical obedience like the one the Son had with his Father. The disciples went around and proclaimed Christ, who builds his church through the transformation of lives.

The early church didn't have the monstrous organizations or the institutions and complex bureaucracies that exist today. Jesus created a culture of multiplication and trained gospel catalysts. The New

---

[1] J. D. Payne, *Discovering Church Planting: An Introduction to the Whats, Whys, and Hows of Global Church Planting* (Colorado Springs, CO: Paternoster, 2009), 11.
[2] Arthur F. Glasser and Donald A. McGavran, *Contemporary Theologies of Mission* (Grand Rapids, MI: Baker Book House, 1983), 26.
[3] Charles L. Chaney, *Church Planting at the End of the Twentieth Century* (Wheaton, IL: Tyndale House Publication Inc., 1986), 20–21.

Testament church wasn't split into denominations as we are fractured today. It was a family, a household of God—men and women from diverse backgrounds, slaves and masters, educated and illiterates, rich and poor, nobles and commons. It was a movement that frightened the established religious leaders, confronted stereotypes, and changed the world.[4] The disciples shared Christ, prayed for the healing of the sick, shared their food and goods, and bridged the sociocultural barriers. The new converts functioned like a household; there was no reticence to hinder their growth. Wherever two or three could gather, they would have church and worship. Even in prison, Paul and Silas could worship and praise God. What a big contrast to our world![5]

Contemporary Culture and Church Planting Strategy

To evangelize and plant churches in the spirit of the New Testament that will transform our culture just like the New Testament Christians did, we must recognize our cultural reality has changed. Church dominance of the American cultural landscape is now a thing of the past. Christian faith henceforth has to justify its claim. Immigrants from other shores other than Europe are here to stay, and a greater percentage of highly skilled professionals are coming from Asia and Africa than from Europe, while low-skilled laborers are coming from countries south of the US border. While the sweeping demographic changes in the United States are significant beyond the shifts as to where people live, and the US is becoming more diverse to the point of being a white-minority nation in a few years, diversity in the population is not the most pressing missiological concern. The diversity that challenges the American evangelical church's missiologically is not primarily racial, although it always has challenged the American churches. The greatest challenge is many of the new immigrants are from non-Christian backgrounds and are adherents of different world religions.[6]

---

[4] Emetuche, *The Future of Church Planting in North America*, 8–10.
[5] Ibid.
[6] Ibid., 30–31.

Therefore, new evangelism strategy that will result in church planting must consider two important factors. First, many non-Christians living in North America today (even some Christians) do not have a biblical worldview, or Anglo-Saxon protestant worldview. In this regard, evangelism that will result in new church plants must be approached with a missionary mindset. The effect of secularization and migration have contributed to North America becoming one of the fastest growing mission fields in the world. Therefore, as we would train our missionaries going to oversee countries to be culturally competent and cross-cultural in their evangelistic outreach, we must train contemporary American churches in cross-cultural outreach within their neighborhoods. Second, our local churches must reflect the diversity of the community in which they are situated. The church must look like the grocery stores, the schools, the community colleges, the neighborhood Laundromats, and the community in the context in which it is planted. In essence, we must not focus on what is easy or simple (looking after people who are like us), we must do all it takes to reach the lost world in our community. Christian faith is countercultural and represents the new humanity in Christ. Peter said of the new community, "But you are a chosen race, a royal priesthood, a holy nation, a people for God's own possession, so that you may proclaim the excellencies of Him who has called you out of darkness into His marvelous light; for you were once not a people, but now you are the people of God; you had not received mercy, but now you have received mercy" (1 Pet 2:9–10). Therefore, a fractured community of faith can never be an instrument in the transformation of a fractured world.

Old Church Planting Strategy Must Be Discarded

One of the most commonly practiced church planting methods promoted today is the homogenous principle, which goes back to Donald McGavran and the Church Growth Movement. As a missionary in India, McGavran became fascinated with church growth, principally in why some churches grow and others do not. In 1957, he returned to the United States where he started the Institute of Church Growth in Eugene, Oregon. Later, he partnered with Alan Tippett, an anthropologist, and their ideas were published in The Church Growth Bulletin. In 1965, McGavran became the dean of the School of World Mission at Fuller Theological Seminary, which provided the platform to popularize his ideas.

McGavran employed social and behavioral sciences in understanding and prescribing his missiological principles. His main emphasis was "the importance of allowing persons to become Christians without forcing them to cross cultural barriers."[7] Many of his ideas can be studied in his two earlier books, *The Bridges of God*, published in 1954, and *Understanding Church Growth*, first published in 1970. Proponents of the homogeneous unit principle argue, "Human beings do build barriers around their own societies,"[8] and therefore, promoted ethnic church planting. The homogeneous unit principle in the United States was embraced by the church partly because of our history.

The sixteenth century through eighteenth century was a volatile time period in Europe, which was divided by religious, ethnic, and civil conflicts. With these divisions in Europe at the time, coupled with a suspicious religious climate between the Catholics and Protestants on one hand and among various Protestant groupings on the other, the new immigrants to the United States were also importing their doctrinal and theological differences. At that period, the overwhelming concern of the initial European immigrants was not evangelism or church planting but escaping persecution and creating a space where they could live, worship, and express their faith as they chose. Although many of these European immigrants established their own churches,

---

[7] Ken Mulholland, "McGavran, Donald A. (1897–1991)," in *Evangelical Dictionary of World Missions*, ed. A. Scott Moreau (Grand Rapids, MI: Baker Books, 2000), 607.

[8] Donald A. McGavran, *Understanding Church Growth*, 3rd ed., ed. C. Peter Wagner (Grand Rapids, MI: Wm. B. Eerdmans Publishing, 1990), 69.

the churches they planted were patterned after European churches with European discriminatory practices.[9]

When these established churches started evangelizing the Native Americans and other immigrant groups that followed the Euro-Americans, these early American churches adopted the homogeneous principle of church planting even when the concept was not known or used because it was rooted in the nature, tradition, culture, and constituency of the American history and migration pattern.[10] In view of this ingrained institutionalized practice of evangelizing and planting churches, the American church believes gathering people who share ethnic backgrounds, political beliefs, social standings, and so on, will be more comfortable with one another and, therefore, more successful together in forming a new congregation.

On the contrary, the apostle Paul, who we often refer to as a model missionary, evangelist, and church planter, never planted a church that was primarily Jewish or gentile, an issue that made some Jewish converts accuse him of subverting cherished Jewish cultural and religious practices (Acts 13:48–51). It is instructive to note it was not only the Jews who opposed Paul; gentiles opposed him too when the gospel he preached was against their cultural and religious practices. They too persecuted him and his missionary team. Paul and Barnabas experienced persecution at Iconium, Lystra, and Derbe (Acts 14:1–23). The cultural design of the church became an issue that the church had to debate and decide in Acts 15. In Galatians 2, the question of personal preference and cultural practice created conflict between Paul and Peter. Paul recounted the incident in these verses:

> But when Cephas came to Antioch, I opposed him to his face, because he stood condemned. For prior to the coming of certain men from James, he used to eat with the Gentiles;

---

[9] Emetuche, *The Future of Church Planting in North America*, 14.
[10] Ibid., 16–18.

but when they came, he began to withdraw and hold himself aloof, fearing the party of the circumcision. The rest of the Jews joined him in hypocrisy, with the result that even Barnabas was carried away by their hypocrisy. But when I saw that they were not straightforward about the truth of the gospel, I said to Cephas in the presence of all, "If you, being a Jew, live like the Gentiles and not like the Jews, how is it that you compel the Gentiles to live like Jews? (Gal 2:11–14)

Therefore, in order to reach our world today, especially North America, the cultural gospel of personal preference and individuality must be discarded, and the church must return to the gospel that is both confrontational and transformational. The gospel proclamation in the New Testament created new communities of faithful followers of Christ Jesus in every city regardless of their racial, sociocultural, educational, and economic standing in their societies. The same should be true in our society today because neither the gospel nor its power has changed. The result is the same wherever Christ is faithfully proclaimed—a transformed life and culture and a new community of diverse, regenerated people in Christ Jesus.[11]

A Case for Multicultural Church Planting

The North American population comes from every ethnolinguistic background, and we can never be like any other nation or people on earth. Apart from immigrants, the Pew Research Center released a report on marriage across racial and ethnic lines in the United States and compared the traits of those who "marry out" with those who "marry in." The research indicated "about 15% of all new marriages in the United States in 2010 were between spouses of a different race or ethnicity from one another, more than double the share in 1980 (6.7%). Among all newlyweds in 2010, 9% of whites, 17% of blacks, 26% of Hispanics and 28%

---

[11] Ibid., 24.

of Asians married out. Looking at all married couples in 2010, regardless of when they married, the share of inter-marriages reached an all-time high of 8.4%. In 1980, that share was just 3.2%."[12]

Similar research carried out in 2006 revealed "more than one-fifth of all American adults (22%) say that they have a close relative who is married to someone of a different race ... That degree of familiarity with—and proximity to—interracial marriage is the latest milestone in what has been a sweeping change in behaviors and attitudes concerning interracial relationships over the past several decades."[13] It is not only multiracial marriages and adoptions that are on the increase; diversity can be seen in most neighborhoods, shopping malls, restaurants, movie theaters, public parks, school districts, colleges, and universities. At the same time, "the growth in the number of white youths slowed sharply in the 1990s, up by just 1 percent in the decade, as the number of white women of childbearing age fell."[14] More recently, that population segment has dipped into a decline.

The number of white Americans under the age of twenty fell by 6 percent between 2000 and 2008. "Instead, growth has come from minorities, particularly Hispanics, as more Latino women enter their childbearing years. Blacks, Asians and Hispanics accounted for about 79 percent of the national population growth between 2000 and 2009."[15] Consequently, "the result has been a changed American landscape, with whites now in minority of the youth population in 10

---

[12] Wendy Wang, "The Rise of Intermarriage: Rates, Characteristics Vary by Race and Gender," Pew Research Center, February 16, 2012, http://www.pewsocialtrends.org/2012/02/16/the-rise-of-intermarriage/.

[13] Pew Research Center, "Guess Who's Coming to Dinner," Pew Research Center, March 14, 2016, https://www.pewresearch.org/wp-content/uploads/sites/3/2010/10/Interracial.pdf.

[14] NewsOne Staff "In Census, Young Americans Increasingly Diverse," News One, February 6, 2011, http://newsone.com/nation/newsone staff4/in-census-young-americans-increasingly-diverse/.

[15] Ibid.

states."¹⁶ What kind of church will resemble this new generation of Americans? As a missionary looking at the New Testament and watching where North American culture is going, I would strongly recommend a multicultural church plant in all our communities.

What Multicultural Church Plant Is Not
Churches Sharing Facilities

In many cities, immigrant churches and new church plants have difficulty getting a good facility where they can worship and organize many of their activities. Often, the church planter or the strategist will negotiate with an existing (often older, Caucasian) congregation for the use of their facilities for a period of time. The church plant could meet in the late afternoon after the host church worship service or in the evening. If the time coincides with the older church's worship time, the new church plant or the immigrant church usually is relegated to a building in the background, basement, or old structure somewhere within the infrastructures of the benevolent church.

Often in this scenario, the two churches have nothing in common except sharing facilities and bills, while the members of the two congregations have nothing in common. Usually if there is any issue, leaders of the two churches will come together to discuss and settle it. Moreover, the new church plant will remain until a more suitable location and facility is found. On a few occasions, the host congregation might invite the new church plant or immigrant church for a program in the main church, and usually they are treated as visitors and accommodated for that particular day.

This example is not a multicultural church because the two churches have separate visions, mission statements, and leadership. They are independent of each other and are not accountable to one another. At best, their relationship is contractual, and the new church plant will

---
¹⁶ Ibid.

leave the venue as soon as they discover a more affordable and better facility that is strategically located. In short, the relationship between the churches is simply a business relationship that can be terminated as soon as it is no longer profitable to the parties involved.[17]

Ministry to an Ethnic or Socioeconomic Group

Another ministry often construed to be a multicultural church plant is when a church is serving a community different from their dominant cultural or economic group in an inner-city context or multi-housing unit. The church may feed the hungry, conduct regular Bible studies in the complex, and distribute leftover food from chain stores or restaurants but have no intention of bringing the new converts to their fold. For example, with the increase in Hispanic immigrants, a good number of churches may have Hispanic ministries to migrants, but there is no real relationship built, and the recipients often are not treated as equals. This kind of ministry is patronizing and lacks the commitment, sacrifice, and humility necessary to building the body of Christ.

When the poor and the rich worship together, they learn from each other and grow together. The rich learn humility, and the presence of the poor is a constant reminder of what James called pure religion: "Pure and undefiled religion in the sight of our God and Father is this: to visit orphans and widows in their distress, and to keep oneself unstained by the world" (Jas 1:27). Stephen Mott and Ronald J. Sider stated, "If we get rich by oppressing the poor, or if we have wealth and do not reach out generously to the needy, the Lord of history moves against us. God judges societies by what they do to the people at the bottom."[18] In the book of Acts, the Bible records the lifestyle of early believers in these words:

---

[17] Emetuche, *The Future of Church Planting in North America*, 45–46.
[18] Stephen Mott and Ronald J. Sider, "Economic Justice: A Biblical Paradigm," in *Toward a Just and Caring Society*. ed. David P. Gushee (Grand Rapids, MI: Baker Books, 1999), 28.

> They were continually devoting themselves to the apostles' teaching and to fellowship, to the breaking of bread and to prayer. Everyone kept feeling a sense of awe; and many wonders and signs were taking place through the apostles. And all those who had believed were together and had all things in common; and they *began* selling their property and possessions and were sharing them with all, as anyone might have need. Day by day continuing with one mind in the temple, and breaking bread from house to house, they were taking their meals together with gladness and sincerity of heart, praising God and having favor with all the people. And the Lord was adding to their number day by day those who were being saved. (Acts 2:42–47)

This passage makes it clear both rich and poor believers were together in one church, and selfishness was eradicated as the haves shared willingly with the have-nots. Craig L. Blomberg observed, "The Pentecostal pilgrims who would have otherwise returned to their homes in the Diaspora may have stayed as part of this fledgling Christian community, creating 'refugees' … Even those local Jerusalemites who joined the first church and who themselves were already impoverished probably cut themselves off from the standard Jewish sources of charity."[19] Whatever the circumstances of the early believers in Jerusalem, they lived, shared, and worshipped God together without the rich patronizing the poor or the natives lording over the Diaspora believers. In Acts 6, when there was a complaint by Hellenists against the Hebrews, it was resolved in the spirit of Christ. Therefore, ministry to the poor, or to a socioeconomic or cultural group in the same community, with no deliberate intention of bringing them to the fold, cannot be said to be a multicultural church plant or ministry.

---

[19] Craig L. Blomberg, *Neither Poverty Nor Riches: A Biblical Theology of Possessions* (Downers Grove, IL: InterVarsity Press, 1999), 162.

Adopting People Groups

Another ministry erroneously associated with a multicultural church plant is a church adopting a people group. Ralph D. Winter defined the concept as "a set of molecules, not atoms, that is an aggregate of peoples, not individuals that make up the population of our planet nor ... geographical territories called countries."[20] In other words, a people group could be a class, caste, tribe, or ethnic unit. The Lausanne Committee for World Evangelization also defined a people group as "a significantly large ethnic or sociological grouping of individuals who perceive themselves to have a common affinity for one another."[21] Mission organizations like the International Mission Board (IMB) of the Southern Baptist Convention adopted this strategy and insist "in a world with dissolving borders, global 'affinity groups'–large groupings of related peoples that share similar origins, languages and cultures—act as a lens through which missionaries view lostness and focus strategy to share the Gospel."[22] Furthermore, the IMB stated, "Focusing strategy through affinity groups gives missionaries a more complete picture of the people they are working to reach as well as the freedom to pursue the lost regardless of their location."[23]

In view of this conviction, the IMB deployed missionaries in North American cities to reach people groups. This strategy is definitely pragmatic and makes evangelistic sense, but it lacks biblical warrant and cannot be applied in North American church planting. First, the United States and Canada are made of a mosaic of peoples from every ethnic group and background. Employing this strategy means we

---

[20] Ralph D. Winter, "Unreached People: The Development of the Concept," in *Reaching the Unreached: The Old-New Challenge*, ed. Harvie M. Conn (Phillipsburg, NJ: Presbyterian and Reformed Publishing Company, 1984), 17.
[21] "Definition: Key Terms in the Cause of Frontier Missions," *Mission Frontiers: Bulletin of the U.S. Centre for World Mission* 16, nos. 1–2 (January/February 1994):10.
[22] "Mapping Resources," People Groups, IMB Global Research. Accessed June 19, 2019, https://www.peoplegroups.org/261.aspx.
[23] Ibid.

have to return to a homogeneous unit principle, which we have argued is not only unbiblical but is a sociocultural perspective contrary to the vision of the church as redeemed people of all races, cultures, and socioeconomic classes coming together in faith in Christ.[24]

Second, in the North American context, the culture is moving toward integration and multiculturalism with increased miscegenation, creating a Samaritan nation. Therefore, the practice amounts to retrogression to the segregation era in the United States, reminiscent of some Jim Crow-era mandates, which leads to the charge that the American church is racist.

Third, people groups or affinity churches are limited in their outreach as the pool of who can join their church is limited to their kind of people. Jesus reminded the Jews of his time, "Is it not written, 'My house shall be called a house of prayer for all the nations?'" (Mark 11:17). Consequently, the concept is not only foreign to the New Testament but also unsustainable in regard to a local church becoming self-sufficient to serve the surrounding community in the Great Commission and Commandment. This lack of inclusiveness is one of the reasons immigrant churches have limited growth because they can have only as many converts as the flow of their type of immigrants into their community.

Fourth, when churches are constituted of only one ethnicity or affinity group, their leadership often defaults to cultural practices in decision-making rather than to the Word of God. For example, an interracial couple was excommunicated on account of racial purity.[25] A church could adopt a group for the purpose of praying and seeing more of that particular population come to faith in Christ, but as they

---

[24] Damian Emetuche, "Avoiding Racism in Starting New Congregations," in *Racism: Christian Reflection* (Waco, TX: Baylor University, 2010).
[25] "Interracial Couple Banned from Kentucky Church," *Huffington Post*, November 30, 2011, http://www.huffingtonpost.com/2011/11/30/interracial-couple-banned-from-kentucky-church_n_1121582.html.

come to Christ in faith, the new converts must be integrated into the local church where they live and work.

Creating a separate congregation for a particular affinity group or people group is contrary to the New Testament church. Paul prayed for the salvation of the Jews (Rom 9—11), but he never planted a church exclusively for the Jews. All his churches were racially, socially, and economically diverse from Antioch to Iconium, Lystra to Derbe, and Corinth to Athens.

Fifth, a church plant in modern North America based on ethnic or affinity groups is dead from the start because it has no future. It is dead from the beginning because after the first-generation immigrants are reached, second and third generations are no longer interested in the primary culture of their parents. The majority of the second and subsequent generations will speak the majority language, become more bicultural, and ultimately become more mainstream American than their parents because of the melding and enculturation within American schools and other institutions. This enculturation is already happening among immigrant churches like Hispanic churches in Miami and other cities where the younger generations are more multicultural, bilingual, and may not want to worship in a traditional Hispanic church.

What about Language Churches or Ministries?

Another ministry often associated with a multicultural church plant is a local church having a separate worship service for a group of believers in the same church in a different language. There are two main arguments for this language service within the North American local church context. The first is many of the immigrants from non-English-speaking countries or cultures do not understand or speak English well enough to worship in English-speaking congregations. The second is people like to hear the gospel in their heart language, and they desire to preserve their culture. While many immigrants coming to America may not speak English fluently, it is not always true they are not interested in learning and worshipping in English. On the contrary, many non-English speakers, as part of their enculturation, may want to worship in English-speaking congregations. A local church may have room for interpreters if the need arises, but the practice of having a little language church ensconced in the basements reduces fellow believers to second-class citizens.

Second, language and culture can be preserved at home in many ways, such as through family, food, clothing, and so forth—different from simply an hour of worship. Interaction with people of other cultures is part of what heaven is about, and it prevents the church from erecting linguistic, cultural, and racial barriers. A local church may provide interpreters as a temporary measure within a context of all believers in the same building worshipping at the same time, but to create a separate worship experience based on language alone does not make a congregation multicultural or multiracial. Again, in the New Testament, local churches worshipped in the language of the majority culture where it was planted. In the gentile world, believers worshipped in Greek or Latin, and in Jerusalem, they worshipped in the Hebrew language, regardless of the converts visiting Jerusalem from over fifteen ethno-linguistic groups. For example, in Acts 2, Peter's message was in Aramaic and not in Greek.

What Is a Multicultural Church?

Multicultural churches in North America must consist of six elements: they must be (1) multiracial, (2) multiethnic, (3) multicultural, (4) multigenerational, (5) multi-socioeconomic, and (6) multi-educational. In one word, a local church must be as diverse as the community in which it is situated and reflect the demography found in the area. Paul's commitment should be the same commitment and conviction of every church planter and pastor in all our communities. God never intended his church to be monocultural but multicultural. He never intended his church to find its identity along bloodlines but through common faith and union in Christ Jesus. The church is, therefore, a new community, a new Israel called out from all the nations of the world.

In *The Essence of the Church: A Community Created by the Spirit*, Craig Van Gelder noted:

> The division of the world along racial or ethnic lines, and institutionalized into national, political units, will no longer exist within God's redemptive reign. For the people of God, there will be a new political reality. The people of God will be formed around a different identity, one that transcends race, ethnicity, and nationalism. It will be an identity rooted in a shared faith and fellowship with the living God. This new community will include people of diverse racial, ethnic, national, and political identities.[26]

As Peter pointed out (1 Pet 2:9-10), the Christian faith is countercultural and represents the new humanity in Christ. Therefore, a fractured community of faith can never be an instrument in the transformation of a fractured world. "It is the nature of the church to live in reconciled relationship with God and one another as a new 'people of God.' This message greatly challenged the Jewish Christians who had to learn to welcome Gentile Christians as full participants in the emerging community of faith."[27]

Furthermore, in the midst of a divided world, the church must find ways to bridge differences in culture because the *ecclesia* of God is composed of people of all cultural, ethnic, racial, economic, and educational backgrounds. Christians in North America have a choice: to plant a church that will look like heaven as painted in the Scriptures or to continue to plant churches according to human traditions and personal choices. Revelation 7:9–12 states:

> After these things I looked, and behold, a great multitude which no one could count, from every nation and *all* tribes

---

[26] Craig Van Gelder, *The Essence of the Church: A Community Created by the Spirit* (Grand Rapids, MI: Baker Books, 2000), 108–109.
[27] Ibid.

and peoples and tongues, standing before the throne and before the Lamb, clothed in white robes, and palm branches were in their hands; and they cry out with a loud voice, saying, "Salvation to our God who sits on the throne, and to the Lamb." And all the angels were standing around the throne and around the elders and the four living creatures; and they fell on their faces before the throne and worshiped God, saying, "Amen, blessing and glory and wisdom and thanksgiving and honor and power and might, be to our God forever and ever. Amen."

If we are willing and obedient, and our answer is yes, we must be willing to plant a true New Testament church of God that will reflect our mosaic nation.

BIBLIOGRAPHY

Blomberg, Craig L. *Neither Poverty nor Riches: A Biblical Theology of Possessions.* Downers Grove, IL: InterVarsity Press, 1999.

Branson, Mark Lau, and Juan F. Martinez. *Churches Culture and Leadership: A Practical Theology of Congregations and Ethnicities.* Downers Grove, IL: IVP Academic, 2011.

Chaney, Charles L. *Church Planting at the End of the Twentieth Century.* Wheaton, IL: Tyndale House Publication Inc., 1986.

Emetuche, Damian. *The Future of Church Planting in North America.* New York: Peter Lang, 2014.

———. "Avoiding Racism in Starting New Congregations." In *Racism: Christian Reflection*, 75–81. Waco, TX: Baylor University, 2010.

Glasser, Arthur F., and Donal A. MacGavran. *Contemporary Theologies of Mission.* Grand Rapids, MI: Baker Book House, 1983.

Huffington Post. "Interracial Couple Banned from Kentucky Church." November 30, 2011. http://www.huffingtonpost.com/2011/11/30/interracial-couple-banned-from-kentucky-church_n_1121582.html.

IMB Global Research. "Mapping Resources." People Groups. Accessed June 19, 2019. https://www.peoplegroups.org/261.aspx.

McGavran, Donald A. *Understanding Church Growth.* 3rd ed. Edited by C. Peter Wagner. Grand Rapids, MI: Wm. B. Eerdmans Publishing, 1990.

Mission Frontiers. "Definition: Key Terms in the Cause of Frontier Missions." *Mission Frontiers: Bulletin of the U.S. Centre for World Mission* 16, nos. 1–2 (January/February 1994): 10.

Mott, Stephen, and Ronald J. Sider, "Economic Justice: A Biblical Paradigm." In *Toward a Just and Caring Society.* Edited by David P. Gushee, 15–45. Grand Rapids, MI: Baker Books, 1999.

Mulholland, Ken. "McGavran, Donald A. (1897–1991)." In *Evangelical Dictionary of World Missions.* Edited by A. Scott Moreau, 607. Grand Rapids, MI: Baker Books, 2000.

NewsOne Staff. "In Census, Young Americans Increasingly Diverse." *News One*, Feburary 6, 2011. http://newsone.com/nation/newsonestaff4/in-census-young-americans-increasingly-diverse/.

Payne, J. D. *Discovering Church Planting: An Introduction to the Whats, Whys, and Hows of Global Church Planting.* Colorado Springs, CO: Paternoster, 2009.

Pew Research Center. "Guess Who's Coming to Dinner." Pew Research Center. March 14, 2006. https://www.pewresearch.org/wp-content/uploads/sites/3/2010/10/Interracial.pdf.

Van Gelder, Craig. *The Essence of the Church: A Community Created by the Spirit.* Grand Rapids, MI: Baker Books, 2000.

Wang, Wendy. "The Rise of Intermarriage: Rates, Characteristics Vary by Race and Gender." Pew Research Center, February 16, 2012. https://www.pewsocialtrends.org/2012/02/16/the-rise-of-intermarriage/.

Winter, Ralph D. "Unreached People: The Development of the Concept." In *Reaching the Unreached: The Old-New Challenge.* Edited by Harvie M. Conn, 17. Phillipsburg, NJ: Presbyterian and Reformed Publishing Company, 1984.

Wright, Christopher J. H. *The Mission of God: Unlocking the Bible's Grand Narrative.* Downers Grove, IL: InterVarsity Press, 2006.

Yamamori, Tetsunao, Bryant L. Myers, and Kenneth L. Luscombe. *Serving with the Urban Poor.* Monrovia, CA: MARC, 1988.

Yancey, George. *One Body One Spirit: Principles of Successful Multiracial Churches.* Downers Grove, IL: InterVarsity Press, 2003.

Multicultural Evangelism

WHAT KIND OF NEIGHBOR AM I?

A Sermon by David Fleming, Pastor of Champion Forest Baptist Church

I am grateful to be with you today, and I love the theme of this month: "Multicultural Leadership in the Church." I suppose that is with the intention of leading our congregations to engage and reach our multicultural communities. I'm sure we all agree this is a conversation we should be having. In fact, we might also agree it is a conversation we have delayed having. We just celebrated the events of Dr. Martin Luther King Jr.'s birthday. Remember when he famously said, "We must face the fact that in America, the church is *still* the most segregated major institution in America. At 11:00 on Sunday morning when we stand and sing, we stand at the most segregated hour in this nation."[1] And he said, "This is tragic."

The tragedy is, it's true now. Still true, although it is sixty years later—still true. Though our workplaces are integrated. Our schools are integrated. Our restrooms and restaurants are integrated. Many, if not all, of our neighborhoods are integrated, multicultural, and multiethnic. We've made some progress, but just not quite enough yet—not

---

This sermon was preached by Dr. David Fleming, senior pastor of Champion Forest Baptist Church, Houston, Texas, on February 5, 2019, in the New Orleans Baptist Theological Seminary chapel service. The transcription was prepared by Dr. Mark Johnson and Dr. Wm. Craig Price.

[1] Martin Luther King Jr., "Prejudice: Speech at Western Michigan University" (lecture, Western Michigan University, Kalamazoo, MI, December 1963).

enough in the church yet. Because, in spite of all of this progress, in our multi-ethnic, multicultural nation, more than eight in ten churches, according to LifeWay, are monocultural churches. According to their research, in fact, 86 percent of our churches, in a multicultural world, are still monocultural.

What's interesting when we think about leadership is that among protestant senior pastors who were surveyed—in other studies and by LifeWay as well—almost 90 percent of us say racial reconciliation is mandated by the gospel. Can I get an "amen" on that? Reconciliation is mandated by the gospel. Almost all of us say that, and yet four out of ten church members think their church should become ethnically diverse. Do you see the leadership gap there? Nine out of ten pastors say this is a gospel issue, but only four out of ten parishioners think their church *should* become more ethnically diverse. In fact, two out of three church members think their church has done enough already to be ethnically diverse. Specifically, in our evangelical conversation, 71 percent of evangelicals believe their church is diverse enough when 86 percent of our churches are still monocultural. Dr. Ed Stetzer, formerly of LifeWay, summarized it this way, "Surprisingly most church goers are content with the ethnic status quo in their churches. In a world where our culture is increasingly diverse and many pastors are talking about diversity, it appears most people are happy where they are and with who they are."[2]

Why is this so important for church leaders? Why is it so important we have this conversation and come to terms with this dilemma? Well, if the little progress we've made over the last fifty years doesn't motivate us, the next fifty years certainly should. Study after study

---

[2] Bob Smietana, "Sunday Morning in America Still Segregated—and That's Ok with Worshipers," LifeWay Research, January 15, 2015, https://lifewayresearch.com/2015/01/15/sunday-morning-in-america-still-segregated-and-thats-ok-with-worshipers/. See also, Bob Smietana, "Sunday morning still segregated, study shows," Baptist Press, January 15, 2015, http://www.bpnews.net/44047/sunday-morning-still-segregated-study-shows. See also Mark Hearn, *Technicolor: Inspiring Your Church to Embrace Multicultural Ministry* (Nashville: TN, B&H Publishing), 2017.

concludes that by 2050 there will not be a single majority of ethnicity in the United States of America. We'll all be minorities. So if discipleship in our churches is important to us—and one would assume it is—and training and equipping our people to live in the real world is important to us, and if mobilizing them to make a difference in that real world is important, then we might want to start asking ourselves tough questions like this one: Can we adequately disciple and deploy our people to thrive in and to engage a largely multicultural world from largely monocultural churches? The answer will depend of course on whether or not our churches are primarily to be training, equipping, and sending stations or retreat centers from an increasingly diverse and increasingly uncomfortable multicultural world.

I've asked a few questions. I want to know why. Why, in fifty years, have we made so little progress—some progress but still so little?

It Could Be Demographics

It could be just as simple as demographics. It could be the practical aspect of who lives where and around whom. In some cases, monocultural churches are monocultural because they're reaching monocultural communities. That makes perfect sense. If a church is reaching its community, it will reflect its community. That makes sense. It would be unreasonable to expect church to be anything but a reflection of its community. If it's monocultural, that would be the expectation.

Having said that, the number of truly monocultural communities is not what it used to be, especially in large cities, in urban centers, and even in suburban areas. It's not what it used to be and, let me tell you something else, it's not what it's going to be. We've got to recognize the changing demographics of the United States of America.

It Could Be Preference

It could be a preference—not so much a demographic issue but a preferential issue. Perhaps this monocultural church experience is an attempt to develop ethnic and cultural identity or perhaps to preserve and to protect it. I would say that would be truer for our minority population because the majority population has many opportunities to develop ethnic and cultural identity, to preserve and protect it. But in the minority community, there are precious few of those opportunities, and it may be that Sunday morning, in a monocultural church context, that is best expressed.

While that is understandable from a cultural and sociological perspective, we have to ask ourselves the question, Is the church the best place—the *right* place—to protect and preserve cultural or ethnic identity in a way that preserves cultural distinctions that ultimately divide the body of Christ? It is just a question. I don't know the answer. But is church the right place to accomplish that goal?

It Could Be the Homogeneous Unit Principle

It could be the homogeneous unit principle I learned years ago here at New Orleans Seminary. This principle states simply that people like to be with people like themselves. We understand that. And we want to associate mostly with people who share our culture, our language, our doctrine, our socioeconomic status, whatever it may be. Of course, you remember that principle was really about missions and evangelism and about how people tend to come to Christ in groups when they don't have to cross cultural boundaries to get to Jesus.

It was descriptive in nature, but unfortunately, too often we take what is descriptive and make it prescriptive. We create church scenarios where we only want to reach people who are like ourselves, if only by default. As one urban professor and church planter in an inner city wrote, "The principle can be used and we could make a good case that it has been used to baptize our desire to turn a blind eye to those on the outside of our own in-group and to affirm our love of comfort and ease within a church made after our own image. However, our society is full of outsiders to communities of grace. How will the insiders welcome the outsiders into their faith communities, which we believe have been called to be shaped by the good news that those who were far from God are now brought near by the grace of Christ?"³

The homogeneous unit principle is certainly descriptive of a natural tendency we probably should all admit we have. We like to be with people who are like ourselves. But the question we should be asking is not, "Is it natural?" We should be asking, "Is it spiritual? Is it supernatural?" I would say, "It is not." There is a higher plain here to which we aspire as church leaders, and that is to be a part of something God is doing, not just something we personally prefer that tends to take the shape of who we are when we look in the mirror. Even though there may be something to this principle, if we aren't careful the very next step in this progression is a far less desirable reality. If we aren't careful, not only do people like to be with people like themselves, but people will *only* like to be with people like themselves, and people who aren't like them won't be welcome. None of us want that. In that case, it's not all that complicated after all. It could be one more little bitty step. It could just simply be—if we're honest—we just don't like people who aren't like us. Maybe that whole "love your neighbor" thing only applies to the right kind of neighbor and only until the wrong neighbor moves in next door. Does that sound familiar to you? You'll find it in Luke, chapter 10, starting with verse 25.

> And a lawyer stood up and put [Jesus] to the test saying, "Teacher, what shall I do to inherit eternal life?" And He said to him, "What is written in the Law? How does it read to you?" And he answered, "You shall love the Lord your God with all your heart, and with all your soul, and with all your strength, and with all your mind; and your neighbor as yourself." And He said to him, "You have answered correctly; do this and you will live." But wishing to justify himself, he said to Jesus, "And who is my neighbor?"

---

[3] Kyuboem Lee, "New Math on the Homogeneous Unit Principle for Church Growth," The Narthex, November 12, 2014, https://medium.com/the-narthex/new-math-on-the-homogeneous-unit-principle-for-church-growth-fe59fa756825.

In the middle of this Bible conversation, there's another predictable conversation going on in the back of our minds—if we are not careful—that sounds a lot like justification for why this is not true of us.

The lawyer should have thrown himself at the mercy of the court and cried, "I can't do that! How can I love God in that comprehensive, total, everything-I've-got, kind of way? How can I love my neighbor as myself? How is that possible?" But, instead, seeking to justify himself, he said, "And who is my neighbor?"

You know what he's doing? He's not asking who can I love? He's not asking who can be or who might be my neighbor? He's asking who isn't. Who's not my neighbor? Who's not in the "in" group? Who can I exclude? Who do I not have to love? By the way, it was a very Jewish, especially a very Pharisaical, even Essene, thing to do, to choose your neighbors, to pick those who were closest to you, and to circle them. They would then exclude those who were not in the "in group" of their neighborhood. Who is my neighbor? That's a way to make a distinction.

Not long ago during one of the upswings in the gun debate, I was called by our local television station wanting me to come into the studio to do an interview on the news to answer a few questions. They asked, "Are you aware there are more handgun licenses per capita in your zip code than anywhere in the State of Texas?"—which means anywhere in the world. At the interview, they asked, "Pastor, how do you feel about your neighbors being armed?" I replied, "Which ones? Which neighbor?" They said, "Does it matter?" And I said, "Well, yeah, if you knew my neighbors it would matter." Now don't look at me like that! I feel the judgment. Don't do that. You know we all make distinctions. I've said it's natural. As a matter of fact, we distinguish one from another. We make these distinctions to define and ultimately to divide us from one another.

It's as simple as our favorite college football team. Are you an LSU Tiger? Are you a Florida Gator? Any Aggies here today? Sometimes that's all it takes right there to define and divide us. That's all it takes.

We can define and divide along national lines: Are you German? Are you French? Are you Russian? Are you Kenyan? Are you American?

We can divide along racial lines: Are you white? Are you black? Are you Hispanic? Are you Asian? Are you multicultural? Interracial?

We can divide over political lines, and we're doing that these days: Are you Democrat, Republican, Independent, Libertarian, or Green?

We can define and divide by socioeconomic class: Are you rich? Poor? Middle-class? If you're middle-class, are you upper-middle, lower-middle, or middle-middle? Or a little bit up toward the lower middle of the middle, middle of the middle? I mean, let's be precise.

We can distinguish along religious lines: Are you Jewish? Are you Muslim? Are you Hindu? Are you Buddhist? Are you atheist? Are you Christian? If you're Christian, we need to know, of course, are you Catholic or Protestant? And if you're Protestant, we'd really like to know if you're Methodist, Presbyterian, or Baptist. And if you're Baptist, are you Northern or Southern Baptist? Are you Independent, Missionary, or Freewill Baptist? If you're Southern Baptist, that's not quite enough. I really need to know if you're reformed, not reformed, or if you have no idea what needs to be reformed. And I really need to know if you're conservative, moderate, or liberal. And shouldn't we also discuss that we can divide by musical styles? I mean, are you traditional, contemporary, or blended? If you're blended, what's the blend? I mean, what's the right blend for you? Is it 50/50? Is it 60/40? 40/60? I don't know, but I care. It's my preference.

And we laugh, but isn't this essentially what the lawyer is trying to do? He's trying to define so that he can divide—to distinguish who he doesn't have to love. Who can I get a pass on? Who do I have the privilege and your permission to exclude as neighbor and who do I need to love?

Jesus answered the lawyer's second question with a parable, which is a very familiar story but with a very unexpected twist, as I'm sure you've studied.

> Jesus replied and said, "A man was going down from Jerusalem to Jericho, and fell among robbers, and they stripped him and

beat him, and went away leaving him half dead. And by chance a priest was going down on that road, and when he saw him, he passed by on the other side. Likewise, a Levite also when he came to the place and saw him, passed by on the other side. But a Samaritan, [and this is the twist] who was on a journey, came upon him; and when he saw him, he felt compassion, and came to him and bandaged up his wounds, pouring oil and wine on them; and he put him on his own beast, and brought him to an inn and took care of him. On the next day he took out two denarii and gave them to the innkeeper and said, 'Take care of him; and whatever more you spend, when I return, I will repay you.' Which of these three do you think proved to be a neighbor to the man who fell into the robbers' hands?" (Luke 10:30–37)

That's not the question. The question is, "Who is not my neighbor?" Who can I exclude from the neighborhood? The answer to the question is a question. Who was neighborly? It wasn't about whether or not the man on the side of the road—probably Jewish, at least from the impression from those who were listening—was a neighbor and deserved love, care, and compassion. But the question was, who will be neighborly to the man who needs a good neighbor? Which of these three do you think proved to be a neighbor to the man who fell among the robber? You'd think he would say, "The Samaritan." But the lawyer said, "The one who showed him mercy." And Jesus said to him the unthinkable: "You go and you do like the good Samaritan did."

Can you imagine the offense that welled up in this good Jewish teacher, keeper of the law, that Jesus would tell him to emulate a Samaritan? That's the twist. You see the point is, this parable is not about the neighbor you have but the neighbor you are. The poor man's neighbors were not very neighborly even though they were neighbors. It was the Samaritan who was a good neighbor to a man who would have never been his neighbor. He was a good neighbor to the man who needed a good neighbor. Here's the real question: *What kind of neighbor am I?*

My wife Beverly and I recently got new neighbors ... finally! We've had an empty lot next to us for years, the whole time we've lived there—thirteen years in that house—there's been an empty lot next to us. A few years ago, someone bought the lot, but they didn't start building right away, so we anticipated and wondered, "Who's moving in next door? Who will be our neighbor?" It's an interesting street we live on. It's a lot like Houston. We have a Vietnamese family on the corner; they're Buddhist. We have a family from India on the other corner; they're Hindu. A family from Pakistan directly across the street; they're Muslim. And then there's us. We're Baptist. We all get along great by the way. So who moves in next door? If that had just been a Jewish family, we'd have it nailed. But, as it turned out, another Christian moved in next door, not from America, but from Central America. And when they moved next door, do you think we breathed a sigh of relief? Whew! Thank goodness! Not another Muslim or Hindu or Buddhist or pagan? You see for the last two or three years, what Beverly and I and our family have been concentrating on is not who will be our neighbor but to whom can we be a good neighbor. That's the question and that's the point of this parable. It's not who my neighbor is but what kind of neighbor I am to those who need a good neighbor.

A neighbor can be next door or across town. A neighbor can be just like me or nothing like me. I mean, if I would give in to my nature, I could tell you who would've moved in next door to me. Me! I mean, think about it. You put you in a funnel and shake it, and see, Who is a perfect neighbor for you? Who would really like what you like? It's you. You would be your perfect neighbor if you gave in to your nature. I'm happy to say we got good neighbors. But regardless of who moved in next to us, I hope the Spirit would win out over the flesh and nature and we would be just as good a neighbor to them that they need us to be regardless of the kind of neighbors they are. By the way, my

Muslim friend across the street has the key and the code to my house, and I have his. He attended all of my kids' graduation parties. It was funny. When he walked in, we offered him some punch, and he said, "No, I can't have that!" I said, "Punch?" He said, "You know Muslims don't drink alcohol." I said, "You're in a Baptist preacher's house. Have some punch! You're safe!" We've had meals at their home, our feet under the same table with a Muslim family from Pakistan. He said, "David, would you ask the blessing?" I said, "You know I pray in Jesus' name?" He said, "I wouldn't expect any less." I prayed over the food. It was Pakistani food, in a Pakistani Muslim's home, in Jesus' name, and we left friends. So it's not about the neighbor you have; it's about the neighbor you are. "Be a good neighbor," Jesus said. Be a good neighbor to anyone anywhere who needs a good neighbor. That's the point of the parable. Let's not miss that.

For the sake of application and the time we have left, let me make three points: How to be a good Samaritan neighbor.

Number 1: See Opportunity

You have to see the opportunities. This man on the side of the road was not the Samaritan's neighbor. The priest and Levite who were the man's neighbors, happily and gladly saw a burden to avoid. But a Samaritan who was not his neighbor saw an opportunity to seize and take advantage of.

The world is changing. What do you think about that? What do you see when you see those changing demographics? What does your mind do when you consider the changing face of our nation? Do you see an opportunity? Do you see a mission?

When Beverly and I came to New Orleans Baptist Theological Seminary in 1991, we sat in this chapel and filled out a card to register with the International Mission Board. We put our yes on the altar saying we would go anywhere with a strong sense we would be "on mission" to the nations somewhere in the world. And God called us to Houston—the mission field of Houston, the most diverse city in

America. I didn't know. I thought I'd end up in Brazil or perhaps Mexico. God sent me to both … in Houston.

We have a saying at Champion Forest. I won't tell you that some didn't react negatively to it, but we say it anyway, in as lovingly a kind way as we can. We say, "You have a choice when you look outside your front door or front window; look left, right, and across the street." When you see your neighborhood changing and the demographics beginning to shift, you have a choice to make. What do you see? Is it, "There goes the neighborhood?" Or is it, "Here come the nations?"

We have signs at our church at every exit on our church property that say, "You are now entering your mission field." By the way, today we are in New Orleans—a wonderfully diverse city otherwise known as "Your Mission Field." Number one: see the opportunity.

Number 2: Care Deeply

That word *compassion* in the parable is a word that comes from deep within. It's an intestinal type of word, and it means to feel deeply, or a gut compassion. Two men were in a hurry. I don't know why they didn't help. It's pointless to speculate. We don't know. Jesus doesn't tell us why they didn't help. We just know they didn't, and that probably reveals the problem. It was a heart problem. Don't you know that if they had cared deeply enough, they would have risked running into those same robbers? Don't you know that if they had cared deeply enough, they would have gone through the provisions for ceremonial cleaning even if he had been deceased and they were defiled? Don't you know that if they had cared deeply enough, supper would have waited? Surely they had been at the temple doing their duties—their job to serve, to minister, to help, and to love. If they had cared about this man, whatever they cared about in Jericho would have waited.

But the Samaritan, who clearly was on a business trip of some kind, had places to be, things to do, and people to see. This was probably going to cost him money. This was certainly going to cost him money. Why was he willing to risk it? Why was he willing to pay the price? Why take the time? It was not his neighbor. It's because when he looked and saw this man, he saw an opportunity to demonstrate what ought to come from the heart, certainly from every Christian. It's called compassion. He cared. And we can surely ask ourselves, "Do we care about the things God cares about?" And can we say, "We are loving God with all we've got," if we aren't compassionately loving the ones God loves?

I can tell you right now I am no Hallmark movie fan. But I watch a lot of Hallmark movies because I am a fan of a woman who is a fan of Hallmark movies. You bet, honey! Let's watch a Hallmark movie. Let's do it! Why? Because I like them? No, because after the Hallmark movie is over, I usually need to see something blown up or cars going too fast, flipping, flying through the air. But because she loves a good Hallmark movie—me too, honey! Because while I'm no fan of Hallmark, I'm a fan of hers.

Let me just suggest if we say we are God's people and we love God, don't we love what and who God loves? Where's the compassion? I get in trouble sometimes when I mention things like caravans headed north through Central America. And not to make any political statement whatsoever, but to simply say, "Can we not empathize to some degree with the plight of those poor people?" Do we not care? Does God not care? Does anybody care? It's not political. It's spiritual. Do we care? Let me tell you the world is changing. What do you think about that? What do you see when you see that? And the world is changing, how do feel about that? Be careful because how you feel might actually be a pop test for whether or not, in fact, we love God as much as we think. See opportunity. Care deeply.

Number 3: Act Responsibly

Two people saw but didn't feel or do anything. One saw, felt, and did something about the situation. The verbs are piled up there, all demonstrating evidence of faith. Not just to say what we believe or to feel strongly about it but to actually put that into action ... to do something about it. That's a test of faith, isn't it? It's not just orthodoxy. It's not just how strongly we feel and convictions. It's about what you do next and if you do anything at all. The Samaritan put it all on the line to do something with compassion given the opportunity that presented itself to him.

The world is changing. The question is not only do we see it and how do we see it, but does it make us feel deeply within, and what are we going to do about it? Hide in our homes? Run for the hills? Or run into the fields? Maybe the harvest isn't as ripe as it once was, but it's still ripe. What are we going to do?

Church leaders, let me say this in closing: Saying, "All are welcome," at your church is not enough. Come on! It's not enough to say the doors are open, the lights are on, everyone's welcome, and we love all people. It's not enough. The "Y'all Come" strategy is not working if they're not coming. And they're not coming. Something is missing. Oh, I know what it is. It's the "Go!" As you go, as you are going, make disciples. Jesus didn't say, "Hiding, make disciples!" He didn't say, "Retreating, make disciples!" He didn't say, "Sheltering, make disciples!" No, Jesus said, "Get out of here! You're going, aren't you? As you go, make disciples." We've got to put the word *go* back into our church mission. *Go* is not just a missionary to the nations, but *go* is a good word for next door, across the street, and across town. *Go* is a good word for a strategy, especially with regards to reflecting a community we are intent upon reaching. What's missing after we address the heart of the issue, whether or not we see opportunity, whether or not we feel love and compassion, whether or not we're willing to do anything, is the real question. Will there be any intentionality? What are we willing to do to help someone come, and when they come, to make them feel welcome so they'll come again and again? And not just so they'll assimilate into our culture and be like us but so they can influence the culture and change the culture so we can be more like Christ together. We're not trying to make one into the other, and the other into the one. We're all trying to be like Jesus, aren't we? Isn't that the goal of the body, to grow up into the Head, to fully mature into who he is? We've got to be strategic. We've got to be more intentional. If the challenge is to reach our community, then we'll reflect our community. And the question is, "If we're not reflecting our community are we reaching our community or just a segment of our community that—not too surprisingly—looks a lot like me?" Intentionality. I would say that has to impact how you present yourselves. From the website to brochures to videos to who is on the platform to who serves in leadership positions, how intentional can we be?

Let me tell you, with a closing story, of a conversation I had with a man who walked with Dr. Martin Luther King Jr. He visited our church with a family who shared with him our vision for a multicultural ministry to reach our whole community. To everyone within the shadow of our steeple, we don't just say they're welcome. We're going after them.

He said, "Let me ask you something, Pastor. What do you do on the weekend of Martin Luther King Jr.'s birthday and celebration?" I said what many of us would say, "We mention it, and sometimes we'll use a quote or tell a story." He smiled very kindly, very saintly, and said, "Well, Pastor, it may be if you're trying to get the attention of a portion of your community, you might want to [value what they value]." And that was the genesis of the *Dream Banquet* seven years ago. On that Sunday night, we clear the deck and have a big get-together, celebrate the dream, and challenge ourselves to keep dreaming, keep the dream alive, and be intentional toward seeing that dream become reality. I don't know a lot of predominantly white, upper-middle class, Republican churches that have a Martin Luther King Jr. Dream Celebration on that Sunday. And I'm not bragging about us, but I do want to say it is a statement of our intentionality to include people who needed us to be a good neighbor to them.

The world is changing.
What do you think about that? What do you see?
The world is changing.
How do you feel about that?
The world is changing.
And the most important question is, "What are you going to do?" What are you going to do about that?

BIBLIOGRAPHY

Hearn, Mark. *Technicolor: Inspiring Your Church to Embrace Multicultural Ministry.* Nashville: TN, B&H Publishing, 2017.

Lee, Kyuboem. "New Math on the Homogeneous Unit Principle for Church Growth." The Narthex, November 12, 2014. https://medium.com/the-narthex/new-math-on-the-homogeneous-unit-principle-for-church-growth-fe59fa756825.

King, Martin Luther, Jr. "Prejudice: Speech at Western Michigan University" Lecture, Western Michigan University. Kalamazoo, M. December 1963.

Smietana Bob. "Sunday Morning in America Still Segregated—and That's Ok with Worshipers." LifeWay Research, January 15, 2015. https://lifewayresearch.com/2015/01/15/sunday-morning-in-america-still-segregated-and-thats-ok-with-worshipers/.

———. "Sunday morning still segregated, study shows." Baptist Press, January 15, 2015. http://www.bpnews.net/44047/sunday-morning-still-segregated-study-shows.

Multicultural Evangelism

TRANSITIONING A MONOCULTURAL CHURCH TO A MULTICULTURAL MINISTRY

An Interview with the Pastor and Executive Team Members of Champion Forest Baptist Church, Houston, Texas

The following interview was conducted March 6, 2019, with Dr. David Fleming, senior pastor of Champion Forest Baptist Church and the following members of his executive team: Dr. Stephen Trammell, global executive pastor and lead pastor of North Klein Campus; Pastor Averri LeMalle, lead pastor of Jersey Village Campus; and Pastor Ramon Medina, lead pastor to Spanish ministry. Interviewees are referred to by their initials. The interview was conducted by Dr. Preston Nix, Dr. Mark Johnson, and Dr. Wm. Craig Price.

Q: How do you and your staff define the terms *multicultural*, *multicultural ministry*, and *multicultural evangelism*?

D.F.: Definitions are moving targets sometimes. I appreciate that you want some precision. We are also willing to adjust our terminology to be clear. Sometimes we have in-house speech, and we want it to be clear. *Multicultural* for us is a representation of more than one culture. That could be ethnic, it could be language, it could be generational, or even a subculture within a culture. Multicultural for us at Champion Forest means not narrowly defining ourselves by one culture. We are not an ethnic church; we are not an old church; we are not an Anglo church; we are not an African-American church. We are a church where anybody could feel welcome and invited to be a part of this culture. Champion Forest is multicultural.

When we use the term *culture*, it means who we are and how we operate. It is our thinking process. It is our paradigm. Our approach to ministry is multicultural. Culture is not something we tolerate. It is something we embrace. I would say *multicultural ministry* is our paradigm for doing church. It is not only who we are as being from different cultures, but our strategy is to be *multicultural*. At the heart of that is *evangelism* because what started all this for us is the desire to reach our community for Christ. We live in Houston—the most diverse city in America, officially. And that's true in the suburbs as much as it is for the inner city, if not more so. If you live in the suburbs or the outer edges of greater Houston, it is a multicultural reality. If we have monocultural churches, that just means we are not reaching our whole community. We are only reaching the segment that looks like us. Our mission and vision from the beginning was to reach our community, which is multicultural. We have used it as a mission. To reach our community, we are going to have to reflect the community, and to reflect it, we will ultimately reach it. So it has always been about missions and evangelism.

The ministry side of it is, "What do you do with them when you've got them?" That creates a different paradigm—a different way of thinking, a different measure of success. It does present some unique challenges monocultural ministry doesn't. We say multicultural ministry is messy. We don't mean that in a derogative or negative sense. We mean it is more complicated because everybody is not the same. They don't think the same, they don't perceive the same, and they don't process the same. Sometimes they have different backgrounds and perspectives, and different filters and lenses. People come from very different places. They see the world in different ways. To do ministry in a multicultural context is a bit more complicated in a wonderful way. And it is definitely more work. It is easier to be monocultural.

I have been a pastor of monocultural churches everywhere except here. So we deal with things here in this context we never dealt with in monocultural settings. That's what we mean by *multicultural* driven by the desire for *evangelism* and reaching our community, and finally, the puzzle that multicultural ministry presents. But it is definitely navigable. You can do it. There is a way through it. You have to be willing to make a few mistakes and say things a few ways you may wish you hadn't said or didn't even know you were saying the wrong way. It takes a lot of grace and a lot of "bearing with one another" to bridge that gap of understanding sometimes with different backgrounds and perspectives.

A.L.: Ultimately the mission is to fulfill the Great Commission by following the Great Commandment. We are drawn by the commission to reach all people for Christ. As a church we have a responsibility for the community we are in to reflect that community. We draw them in with the love of Christ, and that enables us to love all people regardless of differences—and yet highlighting and celebrating those things that make us unique, as well as growing in those things that make us one family, one community of faith.

S.T.: I have pastored monocultural churches in Louisiana before moving here twelve years ago. As Pastor Averri said, "It's all about the Great Commission." In Louisiana, I led our church to go on international mission trips to reach unreached people groups. We targeted Kazakhstan, Honduras, China, and several other countries. What is interesting is that the church was willing to go on mission around the world to reach people they would not welcome in the church I was pastoring. There was a dichotomy of willingness to engage another culture, as long as that culture does not come into our building. What has been so unique in Champion Forest is the intentionality—as Pastor David said so well, and this is what he lives, and that all of us live—and that we have infused this intentionality into our DNA. Our Great Commission consciousness is that we are committed to reaching the people in the shadow of our steeples—plural. So for each campus, the people in the shadow of that new campus or that specific location, we are committed to reaching—they are welcome inside our building. We are going to do everything we can to reach them and to love them.

Q: Is it possible for a church to be involved in multicultural evangelism but not be a multicultural ministry, and certainly not a multicultural church?

R.M.: It's more than having a sign in front of the church that says, "Everybody's Welcome!" It requires someone of another culture being able to come to that church and find a connection with his or her own culture.

A.L.: This requires a level of intentionality where you are willing to do what it takes to embrace all people in that community.

Q: How did you overcome the monocultural barriers to transition the people of Champion Forest into a multicultural mindset? We hear about churches that reach out to people of other cultures across the world, but these same cultures might not be welcome in their church back home.

D.F.: Bear with me and give me some grace to say this straightly: That's just sinful. James says if I prefer one over another, that is sin. If I prefer a rich man and give him the front-row seat or the seat of honor and push the poor man to the fringe, then I have a sinful heart. At some point we must be willing to say this in strong terms—that it is wrong to not be intentional to include. We must make the effort to be more diverse in our outreach.

Let's say there are three zones here:

1. To be intentional to include
2. To be willing to include but to not be intentional
3. To be intentional *not* to include

If you view that on one side, to be intentional not to include—that is, we will go to Africa, Brazil, China, but they are not welcome to come into our church—then we probably ought to approach this from the perspective we are dealing with a sin problem.

The unintentional part is probably where most people are. I want to believe that. I hope it's true most people are willing, and they would in fact embrace and feel great about, including someone of color or a minority in their mostly white church. They are just not going to do what is necessary to create the kind of experience where that is going to happen, more than perhaps the exception to the rule. So for us at Champion Forest Baptist Church, we have always made this a gospel issue. We have always made this a Bible issue. We have never made it a social issue. Of course, there are social implications. There are political implications. There are historical implications. But we just make it about gospel and reach people for Jesus. We really think if you just preach the Bible, and especially if you are talking to Southern Baptists, you know who we are. We are supposed to be people of the book. We are supposed to be people of the Great Commission. So, I have really thought if you connect the Scripture and the heart of God for the nations to the heart of the Southern Baptists, they will get it. You don't have to make it intentionally about social reconciliation or ethnic reconciliation. That's happening, but that's the fruit not the root. The root is a sin issue. We need forgiveness and salvation and reconciliation to God before we can hope to be reconciled to each other.

I talked to an African-American woman here in my office who grew up in the forties and fifties. She told me a story that turned my stomach of how she was mistreated in the State of Florida, the state where I was raised. I told her, "I am surprised pleasantly and blessed that you are here at Champion Forest." Because with the experience she shared with me, most people would be so impacted they could never get over that and could never sit under a white pastor, could never be a part of a predominantly white congregation. They just couldn't do it. She is doing it because of the grace of God. Her heart's been changed, and she sees my heart being changed. And that brings people together. I think it's a mistake to make this a social issue or racial reconciliation issue. Those are wonderful benefits of gospel reconciliation. We just try to preach the word. We try to preach it all, and we don't try to shade it, color it, or shape it to fit our cultural preferences.

Q: At Champion Forest, did you have a specific strategy? Did you get your leadership together, talk about intentionality, and say, "We're going to reach who's around us? Therefore, we are going to have to be multicultural"?

D.F.: The first thing I did was I had a demographics study conducted on the primary area of the church and recognized the transition and the growing diversity. I talked to the search committee from day one: "If God were to call me to Champion Forest, one, would I have the opportunity and, two, would I have your support to reach the whole community for Christ?" Of course, they said yes, and that was absolutely what we would expect, but they are supposed to say yes. The test comes when you actually start doing it. Thank goodness they all were right there. We had an African-American man on the committee. I felt really good about their commitment to support that vision coming in. Through the course of conversations and interviews and meetings with the deacons, I didn't ever surprise them. I never snuck up on them or surprised them. We told them from day one—we're coming to reach people for Christ. We're coming to grow them in their faith—to train, equip, and mobilize them to serve and be on mission for Christ here in our community and around the world. That's what I said coming in the front door. There never really was a time when I got up and made this grand announcement that we are about to start this vision or strategy. I said it in my "view of a call" sermon.

Q: What would you advise pastors to ask who are preparing to be interviewed by a search committee?

D.F.: I think this is an important question. We pastors have a tendency sometimes to say, "Well, if you want me to come, here is what I'm going to do, and if you are not going to do it, then I am not going to come." I won't say my conversation with the Champion Forest search committee was that kind of a conversation. It wasn't an ultimatum. Their answer was not a condition of my coming. Fortunately, it never got to that. I don't know what would have happened if that would have been the case.

But we are doing "heart work" here. That's a process, and it takes time. I'd be afraid for a pastor who came into an all-white, or into an all African-American, or all Hispanic congregation, who from day one said, "We are about to be multicultural." Leaders need to pastor those people, to love those people, to show them a better way, and to soften their hearts and the soil ahead of time.

I might lead with the question to a pastor search committee: "If God opened a door to reach our whole community for Christ, would you all be excited about that? Would this be a good thing?" Because you can't change people in the interview, but you can plant the seed and then begin to cultivate that heart transformation. Certainly, if you have a search committee, presumably they are opinion leaders and influencers in the church. If they are on board, you are way down the road. And that's a good thing. But it does not mean that if they all are not blowing the trumpet from day one that they can't come around. This kind of change requires pastoral leadership. At Champion Forest, the Spanish piece was probably easy initially because we already had a mission. When God gave us the vision to cancel the mission and move them all into one church and be one church in two languages, there was not even a bump in the road. That was low-hanging fruit.

When it came time to hire our first African-American pastor, we had to deal with the issue of whether that decision was reverse discrimination. Were we hiring a guy just because he was black? To which I said, "Yes, what's the problem with that?" We tend to dance around that issue. It's uncomfortable. I just had to get over saying, "Of course, I'm hiring a man because he's African-American. I am doing it on purpose." I called Averri. In my first conversation with Averri I said, "I am looking for an African-American teaching pastor. Do you qualify?" Tell them about that conversation, Averri.

A.L.: I told him, "I've been been a pastor for a long time and an African American all my life. And that I possess the necessary qualifications and specific skill set to pastor in a multicultural context."

D.F.: I don't want to discount the pastoral part. Coming in with the vision is critical, but you must be willing to teach, preach, love, and lead people to embrace that vision. There is a tension for both of those to happen. It's a heart issue. It's a discipleship issue as well as a gospel issue. Being patient as you pastor should be part of the strategy, for sure.

A.L.: What resonates is intentionality. We intentionally value all of the communities represented in the congregation. The make-up of our leadership reflects the make-up of our congregation. This intentionality is of utmost importance for any church leader who is looking to make this kind of impact in the life of a church and community.

Q: You have used the terms *proximity*, *assimilation*, and *accommodation*. Could you define these terms for us?

D.F.: There are important nuances between the definitions. *Proximity* refers to different cultures coming into the same space and is not the goal of multicultural ministry. We are not trying to simply share space and get along. Rather, we're trying to share life. To have a context where people from different cultures gather in the same building is a good start, but that's not the goal. When an African-American family invites a Hispanic, Asian, or Anglo-American family in their home for dinner at their table, now we're getting somewhere. Doing life together is more meaningful than everyone sitting in a church section together. So unity is the goal and the community of faith is built on unity. This is our recurring theme every year at our annual Dream Banquet. We play that sheet of music over and over. Just being here is not the goal. It is what we do when we get here. Do we do mission together? Do we serve together? Are we growing together? That's when we start to feel like we are getting somewhere. When we see people getting together to do life together, then we feel like we are making progress. This goes beyond their particular culture, or ethnicity, or language.

Assimilation is where one culture loses its cultural distinctiveness to become a part of another culture. For example, if a Hispanic family joins a predominantly white church and basically changes to become a part of that larger culture, then that is assimilation.

Accommodation on the other hand is when you retain that cultural distinctive and the greater body accommodates you and does not expect you to lose your identity. We are a welcoming church, and you are welcome to come and be a part of our church. Accommodation says we are going to adjust in order to accommodate you in a Christlike, loving, and fully accepting way that honors you and recognizes your distinctiveness and God's creative genius in you. We don't ignore cultures here; we embrace cultures.

Dr. King said, "I have a dream that my four little children will one day live in a nation where they will not to be judged by the color of their skin but by the content of their character." I think an unintended consequence of that statement for a season was, "Oh, we are not supposed to notice our distinctiveness." We are not supposed to know that I'm white, Pastor Averri is black, Pastor Ramon is Hispanic, or Pastor Stephen is from Louisiana. You are not supposed to know that. I think we are happily moving beyond that. Not only do we notice our cultural differences, but we appreciate God created us this way. *Multicultural* was God's idea, not man's. We see in Rev 7 a multicultural worship service around the throne in heaven. Cultural distinctiveness endures. It is not a product of the fall. It endures into eternity. In our context, to accommodate someone is to say, "Well, of course you are African-American, or you come from South America with a particular cultural distinction or a language need." We want to accommodate that here. We do not want you to disappear in this greater culture. We want the overall culture of Champion Forest to reflect the many cultures that make it up.

Q: Would you say being multicultural is like Neapolitan ice cream where there are three distinctive colors and flavors? Or is it like a blend where you get a new color when you bring them all together?

D.F.: That's a great image. I think maybe it's both. In one setting, those three distinct colors are on display. At other times, for example, for the sake of mission and vision, we don't want three different visions for three different populations. I would say there are times when we want to be something greater together synergistically than the sum of our parts. But that does not mean we want to lose the distinctiveness of the chocolate, the strawberry, or the vanilla.

For example, we have Spanish language services here. Some people might push back and say, "You are not truly multicultural if you have a Spanish-only service." We say, "This is an accommodation to the heart language of the worshipper because they have a need to hear and think theologically in the language of their heart." In this case, it's strawberry, vanilla, and chocolate. But if you saw us out in the neighborhoods on Serve Saturday or after Hurricane Harvey, you would see teams of people from a dozen countries speaking three different languages. But they are all carrying their weight and mudding out a house. That's mixing those colors together for the sake of the community, for unity, for vision, and for mission. Our mission teams are mixed. When we do the Christmas Spectacular for thirty thousand people at Christmas time, the whole choir learns the entire presentation in English and in Spanish. Those are times where you going to see one color and it's all of us. There are other times when we would highlight the distinctions for a reason. We think of it like a stew. Stew is like a soup where it is all a homogenous substance. It's all soup, and then you've got stew with its potatoes, carrots, mushrooms, and beef. We kind of like the stew part. We want to be something together that is greater than the sum of our parts.

Q: Dr. Fleming to Pastor Averri: "Do the African-American churches use these terms *accommodation* and *assimilation* a little differently?"

A.L.: I don't know if that could be applied generally across all African-American contexts and churches. At times, *accommodation* is used more on a limited basis because it may be that there is almost a tolerance of multiculturalism as opposed to truly creating a culture or a space where one who is "different" can fit in. I don't know if that experience is unique to an African-American church or if it is a condition of monoculturalism where one is accustomed to operating in a certain lens of worship that others are invited into. But there's a limitation to the extent that one would be willing to accept them in.

Q: Dr. Fleming to Dr. Trammell: "Stephen, talk about what people look for the first time they walk into any group of people."

S.T.: In September 2012, I wrote out eight integration essentials because we are asked so often how Champion Forest has transitioned to a multicultural reality. Here are eight statements that will address what Pastor David is asking.

1. *Henry Blackaby said, "Look to see where God is at work so you can join him."*

   I think this is a nonnegotiable. Remember Blackaby also taught us, "Pay attention to who God brings to you."

2. *Be sensitive to the first question people ask when they come to your church: "Is there anyone here like me?"*

   This is human nature. When people go to a restaurant or to a ballgame, they are looking for somebody who looks like them. This allows them to have an immediate connection, and it also provides them a sense of security.

3. *Reach your community by reflecting your community.*

This is our theme you have heard the most. If I was sitting down with a pastor anywhere, or if they read this chapter, I would say to them these items: Reach your community by reflecting your community. The goal is that when you go inside of the church, you want the inside of the church to look the way the community looks. You want your church to look (multicultural) like Walmart, or Walgreens, or the movie theater so there is a commonality.

4. *Infuse diversity into the DNA of your local church.*

We are very intentional about infusing diversity into the DNA. This is our fabric of who we are to the core of our local church.

5. *Navigate the friction caused by the motion of integration.*

Motion causes friction. The Holy Spirit is the lubricant. Here's a statement I've used a few times. Champion Forest is for anybody, but it's not for everybody. Not everybody is ready for a multicultural reality because they are still so myopic in their thinking.

6. *Recognize the diversity within diversity.*

Pastor Ramon has taught us this. We thought, "Well, diversity is where you have English, Spanish, or African-American." Pastor Ramon has taught about diversity within diversity. Even within the Spanish culture, there are so many cultural layers, nuances, and uniquenesses that are found there.

7. *Learn to dream within the "vision of house."*

Pastor David establishes and sets our *doctrine and direction, our vision and values.* He's the leader. It is Pastor David's role to establish the "vision of the house." Everything we do is within the vision of the house. What that means is, for each pastor and staff member, we learn to dream within the "vision of the house." We have freedom to dream, but it's going to be consistent with and in alignment to the "vision of the house."

8. *Model what you want to multiply.*

Model what you want to multiply because you will multiply what you model. This is true in parenting, this is true as a professor, it's true of a pastor, it's true of a coach, but it is especially true in multicultural ministry.

R.M.: I receive a lot of people and a lot of pastors here at Champion Forest who want to do what we are doing. Pastor Trammell was talking about the leadership. Always, I say, "If the senior pastor is not on board, this model will not work." Many times, senior pastors send the mission pastor because they want to do something multicultural. But if the senior pastor, as the leader of the church, is not clear about the vision, this model to reach a community that is completely diverse is almost impossible.

A.L.: These eight items have to be at the heart of the leader; otherwise the effort will not make it through the test of time. There are a lot of challenges in ministry alone. One must be true to the Great Commission and Great Commandment. This multicultural vision has to be the conviction of the leader, or he will not be able to withstand the challenges that come with it. It cannot be superficially imposed upon a leader just because it seems to be trending thing.

D.F.: Let me take off on that what Averri is saying. If multicultural ministry or multicultural evangelism is a church growth strategy, I think it is doomed! If it is just about reaching more people just to grow a bigger church, that's ignoble. I mean, I want to reach more people and grow as big a God-sized church as he wants, but a multicultural vision has to come from somewhere else. The reason Averri is here and has stayed as long as he has, the reason Ramon has stayed, and the reason Stephen has stayed, is that the people are buying into a vision that is bigger than, "What does it look like at the end of the year and how hard was it and was it worth it?"

I think it's a moral issue. Certainly, it's an imperative. I cannot go back into a monocultural church. I couldn't. I can't. I just couldn't. Something has changed about me and in me that I couldn't go backwards and be satisfied to exist in a monocultural situation.

Having said that, I think we do need to say one thing. *Monocultural* is not a sinful word. It does not automatically mean you are a bad person or you are a bad church. We want to be careful to reiterate the principle and say a church should reflect its community if it is going to reach its community. And if it reaches its community, it will reflect it. If you are in a monocultural community, then it would make perfect sense your church reflects a monocultural church. That's just natural. So there are still predominantly African-American churches, there will still be Anglo churches, there will still be Hispanic churches, and there will always be Asian churches that are predominantly monocultural. We are really not trying to judge or condemn those churches because they are monocultural. If they are reaching their community they will reflect their community.

But if they are in a large city, that is probably not true. If you are in a suburb, that's probably not true. If you are in Texas, it's not true. The world is changing so quickly that a truly monocultural community is less and less likely to be the reason for a monocultural church. We are not here to make other churches feel bad or look bad. But if a church is in a diverse community, its congregation should reflect that community. That is our important point. I also want to point out a progression that we see in the multicultural setting.

A good first step is to say, "Everyone's welcome." Making them feel welcome is good next step. But at some point, as Averri said, that person is going to shift in their thinking from, "Is there anybody here like me?" to, "Do I belong? Am I safe? Is this a good place for me? Am I welcome?" At some point, that same person is going to start to wonder, "Am I just being tolerated, or am I being included?" They will start looking at the stage to see who's holding the microphone and looking at the choir to see who's singing. They will start looking at the committee line up that we vote on and the deacons and the staff. What they will be looking for is not only, "Are there people like me here, but do people like me have a voice? Are they speaking into the process? Are they speaking into the strategy and to the vision? Am I being represented? Is my particular culture or background being represented in this greater culture?" You have to be very intentional to be able to say yes to those questions. One of the greatest challenges you will encounter is to disciple the church people and move them to make intentional leadership choices that represent and reflect the minority cultures in the church.

S.T.: To tag-team with Pastor David on that, this goes for both multicultural reality and also in our multisite reality. I have been very involved in our committee process over the years. When we are looking at our committees, we are asking, "Is there diversity? Is there male to female ratio? Is there multisite campus representation?" We look at several gauges on the dashboard. And part of the multicultural ministry that is messy, but yet we're intentional, is that we are building a "new vision vocabulary." It is kind of like going to a 3-D movie without 3-D glasses—you just don't see clearly. But once you put those 3-D glasses on, as Pastor David said a moment ago, you see like you have never seen before, and that's why we can't ever go into a monocultural church again because we have 3D glasses on. We have seen what heaven is going to be like, and we can't turn back.

Q: What dangers/challenges/hardships would you tell pastors/ staffs to anticipate and tips to overcome or circumvent them?

D.F.: You have to be willing to put up with the resistance of some. And in some cases, it's coming from a place of, perhaps, a judgment. In other cases, it's just, "I am uncomfortable," or "This makes me uncomfortable." Fortunately, we have had no big movement of people leaving the church over this particular issue. But that's not to say people haven't left the church over this issue. I know of one particular family who pulled out and relocated because one day they picked up their daughter from her Sunday School class, and she was the only white girl. That made them feel uncomfortable. Of course, what do you do? We blessed them, they went away, and six months later they came back. That happens quite a bit. God will get a hold of somebody whose heart may be open but not quite where they want to be. I once said something to one of our key leaders about people leaving the church. He said, "Oh pastor, they heard you coming. If any of them were going to leave over that, they would have already left." So that was kind of good to hear.

No one has ever pitched a fit. No one has ever opposed us. Again, I defer to the Scriptures and to the heart of a Southern Baptist person. It's hard for Southern Baptists to oppose the gospel reaching people and being open to include all people. When you show them right there in the Bible here is what it says, you make it a mission-vision. They might not like it and might even oppose it, but they're probably going to be quiet about it. And of course, if you get your leaders on board and you get everybody leaning in the same direction, saying the same thing, then your deacons and life-group leaders and your key opinion leaders and influencers begin to sing that same song. As soon as somebody pops up that's inconsistent with the vision, immediately somebody's saying, "Hey, you know how it works around here. Let me tell you what's important to us." Once you have that, you have incredible momentum, and you can stop talking because your people are going to say it for you. And that's a real blessing to see that.

Q: Are there culturally specific challenges pertaining to African-American, Latin-American, or Asian-American cultures or congregations as they begin to assimilate?

D.F.: Thinking back over the last ten to twelve years, we've had almost no challenges I can't trace back to or connect to political issues—a change of administration, or somebody waxing all eloquent in a life group about politics, or who's president, or who's doing what, etc. You know that really does create division in the church that we always have to navigate and negotiate. But within the church, if you can just get people to stay on the cross, and on Jesus, and on the gospel, then we just don't have any real challenges. Initially we had to teach our people to stop saying "us" and "them" or "our service" and "their service." The real challenges have been navigating through very divisive political and social issues that surround the church coming inside the church.

A.L.: I was thinking in line with that is also cultural ignorance. Where time has fortified the creation of so many stereotypes of other cultures and ethnicities, the great way that was diffused at CFBC through Pastor David's leadership was by challenging the membership to have cross-cultural relationships. When those socially divisive movements are created in our society, the relationships that have been formed over the years from doing ministry and life together has a way of diffusing that tension by how people value each other on a personal level. So they are gaining insight from one another before they rush to judgment on what's happening or what is being propagated through media in our society.

D.F.: Let me agree with that and say, what Champion Forest was fifteen years ago was a predominantly white, upper middle-class Republican congregation that would have had some definite opinions about caravans coming up through Central America to the borders of the US. Well, that changes when you know someone. When you do life together and pass people in the hall and when you get to know fellow deacons who are from Central America or South America. When you hear their stories and testimonies, you don't think about those people in the same way. We are moving in the direction of recognizing that our need is not to provide a place of retreat for people from all of these struggles out there in the community but to train and equip people in the church with a different mindset: a transformed, paradigm-thinking, biblical worldview. Now they go to their work place, and when somebody starts criticizing and condemning Black Lives Matter or a caravan of people heading up here, they are able to speak truth into that situation based on knowledge and experience. We love to think we are helping our people not simply to navigate but lead others through those conversations.

Q: How do your music ministers overcome the challenges of creating a "new sound"?

D.F.: I don't have much to say about how ministers of music overcome the challenge of creating a new sound. I can tell you the best thing we ever did with regard to music in worship was to say, "Get over it and stop making it an idol." We have gotten to the point where we say, "Look, it is twenty minutes, folks. You have six days, twenty-three hours, and forty minutes minutes every week to sing, worship, and listen to whatever kind of music you want. But for twenty minutes, we are going to try to do something here that's probably not going to touch every person in the same way or check every box. But let's leave behind our individual preferences like Philippians 2 says and try to do something we can all do together."

It's not going to be straight up African-American gospel music or have a Latin feel. We are certainly not going to have one song of one and one song of the other. And we are not going to do European-based background, four-beat sorts of things. We are just asking people not to come expecting what they want and expect but to engage with whatever is put in front of them. So far, most folks are pretty good to do that. And we will do a song that is more on the gospel side and we could probably do better on that and should. It is an ongoing sort of a tension. But boy, music is just complicated. I am glad I am not a minister of music.

Q: What aspects of preaching are different in a multicultural setting? That is, do you preach differently? How do you plan preaching? How is preaching similar or different in a multicultural setting?

D.F.: I'd say, we've added a phrase to Phillips Brook's definition of preaching as "truth through personality." We say preaching is "truth through personality to personalities." We want to take into consideration our context. But Averri preaches like Averri preaches. He doesn't preach like I preach. And I don't try to preach like Averri or Pastor Ramon preaches, because I am not them. We've sort of helped our people understand it's the word, and it's the message, not the messenger. We can slide preachers around. Averri will preach here this Sunday, and people will be thrilled to have him back because he has been in Jersey Village since August. I don't think we really have an issue. I have to be who I am, and Stephen has to be who he is, and Averri has to be who he is. Most of us probably have to navigate that. He probably would still preach differently if he were at Rose of Sharon this Sunday with our friends. But he is not outside of who he is as a preacher and who he is becoming as a communicator of the Bible. Of course, Ramon preaches in Spanish, but in his context, he has to be careful not to use too many words that are Colombian at the expense of the Mexican folks, or the Chilean and Argentinian who are European. We are all just trying to navigate that tension pretty consistently.

A.L.: Because we have the preaching collaboration we do, we are always careful to point out any issue or word choices that would create what we call side energy. We build from each other to help navigate some of the sensitive areas that would take away from our congregation hearing the true message of God. And that is a weekly collaboration.

We have what we call a preaching team meeting at the beginning of the week where we flesh out the big idea as a preaching team. Through the course of the week we begin to share notes with each other via email. Generally, by Thursday we are sharing preliminary notes from the text. By Friday we are really zeroing in and honing down what that message is going to be, but every message is around the central idea that was revealed during our collaborative time.

Q: The term *intentionality* plays a huge part in multicultural ministry. However, there are some instances where intentionality

may seem unnatural. How do you handle that tension when the natural movement of God may seem unnatural to the congregation?

D.F.: If we wanted to use an image, I would think about changing direction in an airplane, a boat, or a car. Going along at sixty miles per hour, there are no g-forces and whatever that word is—it is natural, it feels good, it is comfortable. But suddenly we turn the wheel because we are going to go north to Dallas. Through the turn, it feels unnatural. Now we feel the friction, the g-forces. It's hard on the tires. It is necessary to be a little uncomfortable for a moment before going in the next direction and it starts to feel better again. So, for sure, there is this sense when we are being on the intentional side that it might feel a little uncomfortable, that it might seem a little unnatural. I think that's exactly why you have to have a deep conviction that turbulence is worth it to get you going in the direction you believe the Spirit of God is moving and working. We definitely can tell you stories about living in that tension. My own wife at times had to say to me, "Hey, don't forget you are pastor for white folks too." I was focused on being intentional, but she was being sensitive to the fact the church was feeling the turbulence of turning. Some people were wondering if you wouldn't rather be in an African-American or Hispanic church. So, for sure, there's that turn—tension—friction.

My concern on the other side would be to put all of this on the Lord and to say, "Well, if God wants us to be multicultural, he will make us multicultural." I just would not want to be that spiritual. Because God definitely has ordained the use of people to accomplish his kingdom objectives and projects. We have to do the work. He's the Lord of the harvest, but we have to go into the field; we have to sow that field and cultivate it and work it. So to me, it is the tension between the super and the natural. In any church, you are exactly right. As soon as you say, "We think we should be more intentional so we can reach the whole community," somebody is going to say, "If God is going to save the heathen, he will do it without me!" That statement killed the mission movement for centuries. At some point, you have to embrace the turbulence to change direction. Obviously, the slower the turn, the less the turbulence and tension. You don't want to do any forty-five-degree left turns and throw everybody against the wall. But you can feel that airplane if it turns too quickly. You feel it. If the pilot takes his time and turns it slowly, you barely notice. We control to a degree how quickly we need to get there. Most of the time we turn too sharp, too fast. Stephen's famous saying is, "Slowdown in the turns!"

S.T.: It makes me think of the parallel track with personal soul winning. Personal soul winning is not natural. It is supernatural. You can stay in your zone. You can choose not to engage the waiter or waitress in a spiritual conversation. You can be kind to them, gracious to them, but never take your conversation vertical. You can go the whole month and not have one vertical conversation and be very comfortable in a multicultural reality or in a lost culture. It is natural to not go vertical in your conversation through personal soul winning. So there is really a parallel track here. You have to be willing to look beyond your skin, both to engage a multicultural ministry and personal soul winning.

R.M.: One example I see each Sunday when I am walking in the hallway is a lot of Anglo or African-American people who stop me to say, "Hey, Pastor, I invited somebody—a guy who works with me." Right now, it is completely natural. I think it is in the DNA of the members of Champion Forest now that everybody is welcome. It is so, so natural as the vision of the church.

Q: Why not just plant a multicultural church rather than to go through the hardships of transitioning a monocultural church?

D.F.: Obviously, it is really cool to imagine I would not have to deal with all these pot holes and stumps and avoid all these bad attitudes and "concrete, poured-around" ideas and just go start something new. A lot of young guys prefer that these days. If I were to do that, my core team would be a diverse team. We would start day one with a reflection of a community we are trying to reach. Surely, you would save yourself an awful lot of challenges.

The downside is, there are tens of thousands of monocultural churches of all ethnicities. What about them? We can't just write them off and say it's okay to be whoever you want to be at the expense of your community and the kingdom. I hope you guys at NOBTS are challenging young pastors to take some of these churches and pastor them and lead them and help them through this transition from being monocultural to becoming multicultural.

I am not going to tell anybody this was easy, but it was worth it. I am coming up on twenty-eight years of ministry, and I've had the privilege of serving great churches with great people and have seen incredible things happen. But nothing in my life or ministry compares to watching a predominantly white church transition to a multicultural church happily and (then) thank you for it when you get there. It's incredible, and I wouldn't take anything for the journey. If twelve years ago you had given me all the money I needed, in the best location and a great core team, and said, "You can start from scratch or you can transition Champion Forest Baptist Church," I would choose this transition. I've seen God work in people's lives. I've seen attitudes change that had been set for fifty, sixty, and seventy years. That's a blessing.

I wouldn't want to write off all of these churches who could become effective, kingdom-minded, gospel-centered, whole-community reaching churches if they just had some leadership and pastoral love and care to guide them and lead them through it. We can't afford to write those churches off.

Q: Could you speak to the patience a pastor and congregation need in order to see this transition take place? Speak to the pastoral love and care in allowing the Holy Spirit to work in transforming people's hearts and lives. How does a pastor lead the congregation to embrace "race grace" in this transformational shift? How much time does it take to make a shift to a multicultural church?

D.F.: That's the work of shepherding and pastoring people's hearts, and being an instrument of the Holy Spirit in their lives means you can't force this and probably should not rush this. You have to play the long game. This vision has to be worth waiting for and working slowly and patiently toward. For example: If the first time you meet with a committee, you just tell them how it going to be and that's it, then you will be unemployed; that is what you are going to be. If you can't meet people where they are, then you won't be able to get them to go where they need to go. You have to start where people are.

We are in the spiritual growth and life-change and transformation business. We measure success by progress. It is not about the destination. It's about progress. So some churches may hit a home run in just shifting their thinking. One little shift is a win. Then you set your eyes on the next win. But definitely I've never believed in splitting a church over my particular priorities. I left three monocultural churches, and they are still monocultural. I did not have the opportunity in that context to do there what God is doing here. I could definitely have forced it and been the worse for it, I suspect. Definitely, you are right. It doesn't matter what ethnicity or culture you are, that's deeply engrained in Champion Forest's DNA, and it's a process, a transition to see the world differently.

S.T.: You mentioned *race grace*. That's a great concept. One thing Pastor David models so well is what I call *pace grace*. Pace grace means you have to be willing, first of all, to affirm the congregation where they are. Pastor David not only affirmed the congregation right where it was when he came twelve years ago, but he also honored the previous pastor who had been here twenty-seven years. He honored him, and he acknowledged he was standing on his shoulders. He even said, "The credibility bank I received from Dr. Shook has paved the way for that."

I think it is important for a new pastor to affirm the past of the church. Too frequently, we see pastors come to a new church and they act as though the past doesn't matter, and all of the contributions and sacrifices of the people have no bearing on the future. Conversely, a wise pastor coming to a new church will affirm what the church has done and what it has become. That pastor can start building toward the future. I describe a wise pastor as a leader who knows how to keep "tension on the rubber band" without snapping the rubber band. You have to be a guide. You have to shepherd the flock. If you get too far ahead of the congregation, you are not their shepherd or guide, you are a sojourner. You are over the hill and on your own by yourself. It is then easy to become bitter that the congregation is not with you.

Pastor David is so gifted by God—and Pastor Ramon and Pastor Averri—in not getting too far ahead of the congregation but to walk with the congregation to keep "tension on the rubber band." Leadership is leading people where otherwise they wouldn't go. It is supernatural, and it is intentional. Pastor David has led the church in a direction by default it would have never gone. Because by nature, we prefer what is comfortable, and our default is status quo. Leadership is taking you to a place you really don't want to go or you didn't know you wanted to go. But when you get there you are so thankful you went.

Q: In your multi-campus model, do you find the make-up of the congregation shifts with the ethnicity of the leader when a change in leadership occurs? For example, if an African-American pastor takes the leadership role, does the church then begin to shift toward African-Americans, or Hispanic, or Anglo, etc.?

A.L.: I think the context of Champion Forest has been so well shepherded that part of our DNA is beyond any cultural preferences. In short, even here at Jersey Village, there is not a mass concentration of African-American because I serve Champion Forest Baptist Church at Jersey Village. In fact, it is still predominantly a European-American context, but it is multicultural in understanding as well. I don't think we have that kind of shift in movement primarily because of the teaching that has gone forth before we ever got to this point. It is all about reflecting our community. That is something the congregation knows.

Evangelism Resources

Utilizing Library Resources Effectively for Evangelistic Research, Writing, and Application

Eric Benoy and Jeff Griffin

Libraries and evangelism is not a pairing most people would think to make. On the one hand libraries represent the intellectual side of things, the theory. On the other hand, evangelism represents the epitome of praxis, the doing. Yet these two concepts are closely related. To do something well, to do something effectively, one must be versed in the background, the theory, of whatever it is. Knowledge itself does not guarantee one will be the best practitioner but rather equips the practitioner with more tools that may be implemented in the practice—the doing—thus ensuring a greater probability of success and effectiveness.

Libraries can yield a bounty of information and ideas that will aid each person in becoming more effective in the practice of evangelism. Note the word *can* in the previous sentence. Without some understanding of how to approach and utilize the library's resources in an efficient manner, people can quickly find themselves in unproductive searches. They may then walk away with a poor experience and doubts about the benefits of the library.

A whole field of study exists on the study of information-seeking behavior. There are myriad studies, metrics, and the like that show how people go about finding what they need (or want) to know—whether it is information for a paper or the purchase of a car. Basically, it can be boiled down to a three-step process. First, people will begin the hunt for information by themselves. Not wanting to appear ignorant, they do what they can until they hit a wall. Second, if or when they can go no further, they will ask a friend for some assistance. If no friend is around, they may ask another student or colleague. Third, if or when that avenue is not productive, they then ask a librarian for assistance. The librarian then conducts an interview of sorts to help determine what the person needs.[1]

In ministry, keeping up-to-date on resources available is important as we seek to be effective communicators of the gospel. The gospel itself should not change, but how it is be presented may change. Here, we will present the reader with some techniques and suggestions to make the search for information easier and more productive. This will also enable the reader to more easily and effectively communicate with a librarian about information needs and make better use of limited time. Also, we will address several types of resources available: books (print or electronic), journal articles, electronic resources (internet or multimedia), people, and institutional (to be explained further in that section). Some solutions presented are obvious "no-brainers"; some will be new and create the aha moment of learning.

---

[1] For those interested in learning more about information-seeking behavior, here are a few resources available: Donald Owen Case and Lisa M. Given, *Looking for Information: A Survey of Research on Information Seeking, Needs, and Behavior* (Bingley, UK: Emerald, 2016). Eti Herman and David Nicholas, *Information Science: Critical Concepts in Media and Cultural Studies* (Abingdon, Oxon; New York, NY: Routledge, 2014). James Krikelas, "Information-Seeking Behavior: Patterns and Concepts," *Drexel Library Quarterly* 19, no. 12, no. Spring (1983): 5–20. Angela Weiler, "Information-Seeking Behavior in Generation Y Students: Motivation, Critical Thinking, and Learning Theory," *The Journal of Academic Librarianship* 31, no. 1, no. January (2005): 46–53. Allen Foster, "A Nonlinear Model of Information-Seeking Behavior," *Journal of the American Society for Information Science and Technology* 55 (2004): 228–37, https://doi.org/10.1002/asi.10359.

Searching More Efficiently

TIP 1: Synonyms

Before we get into the various resources and strategies on using those resources, we want to look at searching tips. Whether the source is found in a library catalog, the internet, or other database, there are some basic tools that will help make your search more efficient and effective. The first tip is to keep a thesaurus running in your head at all times. Simply because some terms are used commonly in one denomination does not mean that the same term is used by everyone else. Let's take the term *evangelism*. What other terms communicate this same idea or ideas related to it? *Witnessing? Missions? Preaching? Spreading the word? Proselytize?* You will want to do multiple searches using some of these terms to see if you get any other results that you would have missed by using only *evangelism*. Also, since libraries use Library of Congress subject headings, the term may not be part of their listings. For example, *evangelism* is not preferred by Library of Congress but rather *evangelistic work*.

TIP 2: Truncated Searches

Nearly all databases and the Internet have the ability to accept truncated searches. That is, start spelling a word, stop at any point, and insert an asterisk (a few use a question mark—experimentation will reveal which). This allows a broadening of the inquiry. The partial word becomes a root, and the asterisk represents any possible endings for that root. If you type, "evangel*," the database or system will retrieve all entries that have a word beginning with those letters: *evangel, evangelist, evangelistic, evangelism, evangelical, evangelicalism*. While such a search yields results for *evangelism* and *evangelistic work*, it does yield some results not needed, like *evangelicalism*.

TIP 3: Boolean Operators

The most commonly used Boolean operators are *and, or,* and *not*. Using these operators can either expand or narrow a search. Using *and* will narrow a search down because the word tells the database/system to look for two or more terms used together. For example, "evangelism and church" tells the database/system you only want results with those two exact terms. Of course, you could also use truncation with the operator as well. Typing "evangel* and church*" tells the system you want only results that have words beginning with those roots. Using the operator *or* broadens a single search into a double search: "evangelism or evangelistic work" will yield results for either term. *Not* indicates a desire to exclude some results: "evangelistic work not witnessing." Please note two things: (1) most databases/systems assume *and*, so you can just enter key terms without it, and (2) some require you use Boolean operators for all capital letters or some that you use quotation marks. Only experimentation will let you know which.

TIP 4: Exact Phrases

In most databases, as with the Internet, searching with exact phrases can be just as useful as any other search technique. It lets you know what materials are available that use the exact terminology you use. To do an exact phrase search, simply put the phrase in quotation marks. "Church evangelism" yields results where those two words are together in that order. However, it is possible to still get a few irrelevant results. It may be that one result is actually the word *church* ending one sentence and *evangelism* beginning the next, though not pertaining to "church evangelism."

Resources to Utilize: The Academic

Books

Truly the author of Ecclesiastes is correct in writing, "Be warned: the writing of many books is endless" (Ecc 12:12). Walk into any theological library, and the shelves contain tens of thousands of books. A seasoned pastor's personal library is a copy of those libraries, just not as large. Hundreds of volumes more are published each year in the field of ministry. Each scholar wants to share his or her wisdom and insights with the world. Many thought the invention of e-books would reduce the number of print resources, but that is not the case. Print books will be around for a while. We thus have both to draw upon for our information needs. So where do we begin?

The online catalog is the best place to start. You could go to the section on evangelism in the library stacks (shelves) and peruse the titles on the spines. However, since there is as much art as there is science to the classification and cataloging of materials, such an approach may well result in missing some excellent resources. It can take a bit more time perusing titles in hopes of serendipitous finds because each title has to be noted. Furthermore, bending down and trying to read titles on lower shelves (bifocals do not help a lot) or stretching to read the ones on the top shelves can be frustrating. E-books, meanwhile, are not physically present to peruse. It would then be best to start with the online catalog.

Online catalogs can be searched whether at home, at the office, or at the library itself. This allows you to make better use of your time and library resources when the library is not open. Some library catalogs are strictly bibliographic. That is, no full-text books are available for viewing. Many libraries are cataloging their e-books like they do print books, and those records will provide a link to the text of the e-book. If your catalog does not provide e-books, you will need to use various online services provided by your library to access e-books separately.

Knowing exact titles and authors certainly makes finding what is needed easier. But unless we receive some kind of advertisement or recommendation from a colleague or friend, what is the best way to begin a search? There are two avenues that may be pursued.

The first avenue is a subject search. This allows you to find items related topically. Most of the time these subject searches will also reveal more specific subheadings to help in narrowing down search parameters. It will also show the preferred headings used by the Library of Congress, which most libraries use for their own catalogs. A search for the term *evangelism* yields some results, but the preferred subject heading *evangelistic work* (shown connected to *evangelism*) shows far more results. It takes a while to get used to the controlled vocabulary of catalogers.

The second avenue is the keyword search. This search tells the system to pull any item that has this word as a subject, a word in the title, or in any contents notes. This casts a broad net and usually yields a large number of results, but there will almost always be some titles included that have no bearing on what is needed. A combination of searching while using both of these methods will work well.

Do not forget to include in searches dissertations and theses. Many of these, especially doctor of ministry theses, reflect the author's development and implementation of some aspect of evangelism. Even if the body of these documents is not what you need, at least look at the bibliographies to see what resources each person used. This works with regular books and e-books as well. These authors have already spent time searching for and selecting appropriate resources. There is no need to totally reinvent the wheel.

Journal Articles

Outside of blogs and Internet sites, the most current information in any field of study will be journal articles. Articles are used to communicate ideas on a narrow topic and are presented in a terse format. Journals are indexed once a quarter or every six months. Today, you can access the contents of journals electronically. The most-often used method of accessing them is through some portal such as EBSCOHost, First-Search, J-STOR, etc. Publishers provide databases of the indexed and abstracted articles in their publications, and through cooperative agreements with companies such as those just mentioned, allow those to be searched and, in most cases, accessed online. An advantage of using a portal is the unified searching capability of multiple databases through a single interface. One does not have to "shift gears" switching from database to database.

Some publishers are retrospectively digitizing older materials and some are not. There may be times you will need to access print journals in your library. Some publishers release articles in print format first, with the digital being released at a later date for consumption through the online service mentioned. Since these online services are paid for by your library, no extra fees are involved like ones you would pay to access journal articles on a publisher's website. However, if you were to go straight to the publisher's website, you can access the article there electronically rather than wait for its later release—for a price.

The main databases you will most likely use via these portals that provide access to religious journals and periodic literature are the ATLA Religion Database with ATLASerials (ATLA) database and the Christian Periodical Index (CPI). The American Theological Library Association maintains ATLA and the Association of Christian Librarians maintains CPI. Searching in these online resources is similar to searching an online catalog for books. You can search by author, title, subject, keyword, etc. Remember, as with books, keep a thesaurus running in your head and remember you will be doing multiple searches. Once you access an article online, you are able to utilize various limitation tools to narrow your search: year, language, type of publication, subjects, etc.

Another service that more and more libraries are using is a discovery service. Not to oversimplify what it does, but a discovery service allows you to use one interface to search the library's online catalog (books) and any number of databases (journal articles, essays, papers, etc.) all at the same time. It can save time as you do not have to keep switching between different resources to find them. But, as you have probably guessed, it does yield a lot of results and time that must be spent whittling the results down to a manageable number. Your library can let you know if they use a discovery system.

Online Resources

It can be overwhelming when searching for online resources. The trick is to determine which of the resources are the best and most reliable. When examining Internet sites, take a couple of minutes to scrutinize what is. Always look for an "About Us" section. This reveals what organization or people the site is associated with and usually includes a purpose statement. The issue is to take time to evaluate the resource before simply taking what is presented as being biblically, theologically, or methodologically sound.

Blogs, especially, can be tricky. Anyone can put one up and post whatever they desire. Look for those whose authors list some real credentials (education, ministry experience, publications, or larger entities where they work). Blogs can be merely platforms for opinions on a topic, but they may also give some good insight and advice. Use them judiciously.

Google Scholar is another place to search for materials and information, and this online resource is open to all. Here you can enter your search terms (like other databases) and find books, articles, etc. Some of these have links to full-text PDFs or websites. If not available online, you can then check and see if your library has these resources or if they can obtain these resources for you through interlibrary loans. Please note, however, that few limit tools exist in Google Scholar to limit a search and sort results.

Another online resource not restricted to just libraries is WorldCat. It is a union catalog of thousands of libraries that contains several hundred million bibliographic records. These cover books, dissertations, sheet music, recordings, media, microforms, etc. They are bibliographic, meaning there is no access from that database to digital content of those titles. However, the platform does show which libraries have those in their holdings and how far away those libraries are from you. You can see if your library holds an item or if you need to borrow the item or obtain a photocopy of an article through interlibrary loan.

Document Delivery

If your library does not have what you need in its holdings, you may request the library try to procure the item elsewhere—also known as interlibrary loans. Again, this is when you know specific titles you need; it is not a "just send me whatever you find" kind of request. Document delivery requests are submitted via a union catalog system—World-Cat—which is directed at specific libraries to see if they will loan an item or are willing to make copies of needed articles.

Resources to Utilize: The Applied

People

As you begin to research and read more about evangelism and how to actually engage in evangelism, you start to see a few names occurring frequently. The noted authorities are out there because they possess both the theory and the praxis. Do these two, theory and praxis, sound familiar? They have studied and understand evangelism on the cognitive level, but they have also spent time in the local churches and in the field, testing to see if the theory works and how to improve it. Utilizing people as a resource is profitable but can be fickle. That is, since it requires contacting someone out of the blue you most likely do not know, he or she may or may not respond. Still, authors are usually flattered when people consider them authorities and may be quite willing to give assistance or direction. Those who are quite popular, of course, are harder to contact given the number of people and events that demand their attention. It is not unheard of to get a response a month after the initial contact.

Through your time at the library or in utilizing library resources, you can usually track down these authorities through information gleaned in books or simple Internet searches. Most will have a listed e-mail address, and some will have a telephone number as well. Taking the time to actually write a letter can be good initial contact. In any event, initial contact should be as formal and succinct as possible.

Do not assume familiarity by addressing someone with his or her first name. Let them be the ones in their response to set the tone of how casual you each should be addressed. A paragraph or two can speak far more than two pages.

Institutional Resources

While searching the Internet for resources, make note of institutions and groups that deal with evangelism. As mentioned earlier, make sure the websites are associated with solid organizations, such as academic institutions and denominational offices. Additionally, one of the authorities could have an independent site that is valid as well. Again, one must take time to evaluate the resource before simply accepting what is presented as being biblically, theologically, and methodologically sound.

Some institutions can be helpful in finding pertinent background information on communities before a church develops a plan of evangelistic outreach. For example, the Leavell Center for Evangelism and Church Health of NOBTS can provide customized demographic data for most any community or neighborhood and has programs and people available to assist in equipping church leadership for evangelism. Knowing the community factors such as economics, ethnicity, age, etc. can help a church develop a more meaningful approach to reaching that community. If the church knows it is a working-class community with few children but an increasing population of senior adults, appropriate programs can be developed rather than taking a one-size-fits-all approach.

Another institutional asset is archives. These are rich resources of historical and first-hand information. Sometimes examining the histories of churches or areas around churches will reveal the forces, good and bad, that shaped their communities. Understanding those influential forces will enable a church to better formulate how to reach out to those who live around them and any barriers that need to be overcome. Seminaries and colleges, denominational offices at the state and national level, local organizations, and churches will have these. Accessing archives varies from institution to institution, ranging from boxes of paper files to digitized documents.

Institutions spend a significant amount of time and resources on developing materials for churches to utilize in reaching others. These materials are generally praxis oriented and may focus on training individuals with evangelism skills, or they may be suggested programs that are to be implemented over a period of several weeks. They also provide access to people. It is one thing to read about evangelism, watch videos, or go through a workbook. It is another to have experts available to assist with or perform the training of church members. This allows for dialogue and understanding of specific issues, needs, problems, etc.

After Seminary

Some of you may be saying to yourself that this is the best thing since sliced peanut butter or ketchup caviar (yes, they do exist), but you are not in seminary anymore or will soon graduate and will no longer have access to library materials and databases. Do not fret, and do not fear. You are not bereft of resources or the access to them.

First, remember Internet resources such as Google Scholar and WorldCat are free and open for everyone to use. Second, check with your seminary's library about whether alumni are able to maintain access; most seminaries will indeed grant alumni circulation privileges, and some may provide alumni with access to the ATLA database previously mentioned. You may also ask about interlibrary loans. Third, if you are not serving near the seminary you attended but are near another seminary, ask the same questions. Some will grant circulation privileges to local clergy (please note some may charge a fee). If you are near a Christian college or university, inquire there as well. Their collections may not be as in-depth as your seminary, but some are developing new programs for undergraduates, and they may have some materials there. Finally, a local public library could be helpful.

They can make interlibrary loan requests for you, but be aware you may need to offer to pay for the loans as academic libraries usually do not loan items free to public libraries.

As a minister, you are in an almost constant state of continuing education. There exists an almost unending fount of information and resources to assist you in honing your knowledge, skills, and effectiveness in evangelism. This is what drives us: proclaiming the good news, spreading the good news, and expanding the kingdom of God.

The following is a true story. Most seminary librarians or professors can testify this has been their experience in some way at some point as well:

> A young seminary student was asked to write a research paper in which the professor noted a minimum number of resources to be used. The student wrote his paper, turned it in, and was quite disappointed when he received a rather low grade. In confronting the professor, he was slightly upset. Yes, he had some issues with the paper, but he did not know why points were deducted for resources. The professor explained the student did not use the minimum as required; he had only used the Bible. The student went on to say he was headed to the mission field and most likely would not be able to take a lot of books with him and, besides, all he *needed* was the Bible, so he did not feel as though he should bother with other books.
>
> The professor paused and then asked the student if he felt God had called him to seminary to be trained and prepared for the mission field. He said yes. The professor asked him if he felt God called other people to other fields of ministry. The student replied yes. He told the student that if he was right on both counts, then he should not throw a gift from God back in his face. The student was confused. The

professor explained God had called others to teaching and academic pursuits so as to help train others for ministry—part of that pursuit is book writing. If he, as the student, would say God called him there to learn and be trained, then why ignore the instruction of others God has called? Why throw away an opportunity to soak up all the knowledge possible in the library and its books since he cannot take a library with him on the mission field? Was this not a gift and leading from God to prepare him?

Evangelism is not executed in a vacuum apart from learning, reading, and the continual "renewing of the mind" (to borrow a phrase). Use these suggestions, tips, and resources. Learn them well, and they will serve you in being as effective and efficient as possible in God's kingdom work.

BIBLIOGRAPHY

Case, Donald Owen, and Lisa M. Given. *Looking for Information: A Survey of Research on Information Seeking, Needs, and Behavior.* Bingley, UK: Emerald, 2016.

Foster, Allen. "A Nonlinear Model of Information-Seeking Behavior." *Journal of the American Society for Information Science and Technology* 55 (2004): 228–37.

Herman, Eti, and David Nicholas. *Information Science: Critical Concepts in Media and Cultural Studies.* New York: Routledge, 2014.

Krikelas, James. "Information-Seeking Behavior: Patterns and Concepts." *Drexel Library Quarterly* 19, no. 12, Spring (1983): 5–20.

Weiler, Angela. "Information-Seeking Behavior in Generation Y Students: Motivation, Critical Thinking, and Learning Theory." *The Journal of Academic Librarianship* 31, no. 1, January (2005): 46–53.

PART 4

Preaching and Contemporary Evangelism

The Soul of the Evangelistic Expository Sermon: From Broadus and Criswell to Rogers and Kelley

Adam Hughes

Over the past two to three decades, a clarion call has been issued in the academy to raise up a generation of men who are committed as well as equipped to be faithful expositors of God's word. Perhaps the origin of this call actually began from the needs in the local church. Whether a church explicitly demands systematic expository preaching from its pulpit or not, its spiritual formation, growth, and disciple-making must be founded on the accurate and faithful proclamation of the Bible. Furthermore, God commands pastors to "preach the word" (2 Tim 4:2) and teach those who have come to faith in Christ "all that [Jesus] commanded you" (Matt 28:20).

At the same time, we understand the shepherd must "do the work of an evangelist" (2 Tim 4:5) in order to be faithful in the pulpit and to fulfill his ministry completely. After the example of the apostle Paul and his ministry partners, the pastor aims to "persuade men" (2 Cor 5:11). Throughout the history of the SBC, even though not always identified as expository preaching proper, those in both the academy and church have contributed to or encouraged the integration of these two disciplines. The list includes men such as John A. Broadus, W. A. Criswell, Adrian Rogers, and Charles Kelley. Yet, today by our praxis, nonverbalized and implicit questions seem to have arisen regarding this integration: Can we be both expositional and textually accurate and evangelistic and persuasive in our preaching? Furthermore, do we even need to attempt to do so? The tensions embedded in the questions are often characterized by an imbalance in our ministries, churches, and pulpits on one side of the issue or the other.

In this essay, I will attempt to address this tension and answer these questions by arguing that not only can a pastor be committed to expository and evangelistic preaching simultaneously, but it is a must and biblically consistent that he do so. To begin, I will offer theological and biblical foundations for exposition and evangelism in the pulpit. Next, I will show why evangelistic preaching is consistent with, a necessary component of, and the natural end of biblical exposition. Finally, a simple strategy, based on direct biblical authority and that consistently presents the gospel of Jesus Christ to the lost, will be suggested for being both expositional and evangelistic in the pulpit. But first, let us begin by considering what must be present at a minimum to constitute an expository sermon and an evangelistic sermon.

Descriptions of the Expository and the Evangelistic Sermon

Today the designation "an expository sermon" and the concept of "expository preaching" may not be totally helpful. In some contexts, the discussion surrounding the subject has become fruitless and frustrating because those having the conversation may not be sure what it is. Furthermore, neither preachers nor academicians are talking about it in a monolithic and unified way. Perhaps the designation of expository preaching has become a catchall to the point that almost any and every kind of sermon is placed under this umbrella. In the words of my mentor Dr. David Allen, the term has become so elastic it is not helpful in pinpointing what we are talking about when we use it.[1] In other words, if the goal is to determine what it is and to differentiate

---

[1] David Allen, "Text-Driven Preaching," interviewed by Adam Hughes, NOBTS Conversations, August 14, 2018, https://www.youtube.com/watch?v=LkSYeQRtp40&feature=youtu.be.

expository preaching from the other types of preaching that occur on Sundays in most American churches, a clear distinguishing mark or two may be needed.

One way to provide some marks of expository preaching and thus differentiate between this and other types would be to take a technical approach of sorts. I could give a brief overview of some of the definitions of expository preaching throughout its history before settling on my personal favorites. You would see that some of the descriptions or definitions of exposition have more of a formal feel and may be categorized as academic. Still others are much more casual and practical in nature. However, the purpose of this chapter is not a history of expository preaching or even a precise definition of the term. The purpose essentially is the integration of exposition and evangelism in the pulpit. This approach, then, would be unnecessary and tedious. Therefore, I will begin where I intend to end—my description of the minimum requirements of expository preaching.

An expository sermon is one driven by and thus stays true to the substance, structure, and spirit of the given text of Scripture that has been chosen by the preacher for proclamation.[2] Allow me in my own words to describe what I mean by each of these components and thus bring some clarity to how each functions in a given sermon.

---

[2] This definition is not original with me. I heard it the first time as a masters student and then later as a doctoral student at Southwestern Baptist Theological Seminary in Fort Worth, Texas. At least two foundational books share this definition of expository preaching designated as text-driven preaching. See Steven Smith, *Recapturing the Voice of God: Shaping Sermons Like Scripture* (Nashville, TN: B&H Academic, 2015) and Daniel L. Akin, David L. Allen, and Ned L. Matthews, eds. *Text-Driven Preaching: God's Word at the Heart of Every Sermon* (Nashville, TN: B&H Academic, 2010): "Text-driven preaching is the interpretation and communication of a biblical text in a sermon that represents the substance, structure, and the spirit of the text," Smith, *Recapturing the Voice of God*, 17. "So we use a homiletical method that allows the text to breathe; a method that helps us represent what the text has said: and a method that is driven by the nature of the text itself. This is text-driven preaching," Ibid., 15. "Text-driven preaching stays true to the substance of the text, the structure of the text, and the spirit of the text," Allen, "Introduction," in *Text-Driven Preaching*, 8.

First, substance refers to the subject matter, content, or point(s) of the message. Essentially, it is what a pastor preaches and thus the valid, legitimate, and authoritative applications he can and should make to a contemporary audience. Second, structure indicates the design, flow, or shape of the sermon's outline, design, and argumentation. The arrangement and structure of the text—how the biblical author argued for and designed their subject matter—must inform and guide the sermon. Ultimately, the structure is seen in what is traditionally understood as the outline of the message. Finally, the spirit of the sermon is the tone or the feel (sometimes we might say "emotion") of the text. This often is indicated by genre and should affect delivery (*pathos*).

Perhaps for clarity and simplicity, this description can be distilled even further. The concept of a bank *deposit* is helpful. What is a deposit? What do we do when we make a deposit at the bank? We put in money. The specifics or application may change (cash, checks, or electronic), but we are always putting in. So then, what does it mean to *exposit*? Notice *exposit* has the same root as *deposit*. Therefore, if *deposit* means to put in, *exposit* must mean to take or pull out. In its simplest or most derivate form then, exposition or expository preaching is preaching which pulls out and preaches only what is in the text. This distinction is important. An expository sermon is not one derived from content forced into the text. Nor from content presumed of the text. Nor from content the pastor wishes were in the text. Nor from content perceived from the text.

Practically, this means a sermon that communicates points *from* the text rather than the point or points *of* the text is not an expository sermon.[3] A sermon that uses the text to say what the pastor wants to say or believes rather than allowing the text to use the pastor to communicate its truth is not an expository sermon. A sermon that uses Scripture as a beginning point, an illustration, support for the points of the message, or ammunition to argue for one's personal theological

---

[3] For an excellent explanation and illustration of a type of sermon that takes points from the text rather than majoring on the point(s) of the text, see Steven W. Smith, *Dying to Preach: Embracing the Cross in the Pulpit* (Grand Rapids, MI: Kregel, 2009), 65.

position is not an expository sermon. Furthermore, a sermon that makes application from corrupt or even casual biblical authority is not an expository sermon. Some of these types of preaching may be useful at times, but none of them meet the minimum requirements of what constitutes an expository sermon. An expository sermon is founded on direct biblical authority and driven by what is taken out of the text directly and precisely.

Now that we have a minimum understanding of exposition, what about evangelistic preaching? Is there a clear distinguishing mark or two that constitutes an evangelistic sermon? And if so, what are they? What must be present, at minimum, for a sermon to be considered evangelistic?

Perhaps there is a short answer to this question. An evangelistic sermon essentially is one in which the gospel is explained, and then an appeal is made to the audience for a faith response to Christ based on that gospel explanation.[4] V. L. Stansfield offered an even more precise and detailed definition. He argued, "Evangelistic preaching is presenting 'Jesus Christ in the power of the Holy Spirit, that men may put their trust in God through Him, accept Him as their Savior, and serve Him as their King, in the fellowship of His church.'"[5] However, for the sake of clarity, let us look a little deeper into the question. In order to

---

[4] Emphasizing the necessity of the appeal in an evangelistic sermon, some have used the language of "preaching for a verdict" while others have used the metaphor of "drawing the net." Regardless of the description or verbiage employed, most who have written on the subject do include the concept of calling for a response based on the explanation of the gospel as a consistent and necessary mark of the evangelistic sermon. See Paul W. Powell, *Building an Evangelistic Church* (Dallas: Annuity Board of the Southern Baptist Convention, 1991), 98; O. S. Hawkins, *Drawing the Net: 30 Practical Principles for Leading Others to Christ Publicly and Personally* (Dallas: Annuity Board of the Southern Baptist Convention, 2002), 11–16; and Ken Hemphill, "Preaching and Evangelism," in *Handbook of Contemporary Preaching: A Wealth of Counsel for Creative and Effective Proclamation*, ed. Michael Duduit (Nashville, TN: Broadman and Holman, 1992), 526 respectively.

[5] V. L. Stanfield, *Effective Evangelistic Preaching* (New Orleans, LA: n.p., 1965), 5. This definition of evangelistic preaching is a modification of the definition of evangelism given by the Archbishop's Committee of Inquiry on the Evangelistic Work of the Church in 1918.

do so, we will examine a passage in Acts in which a clear example of an evangelistic sermon is present.

The example in question is Peter's sermon in Acts 2. The context is important. The post-crucified and recently resurrected Lord had given the apostles their mission, namely to give witness to the now realized gospel of Jesus Christ to all nations. Before they took up the task, however, Jesus was going to send help in the person of the Holy Spirit. They were to wait—wait patiently; wait expectantly—for his coming. And wait they did! Then on the day of Pentecost, he arrived. And what an amazing event it was. There were sights and sounds! "And suddenly there came from heaven a noise like a violent rushing wind, and it filled the whole house where they were sitting. And there appeared to them tongues as of fire distributing themselves ... And they were filled with the Holy Spirit and began to speak with other tongues" (Acts 2:2–4). As a result, the residents of Jerusalem heard them and thought they were drunk. And in this moment, Peter stood and preached the first post-resurrection evangelistic sermon.

Three or four components of Peter's message may help describe an evangelistic sermon. First, he drew his sermon from a biblical passage. In fact, even though he quoted three different Old Testament texts (Joel 2:28–32; Ps 16:8–11; and Ps 110:1), I believe the evidence supports that his message came from one passage primarily. The main point of his message appears to be from Ps 16: "God has made Him both Lord and Christ—this Jesus whom you crucified" (Acts 2:36).[6] Notice his content did not originate with him, and therefore the authority of his message and the subsequent appeal came from God's

---

[6] In context, it appears Peter used the other two passages as support to his main point from the primary text. Specifically, he used Joel 2 to address his audience and show there is a biblical rationale for what they were experiencing in order to be able to transition to the content of his message. Essentially, he used it as his "introduction." Furthermore, Ps 110 appears to be argumentation in the sermon. Peter used it to show Ps 16 could not be in reference to David but must be about someone else. The "someone else" has now been revealed. It is Jesus.

word.[7] Second, he explicitly communicated the basics of the gospel founded on the resurrection of Christ from the text. He did this in no less than two places. First, verses 23 and 24 read, "This Man, delivered over by the predetermined plan and foreknowledge of God, you nailed to a cross by the hands of godless men and put Him to death. But God raised Him up again, putting an end to the agony of death." Then again, near the conclusion of his message, he made a similar emphasis. "This Jesus God raised up again, to which we are all witnesses. Therefore having been exalted to the right hand of God, and having received from the Father the promise of the Holy Spirit, He has poured forth this which you both see and hear" (vv. 32–33).

Third, he specifically applied the gospel to the spiritual need of his audience. Throughout the body of the sermon, Peter continued to address them directly. This is evident by his use of the vocative[8] on no less than three occasions: "Men of Judea" (v. 14), "Men of Israel" (v. 22), and "Brethren" (v. 29). Furthermore, Peter consistently called his audience to listen and give heed to the truth of these words: "Let this be known to you and give heed to my words" (v. 14), "listen to these words" (v. 22), and "let all the house of Israel know" (v. 36). This practice would have been a constant reminder that the message was for them and shown the relevance of Jesus's resurrection to their lives.

---

[7] There is not enough space here to take on the discussion of the consistency of the New Testament authors' and apostles' uses of the Old Testament, interpretation methods, and homiletical practices with those on which expository preaching is based. Furthermore, it is beyond the scope of this article to do so. Sufficient for our purposes is Peter clearly believed there was biblical precedent and foundations for the content he presented and the claims he made. At a minimum, his practice indicates he did not believe the sermon's truth originated with him nor was he attempting to pull a message out of "thin air."

[8] See Daniel B. Wallace, *Greek Grammar Beyond the Basics: An Exegetical Syntax of the New Testament* (Grand Rapids, MI: Zondervan, 1996), 65–71. In the syntax of the Greek text of the New Testament, the most common and least disputed designation for the vocative case is simple direct address. Furthermore, even the other categories and subcategories of usage relates to designating the audience. "A substantive in the vocative is used in direct address to designate the addressee," Wallace, 67.

And finally, he gave a passionate appeal for a faith response in Christ based on that gospel application: "Repent, and each of you be baptized in the name of Jesus Christ for the forgiveness of your sins" (v. 38). Notice how the section concludes: "And with many other words he solemnly testified and kept on exhorting them, saying, 'Be saved from this perverse generation!'" (v. 40). "Three-and-a-half years after becoming a follower of Jesus Christ, Simon Peter, the 'big fisherman,' stood on the temple mount in Jerusalem, preached his monumental Pentecostal sermon, and drew the net."[9]

Therefore, from a biblical perspective, a message must include content from a biblical text, an explanation of the basics of the gospel in the context of that biblical text, an application of the connection of the gospel from that biblical text to the spiritual condition of the lost, and an appeal for a faith response in Christ in order to be classified as an evangelistic sermon. "Drawing the net is what the preacher or layman does when he extends the gospel invitation. Drawing the net is what the Christian does when, after presenting the message of salvation, he calls for a decision. Drawing the net is what Peter did at Pentecost."[10]

Now that we have a minimum understanding of both expository and evangelistic preaching, we will focus on a few questions. Are there theological and biblical grounds to be both expositional and evangelistic in our preaching? Does God's word provide a foundation for us to do both simultaneously in a manner that is natural and faithful to the text? Finally, is there a strategy that can help a pastor be a faithful expositor who gives evangelistic appeals in a way that honors the meaning of the text on a consistent basis?

---

[9] Hawkins, *Drawing the Net*, 11.
[10] Ibid., 16.

Theological and Biblical Foundations for Exposition and Evangelism in the Pulpit[11]

As mentioned in the introduction, God commands the pastor in 2 Tim 4:2, "Preach the word." Expository preaching, then, is built on the nature of the word of God itself. As such, a conservative and healthy doctrine of "specific" revelation must include an understanding of the inspiration of Scripture. Perhaps no place in the word of God captures this doctrine better than what Paul wrote in 2 Tim 3:16: "All Scripture is inspired by God and profitable for teaching, for reproof, for correction, for training in righteousness." Specifically, we should understand the Bible is inspired in a way no other text or book has ever been or ever will be. God is the author of the Bible. The Bible has been uniquely authored by God and is the uniquely authored book of God.

The inspiration of the Bible is a, if not the, foundational truth concerning the word of God and thus the expository sermon. And furthermore, since the Bible is inspired, there are at least three other doctrines that derive from the fact that it is inspired—inerrancy, infallibility, and sufficiency. These three doctrines provide the theological underpinning for expository preaching. They show, I believe, that this type of preaching is not simply one method in a sea of many other good methods. Rather, they show that it is a philosophy built on a theology—a clear belief about the Bible itself. For the purpose of space, in this section I will define one of these doctrines and give a brief word of explanation for why it is paramount for preaching.

---

[11] A version of this section first appeared in a blog post on the author's website. "3 Essential Doctrines of Our Bibliology That Are Foundational for Expository Preaching," *Adam L. Hughes Blog* (blog), March 16, 2018, http://adamlhughes.com/3-essential-doctrines-of-our-bibliology-that-are-foundational-for-expository-preaching/.

The Bible Is Sufficient

By sufficient, we understand the Bible is enough. This may lead to a very important question: Enough for what and in what regard? We certainly do not mean enough for anything and everything. (For instance, I am not claiming it is enough in the sense of providing you with all the data you need to replace the alternator on your car or to instruct you how to remove your son's appendix safely.) So in what way is it enough? It is enough for spiritual matters. It is enough to lead us to faith in the Savior who redeems us and to grow us toward Christlikeness in our redemption. Hear the words of David in Ps 19: "The law of the LORD is perfect, restoring the soul" (v. 7).

The word *restore* is not referring to a pick-me-up as when someone is feeling down. A better understanding of *restore* here is *return*. It is the word of the Lord, and the word of the Lord alone, that returns the soul of the one who has wandered far from God back to a relationship with him. This is sufficiency. Of the three doctrines mentioned previously, and of all the components of a robust bibliology, this may be the one that carries the most weight for expository preaching. Here's why. If I really believe the Bible is enough, and that nothing else is, why would I ever dare to mount a pulpit armed with anything else or anything less?

The Bible is sufficient to bring us to the point of salvation: "So faith comes from hearing, and hearing by the word of Christ" (Rom 10:17). Furthermore, the Bible is sufficient to grow us in our salvation: "Like newborn babies, long for the pure milk of the word, so that by it you may grow in respect to salvation" (1 Pet 2:2). What else does the church need? What else does the world need? The word of God is enough for humankind's ultimate need, and thus it is enough for the content of our teaching and preaching. We should not deliver anything less; we cannot deliver anything more. Therefore, from the characteristics of God's word itself, we have a theological foundation for the expository sermon.

We established at the onset, however, that the pastor is not only commanded to preach the word, but he is also called to persuade men

(2 Cor 5:11). He has not fulfilled his vocational mandate if he does anything less than be both biblical and persuasive in his pulpit. Therefore, not only is the nature of the Bible important for our purposes here but also so is what the Bible says directly about preaching and the preaching ministry. One obvious passage to consider is the one we began with (2 Tim 4:1–5), which certainly contains at least an implied connection between honoring the word and evangelism in the preaching ministry. Instead, however, I want us to consider a more obscure passage and one that is not often connected to the pulpit ministry.

Second Corinthians 4:1–6[12] arose out of the description of a dire circumstance. People are lost. The gospel is veiled to them because Satan (i.e., "the god of this age") has blinded them so they will not understand the gospel. They are in the dark (v. 3–4). As it relates to his ministry, however, Paul knew the solution. God can, and is, the only one able to turn on the light from the inside, in the heart. And he does so through Christ (v. 6). Christ is the image (Greek *eikon*) of God (v. 4). That is, he has the same form and is the perfect representation of God.[13] So when Christ is revealed, he reveals God. He always points toward and takes them to the Father.

How has God chosen to enact this process? Through the preaching ministry. The preacher stands in the direct line of God revealing himself to the unredeemed.[14] The preacher proclaims Christ. Christ is the image of God and shows people the Father. And then the Father shines light in the heart and brings people out of darkness (v. 6).[15] But this is only the case if the preacher chooses to preach Christ and not himself. So what does it mean to "preach ourselves"? This question

---

[12] For a fuller examination of this passage's connection to preaching, see Smith, *Dying to Preach*, Part 2 (especially 63–76).

[13] Walter Bauer, *A Greek-English Lexicon of the New Testament and Other Early Christian Literature*, ed. Frederick W. Danker, 3rd ed. (Chicago: University of Chicago Press, 2000), 281–82.

[14] Smith, *Dying to Preach*, 72.

[15] For a visual diagram of this process, see Ibid.

relates closely to two other questions, which form the point for us here: What does this have to do with the preaching ministry? Furthermore, how does it relate specifically to expository preaching?

First, notice again verse five. "For we do not preach ourselves but Christ Jesus as Lord, and ourselves as your bond-servants for Jesus' sake." The word *preach* here is the same term Paul used in 2 Tim 4:2 (Greek *kerusso*), which refers to an official or public announcement.[16] Paul intended for this discussion to be considered in the context of his public or corporate preaching ministry. Second, earlier in the passage, Paul gave us a hint at what it may look like for someone to preach himself: "But we have renounced the things hidden because of shame, not walking in craftiness or *adulterating the word of God*" (2 Cor 4:2, italics added). We know what it means to adulterate something, but for the sake of clarity, understand the word carries the idea of making false by distorting.[17] The opposite of distorting something is to present or represent accurately. Paul in his ministry, his proclamation ministry, was careful to present and represent the word with accuracy. Is that not essentially what we argued constitutes expository preaching?

Paul here was arguing for the presentation of Christ to lost people through a preaching ministry so God may be seen and could turn the light on from the inside. Moreover, whatever other components preaching Christ includes, it must be consistent with accurately presenting the word. To say it in the negative, if the pastor chooses to give people himself and not Christ, what is akin to adulterating that same word, the people will not see and live. Once more, from the Bible, the only logical conclusion is Paul viewed and understood the work of

---

[16] Bauer, *A Greek-English Lexicon*, 543. See also William Perkins, "The Calling of the Ministry" in *The Art of Prophesying and The Calling of Ministry*, rev. ed. (Edinburgh and Carlisle: The Banner of Truth Trust, 1996; reprint, 2002), 85. Although Perkins does not use the same term in his discussion, his metaphor of "angels, ambassadors, and messengers" carrying the message of the lords who sent them is based on the same idea of heralding and is helpful to our understanding here.

[17] Bauer, *A Greek-English Lexicon*, 256.

evangelism to be connected closely to the ministry of proclamation. In more than one place, Paul taught exposition and evangelism are connected, and evangelistic preaching should be a part of faithful and accurate expository preaching.

Now that we see from some key doctrines that expository preaching is consistent with the nature of the Bible and the concepts of expository and evangelistic proclamation are connected closely in a specific text in the Bible, how do we put all of this information together? Can we faithfully exposit the meaning of the word while at the same time having an evangelistic thrust in our pulpits?

The Evangelistic Expository Sermon

In last chapter of Luke's Gospel, the post-resurrected Jesus was on the road to Emmaus with two of his disciples, and yet they did not recognize him. Jesus's timing was impeccable. Before revealing to them who he was, Jesus prepared them to see him in a deeper and clearer way by showing them connections in the Old Testament they apparently had missed previously. "Then beginning with Moses and with all the prophets, he explained to them the things concerning Himself in all the Scriptures" (Luke 24:27). Two ideas are significant in this passage. The first is the word *explained*, which, while it can mean "translate," carries in this context the idea of "to clarify something" or "make it understandable."[18] Jesus made the Old Testament understandable to them. The second significant idea is the designation *all*. Let us be clear on what Luke was saying—Jesus clarified *all* the Scriptures, and when he did, it was he who came into focus. If this is not enough, hear his words once more near the end of the same chapter: "These are My words which I spoke to you while I was still with you, that all things which are written about Me in the Law of Moses and the Prophets and the Psalms must be fulfilled" (v. 44).

---

[18] Ibid., 244.

This narrative begs a question for us: Is it fair to preach evangelistically or, better yet, gospel-centrically from every passage of Scripture? Jesus tells us here. He seems to imply all Scripture relates to Christ: "Every passage either points to Christ futuristically, refers to Christ explicitly, or looks back to Christ reflectively."[19] Let us remember, when Christ is revealed, he always takes people to the Father.[20] Therefore, connecting what we saw in 2 Cor 4:1–6 to what we find in Luke 24, is this not the essence of evangelistic preaching?

It seems clear, then, that we can do faithful expository and evangelistic preaching simultaneously. Furthermore, not only should an accurate understanding of the word lead us to see its connection to Christ and a faithful homiletic lead us to proclaim Christ, but if we do not and it does not, we are neither understanding nor teaching Scripture the way Jesus did. We must preach evangelistically and gospel-centrically from every passage of Scripture. This is how we are the most accurate with the text and the most faithful in our pulpits.

Is there a strategy that allows a pastor to do this well, stay fresh, and does not seem contrived?

Putting It All Together: A Simple Strategy[21]

There is an implied question that underlies this chapter. To this point, it has remained unasked. Essentially the question is, why worry about

---

[19] Jerry Vines and Jim Shaddix, *Power in the Pulpit: How to Prepare and Deliver Expository Sermons*, rev. ed. (Chicago, IL: Moody Publishers, 2017), 37.

[20] Jim Shaddix offers a helpful discussion and explanation of three ways to view Scripture's connections to Christ: Christocentric, Christotelic, and Christoconic. See Jim Shaddix, "Is the Beeline the Best Line" in *Progress in the Pulpit: How to Grow Your Preaching* auths. Jerry Vines and Jim Shaddix (Chicago, IL: Moody Publishers, 2017), 114–21.

[21] A significant portion of this section first appeared in two blog posts on the author's website. "3 Goals I Try to Accomplish in Every Sermon Conclusion," *Adam L. Hughes* (blog), November 9, 2018, http://adamlhughes.com/3-goals-i-try-to-accomplish-in-every-sermon-conclusion/. "My Top 5 Goals for Every Sermon I Preach," *Adam L. Hughes* (blog), April 27, 2018, http://adamlhughes.com/my-top-5-goals-for-every-sermon-i-preach/.

expository preaching and accurate Bible teaching from your pulpit at all? Why not simply and directly present the gospel every week, make an appeal, and enter into a public time of invitation, discarding everything else that does not fit this mold? Why not make the sole subject of every sermon the need of the lost for a Savior and Jesus as the answer to their need? It is not that this would be wrong or all bad. Perhaps the deficiency lies in what would be missing.

Adrian Rogers, the pastor who many Southern Baptists consider to be one of the best ever at preaching evangelistic sermons and giving evangelistic appeals, appears to have wrestled with these same questions: "Most preachers are harming their churches by overemphasizing evangelistic preaching. Pastoral preaching is not the delivery of an evangelistic sermon, but, rather, it is preaching designed to meet the needs of the congregation through a proper feeding of God's Word."[22]

In his philosophy of preaching, Rogers found his answer.

> Yes, preach the gospel. However, preachers who are constantly preaching, "Hell is hot, heaven is sweet, sin is black, judgment is sure, and Jesus saves" are emptying their churches because they are not feeding their sheep. Every sermon may have evangelistic overtones, and every evangelistic message may have therapeutic ideas, but the preacher must be focused in his preaching. … Rather than standing up before hungry sheep and explaining to them why they ought to become a sheep, the preacher should set his priority upon feeding the flock. The primary objective of church preaching is to feed the sheep.[23]

Is there a model that marries all these concepts and the aim of the pastor in a local church? I am not only a major proponent of preaching

---

[22] Joyce Rogers, *Love Worth Finding: The Life of Adrian Rogers and His Philosophy of Preaching* (Nashville, TN: Broadman & Holman Publishers, 2005), 187.
[23] Ibid., 187–88.

the meaning of the text but also preaching the major intent of the text. Passages not only have meaning; they also have intent. Words not only mean something; they also do something. After you summarize the text's content and drive home the main biblical truth of the sermon, the last goal of your conclusion is to make a final appeal. It is in this final appeal based on the meaning and intent of the text that a simple strategy emerges for being both expositional and evangelistic in the pulpit. Here I am not referring to forcing something that is not there or simply tacking on a gospel invitation at the end. The aim should be to reveal what is in the text, then show its relevance to the lives of church members and, having found the legitimate connection to the gospel, make a passionate appeal to the lost based on this connection.

What does this look like practically? Based on the author's intent, which is communicated through the content of the text, I always make two direct applications. First and foremost, I show the redeemed exactly how this teaching is relevant for and in their lives and call them to respond accordingly. I am specific here. I share with them appropriate responses they can make during the time of response. This specific appeal is unique to the text and will differ from week to week depending on the content. It may range anywhere from godly relationships or anger to our place in the body of Christ or disciple-making. The point is always remaining faithful to "pull" or "take out" exactly what is in the passage and make a clear application from it to those who profess to follow Christ.

Second, I tell those who do not know Christ how the text I have finished expositing applies to and matters for them. Regardless of the passage, this appeal is static. I may vary my presentation, but the basic call remains the same. I believe no matter what text I am preaching or what subject it addresses, there is one and exactly one application for every lost person in the room—repent and believe the gospel! I genuinely believe this is the original intent of the divine author, God, for every lost person who hears any portion of his word. Whatever standard set, whatever description of God held up, or whatever action is called for, those who do not have Christ cannot obey.

This is true whether I am preaching on sharing our faith, the mission of God, Christian parenting, marriage, or the qualifications of a pastor. Here's why. Let us take the example of Christian marriage for a moment. What is the key ingredient in a Christian marriage according to Eph 5? Christ and the gospel! As a matter of fact, Paul indicated that the point of his entire teaching on marriage here is the gospel. Are there some good principles for anyone about having a healthy marriage according to Eph 5? Yes, but is this the point? Furthermore, can a lost person who has not been saved by Christ and thus does not have the indwelling Spirit follow these principles? No, and if you tell this person he or she can, you are going to frustrate him or her because they are going to fail trying before they make it to lunch.

My understanding of the application to a lost person from any passage is, "This is God's standard, and you cannot meet it! This is the type of marriage, home, and family God wants for you, but you cannot have it. It is only possible in Christ. Therefore, if you want this reality or to meet this standard in your life, it must start with repenting and accepting the gospel!" It is helpful here to remember Luke 24. There is a legitimate connection to the gospel. My goal is to find it and show it to those who do not know Christ. The point, even if implicit, is they be driven to Christ to whom all the word points and in whom all the word is fulfilled.

I want to model the intent of God as I preach every text. Regarding the unbeliever, I conclude by persuading them to repent and trust Christ. For the believer, I explicitly show them why God gave this passage to us. I believe both of these appeals are worthy, biblical goals. Giving specific appeals for the redeemed and those needing redemption is a great way to end any message, an impactful way to make a lasting impression, and a simple strategy for delivering sermons that capture the soul of the evangelistic expository sermon.

BIBLIOGRAPHY

Akin, Daniel L., David L. Allen, and Ned L. Mathews, eds. *Text-Driven Preaching: God's Word at the Heart of Every Sermon*. Nashville, TN: B&H Academic, 2010.

Allen, David. "Text-Driven Preaching." Interview by Adam Hughes, *NOBTS Conversations*, New Orleans, LA: New Orleans Baptist Theological Seminary, 2017. Accessed June 19, 2019. https://www.youtube.com/watch?v=LkSYeQRtp40&feature=youtu.be.

———. "Introduction." In *Text-Driven Preaching: God's Word at the Heart of Every Sermon*, 1–8. Nashville, TN: B&H Academic, 2010.

Bauer, Walter. *A Greek-English Lexicon of the New Testament and Other Early Christian Literature*. 3rd ed. Chichago, IL: Univeristy Press, 2000.

Hawkins, O. S. *Drawing the Net: 30 Practical Principles for Leading Others to Christ Publicly and Personally*. Dallas, TX: Annuity Board of the Southern Baptist Convention, 2002.

Hemphill, Ken. "Preaching and Evangelism." In *Handbook of Contemporary Preaching: A Wealth of Counsel for Creative and Effective Proclamation*, edited by Michael Duduit, 518–28. Nashville, TN: Broadman and Holman, 1992.

Hughes, Adam L. "3 Essential Doctrines of Our Bibliograpy That Are Foundational for Expository Preaching." *Adam L. Hughes* (blog), March 16, 2018. http://adamlhughes.com/3-essential-doctrines-of-our-bibliology-that-are-foundational-for-expository-preaching/.

———. "3 Goals I Try to Accomplish in Every Sermon Conclusion." *Adam L Hughes* (blog), November 9, 2018. http://adamlhughes.com/3-goals-i-try-to-accomplish-in-every-sermon-conclusion/.

———. "My Top 5 Goals for Every Sermon I Preach." *Adam L. Hughes* (blog). April 27, 2018. http://adamlhughes.com/my-top-5-goals-for-every-sermon-i-preach/.

Perkins, William. "The Calling of the Ministry." In *The Art of Prophesying and The Calling of the Ministry*. Rev. and ed., 80–191. Edinburgh and Carlisle: The Banner of Truth Trust, 1996.

Powell, Paul W. *Building An Evangelistic Church*. Dallas, TX: Annuity Board of the Southern Baptist Convention, 1991.

Rogers, Joyce. *Love Worth Finding: The Life of Adrian Rogers and His Philosophy of Preaching*. Nashville, TN: Broadman & Holman Publishers, 2005.

Shaddix, Jim. "Is the Beeline the Best Line?" In *Progress In The Pulpit: How to Grow Your Preaching*, by Jerry Vines and Jim Shaddix, 107–25. Chicago, IL: Moody Publishers, 2017.

Smith, Steven W. *Dying to Preach: Embracing the Cross in the Pulpit*. Grand Rapids, MI: Kregel, 2009.

———. *Recapturing the Voice of God: Shaping Sermons Like Scripture*. Nashville: B&H Academic, 2015.

Stanfield, V. L. *Effective Evangelistic Preaching*. Grand Rapids, MI: New Orleans, LA: n.p., 1965.

Vines, Jerry, and Jim Shaddix. *Power in the Pulpit: How to Prepare and Deliver Expository Sermons*. Rev. ed. Chicago, IL: Moody Publishers, 2017.

Wallace, Daniel B. *Greek Grammar Beyond the Basics: An Exegetical Syntax of the New Testament*. Grand Rapids, MI: Zondervan, 1996.

DECISIONAL PREACHING: ESSENTIAL ELEMENTS OF THE EVANGELISTIC SERMON

Preston Nix

In his book *Fuel the Fire: Lessons from the History of Southern Baptist Evangelism*, Dr. Charles Kelley identified decisional preaching as one of the four basic methods of evangelism utilized in Southern Baptist churches that contributed to the phenomenal growth of the denomination throughout its history.[1] He described the method of decisional preaching as the utilization of sermons that not only make the gospel known but also declare the demands of the gospel expecting an immediate and public response to the truth preached.[2] The particular type of preaching Southern

---

[1] Charles S. Kelley Jr., *Fuel the Fire: Lessons from the History of Southern Baptist Evangelism*, a Treasury of Baptist Theology, eds. Paige Patterson and Jason G. Duesing (Nashville, TN: B&H Academic, 2018), 51–53. The three other methods Kelley identified and described that contributed to the growth of the Southern Baptist Convention were personal evangelism, Sunday School, and revivalism. See Kelley, *Fuel the Fire*, 69–114. The author wishes to acknowledge the contributions of Dr. Kelley to evangelism in the Southern Baptist Convention through his ministry as a full-time vocational evangelist, a professor of evangelism, and as president of NOBTS in addition to his research and writing in the discipline of evangelism. The author further would like to express his personal appreciation to Dr. Kelley for allowing him to fill the roles at NOBTS that Dr. Kelley himself filled before he became president, including professor of evangelism, director of supervised ministry, director of the Leavell Center for Evangelism and Church Health, and chairman of the pastoral ministries division. From Hurricane Katrina to the Centennial Celebration, being on the team as a NOBTS faculty member under the leadership of Dr. Kelley has been challenging, exciting, and rewarding.

[2] Ibid., 53.

Baptist pastors and evangelists employed that called for immediate decision was evangelistic preaching delivered through evangelistic sermons. In this chapter, those elements essential to an effective evangelistic sermon will be identified and defined in hopes of encouraging the practice of the kind of decisional preaching that has resulted in unprecedented numbers of people coming to faith in Christ through the churches that comprise the Southern Baptist Convention. In addition, the desire is that the content of the chapter will serve to equip today's pastors to be more effective in leading men and women, boys and girls, to place their faith in Jesus as Savior and Lord in this generation. Those essential elements constituting an effective evangelistic sermon that will be examined in this chapter include the content of the evangelistic sermon, which is the gospel, the purpose of the evangelistic sermon, which is salvation, the target of the evangelistic sermon, which is the unsaved, the delivery of the evangelistic sermon, which includes persuasion, the mood of the evangelistic sermon, which is urgency, and the climax of the evangelistic sermon, which is the public invitation.

The Content of the Evangelistic Sermon

The first and foremost essential element of the evangelistic sermon is the content of the sermon. The content of an evangelistic sermon differentiates it from all other types of sermons. In essence, the content of the evangelistic sermon is what makes the sermon evangelistic, and that content should be the gospel. Simply stated, the gospel or *euangelion* is the good news of Jesus Christ. The gospel consists of the life, death, and resurrection of Jesus Christ. The apostle Paul explicitly stated what constituted the gospel when he reminded the Corinthian believers of the gospel he preached to them that had changed their lives. He said the gospel message was "that Christ died for our sins according to the Scriptures, and that He was buried, and that He was raised on the third day according to the Scriptures" (1 Cor 15:3–4). He related that the Corinthians had heard the gospel preached, believed and received the gospel message, and had been saved by the gospel (vv. 1–2).

What makes the facts of the incarnation, the crucifixion, and the resurrection of Jesus Christ good news at any location in the world in any era of history is that, because of who Jesus is and because of what he has done, sinful human beings can be forgiven of their sin, come into right relationship with God, and be given a home in heaven. Dr. Vernon Stanfield recorded what a preacher with whom he was once acquainted said concerning the gospel message he preached, describing it as, "Jesus Christ lived and died and arose, and now lives to save those who will trust him."[3] Stanfield then commented this statement "is the central message of all evangelistic preaching. There will never be another saving message."[4] The focus of the gospel is Jesus and his power to save, and as a result, the content of the evangelistic sermon always should be the gospel of Jesus Christ.[5]

In order to be a true evangelistic sermon, Dr. R. Larry Moyer proposed the preacher must communicate to unbelievers the following three truths:

1. We are sinners
2. Christ died for us and rose again
3. We must trust Christ.[6]

He summarized the three statements as "sin, substitution, and faith."[7] Very few passages of Scripture that can be preached evangelistically contain all three truths, but all three truths need to be

---

[3] As quoted by Vernon L. Stanfield in *Effective Evangelistic Preaching* (Grand Rapids, MI: Baker Book House, 1965), 17.
[4] Ibid.
[5] The message and content of the gospel have been discussed and debated in theological circles in recent years. For an insightful treatment of this topic, see Blake Newsom, "What Is the Gospel?" *Journal for Baptist Theology and Mission* 11 (Fall 2014): 2–15.
[6] R. Larry Moyer, *Show Me How to Preach Evangelistic Sermons* (Grand Rapids, MI: Kregel, 2012), 33, 43, 175, 191.
[7] Ibid., 33.

communicated to unbelievers in order for them to understand the full meaning of the gospel. Therefore, the evangelistic preacher must supply and explain those aspects of the gospel that the passage being preached does not include "at the most natural and appropriate place in the message."[8] In so doing, the preacher fulfills his responsibility to make certain that no portion of the gospel is left out of the evangelistic sermon and that the sermon content includes the complete gospel message that leads to the salvation of sinners.

The Purpose of the Evangelistic Sermon

The second essential element of the evangelistic sermon is the purpose of the sermon. Since the content of the evangelistic sermon is the gospel, then logically the purpose of the evangelistic sermon is the salvation of sinners. The good news of the gospel reveals that because of Christ's substitutionary death upon the cross of Calvary and his bodily resurrection from the dead, he provides forgiveness of sin and access to a right relationship with God to those separated from him due to their sin. The Lord Jesus himself clearly revealed he came to this earth "to seek and to save that which was lost" (Luke 19:10). The apostle Peter boldly declared, "There is salvation in no one else" other than Jesus Christ (Acts 4:12). Titus simply stated the grace of God expressed through Jesus "has appeared, bringing salvation to all men" (Titus 2:11). The apostle Paul strongly articulated the purpose of evangelistic preaching of the gospel when he proudly exclaimed, "For I am not ashamed of the gospel, for it is the power of God for salvation to everyone who believes" (Rom 1:16). Both the purpose and the result of the proclamation of the gospel of Jesus Christ according to Scripture is the salvation of sinners.

---

[8] Ibid., 175.

In speaking of the goals and objectives of evangelistic preaching, Dr. Vernon Stanfield indicated the primary purpose of the evangelistic sermon is the salvation of the lost.

> The first of these is to gain an inner commitment or an inner decision from the unbeliever. After he has preached the gospel, the preacher invites the lost man to believe in Christ, to trust in Christ, or to commit himself to Christ. The unbeliever is asked to believe in what Christ has done for him. Within himself he is consciously to turn to Jesus Christ and to receive him as his Lord and Savior.[9]

Although other purposes or objectives of the evangelistic sermon can be justified, such as encouraging believers to be grateful for their salvation and motivating believers to share their faith with others, the main purpose for preaching evangelistic sermons is for the salvation of unbelievers.

The Target of the Evangelistic Sermon

The third essential element of the evangelistic sermon is the target of the sermon. The target of the evangelistic sermon is those who are unsaved. The evangelistic sermon is directed to a specific audience that consists of those who are unbelievers or non-Christians. Jesus referred to those who needed to respond to the gospel message as the lost and sinners.[10] The apostle Paul declared, "Jesus came into the world to save sinners" (1 Tim 1:15).[11] Clearly the evangelistic sermon should target those in the audience who are lost sinners in need of a Savior. The message is designed to speak to the hearts of those who have yet to make a decision for Jesus Christ and need to do so in order to

---

[9] Stanfield, *Effective Evangelistic Preaching*, 19.
[10] See Matt 9:13; Mark 2:17; Luke 5:32; 15:7, 10, 32; 19:10.
[11] See also Rom 5:8.

experience forgiveness of sin and receive the gift of eternal life. Therefore, the gospel message of the evangelistic sermon "is not directed to the saved, but to the unsaved."[12]

> Therefore, we should speak as though there were no believers in the audience. We don't ask, "Can a Christian identify with what I am saying?" We ask, "Could an unbeliever identify?" [The] ... message should be so focused toward non-Christians that they know they are the ones being addressed. An expository evangelistic message is not prepared for believers and then given to non-Christians. It is prepared for non-Christians and given to non-Christians.[13]

Even though the larger percentage of the audience is already saved, the evangelistic preacher should remember that in the evangelistic sermon, he is preaching to the smaller percentage who are the unsaved who need to hear and respond to the message of the gospel.

The Delivery of the Evangelistic Sermon

The fourth essential element of the evangelistic sermon is the delivery of the evangelistic sermon, which should include persuasion. The utilization of persuasion in the delivery of the evangelistic sermon is not only desirable but also necessary. As previously discussed, the targeted audience of the evangelistic sermon is the unsaved who need to be convinced of their need for salvation. In their natural sinful state, the lost are resistant to the gospel and must be persuaded to repent of their sin and place their faith in the Lord Jesus Christ. The apostle Paul revealed his utilization of persuasion in the preaching of the gospel when he declared, "Knowing the fear of the Lord, we persuade men" (2 Cor 5:11). He further indicated that as an ambassador for Christ

---

[12] Moyer, *Show Me How to Preach Evangelistic Sermons*, 25.
[13] Ibid.

he begged people to be reconciled to God (v. 20). Paul attempted to persuade both Jews and Greeks in the synagogue and the marketplace in Athens to place their faith in Christ. In Corinth, he took a similar approach by "reasoning in the synagogue every Sabbath and trying to persuade Jews and Greeks" to turn to Christ (Acts 18:4, see also Acts 17:17). Clearly the apostle Paul attempted to persuade King Agrippa to repent of his sin and place his faith in Christ, as revealed in the king's reply to Paul, "In a short time you will persuade me to become a Christian" (Acts 26:28).

In the chapter on decisional preaching in his book *Fuel the Fire*, Dr. Kelley discussed the influence of rhetoric on Southern Baptist preaching.[14] He shared the classical definition of rhetoric as the use of all available means of persuasion in any given situation.[15] As Christianity expanded across the Roman Empire, the church became more gentile than Jewish, and its leaders began to be trained in the Greek tradition. As a result, the canons (rules) of Greek and Roman rhetoric began to be applied to the task of preaching and the natural relationship between preaching and rhetoric developed.[16] As Kelley observed,

> Southern Baptists were taught to link biblical proclamation with rhetorical intent. Preachers must proclaim the Word of God with a view to persuading men and women to respond to God's call for repentance, faith, and obedience. Giving hearers the immediate opportunity to respond ... is a logical consequence of the historic emphasis on persuasion in Southern Baptist homiletical theory.[17]

The three means of persuasion identified in classical rhetoric are *ethos*, *pathos*, and *logos*. Although these are not biblical concepts, they

---

[14] Kelley, *Fuel the Fire*, 56–58.
[15] Ibid., 56.
[16] Ibid., 57.
[17] Ibid.

are means of persuasion that operate in any communication setting and are particularly applicable for the evangelistic sermon. The *ethos* or character of the preacher, the *pathos* or passion of the preacher, and the *logos* or logic of the preacher's message all work together in the preaching event to persuade the members of the audience to make a spiritual decision for Christ.[18] Who the audience members perceive the preacher to be, the passion with which he delivers his message, and the logical manner in which the truth is communicated are instrumental in leading people to respond to the message of the gospel. The effective evangelistic preacher must be aware of the available means of persuasion in the preaching event and employ those means competently in the delivery of the evangelistic sermon because the proper utilization of persuasion in the delivery of the evangelistic sermon is critical to the desired response to the gospel message. Craig Loscalzo stated:

> Evangelistic preaching is persuasive preaching: we seek a desired response, and we consciously attempt to influence the attitudes and behaviors of our listeners. That should not surprise us. The gospel itself is inherently persuasive. Its message intends to invoke changes in people's attitudes and to elicit transformation of their behaviors (2 Cor 5:17). Motivated by our love for people, we want to persuade them to accept the gift of new life in Jesus Christ. ... We desperately want others to experience this salvation. We want to persuade them to receive God's offer of life. Persuasive preaching aims at that end.[19]

---

[18] For insight concerning the role of *ethos*, *pathos*, and *logos* in persuasive preaching, see Jerry Vines and Jim Shaddix, *Power in the Pulpit: How to Prepare and Deliver Expository Sermons*, rev. ed. (Chicago, IL: Moody Publishers, 2017), 276–279.

[19] Craig A. Loscalzo, *Evangelistic Preaching that Connects* (Downers Grove, IL: InterVarsity Press, 1995), 28.

Thus far, the discussion of delivery of the evangelistic sermon has focused on the employment of persuasion by the preacher. However, two important truths about persuasive preaching need to be emphasized at this point. First, persuasion never means manipulation or coercion. The way the preacher seeks to persuade people to respond to the gospel "must be in line with the character of the gospel."[20] Jesus, Peter, and Paul clearly attempted to persuade people to respond to the truth of the gospel message, but none of them manipulated or tried to coerce anyone into the kingdom of God. Second, although persuasion makes a significant difference in the communication of the gospel message, no one comes to Christ apart from the influence and power of the Holy Spirit. The preacher must fulfill his role as a persuasive proclaimer of the saving message of Jesus Christ in the delivery of the evangelistic sermon. However, he must acknowledge all of the persuasive ability he possesses ultimately cannot persuade anyone to change his or her life to become a follower of Jesus Christ. The evangelistic preacher must rely upon the power of the Holy Spirit for the desired response to the delivery of his evangelistic sermon because the salvation of the soul ultimately is the result of the work of the Holy Spirit of God.

The Mood of the Evangelistic Sermon

The fifth essential element of an evangelistic sermon is the mood of the evangelistic sermon, which should be characterized by urgency. Mood refers to the emotional quality or the characteristic tone of the message. The message of the gospel deals with serious matters of life and death as well as heaven and hell, and response to the gospel has significance for eternity. As a result, the evangelistic sermon always "should be marked by a sense of urgency."[21] That fact does not mean the sermon should be characterized by "gloom and doom" nor that

---

[20] Ibid., 29.
[21] Stanfield, *Effective Evangelistic Preaching*, 21.

appropriate humor cannot be employed in the delivery of the evangelistic sermon. What that reality means is the evangelistic preacher must be gripped by the seriousness of his task of proclaiming the gospel to those who face the judgment of God for their sin and whose destination is an eternal hell. The evangelistic preacher must communicate clearly and passionately the eternal significance of the gospel message as well as the inevitable consequences both positive and negative of the listener's response to the truth.

The writer of Hebrews emphasized the urgency of responding to the gospel when he shared the truth, "It is appointed for men to die once and after this comes judgment" (Heb 9:27). Jesus dramatically illustrated the urgency of responding to the gospel message in the parable of the rich fool. While the man enjoyed his material wealth and thought he had many more years to live, God said to him, "You fool! This very night your soul is required of you" (Luke 12:20). The apostle Paul emphasized the urgency of responding to the call to salvation when he exclaimed, "Behold, now is 'the acceptable time,' behold, now is 'the day of salvation'" (2 Cor 6:2). Further, prior to the time when Jesus restored the sight of a blind man and led the man to place his faith in him, Jesus related to his disciples the urgency of the task of proclaiming the truth of the gospel. Jesus said, "We must work the works of Him who sent Me as long as it is day; night is coming when no man can work" (John 9:4). The evangelistic sermon must be delivered with a strong sense of urgency because no one knows how much longer he or she will have opportunity in this lifetime to hear and respond to the gospel message, and no evangelistic preacher knows how many more times he will have opportunity to preach the gospel message and call the unsaved to repentance and faith in the Lord Jesus.

The Climax of the Evangelistic Sermon

The sixth and final essential element of the effective evangelistic sermon is the climax of the evangelistic sermon, which is the public invitation. At the close of every evangelistic sermon, an evangelistic appeal should be extended for the listeners to respond both personally and publically to the gospel message. In fact, the evangelistic invitation should be the conclusion of every evangelistic sermon.[22] Since the purpose of the evangelistic sermon is the salvation of sinners, then an appeal for sinners to repent of their sin, believe the gospel, and place their faith in Jesus Christ always should be made. The gospel by its very nature calls for a response.[23] To proclaim the life-transforming message of the gospel and give opportunity for listeners to respond is both logical and biblical. Conversely, to proclaim the message of the gospel and not give opportunity for response is both illogical and unbiblical. As one evangelism professor said to a class of seminary students concerning giving people an opportunity to respond to the gospel after sharing the good news with them, "Impression without expression can lead to depression." When an unsaved person hears an evangelistic sermon in which the gospel message has been communicated but is not given an opportunity to respond to that message, that discrepancy can lead to confusion and frustration. The unsaved individual needs to be instructed as to what he or she needs to do in order to be saved.

Scripture is replete with examples of invitations to respond publically to the Lord. Dr. Vernon Stanfield provided a brief summary of invitations to decide for the Lord recorded both in the Old and New Testaments. He stated:

> When the people had wandered away from God, Moses said to them, "Who is on the LORD's side? let him come unto me" (Exodus 32:26). Joshua challenged the people, "Chose you this day whom ye will serve" (Joshua 24:15). Isaiah invited the people, "Ho, every one that thirsteth come ye to

---

[22] Ibid., 27.
[23] See Loscalzo, *Evangelistic Preaching that Connects*, 157. He wrote, "The gospel, in its essence, is invitational. It calls people to respond; it invites allegiance to its claims." See, also, Moyer, *Show Me How to Preach Evangelistic Sermons*, 191. He stated categorically, "The gospel demands a response."

the waters" (Isaiah 55:1). The word "come" was constantly on the lips of Jesus. This is typified in the great invitation, "Come unto me, all ye that labor and are heavy laden, and I will give you rest" (Matthew 11:28). In the last chapter of the last book of the Bible you will find an all-inclusive invitation, "And the Spirit and the bride say, Come. And let him that heareth say, Come. And let him that is athirst come. And whosoever will, let him take the water of life freely" (Revelation 22:17).[24]

Elijah, in his confrontation with the prophets of Baal on Mount Carmel, demanded the people make a public choice as to whom they would worship. He cried out, "How long will you hesitate between two opinions? If the LORD is God, follow Him; but if Baal, follow him" (1 Kgs 18:21). Ezra the priest revealed to the people they had not fulfilled their covenant responsibility to obey God's law and admonished them to repent publically of their sin (Ezra 10:1–12). John the Baptist preached a message of repentance to be accompanied by public baptism and performance of good deeds that gave evidence of repentance (Luke 3:7–14). Peter, in the sermon he preached at Pentecost, instructed his hearers to repent and be baptized to indicate their commitment to Christ (Acts 2:38).

In addition to the mentioned biblical examples of invitations to respond publically to the Lord, the Bible records admonitions for public response revealing spiritual decisions. Jesus said, "Therefore everyone who confesses Me before men, I will also confess him before My Father who is in heaven" (Matt 10:32). The apostle Paul stated, "If you confess with your mouth Jesus as Lord, and believe in your heart that God raised Him from the dead, you will be saved; for with the heart a person believes, resulting in righteousness, and with the mouth he confesses, resulting in salvation" (Rom 10:9–10). Although the biblical

---

[24] Stanfield, *Effective Evangelistic Preaching*, 27.

examples and biblical admonitions of invitations to respond publically are not exactly the same methodologically as the public invitation is practiced today, nonetheless, public response to the preaching of the gospel has strong biblical precedent.[25]

Besides the biblical and spiritual reasons for the extension of public invitations, practical considerations can be cited as well. The first practical consideration is the public invitation allows the pastor and church to know who has made a decision for Christ. Counsel as to baptism and spiritual growth then can be done. The public invitation also provides a way to discover who is open to the gospel and ready to make a decision for Christ. The pastor, ministerial staff, or other designated decision counselors are able to converse with the inquirers one on one and assist them in trusting Christ for salvation. The public invitation creates the occasion for the pastor to share each week with those present in the worship services how they can become members of the church through a profession of faith and baptism. The public invitation gives opportunity for the congregation to celebrate the salvation decisions and to welcome the new believers into the family of God.

Several types of invitations can be employed at the close of the evangelistic sermon. The first is the verbal appeal for those in the audience to pray a prayer of repentance and faith for salvation where they are seated. The next is the altar call at which those who have prayed to receive Christ come forward to the front of the room in open confession of Christ. The appeal can be made as well to those to come forward who want to talk with someone about their need for Christ. Those who have made decisions for Christ or want to talk with someone further also can be invited to a special room designated for spiritual counsel. Other means such as the raising of hands, looking up at the preacher, filling out a decision card, or coming to a personal meeting with the pastor following the service can be utilized. Although these are not public actions in themselves, they can be coupled with the

---

[25] Kelley, *Fuel the* Fire, 56.

more public methods in a multiple approach to the invitation or what has been called a progressive invitation. For example, the preacher may invite those who are interested in coming to Christ to raise their hands for prayer, lead them in a prayer to trust Christ, ask them to look up at him so he can address them directly, and then invite them to come to the front of the church to make a public decision for Christ.

Whatever the method employed, the evangelistic sermon always should conclude with the extension of a public invitation, giving the listeners opportunity to make decisions for Christ. The climax of an evangelistic sermon, which is the public invitation, is an essential element of the evangelistic sermon. Without the public invitation the evangelistic sermon is incomplete. As Dr. Kelley observed in his discussion of decisional preaching, "Every time an invitation is extended, the pastor is reminding his hearers that a personal relationship with Christ is necessary for one to be right with God," and, "No one is right with God until they 'call upon the name of the Lord.'"[26] The public invitation provides the opportunity for lost sinners to call upon the name of the Lord and be saved, which is the purpose of the evangelistic sermon accomplished at the climax of the evangelistic sermon (Rom 10:13).

Conclusion

Decisional preaching is specifically evangelistic preaching, which has been used of the Lord to reach people with the gospel since the time of Christ. This kind of preaching was identified as one of the four basic methods of evangelism utilized in Southern Baptist churches that contributed to the phenomenal growth of the Southern Baptist Convention throughout its history.[27] As evangelistic preaching in SBC pulpits in recent years has waned, a corresponding decrease in baptisms has been recorded by SBC churches. While a correlation between the

---

[26] Ibid., 67, 53.
[27] Ibid., 51–53.

two appears to exist, any attempt to determine that correlation would be a formidable challenge. However, if more evangelistic sermons incorporating the essential elements as delineated in this chapter were preached in the worship services, then in all likelihood more people would be saved and more people would be baptized in the churches. Encouraging the practice of decisional preaching while equipping pastors to be more effective at preaching evangelistic sermons were the stated outcomes in the ministries of the readers of this chapter. For the glory of God and the growth of the kingdom of God through the salvation of many sinners, the prayer is that these hopes will be realized.

Bibliography

Kelley, Charles S., Jr. *Fuel the Fire: Lessons from the History of Southern Baptist Evangelism.* A Treasury of Baptist Theology, edited by Paige Patterson and Jason G. Duesing. Nashville, TN: B&H Academic, 2018.

Loscalzo, Craig A. *Evangelistic Preaching That Connects.* Downers Grove, IL: InterVarsity Press, 1995.

Moyer, Larry R. *Show Me How to Preach Evangelistic Sermons.* Grand Rapids, MI: Kregel, 2012.

Newsom, Blake. "What Is the Gospel?" *Journal for Baptist Theology and Mission* 11 (Fall 2014).

Stanfield, Vernon L. *Effective Evangelistic Preaching.* Grand Rapids, MI: Baker Book House, 1965.

Vines, Jerry, and Jim Shaddix. *Power in the Pulpit: How to Prepare and Deliver Expository Sermons.* Revised Edition. Chicago, IL: Moody Publishers, 2017.

Invitations with Integrity

Mark Tolbert

I am concerned about a dear friend. God has greatly used this proven friend not only in my life but also in the lives of countless others. This seasoned ally has been an incredible blessing and a vehicle for multitudes to experience comfort, freedom, forgiveness, and untold joy. Although once a very familiar mainstay in evangelical circles, over time this friend has become the victim of misunderstanding, abuse, neglect, ridicule, scorn, slander, and now, near abandonment. This familiar friend is at risk of being portrayed at the least as a marginalized relic or at the worst a dangerous charlatan. That is to say, I am concerned about the current state of public, evangelistic invitations.

One's integrity is crucial. To have your integrity questioned is far more serious than having your competency or skills questioned. There is a serious challenge today concerning the very integrity of the public invitation, not simply the methodology or presentations employed. I would have to agree with those who would charge the public invitation sometimes has been abused or mishandled. Most preachers would support a move to insure invitations are better prepared and extended with more clarity. This chapter addresses that need as well as a more serious issue—the very integrity of the public invitation itself. Is the extending of a public, evangelistic invitation valid? If so, how must we issue invitations with authenticity and integrity?

I came to know Jesus Christ as Savior and Lord in response to a public evangelistic invitation. At the age of sixteen, I attended a Billy Graham movie at a local theater while on a date with my girlfriend. For me, it was just another Friday night at the movies. I did not realize we were attending a religious film, or I probably would not have attended. That movie exposed me to the awareness that although I was a church member, I did not have a relationship with Christ. I was deeply moved and convicted of my sin and need for forgiveness. I understood that I needed Christ's forgiveness and salvation. Sitting in my seat, watching the final scenes of the film, I purposed that I would commit my life to Christ someday.

At the conclusion of that movie, a man gave an appeal for those who wished to make a commitment to Christ to come to the front of the theater and speak with a commitment counselor. Prior to that night, I was unaware of a need to make such a commitment. I had not gone to the movie that night with any intention of coming to Christ. No Christians had talked with me about my need for Christ. I had never been exposed to the message of the gospel. I had never been part of hearing a public evangelistic invitation. A man quoted a scriptural invitation that night as he paraphrased an Old Testament reference (1 Kgs 18:21) that asked, "How long will you hesitate between two opinions? If the LORD is God, follow Him." As the challenge was given, I realized my need to respond to the invitation and to make a commitment to Christ. I went to the front of the theater, and a trained counselor assisted me in making my commitment to Christ. The gospel was made clear, I freely acknowledged my need for Christ, and God wondrously saved me. From personal experience, I bear witness of the legitimate place of extending public evangelistic invitations.

Tragically, the public invitation is in trouble. No longer is the invitation an almost universal part of evangelical worship. What once was a tool that was implemented for the evangelization of the masses is now a mere shadow of the past. Even churches that continue the practice of extending public invitations often do so with little precision or purpose. How could this once mighty and respected evangelistic practice have drifted so far?

Criticisms of the public invitation move along four levels. First, some charge the public invitation is without scriptural warrant. Second, some allege the public invitation is a modern invention. Third, some contend the call for a public response adds man's efforts to salvation coming solely by the grace of God. Still others have eliminated the public proclamation of the gospel with a public invitation in favor of exclusive support of relational evangelism.

In their current form, evangelistic invitations are of relatively recent origin, but the spirit and principle of the public evangelistic invitation is evident in the Bible. There are Old Testament examples. When Moses came down from Mount Sinai, he discovered the people giving themselves over to idolatry and worshipping the golden calf. He confronted the people by asking, "Whoever is for the LORD, come to me!" (Exod 32:26). That was a clear call to the people to make a public declaration and to take a public stand for the Lord. After Moses's death, Joshua was commanded to lead the nation of Israel. The people again lapsed into idolatry. Toward the end of Joshua's life, he called all the tribes together and said, "If it is disagreeable in your sight to serve the LORD, choose for yourselves today whom you will serve: whether the gods which your fathers served which were beyond the River, or the gods of the Amorites in whose land you are living; but as for me and my house, we will serve the LORD" (Josh 24:15). That too was a call for a public commitment of loyalty to God.

Centuries later, idolatry was the issue again. This time Elijah was God's chosen instrument. Standing on Mount Carmel it is recorded, "Elijah came near to all the people and said, 'How long will you hesitate between two opinions? If the LORD is God, follow Him; but if Baal, follow him'" (1 Kgs 18:21). This was a clear, powerful call to public commitment and identification as a follower of God. In Ezra 10:5, Ezra, the great scribe, called upon his contemporaries to swear publicly they would carry out the principles of his reform. Nehemiah's book also indicates the Jewish leaders were required to commit themselves to a covenant of loyalty to the Lord after their revival (Neh 9:39). Hosea urged the people to return to the Lord and receive his forgiveness (Hos 14:2). Throughout the Old Testament is a clear picture of the man of God publicly calling people to make a public commitment to the Lord.

The New Testament records urging people to decide publicly for Christ as well. The apostle Paul announced to the church at Corinth that Christians have been given the ministry of reconciliation (2 Cor 5:18–20). This ministry charges the believer with the task of seeking to join sinful man and holy God together. Further, this ministry compels the Christian to urge the hearer to decide for Christ. The gospel is not to be presented in a casual, perfunctory manner but with a sense of urgency, appeal, and persuasion (v. 11), even as Paul did when he reasoned and persuaded the people of Ephesus (Acts 19:8), and as Jesus charged his disciples to do (Luke 14:23). This urging from the human instrument is to be done while relying on the Spirit of God. The evangelist must do his best to urge men to come to Christ, but there also must be a dependence upon the Holy Spirit to convict and draw people (John 16:8).

Jesus made numerous appeals for people to decide publicly for him. The launching of his ministry included public proclamation of the gospel and public calls to repentance (Matt 4:17). When he called Andrew and John, his first disciples, he extended a public appeal to follow him (Matt 4:19), as he did with the woman of Sychar (John 4:4–42), Philip (John 1:43), Matthew (Luke 5:27), the rich, young ruler (Luke 18:18–34), and Zaccheus (Luke 19:1–10). Jesus also gave general appeals in group settings (Matt 11:28, 29; John 7:37, 38). Jesus gave us a personal example in his extension of public invitations to people to follow him as Lord and Savior.

Other New Testament preachers called for a public decision. Aside from Jesus, the most outstanding example is John the Baptist. John came preaching a message of repentance (Luke 3:23), but the chief characteristic of his ministry was baptizing the people who responded to his message (John 1:28). His ministry, preaching, and appeal were public, and those who responded to his appeal did so publicly.

The followers of Jesus also extended public invitations. Andrew sought out his brother, Peter, and brought him to Jesus (John 1:42). After he went on to become a powerful spokesman for the Lord, Peter called for an immediate, public commitment to Christ—in his sermon on the day of Pentecost (Acts 2:39–40) and in his preaching to the household of Cornelius (Acts 10:28–48). Philip preached to the Ethiopian eunuch and those in his caravan as they traveled along a desert road (Acts 8:26–38). The public proclamation of the gospel was basic to the ministry of the apostle Paul (1 Cor 15:1–11; 1 Thess 1:5–11). His preaching and appeals for Christ were often in a public arena, usually in the setting of the Jewish synagogues, such as: in Pisidian Antioch (Acts 13:14–48), in Iconium (Acts 14:1–7), in Thesalonica (Acts 17:1–4), in Berea (vv. 10–12), in Corinth (Acts 18:1–4), and in Ephesus (Acts 19:1–10). Paul and Silas challenged the jailer at Philippi to place his faith in Christ amid the public spectacle of a crowded jail cell (Acts 16:25–31). The Bible concludes with an invitation to come to Christ (Rev 22:17). Throughout the New Testament is ample evidence for the practice of public proclamation of the gospel, with an appeal for a public declaration of faith in Christ.

This examination of Scripture provides a clear basis for public evangelistic invitations. When the preacher of the gospel makes an appeal for people to decide openly for Christ, he is on solid biblical ground. As the minister of the gospel applies biblical principles of public evangelistic invitations, he can do so with the blessing of heaven.

Critics of the public invitation make the claim the practice started with Charles G. Finney (1792–1875). Although it is true Finney's "new measures" popularized the practice, public evangelistic invitations can be traced back centuries before Finney. The preachers of the first century called upon people to offer themselves as candidates for repentance, faith, and baptism. These invitations continued until AD 324 when Emperor Constantine declared Christianity the state religion of the Roman Empire. In one sudden move, all citizens of

Rome, whether believers or not, were swept into the church, and were proclaimed to be Christians. Adults and infants alike were baptized as they became members of the church. As these infants grew, the need for adult baptism diminished, and the practice of the public invitation declined.

Among Christians who continued to issue a public invitation were the Anabaptists. They opposed the Roman Catholic Church on several issues, including infant baptism. They were faithful in calling for repentance of sins, faith in Christ, and the outward sign of rebaptism. The Anabaptists were opposed by both Catholics and Protestants. Anabaptist reformers proclaimed the message of salvation by grace through faith and believed in the final authority of Scripture, but they opposed the public invitation, believing it to be an addition to faith and, therefore, unbiblical.

Founded by Thomas Helwys in 1609, the Separatists broke away from the Church of England. They believed people must repent and believe on Christ in order to be saved. They invited people to confess Christ publicly through believer's baptism. Famous Separatists include John Bunyan, author of *Pilgrim's Progress*, who advocated a call for a public profession of faith in Christ. The Pilgrims on board the *Mayflower* who came to America in 1620 seeking religious and political liberty were members of a Separatist congregation.

The eighteenth century saw unusually gifted and anointed preachers who employed a variety of public invitations to come to Christ. Jonathan Edwards and George Whitefield would conclude their sermons with an appeal for seekers to meet with them following the service to seek private spiritual guidance. This was the standard invitational model of the eighteenth century. Another of their contemporaries, John Wesley, would also invite seekers to come forward and sit at the "Anxious Seat" where they would receive spiritual counsel. This occurred some fifty years before Finney, who is often cited as the inventor of the modern altar call for the invitation. Noted historian Leon McBeth, in quoting Steve O'Kelly, observes that Separate

Baptists in the southern United States are known to have extended invitations for people to come to the front of the service with the singing of a hymn to make immediate commitments to Christ as early as 1758.[1] In 1799, at a Methodist camp meeting in Red River, Kentucky, a physical altar was erected in front of the pulpit where seekers might come for prayer and instruction. So popular was it that altars became permanent fixtures in many Methodist churches.[2] This is the first record of an "altar call" as a form of the public invitation.

The nineteenth century saw the ministry of Charles G. Finney popularize the modern pattern of coming to the front of the church at the time of invitation to commit to Christ. Charles Haddon Spurgeon employed a type of invitation similar to the eighteenth century model, due in part to the physical limitations of the Metropolitan Tabernacle.[3] Although Finney certainly is credited with the paradigm with which we are now familiar, the spirit and practice of public invitations is well documented in church history.

What about the charge that calling for a response in a public invitation is adding human means to the grace of God? In extending a public invitation, the preacher should make every effort to separate the need for an inner decision to the call for an external expression. A person is justified solely by the grace of God and apart from human effort (Rom 4:1–5). The apostle Paul argued to the Romans that we are right with God based on the inward condition of our hearts (Rom 2:29).

And yet, the one who has a genuine inner relationship of the heart will validate it in an external expression. After Peter's sermon at Pentecost, the people asked, "'What shall we do?' Peter said to them, 'Repent, and each of you be baptized in the name of Jesus Christ

---

[1] H. Leon McBeth, *The Baptist Heritage: Four Centuries of Baptist Witness* (Nashville: Broadman Press, 1987), 231.
[2] Henry B. McLendon, "The Mourner's Bench" (ThD diss., The Southern Baptist Theological Seminary, 1902), 10.
[3] R. Alan Streett, *The Effective Invitation* (Old Tappan, NJ: Fleming H. Revell, 1984), 97.

for the forgiveness of your sins'" (Acts 2:37–38). In his letter to the Romans, Paul described the relationship between inner decision and external expression: "That if you confess with your mouth Jesus as Lord, and believe in your heart that God raised Him from the dead, you will be saved; for with the heart a person believes, resulting in righteousness, and with the mouth he confesses, resulting in salvation" (Rom 10:9–10).

Outward expression is to be evidence of inner grace. To claim inner grace without external expression is to cheapen the gospel of grace. The concept of cheap grace or "easy believism" is often made by those who are of the Reformed persuasion. One is saved not by walking an aisle, raising a hand, or praying a prayer. One is saved by committing oneself to Jesus Christ as Savior and Lord. However, to question the integrity of the public invitation as a means of external expression is to eliminate a legitimate and biblical means of external expression.

Others have abandoned the practice of extending a public invitation in favor of relational evangelism. The preference for relational witness has become an exclusive preference: relational evangelism as the only means of proper witness. Adherents of this position do not merely prefer relational evangelism, they see it as the only legitimate way to evangelize. They do more than merely minimize the legitimacy of the public invitation; they question its very integrity. This view would disparage those who would extend the public invitation as well as those who would practice direct conversational evangelism with a casual acquaintance or a stranger. Although personal relationships can be a valid, perhaps even the preferred means of presenting the gospel, should it be the exclusive approach? It was not the exclusive approach of Jesus Christ, who witnessed to individuals after a brief introduction (John 3:1–21; 4:1–26), as well as to the masses (John 7:37–38).

A public evangelistic invitation may follow various formats. The traditional invitation to walk to the front of the room remains a common and effective form. Other forms are also available that may serve as alternatives. Some settings would suggest using an alternative format for the invitation. Presentations to children, youth, and specialty groups that invite people to raise their hands or make eye contact with the preacher during a closing prayer can sometimes be effective. One can meet privately with those who responded. Encouraging a private conference after the conclusion of the meeting may be used. It is essential that interested people may easily locate the minister and visit in an uninterrupted setting. Providing a response card for people to complete and request later follow-up and conversation has been used with success. Do not make the common mistake of equating a come-forward approach with an evangelistic invitation. Other approaches can and should be used as the context demands.

Making an invitation clear is essential. Do not assume people understand the "language of Zion." Telling people to "make a profession of faith," "to come to the altar," (when you may not actually have an altar) "to get right with God," and "to walk the sawdust trail" (really?) are expressions that are meaningless and perhaps ridiculed by those unfamiliar with church culture. Be crystal clear in your invitation. Make certain you communicate in clear and simple language what you are calling for and how people are to respond. Do not make it difficult for someone to respond; make it easy.

An analogy may prove helpful. How would you invite someone to your home for dinner with you and your family? Would you assume they knew they were welcome and therefore, no invitation is necessary? Of course not. Would you make a vague, meaningless statement, such as "You come see us sometime"? Would you not ensure they knew the details of how to locate your house, the agreed upon date, and the time they would be expected? You might even suggest the dress code for the evening and whether they were expected to bring a side dish. Such details are not considered intrusive or manipulative; rather, they are seen as helpful, courteous, and appreciated when a heartfelt and genuine dinner invitation is extended. Why would we not extend the same courtesies when issuing an invitation to attend, someday, the marriage supper of the Lamb?

Listen to the plea of one being drawn to Christ in the book of Acts. Acts 8 provides the narrative of Phillip's encounter with the Ethiopian eunuch. The royal officer was returning from Jerusalem in order to worship. As Phillip encountered the eunuch's chariot he heard him reading from Isa 53:7–8: "Like a lamb that is led to slaughter, and like a sheep that is silent before its shearers, so He did not open His mouth. By oppression and judgment He was taken away; and as for His generation, who considered that He was cut off out of the land of the living." Upon hearing this, Phillip asked the man if he understood what he was reading. Acts 8:31 records his response: "Well, how could I, unless someone guides me?" This is the silent cry of many: "How can I unless someone guides me?" Here is an individual with whom God seems to have been drawing to himself. He had been to Jerusalem to worship. He was reading a passage of Scripture that seemed to point to a sacrificial lamb. When God sent a surrendered servant named Phillip, he needed only for a God-sent messenger to guide him to Jesus. Today, as on that day, people whom God is drawing are in need of someone to guide them to Jesus.

Consider using a model for your evangelistic invitation. I developed a model for the public invitation as a doctoral student at Southwestern Baptist Theological Seminary. The model can be adapted to various contexts and appeals. My model has four components: a transitional statement, an internal decision, an external expression, and a concluding challenge. Many have found this type of model helpful in extending an invitation.

First, use a transitional statement to begin your invitation. This statement enables the speaker to cross a threshold from message to invitation. It is common for a speaker to have difficulty making the transition into the invitation. Craft a one-sentence statement with which you are comfortable to facilitate this transition. The statement may be a propositional "if/then" statement, with phrasing such as, "If this is what you intend to do, here is what you do." Make it clear and personal. It will help you as well as the hearer move into the opportunity to make a decision.

Next, follow your transition with a call for an internal decision. This is the heart of the invitation, the inner, spiritual response to the working of the Holy Spirit. This should be tied directly or indirectly to the sermon or message that was presented. I am passionate about the invitation, particularly when it is an invitation to respond to the message just preached. Craft this part of the invitation as an appeal to make a response to the inner conviction of the Holy Spirit. This is the part of the invitation that is the most crucial and transformational. I am aware critics of the invitation often accuse an invitational model of placing too much emphasis on outer form, such as walking an aisle or praying a prayer. I agree that simply walking an aisle or praying a prayer may be empty and meaningless without an inner decision and surrender. Call for a sincere inner surrender to the voice of God. Stress this aspect of your invitation above all other components. Use appropriate, Spirit-directed persuasion to urge a sincere surrender of heart and life.

Then, extend an opportunity for an outward expression of one's decision. As previously observed, an inner change should produce outward evidence. Proof of the new birth is new life! James raised serious suspicions about someone who professes to have inner faith without the outward evidence of good works (Jas 2:14–26). An early confessional formula is recorded in Rom 10:8–10. This passage makes clear that heart belief and outward confession are inseparably linked together. Once an inner decision has been settled, an outward expression of the commitment is appropriate and biblical. The outward expression may take one of various forms. At this point make clear that the opportunity to make the outward response is being offered. Let there be no confusion or ambiguity.

Finally, close your invitation with a clear and compelling statement. Be clear and confident by using similar and proven language each time the invitation is given. Give the invitation as an imperative, not a mere suggestion. Make it a real appeal and call for decision. Do not suggest that hearers might come someday; urge them to do so today, now in this moment.

Using the suggested model enables the delivery of both personal as well as public invitations in a clear and confident manner. The four-step formula has proven to be an enormous help in my evangelistic witness. I discovered that having some "tracks to run on" gave me more assurance of what to say in inviting someone to respond to the gospel. I would offer this model for anyone wishing to improve the delivery of an evangelistic invitation. Do not succumb to the trap of evaluating your invitation by the response of the person. Evaluate by whether the invitation is clear and compelling and presented in the power of the Holy Spirit.

I am passionate about the public invitation—God used it the night I came to faith in Christ. I am also passionate in my desire to see it implemented with clarity and integrity. To extend the invitation in an attempt to manipulate or coerce is shameful. I resent coercion and manipulation in any context; I detest it in the setting of a public invitation. At the other extreme is the practice of extending the invitation in a passionless and perfunctory manner. To extend an invitation in a casual, unprepared, and careless manner is another type of abusing the invitation. An invitation to Christ should be done with urgency, passion, and even persuasion. Paul told the Corinthians, "Therefore, knowing the fear of the Lord, we persuade men, but we are made manifest to God; and I hope that we are made manifest also in your consciences. ... Therefore, we are ambassadors for Christ, as though God were making an appeal through us; we beg you on behalf of Christ, be reconciled to God" (2 Cor 5:11, 20).

The church needs a revitalized view and practice of the public evangelistic invitation. We do not need to implement a practice that is dishonoring to God. It is my contention we need to recognize that the public evangelistic invitation is a tool of great integrity, both biblically and historically. Further, when it is implemented properly, its integrity is maintained through the character and methodology of the minister.

May the critics refine our methods and our motives! May God revitalize our passion and our practice! May we stand to proclaim the gospel as God's gracious gift of redemption and salvation, and may God entreat people through us, as we beg the multitudes to be reconciled to God!

BIBLIOGRAPHY

McBeth, H. Leon. *The Baptist Heritage: Four Centuries of Baptist Witness.* Nashville, TN: Broadman Press, 1987.

McLendon, Henry B. "The Mourner's Bench." ThD diss., The Southern Baptist Theological Seminary, 1902.

Streett, R. Alan. *The Effective Invitation.* Old Tappan, NJ: Fleming H. Revell, 1984.

AUTHOR INDEX

A

Absalom, Alex   282, 283, 285, 290, 300
Ackroyd, P. R.   196
Adams, Chris   340, 344
Akin, Daniel L.   462
Aldrich, Joseph C.   249, 257
Alexander, Roberts   27, 87, 102
Allen Jr., John L.   88, 92, 101
Allen, David L.   3, 14, 117, 120, 121, 129, 446, 447, 462
Allison, Gregg R.   229
Amirizadeh, Marzieh   94, 102
Aniol, Scott M.   182, 183, 196
Anthony, Michael J.   299, 323
Armstrong, Richard Stroll   257
Arn, Charles   358
Arn, Win   358
Arturbury, Andrew E.   131, 148
Atkinson, Donald A.   56, 60
Autry, C. E.   108, 129

B

Bailey, Kenneth   47
Bailey, Waylon   6, 14
Baker, Robert A.   68, 80
Balentine, Samuel E.   186, 187, 188, 196
Baptist Press   315, 391, 404
Barna Group   204, 205, 215, 257, 306, 307, 315, 318, 319, 320, 332
Barna Research   332
Barna, George   358
Barnett, Mike   59, 60
Barrett, C. K.   26, 30
Barry, John D.   136, 143, 147, 148
Barth, Karl   193, 196
Bauckham, Richard J.   22, 30
Bauer, Walter   455, 456, 462
Beale, G. K.   142, 147

Bebbington, David W.   74, 80
Bennett, Kay   364, 365, 370
Benoy, Eric   viii, 429
Berg, Ryan   332
Bibi, Asia   94, 95, 101
Bilezikian, Gilbert   299
Bird, Michael F.   143, 147
Bisagno, John   245, 257
Bishop, William Robert   182, 183, 184, 185, 196, 199
Blackaby, Henry   337, 344, 415
Bles, Geoffrey   122, 130
Blomberg, Craig L.   381, 388
Blumhofer, Edith L.   73, 80
Boa, Kenneth D.   192, 193, 194, 196
Boda, Mark J.   186, 188, 196
Boles, John B.   71, 80
Bomar, David   147, 148
Boren, M. Scott   299
Botz, Paschal   187, 197
Bowman, Robert M.   192, 193, 194, 196
Boyd-MacMillan, Ronald   84, 85, 93, 99, 100, 101
Bozeman, Jeanine   viii, 360
BPNews   305, 315, 391, 404
Branson, Mark Lau   388
Breytenbach, Cilliers   139, 147
Bridges, Erich   92, 101
Bright, Bill   8, 14, 75, 249, 257
Bromiley, Geoffrey T.   193, 196
Bromiley, Geoffrey W.   124, 129
Brother Yun   97, 99, 101
Brown, David   16
Brown, Derek R.   147, 148
Brown, K. J.   189, 197
Brown, Richard   326, 327, 334
Brueggemann, Walter   188, 190, 191, 197
Brunson, Mac   257

Brusco, Elizabeth E. 47
Bryant, James W. 257
Buckser, Andrew 47
Burge, Gary M. 47
Burke, Trevor J 30
Burkholder, J. Peter 178, 185, 197
Butterfield, Rosaria 268, 277

C

Cannister, Mark 322, 332
Cannon, Mae Elise 217, 219, 224
Carpenter, Mark Alan 72, 80
Carter, James E. 19
Carter, Joe 342, 344
Carter, Tom 263, 278
Case, Donald Owen 430, 442
Chaney, Charles L. xxvi, 372, 388
Chesterton, G. K. 110, 129
Chitwood, Paul 228, 240
Christensen, Michael J. 145, 147
Christian Job Corps 362, 370
Cline, Stephanie vii, 303
Cloud, Henry 299
Cohick, Lynn H. 47
Coleman, Robert E. 247, 257, 299
Colijn, Brenda B. 131, 133, 135, 147
Comisky, Joel 291, 299
Conant, J. E. 127, 129
Cothen, Joe H. 247, 257
Cowen, Gerald 133, 147
Crawford, Cheryl 321, 333
Crawley, Winston 50, 60
Creech, Joe 73, 80
Crim, Keith R. 188, 199
Crites, Tom 323, 333

D

Dale, Robert D. 249, 257
Danker, Frederick W. 455, 462
Dawson, Scott 12, 14, 339, 344
Day Jr., William H. vii, 346, 348, 358
Dean, Emily vii, 335
Dean, Jody vii, 335
Dean, Kenda Creasy 321, 332
Dempsey, Rod 299
deSilva, David 47
Dever, Mark 77, 80
Dijk, S. J. P. van 187, 197

Dobbins, Gaines 303, 315
Dodd, C. H. 116, 129
Dods, Marcus 87, 102
Donahue, Bill 299
Donaldson, James 87, 102, 103
Douglas Mangum 134, 147, 148
Downey, Murray 249, 257
Drummond, Lewis 108, 129

E

Earls, Aaron 336, 344
Early, David 299
Easley, Kendell H. 18, 30
Edwards, Jonathan 69, 70, 485
Edwards, Steven 319, 332
Edwards, Sue 326
Egli, Jim 290, 299
Elmore, Tim 319, 332
Emetuche, Damian vii, 371, 373, 376, 380, 383, 388
England, Archie vi, 61
Erickson, Millard J. 112, 129, 178, 197
Eskew, Harry 180, 185, 197
Estep, James R. 299, 302
Evans, David 330, 332
Evans, John 356, 358
Evans, Tony 252, 257
Evers, Randy Phillip 358

F

Falk, Daniel K. 186, 196, 197
Farmer, Ben 95, 101,
Farmer, Jeffrey C. vii, 225
Farrar, Steve 254, 257
Fay, William 249, 257
Fields, Doug 326, 332
Finney, Charles G. 71, 74, 80, 179, 484, 485, 486
Fish, Roy 127, 129
Fleener, Lorien vi, 216
Fleming, David vii, 390, 405, 415
Ford, Leighton 262, 277
Foster, Allen 430, 442
Frame, John M. 194, 197
Frend, W. H. C. 93, 101
Friedrich, Gerhard 124, 125, 129
Frost, J. M. 78, 80
Fullerton, W. Y. 266, 277

G

Gallaty, Robby   282, 299
Garland, David   206, 215
Garrett, James Leo, Jr.   133, 137, 147
Garrison, David   91, 101
Geiger, Eric   285, 300, 301
George, Carl F.   285, 300
George, Timothy   xxv
Getty, Keith   185, 197
Getty, Kristyn   185
Gilbert, Lela   86, 88, 89, 92, 102
Given, Lisa M.   430, 442
Gladden, Steve   300
Glasser, Arthur F.   372, 388
Glazier, Stephen   47
Godshall, Matthew Steven   20, 30
Goldingay, John   22, 30
Gonzalez, Justo L.   65, 81
Grace, Meghan   320, 334
Graham, Billy   74, 75, 79, 480
Green, Gene L.   47
Green, Michael   63, 64, 81, 98, 101, 257
Greer, Peter   57, 60
Griffin, Brad   321, 328, 333
Griffin, Jeff   viii, 429
Griffiths, Mark   315
Grout, Donald Jay   178, 185, 197
Grudem, Wayne A.   24, 25, 26, 30, 177, 178, 197
Guder, Darrell   182, 197
Gulledge, J. Kirk   358

H

Habermas, Gary   193, 198
Hadaway, C. Kirk   232, 240
Hallesby, O.   230, 231, 232, 240
Hamme, Joel T.   134, 147
Hammett, Edward H.   358
Hankins, Eric   3, 14, 121, 129
Hannah, John D.   72, 81
Hanson, Paul D.   18, 19, 22, 30
Harrington, Bobby   xix, 282, 283, 285, 290, 300, 301
Harrison, Rodney A.   258
Harvey, Thomas Alan   88, 102
Harwood, Adam   vi, 3, 14, 121, 129, 131, 252, 258
Hassler, Betty   340, 344

Hattaway, Paul   97, 101
Hawkins, O. S.   449, 452, 462
Hearn, Mark   391, 404
Hemphill, Ken   225, 232, 240, 288, 296, 297, 300, 449, 462
Henderson, D. Michael   300
Hendricks, William   303, 315
Henry, Carl F. H.   111, 129
Herman, Eti   430, 442
Hildebrandt, Wilfried   16, 21, 30
Hill, David   22, 30
Hire, L. M.   196
Hobbs, Herschel H.   19
Hobbs, Scott Sterling   74, 81
Horn, F. W.   22, 30
Horst, Chris   57, 60
Houston, James M.   359
Howerton, Rick   286, 287, 298, 300
Hübner, Hans   20, 30
Hughes, Adam L.   viii, 445, 446, 453, 458, 462
Hull, Bill   300
Hull, William E.   260, 277
Hunt, Johnny   79, 81
Hurst, Rebeccah   147
Hurtado, Larry W.   184, 198
Hustad, Don   179, 180, 198
Hyde, Daniel R.   312, 315

I

Icenogle, Gareth Weldom   300
Ingle, Clifford   305, 306, 315, 316

J

Jeremias, Joachim   22, 31
Johnson, Mark   vii, viii, 405
Johnston, Jay   363, 364, 370
Johnston, Thomas   270, 277
Johnston, Thomas P.   4, 13, 14
Johnston, Thomas Paul   75, 81
Johnston, W. B.   193
Jones, Ian   220, 224
Jones, Wayne R.   300
Justin Martyr   64, 81, 87, 91, 98, 99, 102

K

Keehn, Dave   323, 327, 333
Keener, Craig S.   185, 198

Kelley, Charles S., Jr.   viii, xi, xii, xiii, xvii,
    xviii, xxi, xxii, xxiv, xxv, xxvi, xxvii, xxix
    xxx, 29, 31, 61, 78, 79, 81, 177, 179, 184,
    190, 191, 198, 210, 215, 222, 224, 242,
    258, 260, 264, 277, 294, 298, 300, 445,
    464, 470, 476, 477, 479
Kelley, Mark   277
Kelley, Michael   300
Kenney, T.   320, 334
Khan, Sheraz   95, 102
Kilbreth, Leon   258
King, Claude V.   337, 344
King, Kelly D.   341, 344
King, Larry   150, 164
King, Martin Luther, Jr.   390, 403, 404, 413
Kinnaman, David   205, 324, 333
Kittel, Gerhard   124, 125, 129
Klick, Jeffrey A.   258
Klippenstein, Rachel   147, 148
Knight, Harold   193, 196
Koukl, Gregory   174, 176
Koval, Robin   320, 334
Krikelas, James   430, 442
Kuligin, Victor   131, 133, 147
Kuo, Lily   90, 102

L
Land, Richard   xxv, 117, 129
Landers, John M.   68, 80
Langberg, Diane   223, 224
Lawson, Kevin   252, 258
Lee, Kyuboem   393, 404
LeMalle, Averri   405
Lemke, Steve   v, vi, xviii, 107, 117, 120, 129
Lenhart, Amanda   320, 333
Lewis, C. S.   122, 123, 130, 166, 168, 169,
    170, 176, 216, 223, 224
LifeWay Kids   306, 310, 311, 315
Limburg, James   20, 21, 31
Linhart, Terry   327, 333
Litfin, Bryan M.   83, 84, 85, 87, 93, 96, 102
Little, Christopher R.   59, 60
Little, Paul E.   249, 258
Lombard, Peter   121, 130
London, H. B., Jr.   245, 258
Loscalzo, Craig A.   471, 474, 479
Louw, Johannes P.   137,141, 147
Lucado, Max   142, 148
Luscombe, Kenneth L.   389

Luter, Elizabeth   340, 344

M
MacArthur, John   275
Malphurs, Aubrey   260, 277, 338, 345
Malul, Meir   136, 148
Mánek, Jindřich   25, 31
Mangum, Douglas   134, 147, 148
Marshall, Paul   86, 88, 89, 92, 102
Martin, Glen   301
Martin, Lee Roy   17, 31
Martin, Robin   59, 60
Martinez, Juan F.   388
Martyr, Justin   64, 81, 87, 91, 98, 99, 102
Mason, Steven D.   18, 19, 21, 31
Mathews, Ned L.   447, 462
Maxwell, John   244, 258, 319, 333
Mayes, Gary   326, 334
McBeth, H. Leon   485, 486, 492
McBride, Neal F.   301
McComiskey, Thomas   17, 20, 22, 31
McDill, Wayne   249, 258
McElrath, Hugh T.   180, 185, 197
McGavran, Donald A.   76, 81, 372, 374,
    375, 388
McGrath, Alister E.   68, 82
McIntosh, Gary L.   268, 278, 301
McKnight, Scot   47
McLellan, Ronnie   vi, 61
McLendon, Henry B.   486, 492
McRaney, Jr., Will H.   4, 14
Medina, Ramon   405
Melendez, Mario   v, 15
Melick, Shera   301
Metaxas, Eric   189, 198
Miles, Delos   60, 247, 249, 257, 258, 361,
    362, 370
Miles, Jack   136, 148
Miller, Glenn A.   258
Moffett, Samuel Hugh   59, 60
Moody, Dwight Lyman   27, 31, 74, 80, 179
Mooneyham, W. Stanley   51, 52, 56, 60
Moore, Waylon   274, 278
Moreau, A. Scott   375, 388
Morgan, G. Campbell   247, 258
Morley, Patrick   254, 258
Morris, Michelle J.   136, 148
Mosley, Eddie   290, 301, 337, 345
Mott, Stephen   380, 388

Moyer, Larry R.   466, 469, 474, 479
Mulder, Jake   328, 333
Musurillo, Herbert   87, 102
Myers, Bryant L.   389
Myers, Gary   190, 198

N

Nation, Phillip   300
Newman, Judith H.   186, 197
Newsom, Blake   v, xi, 466, 479
Nicholas, David   442
Nicholi, Armand   223, 224
Nida, Eugene Albert   137, 141, 147
Nix, Preston L.   v, viii, 3, 5, 14, 74, 82, 405, 464
North American Mission Board   229, 240

O

O'Brien, Brandon J.   47
O'Donovan, Oliver   170, 176
Odom, David   vii, 317, 323, 333
Ogden, Greg   324, 325, 333
Ogea, Reggie   vii, 241
Olson, Philip N.   50, 60
Osborn, Brooke   vi, 216

P

Palisca, Claude V.   178, 185, 197
Palmer, Jeffrey   57, 60
Parker, T. H. L.   193, 196
Parkinson, Cally   288, 292, 301
Parr, Steve   301, 323, 333
Payne, J. D.   371, 372, 388
Pazmino, Robert E.   301
Peavey, Donna B.   vii, 303, 305
Pennington, Jonathan T.   19, 26, 31
Perkins, William   190, 198, 456, 462
Peters, Chuck   311, 315
Phillips, Jere L.   179, 258
Pierce, James R.   358
Piper, John   182, 198
Plantinga, Cornelius, Jr.   170, 176
Poling, Wayne   287, 301
Powell, Kara   321, 328, 329, 333
Powell, Paul W.   449, 463
Powers, Mark C.   181, 198
Price, Wm. Craig   v, vii, xiii, 15, 405
Putman, Jim   301

Q

Queen, Matt   205, 206, 215

R

Rahn, Dave   327, 333
Rainer, Thom   266, 275, 278
Rankin, Jerry   92, 101
Rankin, Russ   338, 345
Reid, Alvin   4, 5, 9, 14, 108, 130, 192, 266, 278
Reinhardt, Wolfgang   73, 82
Reith, George   87, 102
Rice, Bo   vi, 203
Richards, E. Randolph   47
Richards, Lawrence O.   312, 315
Riley, Jeffrey   vi, 165
Ripken, Nik   98, 100, 102
Ritzema, Elliott   147, 148
Rivers, Loretta   vii, 360
Robbins, Duffy   323, 327, 328, 334
Roberts, Alexander   87, 102, 103
Robertson, Archibald Thomas   11, 14
Robinson, Russ   299
Roesel, Charles L.   49, 56, 60, 250, 259, 269, 278
Rogers, Joyce   459, 463
Ross, Richard   319, 322, 333
Rostampour, Maryam   102
Roudkovski, Jake   vii, 260, 265, 278
Rouse, Ruth   314, 315

S

Sanderson, Leonard   259
Schaeffer, Francis A.   111, 130
Schaff, Philip   64, 65, 66, 81, 82
Scroggins, Jimmy   203, 204, 215
Sedwick, Jay   326, 334
Seemiller, Corey   320, 334
Senter, Mark   322, 334
Shaddix, Jim   270, 278, 458, 463, 471, 478
Sharp, Mary Jo   221, 224
Shea, Nina   86, 88, 89, 92, 102
Shermer, Michael   193, 198
Sider, Ronald J.   50, 55, 60, 380, 388
Silano, G.   121, 130
Sisemore, John T.   283, 301
Skinner, Craig   74, 82
Smietana, Bob   391, 404
Smith, A.   320, 334
Smith, Christian   325, 334
Smith, James E.   19
Smith, Steven W.   447, 448, 455, 463

Soulen, Richard N.   188, 199
Southern Baptist Convention   112, 114, 118, 119, 130, 254, 305, 316, 360, 370
Spader, Dann   326, 334
Sparks and Honey   319, 320, 334
Spurgeon, Charles H.
Stanfield, Vernon L.   259, 449, 463, 466, 468, 472, 474, 475, 479
Stetzer, Ed   182, 183, 198, 285, 301, 391
Stevens, Gerald L.   61, 82
Stier, Greg   324, 334
Stone, Randall   vii, 279, 297, 301, 302
Stott, John   125, 130
Streett, R. Alan   270, 278, 486, 492
Stringer, Martin   178, 198
Stults, Roy   88, 96, 102
Sunday, William Ashley (Billy)   74, 82
Sweeney, Marvin A.   16, 31

T
Talbert, Charles H.   131, 148
Taylor, Allan   288, 302
Taylor, Bill   293
Taylor, Ken   v, 48
Terry, John Mark   6, 8, 12, 14, 57, 60, 65, 67, 68, 69, 71, 82
Tertullian   83, 84, 85, 97, 98, 103, 193
Thelwall, S.   103
Thiselton, Anthony C.   27, 28, 29, 31
Thompson, W. Oscar   295, 302
Tillman, Don   299
Tolbert, Mark   viii, 248, 480
Tollet, Anne-Isabelle   95, 101
Torrance, Thomas F.   193, 196
Townsend, John   299
Tozer, A.W.   180, 182, 198
Trammell, Stephen   405, 415, 417
Trueblood, Ben   319, 321, 324, 334
Turner, Anthony   320, 334
Turner, Max   22, 23, 24, 25, 26, 31

U
Unruh, Heidi Rolland   50, 60

V
Vallone, Donna   320, 334
Van Gelder, Craig   386, 388
Van Til, Cornelius   192, 193, 199
Vanderbloemen   298, 302
Vandergriff, Steve   326, 327, 334

Vines, Jerry   247, 259, 270, 278, 458, 463, 471, 479

W
Wagner, C. Peter   76, 81, 375, 388
Waldvogel, Edith   80
Wallace, Daniel B.   451, 463
Wamble, Hugh   305, 306, 316
Warren, Bill   v, 33
Warren, Rick   76, 82
Warrington, Keith   30
Watson, David   33, 47
Watt, Jan G. van der   131, 147, 148
Weiler, Angela   430, 442
Welch, Bobby H.   302
Wentz, Lazarus   147, 148
Werline, Rodney A.   186, 196, 197
Wesley, John   68, 69, 300, 485
Westerman, Claus   188, 199
Whaley, Vernon M.   181, 199
Wheeler, David   181, 199
White, Ellen Gould   66, 82
Whitefield, George   68, 69, 70, 485
Whitlark, Jason A.   131, 148
Widder, Wendy   147, 148
Wilken, Robert   83, 103
Wilson, Darryl H.   282, 302
Winter, Ralph D.   382, 389
Wirt, Sherwood Eliot   51, 60
Wiseman, Neil B.   245, 258
Witherington, Ben   184, 199
Wittung, Jeffrey A.   145, 147
Wolcott, Carrie Sinclair   147, 148
Wood, Leon James   32
Woodward, Greg   vi, 177, 183, 184, 185, 192, 194, 199
Wright, Christopher J. H.   32, 133, 134, 148, 389
Wright, N. T.   184, 185, 186, 187, 199
Wright, Norman   217, 224
Wright, Steve   203, 215
Wurmbrand, Richard   86, 87, 95, 103

Y
Yamamori, Tetsunao   389
Yancey, George   389
Yessick, Tommy   245, 259

Z
Zacharias, Ravi   200

Scripture Index

1

1 Cor 1:18–21   124
1 Cor 1:18–25   123
1 Cor 1:2   117, 123, 141
1 Cor 1:23   117, 123
1 Cor 1:23–24   117
1 Cor 15:1–11   116, 484
1 Cor 15:1–5   263
1 Cor 15:3–4   209, 465
1 Cor 15:3–4   209, 465
1 Cor 2:2   116
1 Cor 3:5–8   268
1 Cor 6:9–10   135, 169
1 Cor 9:20–23   128
1 John 1:8–10   119, 137
1 John 2:2   113, 116, 121, 321
1 John 3:1   137
1 John 3:2   120, 143
1 John 3:23   120, 143
1 John 4:19   126
1 John 4:7–10   113
1 John 5:14–15   226
1 Kgs 17   25
1 Kgs 18:21, 36–39   330, 475, 481, 482
1 Pet 1:1–2   121
1 Pet 1:15–16   141
1 Pet 1:3–5   126
1 Pet 2:2   209, 454
1 Pet 2:22   209
1 Pet 2:24   209
1 Pet 2:9–10   374, 386
1 Pet 2:9–10   374, 386
1 Pet 3:15   209, 311
1 Pet 3:15–6   175
1 Pet 3:18   141
1 Pet 3:18   209, 311
1 Pet 5:2   126
1 Sam 1:10–11   133
1 Sam 10:6, 10   17

1 Sam 11:6   17
1 Sam 19:20, 23   17
1 Sam 2:1   133
1 Thess 1:5–11   484
1 Tim 1:15   468
1 Tim 2:1–8   226, 468
1 Tim 2:2   228
1 Tim 2:24   226
1 Tim 2:3–4   247
1 Tim 2:3–6   116, 120, 121
1 Tim 2:8   228
1 Tim 3   245
1 Tim 3:2   126
1 Tim 4:1–16, 6:1–4   108
1 Tim 4:1–4   226
1 Tim 4:10   321
1 Tim 4:11–16   226
1 Tim 4:13   126
1, 2, and 3 John   38

2

2 Chron 36:22   20
2 Cor 3:18   142
2 Cor 3:7–8   142
2 Cor 4:1–6   123, 458
2 Cor 4:2   110, 456
2 Cor 4:3–4   165
2 Cor 4:5   114
2 Cor 4:7   124
2 Cor 5:10–11   125
2 Cor 5:11   119, 206, 445, 455, 469, 491
2 Cor 5:11–20   119, 206, 445, 455, 469, 491
2 Cor 5:11, 20   206, 491
2 Cor 5:14   9
2 Cor 5:17   136, 142, 471
2 Cor 5:18–20   45, 483
2 Cor 5:18–20   45, 483, 491
2 Cor 5:20   108, 369
2 Cor 5:21   209, 311

2 Cor 5:21   209, 311
2 Cor 6:2   473
2 Corinthians   206
2 Pet 1:21   108, 117
2 Pet 1:4   145
2 Pet 2:1–22   108
2 Pet 2:4–10   127
2 Pet 3:18   120
2 Pet 3:9   113, 116, 121, 247, 321
2 Sam 23:2   17
2 Tim 2:15   110
2 Tim 2:15–19; 3:13; 4:3–4   108
2 Tim 2:2   338
2 Tim 2:24   126
2 Tim 2:24, 4:1–4   126
2 Tim 2:3–4   321
2 Tim 3:15   266
2 Tim 4:1–5   241, 455
2 Tim 4:2   445, 453, 456
2 Tim 4:2–5   109
2 Tim 4:5   xvii, 124, 265, 445
2 Tim 4:5   xvii, 124, 265, 445
2 Timothy 4   242

A

Acts 1:16   24, 62
Acts 1:16–20   62
Acts 1:8   3, 26, 27, 124, 126, 203, 263, 366, 371
Acts 10   38, 44, 162, 247
Acts 10:22   144
Acts 10:28–48   484
Acts 10:38   28
Acts 11:20–21   63
Acts 11:23   124
Acts 13:14–48   484
Acts 13:3   228
Acts 13:48–51   376
Acts 14:1–23   376
Acts 14:1–7   484
Acts 14:8–20   63
Acts 15   43, 376
Acts 16:14–15   63
Acts 16:25–31   484
Acts 16:31   266
Acts 17:1–4   330, 484
Acts 17:17   470
Acts 17:22–34   63
Acts 18:4   63
Acts 19:1–10   484
Acts 19:8   483
Acts 19:9–10   63
Acts 2   204, 385, 450
Acts 2:1–4   61
Acts 2:14–41   127
Acts 2:17   26 Acts 2:17–21   15
Acts 2:2–4   450
Acts 2:22–24   120
Acts 2:22–39, 3:13–26, 4:10–12, 10:36–43, 13:17–41   116
Acts 2:22, 8   28
Acts 2:27, 31   126
Acts 2:36   450
Acts 2:36–39   330
Acts 2:37–38   486
Acts 2:37–41, 47   127
Acts 2:38   114, 120, 208, 475
Acts 2:38, 16:31   114
Acts 2:38, 4:12, 16:31   114, 121
Acts 2:39–40   484
Acts 2:4   118
Acts 2:40–41   124
Acts 2:41   63, 118
Acts 2:42   126, 127
Acts 2:42–47   381
Acts 2:47   98
Acts 20:27, 31   126
Acts 21:8   242
Acts 21:8   242
Acts 24–26   247
Acts 26:18   28
Acts 26:28   470
Acts 27:33   124–25
Acts 3:22; 7:37   25, 54
Acts 4:11–12   246
Acts 4:12   115, 467
Acts 4:12, 16:31   116
Acts 4:13   203
Acts 7:51   121, 123
Acts 8   38, 43, 135, 162, 247, 488
Acts 8–12   38
Acts 8:26–38   484
Acts 8:31   489
Acts 8:33   135
Acts 9:10–18   63

Acts 9:18   28
Acts 9:31   28   Chron 24:20   16

C
Col 1:13   135
Col 1:16–17   310
Col 1:19–21   119
Col 1:9   226
Col 3:18–21   254

D
Dan 9:14   143
Deut 32:39   132
Deut 32:4   143
Deut 6:25   143
Deut 6:4–5   304
Deut 6:4–9   110

E
Eccl 1:9   166
Eccl 12:12   432
Ecclesiastes   432
Eph 1:13–14   126
Eph 1:17–19   226
Eph 1:5   137
Eph 1:7   137, 139
Eph 2:1   12, 172
Eph 2:1–4, 4:17–19   226
Eph 2:1, 3, 5   12
Eph 2:10   136
Eph 2:14   46
Eph 2:16   114, 119
Eph 2:8–10   123
Eph 2:8–9   126, 311
Eph 4:11   126, 242
Eph 4:13–16   326
Eph 4:17–19   121
Eph 4:17–20   172
Eph 4:30   123, 139
Eph 5   461
Eph 5:1   173
Eph 5:21–33   254
Eph 5:22–33   136
Eph 5:5   135
Eph 6:10–20   226
Ephesians   322, 325
Esth 4:14   140
Esther   140
Exod 32:26   482

Exod 33:17   226   Exod 13:13   139
Exod 14:13   133
Exod 15:8   16
Exod 29:21   141
Exod 3:7–8   134, 140
Exodus   25, 31, 474
Ezek 10:18–19   22
Ezek 16:20   136
Ezek 18:5–9   144
Ezekiel   18, 19, 21, 136, 145, 148
Ezra   186, 188, 475, 482
Ezra 10:1–12   475
Ezra 10:5   482

G
Gal 1:6–9   107
Gal 1:7   309
Gal 2   376
Gal 2:11–14   377
Gal 2:15–16   42
Gal 3:13   139
Gal 3:21–22   144
Gal 3:26   137
Gal 3:28   335
Gal 3:6   144
Gal 4:4–7   137
Gal 4:5, 7   137
Gal 4:6   137
Gal 5:1   141
Gal 5:19–21   173
Gal 5:21   135
Galatians   173
Gen 1:1   310
Gen 1:27   118, 366
Gen 15   42, 43
Gen 15:6   42, 143
Gen 17   42, 43
Gen 25–50   xxix
Gen 32:11   140
Gen 45:7   140
Gen 49:18   133
Gen 7:1   143

H
Heb 11   79
Heb 11:7   143
Heb 13:3   87   Heb 2:11   137
Heb 2:14   144

Heb 2:17   137
Heb 2:9   321
Heb 7:27, 9:28, 10:10   120
Heb 9:15   139
Heb 9:22   137
Heb 9:27   10, 473
Heb 9:28   134
Hebrews   25, 134, 143, 144, 381, 473
Hosea 14:2   482

I

Isa 11:1–5; 42:1; 61:1–5   20
Isa 38:20   134
Isa 4:4   20
Isa 42:1–9; 49:1–13; 50:4–11; 52:13–53:12   19
Isa 43:1   226
Isa 45:1   20
Isa 55:11   110
Isa 55:6–11   175
Isa 55:8–9   111
Isa 59:1   247
Isa 6:1–5   137
Isa 61:1–2   19
Isaiah   17, 18, 19, 20, 62, 134, 162, 474
Isaiah 11   19
Isaiah 40–66   18, 19
Isaiah 61   19

J

James   31, 32, 34, 38, 39, 40, 42, 45, 376, 380, 408, 490
Jas 1:27   380
Jas 1:5   166
Jas 2:14–26   490
Jas 2:26   39
Jas 3:1   108
Jas 4:4   136
Jer 12:1   143
Jer 15:20–21   134
Jer 4:3   262
Jeremiah   19, 134
Job 42:7–8   107
Joel 2   20, 21, 22, 450
Joel 2:28–32   15, 17, 26, 450
Joel 3:1   17
John   10, 27, 38, 135, 143, 171
John 1:1–3, 4   208

John 1:11–12, 3:14–17, 10:1–10, 14:6   119, 121
John 1:11–12, 3:16–17   115, 119
John 1:11–12, 3:16–18, 14:6   115, 120
John 1:12   137
John 1:14   111
John 1:17   172
John 1:28   483
John 1:29   139
John 1:42   483
John 1:43   62, 483
John 1:8–12   115, 137, 171
John 1:9   171
John 10:1–2, 7–8   120
John 10:10   135
John 10:27–28   252
John 10:27–28   252
John 11:12   134
John 12:31–33   114
John 14:1–6   59, 115, 127, 160, 246, 311
John 14:15   7, 172
John 14:23–4   172
John 15:13   8
John 15:16, 10:27–29   126
John 15:4–6   226
John 16:33   216
John 16:33   216
John 16:5–15   169
John 16:7   28
John 16:7–10   264
John 16:7–14   117
John 16:8   314
John 16:8   226, 263, 483
John 16:8–11   117, 123, 283
John 16:8–11   117, 123, 283
John 18   262
John 20:21   3, 280
John 20:21–23   263, 371
John 21:15–17   7
John 3   135, 262
John 3:1–16   62
John 3:1–21   487
John 3:1–6   62, 263
John 3:14–15   114
John 3:14–17   115
John 3:16   9, 12, 114, 266, 311
John 3:16–17   112

John 3:16–18   280
John 3:17   321
John 3:17–21   171
John 3:18   12
John 3:3   136
John 3:3, 5   135
John 3:36   12
John 4:1–42   62, 262, 483
John 4:34–38   269
John 4:7–8   112
John 5:14–15   226
John 6   53
John 6:51   53
John 6:60–71   62
John 7:37–38   487
John 7:37, 38   483
John 8:12   171
John 8:3–11   138
John 8:31–58   172
John 8:32   140
John 9:38   262
John 9:4   473
Jonah   330
Jonah 1:1–2; 3:4–5; 4:1–2   330
Jonah 1:4   16
Joshua   16, 134, 482
Joshua 24:15   474
Jude 1:24–25   126
Jude 3   120

L

Lev 19:2   141
Lev 4–5   137
Lev 8:2–30   16
Luke   xvi, 15
Luke 1:15   23
Luke 1:28–35; 2:9–20   61
Luke 1:47   134
Luke 1:5–6   144
Luke 10   361, 394
Luke 10:1–12   262
Luke 10:20   28
Luke 10:25–37   38, 52, 226, 397
Luke 11:1   226
Luke 12:20   473
Luke 13:11   28
Luke 13:12–14   28
Luke 14:23   3, 483

Luke 15   35
Luke 15:10   294
Luke 15:11–24   138
Luke 15:28   124
Luke 15:3–7   7
Luke 16:19–31   127
Luke 17:11—18   62, 251
Luke 18:1–8   226
Luke 18:18–34   483
Luke 18:35   28
Luke 18:9–14   144
Luke 19:1–10   280, 483
Luke 19:1–11   62, 467
Luke 19:1–6, 8–10   330
Luke 19:10   7
Luke 19:38   25
Luke 2:11   134
Luke 2:21–22; Acts 2:1–4   61
Luke 2:25   144
Luke 2:25–27   23
Luke 22:20   137
Luke 22:70   25
Luke 23:2   25
Luke 23:2–3, 7   25
Luke 23:32–43   62
Luke 23:35–39   25, 134
Luke 23:45   25
Luke 23:50   144
Luke 24   458, 461
Luke 24:27   457
Luke 24:44–48   280
Luke 24:45–47   371
Luke 24:46–48   3
Luke 24:46–49   263
Luke 3:16   23
Luke 3:18   61
Luke 3:23   483
Luke 3:6   134
Luke 3:7–14   475
Luke 4:1   23
Luke 4:18   25, 28
Luke 4:18–19   15, 62
Luke 4:19   28
Luke 4:36   28
Luke 5   361
Luke 5:27   483
Luke 5:32   144, 468
Luke 5:32; 15:7, 10, 32;

19:10   468
Luke 6:18   28
Luke 6:27   92
Luke 6:27–28   99
Luke 7:11–23   24
Luke 7:21–22   28
Luke 8:2   28
Luke 8:4–15   264
Luke 9   25, 361
Luke 9:42   28
Luke 9:57–62   367

M

Mark 1:14–15   34, 62, 262
Mark 1:15   208
Mark 1:16–20   35
Mark 1:38   53
Mark 10:14   266
Mark 10:15   135, 251
Mark 10:17–23   135
Mark 10:24–26   135
Mark 11:17   383
Mark 11:24   226
Mark 12:29–31   52
Mark 16:15   3, 5, 263
Mark 2:13–14   330
Mark 2:17   144, 468
Mark 4:14   109
Mark 5   124
Mark 5:1–5   140
Mark 5:10   124
Mark 5:18   124
Mark 5:19   5
Mark 5:20   140
Mark 7:14–23   167
Mark 7:20–23   167
Mark 9:42–48, 13:24–30   127
Mark 9:43   135
Matt28:20   445
Matt 1:20–21; 2:2   61
Matt 1:21   134
Matt 1:31   121
Matt 10:32   475
Matt 11:28   483
Matt 11:28, 29   483
Matt 12:33–37   167
Matt 13:1–23   274

Matt 16:16   120
Matt 18:19–20   226
Matt 18:29   124
Matt 18:6   266
Matt 19:13–15   303
Matt 19:14   251
Matt 19:16–26   367
Matt 19:22   62
Matt 19:28   136
Matt 21:13   187
Matt 21:22   226
Matt 23:37   123
Matt 25   9, 52, 135, 250
Matt 25:1–13   135
Matt 25:31–33, 41   9
Matt 25:31–46   127, 250
Matt 25:35–36   52
Matt 26:28   137
Matt 26:47–56   62
Matt 28:18–20   3, 5, 263, 280, 371
Matt 4:12–22   62, 324, 330, 367, 483
Matt 4:19; 9:9   62, 367
Matt 4:23; 9:35   62
Matt 5   54
Matt 5–7   167
Matt 5:14–16   239
Matt 5:14, 16   175
Matt 5:16   54
Matt 5:20   36
Matt 5:48   113
Matt 5:6   144
Matt 6:1–18   37
Matt 6:10   135
Matt 6:13   140
Matt 7:13–14   120
Matt 7:13–23   127
Matt 7:14   135
Matt 7:15–20; 12:33–37; 15:15–20   167
Matt 7:24–29   110
Matt 8:12   12
Matt 8:24–25   134
Matt 8:3   341
Matt 9:13   144, 468
Matt 9:21–22   134
Matt 9:35   53
Matt 9:36   8, 11
Matt 9:38   228

N

Neh 9:39   482
Num 11–12   17
Num 11:25–29   17
Num 11:25; 12:6   17
Num 11:28   17
Num 11:29   16, 22
Num 18:15–16   139

P

Phil 2   422
Phil 2:12–13   141
Phil 2:6–7   209
Phil 2:8–9   209
Phil 3:20–21   135
Phil 3:8   175
Phlm 1:6   318
Ps 11:7   143
Ps 110   184, 450
Ps 110:1   450
Ps 118:38   25
Ps 126:5–6   264
Ps 16   450
Ps 16:8–11   450
Ps 97:1   135
Pss. 25:20; 143:9   140

R

Rev 20:11–12, 15   10
Rev 20:11–15   127
Rev 22:17   484
Rev 4:11   310
Rev 7:10   140
Rev 7:9   139
Rev 7:9–12   386
Rom 1: 24–32   168
Rom 1:13–17   128
Rom 1:16   114, 120, 175, 204, 210, 309, 368, 467
Rom 1:18–21   108
Rom 1:18–24   121
Rom 1:20–21   210
Rom 10:1–3   226
Rom 10:13   26, 321, 477
Rom 10:13–15   123, 212
Rom 10:13–17   246
Rom 10:14   205

Rom 10:17   205
Rom 10:8–10   490
Rom 10:9   208
Rom 10:9–10   114, 212, 228, 230, 266, 475, 487
Rom 10:9–10, 13   120, 311
Rom 10:9–13   120
Rom 10:9–15   121
Rom 12:1–2   213
Rom 12:2   113
Rom 14:10, 12   10
Rom 2:12–16   108, 166
Rom 2:4   211
Rom 3:10   144
Rom 3:23   12, 35, 118, 211, 311
Rom 3:23–6   168
Rom 3:9, 23   137
Rom 4:1–5   486
Rom 4:24   144
Rom 4:3, 9, 22   144
Rom 5:10   110, 135
Rom 5:6–11   138
Rom 5:8   328
Rom 6:10   120
Rom 6:18, 20, 22   141
Rom 6:23   12, 208, 211, 212, 311, 328
Rom 8:14, 16   137
Rom 8:15   137
Rom 8:16   137
Rom 8:16–17, 38–39   213
Rom 8:23   139
Rom 8:26–27   235
Rom 8:29–30   121, 126
Rom 8:29–30, 11:2   121
Rom 8:30   143
Rom 9–11   384
Rom 9:4   137
Rom 9:9–10   328
Ruth 2:20   139

T

Titus 1:9–6, 2:1   126
Titus 2   343
Titus 2:11   467
Titus 2:3–5   341
Titus 3:5   136

SUBJECT INDEX

A

accommodation   413, 414, 415
adoption   136, 137, 148, 362, 378
African-American   73, 405, 409, 410, 411, 412, 413, 415, 416, 418, 420, 422, 424, 425, 428
American Theological Library   435
Amirizadeh, Marzieh   94, 102
Anglo   374, 405, 412, 418, 425, 428
Annual Church Profile   346
anoint   16, 17, 19, 20, 21, 23, 24, 25, 26, 27, 28, 29, 62, 295, 485
anthropology   33, 47, 108, 118, 152
apologetics   87, 98, 99, 152, 153, 174, 184, 191, 192, 193, 194
assimilation   275, 288, 412, 413, 415
atheist   193, 320, 396
ATLA   72, 73, 74, 80, 81, 82
Augustine, Saint   65, 93, 94, 96
awakening   xii, 68, 69, 70, 71, 72, 74
Awana   267, 276
Azusa Street   72, 73, 80

B

Babylonian   17, 18
Baptist Faith and Message   xxv, 112, 114, 117, 118, 119, 130, 254, 305, 316, 360
Barna   124, 204, 205, 215, 257, 306, 307, 315, 318, 319, 320, 332, 358, 376, 377
basar   190
being included   137, 418
BFH (Baptist Frienship House)   364, 365
Bibi, Asia   94, 95, 101
bicultural   384
Blackaby, Henry   337, 344, 415
Boniface   65
boolean operators   431, 432
Broadus   vii, 445
Buddhist   158, 396, 398
business revulsion   72

C

Caesar   25, 86
Calvin, John   66, 67, 68, 185
Champion Forest   vii, viii, 400, 405, 406, 407, 408, 409, 410, 411, 413, 415, 416, 417, 421, 425, 426, 427, 428
children   vii, xv, xviii, xix, xxvi, xxix, 23, 58, 90, 115, 122, 137, 143, 144, 170, 173, 191, 213, 218, 234, 244, 245, 250, 251, 252, 253, 254, 255, 258, 266, 267, 268, 272, 276, 284, 288, 303, 304, 305, 306, 307, 308, 309, 310, 311, 312, 313, 314, 315, 316, 323, 325, 333, 338, 346, 347, 355, 357, 359, 362, 364, 371, 413, 438, 487
Christiansuffering   vi, 84, 94, 97, 100
Christmasspectacular   414
christology   108, 114, 185
church growth   xxii, xxvi, 76, 77, 81, 82, 84, 89, 97, 98, 99, 232, 240, 265, 278, 283, 288, 301, 349, 352, 358, 371, 374, 375, 388, 393, 404, 417
church growth movement   76, 77, 374
church growth strategy   417
church planting   vii, xvi, 182, 371, 372, 373, 374, 375, 376, 377, 380, 382, 388
college students   vii, 317, 318, 319, 321, 324, 325, 326, 327, 329
Columba   65
communist   84, 86, 88, 89, 90, 95, 96,97
community   xi, xv, xxii, 19, 20, 50, 56, 60, 76, 85, 98, 168, 171, 178, 190, 234, 235, 236, 237, 255, 256, 261, 262, 263, 264, 269, 272, 273, 280, 281, 288, 293, 299, 301, 312, 326, 328, 336, 337, 340, 345, 348, 349, 352, 355, 357, 363, 364, 372, 374, 377 380, 381, 383, 385, 386, 388, 392, 402, 403, 406, 407, 410, 411, 412, 414, 415, 416, 418, 421, 424, 426, 428, 438
community widows/widowers banq 274

compassion 7, 8, 9, 11, 13, 19, 53, 217, 218, 225, 236, 244, 262, 265, 269, 297, 400, 401, 402
Constantine 83, 484
context v, xiii, xiv, xvii, 17, 20, 22, 33, 34, 35, 36, 37, 38, 39, 40, 41, 45, 46, 47, 76, 132, 150, 182, 184, 187, 188, 196, 198, 207, 216, 237, 238, 241, 244, 249, 251, 255, 260, 261, 262, 264, 269, 274, 275, 307, 324, 329, 343, 348, 355, 358, 361, 366, 372, 374, 380, 383, 384, 385, 393, 406, 407, 412, 413, 415, 423, 427, 428, 446, 450, 452, 456, 457, 488, 489, 491
conversionist theology 303
counseling vi, 216, 217, 218, 220, 221, 222, 223, 224, 250, 294, 307, 330
covenant 17, 18, 20, 21, 26, 42, 43, 59, 90, 131, 136, 137, 138, 139, 141, 144, 172, 186, 275, 475, 482
CPI (Christian Periodical Index) 435
Criswell, W. A. 79, 445
cross-cultural 374, 421
Cyrus the Great 20

D

database 284, 285, 431, 432, 434, 435, 436, 439
Day of Pentecost 44, 118, 120, 127, 450, 484
dean of house churches 88
decisional preaching viii, xvii, 260, 464, 465, 470, 477, 478
Deism 111
deliverance 19, 140, 145, 211, 231, 280
demographics xi, xvi, 77, 244, 250, 261, 348, 373, 392, 399, 400, 410, 438
demography 385
development ministries 57
DNA 407, 416, 425, 427, 428
doing life 412

E

EBSCOhost 434
ecclesiology 108, 126, 246
Edwards, Jonathan 69, 70, 485
ekklesia 372
elderly 84, 85, 350, 352, 356
Elijah 23, 25, 330, 475, 482
enculturation 384, 385

English as a second language 49, 364
Ephesus 63, 126, 172, 483, 484
ERLC (Ethics and Religious Liberty 363, 370
ethics 156, 166, 167, 170, 174, 176, 194
ethnic 250, 375, 376, 377, 380, 382, 384, 386, 390, 391, 392, 393, 405, 409,
ethnicity(s) 377, 383, 386, 388, 391, 413, 421, 426, 427, 428, 438
euangelion 242, 262, 465
evangelism xi, xiii, xiv, xv, xvi, xvii, xx, xxi, xxii, 4, 5, 6, 8, 9, 12, 13, 14, 15, 26, 27, 28, 29, 31, 33, 37, 38, 40, 42, 44, 45, 46, 47, 48, 49, 50, 51, 52, 53, 55, 56, 57, 59, 60, 61, 62, 63, 64, 65, 67, 68, 69, 71, 72, 75, 76, 77, 78, 79, 81, 83, 84, 91, 97, 98, 99, 100, 101, 105, 107, 108, 109, 110, 111, 114, 117, 118, 119, 125, 126, 127, 128, 129, 153, 160, 165, 166, 177, 178, 179, 181, 183, 184, 185, 189, 191, 195, 198, 199, 201, 204, 205, 206, 207, 208, 214, 215, 216, 220, 225, 226, 229, 232, 237, 241, 242, 246, 247, 248, 249, 250, 257, 258, 259, 260, 261, 263, 264, 265, 266, 269, 270, 274, 275, 276, 277, 278, 279, 280, 281, 282, 284, 286, 288, 289, 294, 295, 298, 299, 300, 302, 303, 304, 305, 312, 313, 314, 315, 317, 318, 319, 321, 322, 323, 324, 325, 326, 327, 328, 329, 330, 331, 323, 333, 335, 336, 337, 339, 341, 342, 343, 344, 346, 347, 348, 349, 350, 351, 352, 353, 354, 355, 356, 357, 358, 360, 361, 363, 364, 365, 366, 368, 369, 370, 371, 372, 374, 375, 390, 393, 405, 406, 407, 408, 417, 429, 431, 432, 433, 434, 437, 438, 439, 440, 441, 443, 446, 447, 449, 453, 455, 457, 462, 464, 474, 477, 479, 482, 487
evangelism explosion 77, 248
evangelist vii, xiii, xiv, xvii, xix, 26, 28, 65, 66, 71, 72, 73, 74, 75, 79, 85, 98, 124, 170, 179, 190, 229, 241, 242, 246, 248, 250, 253, 254, 256, 257, 271, 295, 307, 308, 309, 310, 314, 322, 376, 464
evangelistic preaching xvii, 74, 259, 446, 449, 452, 457, 458, 459, 463, 465, 466, 467, 468, 471, 472, 474, 475, 477
evidentialism 192, 194
evidentialists 193

Exodus   140, 186
exposition   125, 445, 446, 447, 448, 449, 452, 453, 457, 460
expository sermon   viii, 270, 278, 445, 446, 447, 448, 449, 453, 454, 457, 458, 461, 463, 471, 479

F

facilities   275, 291, 379
FAITH (acronym)   328
faith-based   250, 256, 361, 362, 364, 366
fasting   37, 233
fathers.com   338, 344
Felicitas   93, 94, 96
Felix, Minucius   98
fideism   192, 193, 194
Finney, Charles   71, 74, 80, 179, 484, 485, 486
firstsearch   434
follow-up   39, 272, 273, 274, 275, 276, 278, 282, 286, 288, 300, 330, 488
followers   3, 5, 35, 37, 42, 43, 45, 50, 53, 54, 66, 67, 84, 93, 135, 170, 214, 223, 225, 227, 228, 229, 230, 231, 237, 238, 239, 262, 274, 275, 280, 281, 282, 283, 284, 294, 297, 304, 327, 361, 367, 377, 483
forgiveness   11, 63, 92, 116, 119, 120, 123, 137, 138, 145, 168, 208, 209, 211, 212, 228, 229, 230, 280, 311, 328, 409, 452, 467, 469, 480, 481, 482, 486
Frelinghuysen, Theodore   69
friction   416, 424
friendship   249, 255, 269, 290, 320, 333, 352, 364, 365
fullness   22, 118, 325

G

Galilee   7, 8, 23, 34, 40, 45
Generation Z/Gen Z   257, 318, 319, 320, 332, 334
Genesis   136, 187, 281, 403
God-breathed   108
God's family   136, 137, 145
God's kingdom   135, 145, 441
going vertical   425
good Samaritan   38, 39, 45, 52, 361, 397, 399
Gospel Coalition, The   342, 344
gospel conversation   174, 192, 203, 207, 208, 209, 210, 215, 219, 220, 225, 238, 239, 255, 256, 283, 328, 329, 331, 337

gospel of Yahweh   191
Graham, Billy   74, 75, 79, 81, 480
Great Commission   v, vi, xi, xiv, xv, xvi, xxii, xxiii, xxvii, xxviii, 3, 4, 5, 6, 7, 8, 9, 11, 13, 14, 79, 81, 98, 125, 181, 191, 199, 203, 214, 222, 223, 263, 270, 277, 279, 280 299, 304, 312, 321, 360, 371, 372, 383, 407, 409, 417

H

Harrington, Bobby   xix, xx
harvest/harvesting   4, 14, 53, 75, 127, 228, 261, 262, 263, 264, 265, 269, 270, 273, 276, 277, 324, 358, 402
Helwys, Thomas   485
Helwys, Thomas   485
hermeneutics   110, 111, 184, 199
Hindu   50, 158 396, 398
Hispanic-American   250, 378, 380, 384, 395, 411, 412, 413, 418,
holistic ministry   50
Holy Spirit   v, xiv, 4, 13, 15, 19, 20, 22, 23, 26, 27, 28, 29, 30, 44, 50, 61, 63, 69, 70, 73, 89, 97, 108, 109, 110, 111, 112, 117, 118, 119, 120, 121, 123, 137, 144, 169, 203, 206, 207, 208, 210, 213, 225, 226, 228, 235, 236, 237, 263, 264, 265, 266, 273, 275, 276, 282, 283, 304, 309, 310, 312, 314, 315, 330, 361, 371, 372, 416, 426, 427, 449, 450, 451, 472, 483, 489, 490, 491
home-based groups   291, 292
homogeneous unit principle   76, 375, 383, 393, 394, 404
Hurricane Harvey   414
Huss, John   66

I

inerrancy   109, 110, 453
inspiration   xvii, 108, 109, 110, 265, 269, 453
integrity   viii, xvii, xxii, 41, 167, 175, 189, 289, 366, 480, 487, 491
intentionality   xv, 4, 14, 19, 38, 68, 151, 207, 230, 233, 249, 250, 254, 256, 260, 261, 263, 265, 266, 268, 269, 275, 276, 278, 281, 286, 287, 288, 292, 294, 303, 307, 323, 324, 325, 337, 339, 341, 350, 352, 362, 367, 368, 402, 403, 407, 408, 409, 410, 416, 419, 423, 424, 428

Subject Index 509

International Mission Board 56, 78, 92, 101, 382, 399
invitation viii, xx, xxi, 62, 78, 125, 169, 179, 192, 217, 222, 251, 270, 272, 274, 278, 283, 284, 294, 307, 323, 324, 326, 330, 334, 341, 452, 459, 460, 465, 473, 474, 475, 476, 477, 480, 481, 482, 483, 484, 485, 486, 487, 488, 489, 490, 491, 492

J
J-STOR 434
Jesus movement 75
Jewish 25, 33, 34, 35, 36, 37, 38, 39, 40, 41, 42, 43, 44, 45, 52, 63, 138, 150, 186, 187, 376, 381, 386, 395, 396, 397, 398, 470, 482, 484
Jewish culture 33, 34, 35, 38, 41, 42, 43, 45
Jibla Baptist Hospital 92
Jingwen, Liu 94
Jinping, Xi 89, 90
justification 125, 143, 174, 175, 189, 371, 394

K
kavod 18
Kelley, Rhonda Harrington xviii, xix, xx, xxi
King Ethelbert 65
King, Martin Luther, Jr. 390, 403, 404
kyrie 187, 197

L
language of Zion 308, 488
Laurie, Greg 75
leadership xviii, xx, xxii, xxiii, xxix, xxx, 41, 49, 68, 78, 79, 81, 85, 137, 179, 233, 234, 241, 242, 243, 244, 245, 253, 256, 258, 260, 261, 263, 264, 267, 270, 271, 272, 273, 274, 275, 276, 277, 283, 285, 287, 295, 297, 300, 301, 309, 319, 323, 326, 333, 349, 355, 379, 383, 388, 390, 391, 403, 410, 411, 412, 417, 419, 421, 426, 428, 438, 464
Leavell Center xxii, 261, 438, 464
Lewis, C. S. 122, 166, 168, 216, 223, 224
library viii, xvi, xxv, 64, 65, 66, 78, 80, 81, 82, 347, 359, 429, 430, 431, 432, 433, 435, 436, 437, 439, 440, 441, 442
LifeWay 321, 338, 340, 341, 390, 391

liturgists 183, 187
liturgy 178, 179, 187, 188, 192, 194
location 33, 63, 87, 91, 220, 291, 350, 379, 382, 408, 426, 466
Luther, Martin 66, 67, 156, 178, 193

M
ma'al 186, 187
marching orders 3, 4, 13
Martyr, Justin 64, 87, 91, 98, 99, 102
martyrs 64, 84, 87, 91, 92, 93, 94, 96, 97, 101, 102
martyrs of Lyons and Vienne 91, 93
masiah 16
mass evangelism 229, 270
Mayflower 485
McGavran, Donald 76, 81, 372, 374, 375, 388
mcgready 70
mentor xxii, 249, 253, 269, 285, 325, 336, 337, 338, 341, 343, 362, 446
mentoring 269, 336, 337, 338, 341, 343, 362
Methodist 69, 70, 72, 222, 224, 396, 486
Mingdao, Wang 88, 96, 102
missing jewel 180, 198
mission drift 57, 58, 60
missional culture 322, 323
Mississippi 363, 370
modeling 232, 233, 296, 319, 327
monocultural vii, xvi, 385, 390, 391, 392, 393, 405, 406, 407, 408, 415, 418, 419, 425, 426, 427
moral transformation 169, 170
morality vi, xi, 165, 167, 169, 173, 174, 175
motivations v, 3, 4, 13, 127, 257, 296, 318, 332
movements 65, 73, 90, 91, 371, 421
multi-educational 385
multi-socioeconomic 385
multicultural vii, xvi, 371, 377, 379, 380, 381, 382, 383, 384, 385, 390, 391, 392, 403, 404, 405, 406, 407, 408, 410, 411, 412, 413, 414, 415, 416, 417, 418, 419, 422, 423, 424, 425, 426, 427, 428
multiethnic 385
multigenerational 385
musical 182, 196, 396
Muslim 84, 91, 92, 94, 97, 101, 158, 396, 398, 399

N

Nettleton 179
new groups 286, 287, 295, 342
new life 135, 136, 145, 229, 287, 471, 490
New Methodists, The 222, 224
NOBTS (New Orleans Baptist Theo xi, xiii, xvii, xx, xxi, xxii, xxiii, xxiv, xxvii,xxviii, 84, 155, 174, 177, 179, 189, 190, 191, 193, 195, 198, 222, 242, 245, 248, 261, 305, 426, 438, 446, 464
nones 336
North AmericanMission Board 78, 79, 229, 240, 262, 364

O

O'Kelly, Steve 485
obedience 5, 37, 63, 86, 90, 98, 100, 102, 208, 212, 304, 305, 367, 372, 470
oikos 237, 239
omnibenevolent 112
omnipresent 111
omnisapient 112
omniscient 111
ordain 16, 163, 190, 232, 424
organization xix, 49, 51, 57, 74, 82, 87, 217, 218, 220, 250, 255, 256, 260, 267, 279, 284, 288, 289, 294, 298, 352, 372, 382, 436, 438, 439
origin 26, 31, 136, 184, 186, 188, 196, 198, 199, 382, 445, 447, 482
overseer 243

P

pace grace 427
Paedobaptists 306
parakaleō 28
participation 144, 145, 261, 272, 289, 297, 327
pastoral vision 349
Patrick, Scot 65
peithomen 125
pentecostals 73
people groups 247, 382, 383, 407
Perpetua 86, 93, 94, 96, 97, 98, 99,100
persecution xiv, 28, 63, 64, 65, 68, 83, 84, 87, 88, 89,90, 91, 92, 93, 95, 97, 98, 99, 100, 101, 102, 375, 376
PewResearch Center 335, 344, 345, 377, 378
Pietism 67, 68
Pilgrim's Progress 485
plenary verbal 109
plērēs 22
pneumatology v, 15, 108, 117
Polycarp 64, 85, 86, 87,98
prayer walking 231, 233, 234, 235, 236, 237
presuppositionalism 192, 194
prioritism 59
promise 21, 25, 27, 35, 77, 113, 114, 116, 126, 127, 134, 143, 145, 186, 203, 208, 225, 226, 235, 240, 247, 451
prospects 269, 273, 284, 285, 287, 288, 291, 293, 294, 305
Protestant 49, 88, 92, 306, 346, 374, 375, 391, 396, 485
proximity 186, 189, 290, 278, 412
Pudens 96
Puritanism 67, 68

R

race grace 427
reaching men 249, 254, 255, 336
reconciliation 108, 125, 138, 139, 145, 147, 190, 209, 221, 281, 303, 391, 409, 410, 483
redemption 118, 120, 132, 139, 140, 145, 166, 169, 222, 226, 281, 295, 454, 461, 491
reformation 47, 65, 66, 67, 81, 180, 187, 197
repentance 36, 38, 40, 44, 45, 62, 113, 116, 169, 173, 189, 208, 211, 212, 247, 266, 280, 303, 304, 470, 473, 475, 476, 483, 484, 485
resistance 88, 253, 419
restore 7, 20, 36, 139, 188, 222, 223, 224, 454, 473
revelation 10, 108, 111, 114, 129, 131, 163, 193, 228, 264, 303, 386, 453, 475
revival xx, xxii, xxv, xxvii, 61, 64, 69, 70, 71, 72, 73, 74, 75, 78, 80, 82, 84, 85, 184, 228, 234, 252, 260, 270, 271, 272, 273, 278, 340, 345, 350, 355, 356, 357, 464, 482
righteousness 17, 19, 36, 42, 112, 113, 114, 117, 120, 141, 143, 144, 145, 147, 160, 162, 163, 167, 168, 169, 173, 209, 212, 226, 228, 230, 283, 314, 453, 475, 487
Rogers, Adrian 79, 445, 459, 463
Roman Catholic Church 67, 485

Roman Empire 33, 34, 65, 83, 470, 484
Roman Road xxvi, xxx, 210, 248, 264, 277, 328, 329
Romania 86, 87, 95
Rong, Jiang 90
Rustampoor, Maryam 94

S

Saddleback Church 76, 280
SAE (senior adult evangelism) 348, 349, 350, 351, 352, 353, 354, 355, 356
salvation vi, xiv, xxix, 9, 10, 11, 22, 23, 27, 43, 45, 48, 49, 50, 62, 67, 111, 114, 115, 117, 118, 119, 120, 121, 123, 125, 126, 127, 129, 131, 132, 133, 134, 135, 136, 137, 138, 139, 140, 142, 143, 144, 145, 146, 147, 148, 158, 162, 169, 175, 178, 182, 190, 191, 204, 207, 208, 209, 210, 211, 212, 213, 214, 2228, 229, 230, 232, 233, 242, 246, 247, 248, 251, 252, 253, 256, 263, 264, 273, 275, 280, 295, 303, 304, 305, 306, 307, 309, 310, 313, 318, 328, 329, 330, 331, 335, 362, 368, 372, 384, 387, 409, 452, 454, 465, 467, 468, 469, 471, 472, 473, 474, 475, 476, 481, 482, 485, 487, 491
salvation history 22
sanctification 117, 125, 141, 144, 145, 217, 227
Saturus 96, 97, 100
Savonarola, Jerome 66
sawdust trail 488 SBC (Southern Baptist Convention) xxii, xxiii, xxv, xvi, xxvii, xxiii, xxiv, xxvi, xxx, 29, 61, 77, 78, 79, 80, 92, 112, 114, 118, 119, 130, 241, 242, 253, 254, 264, 277, 282, 305, 306, 315, 316, 342, 345, 346, 347, 348, 349, 352, 353, 356, 357, 358, 360, 363, 370, 382, 445, 449, 462, 463, 464, 465, 477
searching 11, 220, 221, 234, 283, 431, 432, 434, 435, 436, 438
seed vi, 83, 84, 97, 109, 262, 264, 265, 268, 294, 411
self-revealing 111
senior adults vii, xv, 346, 347, 348, 349, 350, 351, 352, 353, 354, 355, 356, 357, 358, 438
Separatist 68, 485
Serve Saturday 414

shadow of our steeple xvi, 403, 408
Shema 304
shepherd, shepherding 7, 8, 9, 11, 53, 61, 243, 244, 247, 427, 248, 445
side energy 423
small group vii, xv, 78, 99, 118, 233, 253, 268, 274, 279, 280, 281, 282, 283, 284, 285, 186, 287, 288, 289, 290, 291, 292, 294, 296, 297, 298, 299, 300, 301, 302, 329, 337, 338, 345
social action 50, 51, 55, 56, 59, 60, 189, 361
Social Gospel Movement 48, 49
social work vii, 189, 197, 360, 361, 362, 363, 364, 366, 369
sociological 178, 198, 289, 382, 393
Son of God 23, 25, 114, 116, 122, 171, 209, 325
soteriology 108, 119, 121, 124, 129, 131, 148, 246
soul-winning xxv, 248, 249, 257, 259, 356, 358
Southern Baptist Convention Execu 345
sowing 36, 261, 262, 264, 266, 267, 276
Spirit of the Lord 15, 17, 19, 21, 23, 31, 62
Spirit of Yahweh 16, 17, 20, 21, 30
Spurgeon, Charles Haddon 74, 82, 225, 262, 266, 277, 278, 486
strategize vii, 260
strategy vi, 13, 78, 225, 237, 239, 241, 246, 248, 249, 260, 261, 262, 263, 264, 266, 267, 268, 269, 270, 271, 273, 274, 275, 276, 279, 285, 287, 288, 289, 298, 300, 301, 323, 324, 326, 363, 373, 374, 382, 402, 406, 410, 412, 417, 419, 446, 452, 458, 460, 461
Sunday School vii, xv, xix, xxx, 68, 78, 80, 180, 267, 276, 279, 281, 282, 283, 286, 287, 288, 290, 293, 294, 296, 297, 298, 300, 301, 302, 351, 352, 353, 420, 464
Sunday, Billy 74, 82

T

Tatian 98
temple 17, 18, 21, 22, 23, 25, 37, 54, 133, 184, 185, 186, 187, 188, 196, 292, 381, 400, 452
Tertullian 83, 84, 85, 97, 98, 103, 193
Theophilus 98

theopneustos 108, 119, 121, 124, 129, 131, 148, 246
Thor 65
Torah 35, 36, 38, 39, 186
Tozer, A. W. 180, 182, 198
transcendence 194
transformation xxiv, 59, 142, 143, 144, 145, 169, 170, 285, 300, 301, 342, 372, 374, 377, 386, 411, 427, 471, 490
trauma 217, 219, 220, 221, 223, 224, 265
Trinitarian 29, 158
Trinity 111, 112, 122, 158, 208
turbulence 424, 425

U

United States Bureau 347
Upward Sports 267, 276
urgency 246, 247, 248, 465, 472, 473, 483, 491

V

VBS (Vacation Bible School) 253, 267, 276, 284, 307, 308, 312
vision of the house 416
visitation 69, 72, 78, 294, 297
von Zinzendorf, Nickolaus 68

W

Webber, Robert E. 180
wellness 245, 246
Welsh revival 72, 73, 82
Wesley, John 68, 69, 300, 485
Whitefield, George 68, 69, 70, 485
Wiersbe, Warren 180

wild game supper 255, 273
WMU (Woman's Missionary Union 314, 362, 370
women vii, xiii, xv, xxi, 79, 93, 94, 95, 96, 98, 221, 224, 287, 235, 336, 338, 340, 341, 342, 343, 344, 362, 373, 378, 470
worldcat 436, 437, 439
worship vi, xv, xxii, 17, 18, 25, 37, 39, 43, 44, 45, 73, 76, 86, 87, 91, 93, 99, 101, 118, 133, 141, 142, 147, 162, 163, 177, 178, 179, 180, 181, 182, 183, 184, 185, 187, 188, 189, 190, 191, 192, 194, 195, 196, 197, 198, 199, 213, 231, 234, 237, 251, 253, 261, 270, 272, 284, 285, 291, 292, 294, 307, 312, 315, 322, 329, 337, 353, 367, 373, 375, 379, 380, 381, 384, 385, 387, 391, 404, 413, 414, 415, 422, 475, 476, 478, 481, 482, 489
Wurmbrand, Richard 86, 87
Wurmbrand, Sabina 86, 95

Y

Yi, Wang 90
youth vii, xv, xx, xxvi, xxx, 58, 77, 182, 196, 253, 266, 267, 268, 276, 284, 317, 318, 319, 321, 322, 323, 324, 325, 326, 327, 329, 330, 332, 333, 334, 346, 347, 355, 357, 378, 487
Yun, Brother 97, 99, 101

Z

Zionese 308
Zwingli, Ulrich 66, 67

CONTRIBUTOR BIOGRAPHIES

Eric Benoy (ThM, MDiv, MACE, New Orleans Baptist Theological Seminary; MLIS, Louisiana State University; MEd, University of New Orleans) is reference librarian and collection development librarian of the John T. Christian Library and director of the Martin Music Library at New Orleans Baptist Theological Seminary. He is senior minister of Airline Baptist Church, Metairie, Louisiana.

Jeanine C. Bozeman (PhD, MRE, New Orleans Baptist Theological Seminary; MSW, Tulane University) is distinguished professor of social work at New Orleans Baptist Theological Seminary.

Dr. Rex D. Butler (PhD, Southwestern Baptist Theological Seminary; MA, Wayland Baptist University) is professor of church history and patristics, occupying the John T. Westbrook Chair of Church History at New Orleans Baptist Theological Seminary.

Stephanie Cline (ThM, MACE, New Orleans Baptist Theological Seminary) is minister to families at First Baptist Church, Center, Texas.

Bill Day (PhD, New Orleans Baptist Theological Seminary; MDiv, The Southern Baptist Theological Seminary) is distinguished research professor, occupying the Gurney Chair of Evangelism and Church Health, and associate director of the Leavell Center for Evangelism and Church Health at New Orleans Baptist Theological Seminary.

Emily Dean (PhD, MDiv, New Orleans Baptist Theological Seminary) is director of women's academics and organizations and adjunct faculty at New Orleans Baptist Theological Seminary.

Jody Dean (PhD, MDiv, New Orleans Baptist Theological Seminary) is associate professor of Christian education and senior regional associate dean for extension centers at New Orleans Baptist Theological Seminary.

Damian Emetuche (PhD, The Southern Baptist Theological Seminary; ThM, BTh, Nigerian campus of The Southern Baptist Theological Seminary) served as assistant professor and past director of the Nehemiah Project at NOBTS. He is chaplain for Tampa General Hospital and pastor of Clermont Central Church, Clermont, Florida. He is a board-certified chaplain with the Association of Professional Chaplains and an adjunct professor with New Orleans Baptist Theological Seminary.

Archie W. England (PhD, Mid-America Baptist Theological Seminary; MDiv, Golden Gate Baptist Theological Seminary) is professor of Old Testament and Hebrew, occupying the J. Wash Watts Chair of Old Testament and Hebrew, and chairman of the Division of Biblical Studies at New Orleans Baptist Theological Seminary.

Jeffrey Farmer (PhD, ThM, MDiv, New Orleans Baptist Theological Seminary) is associate professor of church ministry and evangelism and associate director of the Caskey Center for Church Excellence at New Orleans Baptist Theological Seminary.

Lorien Fleener (ThM, MAMFC, New Orleans Baptist Theological Seminary) is adjunct online professor of psychology and counseling at Leavell College for New Orleans Baptist Theological Seminary.

Jeff Griffin (MDiv, PhD, Mid-America Baptist Theological Seminary; MLIS, University of North Texas) is dean of libraries and professor of Old Testament and Hebrew at New Orleans Baptist Theological Seminary.

Adam Harwood (PhD, MDiv, Southwestern Baptist Theological Seminary) is associate professor of theology, occupying the McFarland Chair of Theology, director of the Baptist Center for Theology and Ministry, and editor of the *Journal for Baptist Theology and Ministry* at New Orleans Baptist Theological Seminary.

Adam Hughes (PhD, MDiv, Southwestern Baptist Theological Seminary) is assistant professor of expository preaching, dean of the chapel, director of the Adrian Rogers Center for Expository Preaching, and director of mentoring programs in pastoral ministries at New Orleans Baptist Theological Seminary.

Mark Louis Johnson Sr. (DMin, New Orleans Baptist Theological Seminary; MDiv, ThM, Princeton Theological Seminary) is adjunct professor in leadership and administration at New Orleans Baptist Theological Seminary and is pursuing a PhD in evangelism.

Steve Lemke (MDiv, MRE, PhD, Southwestern Baptist Theological Seminary) is professor of philosophy and ethics, provost emeritus, and vice president for institutional assessment at New Orleans Baptist Theological Seminary.

Ronnie McLellan (ThM, MDiv, New Orleans Baptist Theological Seminary) is pursuing a PhD in evangelism and is pastor of First Baptist Church of Marrero, Louisiana.

Mario M. C. Melendez (PhD, New Orleans Baptist Theological Seminary; M.C.S. Union University) is a pastor in the New Orleans area and has served at four institutions of higher education.

Blake Newsom (MDiv, ThM, PhD, New Orleans Baptist Theological Seminary) is senior pastor of Dauphin Way Baptist Church, Mobile, Alabama, and associate professor of expository preaching at New Orleans Baptist Theological Seminary.

Preston Nix (PhD, MDiv, Southwestern Baptist Theological Seminary) is professor of evangelism and evangelistic preaching, occupying the Roland Q. Leavell Chair of Evangelism, chairman of the Pastoral Ministries division, director of the Leavell Center for Evangelism and Church Health, and director of supervised ministry at New Orleans Baptist Theological Seminary.

David Odom (PhD, MACE, Southwestern Baptist Theological Seminary) is associate professor of student ministry and director of the Youth Ministry Institute at New Orleans Baptist Theological Seminary.

Reggie Ogea (ThD, MDiv, New Orleans Baptist Theological Seminary) is professor of leadership and pastoral ministry, occupying the Perry Sanders Chair of Pastoral Leadership, and associate dean for the professional doctoral programs at New Orleans Baptist Theological Seminary.

Brooke Osborn (PhD, MAMFC, New Orleans Baptist Theological Seminary) is assistant professor of psychology and counseling at Leavell College for New Orleans Baptist Theological Seminary.

Donna B. Peavey (PhD, ThM, MRE, New Orleans Baptist Theological Seminary) is professor of Christian education, director of Children's Ministry Institute, director of Innovative Learning, and director of management and training for the Early Learning Center at New Orleans Baptist Theological Seminary.

Wm. Craig Price (PhD, MDiv, Southwestern Baptist Theological Seminary) is professor of Greek and New Testament, occupying the Robert Hamblin Chair of Biblical Exposition, and associate dean of online learning at New Orleans Baptist Theological Seminary.

Bo Rice (PhD, ThM, MDiv, New Orleans Baptist Theological Seminary) is associate professor of evangelism and preaching, dean of graduate studies, and director of the Entrust mentoring program at New Orleans Baptist Theological Seminary.

Jeffrey B. Riley (PhD, MDiv, Southwestern Baptist Theological Seminary) is professor of ethics and associate dean of research doctoral programs at New Orleans Baptist Theological Seminary and is a research fellow of the Ethics and Religious Liberty Commission of the Southern Baptist Convention.

Loretta Rivers (PhD, Tulane University; MSW, Louisiana State University; MACE, New Orleans Baptist Theological Seminary) is associate dean of graduate studies and professor of social work at New Orleans Baptist Theological Seminary.

Jake Roudkovski (PhD, ThM, MDiv, New Orleans Baptist Theological Seminary) is professor of evangelism and pastoral leadership, occupying the Max and Bonnie Thornhill Chair of Evangelism, and director of the doctor of ministry program at New Orleans Baptist Theological Seminary.

Robert B. Stewart (PhD, MDiv, Southwestern Baptist Theological Seminary) is professor of philosophy and theology, occupying the Greer-Heard Chair of Faith and Culture, and director of the Christian apologetics program at New Orleans Baptist Theological Seminary.

Randall L. Stone (PhD, ThM, New Orleans Baptist Seminary; MRE, Midwestern Baptist Theological Seminary) is professor of Christian education, occupying the John T. Sisemore Chair of Christian Education, the chairman of the Discipleship and Ministry Leadership division, and director of the EdD and DEdMin programs at New Orleans Baptist Theological Seminary.

Ken Taylor (PhD, MDiv, New Orleans Baptist Theological Seminary) is professor of urban missions, occupying the Chester L. Quarles Chair of Urban Missions, and the codirector of the Global Missions Center at New Orleans Baptist Theological Seminary.

Mark Tolbert (DMin, MDiv, Southwestern Baptist Theological Seminary) is professor of preaching and pastoral ministry, occupying the Caskey Chair of Church Excellence, and founding director of the Caskey Center for Church Excellence at New Orleans Baptist Theological Seminary.

William Warren (PhD, MDiv, New Orleans Baptist Theological Seminary) is professor of New Testament and Greek, occupying the Landrum P. Leavell, II, Chair of New Testament, director of the H. Milton Haggard Center for New Testament Textual Studies, and director of the online Spanish master of theological studies degree at New Orleans Baptist Theological Seminary.

Gregory A. Woodward (PhD, Florida State University; MME, University of Southern Mississippi; post-grad. study in biblical languages and theology, New Orleans Baptist Theological Seminary) is associate professor of conducting and worship, occupying the Lallage Feazell Chair of Church Music, and the chairperson of the Division of Church Music.

www.ingramcontent.com/pod-product-compliance
Lightning Source LLC
Chambersburg PA
CBHW071009140426
42814CB00004BA/172